T0211282

Lecture Notes in Computer Science 10227

Commenced Publication in 1973
Founding and Former Series Editors:
Gerhard Goos, Juris Hartmanis, and Jan van Leeuwen

Formal Methods

Subline of Lectures Notes in Computer Science

More information about this series at http://www.springer.com/series/7408

Clark Barrett · Misty Davies
Temesghen Kahsai (Eds.)

NASA
Formal Methods

9th International Symposium, NFM 2017
Moffett Field, CA, USA, May 16–18, 2017
Proceedings

 Springer

Editors
Clark Barrett (iD)
Stanford University
Palo Alto, CA
USA

Temesghen Kahsai
NASA Ames Research Center
Moffett Field, CA
USA

Misty Davies
NASA Ames Research Center
Moffett Field, CA
USA

ISSN 0302-9743   ISSN 1611-3349   (electronic)
Lecture Notes in Computer Science
ISBN 978-3-319-57287-1   ISBN 978-3-319-57288-8   (eBook)
DOI 10.1007/978-3-319-57288-8

Library of Congress Control Number: 2017937299

LNCS Sublibrary: SL2 – Programming and Software Engineering

Printed on acid-free paper

This Springer imprint is published by Springer Nature
The registered company is Springer International Publishing AG
The registered company address is: Gewerbestrasse 11, 6330 Cham, Switzerland

Preface

The NASA Formal Methods (NFM) Symposium is a forum to foster collaboration between theoreticians and practitioners from NASA, academia, and industry, with the goal of identifying challenges and providing solutions to achieving assurance in mission- and safety-critical systems. Examples of such systems include advanced separation assurance algorithms for aircraft, next-generation air transportation, autonomous rendezvous and docking for spacecraft, autonomous on-board software for unmanned aerial systems (UAS), UAS traffic management, autonomous robots, and systems for fault detection, diagnosis, and prognostics. The topics covered by the NASA Formal Methods Symposia include: model checking, theorem proving, SAT and SMT solving, symbolic execution, automated testing and verification, static and dynamic analysis, model-based development, runtime verification, software and system testing, safety assurance, fault tolerance, compositional verification, security and intrusion detection, design for verification and correct-by-design techniques, techniques for scaling formal methods, formal methods for multi-core GPU-based implementations, generation, specification, and validation of requirements, human–machine interaction analysis, certification, and applications of formal methods in systems development.

This volume contains the papers presented at NFM 2017, the 9th NASA Formal Methods Symposium, held at the NASA Ames Research Center, Moffett Field, CA, during May 16–18, 2017. Previous symposia were held in Minneapolis, MN (2016), Pasadena, CA (2015), Houston, TX (2014), Moffett Field, CA (2013), Norfolk, VA (2012), Pasadena, CA (2011), Washington, DC (2010), and Moffett Field, CA (2009). The series started as the Langley Formal Methods Workshop, and was held under that name in 1990, 1992, 1995, 1997, 2000, and 2008. Papers were solicited for NFM 2017 under two categories: regular papers describing fully developed work and complete results, and short papers describing tools, experience reports, or work in progress with preliminary results. The symposium received 77 submissions for review (60 regular papers and 17 short papers) out of which 31 were accepted for publication (23 regular papers and eight short papers). These submissions went through a rigorous reviewing process, where each paper was first independently reviewed by at least three reviewers and then subsequently discussed by the Program Committee.

In addition to the refereed papers, the symposium featured five invited presentations: "Formal Methods for the Informal World," by Michael Wagner, Senior Commercialization Specialist at the Robotics Institute at Carnegie Mellon University, Pittsburgh, PA; "Agile Aerospace at Planet," by Ben Haldeman, Technologist and Program Manager at Planet, San Francisco, CA; "Moving Fast with High Reliability: Static Analysis at Uber," by Manu Sridharan, Senior Software Engineer at Uber, Palo Alto, CA; "Challenges in Designing for the Next Era of Human Space Exploration," by Jason Crusan, Director of the Advanced Exploration Systems Division within the Human Exploration and Operations Mission Directorate at NASA, Washington, DC; and "A Tour of Formal Methods in Support of Aerospace Products Development," by

Alexandre Arnold, Research Engineer at Airbus. The symposium also featured a panel that discussed how to make more real problems and case studies from NASA and the aerospace industry available to researchers.

The organizers are grateful to the authors for submitting their work to NFM 2017 and to the invited speakers for sharing their insights. NFM 2017 would not have been possible without the collaboration of the outstanding Program Committee and additional reviewers, the support of the Steering Committee, the efforts of the staff at the NASA Ames Research Center, and the general support of the NASA Formal Methods community. The NFM 2017 website can be found at: https://ti.arc.nasa.gov/events/nfm-2017.

May 2017

Clark Barrett
Misty Davies
Temesghen Kahsai

Organization

Program Committee

Ella Atkins	University of Michigan, USA
Domagoj Babic	Google, USA
Julia Badger	NASA Johnson Space Center, USA
Clark Barrett	Stanford University, USA
Kirstie Bellman	The Aerospace Corporation, USA
Dirk Beyer	LMU Munich, Germany
Nikolaj Bjorner	Microsoft Research, USA
Kalou Cabrera Castillos	LAAS-CNRS, France
Alessandro Cimatti	FBK-IRST, Italy
Misty Davies	NASA Ames Research Center, USA
Ewen Denney	Stinger Ghaffarian Technologies and NASA Ames Research Center, USA
Dino Distefano	Facebook, UK
Eric Feron	Georgia Institute of Technology, USA
Pierre-Loic Garoche	ONERA, France
Patrice Godefroid	Microsoft Research, USA
Alwyn Goodloe	NASA Langley Research Center, USA
Alberto Griggio	FBK-IRST, Italy
Aarti Gupta	Princeton University, USA
Arie Gurfinkel	University of Waterloo, Canada
John Harrison	Intel Corporation, USA
Klaus Havelund	Jet Propulsion Laboratory, California Institute of Technology, USA
Kelly Hayhurst	NASA Langley Research Center, USA
Mats Heimdahl	University of Minnesota, USA
Mike Hinchey	Lero-the Irish Software Engineering Research Centre, Ireland
Susmit Jha	SRI International, USA
Rajeev Joshi	Laboratory for Reliable Software, Jet Propulsion Laboratory, USA
Dejan Jovanović	SRI International, USA
Temesghen Kahsai	NASA Ames Research Center/CMU, USA
Gerwin Klein	Data61, CSIRO, Australia
Daniel Kroening	University of Oxford, UK
Wenchao Li	Boston University, USA
Lowry Michael	NASA Ames Research Center, USA
Jorge A Navas	SRI International, USA
Natasha Neogi	NASA Langley Research Center, USA
Meeko Oishi	University of New Mexico, USA

Lee Pike	Galois, Inc., USA
Zvonimir Rakamaric	University of Utah, USA
Murali Rangarajan	The Boeing Company, USA
Kristin Yvonne Rozier	Iowa State University, USA
Lael Rudd	Draper, USA
Philipp Ruemmer	Uppsala University, Sweden
Neha Rungta	Amazon Web Services, USA
John Rushby	SRI International, USA
Sriram Sankaranarayanan	University of Colorado, Boulder, USA
Martin Schäf	SRI International, USA
Cesare Tinelli	The University of Iowa, USA
Christoph Torens	German Aerospace Center, Institute of Flight Systems, Germany
Virginie Wiels	ONERA/DTIM, France

Additional Reviewers

Backeman, Peter	Hamon, Arnaud
Backes, John	He, Shaobo
Bittner, Benjamin	Hendrix, Joe
Blackshear, Sam	Howar, Falk
Calderón Trilla, José Manuel	Luckow, Kasper
Cattaruzza, Dario	Mattarei, Cristian
Chowdhury, Omar	Mercer, Eric
Cohen, Raphael	Mote, Mark
Dangl, Matthias	Mukherjee, Rajdeep
Dimjasevic, Marko	Poetzl, Daniel
Elliott, Trevor	Reynolds, Andrew
Erkok, Levent	Sanchez, Huascar
Galea, John	Sun, Youcheng
Gay, David	Tkachuk, Oksana
Gross, Kerianne	Zeljić, Aleksandar

Contents

An Automata-Theoretic Approach to Modeling Systems and Specifications over Infinite Data

Hadar Frenkel[1]([✉]), Orna Grumberg[1], and Sarai Sheinvald[2]

[1] Department of Computer Science, The Technion, Haifa, Israel
hfrenkel@cs.technion.ac.il
[2] Department of Software Engineering, ORT Braude Academic College,
Karmiel, Israel

Abstract. Data-parameterized systems model finite state systems over an infinite data domain. VLTL is an extension of LTL that uses variables in order to specify properties of computations over infinite data, and as such VLTL is suitable for specifying properties of data-parameterized systems. We present *Alternating Variable Büchi Word Automata* (AVBWs), a new model of automata over infinite alphabets, capable of modeling a significant fragment of VLTL. While alternating and non-deterministic Büchi automata over finite alphabets have the same expressive power, we show that this is not the case for infinite data domains, as we prove that AVBWs are strictly stronger than the previously defined Non-deterministic Variable Büchi Word Automata (NVBWs). However, while the emptiness problem is easy for NVBWs, it is undecidable for AVBWs. We present an algorithm for translating AVBWs to NVBWs in cases where such a translation is possible. Additionally, we characterize the structure of AVBWs that can be translated to NVBWs with our algorithm, and identify fragments of VLTL for which a direct NVBW construction exists. Since the emptiness problem is crucial in the automata-theoretic approach to model checking, our results give rise to a model-checking algorithm for a rich fragment of VLTL and systems over infinite data domains.

1 Introduction

Infinite data domains become increasingly relevant and wide-spread in real-life systems, and are integral in communication systems, e-commerce systems, large databases and more. Systems over infinite data domains were studied in several contexts and especially in the context of datalog systems [4] and XML documents [5,7], that are the standard of web documents.

Temporal logic, particularly LTL, is widely used for specifying properties of ongoing systems. However, LTL is unable to specify computations that handle infinite data. Consider, for example, a system of processes and a scheduler. If the set of processes is finite and known in advance, we can express and verify properties such as "every process is eventually active". However, if the system is dynamic, in which new processes can log in and out, and the total number of processes is unbounded, LTL is unable to express such a property.

© Springer International Publishing AG 2017
C. Barrett et al. (Eds.): NFM 2017, LNCS 10227, pp. 1–18, 2017.
DOI: 10.1007/978-3-319-57288-8_1

VLTL (LTL with variables) [11] extends LTL with variables that range over an infinite domain, making it a natural logic for specifying ongoing systems over infinite data domains. For the example above, a VLTL formula can be $\varphi_1 = \forall x : \ \mathsf{G}\,(loggedIn(x) \ \rightarrow \ \mathsf{F}\,(active(x)))$, where x ranges over the process IDs. Thus, the formula specifies that for every process ID, once it is logged in, it will eventually be active. Notice that this formula now specifies this property for an unbounded number of processes. As another example, the formula $\varphi_2 = \mathsf{G}\,\exists x(send(x) \wedge \mathsf{F}\,receive(x))$, where x ranges over the message contents (or message IDs), specifies that in every step of the computation, some message is sent, and this particular message is eventually received. Using variables enables handling infinitely many messages along a single computation.

In the *automata-theoretic approach to model checking* [18,19], both the system and the specification are modeled by automata whose languages match the set of computations of the system and the set of satisfying computations of the formula. Model-checking is then reduced to reasoning about these automata. For ongoing systems, automata over infinite words, particularly nondeterministic and alternating Büchi automata (NBWs and ABWs, respectively) are used [18]. Thus, for ongoing systems with infinite data and VLTL, a similar model is needed, capable of handling infinite alphabets. In [10,11], the authors suggested *nondeterministic variable Büchi word automata* (NVBWs), a model that augments NBWs with variables, and used it to construct a model-checking algorithm for a fragment of VLTL that is limited to $\exists$-quantifiers that appear only at the head of the formula.

The emptiness problem for NVBWs is NLOGSPACE-complete. Since the emptiness problem is crucial for model checking, NVBWs are an attractive model. However, they are quite weak. For example, NVBWs are unable to model the formula φ_2 above.

In this work, we present a new model for VLTL specifications, namely *alternating variable Büchi word automata* (AVBWs). These are an extension of NVBWs, which we prove to be stronger and able to express a much richer fragment of VLTL. Specifically, we show that AVBWs are able to express the entire fragment of $\exists^*$-VLTL, which is a fragment of VLTL with only $\exists$-quantifiers, whose position in the formula is unrestricted.

We now elaborate more on NVBWs and AVBWs. As mentioned, an NVBW $\mathcal{A}$ uses variables that range over an infinite alphabet Γ. A run of $\mathcal{A}$ on a word w assigns values to the variables in a way that matches the letters in w. For example, if a letter $a.8$ occurs in w, then a run of $\mathcal{A}$ may read $a.x$, where x is assigned 8. In addition, the variables may be reset at designated states along the run, and so $a.x$ can be later used for reading another letter $a.5$, provided that x has been reset. Resetting then allows reading an unbounded number of letters using a fixed set of variables. Another component of NVBWs is an inequality set E, that allows restricting variables from being assigned with the same value. Our new model of AVBWs extends NVBWs by adding *alternation*. An alternating automaton may split its run and continue reading the input along several different paths simultaneously, all of which must accept.

There is a well-known translation from LTL to ABW [18]. Thus, AVBWs are a natural candidate for modeling VLTL. Indeed, as we show, AVBWs are able to express all ∃*-VLTL, following a translation that is just as natural as the LTL to ABW translation. Existential quantifiers (anywhere) in the formula are translated to corresponding resets in the automaton. Moreover, unlike the finite alphabet case, in which NBWs and ABWs are equally expressive, in the infinite alphabet case alternation proves to be not only syntactically stronger but also semantically stronger, as we show that AVBWs are more expressive than NVBWs.

As we have noted, our goal is to provide a model which is suitable for a model-checking algorithm for VLTL, and that such a model should be easily tested for emptiness. However, we show that the strength of AVBWs comes with a price, and their emptiness problem is unfortunately undecidable. To keep the advantage of ease of translation of VLTL to AVBWs, as well as the ease of using NVBWs for model-checking purposes, we would then like to translate AVBWs to NVBWs, in cases where such a translation is possible. This allows us to enjoy the benefit of both models, and gives rise to a model-checking algorithm that is able to handle a richer fragment of VLTL than the one previously studied.

We present such a translation algorithm, inspired by the construction of [14]. As noted, such a translation is not always possible. Moreover, we show that there is no algorithm that is both sound and complete, even if we restrict completeness to require returning "no translation possible". Our algorithm is then sound but incomplete, and we present an example for which it will not halt. However, we give a characterization for AVBWs for which our algorithm does halt, relying on the graphical structure of the underlying automaton. The essence of the characterization is that translatable AVBWs do not have a cycle that contains a reset action which leads to an accepting state. Consider once again $\varphi_2 = G \exists x(send.x \land F\ receive.x)$. Here, we keep sending messages that must arrive eventually. However, there is no bound on when they will arrive. Since this is a global requirement, there must be some cycle that verifies it, and such cycles are exactly the ones that prevent the run of the translation algorithm from halting.

The importance of our algorithm and structural characterization is a twofold: (1) given an AVBW $\mathcal{A}$, one does not need to know the semantics of $\mathcal{A}$ in order to know if it is translatable, and to automatically translate $\mathcal{A}$ to an equivalent NVBW; and (2) Given a general ∃*-VLTL formula, one can easily construct an equivalent AVBW $\mathcal{A}$, use our characterization to check whether it is translatable, and continue with the NVBW that our translation outputs.

In addition to the results above, we also study fragments of ∃*-VLTL that have a direct construction to NVBWs, making them an "easy" case for modeling and model checking.

Related Work. Other models of automata over infinite alphabets have been defined and studied. In [13] the authors define *register automata over infinite alphabets*, and study their decidability properties. [16] use register automata as well as *pebble automata* to reason about first order logic and monadic second order logic, and to describe XML documents. [3] limit the number of variables and use extended first order logic to reason about both XML and some verification properties. In [4] the authors model infinite state systems as well as infinite data domains, in order to express some extension of monadic first order logic. Our model is closer to finite automata over infinite words than the models above, making it easier to understand. Moreover, due to their similarity to ABWs, we were able to construct a natural translation of $\exists^*$-VLTL to AVBWs, inspired by [18]. We then translate AVBWs to NVBWs. Our construction is consistent with [14] which provides an algorithm for translating ABWs to NBWs. However, in our case additional manipulations are needed in order to handle the variables and track their possible assignments.

The notion of LTL over infinite data domains was studied also in the field of runtime verification (RV) [1,2,8]. Specifically, in [1], the authors suggest a model of quantified automata with variables, in order to capture traces of computations with different data values. The purpose in RV is to check whether a single given trace satisfies the specification. Moreover, the traces under inspection are finite traces. This comes into play in [1] where the authors use the specific data values that appear on such a trace in order to evaluate satisfiability. In [2] the authors suggest a 3-valued semantics in order to capture the uncertainty derived from the fact that traces are finite. Our work approaches infinite data domains in a different manner. Since we want to capture both infinite data domains and infinite traces, we need a much more expressive model, and this is where AVBWs come into play.

2   Preliminaries

Given a finite set of directions D, a *D-tree* T is a set $T \subseteq D^*$. The root of T is the empty word ϵ. A node x of T is a word over D that describes the path from the root of T to x. That is, for a word $d = d_1, d_2, \cdots, d_n$ there is a path in the tree $\pi = \epsilon, d_1, d_1d_2, \cdots, d_1d_2 \cdots d_n$ such that every word $d'd_i$ is a successor of the previous word d'. For a word $w \cdot x \in D^*$ where $w \in D^*$ and $x \in D$, if $w \cdot x \in T$ then $w \in T$, i.e. the tree is prefix closed. A successor of a node $w \in T$ is of the form $w \cdot x$ for $x \in D$.

Given a set L, an *L-labeled D-tree* is a pair $\langle T, f \rangle$ where T is a D-tree, and $f : T \rightarrow L$ is a labeling function that labels each node in T by an element of L.

A *non-deterministic Büchi automaton* over infinite words (NBW) [6] is a tuple $\mathcal{B} = \langle \Sigma, Q, q_0, \delta, \alpha \rangle$ where Σ is a finite alphabet; Q is a finite set of states; $q_0 \in Q$ is the initial state; $\alpha \subseteq Q$ is a set of accepting states; and $\delta : Q \times \Sigma \rightarrow 2^Q$ is the transition function. For a word $\rho \in \Sigma^\omega$, we denote by ρ_i the letter of ρ in position i.

A *run* of $\mathcal{B}$ on a word $\rho \in \Sigma^\omega$ is an infinite sequence of states $q_0, q_1, q_2, \cdots \in Q^\omega$, that is consistent with δ, i.e., q_0 is the initial state and $\forall i > 0 : q_i \in \delta(q_{i-1}, \rho_i)$. A run of $\mathcal{B}$ is *accepting* if it visits some state of α infinitely often. We say that $\mathcal{B}$ *accepts* a word ρ if there exists an accepting run of $\mathcal{B}$ on ρ. The *language* of $\mathcal{B}$, denoted $\mathcal{L}(\mathcal{B})$, is the set of words accepted by $\mathcal{B}$.

An *alternating Büchi automaton* over infinite words (ABW) [15] is a tuple $\mathcal{B}_A = \langle \Sigma, Q, q_0, \delta, \alpha \rangle$ where Σ, Q, q_0 and α are as in NBW. The transition relation is $\delta : Q \times \Sigma \to B^+(Q)$, where $B^+(Q)$ is the set of positive boolean formulas over the set of states, i.e. formulas that include only the boolean operators $\wedge$ and $\vee$[1]. For example, if $\delta(q, a) = (q_1 \wedge q_2) \vee q_3$, then, by reading a from q, the ABW $\mathcal{B}_A$ moves to either both q_1 and q_2, or to q_3. We assume that δ is given in a disjunctive normal form (DNF).

A *run* of an ABW is a Q-labeled Q-tree. Disjunctions are equivalent to nondeterministic choices, and so every disjunct induces a tree. A conjunction induces a split to two or more successors. For example, $\delta(q, a) = (q_1 \wedge q_2) \vee q_3$ induces two trees. In the first, q has two successors, q_1 and q_2. In the second tree the only successor of q is q_3. A run is *accepting* if every infinite path in the corresponding tree visits a state from α infinitely often, and every finite path ends with *true*. The notions of acceptance and language are as in NBWs.

We say that an automaton (either NBW or ABW) is a *labeled automaton* if its definition also includes a labeling function $\mathscr{L} : Q \to L$ for its states, where L is a set of labels. We use this notion to conveniently define variable automata later on.

We assume that the reader is familiar with the syntax and semantics of LTL.

Variable LTL, or *VLTL*, as defined in [11], extends LTL by augmenting atomic propositions with variables. Let AP be a set of parameterized atomic propositions, let X be a finite set of variables, and let $\bar{x}$ be a vector of variables. Then, the formulas in VLTL are over $AP \times X$, thus allowing the propositions to carry data from an infinite data domain. We inductively define the syntax of VLTL.

– For every $a \in AP$ and $x \in X$ the formulas $a.x$ and $\neg a.x$ are VLTL formulas[2].
– For a VLTL formula $\varphi(\bar{x})$ and $x \in X$, the formulas $\exists x \varphi(\bar{x})$ and $\forall x \varphi(\bar{x})$ are in VLTL.
– If $\varphi_1(\bar{x})$ and $\varphi_2(\bar{x})$ are VLTL formulas, then so are $\varphi_1(\bar{x}) \vee \varphi_2(\bar{x})$; $\varphi_1(\bar{x}) \wedge \varphi_2(\bar{x})$; $\mathsf{X}\varphi(\bar{x})$; $\mathsf{F}\varphi_1(\bar{x})$; $\mathsf{G}\varphi_1(\bar{x})$; $\varphi_1(\bar{x}) \mathsf{U} \varphi_2(\bar{x})$; and $\varphi_1(\bar{x}) \mathsf{V} \varphi_2(\bar{x})$, where V is the release operator, which is the dual operator of U.

Given an alphabet Γ, an assignment $\theta : X \to \Gamma$, and a word $\rho \in (2^{AP \times \Gamma})^\omega$, we denote $\rho \vDash_\theta \varphi(\bar{x})$ if $\rho \vDash \varphi(\bar{x})_{[\bar{x} \leftarrow \theta(\bar{x})]}$ under the standard semantics of LTL. For example, for $\rho = \{p.1\}^\omega$ it holds that $\rho \vDash_\theta \mathsf{G}p.x$ for $\theta(x) = 1$.

We denote $\rho \vDash_\theta \exists x \varphi(\bar{x})$ if there exists an assignment $x \leftarrow d$ to the variable x such that $\rho \vDash_\theta \varphi(\bar{x})_{[x \leftarrow d]}$, where $\vDash_\theta$ is as defined before. We denote $\rho \vDash_\theta \forall x \varphi(\bar{x})$ if for every assignment $x \leftarrow d$ to the variable x, it holds that $\rho \vDash_\theta \varphi(\bar{x})_{[x \leftarrow d]}$.

We say that a formula φ is *closed* if every occurrence of a variable in φ is under the scope of a quantifier. Notice that the satisfaction of closed formulas is independent of specific assignments. For a closed formula φ over $\bar{x}$, we then write $\rho \vDash \varphi(\bar{x})$.

The logic $\exists^*$-VLTL is the set of all closed VLTL formulas in negation normal form (NNF) that only use the $\exists$-quantifier. Note that the $\exists$-quantifier may appear

---

[1] In particular, the negation operator is not included.
[2] The semantics of $\neg a.x$ is regarding a specific value. I.e., if $x = d$ then $a.d$ does not hold, but $a.d'$ for $d \neq d'$ may hold.

anywhere in the formula. The logic $\exists^*_{pnf}$-VLTL is the set of all $\exists^*$-VLTL formulas in prenex normal form, i.e., $\exists$-quantifiers appear only at the beginning of the formula.

The *language* of a formula φ, denoted $\mathcal{L}(\varphi)$, is the set of computations that satisfy φ.

We now define *non-deterministic variable Büchi automata* over infinite words (NVBWs). Our definition is tailored to model VLTL formulas, and thus is slightly different from the definition in [10]. Specifically, the alphabet consists of subsets of $AP \times X$, where AP is a finite set of parameterized atomic propositions.

An NVBW is a tuple $\mathcal{A} = \langle \mathcal{B}, \Gamma, E \rangle$, where $\mathcal{B} = \langle 2^{AP \times X}, Q, q_0, \delta, reset, \alpha \rangle$ is a labeled NBW, X is a finite set of variables, $reset : Q \rightarrow 2^X$ is a labeling function that labels each state q with the set of variables that are reset at q, the set $E \subseteq \{x_i \neq x_j | x_i, x_j \in X\}$ is an inequality set over X, and Γ is an infinite alphabet.

A *run* of an NVBW $\mathcal{A} = \langle \mathcal{B}, \Gamma, E \rangle$ on a word $\rho \in (2^{AP \times \Gamma})^\omega$, where $\rho = \rho_1 \rho_2 \cdots$ is a pair $\langle \pi, r \rangle$ where $\pi = (q_0, q_1, q_2, \cdots)$, is an infinite sequence of states, and $r = (r_0, r_1, \cdots)$ is a sequence of mappings $r_i : X \rightarrow \Gamma$ such that:

1. There exists a word $z \in (2^{AP \times X})^\omega$ such that $\forall i : r_i(z_i) = \rho_i$ and π is a run of $\mathcal{B}$ on z. We say that z is a *symbolic word* that is consistent on $\langle \pi, r \rangle$ with the *concrete word* ρ.
2. The run respects the reset actions: for every $i \in \mathbb{N}, x \in X$, if $x \notin reset(q_i)$ then $r_i(x) = r_{i+1}(x)$.
3. The run respects E: for every $i \in \mathbb{N}$ and for every inequality $(x_m \neq x_l) \in E$ it holds that $r_i(x_l) \neq r_i(x_m)$.

A run $\langle \pi, r \rangle$ on ρ is *accepting* if π is an accepting run of $\mathcal{B}$ on a symbolic word z that corresponds to ρ on $\langle \pi, r \rangle$, i.e. π visits α infinitely often. The notion of acceptance and language are as in NBWs.

Intuitively, a run of an NVBW $\mathcal{A}$ on a word ρ assigns each occurrence of a variable a letter from Γ. A variable can "forget" its value only if a reset action occurred. The inequality set E prevents from certain variables to be assigned with the same value.

We say that an NVBW $\mathcal{A}$ *expresses* a formula φ if $\mathcal{L}(\mathcal{A}) = \mathcal{L}(\varphi)$.

Example 1. Consider the concrete word $\rho = \{send.1\}, (\{send.2, rec.1\}, \{send.1, rec.2\})^\omega$. In an NVBW $\mathcal{A}$, a corresponding symbolic word can be $z = \{send.x_1\}, (\{send.x_2, rec.x_1\}, \{send.x_1, rec.x_2\})^\omega$. If $\mathcal{A}$ includes reset actions for x_1 and x_2 in every even state in some path of $\mathcal{A}$, then another concrete word consistent with z can be $\rho' = \{send.1\}, \{send.2, rec.1\}, \{send.3, rec.4\}, \{send.4, rec.3\}, \{send.5, rec.6\}, \cdots$, since the values of x_1 and x_2 can change at every even state.

3 Variable Automata: Non-determinism Vs. Alternation

In Sect. 5 we show that NVBWs are useful for model checking in our setting, since they have good decidability properties. In particular, there is a polynomial construction for intersection of NVBWs, and their emptiness problem is

NLOGSPACE-complete [10]. In Sect. 4 we describe a translation of $\exists^*_{pnf}$-VLTL formulas to NVBWs. We now show that NVBWs are too weak to express all VLTL formulas, or even all $\exists^*$-VLTL formulas. It follows that $\exists^*$-VLTL is strictly more expressive than $\exists^*_{pnf}$-VLTL. Nevertheless, we use NVBWs for model checking at least for some fragments of $\exists^*$-VLTL.

Before discussing the properties of variable automata, we first give some motivation for their definition, as given in Sect. 2. In particular, we give motivation for the *reset* labeling function and for E, the inequity set.

Example 2. We begin with resets. Consider the $\exists^*$-VLTL formula $\varphi_1 = G\exists x(a.x)$. One possible computation satisfying φ_1 is $\rho = a.1, a.2, a.3, \cdots$. No NVBW with a finite number of variables can read ρ, unless some variable is reassigned. The reset action allows these reassignments.

Example 3. To see the necessity of the inequality set E, consider the $\exists^*$-VLTL formula $\varphi_2 = \exists x(G\neg a.x)$. We can use a variable x to store a value that never appears along the computation with a. Imposing inequality restrictions on x with all other variables makes sure that the value assigned to x does not appear along the computation via assignments to other variables. Note that if the logic does not allow negations at all, the inequality set is not needed.

3.1 NVBWs Are Not Expressive Enough for $\exists^*$-VLTL

We first show that NVBWs cannot express every $\exists^*$-VLTL formula.

Lemma 1. *The formula $\varphi_{G\exists} = G\exists x(b.x \wedge Fa.x)$ cannot be expressed by an NVBW.*

Proof. Consider the following word ρ over $AP = \{a, b\}$ and $\Gamma = \mathbb{N}$.

$$\rho = \{a.1, b.1\}, \{a.2, b.2\}, \{a.2, b.3\}, \{a.3, b.4\}, .., \{a.4, b.8\}.., \{a.(k+1), b.2^k\}, \cdots$$

i.e., $b.(i)$ occurs in ρ_i, and $a.(i+1)$ occurs for the first time in ρ_{2^i} and continues until $\rho_{2^{i+1}-1}$.

It is easy to see that ρ satisfies $\varphi_{G\exists}$ since at step t for $x = t$ we have that $b.t$ holds, and at some point in the future, specifically at step 2^{t-1}, the proposition $a.t$ will hold.

Assume, by way of contradiction, that $\mathcal{A}$ is an NVBW with m variables that expresses $\varphi_{G\exists}$. Then over a sub-word with more than m values for b, one variable must be reset and used for two different values. We can then create a different computation in which the value that was "forgotten" never appears with a, thus not satisfying $\varphi_{G\exists}$, but accepted by $\mathcal{A}$, a contradiction. $\square$

Not only $\exists$-quantifiers are problematic for NVBWs. NVBWs cannot handle $\forall$-quantifiers, even in PNF. The proof of the following Lemma is almost identical to the proof of Lemma 1.

Lemma 2. *The formula $\varphi = \forall x : G(a.x \rightarrow Fb.x)$ cannot be expressed by an NVBW.*

3.2 Alternating Variable Büchi Automata

In Sect. 3.1 we have shown that NVBWs are not expressive enough, even when considering only the fragment of $\exists^*$-VLTL. We now introduce *alternating variable Büchi automata* over infinite words (AVBW), and show that they can express all of $\exists^*$-VLTL. We study their expressibility and decidability properties.

Definition 1. *An AVBW is a tuple $\mathcal{A} = \langle \mathcal{B}_A, \Gamma, E \rangle$ where $\mathcal{B}_A = \langle 2^{AP \times X}, Q, q_0, \delta, reset, \alpha \rangle$ is a labeled ABW, X is a finite set of variables, $reset : Q \to 2^X$ is a labeling function that labels every state q with the set of variables that are reset at q, the set E is an inequality set, and Γ is an infinite alphabet. We only allow words in which a proposition $a.\gamma$ for $\gamma \in \Gamma$ appears at most once in every computation step, i.e., no word can contain both $a.\gamma$ and $a.\gamma'$ for $\gamma \neq \gamma'$ at the same position.*

A *run* of an AVBW $\mathcal{A}$ on a word $\rho \in (2^{AP \times \Gamma})^\omega$ is a pair $\langle T, r \rangle$ where T is a Q-labeled Q-tree and r labels each node t of T by a function $r_t : X \to \Gamma$ such that:

1. The root of T is labeled with q_0.
2. For each path π on T there exists a symbolic word $z_\pi \in (2^{AP \times X})^\omega$ such that $r_{\pi_i}((z_\pi)_i) = \rho_i$.
3. The run respects δ: for each node $t \in T$ labeled by q of depth i on path π, the successors of t are labeled by $q_1, \cdots, q_t$ iff one of the conjuncts in $\delta(q, (z_\pi)_i)$ is exactly $\bigwedge_{j=1..t} q_j$.
4. The run respects the reset actions: if t' is a child node of t labeled by q and $x \notin reset\,(q)$, then $r_t(x) = r_{t'}(x)$.
5. The run respects E: for every $(x_i \neq x_j) \in E$ and for every node $t \in T$ it holds that $r_t(x_i) \neq r_t(x_j)$.

Intuitively, much like in NVBWs, the variables in every node in the run tree are assigned values in a way that respects the resets and the inequality set.

A run $\langle T, r \rangle$ on ρ is *accepting* if every infinite path π is labeled infinitely often with states in α. The notion of acceptance and language are as usual. Note that the same variable can be assigned different values on different paths.

Just like ABWs, AVBWs are naturally closed under union and intersection. However, unlike ABWs, they are not closed under complementation. We prove this in Sect. 3.4.

3.3 AVBWs Can Express All of $\exists^*$-VLTL

We now show that AVBWs can express $\exists^*$-VLTL. Together with Lemma 1, we reach the following surprising theorem.

Theorem 1. *AVBWs are strictly more expressive than NVBWs.*

This is in contrast to the finite alphabet case, where there are known algorithms for translating ABWs to NBWs [14].

Theorem 2. *Every $\exists^*$-VLTL φ formula can be expressed by an AVBW $\mathcal{A}_\varphi$.*

We start with an example AVBW for $\varphi_{G\exists} = \mathsf{G}\,\exists x(b.x \wedge \mathsf{F}\,a.x)$ from Lemma 1.

Example 4. Let $\mathcal{A} = \langle \mathcal{B}, \mathbb{N}, \emptyset \rangle$ where $\mathcal{B} = \langle 2^{AP \times \{x_1, x_2, x_3\}}, \{q_0, q_1\}, q_0, \delta, reset, \{q_0\}\rangle$.

- $reset(q_0) = \{x_1, x_2\}$, $reset(q_1) = \{x_2, x_3\}$
- $\delta(q_0, \{b.x_1\}) = \delta(q_0, \{a.x_2, b.x_1\}) = q_0 \wedge q_1$
  $\delta(q_0, \{b.x_1, a.x_1\}) = true$
  $\delta(q_1, \{b.x_2\}) = \delta(q_1, \{a.x_2\}) = \delta(q_1, \{a.x_2, b.x_3\}) = q_1$
  $\delta(q_1, \{a.x_1\}) = \delta(q_1, \{a.x_1, b.x_2\}) = true$

Intuitively, q_0 makes sure that at each step there is some value with which b holds. The run then splits to both q_0 and q_1. The state q_1 waits for a with the same value as was seen in q_0 (since x_1 is not reset along this path, it must be the same value), and uses x_2, x_3 to ignore other values that are attached to a, b. The state q_0 continues to read values of b (which again splits the run), while using x_2 to ignore values assigned to a. See Fig. 1 for a graphic representation of $\mathcal{A}$.

We now proceed to the proof of Theorem 2.

Proof. Let φ be an $\exists^*$-VLTL formula. We present an explicit construction of $\mathcal{A}_\varphi$, based on the construction of [18] and by using resets to handle the $\exists$-quantifiers, and inequalities to handle negations. First, we rename the variables in φ and get an equivalent formula φ', where each existential quantifier bounds a variable with a different name. For example, if $\varphi = \exists x(a.x\,\mathsf{U}\,\exists x(b.x))$ then $\varphi' = \exists x_1(a.x_1\,\mathsf{U}\,\exists x_2(b.x_2))$. Let $sub(\varphi)$ denote all sub-formulas of φ and let $var(\varphi)$ denote the set of variables that appear in φ.

Let $\mathcal{A}_\varphi = \langle \mathcal{B}, \Gamma, E \rangle$ where $\mathcal{B} = \langle 2^{AP \times X}, Q, q_0 = \varphi', \delta, reset, \alpha \rangle$ and where

- $X = var(\varphi') \cup \{x_p | p \in AP\}$

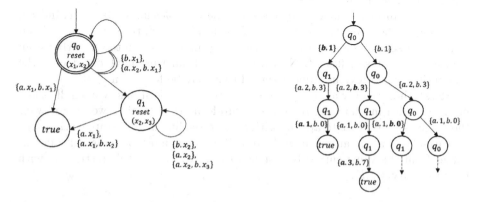

Fig. 1. The AVBW $\mathcal{A}$ described in Example 4 and an example of a run. The double arch between transitions represents an "and" in δ.

- $Q = sub(\varphi')$
- $\forall q \in Q : \{x_p | p \in AP\} \subseteq reset(q)$ and, for $q = \exists x_1, \cdots, \exists x_n \eta$, we have $\{x_1, \cdots, x_n\} \subseteq reset(q)$.
- $E = \{x \neq x' | x' \in X, \exists a : \neg a.x \in sub(\varphi')\}$.
- α consists of all states of the form $\eta \vee \psi$.

The set of states Q consists of all sub-formulas of φ'. Intuitively, at every given point there is an assignment to the variables, that may change via resets. If an accepting run of $\mathcal{A}$ on ρ visits a state ψ, then the suffix of ρ that is read from ψ satisfies ψ under the current assignment to the variables. The set of variables X consists of all variables in φ', as well as a variable x_p for every atomic proposition $p \in AP$. The additional variables enable the run to read and ignore currently irrelevant inputs. For example, for $\varphi = \exists x F\ (b.x \wedge a.x)$, we want to read (and ignore) values of a and b until $a.\gamma \wedge b.\gamma$ occurs with some γ.

Let A be a subset of $AP \times X$ (recall that $\mathcal{B}$ is defined over the alphabet $2^{AP \times X}$). We define δ as follows.

- $\delta(a.x, A) = true$ if $a.x \in A$ and $\delta(a.x, A) = false$ if $a.x \notin A$
- $\delta(\neg a.x, A) = true$ if $a.x \notin A$ and $\delta(\neg a.x, A) = false$ if $a.x \in A$
- $\delta(\eta \wedge \psi, A) = \delta(\eta, A) \wedge \delta(\psi, A)$.
- $\delta(\eta \vee \psi, A) = \delta(\eta, A) \vee \delta(\psi, A)$
- $\delta(X \eta, A) = \eta$
- $\delta(\eta \cup \psi, A) = \delta(\psi, A) \vee (\delta(\eta, A) \wedge \eta \cup \psi)$
- $\delta(\eta \vee \psi, A) = \delta(\eta \wedge \psi, A) \vee (\delta(\psi, A) \wedge \eta \vee \psi)$
- $\delta(\exists x \eta, A) = \delta(\eta, A)$

Note that since we only use formulas in NNF, we define δ for both *"and"* and *"or"*, as well as for $\cup$ (until) and $\vee$ (release) operators.

Correctness. It can be shown that a word ρ is accepted from a state ψ with a variable assignment r iff $\rho \models_r \psi$. We elaborate on how the construction handles the $\exists$-quantifier and negations.

The $\exists$-quantifier is handled by resetting the variables under its scope. Indeed, according to the semantics of $\exists$, for ψ of the form $\exists x : \psi'$, the suffix of ρ holds if ψ' holds for some assignment to x. Resetting x allows the run to correctly assign x in a way that satisfies ψ'. Notice also that from this point on, due to the $\exists$ quantifier, the previous value assigned to x may be forgotten.

Recall that we only allow negations on atomic propositions. We handle these negations with inequalities. If $\neg a.x$ is a sub-formula of φ, then we do not want the value assigned to x to appear with a when reading a from state $\neg a.x$. Thus, all variables that a can occur with from state $\neg a.x$ must be assigned different values from the value currently assigned to x. We express this restriction with the inequality set E.   □

3.4   AVBWs Are Not Complementable

As mentioned before, unlike ABWs, AVBWs are not complementable. To prove this, we show that $\forall^*$-VLTL cannot generally be expressed by AVBWs. Since negating an $\exists^*$-VLTL formula produces a $\forall^*$-VLTL formula, the result follows.

Theorem 3. *There is no AVBW that expresses $\varphi_\forall = \forall x F a.x$.*

Proof. Obviously, if the alphabet is not countable, then it cannot be enumerated by a computation. However, the claim holds also for countable alphabets. Assume by way of contradiction that there exists an AVBW $\mathcal{A}$ that expresses $\varphi_\forall$ for $\Gamma = \mathbb{N}$. Then $\mathcal{A}$ accepts $w = a.0a.1a.2\cdots$. Since the variables are not sensitive to their precise contents but only to inequalities among the values, it is easy to see that the accepting run of $\mathcal{A}$ on w can also be used to read $w^1 = a.1a.2\cdots$, in which the value 0 never occurs.   □

The negation of the above $\varphi_\forall$ is in $\exists^*$-VLTL, thus there is an AVBW that expresses it.

Corollary 1. *AVBWs are not complementable.*

Corollary 2. $\forall^*$-*VLTL is not expressible by AVBWs.*

3.5   Variable Automata: From AVBW to NVBW

The emptiness problem for NVBWs is NLOGSPACE-complete [10]. In the context of model checking, this is an important property. We now show that for AVBWs, the emptiness problem is undecidable.

Lemma 3. *The emptiness problem for AVBWs is undecidable.*

Proof. According to [17], the satisfiability problem for $\exists^*$-VLTL is undecidable. The satisfiability of a formula φ is equivalent to the nonemptiness of an automaton that expresses φ. Since we have showed that every $\exists^*$-VLTL formula can be expressed by an AVBW, the proof follows.   □

Since the emptiness problem for NVBWs is easy, we are motivated to translate AVBWs to NVBWs in order to model check properties that are expressed by AVBWs. In particular, it will enable us to model check $\exists^*$-VLTL properties. This, however, is not possible in general since AVBWs are strictly more expressive than NVBWs (Theorem 1).

In this section we present an incomplete algorithm, which translates an interesting subset of AVBWs to equivalent NVBWs. We later give a structural characterization for AVBWs that can be translated by our algorithm to NVBWs.

3.5.1   From AVBW to NVBW

Our algorithm is inspired by the construction of [14] for translating ABW to NBW. In [14] the states of the NBW are of the form $\langle S, O \rangle$ where S is the set of the states the ABW is currently at, and O is the set of states from paths that "owe" a visit to an accepting state. While running the NBW on a word ρ, accepting states are removed from O, until $O = \emptyset$. Thus, when $O = \emptyset$, all paths have visited an accepting state at least once. Now, O is again set to be S, and a new round begins. The accepting states of the NBW are states of the form $\langle S, \emptyset \rangle$.

Here, we wish to translate an AVBW $\mathcal{A}$ to an NVBW $\mathcal{A}'$. For simplicity, we assume that $E = \emptyset$. The changes for the case where $E \neq \emptyset$ are described later.

In our case, the variables make the translation harder, and as shown before, even impossible in some cases. In addition to S, O we must also remember which variables are currently in use, and might hold values from previous states. In our translation, the states of the NBW are tuples containing S, O and the sets of variables in use. Since AVBWs allow different paths to assign different values to the same variable, the translation to an NVBW must allocate a new variable for each such assignment. We also need to release variables that were reset in the AVBW, in order to reuse them in the NVBW to avoid defining infinitely many variables. Since we need to know which variables are in use at each step of a run of $\mathcal{A}$, we dynamically allocate both the states and the transitions of $\mathcal{A}'$.

Thus, δ', the transition function of $\mathcal{A}'$, is defined dynamically during the run of our algorithm, as do the states of $\mathcal{A}'$. Moreover, since each path may allocate different values to the same variable, it might be the case that the same variable holds infinitely many values (from different paths). Such a variable induces an unbounded number of variables in $\mathcal{A}'$. Our algorithm halts when no new states are created, and since the fresh variables are part of the created states, creating infinitely many such variables causes our algorithm not to halt. Therefore, the algorithm is incomplete.

Algorithm AVBWtoNVBW: Let $\mathcal{A} = \langle \mathcal{B}_\mathcal{A}, \Gamma, E \rangle$ be an AVBW, where $\mathcal{B}_\mathcal{A} = \langle 2^X, Q, q_0, \delta, reset, \alpha \rangle$. For simplicity we assume that $\mathcal{B}_\mathcal{A}$ is defined over the alphabet 2^X instead of $2^{AP \times X}$. Recall that we assume that $\delta(q, X')$ is in DNF for all $q \in Q, X' \subseteq X$. Let $\mathcal{A}' = \langle \mathcal{B}', \Gamma, E' \rangle$ be an NVBW where $\mathcal{B}' = \langle 2^Z, Q', q_0', \delta', reset', \alpha' \rangle$, and[3]:

- $Z = \{z_i | i = 0..k\}$ is the set of variables. k can be finite or infinite, according to the translation. If $|Z| < \infty$ then the AVBW is translatable to an NVBW.
- $Q' \subseteq 2^{Q \times 2^{X \times Z}} \times 2^{Q \times 2^{X \times Z}}$. The states of $\mathcal{A}'$ are pairs $\langle S, O \rangle$. Each of S, O is a set of pairs of type $\langle q, f_q \rangle$ where $q \in Q$, and $f_q : X \to Z$ is a mapping from the variables of $\mathcal{A}$ to the variables of $\mathcal{A}'$. At each state we need to know how many different values can be assigned to a variable $x \in X$ by $\mathcal{A}$, and create variables $z_i \in Z$ accordingly, in order to keep track of the different values of x.
- $q_0' = \langle \{(q_0, \emptyset)\}, \emptyset \rangle$. The initial state of $\mathcal{A}'$ is the initial state of $\mathcal{A}$ with no additional mappings.
- $\alpha' = 2^{Q \times 2^{X \times Z}} \times \emptyset$. The accepting states of $\mathcal{A}'$ are states for which $O = \emptyset$, i.e., all paths in $\mathcal{A}$ have visited an accepting state.

---

[3] Comments to the algorithm are given in gray.

1. Preprocessing: For each $q \in Q$: if there is no accepting state or *true* reachable from q then replace q with *false*. This is in order to remove loops that may prevent halting, but, in fact, are redundant since they do not lead to an accepting state.
2. Initiation: set $S = \{\langle q_0, \emptyset \rangle\}, O = \emptyset, Q_{\text{new}} = \{\langle S, O \rangle\}, Q_{\text{old}} = \emptyset, \text{vars} = \emptyset, Z = \emptyset$. The purpose of S, O is as explained above; $Q_{\text{new}}, Q_{\text{old}}$ keep track of the changes in the states that the algorithm creates, in order to halt when no new states are created; *vars* holds variables of Z that are currently in use.
3. We iteratively define $\delta'(\langle S, O \rangle, X')$ for $\langle S, O \rangle \in Q_{\text{new}}$, as long as new states are created, i.e. while $Q_{\text{new}} \not\subseteq Q_{\text{old}}$
   (a) Set: $S' = O' = \emptyset, Z' = \emptyset, Z_{\text{reset}} = \emptyset$. The purpose of Z_{reset} is to reset fresh variables, in order to reduce the number of states; at each step, Z' holds the variables in Z which label the current edge (and are the image of the variables in X which label the corresponding edges in $\mathcal{A}$). The group Z_{reset} is initialized at every iteration of the algorithm.
   (b) $Q_{\text{old}} = Q_{\text{old}} \cup \{\langle S, O \rangle\}$
   (c) $Q_{\text{new}} = Q_{\text{new}} \setminus \{\langle S, O \rangle\}$
   (d) For each $\langle q, f_q \rangle \in S$ and $X' \subseteq X$, let $P_q \subseteq Q$ be a minimal set of states with $P_q \models \delta(q, X')$.
      i. Create a state $\langle p, f_p \rangle$ for each $p \in P_q$. The function f_p is initialized to $f_p(x) = f_q(x)$ for $x \notin \text{reset}(p)$. I.e., every successor state p of q remembers the same assignments to variables as in q, but releases the assignments to variables that were reset in p.
      ii. For $x \in X'$ with $x \in \text{dom}(f_q)$, update $Z' = Z' \cup \{f_q(x)\}$
      iii For each $x \in X'$ with $x \notin \text{dom}(f_q)$, let $i \in \mathbb{N}$ be the minimal index for which $z_i \notin \text{vars}$.
         A. Add to f_p the mapping $f_p(x) = z_i$ if $x \notin \text{reset}(p)$.
         B. Update $\text{vars} = \text{vars} \cup \{z_i\}, Z' = Z' \cup \{z_i\}, Z_{\text{reset}} = Z_{\text{reset}} \cup \{z_i\}, Z = Z \cup \{z_i\}. z_i$ may already be in Z, if it was introduced earlier.
      iv. Define $S_{P_q} = \{\langle p, f_p \rangle\}_{p \in P_q}$
      v. If $O \neq \emptyset$: define $O_{P_q} = S_{P_q}$ if $\langle q, f_q \rangle \in O$. I.e., add to O' only successors states of states from O.
      vi. If $O = \emptyset$: define $O_{P_q} = S_{P_q}$
   (e) Define $S' = \bigcup_{\langle q, f_q \rangle \in S} S_{P_q}, O' = \left(\bigcup_{\langle q, f_q \rangle \in O} O_{P_q} \right) \setminus \{\langle p, f_p \rangle\}_{p \in \alpha}$
   (f) Add $\{z_i | z_i \in Z_{\text{reset}}\}$ to the reset function of previous state, $\langle S, O \rangle$. I.e., $\text{reset}'(\langle S, O \rangle) = \text{reset}'(\langle S, O \rangle) \cup \{z_i | z_i \in Z_{\text{reset}}\}$.
   (g) Define $\langle S', O' \rangle \in \delta'(\langle S, O \rangle, Z')$
   (h) Update $Q_{\text{new}} = Q_{\text{new}} \cup \{\langle S', O' \rangle\}$
   (i) If for $z_i \in \text{vars}$ it holds that for all $\langle S, O \rangle \in Q_{\text{new}}$, for all $\langle p, f_p \rangle \in S$ we have $z_i \notin \text{range}(f_q)$, then:
      i. $\text{vars} = \text{vars} \setminus \{z_i\}$.
      ii. add z_i to $\text{reset}'(\langle S', O' \rangle)$
      Here we release variables of Z that are no longer in use. The way to do so is to reset them, thus $\mathcal{A}'$ can assign them a new value, and to delete them from *vars* so they can be in use in following transitions.
4. Set $Q' = Q_{\text{old}}$

To handle cases where $E \neq \emptyset$, instead of mapping x to any unmapped variable $z_i \in Z$, each variable x may be mapped only to a unique set $\{z_{x_i}\}_{i \in I_x}$. Then, we define $E' = \{z_{x_i} \neq z_{x'_j} | i \in I_x, j \in I_{x'}, (x \neq x') \in E\}$. Notice that this does not change the cardinality of Z.

3.5.2   A Structural Characterization of Translatable AVBWs

In order to define a structural characterization, we wish to refer to an AVBW $\mathcal{A}$ as a directed graph $G_\mathcal{A}$ whose nodes are the states of $\mathcal{A}$. There is an edge from q to q' iff q' is in $\delta(q, A)$ for some $A \subseteq X$. For example, if $\delta(q, x) = q_1 \vee (q_2 \wedge q_3)$ then there are edges from q to q_1, q_2 and q_3.

Definition 2. An x-cycle in an AVBW A is a cycle $q^0, q^1, \cdots, q^k, q^{k+1}$ where $q^{k+1} = q^0$, of states in $G_\mathcal{A}$ such that:

1. For all $1 \leq i \leq k+1$ it holds that q^i is in $\delta(q^{i-1}, A)$ for some $A \subseteq X$.
2. There exists $1 \leq i \leq k+1$ such that q^i is in $\delta(q^{i-1}, A)$ for $A \subseteq X$ and $x \in A$.
   i.e. there is an edge from one state to another on the cycle, labeled x.

Theorem 4. Assume the preprocessing of stage 1 in the algorithm has been applied, resulting in an AVBW $\mathcal{A}$. Algorithm AVBWtoNVBW halts on $\mathcal{A}$ and returns an equivalent NVBW iff for every x-cycle $\mathcal{C}$ in $G_\mathcal{A}$ one of the following holds:

1. For every q on $\mathcal{C}$ it holds that $x \notin reset(q)$.
2. For every state q on a path from the initial state to $\mathcal{C}$ with $q_1 \wedge q_2 \in \delta(q, A)$ for $x \in A$, such that q_1 is on the cycle $\mathcal{C}$ and q_2 leads to an accepting state, it holds that every x-cycle $\mathcal{C}' \neq \mathcal{C}$ on a path from q_2 to an accepting state contains a state q' with $x \in reset(q')$.

Proof. First, notice that Algorithm AVBWtoNVBW halts iff Z is of a finite size, i.e., the number of variables it produces is finite.

For the first direction we show that running AVBWtoNVBW on an AVBW $\mathcal{A}$ with the above properties results in an NVBW with Z of a finite size. In each of the two cases, we can bound the distance between two reset actions for the same variable, or between a reset action and an accepting state, along every possible run. This, since we can bound the length of the longest path from a state on an x-cycle to an accepting state. Thus all variables in X induce a finite number of variables in Z.

For the other direction, since 1–2 do not hold, there exists a state q that leads both to an x-cycle $\mathcal{C}$ on which x is reset, and to an x-cycle $\mathcal{C}'$ with no $reset(x)$, on a way to an accepting state. While running our algorithm, a new mapping $x \to z_i$ is introduced at every visit to $reset(x)$ on $\mathcal{C}$. At the same time, z_i cannot be removed from $vars$, because of the visits to $\mathcal{C}'$, which does not reset x, and thus its value must be kept. Therefore, the algorithm continuously creates new assignments $x \to z_j$ for $j \neq i$. Thus $vars$ contains an unbounded set of variables. The fact that there is a path to an accepting state is needed in order for this cycle to "survive" the preprocessing. $\square$

3.5.3   Completeness and Soundness

As we mentioned before, no translation algorithm from AVBWs to NVBWs can be both sound and complete, and have a full characterization of inputs for which the algorithm halts. We now prove this claim.

Theorem 5. *There is no algorithm $\mathcal{E}$ that translates AVBWs into NVBWs such that all the following hold.*

1. *Completeness - for every $\mathcal{A}$ that has an equivalent NVBW, $\mathcal{E}(\mathcal{A})$ halts and returns such an equivalent NVBW.*
2. *Soundness - If $\mathcal{E}(\mathcal{A})$ halts and returns an NVBW $\mathcal{A}'$, then $\mathcal{A}'$ is equivalent to $\mathcal{A}$.*
3. *There is a full characterization of AVBWs for which $\mathcal{E}$ halts.*

Proof. As we have shown in Lemma 3, the emptiness problem of AVBWs is undecidable. Assume there is a translation algorithm $\mathcal{E}$ as described in Theorem 5. Then consider the following procedure. Given an AVBW $\mathcal{A}$, if $\mathcal{E}$ halts, check if $\mathcal{E}(\mathcal{A})$ is empty. If $\mathcal{E}$ does not halt on input $\mathcal{A}$, we know it in advance due to the full characterization. Moreover, we know that $\mathcal{L}(\mathcal{A})$ is not empty (otherwise, since $\mathcal{E}$ is complete, $\mathcal{E}$ would halt on $\mathcal{A}$, since there is an NVBW for the empty language). Hence, a translation algorithm as described in Theorem 5 gives us a procedure to decide the emptiness problem for AVBWs, a contradiction.   □

For our algorithm, we have shown a full characterization for halting. Now we prove that our algorithm is sound, and demonstrate its incompleteness by an example of an AVBW for the empty language, for which our algorithm does not halt.

Theorem 6. *Algorithm AVBWtoNVBW is sound.*

Proof. First we show that the definition of E' is correct. Indeed, every $(z_{x_i} \neq z_{x'_j}) \in E'$ is derived from $(x \neq x') \in E$, and each z_{x_i} is induced from only one variable, $x \in X$. Therefore, E' preserves exactly the inequalities of E. Now, $reset'$ is defined according to $reset$ such that if z_i is induced from x, and x is reset in a state q then z_i is reset in states that include q. Therefore $reset'$ allows fresh values only when $reset$ does. The correctness of the rest of the construction follows from the correctness of [14] and from the explanations in the body of the algorithm.   □

Example 5. Incompleteness of the algorithm Let $\mathcal{A} = \langle \mathcal{B}, \Gamma, \emptyset \rangle$ where $\mathcal{B} = \langle \{a.x, b.x\}, \{q_0, q_1\}, q_0, \delta, reset, \{q_0\} \rangle$ and $reset(q_0) = \{x\}, reset(q_1) = \emptyset$. The definition of δ is: $\delta(q_0, \{a.x\}) = q_0 \wedge q_1, \delta(q_1, \{a.x\}) = q_1, \delta(q_1, \{b.x\}) = true$. The language of $\mathcal{A}$ is empty, since in order to reach an accepting state on the path from q_1, the input must be exactly $\{b.i\}$ for some $i \in \Gamma$, but the cycle of q_0 only allows to read $\{a.j\}$, without any $b.i$. Although there is an NVBW for the empty language, our algorithm does not halt on $\mathcal{A}$: it keeps allocating new variables to x, thus new states are created and the algorithm does not reach a fixed point.

4   Fragments of ∃*-VLTL Expressible by NVBWs

We now present several sub-fragments of ∃*-VLTL with a direct NVBW construction.

We can construct an NVBW for ∃*-VLTL formula in prenex normal form, denoted $\exists^*_{pnf}$-*VLTL*. The construction relies on the fact that variables cannot change values throughout the run. Since every $\exists^*_{pnf}$-VLTL formula is expressible with an NVBW, together with Lemma 1, we have the following corollary.

Corollary 3. ∃*-*VLTL is stronger than* $\exists^*_{pnf}$-*VLTL*.[4].

Another easy fragment is ∃*-(X,F)-*VLTL*, which is ∃*-VLTL with only the X,F temporal operators, similar to the definitions of [9]. ∃ and X,F are interchangeable. Thus, every ∃*-(X,F)-VLTL formula is equivalent to an $\exists^*_{pnf}$-VLTL, which has a direct construction to an NVBW.

A direct construction from VLTL to NVBWs exists also for ∃*-VLTL formulas in which all quantifiers are either at the beginning of the formula, or adjacent to a parameterized atomic proposition. This extends the construction for $\exists^*_{pnf}$-VLTL by adding resets to some of the states.

5   Model Checking in Practice

The model-checking problem over infinite data domains asks whether an NVBW $\mathcal{A}_M$ accepts a computation that satisfies an ∃*-VLTL formula φ, which specifies "bad" behaviors. If φ is one of the types mentioned in Sect. 4, we can build an equivalent NVBW $\mathcal{A}_\varphi$ for φ. For a general φ, we build an equivalent AVBW $\mathcal{A}$ according to Sect. 3.3 and if the structure of $\mathcal{A}$ agrees with the structural conditions of Theorem 4, we translate $\mathcal{A}$ to an equivalent NVBW $\mathcal{A}_\varphi$ according to Sect. 3.5.1. Now, if $\mathcal{A}_\varphi$ exists, the intersection $\mathcal{A}_\varphi \cap \mathcal{A}_M$ includes all computations of $\mathcal{A}_M$ that are also computations of $\mathcal{A}_\varphi$. Checking the emptiness of the intersection decides whether $\mathcal{A}_M$ has a "bad" behavior that satisfies φ.

6   Conclusions and Future Work

We defined AVBWs, a new model of automata over infinite alphabets that describes all ∃*-VLTL formulas. We showed that AVBWs, unlike ABWs, are not complementable and are stronger than NVBWs. Nevertheless, we presented an algorithm for translating AVBWs to NVBWs when possible, in order to preform model checking. Moreover, we defined a structural characterization of translatable AVBWs. Finally, we presented the full process of model checking a model M given as an NVBW against an ∃*-VLTL formula. A natural extension of our work is to use the techniques presented in this paper in order to preform model checking for VCTL [12] formulas as well.

---

[4] In [17] the authors conjecture without proof that the formula $G \exists x : a.x$ does not have an equivalent in *PNF*. In Lemma 1 we showed $G \exists x(b.x \wedge F a.x)$ does not have an equivalent NVBW, thus it does not have an equivalent $\exists^*_{pnf}$-VLTL formula. This is a different formula from $G \exists x : a.x$, but the conclusion remains the same.

References

1. Barringer, H., Falcone, Y., Havelund, K., Reger, G., Rydeheard, D.: Quantified event automata: towards expressive and efficient runtime monitors. In: Giannakopoulou, D., Méry, D. (eds.) FM 2012. LNCS, vol. 7436, pp. 68–84. Springer, Heidelberg (2012). doi:10.1007/978-3-642-32759-9_9

2. Bauer, A., Leucker, M., Schallhart, C.: Runtime verification for LTL and TLTL. ACM Trans. Softw. Eng. Methodol. **20**(4), 14:1–14:64 (2011)

3. Bojańczyk, M., Muscholl, A., Schwentick, T., Segoufin, L., David, C.: Two-variable logic on words with data. In: 21st IEEE Symposium on Logic in Computer Science (LICS 2006), 12–15, Seattle, WA, USA, Proceedings, pp. 7–16. IEEE Computer Society, 2006, August 2006

4. Bouajjani, A., Habermehl, P., Jurski, Y., Sighireanu, M.: Rewriting systems with data. In: Csuhaj-Varjú, E., Ésik, Z. (eds.) FCT 2007. LNCS, vol. 4639, pp. 1–22. Springer, Heidelberg (2007). doi:10.1007/978-3-540-74240-1_1

5. Brambilla, M., Ceri, S., Comai, S., Fraternali, P., Manolescu, I.: Specification and design of workflow-driven hypertexts. J. Web Eng. **1**(2), 163–182 (2003)

6. J. R. Buechi. On a decision method in restricted second-order arithmetic. In International Congress on Logic, Methodology, and Philosophy of Science, pp. 1–11. Stanford University Press, (1962)

7. Ceri, S., Matera, M., Rizzo, F., Demaldé, V.: Designing data-intensive web applications for content accessibility using web marts. Commun. ACM **50**(4), 55–61 (2007)

8. Colin, S., Mariani, L.: Run-time verification. In: Broy, M., Jonsson, B., Katoen, J.-P., Leucker, M., Pretschner, A. (eds.) Model-Based Testing of Reactive Systems. LNCS, vol. 3472, pp. 525–555. Springer, Heidelberg (2005). doi:10.1007/11498490_24

9. Emerson, E.A., Halpern, J.Y.: "sometimes" and "not never" revisited: on branching versus linear time temporal logic. J. ACM **33**(1), 151–178 (1986)

10. Grumberg, O., Kupferman, O., Sheinvald, S.: Variable Automata over Infinite Alphabets. In: Dediu, A.-H., Fernau, H., Martín-Vide, C. (eds.) LATA 2010. LNCS, vol. 6031, pp. 561–572. Springer, Heidelberg (2010). doi:10.1007/978-3-642-13089-2_47

11. Grumberg, O., Kupferman, O., Sheinvald, S.: Model checking systems and specifications with parameterized atomic propositions. In: Chakraborty, S., Mukund, M. (eds.) ATVA 2012. LNCS, pp. 122–136. Springer, Heidelberg (2012). doi:10.1007/978-3-642-33386-6_11

12. Grumberg, O., Kupferman, O., Sheinvald, S.: A game-theoretic approach to simulation of data-parameterized systems. In: Cassez, F., Raskin, J.-F. (eds.) ATVA 2014. LNCS, vol. 8837, pp. 348–363. Springer, Cham (2014). doi:10.1007/978-3-319-11936-6_25

13. Kaminski, M., Francez, N.: Finite-memory automata. Theor. Comput. Sci. **134**(2), 329–363 (1994)

14. Miyano, S., Hayashi, T.: Alternating finite automata on omega-words. Theor. Comput. Sci. **32**, 321–330 (1984)

15. Muller, D., Schupp, P.E.: Alternating automata on infinite objects, determinacy and Rabin's theorem. In: Nivat, M., Perrin, D. (eds.) LITP 1984. LNCS, vol. 192, pp. 99–107. Springer, Heidelberg (1985). doi:10.1007/3-540-15641-0_27

16. Neven, F., Schwentick, T., Vianu, V.: Towards regular languages over infinite alphabets. In: Sgall, J., Pultr, A., Kolman, P. (eds.) MFCS 2001. LNCS, vol. 2136, pp. 560–572. Springer, Heidelberg (2001). doi:10.1007/3-540-44683-4_49

17. Song, F., Wu, Z.: Extending temporal logics with data variable quantifications. In: Raman, V., Suresh, S.P. (eds.) 34th International Conference on Foundation of Software Technology and Theoretical Computer Science, FSTTCS 15–17, 2014, New Delhi, India, vol. 29 of LIPIcs, pp. 253–265. Schloss Dagstuhl - Leibniz-Zentrum fuer Informatik, 2014, December 2014

18. Vardi, M.Y.: An automata-theoretic approach to linear temporal logic. In: Moller, F., Birtwistle, G. (eds.) Logics for Concurrency. LNCS, vol. 1043, pp. 238–266. Springer, Heidelberg (1996). doi:10.1007/3-540-60915-6_6

19. Vardi, M.Y., Wolper, P.: An automata-theoretic approach to automatic program verification (preliminary report). In: Proceedings of the Symposium on Logic in Computer Science (LICS 1986), Cambridge, Massachusetts, USA, June 16–18, pp. 332–344. IEEE Computer Society (1986)

Learning from Faults: Mutation Testing in Active Automata Learning

Bernhard K. Aichernig and Martin Tappler[(⊠)]

Institute of Software Technology, Graz University of Technology, Graz, Austria
{aichernig,martin.tappler}@ist.tugraz.at

Abstract. System verification is often hindered by the absence of formal models. Peled et al. proposed black-box checking as a solution to this problem. This technique applies active automata learning to infer models of systems with unknown internal structure.

This kind of learning relies on conformance testing to determine whether a learned model actually represents the considered system. Since conformance testing may require the execution of a large number of tests, it is considered the main bottleneck in automata learning.

In this paper, we describe a randomised conformance testing approach which we extend with fault-based test selection. To show its effectiveness we apply the approach in learning experiments and compare its performance to a well-established testing technique, the partial W-method. This evaluation demonstrates that our approach significantly reduces the cost of learning – in one experiment by a factor of more than twenty.

Keywords: Conformance testing · Mutation testing · FSM-based testing · Active automata learning · Minimally adequate teacher framework

1 Introduction

Since Peled et al. [21] have shown that active automata learning can provide models of black-box systems to enable formal verification, this kind of learning has turned into an active area of research in formal methods. Active learning of automata in the minimally adequate teacher (MAT) framework, as introduced by Angluin [2], assumes the existence of a teacher. In the non-stochastic setting, this teacher must be able to answer two types of queries, *membership* and *equivalence queries*. The former corresponds to a single test of the system under learning (SUL) to check whether a sequence of actions can be executed or to determine the outputs produced in response to a sequence of inputs. Equivalence queries on the other hand correspond to the question whether a hypothesis model produced by the learner represents the SUL. The teacher either answers affirmatively or with a counterexample showing non-equivalence between the SUL and the hypothesis.

The first type of query is simple to implement for learning black-box systems. It generally suffices to reset the system, execute a single test and record

C. Barrett et al. (Eds.): NFM 2017, LNCS 10227, pp. 19–34, 2017.
DOI: 10.1007/978-3-319-57288-8_2

observations. Equivalence queries however, are more difficult to implement. Peled et al. [21], as one of the first to combine learning and formal verification, proposed to implement these queries via conformance testing. In particular, they suggested to use the conformance testing algorithm by Vasilevskii [30] and Chow [6].

This method is also referred to as W-method and there exist optimisations of it, like the partial W-method [11] or an approach by Lee and Yannankakis [16], but all have the same worst-case complexity [4]. All three methods share two issues. They require a fixed upper bound on the number of states of the black-box system which is generally unknown. Additionally, the size of the constructed test suite is exponential in this bound. Therefore, implementing the equivalence oracle can be considered "the true bottleneck of automata learning" [4].

In practice, there is limited time for testing and thereby also for learning. The ZULU challenge [7] addressed this issue by limiting the number of tests to be executed [12]. More concretely, competitors learned finite automata from a limited number of membership queries without explicit equivalence queries. Equivalence queries thus had to be approximated through clever selection of membership queries. This led to a different view of the problem: rather than "trying to prove equivalence", the new target was "finding counterexamples fast" [12].

In this paper we propose an implementation of equivalence queries based on mutation testing [15], more specifically on model-based mutation testing [1]. This approach follows the spirit of the ZULU challenge by trying to minimise the number of tests for executing equivalence queries. We use a combination of random testing, to achieve high variability of tests, and mutation analysis, to address coverage appropriately. To illustrate the effectiveness of our approach, which has been implemented based on the LearnLib library [14], we will mainly compare it to the partial W-method [11] and show that the cost of testing can be significantly reduced while still learning correctly. In other words, our method reliably finds counterexamples with less testing. In addition to that, we also compare it to purely random testing and to an effective implementation of a randomised conformance testing method described by Smeenk et al. [26].

We target systems which can be modelled with a moderately large number of states, i.e. with up to fifty states. This restriction is necessary, because mutation analysis is generally a computationally intensive task for large systems. Nevertheless, there exists a wealth of non-trivial systems, such as implementations of communication protocols, which can be learned nonetheless. The rest of this paper is structured as follows. Section 2 discusses related work and Sect. 3 introduces preliminaries. The main parts, the test-suite generation approach and its evaluation, are presented in Sects. 4 and 5. We conclude the paper in Sect. 6. The implementation used in our evaluation is available at [27].

2 Related Work

We address conformance testing in active automata learning. Hence, there is a relationship to the W-method [6,30] and the partial W-method [11], two conformance testing methods implemented in LearnLib [14]. However, we handle fault coverage differently. By generating tests to achieve transition coverage, we also test for "output" faults, but do not check for "transfer" faults. Instead we present a fault model directly related to the specifics of learning in Sect. 4.3.

We combine model-based mutation testing and random testing, which we discussed in previous work [1]. Generally, random testing is able to detect a large number of mutants fast, such that only a few subtle mutants need to be checked with directed search techniques. While we do not aim at detecting all mutants, i.e. we do not apply directed search, this property provides a certain level of confidence. By analysing mutation coverage of random tests, we can guarantee that detected mutations do not affect the learned model.

Howar et al. noted that it is necessary to find counterexamples with few tests for automata learning to be practically applicable [12]. We generally follow this approach. Furthermore, one of the heuristics described in [12] is based on Rivest and Schapire's counterexample processing [23], similar to the fault model discussed in Sect. 4.3. More recent work in this area has been performed by Smeenk et al. [26], who implemented a partly randomised conformance testing technique. In order to keep the number of tests small, they applied a technique to determine an adaptive distinguishing sequence described by Lee and Yannakakis [17]. With this technique and domain-specific knowledge, they succeeded in learning a large model of industrial control software. The same technique has also been used to learn models of Transmission Control Protocol (TCP) implementations [10].

3   Preliminaries

3.1   Mealy Machines

We use Mealy machines because they are well-suited to model reactive systems and they have successfully been used in contexts combining learning and some form of verification [10, 18, 24, 28]. In addition to that, the Java-library Learn-Lib [14] provides efficient algorithms for learning Mealy machines.

Basically, Mealy machines are finite state automata with inputs and outputs. The execution of such a Mealy machine starts in an initial state and by executing inputs it changes its state. Additionally, exactly one output is produced in response to each input. Formally, Mealy machines can be defined as follows.

Definition 1. *A Mealy machine $\mathcal{M}$ is a 6-tuple $\mathcal{M} = \langle Q, q_0, I, O, \delta, \lambda \rangle$ where*

- *Q is a finite set of states*
- *q_0 is the initial state,*
- *I/O is a finite set of input/output symbols,*
- *$\delta : Q \times I \to Q$ is the state transition function, and*
- *$\lambda : Q \times I \to O$ is the output function.*

We require Mealy machines to be input-enabled and deterministic. The former demands that outputs and successor states must be defined for all inputs and all states, i.e. δ and λ must be surjective. A Mealy machine is deterministic if it defines at most one output and successor state for every pair of input and state, i.e. δ and λ must be functions in the mathematical sense.

Notational Conventions. Let $s, s' \in S^*$ be two sequences of input/output symbols, i.e. $S = I$ or $S = O$, then $s \cdot s'$ denotes the concatenation of these sequences. The empty sequence is represented by ϵ. The length of a sequence is given by $|s|$. We implicitly lift single elements to sequences, thus for $e \in S$ we have $e \in S^*$ with $|e| = 1$. As a result, the concatenation $s \cdot e$ is also defined.

We extend δ and λ to sequences of inputs in the standard way. Let $s \in I^*$ be an input sequence and $q \in Q$ be a state, then $\delta(q, s) = q' \in Q$ is the state reached by executing s starting in state q. For $s \in I^*$ and $q \in Q$, the output function $\lambda(q, s) = t \in O^*$ returns the outputs produced in response to s executed in state q. Furthermore, let $\lambda(s) = \lambda(q_0, s)$. For state q the set $acc(q) = \{s \in I^* | \delta(q_0, s) = q\}$ contains the access sequences of q, i.e. the sequences leading to q. Note that other authors define a unique access sequence $s \in I^*$ for each q [13].

Finally we need a basis for determining whether two Mealy machines are equivalent. Equivalence is usually defined with respect to outputs [10], i.e. two deterministic Mealy machines are equivalent if they produce the same outputs for all input sequences. A Mealy machine $\langle Q_1, q_{01}, I, O, \delta_1, \lambda_1 \rangle$ is equivalent to another Mealy machine $\langle Q_2, q_{02}, I, O, \delta_2, \lambda_2 \rangle$ iff $\forall s \in I^* : \lambda_1(q_{01}, s) = \lambda_2(q_{02}, s)$. A counterexample to equivalence is thus an $s \in I^*$ such that $\lambda_1(q_{01}, s) \neq \lambda_2(q_{02}, s)$.

3.2   Active Automata Learning

We consider learning in the minimally adequate teacher (MAT) framework [2]. Algorithms in this framework infer models of black-box systems, also referred to as SULs, through interaction with a so-called teacher.

Minimally Adequate Teacher Framework. The interaction is carried out via two types of queries posed by the learning algorithm and answered by a MAT. These two types of queries are usually called *membership queries* and *equivalence queries*. In order to understand these basic notions of queries consider that Angluin's original L^* algorithm is used to learn a deterministic finite automaton (DFA) representing a regular language known to the teacher [2]. Given some alphabet, the L^* algorithm repeatedly selects strings and asks membership queries to check whether these strings are in the language to be learned. The teacher may answer either *yes* or *no*.

After some queries the learning algorithm uses the knowledge gained so far and forms a hypothesis, i.e. a DFA consistent with the obtained information which should represent the regular language under consideration. The algorithm presents the hypothesis to the teacher and issues an equivalence query in order to check whether the language to be learned is equivalent to the language represented by the hypothesis automaton. The response to this kind of query is either *yes* signalling that the correct DFA has been learned or a counterexample to equivalence. Such a counterexample is a witness showing that the learned model is not yet correct, i.e. it is a word from the symmetric difference of the language under learning and the language accepted by the hypothesis.

After processing a counterexample, learning algorithms start a new *round* of learning. The new round again involves membership queries and a concluding equivalence query. This general mode of operation is used by basically all algorithms in the MAT framework with some adaptations. These adaptations may for instance enable the learning of Mealy machines as described in the following.

Learning Mealy Machines. Margaria et al. [18] and Niese [20] were one of the first to infer Mealy-machine models of reactive systems using an L^*-based algorithm. Another L^*-based learning algorithm for Mealy machines has been presented by Shahbaz and Groz [25]. They reuse the structure of L^*, but substitute membership queries for *output queries*. Instead of checking whether a string is accepted, they provide inputs and the teacher responds with the corresponding outputs. For a more practical discussion, consider the instantiation of a teacher. Usually we want to learn the behaviour of a black-box SUL of which we only know the interface. Hence, output queries are conceptually simple: provide inputs to the SUL and observe produced outputs. However, there is a slight difficulty hidden. Shahbaz and Groz [25] assume that outputs are produced in response to inputs executed from the **initial** state. Consequently, we need to have some means to reset a system. As discussed in the introduction, we generally cannot check for equivalence. It is thus necessary to approximate equivalence queries, e.g., via conformance testing as implemented in LearnLib [14]. To summarise, a learning algorithm for Mealy machines relies on three operations:

reset: resets the SUL
output query: performs a single test executing inputs and recording outputs
equivalence query: conformance testing between SUL and hypothesis.

As shown in Fig. 1, the teacher is usually a component communicating with the SUL. An equivalence query results in a positive answer if all conformance tests pass, i.e. the SUL produces the same outputs as the hypothesis. If there is a failing test, the corresponding input sequence is returned as counterexample.

Due to the incompleteness of testing, learned models may be incorrect. If, e.g., the W-method [6,30] is used for testing, the learned model may be incorrect if assumptions placed on the maximum number of states of the SUL do not hold.

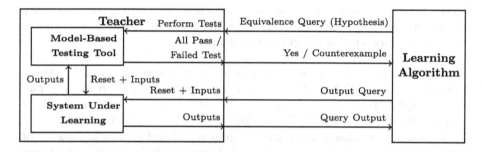

Fig. 1. The interaction between SUL, teacher and learning algorithm (based on [26]).

Algorithm 1. The test-case generation algorithm.

1: $state \leftarrow s_{0h}$	13: $test \leftarrow test \cdot p \cdot rI \cdot rSteps$
2: $test \leftarrow \epsilon$	14: $state \leftarrow \delta(\delta(rS, rI), rSteps)$
3: **if** $coinFlip(0.5)$ **then**	15: **if** $|test| > maxSteps$ **then**
4: $test \leftarrow rSeq(I, l_{\text{infix}})$	16: **break**
5: $state \leftarrow \delta(state, test)$	17: **else if** $coinFlip(p_{\text{stop}})$ **then**
6: **end if**	18: **break**
7: **loop**	19: **end if**
8: $rS \leftarrow rSel(S_h)$ ▷ (rS, rI) defines	20: **else if** $\neg coinFlip(p_{\text{retry}})$ **then**
9: $rI \leftarrow rSel(I)$ ▷ a transition	21: **break**
10: $p \leftarrow path(state, rS)$	22: **end if**
11: **if** $p \neq None$ **then**	23: **end loop**
12: $rSteps \leftarrow rSeq(I, l_{\text{infix}})$	

---

4 Test-Suite Generation

We had shown previously "that by adding mutation testing to a random testing strategy approximately the same number of bugs were found with fewer test cases" [1]. Motivated by this, we developed a simple and yet effective test-suite generation technique. The test-suite generation has two parts, (1) generating a large set of tests T and (2) selecting a subset $T_{\text{sel}} \subset T$ to be run on the SUL.

4.1 Test-Case Generation

The goal of the test-case generation is to achieve high coverage of the model under consideration combined with variability through random testing. The test-case generation may start with a random walk through the model and then iterates two operations. First, a transition of the model is chosen randomly and a path leading to it is executed. If the transition is not reachable, another target transition is chosen. Second, another short random walk is executed. These two operations are repeated until a stopping criterion is reached.

Stopping. Test-case generation stops as soon as the test has a length greater than a maximum number of steps *maxSteps*. Alternatively, it may also stop dependent on probabilities p_{retry} and p_{stop}. The first one controls the probability of continuing in case a selected transition is not reachable while the second one controls the probability of stopping prematurely.

Random Functions. The generation procedure uses three random functions. A function *coinFlip* defined for $p \in [0, 1]$ by $\mathbb{P}(coinFlip(p) = true) = p$ and $\mathbb{P}(coinFlip(p) = false) = 1 - p$. The function *rSel* selects a single sample from a set according to a uniform distribution, i.e. $\forall e \in S: \mathbb{P}(rSel(S) = e) = \frac{1}{|S|}$. The function *rSeq* takes a set S and a bound $b \in \mathbb{N}$ and creates a sequence of length $l \leq b$ consisting of elements from S chosen via *rSel*, whereby l is chosen uniformly from $[0..b]$.

We assume a given Mealy machine $\mathcal{M}_h = \langle S_h, s_{0h}, I, O, \lambda_h, \delta_h \rangle$ in the following. Algorithm 1 realises the test-case generation based on $\mathcal{M}_h$. As additional inputs, it takes stopping parameters and $l_{\text{infix}} \in \mathbb{N}$, an upper bound on the number of steps executed between visiting two transitions. The function *path* returns a path leading from the current state to another state. Currently, this is implemented via breadth-first exploration but other approaches are possible as long as they satisfy $path(s, s') = \text{None}$ iff $\nexists \bar{i} \in I^* : \delta(s, \bar{i}) = s'$ and $path(s, s') = \bar{i} \in I^*$ such that $\delta(s, \bar{i}) = s'$, where $\text{None} \notin I$ denotes that no such path exists.

4.2   Test-Case Selection

To account for variations in the quality of randomly generated tests, not all generated tests are executed on the SUL, but rather a selected subset. This selection is based on coverage, e.g. transition coverage.

For the following discussion, assume that a set of tests T_{sel} of fixed size n_{sel} should be selected from a previously generated set T to cover elements from a set C. In a simple case, C can be instantiated to the set of all transitions, i.e. $C = S_h \times I$ as $(s, i) \in S_h \times I$ uniquely identifies a transition because of determinism. The selection comprises the following three steps:

1. The coverage of single test cases is analysed, i.e. each test case $t \in T$ is associated with a set $C_t \subseteq C$ covered by t.
2. The actual selection has the objective of optimising the overall coverage of C. We greedily select test cases until either the upper bound n_{sel} is reached, all elements in C are covered, or we do not improve coverage. More formally:

```
1: T_sel ← ∅                              6:     end if
2: while |T_sel| < n_sel ∧ C ≠ ∅ do       7:         T_sel ← T_sel ∪ {t_opt}
3:     t_opt ← argmin_{t∈T} |C \ C_t|     8:         C ← C \ C_{t_opt}
4:     if C ∩ C_{t_opt} = ∅ then          9: end while
5:         break  ▷ no improvement
```

3. If n_{sel} tests have not yet been selected, then further tests are selected which individually achieve high coverage. For that $t \in T \setminus T_{\text{sel}}$ are sorted in descending size of C_t and the first $n_{\text{sel}} - |T_{\text{sel}}|$ tests are selected.[1]

4.3   Mutation-Based Selection

A particularly interesting selection criterion is mutation-based selection. The choice of this criterion is motivated by the fact that model-based mutation testing can effectively be combined with random testing [1]. Generally, in this fault-based test-case generation technique, known faults are injected into a model creating so-called mutants. Test cases are then generated which distinguish these mutants from the original model and thereby test for the corresponding faults.

---

[1] Note that more sophisticated test suite reduction/prioritisation strategies could be used. However, this is beyond the scope of this paper.

Thus, in our case we alter the hypothesis $\mathcal{M}_h$, creating a set of mutants $\mathcal{MS}_{mut}$. The objective is now to distinguish mutants from the hypothesis, i.e. we want tests that show that mutants are observably different from the hypothesis. Hence, we can set $C = \mathcal{MS}_{mut}$ and $C_t = \{\mathcal{M}_{mut} \in \mathcal{MS}_{mut} \mid \lambda_h(t) \neq \lambda_{mut}(t)\}$.

Type of Mutation. The type of faults injected into a model is governed by mutation operators, which basically map a model to a set of mutated models (mutants). There is a variety of operators for programs [15] and also finite-state machines [9]. As an example, consider a mutation operator *change output* which changes the output of each transition and thereby creates one mutant per transition. Since there is exactly one mutant that can be detected by executing each transition, selection based on such mutants is equivalent to selection with respect to transition coverage. Hence, mutation can simulate other coverage criteria. In fact, for our evaluation we implemented transition coverage via mutation.

Blindly using all available mutation operators may not be effective. Fault-based testing should rather target faults likely to occur in the considered application domain [22]. Thus, we developed a family of mutation operators, called *split-state* operators, directly addressing active automata learning.

Split-State Operator Family. There are different ways to process counterexamples in the MAT framework, such as by adding all prefixes to the used data structures [2]. An alternative technique due to Rivest and Schapire [23] takes the "distinguishing power" of a counterexample into account. The basic idea is to decompose a counterexample into a prefix u, a single action a and a suffix v such that v is able to distinguish access sequences in the current hypothesis. In other words, the distinguishing sequence v shows that two access sequences, which were hypothesised to lead to the same state, actually lead to observably nonequivalent states. This knowledge is then integrated into the data structures.

Since it is an efficient form of processing counterexamples, adaptations of it have been used in other learning algorithms such as the TTT algorithm [13]. This algorithm makes the effect of this decomposition explicit. It *splits* a state q reached by an access sequence derived from u and a. The splitting further involves (1) adding a new state q' reached by another access sequence derived from u and a (which originally led to q) and (2) adding sequences to the internal data structures which can distinguish q and q'.

The development of the *split-state* family of mutation operators is motivated by the principle underlying the TTT and related algorithms. Basically, we collect pairs (u, u') of access sequences of a state q, add a new state q' and redirect u' to q'. Furthermore, we add transitions such that q' behaves the same as q except for a distinguishing sequence v. Example 1 illustrates this mutation operator.

Example 1. (Split State Mutation). A hypothesis produced by a learning algorithm may be of the form shown in Fig. 2a. Note that not all edges are shown in the figure and dashed edges represent sequences of transitions. The access sequences $acc(q_{h3})$ of q_{h3} thus include $\bar{i} \cdot i_1$ and $\bar{i}' \cdot i_1'$. A possible corresponding black-box SUL is shown in Fig. 2b. In this case, the hypothesis incorrectly

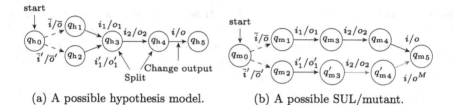

(a) A possible hypothesis model.   (b) A possible SUL/mutant.

Fig. 2. Demonstration of split state.

assumes that $\bar{i} \cdot i_1$ and $\bar{i}' \cdot i_1'$ lead to the same state. We can model a transformation from the hypothesis to the SUL by splitting q_{h3} and q_{h4} and changing the output produced in the new state q_{m4}' as indicated in Fig. 2b. State q_{h4} has to be split as well to introduce a distinguishing sequence of length 2 while still maintaining determinism. A test case covering the mutation is $\bar{i}' \cdot i_1' \cdot i_2 \cdot i$.

A mutant models a SUL containing two different states q and q' which are assumed to be equivalent by the hypothesis. By executing a test covering a mutant $\mathcal{M}_{\mathrm{mut}}$, we either find an actual counterexample to equivalence between SUL and hypothesis or prove that the SUL does not implement $\mathcal{M}_{\mathrm{mut}}$. Hence, it is possible to guarantee that the SUL possesses certain properties. This is similar to model-based mutation testing in general, where the absence of certain faults, those modelled by mutation operators, can be guaranteed [1].

Split state is a family of mutation operators as the effectiveness of the approach is influenced by several parameters, such that the instantiation of parameters can be considered a unique operator. The parameters are:

Max. number of sequences n_{acc}: an upper bound on the number of mutated access sequences leading to a single state.

Length of distinguishing sequences k: for each splitting operation we create $|I|^k$ mutants, one for each sequence of length k. Note that this requires the creation of k new states. Coverage of all mutants generated with length k implies coverage of all mutants with length $l < k$.

Split at prefix flag: redirecting a sequence $u' \cdot a$ from q to q' usually amounts to changing $\delta(\delta(s_{0h}, u'), a) = q$ to $\delta(\delta(s_{0h}, u'), a) = q'$. However, if the other access sequence in the pair is $u \cdot a$ with $\delta(s_{0h}, u') = \delta(s_{0h}, u)$, this is not possible because it would introduce non-determinism. This flag specifies whether the access sequence pair $(u \cdot a, u' \cdot a)$ is ignored or whether further states are added to enable redirecting $u' \cdot a$. We generally set it to *true*.

Efficiency Considerations. While test-case generation can efficiently be implemented, mutation-based selection is computationally intensive. It is necessary to check which of the mutants is covered by each test case. Since the number of mutants may be as large as $|S| * n_{\mathrm{acc}} * |I|^k$, this may become a bottleneck.

Consequently, cost reduction techniques for mutation [15] need to be considered. We reduce execution cost by avoiding the explicit creation of mutants.

Essentially only the difference to the hypothesis is stored and executed. Since this does not solve the problem completely, mutant reduction techniques need to be considered as well. Jia and Harman identify four techniques to reduce the number of mutants [15]. We use two of them: *Selective Mutation* applies only a subset of effective mutation operators. In our case, we apply only one mutation operator. With *Mutant Sampling* only a subset of mutants is randomly selected and analysed while the rest is discarded.

In essence, the choice of the bound on the number of access sequences, the number of selected tests, the sample size, etc. needs to take the cost of executing tests on the SUL into account. Thus, it is tradeoff between the cost of mutation analysis and testing, as a more extensive analysis can be assumed to produce better tests and thereby require fewer test executions. Additionally, the number of mutants may be reduced as follows.

Mutation analysis of executed tests: we keep track of all tests executed on the SUL. Prior to test-case selection, these test cases are examined to determine which mutants are covered by the tests. These mutants can be discarded because we know for all executed tests t and covered mutants $\mathcal{M}_{mut}$ that $\lambda_h(t) = \lambda_{sul}(t)$ and $\lambda_h(t) \neq \lambda_{mut}(t)$ which implies $\lambda_{sul}(t) \neq \lambda_{mut}(t)$, i.e. the mutants are not implemented by the SUL. This extension prevents unnecessary coverage of already covered mutants and reduces the number of mutants to be analysed. This takes the iterative nature of learning into account as suggested in [12] in the context of equivalence testing.

Adapting to learning algorithm: by considering the specifics of a learning algorithm, the number of access sequences could be reduced. For instance in discrimination-tree-based approaches [13], it would be possible to create mutants only for access sequences S stored in the discrimination tree and for their extensions $S \cdot I$. However, this has not been implemented yet.

5   Evaluation

In the following, we evaluate two variations of our new test-suite generation approach. We will refer to test-case generation with transition-coverage-based selection as *transition coverage*. The combination with mutation-based selection will be referred to as *split state*. We compare these two techniques to alternatives in the literature: the partial W-method [11] and the random version of the approach discussed in [26] available at [19]. We refer to the latter as *random L & Y*. Note that this differs slightly from [10, 26] in which also non-randomised test, i.e. complete up to some bound, were generated.

We evaluate the different conformance testing methods based on two case studies from the domain of communication protocols. The examined systems are given in Table 1. This table includes the number of states and inputs of the true Mealy machine model and a short description of each system. Due to space limitations, we refer to other publications for in-depth descriptions.

Table 1. A short description of examined systems.

System	# States	# Inputs	Short description
TCP server (Ubuntu)	57	12	Models of TCP server/client implementations from three different vendors have been learned and analysed by Fiterău-Broştean et al. [10]. We simulated the server model of Ubuntu available at [29].
MQTT broker (emqtt [8])	18	9	Model of an MQTT [3] broker interacting with two clients. We discussed the learning setup in [28].

5.1 Measurement Setup

To objectively evaluate randomised conformance testing, we investigate the probability of learning the correct model with a limited number of interactions with the SUL, i.e. only a limited number of tests may be executed. We generally base the cost of learning on the number of executed inputs rather than on the number of tests/resets. This decision follows from the observation that resets in the target application area, protocols, can be done fast (simply start a new session), whereas timeouts and quiescent behaviour cause long test durations [24,28]. Note that we take previously learned models as SULs. Their simulation ensures fast test execution which enables a thorough evaluation.

To estimate the probability of learning the correct models, we performed each learning run 50 times and calculated the relative frequency of learning the correct model. In the following, we refer to such a repetition as a single experiment. Note that given the expected number of states of each system, we can efficiently determine whether the correct model has been learned, since learned models are minimal with respect to the number of states [2].

In order to find a lower limit on the number of tests required by each method to work reliably, we bounded the number of tests executed for each equivalence query and gradually increased this bound. Once all learning runs of an experiment succeeded we stopped this procedure. For learning with the partial W-method [11] we gradually increased the depth parameter implemented in LearnLib [14] until we learned the correct model. Since this method does not use randomisation, we did not run repeated experiments and report the measurement results for the lowest possible depth-parameter value.

As all algorithms can be run on standard notebooks, we will only exemplarily comment on runtime. For a fair comparison, we evaluated all equivalence-testing approaches in combination with the same learning algorithm, i.e. L^* with Rivest and Schapire's counterexample-handling implemented by LearnLib 0.12 [14].

TCP – Ubuntu. The number of tests and steps required to reliably learn the Ubuntu TCP-server are given in Table 2. In order to perform these experiments, we generated 100,000 tests and selected the number of tests given in the first line

Table 2. Performance measurements for learning an Ubuntu TCP-server-model.

	Transition coverage	Split state	Partial W-method	Random L & Y
Bound on # equivalence tests/depth parameter	10,000	4,000	2	46,000
Mean # tests [equivalence]	12,498	4,786	793,939	71,454
Mean # steps [equivalence]	239,059	138,840	7,958,026	823,623
Mean # tests [membership]	9,633	10,017	13,962	11,445
Mean # steps [membership]	127,684	129,214	147,166	136,827

of Table 2 to perform each equivalence query. For the partial W-method this line includes the depth-parameter value. Note that the mean values of tests/steps represent the numbers summed over all rounds of learning (but averaged over 50 runs), while the bound on the number of tests applies to only a single round. The test-case generation with Algorithm 1 has been performed with parameters $maxSteps = 40$, $p_{retry} = 0.9$, $p_{stop} = 0.1$, and $l_{infix} = 6$. The chosen parameters for *split state* selection are $n_{acc} = 100$ (max. access sequences per state) and $k = 2$ (length of distinguishing sequence). Additionally, we performed mutant sampling by first reducing the number of mutants to one quarter of the original mutants and then to 10,000 if necessary.

We see in the table that the average number of tests and steps required for membership queries is roughly the same for all techniques. This is what we expected as the same learning algorithm is used in all cases, but the numbers shall demonstrate that techniques requiring less tests do not trade membership for equivalence tests. With this out of the way, we can concentrate on equivalence testing. We see that *split state* pays off in this experiment with *transition coverage* requiring 1.7 times as many steps. The average cost of test selection is 104 seconds for *split state* and 4 seconds for *transition coverage*. However, considering the large savings in actual test execution, *split state* performs better.

We also evaluated *random L & Y* with a middle sequence of expected length 4 (similar to [10]). For this setup, *random L & Y* requires significantly more steps and tests than both alternatives. There may be more suitable parameters, however, which would improve the performance of *random L & Y*. Nevertheless, the model structure of Ubuntu's TCP-server seems to be beneficial for our approach.

All randomised approaches outperformed the partial W-method. In particular *split state* is able to reduce the number of test steps by a factor of 57. Taking the membership queries into account, the overall cost of learning is reduced by a factor of about 22. The relative gap between tests, a reduction by a factor of 166, is even larger. This is an advantage of our approach as we can flexibly control test length and thereby account for systems with expensive resets. Purely random testing is not a viable choice in this case. An experiment with 1,000,000 tests per equivalence query succeeded in learning correctly in only 4 of 50 runs.

MQTT – emqtt. The number of tests and steps required to reliably learn models of the emqtt broker are given in Table 3. In order to perform these experiments, we used largely the same setup and the same sampling strategy as for the TCP experiments, but generated only 10,000 tests as a basis for selection. Furthermore, we set $p_{\text{retry}} = 0.95$, $p_{\text{stop}} = 0.05$, $l_{\text{infix}} = 6$, $n_{\text{acc}} = 300$, and $k = 3$.

In Table 3, we see a similarly large improvement with respect to the partial W-method. The partial W-method requires about 52 times as many test steps as *split state*. Other than that, we see that the improvement of *split state* over *transition coverage* is not as drastic as for the Ubuntu TCP-server and testing with *random L & Y* also performs well. Figure 3 depicts the learning performance of the three different approaches and undirected random testing. It shows the dependency between the average number of equivalence-test steps and the estimated probability $\mathbb{P}_{\text{est}}(correct)$ of learning the correct model. The graph shows that significantly more testing is required by random testing.

Table 3. Performance measurements for learning an emqtt-broker model.

	Transition coverage	Split state	Partial W-method	Random L & Y
Bound on # equivalence tests/depth parameter	275	125	2	1100
Mean # tests [equivalence]	345	182	72,308	1,679
Mean # steps [equivalence]	13,044	7,755	487,013	11,966
Mean # tests [membership]	1,592	1,623	1,808	1,683
Mean # steps [membership]	12,776	13,160	11,981	12,005

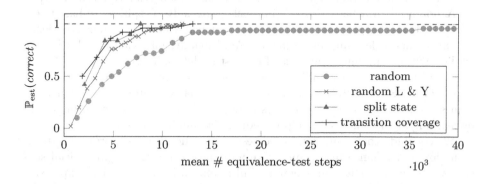

Fig. 3. Average number of equivalence-test steps required to reliably learn the correct emqtt-broker model.

Discussion and Threats to Validity. The results shown above suggest that *transition coverage* and especially *split state* perform well. However, the performance depends on the system structure. There are systems for which *transition* *coverage* performs slightly better with regard to the required number of steps than *split state*, as the latter favours longer tests. In these cases, *split state* may simply add no value because *transition coverage* already performs well.

For the TCP-server case study, we report effectiveness superior to that of *random L & Y*. The performance of our technique depends on the concrete instantiation of more parameters than the performance of *random L & Y*. Finding suitable parameters is thus more difficult for our approach and relative performance gains may decrease for unsuitable choices. Additionally, *random L & Y* generates tests much more efficiently than *split state*. Split-state mutation analysis is only feasible for moderate-sized models, whereas *random L & Y* has successfully been applied for learning of a system with more than 3,000 states [26]. Mutation-based test-case selection would be hindered by the large number of mutants and tests forming the basis for selection – to our experience the number of tests should be increased with model size. More concretely, applying the technique to systems with significantly more than 100 states would likely not pay off. Aggressive mutant sampling would be necessary, rendering the mutation-based selection less effective. Without sampling, the decreased testing duration would not compensate for the cost of mutation analysis.

6 Conclusion

We presented a simple test-case generation technique which accompanied with appropriate test-case selection yields effective test suites. In particular, we further motivated and described a fault-based test selection approach with a fault model tailored towards learning. First experiments showed it is possible to reliably learn system models with a significantly lower number of test cases as compared to complete conformance testing with, e.g., the partial W-method [11].

A potential drawback of our approach, especially of split-state-based test selection, is the large number of parameters, which according to our experience heavily influence learning performance. Additionally, mutation-based selection applies mutant sampling, thus it is of interest to determine the influence of sampling and whether corresponding observations made for program mutation [15] also hold for FSM mutation. Nevertheless, alternative mutant reduction techniques are not entirely exhausted. As indicated in Sect. 4.3, information stored by learning algorithms could help to reduce the number of mutants.

We conclude that mutation-based test-suite generation is a promising technique for conformance testing in active automata learning. Despite initial success, we believe that it could show its full potential for testing more expressive types of models like extended finite state machines [5]. This would enable the application of more comprehensive fault models. Finally, alternatives to the simple greedy test-selection may also provide benefits.

Acknowledgment. This work was supported by the TU Graz LEAD project "Dependable Internet of Things in Adverse Environments". We would also like to thank the developers of LearnLib and of the test-case generator available at [19].

References

1. Aichernig, B.K., Brandl, H., Jöbstl, E., Krenn, W., Schlick, R., Tiran, S.: Killing strategies for model-based mutation testing. Softw. Test. Verif. Reliab. **25**(8), 716–748 (2015)
2. Angluin, D.: Learning regular sets from queries and counterexamples. Inf. Comput. **75**(2), 87–106 (1987)
3. Banks, A., Gupta, R. (eds.): MQTT Version 3.1.1. OASIS Standard, October 2014. Latest version: http://docs.oasis-open.org/mqtt/mqtt/v3.1.1/os/mqtt-v3.1.1-os.html
4. Berg, T., Grinchtein, O., Jonsson, B., Leucker, M., Raffelt, H., Steffen, B.: On the correspondence between conformance testing and regular inference. In: Cerioli, M. (ed.) FASE 2005. LNCS, vol. 3442, pp. 175–189. Springer, Heidelberg (2005). doi:10.1007/978-3-540-31984-9_14
5. Cassel, S., Howar, F., Jonsson, B., Steffen, B.: Active learning for extended finite state machines. Formal Asp. Comput. **28**(2), 233–263 (2016)
6. Chow, T.S.: Testing software design modeled by finite-state machines. IEEE Trans. Softw. Eng. **4**(3), 178–187 (1978)
7. Combe, D., de la Higuera, C., Janodet, J.-C.: Zulu: an interactive learning competition. In: Yli-Jyrä, A., Kornai, A., Sakarovitch, J., Watson, B. (eds.) FSMNLP 2009. LNCS (LNAI), vol. 6062, pp. 139–146. Springer, Heidelberg (2010). doi:10.1007/978-3-642-14684-8_15
8. emqtt. http://emqtt.io/. Accessed 29 Nov 2016
9. Fabbri, S., Delamaro, M.E., Maldonado, J.C., Masiero, P.C.: Mutation analysis testing for finite state machines. In: ISSRE 1994, pp. 220–229. IEEE (1994)
10. Fiterău-Broștean, P., Janssen, R., Vaandrager, F.: Combining model learning and model checking to analyze TCP implementations. In: Chaudhuri, S., Farzan, A. (eds.) CAV 2016. LNCS, vol. 9780, pp. 454–471. Springer, Cham (2016). doi:10.1007/978-3-319-41540-6_25
11. Fujiwara, S., von Bochmann, G., Khendek, F., Amalou, M., Ghedamsi, A.: Test selection based on finite state models. IEEE Trans. Softw. Eng. **17**(6), 591–603 (1991)
12. Howar, F., Steffen, B., Merten, M.: From ZULU to RERS - lessons learned in the ZULU challenge. In: Margaria, T., Steffen, B. (eds.) ISoLA 2010. LNCS, vol. 6415, pp. 687–704. Springer, Heidelberg (2010). doi:10.1007/978-3-642-16558-0_55
13. Isberner, M., Howar, F., Steffen, B.: The TTT algorithm: a redundancy-free approach to active automata learning. In: Bonakdarpour, B., Smolka, S.A. (eds.) RV 2014. LNCS, vol. 8734, pp. 307–322. Springer, Cham (2014). doi:10.1007/978-3-319-11164-3_26
14. Isberner, M., Howar, F., Steffen, B.: The open-source LearnLib. In: Kroening, D., Păsăreanu, C.S. (eds.) CAV 2015. LNCS, vol. 9206, pp. 487–495. Springer, Cham (2015). doi:10.1007/978-3-319-21690-4_32
15. Jia, Y., Harman, M.: An analysis and survey of the development of mutation testing. IEEE Trans. Softw. Eng. **37**(5), 649–678 (2011)
16. Lee, D., Yannakakis, M.: Principles and methods of testing finite state machines - a survey. Proc. IEEE **84**(8), 1090–1123 (1996)
17. Lee, D., Yannakakis, M.: Testing finite-state machines: state identification and verification. IEEE Trans. Comput. **43**(3), 306–320 (1994)
18. Margaria, T., Niese, O., Raffelt, H., Steffen, B.: Efficient test-based model generation for legacy reactive systems. In: Ninth IEEE International High-Level Design Validation and Test Workshop 2004, pp. 95–100. IEEE Computer Society (2004)

19. Moerman, J.: Yannakakis - test-case generator. https://gitlab.science.ru.nl/moerman/Yannakakis. Accessed 30 Nov 2016
20. Niese, O.: An integrated approach to testing complex systems. Ph.D. thesis, Dortmund University of Technology (2003)
21. Peled, D., Vardi, M.Y., Yannakakis, M.: Black box checking. In: Wu, J., Chanson, S.T., Gao, Q. (eds.) FORTE XII/PSTV XIX 1999. IFIP AICT, vol. 28, pp. 225–240. Springer, Boston (1999). doi:10.1007/978-0-387-35578-8_13
22. Pretschner, A.: Defect-based testing. In: Dependable Software Systems Engineering, NATO Science for Peace and Security Series, D: Information and Communication Security, vol. 40, pp. 224–245. IOS Press (2015)
23. Rivest, R.L., Schapire, R.E.: Inference of finite automata using homing sequences. Inf. Comput. **103**(2), 299–347 (1993)
24. de Ruiter, J., Poll, E.: Protocol state fuzzing of TLS implementations. In: USENIX Security 15, pp. 193–206. USENIX Association (2015)
25. Shahbaz, M., Groz, R.: Inferring Mealy machines. In: Cavalcanti, A., Dams, D.R. (eds.) FM 2009. LNCS, vol. 5850, pp. 207–222. Springer, Heidelberg (2009). doi:10.1007/978-3-642-05089-3_14
26. Smeenk, W., Moerman, J., Vaandrager, F., Jansen, D.N.: Applying automata learning to embedded control software. In: Butler, M., Conchon, S., Zaïdi, F. (eds.) ICFEM 2015. LNCS, vol. 9407, pp. 67–83. Springer, Cham (2015). doi:10.1007/978-3-319-25423-4_5
27. Tappler, M.: mut-learn - randomised mutation-based equivalence testing. https://github.com/mtappler/mut-learn. Accessed 07 Dec 2016
28. Tappler, M., Aichernig, B.K., Bloem, R.: Model-based testing IoT communication via active automata learning. In: ICST 2017. IEEE Computer Society (2017)
29. TCP models. https://gitlab.science.ru.nl/pfiteraubrostean/tcp-learner/tree/cav-aec/models. Accessed 14 Nov 2016
30. Vasilevskii, M.P.: Failure diagnosis of automata. Cybernetics **9**(4), 653–665 (1973)

Parametric Model Checking Timed Automata Under Non-Zenoness Assumption

Étienne André[1], Hoang Gia Nguyen[1(✉)], Laure Petrucci[1], and Jun Sun[2]

[1] LIPN, CNRS UMR 7030, Université Paris 13, Sorbonne Paris Cité,
Villetaneuse, France
`hoanggia.nguyen@lipn.univ-paris13.fr`
[2] ISTD, Singapore University of Technology and Design, Singapore, Singapore

Abstract. Real-time systems often involve hard timing constraints and concurrency, and are notoriously hard to design or verify. Given a model of a real-time system and a property, parametric model-checking aims at synthesizing timing valuations such that the model satisfies the property. However, the counter-example returned by such a procedure may be *Zeno* (an infinite number of discrete actions occurring in a finite time), which is unrealistic. We show here that synthesizing parameter valuations such that at least one counterexample run is non-Zeno is undecidable for parametric timed automata (PTAs). Still, we propose a semi-algorithm based on a transformation of PTAs into *Clock Upper Bound PTAs* to derive all valuations whenever it terminates, and some of them otherwise.

1 Introduction

Timed automata (TAs) [1] are a popular formalism for real-time systems modeling and verification, providing explicit manipulation of clock variables. Real-time behavior is captured by clock constraints on system transitions, setting or resetting clocks, etc. TAs have been studied in various settings (such as planning [19]) and benefit from powerful tools such as Uppaal [21] or PAT [24].

Model checking TAs consists of checking whether there exists an accepting cycle (i.e. a cycle that visits infinitely often a given set of locations) in the automaton made of the product of the TA modeling the system with the TA representing a violation of the desired property (often the negation of a property expressed, e.g. in CTL). However, such an accepting cycle does not necessarily mean that the property is violated: indeed, a known problem of TAs is that they allow Zeno behaviors. An infinite run is non-Zeno if it takes an unbounded amount of time; otherwise it is Zeno. Zeno runs are infeasible in reality and thus must be pruned during system verification. That is, it is necessary to check whether a run is Zeno or not so as to avoid presenting Zeno runs as counterexamples. The problem of checking whether a timed automaton accepts at least one

This work is partially supported by the ANR national research program PACS (ANR-14-CE28-0002).

C. Barrett et al. (Eds.): NFM 2017, LNCS 10227, pp. 35–51, 2017.
DOI: 10.1007/978-3-319-57288-8_3

non-Zeno run, i. e. the emptiness checking problem, has been tackled previously (e. g. [11,15,16,25–27]).

It is often desirable not to fix *a priori* all timing constants in a TA: either for tuning purposes, or to evaluate robustness when clock values are imprecise. For that purpose, parametric timed automata (PTAs) extend TAs with parameters [2]. Although most problems of interest are undecidable for PTAs [3], some (semi-)algorithms were proposed to tackle practical parameter synthesis (e. g. [4,9,18,20]). We address here the synthesis of parameter valuations for which there exists a non-Zeno cycle in a PTA; this is highly desirable when performing parametric model-checking for which the parameter valuations violating the property should not allow only Zeno-runs. As far as the authors know, this is the first work on parametric model checking of timed automata with the non-Zenoness assumption. Just as for TAs, the parametric zone graph of PTAs (used in e. g. [4,17,18]) cannot be used to check whether a cycle is non-Zeno. Therefore, we propose here a technique based on *clock upper bound PTAs* (CUB-PTAs), a subclass of PTAs satisfying some syntactic restriction, and originating in CUB-TAs for which the non-Zeno checking problem is most efficient [27]. In contrast to regular PTAs, we show that synthesizing valuations for CUB-PTAs such that there exists an infinite non-Zeno cycle can be done based on (a light extension of) the parametric zone graph. We make the following technical contributions:

1. We show that the parameter synthesis problem for PTAs with non-Zenoness assumption is undecidable.
2. We show that any PTA can be transformed into a finite list of CUB-PTAs;
3. We develop a semi-algorithm to solve the non-Zeno synthesis problem using CUB-PTAs, implemented in IMITATOR and validated using benchmarks.

Outline. Section 2 recalls the necessary preliminaries. Section 3 shows the undecidability of non-Zeno-Büchi emptiness. We then present the concept of CUB-PTAs (Sect. 4), and show how to transform a PTA into a list of CUB-PTAs. Zeno-free parametric model-checking of CUB-PTA is addressed in Sect. 5, and experiments reported in Sect. 6. Finally, Sect. 7 concludes and gives perspectives for future work.

2   Preliminaries

Throughout this paper, we assume a set $X = \{x_1, \ldots, x_H\}$ of *clocks*, i. e. real-valued variables that evolve at the same rate. A clock valuation is a function $w : X \to \mathbb{R}_{\geq 0}$. We write $X = 0$ for $\bigwedge_{1 \leq i \leq H} x_i = 0$. Given $d \in \mathbb{R}_{\geq 0}$, $w + d$ denotes the valuation such that $(w + d)(x) = w(x) + d$, for all $x \in X$.

We assume a set $P = \{p_1, \ldots, p_M\}$ of *parameters*, i. e. unknown constants. A parameter *valuation* v is a function $v : P \to \mathbb{Q}_{\geq 0}$. A *strictly positive* parameter valuation is a valuation $v : P \to \mathbb{Q}_{>0}$.

In the following, we assume $\lhd \in \{<, \leq\}$ and $\bowtie \in \{<, \leq, \geq, >\}$. Throughout this paper, *lt* denotes a linear term over $X \cup P$ of the form $\sum_{1 \leq i \leq H} \alpha_i x_i +$

$\sum_{1 \le j \le M} \beta_j p_j + d$, with $\alpha_i, \beta_j, d \in \mathbb{N}$. Similarly, *plt* denotes a parametric linear term over P, that is a linear term without clocks ($\alpha_i = 0$ for all i). A *constraint* C (i. e. a convex polyhedron) over $X \cup P$ is a set of inequalities of the form $lt \bowtie lt'$, with lt, lt' two linear terms. We denote by *true* (resp. *false*) the constraint that corresponds to the set of all possible (resp. the empty set of) valuations. Given a parameter valuation v, $v(C)$ denotes the constraint over X obtained by replacing each parameter p in C with $v(p)$. Likewise, given a clock valuation w, $w(v(C))$ denotes the expression obtained by replacing each clock x in $v(C)$ with $w(x)$. We say that v *satisfies* C, denoted by $v \models C$, if the set of clock valuations satisfying $v(C)$ is non-empty. We say that C is *satisfiable* if $\exists w, v$ s.t. $w(v(C))$ evaluates to true. We define the *time elapsing* of C, denoted by $C^\nearrow$, as the constraint over X and P obtained from C by delaying all clocks by an arbitrary amount of time. Given $R \subseteq X$, we define the *reset* of C, denoted by $[C]_R$, as the constraint obtained from C by resetting the clocks in R, and keeping the other clocks unchanged. We denote by $C{\downarrow}_P$ the projection of C onto P, i. e. obtained by eliminating the clock variables using existential quantification.

A *guard* g is a constraint over $X \cup P$ defined by inequalities of the form $x \bowtie plt$. We assume w.l.o.g. that, in each guard, given a clock x, at most one inequality is in the form $x \lhd plt$, that is a clock has a single upper bound (or none). A non-parametric guard is a guard over X, i. e. with inequalities $x \bowtie z$, with $z \in \mathbb{N}$. A *parametric zone* C is a constraint over $X \cup P$ defined by inequalities of the form $x_i - x_j \bowtie plt$. A *parametric constraint* K is a constraint over P defined by inequalities of the form $plt \bowtie plt'$, with plt, plt' two parametric linear terms. We use the notation $v \models K$ to indicate that valuating parameters p with $v(p)$ in K evaluates to true. We denote by $\top$ (resp. $\bot$) the parametric constraint that corresponds to the set of all possible (resp. the empty set of) parameter valuations. Given two parametric constraints K_1 and K_2, we write $K_1 \subseteq K_2$ whenever for all v, $v \models K_1 \Rightarrow v \models K_2$.

Definition 1. *A PTA $\mathcal{A}$ is a tuple $\mathcal{A} = (\Sigma, L, l_0, X, P, K_0, I, E)$, where: (i) Σ is a finite set of actions, (ii) L is a finite set of locations, (iii) $l_0 \in L$ is the initial location, (iv) X is a set of clocks, (v) P is a set of parameters, (vi) K_0 is the initial parameter constraint, (vii) I is the invariant, assigning to every $l \in L$ a guard $I(l)$, (viii) E is a set of edges $e = (l, g, a, R, l')$ where $l, l' \in L$ are the source and target locations, $a \in \Sigma$, $R \subseteq X$ is a set of clocks to be reset, and g is a guard.*

The initial constraint K_0 is used to constrain some parameters (as in, e. g. [4,17]); in other words, it defines a domain of valuation for the parameters. For example, given two parameters $p_{\min}$ and $p_{\max}$, we may want to ensure that $p_{\min} \le p_{\max}$. Given $\mathcal{A} = (\Sigma, L, l_0, X, P, K_0, I, E)$, we write $\mathcal{A}.K_0$ as a shortcut for the initial constraint of $\mathcal{A}$. In addition, given K_0', we denote by $\mathcal{A}(K_0')$ the PTA where $\mathcal{A}.K_0$ is replaced with K_0'.

Observe that, as in [27], we do not define accepting locations. In our work, we are simply interested in computing valuations for which there is a non-Zeno cycle. A more realistic parametric model checking approach would require additionally that the cycle is accepting, i. e. it contains at least one accepting location.

However, this has no specific theoretical interest, and would impact the readability of our exposé.

Given a parameter valuation $v \models \mathcal{A}.K_0$, we denote by $v(\mathcal{A})$ the nonparametric TA where all occurrences of a parameter p_i have been replaced by $v(p_i)$.

Definition 2 (Concrete semantics of a TA). *Given a PTA $\mathcal{A} = (\Sigma, L, l_0, X, P, K_0, I, E)$, and a parameter valuation v, the concrete semantics of $v(\mathcal{A})$ is given by the timed transition system $(S, s_0, \rightarrow)$, with $S = \{(l, w) \in L \times \mathbb{R}_{\geq 0}^H \mid w(v(I(l)))$ is true\}, $s_0 = (l_0, \mathbf{0})$, and $\rightarrow$ consists of the discrete and (continuous) delay transition relations:*

- *discrete transitions: $(l, w) \xrightarrow{e} (l', w')$, if $(l, w), (l', w') \in S$, there exists $e = (l, g, a, R, l') \in E$, $w' = [w]_R$, and $w(v(g))$ is true.*
- *delay trans.: $(l, w) \xrightarrow{d} (l, w + d)$, with $d \in \mathbb{R}_{\geq 0}$, if $\forall d' \in [0, d], (l, w + d') \in S$.*

A *(concrete) run* is a sequence $r = s_0 \alpha_0 s_1 \alpha_1 \cdots s_n \alpha_n \cdots$ s.t. $\forall i, (s_i, \alpha_i, s_{i+1}) \in \rightarrow$. We consider as usual that concrete runs strictly alternate delays d_i and discrete transitions e_i and we thus write concrete runs in the form $r = s_0 \xrightarrow{(d_0, e_0)} s_1 \xrightarrow{(d_1, e_1)} \cdots$. We refer to a state of a run starting from the initial state of a TA $\mathcal{A}$ as a *concrete state* of $\mathcal{A}$. Note that when a run is finite, it must end with a concrete state. Given a concrete state $s = (l, w)$, we say that s is reachable (or that $v(\mathcal{A})$ reaches s) if s belongs to a run of $v(\mathcal{A})$. By extension, we say that l is reachable in $v(\mathcal{A})$, if there exists a concrete state (l, w) that is reachable.

An infinite run is said to be *Zeno* if it contains an infinite number of discrete transitions within a finite delay, i.e. if the sum of all delays d_i is bounded.

Symbolic Semantics. Let us recall the symbolic semantics of PTAs (as in e.g. [4,18]). A symbolic state is a pair $\mathbf{s} = (l, C)$ where $l \in L$ is a location, and C its associated parametric zone. The initial symbolic state of $\mathcal{A}$ is $\mathbf{s}_0 = \left(l_0, (\{\mathbf{0}\} \wedge I(l_0))^{\nearrow} \wedge I(l_0) \wedge K_0\right)$. That is, the initial state corresponds to all clocks equal to 0 followed by time-elapsing, intersected with the initial invariant and the initial parameter constraint. The symbolic semantics relies on the Succ operation. Given a symbolic state $\mathbf{s} = (l, C)$ and an edge $e = (l, g, a, R, l')$, $\mathsf{Succ}(\mathbf{s}, e) = (l', C')$, with $C' = \left([(C \wedge g)]_R\right)^{\nearrow}$. The Succ operation is effectively computable, using polyhedra operations: note that the successor of a parametric zone C is a parametric zone. A symbolic run of a PTA is an alternating sequence of symbolic states and edges starting from the initial symbolic state, of the form $\mathbf{s}_0 \xRightarrow{e_0} \mathbf{s}_1 \xRightarrow{e_1} \cdots \xRightarrow{e_{m-1}} \mathbf{s}_m$, such that for all $i = 0, \ldots, m-1$, we have $e_i \in E$, and $\mathbf{s}_{i+1} = \mathsf{Succ}(\mathbf{s}_i, e_i)$. The symbolic semantics is often given in the form of a *parametric zone graph*, i.e. symbolic states of $\mathcal{A}$ and transitions $(\mathbf{s}, e, \mathbf{s}')$ whenever $\mathbf{s}' = \mathsf{Succ}(\mathbf{s}, e)$. Given a symbolic run $(l_0, C_0) \xRightarrow{e_0} (l_1, C_1) \xRightarrow{e_1} \cdots \xRightarrow{e_{n-1}} (l_n, C_n) \cdots$, its *untimed support* is the sequence $l_0 e_0 l_1 \cdots e_{n-1} l_n \cdots$. Two runs (symbolic or concrete) are *equivalent* if they have the same untimed support.

Let us recall a lemma relating concrete and symbolic runs.

Lemma 1. *Let $\mathcal{A}$ be a PTA, and let $\mathbf{r}$ be a symbolic run of $\mathcal{A}$ reaching (l, C). Let $v \models \mathcal{A}.K_0$. There exists an equivalent concrete run in $v(\mathcal{A})$ iff $v \models C{\downarrow}_P$.*

Proof. From [17, Propositions 3.17 and 3.18]. ∎

Given a symbolic run $\mathbf{r}$ reaching (l, C), we call the *concrete runs associated with $\mathbf{r}$* the concrete runs equivalent to $\mathbf{r}$ in $v(\mathcal{A})$, for all $v \models C{\downarrow}_P$.

Problems. In this paper, we aim at addressing the following two problems.

> **non-Zeno emptiness problem:**
> INPUT: A PTA $\mathcal{A}$
> PROBLEM: Is the set of parameter valuations v for which there exists a non-Zeno infinite run in $v(\mathcal{A})$ empty?

> **non-Zeno synthesis problem:**
> INPUT: A PTA $\mathcal{A}$
> PROBLEM: Synthesize the set of parameter valuations v for which there exists an infinite non-Zeno run in $v(\mathcal{A})$.

3   Undecidability of the Non-Zeno Emptiness Problem

As reachability is undecidable for PTAs [2], it is unsurprising that the existence of a valuation for which there exists a non-Zeno infinite run is undecidable too.

Theorem 1. *The non-Zeno emptiness problem is undecidable for PTAs.*

Proof. By reduction from the halting problem of a deterministic 2-counter-machine, which is undecidable [22]. We encode a 2-counter machine (2CM) using PTAs, following an encoding in [8]. This encoding is such that the location $l_{\mathtt{halt}}$ encoding the halting state of the 2CM is reachable iff the 2CM halts, and for valuations of the (unique) parameter v such that $v(p)$ is larger than or equal to the maximum value of the counters along the (unique) run of the machine. Then, since this encoding is such that for any parameter valuation, the encoding stops after $v(p)$ discrete steps, the encoding has no infinite run for any valuation.

Then, from the location encoding the halting location (i.e. $l_{\mathtt{halt}}$), we add a transition resetting x to a new location l_f. This location has a self-loop guarded with $x = 1$ and resetting x (where x is any of the four clocks used in the encoding in [8]). Hence whenever $l_{\mathtt{halt}}$ is reachable, there is an infinite non-Zeno run looping on l_f. That is, there is an infinite non-Zeno run iff the 2CM halts. ∎

Since the emptiness problem is undecidable, the synthesis problem becomes intractable. In the remainder of this paper, we will devise a *semi-algorithm* to address non-Zeno synthesis, i.e. an algorithm that computes the exact solution if it terminates. Otherwise, we compute an under-approximation of the result.

4   CUB-Parametric Timed Automata

It has been shown (e.g. [11,25]) that checking whether a run of TA is infeasible based on the symbolic semantics alone. In [27], the authors identified a subclass of TAs called CUB-TAs for which non-Zenoness checking based on the symbolic semantics is feasible. Furthermore, they show that an arbitrary TA can be transformed into a CUB-TA. Based on their work, we first show that arbitrary PTAs can be transformed into a parametric version of CUB-TAs, and then solve the non-Zeno synthesis problem based on parametric CUB-TAs.

As defined in [27], a clock upper bound is either ∞ or a pair $(n, \lhd)$ where $n \in \mathbb{Q}$ (recall that $\lhd$ is either $<$ or $\leq$). We write $(n_1, \lhd_1) = (n_2, \lhd_2)$ to denote $n_1 = n_2$ and $\lhd_1 = \lhd_2$; $(n_1, \lhd_1) \leq (n_2, \lhd_2)$ to denote $n_1 < n_2$, or if $n_1 = n_2$, then either $\lhd_2$ is $\leq$ or both $\lhd_1$ and $\lhd_2$ are $<$. Further, we write $(n, \lhd) > d$ where d is a constant to denote $n > d$. We define $\min((n, \lhd_1), (m, \lhd_2))$ to be $(n, \lhd_1)$ if $(n, \lhd_1) \leq (m, \lhd_2)$, and $(m, \lhd_2)$ otherwise. Given a clock x and a non-parametric guard g, we write $ub(g, x)$ to denote the upper bound of x given g. Formally,

$$
ub(g, x) = \begin{cases}
(n, \lhd) & \text{if } g \text{ is } x \lhd n \\
\infty & \text{if } g \text{ is } x > n \text{ or } x \geq n \\
\infty & \text{if } g \text{ is } x' \bowtie n \text{ and } x' \neq x \\
\infty & \text{if } g \text{ is } true \\
\min(ub(g_1, x), ub(g_2, x)) & \text{if } g \text{ is } g_1 \wedge g_2
\end{cases}
$$

Definition 3. *A TA is a* CUB-TA *if for each edge* (l, g, a, R, l'), *for all clocks* $x \in X$, *we have (i)* $ub(I(l), x) \leq ub(g, x)$, *and (ii) if* $x \notin R$, *then* $ub(I(l), x) \leq ub(I(l'), x)$.

Intuitively, every clock in a CUB-TA has a non-decreasing upper bound along any path until it is reset.

4.1   Parametric Clock Upper Bounds

Let us define clock upper bounds in a parametric setting. A *parametric clock upper bound* is either ∞ or a pair $(plt, \lhd)$.

Given a clock x and a guard g, we denote by $pub(g, x)$ the parametric upper bound of x given g. This upper bound is a parametric linear term. Formally,

$$
pub(g, x) = \begin{cases}
(plt, \lhd) & \text{if } g \text{ is } x \lhd plt \\
\infty & \text{if } g \text{ is } x > plt \text{ or } x \geq plt \\
\infty & \text{if } g \text{ is } x' \bowtie plt \text{ and } x' \neq x \\
\infty & \text{if } g \text{ is } true \\
\min(pub(g_1, x), pub(g_2, x)) & \text{if } g \text{ is } g_1 \wedge g_2
\end{cases}
$$

Recall that, in each guard, given a clock x, at most one inequality is in the form $x \lhd plt$. In that case, at most one of the two terms is not ∞ and therefore the minimum is well-defined (with the usual definition that $\min(plt, \infty) = plt$).[1]

---

[1] Note that if a clock has more than a single upper bound in a guard, then the minimum can be encoded as a disjunction of constraints, and our results would still apply with non-convex constraints (that can be implemented using a finite list of convex constraints).

We write $(plt_1, \lhd_1) \leq (plt_2, \lhd_2)$ to denote the constraint

$$\begin{cases} plt_1 < plt_2 \text{ if } \lhd_1 = \leq \text{ and } \lhd_2 = < \\ plt_1 \leq plt_2 \text{ otherwise.} \end{cases}$$

That is, we constrain the first parametric clock upper bound to be smaller than or equal to the second one, depending on the comparison operator.

Given two parametric clock upper bounds $pcub_1$ and $pcub_2$, we write $pcub_1 \leq pcub_2$ to denote the constraint

$$\begin{cases} (plt_1, \lhd_1) \leq (plt_2, \lhd_2) \text{ if } pcub_1 = (plt_1, \lhd_1) \text{ and } pcub_2 = (plt_2, \lhd_2) \\ \top \qquad\qquad\qquad\quad \text{ if } pcub_2 = \infty \\ \bot \qquad\qquad\qquad\quad \text{ otherwise.} \end{cases}$$

This yields an inequality constraining the first parametric clock upper bound to be smaller than or equal to the second one.

4.2 CUB Parametric Timed Automata

We extend the definition of CUB-TAs to parameters as follows:

Definition 4. *A PTA is a CUB-PTA if for each edge (l, g, a, R, l'), for all clocks $x \in X$, the following conditions hold: (i) $\mathcal{A}.K_0 \subseteq \big(pub(I(l), x) \leq pub(g, x)\big)$, and (ii) if $x \notin R$, then $\mathcal{A}.K_0 \subseteq \big(pub(I(l), x) \leq pub(I(l'), x)\big)$.*

Hence, a PTA is a *CUB-PTA* iff every clock has a non-decreasing upper bound along any path before it is reset, for all parameter valuations satisfying the initial constraint $\mathcal{A}.K_0$.

Note that, interestingly enough, the class of hardware circuits modeled using a bi-bounded inertial delay[2] fits into CUB-PTAs (for all parameter valuations).

Example 1. Consider the PTA $\mathcal{A}$ in Fig. 1a s.t. $\mathcal{A}.K_0 = \top$. Then $\mathcal{A}$ is not CUB: for x, the upper bound in l_0 is $x \leq 1$ whereas that of the guard on the transition outgoing l_0 is $x \leq p$. $(1, \leq) \leq (p, \leq)$ yields $1 \leq p$. Then, $\top \not\subseteq \big(1 \leq p\big)$; for example, $p = 0$ does not satisfy $1 \leq p$.

Consider again the PTA $\mathcal{A}$ in Fig. 1a, this time assuming that $\mathcal{A}.K_0 = (p = 1 \wedge 1 \leq p' \wedge p' \leq p'')$. This PTA is a CUB-PTA. (The largest constraint K_0 making this PTA a CUB will be computed in Example 2.) □

Lemma 2. *Let $\mathcal{A}$ be a CUB-PTA. Let $v \models \mathcal{A}.K_0$. Then $v(\mathcal{A})$ is a CUB-TA.*

Proof. Let $v \models \mathcal{A}.K_0$. Let $e = (l, g, a, R, l')$ be an edge. Given a clock $x \in X$, from Definition 4, we have that $v \models \big(pub(I(l), x) \leq pub(g, x)\big)$, and therefore $v(pub(I(l), x)) \leq v(pub(g, x))$. This matches the first case of Definition 3. The second case $(x \notin R)$ is similar. ∎

---

[2] This model assumes that, after the change of a signal in the input of a gate, the output changes after a delay which is modeled using a parametric closed interval.

(a) CUB for some valuations   (b) CUB for no valuations

Fig. 1. Examples of PTAs to illustrate the CUB concept

Algorithm 1. CUBdetect($\mathcal{A}$)

Input: PTA $\mathcal{A} = (\Sigma, L, l_0, X, P, K_0, I, E)$
Output: A constraint K ensuring the PTA is a CUB-PTA
1 $K \leftarrow K_0$
2 **foreach** *edge* (l, g, a, R, l') **do**
3   **foreach** *clock* $x \in X$ **do**
4      $K \leftarrow K \wedge \big(pub(I(l), x) \leq pub(g, x)\big)$
5   **if** $x \notin R$ **then** $K \leftarrow K \wedge \big(pub(I(l), x) \leq pub(I(l'), x)\big)$

6 **return** K

4.3 CUB PTA Detection

Given an arbitrary PTA, our approach works as follows. Firstly, we check whether it is a CUB-PTA for some valuations. If it is, we proceed to the synthesis problem, using the cycle detection synthesis algorithm (Sect. 5); however, the result may be partial, as it will only be valid for the valuations for which the PTA is CUB. This incompleteness may come at the benefit of a more efficient synthesis. If it is CUB for no valuation, it has to be transformed into an equivalent CUB-PTA (which will be considered in Sect. 4.4).

Our procedure to detect whether a PTA is CUB for some valuations is given in Algorithm 1. For each edge in the PTA, we enforce the CUB condition on each clock by constraining the upper bound in the invariant of the source location to be smaller than or equal to the upper bound of the edge guard (line 4). Additionally, if the clock is not reset along this edge, then the upper bound of the source location invariant should be smaller than or equal to that of the target location (line 5). If the resulting set of constraints accepts parameter valuations (i. e. is not empty), then the PTA is a CUB-PTA for these valuations.

Example 2. Consider again the PTA $\mathcal{A}$ in Fig. 1a, assuming that $\mathcal{A}.K_0 = \top$. This PTA is CUB for $1 \leq p \wedge 1 \leq p' \wedge p' \leq p''$.

Consider the PTA $\mathcal{A}$ in Fig. 1b, with $\mathcal{A}.K_0 = \top$. When handling location l_0 and clock x, line 4 yields $\mathcal{A}.K = \top \wedge [(p, \leq) \leq (1, \leq)] = p \leq 1$ and then, from line 5, $\mathcal{A}.K = p \leq 1 \wedge [(p, \leq) \leq (p, <)] = p \leq 1 \wedge p < p = \bot$. Hence, there is no valuation for which this PTA is CUB.   □

Proposition 1. *Let* $K = $ CUBdetect$(\mathcal{A})$. *Then* $\mathcal{A}(K)$ *is a CUB-PTA.*

Proof. From the fact that Algorithm 1 gathers constraints to match Definition 4.   ■

4.4   Transforming a PTA into a Disjunctive CUB-PTA

In this section, we show that an arbitrary PTA can be transformed into an extension of CUB-PTAs (namely *disjunctive CUB-PTA*), while preserving the symbolic runs.

For non-parametric TAs, it is shown in [27] that any TA can be transformed into an equivalent CUB-TA. This does not lift to CUB-PTAs.

Example 3. No equivalent CUB-PTA exists for the PTA in Fig. 2b where $K_0 = \top$. Indeed, the edge from l_1 to l_2 (resp. l_3) requires $p_1 \leq p_2$ (resp. $p_1 > p_2$). It is impossible to transform this PTA into a PTA where K_0 (which is $\top$) is included in both $p_1 \leq p_2$ and $p_1 > p_2$.   □

Therefore, in order to overcome this limitation, we propose an alternative definition of *disjunctive CUB-PTAs*. They can be seen as a union (as defined in the timed automata patterns of, e.g. [13]) of CUB-PTAs.

Definition 5. *A* disjunctive CUB-PTA *is a list of CUB-PTAs.*

Given a disjunctive CUB-PTA $\mathcal{A}_1, \ldots, \mathcal{A}_n$, *with* $\mathcal{A}_i = (\Sigma_i, L_i, l_0^i, X_i, P_i, K_0^i, I_i, E_i)$, *the PTA associated with* this disjunctive PTA *is* $\mathcal{A} = (\bigcup_i \Sigma_i, \bigcup_i L_i \cup \{l_0\}, l_0, \bigcup_i X_i, \bigcup_i P_i, \bigcup_i K_0^i, \bigcup_i I_i, E)$, *where* $E = \bigcup_i E_i \cup E'$ *with* $E' = \bigcup_i (l_0, K_0^i, \epsilon, X, l_0^i)$.

Basically, the PTA associated with a disjunctive CUB-PTA is just an additional initial location that connects to each of the CUB-PTAs initial locations, with its initial constraint on the guard.[3]

Example 4. In Fig. 2d (without the dotted, blue elements), two CUB-PTAs are depicted, one (say $\mathcal{A}_1$) on the left with locations superscripted by 1, and one (say $\mathcal{A}_2$) on the right superscripted with 2. Assume $\mathcal{A}_1.K_0$ is $p_1 \leq p_2$ and $\mathcal{A}_2.K_0$ is $p_1 > p_2$. Then the full Fig. 2d (including dotted elements) is the PTA associated with the disjunctive CUB-PTA made of $\mathcal{A}_1$ and $\mathcal{A}_2$.   □

The key idea behind the transformation from a TA into a CUB-TA in [27] is as follows: whenever a location l is followed by an edge e and a location l' for which $ub(g, x) < ub(l, x)$ or $ub(l', x) < ub(l, x)$ for some x if $x \notin R$, otherwise $ub(g, x) < ub(l, x)$, location l is split into two locations: one (say l_1) with a "decreased upper bound", i.e. $x \lhd ub(l', x)$, that is then connected to l'; and one (say l_2) with the same invariant as in l, and with no transition to l'. Therefore, the original behavior is maintained. Note that this transformation induces some non-determinism (one must non-deterministically choose whether one enters l_1 or l_2, which will impact the future ability to enter l') but this has no impact on the existence of a non-Zeno cycle.

Here, we extend this principle to CUB-PTAs. A major difference is that, in the parametric setting, comparing two clock upper bounds does not give a

---

[3] A purely parametric constraint (e.g. $p_1 > p_2 \land p_3 = 3$) is generally not allowed by the PTA syntax, but can be simulated using appropriate clocks (e.g. $p_1 > x > p_2 \land p_3 = x' = 3$). Such parametric constraints are allowed in the input syntax of IMITATOR.

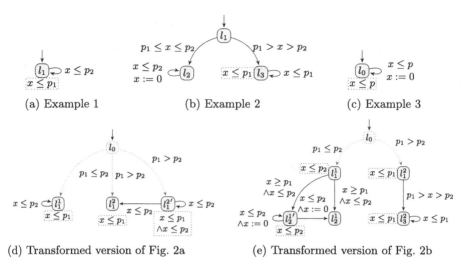

Fig. 2. Examples: detection of and transformation into CUB-PTAs

Boolean answer but a parametric answer. For example, in a TA, $(2, \leq) \leq (3, <)$ holds (this is true), whereas in a PTA $(p_1, \leq) \leq (p_2, <)$ denotes the *constraint* $p_1 < p_2$. Therefore, the principle of our transformation is that, whenever we have to compare two parametric clock upper bounds, we consider both cases: here either $p_1 < p_2$ (in which case the first location does not need to be split) or $p_1 \geq p_2$ (in which case the first location shall be split). This yields a finite list of CUB-PTAs: each of these CUB-PTAs consists in one particular ordering of all parametric linear terms used as upper bounds in guards and invariants. (In practice, in order to reduce the complexity, we only define an order on the parametric linear terms the comparison of which is needed during the transformation.)

Example 5. Let us transform the PTA in Fig. 2a: if $p_1 \leq p_2$ then the PTA is already CUB, and l_1 does not need to be split. This yields a first CUB-PTA, depicted on the left-hand side of Fig. 2d. However, if $p_1 > p_2$, then l_1 needs to be split into $l_1^{2'}$ (where time cannot go beyond p_2) and into l_1^2 (where time can go beyond p_2, until p_1), but the self-loop cannot be taken anymore (otherwise the associated guard makes the PTA not CUB). This yields a second CUB-PTA, depicted on the right-hand side of Fig. 2d. Both make a disjunctive CUB-PTA equivalent to Fig. 2a.

Similarly, we give the transformation of Fig. 2b in Fig. 2e.   □

5   Zeno-Free Cycle Synthesis in CUB-PTAs

Taking a disjunctive CUB-PTA as input, we show in this section that synthesizing the parameter valuations for which there exists at least one non-Zeno cycle (and therefore an infinite non-Zeno run) reduces to an SCC (strongly connected component) synthesis problem.

First, we define a light extension of the parametric zone graph as follows. The *extended parametric zone graph* of a PTA $\mathcal{A}$ is identical to its parametric zone graph, except that any transition $(\mathbf{s}, e, \mathbf{s}')$ is replaced with $(\mathbf{s}, (e, b), \mathbf{s}')$, where b is a Boolean flag which is true if time can *potentially* elapse between $\mathbf{s}$ and $\mathbf{s}'$. In practice, b can be computed as follows, given $\mathbf{s} = (l, C)$ and edge e:

1. add a fresh extra clock x_0 to the constraint C, i.e. compute $C \wedge x_0 = 0$
2. compute the successor $\mathbf{s}' = (l', C')$ of $(l, C \wedge x_0 = 0)$ via edge e
3. check whether $C' \Rightarrow x_0 = 0$: if so, then $b = \text{false}$; otherwise $b = \text{true}$.

Introducing such a clock is cheap: the check is not expensive, and the extra clock does not impact the size of the parametric zone graph: x_0 is 0 in all nodes of the zone graph and can be eliminated from the memory, therefore not requiring more space nor extra states.

In contrast to non-parametric TAs, the flag b does not necessarily mean that time can necessarily elapse for *all* parameter valuations. Consider the example in Fig. 2c. After taking one loop, we have that $x_0 \leq p$: therefore, x_0 is not necessarily 0, and b is true. But consider v such that $v(p) = 0$: then in l_1 time can never elapse. However, we show in the following lemma that the flag b *does* denote time elapsing for *strictly positive* parameters.

Lemma 3. *Let* $(l, C) \overset{e,b}{\Rightarrow} (l', C')$ *be a transition of the extended parametric zone graph of a PTA $\mathcal{A}$. Then, for any strictly positive parameter valuation in $C'\!\downarrow_P$, there exists an equivalent transition in $v(\mathcal{A})$ in which time can elapse.*

Proof. First note that, for any $v \models C'\!\downarrow_P$, an equivalent concrete transition exists in $v(\mathcal{A})$, from Lemma 1. Now, since b is true, the extra clock x_0 in the state of the extended parametric zone graph corresponding to (l, C') is either unbounded, or bounded by some parametric linear term plt. If it is unbounded, then time can elapse for any valuation, and the lemma holds trivially. Assume $x_0 \leq plt$ for some plt. As our parameters are strictly positive, then for any valuation v, $v(plt)$ evaluates to a strictly positive rational, and therefore time can elapse along this transition in $v(\mathcal{A})$. $\blacksquare$

Definition 6. *An infinite symbolic run* $\mathbf{r}$ *is non-Zeno if all its associated concrete runs are non-Zeno.*

In the remainder of this section, given an edge $e = (l, g, a, R, l')$, $e.R$ denotes that the clocks in R reset along e.

The following theorem states that an infinite symbolic run is non-Zeno iff the time can (potentially) elapse along infinitely many edges and, whenever a clock is bounded from above, then eventually either this clock is reset or it becomes unbounded.

Theorem 2. *Let* $\mathbf{r} = \mathbf{s}_0 \overset{(e_0,b_0)}{\Rightarrow} \mathbf{s}_1 \overset{(e_1,b_1)}{\Rightarrow} \cdots$ *be an infinite symbolic run of the extended parametric zone graph of a CUB-PTA $\mathcal{A}$.* $\mathbf{r}$ *is non-Zeno if and only if*

∗ *there exist infinitely many k such that $b_k = \text{true}$; and*

⋆ *for all $x \in X$, for all $i \geq 0$, given $\mathbf{s}_i = (l_i, C_i)$, if $pub(l_i, x) \neq \infty$, there exists j such that $j \geq i$ and $x \in e_j.R$ or $pub(l_j, x) = \infty$.*

We now show that synthesizing parameter valuations for which there exists a non-Zeno infinite run reduces to an SCC searching problem.

First, given an SCC scc, we denote by $scc.K$ the parameter constraint associated with scc, i.e. $C{\downarrow}_P$, where (l, C) is any state of the SCC.[4]

Theorem 3. *Let $\mathcal{A}$ be a CUB-PTA of finite extended parametric zone graph $\mathcal{G}$. Let v be a strictly positive parameter valuation. $v(\mathcal{A})$ contains a non-Zeno infinite run if and only if $\mathcal{G}$ contains a reachable SCC scc such that $v \models scc.K$ and*

† *scc contains a transition $\mathbf{s} \overset{(e,b)}{\Rightarrow} \mathbf{s}'$ such that $b = true$; and*
‡ *for every clock x in X, given $\mathbf{s} = (l, C)$, if $pub(l, x) \neq \infty$ for some state $\mathbf{s}$ in scc, there exists a transition in scc with label (e, b) such that $x \in e.R$.*

Therefore, from Theorem 3, synthesizing valuations yielding an infinite symbolic run reduces to an SCC searching problem in the extended parametric zone graph. Then, we need to test each SCC against two conditions: whether it contains a transition which can be locally delayed (i.e. whether it contains a transition where $b = true$); and whether every clock having an upper bound other than ∞ at some state is reset along some transition in the SCC. Then, for all SCCs matching these two conditions, we return the associated parameter constraint.

We give in Algorithm 2 an algorithm synthNZ to solve the non-Zeno synthesis problem for CUB-PTAs. synthNZ simply iterates on the SCCs, and gathers their associated parameter constraints whenever they satisfy the conditions in Theorem 3.

Algorithm 2. CUB-PTA non-Zeno synthesis algorithm synthNZ($\mathcal{A}$)

Input: CUB-PTA $\mathcal{A}$ and its extended parametric zone graph $\mathcal{G}$
Output: constraint K_{NZ} for which there is a non-Zeno infinite run
1 $K_{NZ} \leftarrow \bot$ **while** *there are un-visited states in $\mathcal{G}$* **do**
2 | find a new SCC scc;
3 | mark all states in scc as visited;
4 | **if** *scc satisfies † and ‡* **then**
5 | | $K_{NZ} \leftarrow K_{NZ} \vee scc.K$;

6 **return** K_{NZ};

If $\mathcal{G}$ is finite, then the correctness and completeness of synthNZ immediately follow from Theorem 3. If only an incomplete part of $\mathcal{G}$ is computed (e.g. by bounding the exploration depth, or the number of explored states, or the

---
[4] Following a well-known result for PTAs, all symbolic states belonging to a same cycle in a parametric zone graph have the same parameter constraint.

execution time) then only the $\Leftarrow$ direction of Theorem 3 holds: in that case, the result of synthNZ is correct but non-complete, i.e. it is a valid under-approximation. In the context of parametric model checking, knowing which parameter valuations violate the property is already very helpful to the designer, as it helps to discard unsafe valuations, and to refine the model.

6 Experiments

We implemented our algorithms in IMITATOR [5].[5] The Parma Polyhedra Library (PPL) [10] is integrated inside the core of IMITATOR in order to solve mainly linear inequality system problems. Experiments were run on an Intel Core 2 Duo P8600 at 2.4 GHz and 4 GiB of memory.

We compare three approaches: (1) A cycle detection synthesis without the non-Zenoness assumption (called synthCycle). The result may be an over-approximation of the actual result, as some of the parameters synthesized may yield only Zeno cycles. If synthCycle does not terminate, its result is an under-approximation of an over-approximation, therefore considered as potentially invalid; that is, there is no guarantee of correctness for the synthesized constraint. (2) Our CUB-detection (Algorithm 1) followed by synthesis (Algorithm 2): the result may be under-approximated, as only the valuations for which the PTA is CUB are considered. (3) Our CUB-transformation (CUBtrans) followed by synthesis (Algorithm 2) on the resulting disjunctive CUB-PTA. If the algorithm terminates, then the result is exact, otherwise it may be under-approximated.

We consider various benchmarks: protocols (CSMA/CD, Fischer [2], RCP, WFAS), hardware circuits (And-Or, flip-flop), scheduling problems (Sched5), a networked automation system (simop) and various academic benchmarks.

We give from left to right in Table 1 the case study name and its number of clocks, parameters and locations. For synthCycle, we give the computation time (TO denotes a time-out at 3600 s), the constraint type ($\bot$, $\top$ or another constraint) and the validity of the result: if synthCycle terminates, the result is an over-approximation, otherwise it is potentially invalid. For CUBdetect (resp. CUBtrans) we give the detection (resp. transformation) time, the total time (including synthNZ), the result, and whether it is an under-approximation or an exact result. We also mention whether CUBdetect outputs that all, none or some valuations make the PTA CUB; and we give the number of locations in the transformed disjunctive CUB-PTA output by CUBtrans. The percentage is used to compare the number of valuations (comparison obtained by discretization) output by the algorithms, with CUBtrans as the basis (as the result is exact).

The toy benchmark CUBPTA1 is a good illustration: CUBtrans terminates after 0.073 s (and therefore its result is exact) with some constraint. CUBdetect is faster (0.015 s) but infers that only some valuations are CUB and analyzes

---

[5] For experimental data including source and binary, see http://imitator.fr/static/NFM17.

Table 1. Experimental comparison of the three algorithms

Model				synthCycle			CUBdetect					CUBtrans				
Name	#X	#P	#L	t (s)	Result	Appr.	Detec t (s)	Total t (s)	CUB for	Result	Appr.	Trans t (s)	Total t (s)	#L CUB	Result	Appr.
CSMA/CD	3	3	28	TO	⊤	invalid?	0.013	0.013	⊥	-	-	0.300	TO	74	⊤	exact
Fischer	2	4	13	TO	⊤	invalid?	0.003	0.003	⊥	-	-	0.012	TO	20	⊤	exact
RCP	6	5	48	TO	Some	invalid?	0.013	0.013	⊥	-	-	0.348	TO	71	⊥	under
WFAS	4	2	10	TO	Some 102%	invalid?	0.009	0.009	⊥	-	-	0.246	1848	40	Some 100%	exact
AndOr	4	4	27	TO	Some 166%	invalid?	0.012	0.012	⊥	-	-	0.059	TO	34	Some 100%	under
Flip-flop	5	2	52	0.058	⊥	exact	0.002	0.086	⊤	⊥	exact	0.010	0.972	58	⊥	exact
Sched5	21	2	153	190	⊥	exact	0.051	0.051	⊥	-	-	1.180	TO	180	⊥	under
simop	8	2	46	TO	⊥	invalid?	0.012	0.012	⊥	-	-	0.219	TO	81	⊥	under
train-gate	5	9	11	TO	⊥	invalid?	0.000	TO	Some	⊥	under	0.059	TO	23	⊥	under
coffee	2	3	4	TO	Some 100%	invalid?	0.000	TO	Some	Some 100%	under	0.012	TO	10	Some 100%	under
CUBPTA1	1	3	2	0.006	⊤ 208%	over	0.000	0.015	Some	Some 69%	under	0.006	0.073	6	Some 100%	exact
JLR13	2	2	2	TO	⊥	invalid?	0.000	TO	⊤	⊥	under	0.000	TO	3	⊥	under

only these valuations; the synthesized result is only 69% of the expected result. In contrast, synthCycle is much faster (0.006 s) but obtains too many valuations (208% of the expected result) as it infers many Zeno valuations.

Let us discuss the results. First, synthCycle almost always outputs a possibly invalid result (neither an under- nor an over-approximation), which justifies the need for techniques handling non-Zeno assumptions. In only one case (CUBPTA1), it outputs a non-trivial over-approximation. In two cases, it happens to give an exact answer, as the over-approximation of ⊥ necessarily means that ⊥ is the exact result. In contrast, CUBtrans gives an exact result in five cases, a non-trivial under-approximation in two cases; the five remaining cases are a disappointing result in which ⊥ is output as an under-approximation. By studying the model manually, we realized that some non-Zeno cycles actually exist for some valuations, but our synthesis algorithm was not able to derive them. Only in one of these cases (Sched5), synthCycle outputs a more interesting result than CUBtrans.

The transformation is relatively reasonable both in terms of added locations (in the worst case, there are 40 instead of 10 locations, hence four times more, for WFAS) and in terms of transformation time (the worst case is 1.2 s for Sched5). Our experiments do not allow us to fairly compare the time of synthCycle (without non-Zenoness) and synthNZ (with non-Zenoness assumption) as, without surprise due to the undecidability, most analyses do not terminate. Only two benchmarks terminate for both algorithms, but are not significant (<1 s).

Note that flip-flop is a hardware circuit modeled using a bi-bounded inertial delay, and is therefore CUB for all valuations.

An interesting benchmark is WFAS, for which our transformation procedure terminates whereas synthCycle does not. Therefore, we get an exact result while the traditional procedure cannot produce any valuable output.

As a conclusion, CUBdetect seems to be faster but less complete than CUBtrans. As for CUBtrans, its result is almost always more valuable than synthCycle, and therefore is the most interesting algorithm.

7 Conclusion

We proposed a technique to synthesize valuations for which there exists a non-Zeno infinite run in a PTA. By adding accepting states, this allows for parametric model checking with non-Zenoness assumption. Our techniques rely on a transformation to a disjunctive CUB-PTA (or in some cases on a simple detection of the valuation for which the PTA is already CUB), and then on a dedicated cycle synthesis algorithm. We implemented our techniques in IMITATOR and compared our algorithms on a set of benchmarks.

Future Works. Our technique relying on CUB-PTAs extends the technique of CUB-TAs: this technique is shown in [27] to be the most efficient for performing non-Zeno model checking for TAs. However, for PTAs, other techniques (such as yet to be defined parametric extensions of strongly non-Zeno TAs [26] or guessing zone graph [16]) could turn more efficient and should be investigated.

In addition, parametric stateful timed CSP (PSTCSP) [7] is a formalism for which the CUB assumption seems to be natively verified. Therefore, studying non-Zeno parametric model checking for PSTCSP, as well as transforming PTAs into PSTCSP models, would be an interesting direction of research.

Studying the decidability of the underlying decision problem should be done for famous subclasses of PTAs constraining the use of parameters (namely L/U-PTAs, L-PTAs and U-PTAs [17]) as well as for new semantic subclasses that we recently proposed and that benefit from decidability results (namely integer-point PTAs and reset-PTAs [6]).

An interesting future will be to design a multi-core extension of our non-Zeno synthesis algorithm; this could be done by reusing parallel depth first search algorithms for finding cycles [14].

Finally, combining our synthesis algorithms with IC3 [12], as well as extending them to hybrid systems [23] is also of high practical interest.

References

1. Alur, R., Dill, D.L.: A theory of timed automata. Theoret. Comput. Sci. **126**(2), 183–235 (1994)
2. Alur, R., Henzinger, T.A., Vardi, M.Y.: Parametric real-time reasoning. In: STOC, pp. 592–601. ACM (1993)
3. André, É.: What's decidable about parametric timed automata? In: Artho, C., Ölveczky, P.C. (eds.) FTSCS 2015. CCIS, vol. 596, pp. 52–68. Springer, Cham (2016). doi:10.1007/978-3-319-29510-7_3
4. André, É., Chatain, T., Encrenaz, E., Fribourg, L.: An inverse method for parametric timed automata. IJFCS **20**(5), 819–836 (2009)

5. André, É., Fribourg, L., Kühne, U., Soulat, R.: IMITATOR 2.5: a tool for analyzing robustness in scheduling problems. In: Giannakopoulou, D., Méry, D. (eds.) FM 2012. LNCS, vol. 7436, pp. 33–36. Springer, Heidelberg (2012). doi:10.1007/978-3-642-32759-9_6

6. André, É., Lime, D., Roux, O.H.: Decision problems for parametric timed automata. In: Ogata, K., Lawford, M., Liu, S. (eds.) ICFEM 2016. LNCS, vol. 10009, pp. 400–416. Springer, Cham (2016). doi:10.1007/978-3-319-47846-3_25

7. André, É., Liu, Y., Sun, J., Dong, J.S.: Parameter synthesis for hierarchical concurrent real-time systems. Real-Time Syst. **50**(5–6), 620–679 (2014)

8. André, É., Markey, N.: Language preservation problems in parametric timed automata. In: Sankaranarayanan, S., Vicario, E. (eds.) FORMATS 2015. LNCS, vol. 9268, pp. 27–43. Springer, Cham (2015). doi:10.1007/978-3-319-22975-1_3

9. Aştefănoaei, L., Bensalem, S., Bozga, M., Cheng, C.-H., Ruess, H.: Compositional parameter synthesis. In: Fitzgerald, J., Heitmeyer, C., Gnesi, S., Philippou, A. (eds.) FM 2016. LNCS, vol. 9995, pp. 60–68. Springer, Cham (2016). doi:10.1007/978-3-319-48989-6_4

10. Bagnara, R., Hill, P.M., Zaffanella, E.: The Parma Polyhedra Library: toward a complete set of numerical abstractions for the analysis and verification of hardware and software systems. Sci. Comput. Program. **72**(1–2), 3–21 (2008)

11. Bowman, H., Gómez, R.: How to stop time stopping. Formal Aspects Comput. **18**(4), 459–493 (2006)

12. Cimatti, A., Griggio, A., Mover, S., Tonetta, S.: Parameter synthesis with IC3. In: FMCAD, pp. 165–168. IEEE (2013)

13. Dong, J.S., Hao, P., Qin, S., Sun, J., Yi, W.: Timed automata patterns. IEEE Trans. Softw. Eng. **34**(6), 844–859 (2008)

14. Evangelista, S., Laarman, A., Petrucci, L., van de Pol, J.: Improved multicore nested depth-first search. In: Chakraborty, S., Mukund, M. (eds.) ATVA 2012. LNCS, vol. 7561, pp. 269–283. Springer, Heidelberg (2012). doi:10.1007/978-3-642-33386-6_22

15. Gómez, R., Bowman, H.: Efficient detection of Zeno runs in timed automata. In: Raskin, J.-F., Thiagarajan, P.S. (eds.) FORMATS 2007. LNCS, vol. 4763, pp. 195–210. Springer, Heidelberg (2007). doi:10.1007/978-3-540-75454-1_15

16. Herbreteau, F., Srivathsan, B., Walukiewicz, I.: Efficient emptiness check for timed Büchi automata. Formal Methods Syst. Des. **40**(2), 122–146 (2012)

17. Hune, T., Romijn, J., Stoelinga, M., Vaandrager, F.W.: Linear parametric model checking of timed automata. JLAP **52–53**, 183–220 (2002)

18. Jovanović, A., Lime, D., Roux, O.H.: Integer parameter synthesis for timed automata. Trans. Softw. Eng. **41**(5), 445–461 (2015)

19. Khatib, L., Muscettola, N., Havelund, K.: Mapping temporal planning constraints into timed automata. In: TIME, pp. 21–27. IEEE Computer Society (2001)

20. Knapik, M., Penczek, W.: Bounded model checking for parametric timed automata. Trans. Petri Nets Models Concurr. **5**, 141–159 (2012)

21. Larsen, K.G., Pettersson, P., Yi, W.: UPPAAL in a nutshell. Int. J. STTT **1**(1–2), 134–152 (1997)

22. Minsky, M.L.: Computation: Finite and Infinite Machines. Prentice-Hall, Inc., Upper Saddle River (1967)

23. Schupp, S., Ábrahám, E., Chen, X., Makhlouf, I.B., Frehse, G., Sankaranarayanan, S., Kowalewski, S.: Current challenges in the verification of hybrid systems. In: Berger, C., Mousavi, M.R. (eds.) CyPhy 2015. LNCS, vol. 9361, pp. 8–24. Springer, Cham (2015). doi:10.1007/978-3-319-25141-7_2

24. Sun, J., Liu, Y., Dong, J.S., Pang, J.: PAT: towards flexible verification under fairness. In: Bouajjani, A., Maler, O. (eds.) CAV 2009. LNCS, vol. 5643, pp. 709–714. Springer, Heidelberg (2009). doi:10.1007/978-3-642-02658-4_59
25. Tripakis, S.: Verifying progress in timed systems. In: Katoen, J.-P. (ed.) ARTS 1999. LNCS, vol. 1601, pp. 299–314. Springer, Heidelberg (1999). doi:10.1007/3-540-48778-6_18
26. Tripakis, S., Yovine, S., Bouajjani, A.: Checking timed Büchi automata emptiness efficiently. Formal Methods Syst. Des. 26(3), 267–292 (2005)
27. Wang, T., Sun, J., Wang, X., Liu, Y., Si, Y., Dong, J.S., Yang, X., Li, X.: A systematic study on explicit-state non-Zenoness checking for timed automata. IEEE Trans. Softw. Eng. 41(1), 3–18 (2015)

Multi-timed Bisimulation for Distributed Timed Automata

James Ortiz, Moussa Amrani$^{(\boxtimes)}$, and Pierre-Yves Schobbens

Computer Science Faculty, University of Namur, Namur, Belgium
{james.ortizvega,moussa.amrani,pierre-yves.schobbens}@unamur.be

Abstract. Timed bisimulation is an important technique which can be used for reasoning about behavioral equivalence between different components of a complex real-time system. The verification of timed bisimulation is a difficult and challenging problem because the state explosion caused by both functional and timing constraints must be taken into account. Timed bisimulation was shown decidable for Timed Automata (TA). Distributed TA and TA with Independent Clocks (icTA) were introduced to model Distributed Real-time Systems. They are a variant of TA with local clocks that may not run at the same rate. In this paper, we first propose to extend the theory of Timed Labeled Transition Systems to Multi-Timed Labeled Transition Systems, and relate them by an extension of timed bisimulation to multi-timed bisimulation. We prove the decidability of multi-timed bisimulation and present an EXPTIME algorithm for deciding whether two icTA are multi-timed bisimilar. For multi-timed bisimilarity, an extension of the standard refinement algorithm is described.

1 Introduction

Distributed Real-Time Systems (DTS) are increasing with the scientific and technological advances of computer networks. The high demand for computer networks has caused the development of new complex applications which benefit from the high performance and resources offered by modern telecommunications networks. Current researches in the area of DTS have emerged from the need to specify and analyze the behavior of these systems, where both distributed behavior and timing constraints are present. Formal verification methods, such as model checking, have been used to verify the correctness of complex DTS. Model checking over DTS becomes rapidly intractable because the state space often grows exponentially with the number of components considered. A technique to reduce the state space is to merge states with the same behaviour. For untimed systems, the notion of *bisimulation* [13] is classically used to this end, and its natural extension for real-time systems, *timed bisimulation*, was already shown decidable for Timed Automata (TA) [2,12]. A timed automaton is a finite automaton augmented with real-valued clocks, represented as variables that increase at the same rate as time progresses. TA assume perfect clocks: all clocks have infinite precision and are perfectly synchronized. In this paper,

© Springer International Publishing AG 2017
C. Barrett et al. (Eds.): NFM 2017, LNCS 10227, pp. 52–67, 2017.
DOI: 10.1007/978-3-319-57288-8_4

we study two variants of TA called Distributed Timed Automata (DTA) and Timed Automata with Independent Clocks (icTA) proposed by [1,11,16] to model DTS, where the clocks are not necessarily synchronized. TA have been used to model DTS such as Controller Area Network [14] and WirelessHART Networks [10]. But, TA, icTA and timed bisimulation are based on a sequential semantics of a Timed Labelled Transition Systems (TLTS), i.e., a run of a TLTS is given by a sequence of actions and timestamps.

Unfortunately, a sequential semantics does not describe completely the behavior of the DTS, because interactions between processes with their associated local clocks that are running at the same rate and distribution of the actions over the components are not considered. Also, model-checking and bisimulation equivalence algorithms have been implemented in tools [19,20] for the sequential semantics used by the model (e.g., TA, TLTS, etc.). In contrast, behavioral equivalences for DTS have only been introduced in [3]. It is, however, not clear whether such equivalences agree with the distributed timed properties in DTS. Therefore, we propose an alternative semantics to the classical sequential semantics for TLTS and icTA: specifically, a run of a system in our alternative semantics is given by the sequences of pairs (action, tuples of timestamps). We propose an alternative semantics in order to be able to consider a semantics which expresses the distribution of the actions and timestamps over the components. With this alternative, it becomes possible to analyze the local behavior of the components *independently*, thus enhancing the expressiveness of the TLTS (and icTA). We introduce Multi-Timed Labelled Transition Systems (MLTS), an extension of classical TLTS in order to cope with the notion of multiple local times, and we propose efficient algorithms using refinement techniques [17].

Contributions. One of our main contributions is to incorporate a alternative semantics over sequential semantics for TLTS and icTA. Also, we extend the classical theory of timed bisimulation with the notion multi-timed bisimulation and their corresponding decision algorithms. We also present two algorithms: (i) a forward reachability algorithm for the parallel composition of two icTA, which will help us to minimize the state space exploration by our second algorithm, and (ii) a decision algorithms for multi-timed bisimulation using the zone-based technique [5]. Multi-timed bisimulation is a relation over local clocks (and processes), and cannot be computed with the standard partition refinement algorithm [17]. Instead, our algorithm successively refines a set of zones such that ultimately each zone contains only multi-timed bisimilar pairs of states. Furthermore, we show that our algorithm is EXPTIME-complete. Since TA are a special variant of icTA, our work conservatively extends the expressiveness of TA and TLTS; and since timed bisimulation over TA [19,20] can be regarded as a special case of multi-timed bisimulation, our decision algorithms could potentially be used to analyze complex DTS.

Structure of the Paper. After recalling preliminary notions in Sect. 2, we introduce our alternative semantics for icTA in Sect. 3, based on multi-timed words consumed by MLTS. Section 4 deals with bisimulation: we first define multi-timed bisimulation, by adapting the classical definition to MLTS, then show its decidability by exhibiting an EXPTIME algorithm. Finally, Sect. 5 compares our work with existing contributions, and Sect. 6 concludes. Due to space constraints, some proofs are not given here, but stay available in a Technical Report available online [15].

2   Preliminaries

We describe in this section the notations needed for formally defining Timed Labelled Transition Systems (TLTS) and Timed Automata TA.

Timed Words. The set of all *finite words* over a finite alphabet of actions Σ is denoted by Σ^*. Let $\mathbb{N}$, $\mathbb{R}$ and $\mathbb{R}_{\geq 0}$ respectively denote the sets of natural, real and nonnegative real numbers. A timed word [2] over Σ is a finite sequence $\theta = ((\sigma_1, t_1), (\sigma_2, t_2) \ldots (\sigma_n, t_n))$ of actions paired with nonnegative real numbers (i.e., $(\sigma_i, t_i) \in \Sigma \times \mathbb{R}_{\geq 0}$) such that the timestamped sequence $t = t_1 \cdot t_2 \cdots t_n$ is nondecreasing (i.e., $t_i \leq t_{i+1}$). We sometimes define θ as the pair $\theta = (\sigma, t)$ with $\sigma \in \Sigma^*$ and t a sequence of timestamps with the same length.

Clocks. A clock is a real positive variable that increases with time. Let X be a finite set of clock names. A clock constraint $\phi \in \Phi(X)$ is a conjunction of comparisons of a clock with a natural constant c: with $x \in X$, $c \in \mathbb{N}$, and $\sim \in \{<, >, \leq, \geq, =\}$, ϕ is defined by

$$\phi ::= true \mid x \sim c \mid \phi_1 \wedge \phi_2$$

A clock valuation $\nu \in \mathbb{R}_{\geq 0}^X$ over X is a mapping $\nu : X \to \mathbb{R}_{\geq 0}$. For a time value $t \in \mathbb{R}_{\geq 0}$, we note $\nu + t$ the valuation defined by $(\nu + t)(x) = \nu(x) + t$. Given a clock subset $Y \subseteq X$, we note $\nu[Y \to 0]$ the valuation defined as follows: $\nu[Y \leftarrow 0]$ $(x) = 0$ if $x \in Y$ and $\nu[Y \leftarrow 0](x) = \nu(x)$ otherwise. The projection of ν on Y, written $\nu \rfloor_Y$, is the valuation over Y containing only the values in ν of clocks in Y.

Timed Automata (TA). A TA is a tuple $\mathcal{B} = (\Sigma, X, S, s_0, \to_{ta}, I, F)$ where Σ is a finite alphabet, X a clock set, S a set of locations with $s_0 \in S$ the initial location and $F \subseteq S$ the set of (sink) final states, $\to_{ta} \subseteq S \times \Sigma \times \Phi(X) \times 2^X \times S$ is the automaton's transition relation, $I : S \to \Phi(X)$ associates to each location a clock constraint as invariant. For a transition $(s, \phi, a, Y, s') \in \to_{ta}$, we classically write $s \xrightarrow{\phi, a, Y} s'$ and call s and s' the source and target location, ϕ is the guard, a the action or label, Y the set of clocks to be reset. During the execution of a TA $\mathcal{B}$, a *state* is a pair $(s, \nu) \in S \times \mathbb{R}_{\geq 0}^X$, where s denotes the current state with its accompanying clock valuation ν, starting at s_0, ν_0 where ν_0 maps each clock to 0. We only consider *legal* states, i.e. states that satisfy $\nu \models I(s)$ (i.e. valuations that map clocks to values that satisfy the current state's invariant).

Timed Transition System (TLTS). The transition system TLTS($\mathcal{B}$) generated by $\mathcal{B}$ is defined by TLTS($\mathcal{B}$) $= (Q, q_0, \Sigma, \to_{tlts})$, where Q is a set of legal states over $\mathcal{B}$ with initial state $q_0 = (s_0, \nu_0)$, Σ a finite alphabet and $\to_{tlts} \subseteq Q \times$

$(\Sigma \uplus \mathbb{R}_{\geq 0}) \times Q$ is the TLTS transition relation defined by: (a) Delay transition: $(s, \nu) \xrightarrow{t} (s, \nu + t)$ for some $t \in \mathbb{R}_{\geq 0}$, iff $\nu + t \vDash I(s)$, (b) Discrete transition: $(s, \nu) \xrightarrow{a} (s', \nu')$, iff $s \xrightarrow{\phi, a, Y} s'$, $\nu \vDash \phi$, $\nu' \vDash \nu[Y \rightarrow 0]$ and $\nu' \vDash I(s')$.

3   An Alternative Semantics for DTA

In this section, we define an alternative semantics (which we will call multi-timed semantics) for icTA as opposed to the mono-timed semantics of [1]. The main problem with the semantics of [1] is that they use the reference time. The benefits of this new definition are threefold. First, the multi-timed semantics preserves the untimed language of the icTA. Second, the multi-timed semantics can work with multi-timed words. Third, the region equivalence defined in [1] could form a finite time-abstract bisimulation on the multi-timed semantics. Hence, the multi-timed semantics allows to build a region automaton that accepts exactly Untime($\mathcal{L}(\mathcal{A})$) for all icTA $\mathcal{A}$ [1]. Thus, we extend TLTS and icTA to their multi-timed version.

3.1   Multi-timed Actions

Let $Proc$ be a non-empty set of processes, then, we denote by $\mathbb{R}_{\geq 0}^{Proc}$ the set of functions from $Proc$ to $\mathbb{R}$, that we call $tuples$. A tuple $\boldsymbol{d} \in \mathbb{R}_{\geq 0}^{Proc}$ is smaller that $\boldsymbol{d}'$, noted, $\boldsymbol{d} < \boldsymbol{d}'$ iff $\forall i \in Proc$ $\boldsymbol{d}_i \leq \boldsymbol{d}_i'$ and $\exists i \in Proc$ $\boldsymbol{d}_i < \boldsymbol{d}_i'$. A Monotone Sequence of Tuples (MST) is a sequence $\boldsymbol{d} = \boldsymbol{d}_1 \boldsymbol{d}_2 \cdots \boldsymbol{d}_n$ of tuples of $\mathbb{R}_{\geq 0}^{Proc}$ where: $\forall j \in 1 \cdots n - 1$, $\boldsymbol{d}_j \leq \boldsymbol{d}_{j+1}$. A multi-timed word on Σ is a pair $\theta = (\sigma, \boldsymbol{d})$ where $\sigma = \sigma_1 \sigma_2 \ldots \sigma_n$ is a finite word $\sigma \in \Sigma^*$, and $\boldsymbol{d} = \boldsymbol{d}_1 \boldsymbol{d}_2 \ldots \boldsymbol{d}_n$ is a MST of the same length. This is the analog of a $timed$ $word$ (or $multi$-$timed$ $action$) [2]. A $multi$-$timed$ $word$ can equivalently be seen as a sequence of pairs in $\Sigma \times \mathbb{R}_{\geq 0}^{Proc}$.

3.2   Multi-timed Labeled Transition Systems

Our multi-timed semantics is defined in terms of $runs$ that record the state and clock values at each transition points traversed during the consumption of a $multi$-$timed$ word. Instead of observing actions at a global time, a multi-timed word allows to synchronise processes on a common action that may occur at a specific process time.

Definition 1 (Multi-timed Labelled Transition System). *A Multi-Timed Labelled Transition System (MLTS) over a set of processes $Proc$ is a tuple $\mathcal{M} = (Q, q_0, \Sigma, \rightarrow_{mlts})$ such that: (i) Q is a set of states. (ii) $q_0 \in Q$ is the initial state. (iii) Σ is a finite alphabet. (v) $\rightarrow_{mlts} \subseteq Q \times (\Sigma \uplus \mathbb{R}_{\geq 0}^{Proc}) \times Q$ is a set of transitions.*

The transitions from state to state of a MLTS are noted in the following way: (i) A transition (q, a, q') is denoted $q \xrightarrow{a} q'$ and is called a $discrete$ $transition$, if $a \in \Sigma$ and $(q, a, q') \in \rightarrow_{mlts}$, (ii) A transition $(q, \boldsymbol{d}, q')$ is denoted $q \xrightarrow{\boldsymbol{d}} q'$ and is called a $delay$ $transition$, if $\boldsymbol{d} \in \mathbb{R}_{\geq 0}^{Proc}$ and $(q, \boldsymbol{d}, q') \in \rightarrow_{mlts}$.

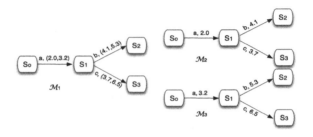

Fig. 1. Multi-timed and Timed Labelled Transition Systems

A run of $\mathcal{M}$ can be defined as a finite sequence of moves, where discrete and continuous transitions alternate: $\rho = q_0 \xrightarrow{d_1} q_0' \xrightarrow{a_1} q_1 \xrightarrow{d_2} q_1' \xrightarrow{a_2} q_2 \ldots$ $q_{n-1} \xrightarrow{d_{n-1}} q_{n-1}' \xrightarrow{a_{n-1}} q_n$, where $\forall 0 \leq i \leq n-1, q_i \in Q, \forall j \leq n - 1, d_j \in \mathbb{R}_{\geq 0}^{Proc}, q_j' \in Q$ and $a_j \in \Sigma$. The *multi-timed word* of ρ is $\theta = ((a_1, t_1), (a_2, t_2) \ldots, (a_n, t_n))$, where $t_i = \sum_{j=1}^{i} d_j$. A multi-timed word θ is *accepted* by $\mathcal{M}$ iff there is a maximal initial run whose multi-timed word is θ. The *language* of $\mathcal{M}$, denoted $\mathcal{L}(\mathcal{M})$, is defined as the set of multi-timed words accepted by some run of $\mathcal{M}$. Note that MLTS are a proper generalisation of TLTS: each TLTS can be seen as a MLTS with a single process and conversely.

For example, consider the two transition systems in Fig. 1: a MLTS on the left ($\mathcal{M}_1$) and two TLTS on the right ($\mathcal{M}_2$ and $\mathcal{M}_3$) with the finite input alphabet $\Sigma = \{a, b, c\}$. In brief, $\mathcal{M}_2$ and $\mathcal{M}_3$ could be considered as the projection of $\mathcal{M}_1$ on the case of process 1 and 2.

3.3   A Multi-timed Semantics for icTA

DTA [1,11] consist of a number of local timed automata. In [1], DTA are not much studied. Instead, their product is first computed, giving rise to the class of icTA ($\mathcal{A} = (\mathcal{B}, \pi)$, where $\mathcal{B}$ is a TA and π is a function maps each clock to a process).

Given $\pi : X \rightarrow Proc$, a clock valuation $\nu : X \rightarrow \mathbb{R}_{\geq 0}$ and $d \in \mathbb{R}_{\geq 0}^{Proc}$: the valuation $\nu +_\pi d$ is defined by $(\nu +_\pi d)(x) = \nu(x) + d_{\pi(x)}$ for all $x \in X$. A Rate is a tuple $\tau = (\tau_q)_{q \in Proc}$ of local time functions. Each local time function τ_q maps the reference time to the time of process q, i.e., $\tau_q : \mathbb{R}_{\geq 0} \rightarrow \mathbb{R}_{\geq 0}$. The functions τ_q must be continuous, strictly increasing, divergent, and satisfy $\tau_q(0) = 0$. The set of all these tuples τ is denoted by *Rates*.

The operational semantics of an icTA has been associated to a sequential semantics. A run of an icTA $\mathcal{A}$ for $\tau \in Rates$ with a sequential semantics as a sequence $(s_1, \nu_1) \xrightarrow{t_1, a_1} (s_2, \nu_2) \xrightarrow{t_2, a_2} (s_2, \nu_3) \ldots (s_{n-1}, \nu_{n-1}) \xrightarrow{t_{n-1}, a_{n-1}} (s_n, \nu_n)$ where $\forall 1 \leq i \leq n, s_i \in S$ and $\forall j \leq n - 1, t_j \in \mathbb{R}_{\geq 0}$ and $a_j \in \Sigma$. Here, we want to associate operational semantics of a icTA to a MLTS.

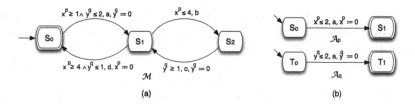

Fig. 2. (a) An icTA $\mathcal{M}$, (b) An counter example of Multi-timed bisimulation

Definition 2. *Let $\mathcal{A}$ be an icTA and $\tau \in Rates$. Our **multi-timed semantics** of the icTA $\mathcal{A}$ is given by a MLTS over Proc, denoted by $MLTS(\mathcal{A}, \tau) = (Q, q_0, \Sigma, \rightarrow_{mlts})$. The set of states Q consists of triples composed of a location, a clock valuation and lastly the reference time: $Q = \{(s, \nu, t) \in S \times \mathbb{R}^X_{\geq 0} \times \mathbb{R}_{\geq 0} \mid \nu \models I(s)\}$. The starting state is $q_0 = (s_0, \nu_0, 0)$, where ν_0 is the valuation that assigns 0 to all the clocks. Σ is the alphabet of $\mathcal{A}$. The transition relation $\rightarrow_{mlts}$ is defined by:*

(i) A transition $(q_i, \boldsymbol{d}, q'_i)$ is denoted $q_i \xrightarrow{\boldsymbol{d}} q'_i$, and is called a *delay transition*, where $q_i = (s_i, \nu_i, t_i)$, $q'_i = (s_i, \nu_i +_\pi \boldsymbol{d}, t_{i+1})$, $\boldsymbol{d} = \tau(t_{i+1}) - \tau(t_i)$ and $\forall t \in [t_i, t_{i+1}] : \nu_i +_\pi (\tau(t) - \tau(t_i)) \models I(s_i)$.

(ii) A transition (q_i, a, q_{i+1}) is denoted $q_i \xrightarrow{a} q_{i+1}$, and is called a *discrete transition*, where $q_i = (s_i, \nu_i, t_i)$, $q_{i+1} = (s_{i+1}, \nu_{i+1}, t_{i+1})$, $a \in \Sigma$, there exists a transition $(s_i, a, \phi, Y, s_{i+1}) \in \rightarrow_{ic}$, such that $\nu_i \models \phi$, $\nu_{i+1} = \nu_i[Y \to 0]$, $\nu_{i+1} \models I(s_{i+1})$, $t_i = t_{i+1}$.

In Definition 2, we have introduced a multi-timed semantics for icTA, following ideas of [1]. A run of an icTA $\mathcal{A}$ for $\tau \in Rates$ with our multi-timed semantics is an initial path in $MLTS(\mathcal{A}, \tau)$ where discrete and continuous transition alternate. A multi-timed word is accepted by $\mathcal{A}$ for $\tau \in Rates$ iff it is accepted by $MLTS(\mathcal{A}, \tau)$.

Example 1. The Fig. 2(a) shows an icTA $\mathcal{M}$ with the finite input alphabet $\Sigma = \{a, b, c, d\}$, the set of processes $Proc = \{p, q\}$, the set of clocks $X = \{x^p, y^q\}$ and $\tau = (2t, t)$ i.e. $\tau_p(t) = 2t$ and $\tau_q(t) = t$. A run of $\mathcal{M}$ on multi-timed word $\theta = ((a, (2.0, 1.0))(b, (3.0, 1.5))(c, (4.2, 2.1))(d, (6.0, 3.0)))$ is given by ρ $(S_0, [x^p = 0.0, y^q = 0.0], 0.0) \xrightarrow{(2.0, 1.0)} (S_0, [x^p = 2.0, y^q = 1.0], 1.0) \xrightarrow{a} (S_1, [x^p = 2.0, y^q = 0.0], 1.0) \xrightarrow{(1.0, 0.5)} (S_1, [x^p = 3.0, y^q = 1.5], 1.5) \xrightarrow{b} (S_2, [x^p = 3.0, y^q = 1.5], 1.5) \xrightarrow{(1.2, 0.6)} (S_2, [x^p = 4.2, y^q = 1.1], 2.1) \xrightarrow{c} (S_1, [x^p = 4.2, y^q = 0.0], 2.1) \xrightarrow{(1.8, 0.9)} (S_1, [x^p = 6.0, y^q = 0.9], 3.0) \xrightarrow{c} (S_0, [x^p = 0.0, y^q = 0.9], 3.0)$.

4 Multi-timed Bisimulation

From a distributed approach, a DTS consist of several processes with their associated local clocks that are not running at the same rate. Thus, in order to formalize preservation of distributed timed behavior, we extend the classical definition of timed bisimulation [9] towards a multi-timed semantics. Our motivation for extending the classical definition of timed bisimulation is twofold: first, efficient algorithms checking for timed and time-abstract bisimulation have been discovered [12,19]. Nonetheless, these algorithms are based on sequential semantics (i.e., TLTS and TA). Second, verifying the preservation of distributed timed behavior in DTS could be used to master the combinatorial explosion of the size of the model due to the composition of the processes.

4.1 Strong Multi-timed Bisimulation

Let $\mathcal{M}_1$ and $\mathcal{M}_2$ be two MLTS over the same set of actions Σ and processes $Proc$. Let $Q_{\mathcal{M}_1}$ (resp., $Q_{\mathcal{M}_2}$) be the set of states of $\mathcal{M}_1$ (resp., $\mathcal{M}_2$). Let $\mathcal{R}$ be a binary relation over $Q_{\mathcal{M}_1} \times Q_{\mathcal{M}_2}$. We say that $\mathcal{R}$ is a strong multi-timed bisimulation whenever the following transfer property holds (note that technically this is simply strong bisimulation over $\Sigma \uplus \mathbb{R}_{\geq 0}^{Proc}$):

Definition 3. *A strong multi-timed bisimulation over MLTS $\mathcal{M}_1$, $\mathcal{M}_2$ is a binary relation $\mathcal{R} \subseteq Q_{\mathcal{M}_1} \times Q_{\mathcal{M}_2}$ such that, for all $q_{\mathcal{M}_1} \mathcal{R} q_{\mathcal{M}_2}$, the following holds:*

(i) *For every $a \in \Sigma$ and for every discrete transition $q_{\mathcal{M}_1} \xrightarrow{a}_{\mathcal{M}_1} q'_{\mathcal{M}_1}$, there exists a matching discrete transition $q_{\mathcal{M}_2} \xrightarrow{a}_{\mathcal{M}_2} q'_{\mathcal{M}_2}$ such that $q'_{\mathcal{M}_1} \mathcal{R} q'_{\mathcal{M}_2}$ and symmetrically.*

(ii) *For every $\boldsymbol{d} = (d_1, \ldots, d_n) \in \mathbb{R}_{\geq 0}^{Proc}$, for every delay transition $q_{\mathcal{M}_1} \xrightarrow{\boldsymbol{d}}_{\mathcal{M}_1} q'_{\mathcal{M}_1}$, there exists a matching delay transition $q_{\mathcal{M}_2} \xrightarrow{\boldsymbol{d}}_{\mathcal{M}_2} q'_{\mathcal{M}_2}$ such that $q'_{\mathcal{M}_1} \mathcal{R} q'_{\mathcal{M}_2}$ and symmetrically.*

Two states $q_{\mathcal{M}_1}$ and $q_{\mathcal{M}_2}$ are multi-timed bisimilar, written $q_{\mathcal{M}_1} \approx q_{\mathcal{M}_2}$, iff there is a multi-timed bisimulation that relates them. $\mathcal{M}_1$ and $\mathcal{M}_2$ are multi-timed bisimilar, written $\mathcal{M}_1 \approx \mathcal{M}_2$, if there exists a multi-timed bisimulation relation $\mathcal{R}$ over $\mathcal{M}_1$ and $\mathcal{M}_2$ containing the pair of initial states.

As a consequence of Definition 3, the notion of multi-timed bisimulation extends to icTA and we have the following definition:

Definition 4. *Let $\mathcal{A}$ and $\mathcal{B}$ be two icTA. We say the automata $\mathcal{A}$ and $\mathcal{B}$ are multi-timed bisimilar, denoted $\mathcal{A} \approx \mathcal{B}$, iff $\forall \tau \in Rates$ $MLTS(\mathcal{A}, \tau) \approx MLTS(\mathcal{B}, \tau)$.*

When there is only one process, the multi-timed bisimulation is the usual timed bisimulation. Consider the two icTA $\mathcal{A}_p$ (top) and $\mathcal{A}_q$ (bottom) in Fig. 2(b) with the alphabet $\Sigma = \{a\}$, the set of processes $Proc = \{p, q\}$, the set of clocks $X = \{x^p, y^q\}$ and $\tau = (t^2, 3t)$ i.e. $\tau_p(t) = t^2$ and $\tau_q(t) = 3t$. $\mathcal{A}_p$ and $\mathcal{A}_q$ in Fig. 2(b) depicts an icTA. $\mathcal{A}_p$ performs nondeterministically the transition with the guard $x^p \leq 2$, the action a, resets clock x^p to 0 and enters location s_1. Similarly, $\mathcal{A}_q$ performs nondeterministically the transitions with the guard $y^q \leq 2$, the action

a, resets clock y^q to 0 and enters location t_1. We will show that these icTA are not multi-timed bisimilar (Definition 3) ever if their underling TA are bisimilar (and ever isomorphic): We have $(S_0, [x^p = 0], 0)$ in $\mathsf{MLTS}(\mathcal{A}_p, \tau_p)$ and $(T_0, [y^q = 0], 0)$ since $\mathcal{A}_p$ can run the delay transition $(S_0, [x^p = 0], 0) \xrightarrow{(1,3)} (S_0, [x^p = 1.0], 1)$ and $\mathcal{A}_q$ in $\mathsf{MLTS}(\mathcal{A}_q, \tau_q)$. We have $(S_0, [x^p = 0], 0) \not\approx (T_0, [y^q = 0], 0)$ can only match this transition with $(T_0, [y^q = 0], 0) \xrightarrow{(1,3)} (T_0, [y^q = 3], 1)$. From these states $\mathsf{MLTS}(\mathcal{A}_p, \tau_p)$ can fire a while $\mathsf{MLTS}(\mathcal{A}_q, \tau_q)$ cannot.

4.2 Decidability

Inspired by [12], we show that for given icTA $\mathcal{A}$, $\mathcal{B}$, checking whether $\mathcal{A} \approx \mathcal{B}$ is decidable via a suitable zone graph [12]. In order to define the notion of clock zone over a set of clocks X, we need to consider the set $\Phi^+(X)$ of extended clock constraints.

Definition 5. *A clock constraint ϕ is a conjunction of comparisons of a clock with a constant c, given by the following grammar, where ϕ ranges over $\Phi^+(X)$, $x_i, x_j \in X$, $c \in \mathbb{N}$, and $\sim \in \{<, >, \leq, \geq, =\}$:*

$$\phi ::= true \mid x_i \sim c \mid x_i - x_j \sim c \mid \phi_1 \wedge \phi_2.$$

A clock constraint of the form $x_i - x_j \sim c$ is called diagonal constraint and x_i, x_j must belong to the same process. The notion of satisfaction of a clock constraint $\phi \in \Phi^+(X)$ by a valuation is given by the clause $\nu \models x_i - x_j \sim c$ iff $\nu(x_i) - \nu(x_j) \sim c$.

Informally, a clock zone $\mathcal{Z}$ is a conjunction of extended clock constraints $\phi \in \Phi^+(X)$ with inequalities of clock differences and its semantics is the set of clock valuations that satisfy it $[\![\mathcal{Z}]\!] = \{\nu \mid \nu \models \phi\}$. We omit the semantics brackets $([\![\mathcal{Z}]\!])$ when obvious. For any clock zones $\mathcal{Z}$, $\mathcal{Z}'$ and finite set of clocks X, the semantics of the intersection, clock reset, inverse clock reset, time successor and time predecessor events on clock zone can be defined as: (i) $\mathcal{Z} \cap \mathcal{Z}' = \{\nu \mid \nu \in \mathcal{Z} \wedge \nu \in \mathcal{Z}'\}$, (ii) $\mathcal{Z} \downarrow_X = \{\nu[X \to 0] \mid \nu \in \mathcal{Z}\}$, (iii) $\mathcal{Z} \uparrow_X = \{\nu \mid \nu[X \to 0] \in \mathcal{Z}\}$, (iv) $\mathcal{Z} \uparrow = \{\nu +_\pi d \mid \nu \in \mathcal{Z} \text{ and } d \in \mathbb{R}^{Proc}_{>0}\}$, (v) $\mathcal{Z} \downarrow = \{\nu -_\pi d \mid \nu \in \mathcal{Z} \text{ and } d \in \mathbb{R}^{Proc}_{>0}\}$.

A zone graph [12] is similar to a region graph [2] with the difference that each node consists of pair (called a zone) of a location s and a clock zone $\mathcal{Z}$ (i.e., $q = (s, \mathcal{Z})$). For $q = (s, \mathcal{Z})$, we write $(s', \nu) \in q$ if $s = s'$ and $\nu \in \mathcal{Z}$, indicating that a state is included in a zone. Analogously, we can write $(s, \mathcal{Z}) \subseteq (s', \mathcal{Z}')$ to indicate that $s = s'$ and $\mathcal{Z} \subseteq \mathcal{Z}'$. We will use the notation $\mathsf{Action}(e)$ to denote the action a of the edge e. Furthermore, we extend the zone operations for an icTA $\mathcal{A}$ in the following way:

Definition 6. *Let $q = (s, \mathcal{Z})$ be a zone and $e = (s, a, \phi, Y, s') \in \to_{icta}$ be a transition of $\mathcal{A}$, then $post(\mathcal{Z}, e) = \{\nu' \mid \exists \nu \in \mathcal{Z}, \exists \tau \in Rates, \exists t \in \mathbb{R}_{\geq 0}, (s, \nu, t) \xrightarrow{e}_{mlts(\mathcal{A}, \tau)} (s', \nu', t)\}$ is the set of valuations that q can reach by taking the transition e.*

Definition 7. *Let $q = (s, \mathcal{Z}')$ be a zone and $e = (s, a, \phi, Y, s') \in \rightarrow_{icta}$ be a transition of $\mathcal{A}$, then $\mathsf{pred}(\mathcal{Z}', e) = \{\nu | \exists \nu' \in \mathcal{Z}', \exists \tau \in Rates, \exists t \in \mathbb{R}_{\geq 0}, (s, \nu, t) \xrightarrow{e}_{mlts(\mathcal{A}, \tau)} (s', \nu', t)\}$ is the set of valuations that q can reach by executing the transition e.*

Intuitively, the zone $(s', \mathsf{post}(\mathcal{Z}, e))$ describes the discrete successor of the zone $(s, \mathcal{Z})$ under the transition e, and the zone $(s, \mathsf{pred}(\mathcal{Z}', e))$ describes the discrete predecessor of the zone $(s', \mathcal{Z}')$ under the transition e.

Definition 8 (Multi-timed Zone Graph). *Given an icTA $\mathcal{A} = (\Sigma, X, S, s_0, \rightarrow_{icta}, I, F, \pi)$, its symbolic multi-timed zone graph $(ZG(\mathcal{A}))$ is a transition system $ZG(\mathcal{A}) = (Q, q_0, (\Sigma \cup \{\uparrow\}), \rightarrow_{ZG})$, where: (i) Q consists of pairs $q = (s, \mathcal{Z})$ where $s \in S$, and $\mathcal{Z} \in \Phi^+(X)$ is a clock zone with $\mathcal{Z} \subseteq I(s)$. (ii) $q_0 \in Q$ is the initial zone $q_0 = (s_0, \mathcal{Z}_0)$ with $\mathcal{Z}_0 = [\![\bigwedge_{x \in X} x = 0]\!]$. (iii) Σ is the set of labels of $\mathcal{A}$. (iv) $\rightarrow_{ZG} \subseteq Q \times (\rightarrow_{icta} \cup \{\uparrow\}) \times Q$ is a set of transitions, where each transition in $ZG(\mathcal{A})$ is a labelled by a transition $e = (s, a, \phi, Y, s') \in \rightarrow_{icta}$, where s and s' are the source and target locations, ϕ is a clock constraint defining the guard of the transition, a is the action of the edge and Y is the set of clocks to be reset by the transition in the icTA $\mathcal{A}$. For each $e \in \Sigma$, transitions are defined by the rules:*

(i) For every $e = (s, a, \phi, Y, s')$ and clock zone $\mathcal{Z}$, there exists a discrete transition (q, e, q'), where $q = (s, \mathcal{Z}) \xrightarrow{e}_{ZG} q' = (s', \mathsf{post}(\mathcal{Z}, e))$ if $\mathsf{post}(\mathcal{Z}, e) \neq \emptyset$.
(ii) For a clock zone $\mathcal{Z}$, there exists a delay transition $(q, \uparrow, q')$, where $q = (s, \mathcal{Z}) \xrightarrow{\uparrow}_{ZG} q' = (s, \mathcal{Z}')$ and $\mathcal{Z}' = \mathcal{Z} \uparrow \cap I(s)$.

Note that $\uparrow$ is used here as a symbol to represent symbolic positive delay transitions. Only the reachable part is constructed.

Lemma 1. *Let $(s, \mathcal{Z})$ be a zone and $e = (s, a, \phi, Y, s') \in \rightarrow_{icta}$ be a transition of an icTA $\mathcal{A}$, then $\mathcal{Z} \uparrow$, $\mathcal{Z} \uparrow_x$, $\mathcal{Z} \downarrow$, $\mathsf{post}(\mathcal{Z}, e)$ and $\mathsf{pred}(\mathcal{Z}', e)$ are also zones.*

Multi-timed Zone Graph Algorithm: In Algorithm 1, we build a reachable multi-timed zone graph $(ZG(\mathcal{A} \parallel \mathcal{B}))$ for the parallel composition of two icTA ($\mathcal{A}$ and $\mathcal{B}$). Algorithm 1 build a multi-timed zone graph, starting with the pair $(s_0, \mathcal{Z}_0)$ (s_0 initial location of the automaton $\mathcal{A}$ with $\mathcal{Z}_0 = [\![\bigwedge_{x \in X} x = 0]\!]$ represents the initial zone). However, the multi-timed zone graph can be infinite, because constants used in zones may grow for ever. Therefore, we use a technique called extrapolation abstraction ($Extra^+_{LU_{(s)}}$ (LU-bound)) [4,7], where L is the maximal lower bound and U is the maximal upper bounds. For every location s of a $ZG(\mathcal{A})$, there are bound functions LU and the symbolic zone graph using $Extra^+_{LU_{(s)}}$. Then, we build zones of the form $q_{ZG} = (s, Extra^+_{LU_{(s)}}(\mathsf{post}(\mathcal{Z}, e)))$.

Lemma 2 (Completeness). *Let $\theta = (s_0, \nu_0, t_0) \xrightarrow{d_0, a_0} (s_1, \nu_1, t_1) \xrightarrow{d_1, a_1} \dots \xrightarrow{d_{n-1}, a_{n-1}} (s_n, \nu_n, t_n)$ be a run of $MLTS(\mathcal{A}, \tau)$, for some $\tau \in Rates$. Then, for any state (s_i, ν_i, t_i) where $0 \leq i \leq n$, there exists a symbolic zone $(s_i, \mathcal{Z}_i)$ added in Q such that $\nu_i \in \mathcal{Z}_i$.*

The above lemma tells that the Algorithm 1 over-approximates reachability. Now, we can establish the termination of the Algorithm 1, because there are finitely many $Extra^+_{LU_{(s)}}$ zones. Here, we will use Algorithm 1 to over-approximate the co-reachable state space of the two icTA $\mathcal{A}$ and $\mathcal{B}$, on the strongly synchronized product of $\mathcal{A}$ and $\mathcal{B}$. The time complexity of this algorithm is given in terms of the number of clocks, the number of clocks and the number of transitions of the icTA: $O(|S| \times | \rightarrow_{\text{icTA}} | \times |X|^2))$ where $|S|$ represent the number of states in the icTA $\mathcal{A}$, $|X|$ the number of clocks in $\mathcal{A}$ and $| \rightarrow_{\text{icTA}} |$ the number of transitions in $\mathcal{A}$.

Algorithm 1. Reachable Multi-timed Zone Graph with subsumption

---

Input : An icTA $\mathcal{C} = (\Sigma, X, S, s_0, \rightarrow_{icta}, I, F, \pi)$.
Output: A reachable zone graph $\text{ZG}(\mathcal{C}) = (Q, q_0, \Sigma, \rightarrow_{\text{ZG}})$.
1 // $s \in S$ is a location of $\mathcal{C}$, $\mathcal{Z}_{1 \leq i \leq 3}$ are clock zones.
2 // T_{ZG} is a set of transitions (i.e. $\rightarrow_{\text{ZG}} = T_{\text{ZG}}$), E_{ZG} is a set of labels.
3 // D and Q are a set of pairs $S \times \mathcal{Z}$, D is the set of open states.
4 **Function** *BuildSymbZoneGraph($\mathcal{C}$)*
5 $\quad$ $q_0 = (s_0, \mathcal{Z}_0)$ such that for all $x \in X$ and $\nu \in \mathcal{Z}_0$, $\nu(x) = 0$;
6 $\quad$ Q, D $\leftarrow \{q_0\}$, $T_{\text{ZG}} \leftarrow \emptyset$, M $\leftarrow \emptyset$;
7 $\quad$ **while** $D \neq \emptyset$ **do**
8 $\quad\quad$ Choose and Remove $(s, \mathcal{Z}_1)$ from D ;
9 $\quad\quad$ **for** *each transition* $e = (s, a, \phi, Y, s') \in \rightarrow_{icta}$ *such that* $\mathcal{Z}_1 \wedge \phi \neq \emptyset$ **do**
10 $\quad\quad\quad$ // $\mathcal{Z}_2$ is the successor
11 $\quad\quad\quad$ $\mathcal{Z}_2 \leftarrow Extra^+_{LU_{(s)}}(\text{post}(\mathcal{Z}_1, e))$;
12 $\quad\quad\quad$ $E_{\text{ZG}} \leftarrow E_{\text{ZG}} \cup \{e\}$;
13 $\quad\quad\quad$ **if** *exists* $(s', \mathcal{Z}_4) \in Q$ *such that* $\mathcal{Z}_2 \subseteq \mathcal{Z}_4$ **then**
14 $\quad\quad\quad\quad$ $T_{\text{ZG}} \leftarrow T_{\text{ZG}} \cup \{(s, \mathcal{Z}_1) \xrightarrow{e}_{\text{ZG}} (s', \mathcal{Z}_3)\}$;
15 $\quad\quad\quad$ **else**
16 $\quad\quad\quad\quad$ $T_{\text{ZG}} \leftarrow T_{\text{ZG}} \cup \{(s, \mathcal{Z}_1) \xrightarrow{e}_{\text{ZG}} (s', \mathcal{Z}_2)\}$;
17 $\quad\quad\quad\quad$ Q $\leftarrow$ Q $\cup \{(s', \mathcal{Z}_2)\}$, D $\leftarrow$ D $\cup \{(s', \mathcal{Z}_2)\}$;
18 $\quad\quad\quad$ **end**
19 $\quad\quad$ **end**
20 $\quad\quad$ $\mathcal{Z}_2 \leftarrow \mathcal{Z}_1 \uparrow \wedge I(s)$;
21 $\quad\quad$ **if** *exists* $(s, \mathcal{Z}_3) \in Q$ *such that* $\mathcal{Z}_2 \subseteq \mathcal{Z}_3$ **then**
22 $\quad\quad\quad$ $T_{\text{ZG}} \leftarrow T_{\text{ZG}} \cup \{(s, \mathcal{Z}_1) \xrightarrow{\uparrow}_{\text{ZG}} (s, \mathcal{Z}_3)\}$;
23 $\quad\quad$ **else**
24 $\quad\quad\quad$ $T_{\text{ZG}} \leftarrow T_{\text{ZG}} \cup \{(s, \mathcal{Z}_1) \xrightarrow{\uparrow}_{\text{ZG}} (s', \mathcal{Z}_2)\}$;
25 $\quad\quad\quad$ Q $\leftarrow$ Q $\cup \{(s, \mathcal{Z}_2)\}$, D $\leftarrow$ D $\cup \{(s, \mathcal{Z}_2)\}$;
26 $\quad\quad$ **end**
27 $\quad$ **end**
28 $\quad$ **return** $(Q, q_0, \Sigma, \rightarrow_{\text{ZG}})$;
29 **end**

Refinement Algorithm: Now, we describe a refinement algorithm with signature to compute the multi-timed bisimulation from their zone graph of their strong product $\text{ZG}(\text{ZG}(\mathcal{A} \parallel \mathcal{B}))$. The passage of arbitrary local times are abstracted by time elapse $\uparrow$ transitions from a zone to successor zones, and discrete transitions. Essentially, our algorithm is based on the refinement technique [6,17,19]. The state space Q of $\text{ZG}(\mathcal{A} \parallel \mathcal{B})$ is divided in zones that initially over-approximate the co-reachable states of $\mathcal{A}$ and $\mathcal{B}$. Algorithm 2 starts from an initial set of zones Π_0 and successively refines these sets such that ultimately each zone contains only bisimilar state pairs.

The runs of a zone graph involve a sequence of moves with discrete and time-elapse ↑ transitions. The refinement algorithm has thus to deal with the following difficulties: when taking a ↑ transition, where the clocks in different processes are not perfectly synchronous, it should take into consideration that the time elapse traverses continuously diagonal, almost vertical and horizontal time successor zones. Conversely, when the clocks belonging to the same process (i.e., perfectly synchronous), the time elapsing traverses only continuously diagonal time successor zones. Thus, the time refinement operator presented in [19] is not applicable within our Algorithm 2. Figure 3 presents an example: (a) a time elapsing traversing the clock regions 1 to 3 for synchronous clocks, (b) a time elapsing traversing continuously diagonal, almost horizontal and vertical time successor zones for asynchronous clocks.

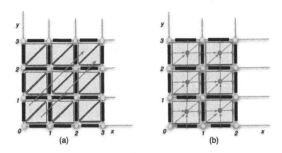

Fig. 3. (a) A time elapsing traversing 0 to 3, (b) Multi-timed time successors.

The discrete refinement operator presented in [19] is also not applicable within our Algorithm 2. Therefore, our algorithm adopts the idea of the signature-based technique [6], which assigns states to equivalence blocks according to a characterizing signature. In each refinement iteration, the set of zones are refined according to a signature. The algorithm in [6], cannot be applied in our setting in a straightforward way, due to its untimed characteristic, while in our case, the time and discrete characteristics should be considered. Based on [6], we introduce a signature refinement operator which refine the set of zones until a fixed point is reached, which is the complete multi-timed bisimulation. Thus, we introduce the timed and discrete predecessor operators.

Definition 9. *Let* $q = (s, \mathcal{Z})$ *and* $q' = (s, \mathcal{Z}')$ *be two zones, then:* $\mathsf{TimePred}_{\uparrow}(\mathcal{Z}, \mathcal{Z}') = \{\nu \in \mathcal{Z} \mid \exists\, \boldsymbol{d} \in \mathbb{R}_{>0}^{Proc}, \exists\, \tau \in Rates, \exists\, t, t'' \geq 0, t \leq t''$ *and* $\forall t', t \leq t' \leq t''$, *and* $\boldsymbol{d} = \tau(t'') - \tau(t), (\nu +_{\pi} \boldsymbol{d}) \in \mathcal{Z}'$, *and* $\boldsymbol{d}' = \tau(t') - \tau(t)$ *then* $(\nu +_{\pi} \boldsymbol{d}') \in (\mathcal{Z} \cup \mathcal{Z}')\}$ *is the set of valuations in the zone* $\mathcal{Z}$ *from which a valuation of* $\mathcal{Z}'$ *can be reached through the elapsing of time, without entering any other zones besides* $\mathcal{Z}$ *and* $\mathcal{Z}'$ *(i.e.,* $\mathcal{Z} \cup \mathcal{Z}'$*).*

The $\mathsf{TimePred}_{\uparrow}(\mathcal{Z}, \mathcal{Z}')$ operator refines $\mathcal{Z}$ selecting the states that can reach $\mathcal{Z}'$.

Lemma 3. *Let $q = (s, \mathcal{Z})$, $q' = (s, \mathcal{Z}') \in Q$ be two zones, then TimePred$_\uparrow$ $(\mathcal{Z}, \mathcal{Z}')$ is a clock zone.*

We use as signature of a state (s, ν) the set of outgoing transitions from (s', ν'). Then, a refinement of a zone can be computed by grouping states that have the same signature. The resulting set of zones then represents the multi-timed bisimulation relation: two states (s, ν) and (s', ν') are multi-timed bisimilar iff they are in the same zone with similar outgoing transitions. Formally, this is captured in the following definition:

Definition 10. *Let $q = (s, \mathcal{Z})$ be a zone, then the signature of a state $(s, \nu) \in q$ formed by the set of labels of all the edges starting from (s, ν) is defined as:*
$ActionSigPred_q(s, \nu) = \{(Action(e)) \mid \exists \mathcal{Z}', \exists \nu' \in \mathcal{Z}', (s, \nu) \xrightarrow{Action(e)}_{icTA} (s', \nu')\}$. *Also, the signature of the zone q is defined as: $ActionSig(q) = \bigcup_{(s,\nu)\in q} ActionSigPred_q(s, \nu)$.*

$ActionSigPred_q(s, \nu)$ operator is used to compute the signatures of a state into a zone. Our Algorithm 2 consists of two steps: The initial phase, is responsible for keeping a pair of states in q into zones so that every pair of states ($i.e.$, $((s_\mathcal{A}, s_\mathcal{B})$, $(\nu_\mathcal{A}, \nu_\mathcal{B})))$ from the same zone q have the same signature $ActionSigPred_q$ $(s_\mathcal{A}, \nu_\mathcal{A}) = ActionSigPred_q(s_\mathcal{B}, \nu_\mathcal{B})$. The refinement phase, consists of computing the timed predecessors (see Definition 11 below) and the discrete signature predecessors (see Definition 12 below) until a stable set of zones is reached. Stable zone are a multi-timed bisimulation relation if every pair of states of every zone in the set have the same signature with respect to every computed refinement. A detailed explication about building a stable zones follows:

- **Initial phase:** Let $\Pi_0 = Q$ be the initial set of zones, where Q is given by Algorithm 1. After the initial phase, the set Π contains zones consisting of states with unique signatures, $ActionSigPred_q(s_\mathcal{A}, \nu_\mathcal{A}) = ActionSigPred_q(s_\mathcal{B}, \nu_\mathcal{B})$.
- **Refinement phase:** An existing set of zones are iteratively refined until all zones becomes stable simultaneously with respect to all their timed predecessors and discrete predecessors. For simplicity, we will write $(s, \mathcal{Z})$ to denote the pairs $((s_\mathcal{A}, s_\mathcal{B}), \mathcal{Z})$.

Definition 11. *Let Π be a set of zones and $q = (s, \mathcal{Z})$, $q' = (s', \mathcal{Z}')$ be two zones in Π. Then for the delay transitions, the refinement function is defined as follows:*
$$TimeRefine(\mathcal{Z}, \Pi) = \{TimePred_\uparrow(\mathcal{Z}, \mathcal{Z}') \mid \mathcal{Z}' \in \Pi, q \xrightarrow{\uparrow}_\Pi q'\}.$$

Definition 12. *Let Π be a set of zones and $q = (s, \mathcal{Z})$, $q' = (s', \mathcal{Z}')$ be two zones in Π. Let $q = (s, \mathcal{Z})$ be the currently examined zone and $ActionSig(q)$ be the signatures of the set of states into the zone q. Let $e_\mathcal{A}$ and $e_\mathcal{B}$ be the transitions of the icTAs $\mathcal{A}$ and $\mathcal{B}$. Then the refinement of a zone q is defined as follows:*
$$DiscreteSigRefine(\mathcal{Z}, \Pi) = \bigcap_{a \in ActionSig(q)}((\bigcap_{\{e_\mathcal{A}|Action(e_\mathcal{A})=a\}} \bigcup_{\{e_\mathcal{B}|Action(e_\mathcal{B})=a\}}$$
$$pred(\mathcal{Z}', (e_\mathcal{A}, e_\mathcal{B}))) \cap (\bigcap_{\{e_\mathcal{B} \mid Action(e_\mathcal{B})=a\}} \bigcup_{\{e_\mathcal{A} \mid Action(e_\mathcal{A})=a\}} pred(\mathcal{Z}', (e_\mathcal{A}, e_\mathcal{B})))).$$

Lemma 4. *Let $(s, \mathcal{Z})$ be a class of Π and let e be an edge of the $ZG(\mathcal{C})$, then each of* TimeRefine$(\mathcal{Z}, \Pi)$ *and* DiscreteSigRefine$(\mathcal{Z}, \Pi)$ *forms a partition of $\mathcal{Z}$ in zones.*

The correctness of the Algorithm 2 follows from the algorithm in [6,17]. The definition TimeRefine$(\mathcal{Z}, \Pi)$ above to generate a finer set of zones, which deals with delay transitions. The definition of DiscreteSigRefine$(\mathcal{Z}, \Pi)$, generate also a finer set of zones and distinguishes the states with discrete transitions. Termination is ensured by Lemma 4. Algorithm 2 describes the main steps of the decision procedure for multi-timed bisimulation checking. It is based on the function BuildSymbZoneGraph (i.e., Algorithm 1). The function PartitionZoneGraph returns stable set of zones Π. Given a set of zones Π, the Algorithm 2 computes the states $((s_{\mathcal{A}}, s_{\mathcal{B}}), \mathcal{Z})$ from Π that are bisimilar up to the desired initial state $((s_{\mathcal{A}}^0, s_{\mathcal{B}}^0), \mathcal{Z}_0)$.

Algorithm 2. The partition refinement algorithm for a reachable ZG

```
   Input  : A ZG(C) = (Q = Q_A × Q_B, q_0 = (q_A^0, q_B^0), Σ = Σ_A ∪ Σ_B, →_ZG), Π.
   Output: A coarsest partition Π.
1  // q ∈ Q is a zone of ZG(C), Π is a set of zones, Z, Z' are clock zones.
2  // Q is a set of pairs S × Z.
3  Function PartitionZoneGraph(ZG(C), Π)
4  |    // Phase I - Get the input partition Π
5  |    Π' ← Π ;
6  |    Repeat
7  |    |    // Phase II - Refine Π' by delay transitions:
8  |    |    for each zone (or block) Z ∈ Π' do
9  |    |    |    Π' ← TimeRefine(Z, Π') ;
10 |    |    end
11 |    |    // Phase III - Refine Π' by discrete transitions:
12 |    |    for each zone (or block) Z ∈ Π' do
13 |    |    |    Π' ← DiscreteSigSplit(Z, Π') ;
14 |    |    end
15 |    Until Π' does not change;
16 |    Return Π' ;
17 end
```

Proposition 1. *Let $q = (s, \mathcal{Z})$ be a zone. Let $(s_{\mathcal{A}}, \nu_{\mathcal{A}})$ and $(s_{\mathcal{B}}, \nu_{\mathcal{B}})$ be two states in q, then $(s_{\mathcal{A}}, \nu_{\mathcal{A}}) \approx (s_{\mathcal{B}}, \nu_{\mathcal{B}})$ iff $((s_{\mathcal{A}}, s_{\mathcal{B}}), \nu_{\mathcal{A}} \cup \nu_{\mathcal{B}}) \in \mathcal{Z}$.*

Theorem 1. *Deciding multi-timed bisimulation between two icTA is EXPTIME-complete.*

An example of the zone graph, partition and multi-timed bisimulation computed by our algorithms can be found in Fig. 4. The Fig. 4(a) shows two icTA $\mathcal{A}$ and $\mathcal{B}$ with the finite input alphabet $\Sigma = \{a, b\}$, the set of processes $Proc = \{p, q\}$, the set of clocks $X = \{x^p, y^q\}$ and $\tau_p > \tau_q$. The Fig. 4(b) shows the zone graph computed by Algorithm 1. The Fig. 4(c) shows the multi-timed bisimulation for $\mathcal{A}$ and $\mathcal{B}$.

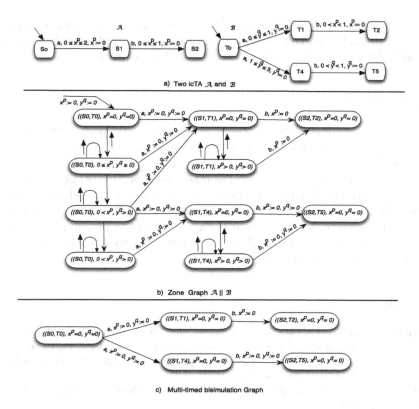

Fig. 4. (a) Composition of icTAs; (b) Zone graph; (c) bisimulation

5   Related Work

Because TA are a general-purpose formalism, several implementations and extensions have been considered. For example, Puri [18] studied the semantics of
robustness timed automata where clocks can drift in a bounded way, i.e. clocks
may grow at independent rates in the interval $1 \pm \epsilon$. Krishnan [11] considered
asynchronous distributed timed automata, where clocks evolve independently in
each component. Akshay *et al.* concentrate on the untimed language of DTA. In
a previous work [16], we suggested a model that has the same expressive power
as event clock automata [2], but without studied possible simulation algorithms.

The notion of bisimulation for TA is studied in various contributions
[4,8,9,19,20]. Cerans [9] gives a proof of decidability for timed bisimulation.
Several techniques are used in the literature for providing algorithms capable of
checking (bi-)simulation: Weise and Lenzkes [20] rely on a zone-based algorithm
for weak bisimulation over TA, but no implementation is provided; Bulychev
et al. [8] study timed simulation for simulation-checking games, for which an
implementation is available from [4]; region construction for timed bisimulation
was also considered by Akshay *et al.* [1], but never implemented; and more closely

to our work, Tripakis and Yovine proposed a time-abstract bisimulation over TA in [19]. Krishnan [11] and our previous work [16] manipulated clock drifts as well for manipulating DTA, but without considering bisimulation.

6 Conclusions

Bisimulation is a common technique to reduce the state space explosion issue encountered during model-checking of real-time systems. To enable the application of this technique for DTS modelled by icTA, we proposed an alternative semantics for capturing the execution of icTA, based on multi-timed words running over Multi-Timed Labelled Transition Systems. We extended the notion of bisimulation to such structures, and proposed an EXPTIME algorithm for checking decidability. We are now studying how to efficiently implement such structures and decidability algorithm, and plan to compare their performance against classical work as proposed in [4,19].

References

1. Akshay, S., Bollig, B., Gastin, P., Mukund, M., Narayan Kumar, K.: Distributed timed automata with independently evolving clocks. In: Breugel, F., Chechik, M. (eds.) CONCUR 2008. LNCS, vol. 5201, pp. 82–97. Springer, Heidelberg (2008). doi:10.1007/978-3-540-85361-9_10

2. Alur, R., Dill, D.L.: A theory of timed automata. Theor. Comput. Sci. **126**(2), 183–235 (1994)

3. Balaguer, S., Chatain, T.: Avoiding shared clocks in networks of timed automata. In: Koutny, M., Ulidowski, I. (eds.) CONCUR 2012. LNCS, vol. 7454, pp. 100–114. Springer, Heidelberg (2012). doi:10.1007/978-3-642-32940-1_9

4. Behrmann, G., Bouyer, P., Larsen, K.G., Pelánek, R.: Lower and upper bounds in zone-based abstractions of timed automata. STTT **8**(3), 204–215 (2006)

5. Bengtsson, J., Yi, W.: Timed automata: semantics, algorithms and tools. In: Desel, J., Reisig, W., Rozenberg, G. (eds.) ACPN 2003. LNCS, vol. 3098, pp. 87–124. Springer, Heidelberg (2004). doi:10.1007/978-3-540-27755-2_3

6. Blom, S., Orzan, S.: A distributed algorithm for strong bisimulation reduction of state spaces. Electr. Notes Theor. Comput. Sci. **68**(4), 523–538 (2002)

7. Bouyer, P.: Forward analysis of updatable timed automata. Form. Methods Syst. Des. **24**(3), 281–320 (2004)

8. Bulychev, P., Chatain, T., David, A., Larsen, K.G.: Efficient on-the-fly algorithm for checking alternating timed simulation. In: Ouaknine, J., Vaandrager, F.W. (eds.) FORMATS 2009. LNCS, vol. 5813, pp. 73–87. Springer, Heidelberg (2009). doi:10.1007/978-3-642-04368-0_8

9. Čerāns, K.: Decidability of bisimulation equivalences for parallel timer processes. In: Bochmann, G., Probst, D.K. (eds.) CAV 1992. LNCS, vol. 663, pp. 302–315. Springer, Heidelberg (1993). doi:10.1007/3-540-56496-9_24

10. De Biasi, M., Snickars, C., Landernäs, K., Isaksson, A.: Simulation of process control with WirelessHART networks subject to clock drift. In: COMPSAC (2008)

11. Krishnan, P.: Distributed timed automata. In: Workshop on Distributed Systems (1999)

12. Laroussinie, F., Larsen, K.G., Weise, C.: From timed automata to logic — and back. In: Wiedermann, J., Hájek, P. (eds.) MFCS 1995. LNCS, vol. 969, pp. 529–539. Springer, Heidelberg (1995). doi:10.1007/3-540-60246-1_158
13. Milner, R.: Communication and Concurrency. Prentice Hall, Upper Saddle River (1989)
14. Monot, A., Navet, N., Bavoux, B.: Impact of clock drifts on CAN frame response time distributions. In: ETFA, Toulouse, France (2011)
15. Ortiz, J., Schobbens, P.-Y.: Extending timed bisimulation for distributed timed systems. Technical report, University of Namur (2016). http://www.info.fundp.ac.be/~jor/Multi-TimedReport/
16. Ortiz, J., Legay, A., Schobbens, P.-Y.: Distributed event clock automata. In: Bouchou-Markhoff, B., Caron, P., Champarnaud, J.-M., Maurel, D. (eds.) CIAA 2011. LNCS, vol. 6807, pp. 250–263. Springer, Heidelberg (2011). doi:10.1007/978-3-642-22256-6_23
17. Paige, R., Tarjan, R.E.: Three partition refinement algorithms. SIAM J. Comput. 16(6), 973–989 (1987)
18. Puri, A.: Dynamical properties of timed automata. In: Ravn, A.P., Rischel, H. (eds.) FTRTFT 1998. LNCS, vol. 1486, pp. 210–227. Springer, Heidelberg (1998). doi:10.1007/BFb0055349
19. Tripakis, S., Yovine, S.: Analysis of timed systems using time-abstracting bisimulations. Form. Methods Syst. Des. 18(1), 25–68 (2001)
20. Weise, C., Lenzkes, D.: Efficient scaling-invariant checking of timed bisimulation. In: Reischuk, R., Morvan, M. (eds.) STACS 1997. LNCS, vol. 1200, pp. 177–188. Springer, Heidelberg (1997). doi:10.1007/BFb0023458

Auto-Active Proof of Red-Black Trees in SPARK

Claire Dross$^{(\boxtimes)}$ and Yannick Moy

AdaCore, 75009 Paris, France
dross@adacore.com

Abstract. Formal program verification can guarantee that a program is free from broad classes of errors (like reads of uninitialized data and run-time errors) and that it complies with its specification. Tools such as SPARK make it cost effective to target the former in an industrial context, but the latter is much less common in industry, owing to the cost of specifying the behavior of programs and even more the cost of achieving proof of such specifications. We have chosen in SPARK to rely on the techniques of auto-active verification for providing cost effective formal verification of functional properties. These techniques consist in providing annotations in the source code that will be used by automatic provers to complete the proof. To demonstrate the potential of this approach, we have chosen to formally specify a library of red-black trees in SPARK, and to prove its functionality using auto-active verification. To the best of our knowledge, this is the most complex use of auto-active verification so far.

1 Introduction

Formal program verification allows programmers to guarantee that the programs they write have some desired properties. These properties may simply be that the program does not crash or behave erratically, or more complex critical properties related to safety or security. Being able to guarantee such properties will be essential for high assurance software as requirements are increasingly complex and security attacks more pervasive.

SPARK is a subset of the Ada programming language targeted at safety- and security-critical applications. GNATprove is a tool that analyzes SPARK code and can prove absence of run-time errors and user-specified properties expressed as contracts. GNATprove is based on modular deductive verification of programs, analyzing each function in isolation based on its contract and the contracts of the functions it calls. The main benefit of this approach is that it allows using very precise semantics of programming constructs and powerful automatic provers. The main drawback is that top-level specifications are not sufficient.

Work partly supported by the Joint Laboratory ProofInUse (ANR-13-LAB3-0007, http://www.spark-2014.org/proofinuse) and project VECOLIB (ANR-14-CE28-0018) of the French national research organization.

C. Barrett et al. (Eds.): NFM 2017, LNCS 10227, pp. 68–83, 2017.
DOI: 10.1007/978-3-319-57288-8_5

Programmers need to provide many intermediate specifications in the form of additional contracts, loop invariants and assertions.

Providing the right intermediate specifications is a difficult art, but progress has been achieved in recent years through a method known as auto-active verification. Various languages and tools now provide features for effective auto-active verification. SPARK is among these. In this paper, we explore the capabilities of auto-active verification for automatically proving complex algorithms. We have chosen to target red-black trees because they are well-known, commonly used in practice, and yet sufficiently complex that no implementation of imperative red-black trees has been formally verified using auto-active verification. Our implementation of red-black trees, with all the code for auto-active verification, is publicly available in the repository of SPARK.[1]

2   Preliminaries

2.1   SPARK 2014

SPARK is a subset of the Ada programming language targeted at safety- and security-critical applications. SPARK builds on the strengths of Ada for creating highly reliable and long-lived software. SPARK restrictions ensure that the behavior of a SPARK program is unambiguously defined, and simple enough that formal verification tools can perform an automatic diagnosis of conformance between a program specification and its implementation. The SPARK language and toolset for formal verification have been applied over many years to on-board aircraft systems, control systems, cryptographic systems, and rail systems [18].

In the versions of SPARK up to SPARK 2005, specifications are written as special annotations in comments. Since version SPARK 2014 [17], specifications are written as special Ada constructs attached to declarations. In particular, various contracts can be attached to subprograms: data flow contracts, information flow contracts, and functional contracts (preconditions and postconditions, introduced respectively by `Pre` and `Post`). An important difference between SPARK 2005 and SPARK 2014 is that functional contracts are executable in SPARK 2014, which greatly facilitates the combination of test and proof. The definition of the language subset is motivated by the simplicity and feasibility of formal analysis and the need for an unambiguous semantics. Tools are available that provide flow analysis and proof of SPARK programs.

Flow analysis checks correct access to data in the program: correct access to global variables (as specified in data and information flow contracts) and correct access to initialized data. Proof is used to demonstrate that the program is free from run-time errors such as arithmetic overflow, buffer overflow and division-by-zero, and that the functional contracts are correctly implemented. GNATprove is the tool implementing both flow analysis and proof of SPARK code.

---

[1] https://github.com/AdaCore/spark2014/tree/master/testsuite/gnatprove/tests/red _black_trees.

2.2 Auto-Active Verification

The term *auto-active verification* was coined in 2010 by researcher Rustan Leino [15] to characterise *tools where user input is supplied before VC gener-ation [and] therefore lie between automatic and interactive verification* (hence the name auto-active). This is in contrast to fully automatic verifiers for which *the specification is fixed* and interactive verifiers for which *the user input is sup-plied after VC generation, which is the typical case when the reasoning engine is an interactive proof assistant.* Auto-active verification is at the center of the academic formal program verification toolsets Dafny [14], the Eiffel Verification Environment (EVE) [9], Why3 [8] as well as the industrial formal program ver-ification toolsets Frama-C[2] and SPARK[3].

In all these toolsets, auto-active verification consists in a set of specification features at the level of the source language, and a set of tool capabilities to interact with users at the level of the source code. The specification features consist at least in constructs to specify function contracts (preconditions and postconditions) and data invariants, as well as specialized forms of assertions (loop invariants and loop variants, assumptions and assertions). All the toolsets mentioned above also support *ghost code*, a feature to instrument code for ver-ification. Ghost functions are also called lemmas when their main purpose is to support the proof of a property that is later used at the point where the function is called. See [12] for a comparison of how ghost code differs between Why3, Frama-C and SPARK. Various tool capabilities facilitate user interac-tion at source level: fast running time that exploits multiprocessor architectures and minimizes rework between runs, the ability to trade running time for more verification power, feedback from the toolset when verification is unsuccessful (counterexamples in particular).

Auto-active verification in the above toolsets has been used to fully verify algorithms, libraries and even full applications: examples include a container library in Eiffel [19], distributed systems in Dafny [10], secure execution of apps in Dafny [11], binary heaps in Why3 [21], allocators in SPARK [5].

2.3 Red-Black Trees

Red-black trees are a kind of self-balancing binary search trees. Nodes in the tree are colored red or black, and balance is maintained by ensuring that two prop-erties are preserved: (1) a red node can only have black children, and (2) every path from the root to a leaf has the same number of black nodes. The conse-quence of these two properties is that the path from the root to a leaf can be at most twice as long as the path from the root to another leaf.

Implementations of red-black trees are used in the Linux kernel (in C) and standard container libraries for various languages (C++ STL, Java.util, Ada). The insertion and deletion algorithms work by inserting or deleting the node as in a binary search tree, which may violate properties (1) and (2) above, and

---

[2] http://frama-c.com/.
[3] http://www.adacore.com/sparkpro/.

then restoring the balance by working their way up on the path from the root to the point of insertion or deletion. At every node on this path, the algorithms may *rotate* the subtree, which consists in a local rearrangement of nodes to restore properties (1) and (2). These algorithms are sufficiently complex that no implementation of imperative red-black trees has been formally verified in Dafny, Eiffel or Why3. See Sect. 5 for a list of the closest works, including some using auto-active verification. We are following the algorithm from Cormen et al. [4] for insertion in a red-black tree. We did not implement the deletion algorithm, which would be very similar to insertion. In the same way, we did not verify that every branch in a red-black tree contains the same number of black nodes.

3   Red-Black Trees in SPARK

3.1   Invariants and Models

Implementing red-black trees correctly from the pseudo-code algorithm in a text-book is straightforward, but understanding why the algorithm is correct is tricky, and thus the implementation is hard to verify formally. The main point of complexity is that it forces one to reason about different levels of properties all at once. Instead, we have divided the implementation into three distinct parts, each one concerned with one property level: binary trees, search trees and red-black trees. Binary trees maintain a tree structure on the underlying memory. Search trees build on binary trees by associating values to tree nodes and maintain the order of values in the tree. Red-black trees build on search trees and enforce balancing using the classical red-black tree coloring mechanism.

The property enforced at each level is expressed in a type invariant. In SPARK, the invariant may be temporarily violated inside the implementation of the functions that operate on the type, but are guaranteed to hold for external users of objects of that type. More precisely, functions that operate on a type can assume the invariant on entry and must restore it on exit (which leads to verification conditions in SPARK).

Binary Trees: As explained in Sect. 3.2, binary trees are implemented as arrays, using the representation described in Fig. 1. Each node contains a reference to its left and right children, if any, as well as a reference to its parent and a position, which may be Top for the root, Right or Left otherwise depending on the node position with respect to its parent. The invariant of binary trees states that values of these fields are consistent across the tree. For example, the left child of a node has position Left and the node as parent.

To reason about the tree structure at a higher level, we provide a model (an abstract representation) of binary trees which makes explicit the *access paths* from the root to every node in the tree. It associates a sequence of directions, namely Right or Left, with each node in the binary tree, corresponding to the path from the root to the node. As the underlying array also contains unused cells that do not correspond to tree nodes, an additional boolean encodes whether the node belongs to the tree. Figure 2 gives the model of the binary tree presented

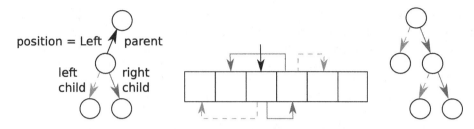

Fig. 1. (from left to right) Representation of nodes in binary trees. Example of a binary tree, for readability, parents and positions are not represented. A higher level view of the same binary tree.

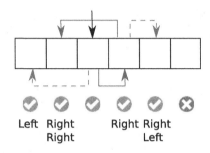

Left Right   Right Right
      Right   Left

Fig. 2. Example of model of a binary tree.

in Fig. 1. In this example, all the nodes belong to the tree except the last one. The access paths written below each node can be used to reconstruct easily the high level view of the tree.

Search Trees: The invariant of search trees states that the value stored in each node of the tree is larger than all the values stored in the subtree rooted at its left child and smaller than all the values stored in the subtree rooted at its right child. It is given in Fig. 3, together with an example of values that would fit the

```
(for all I in Index_Type ⇒
  (for all J in Index_Type ⇒
    (if Model (T) (I).Reachable
      and Model (T) (J).Reachable
      and Model (T) (I).Path < Model (T) (J).Path
    then (if Get (Model (T) (J).Path,
                 Length (Model (T) (I).Path) + 1) = Left
          then Values (J) < Values (I)
          else Values (J) > Values (I)))))
```

Fig. 3. Type invariant of search trees. For a search tree T, Model (T) returns the model of the underlying binary tree of T. For each index I in the underlying array, if Model (T) (I).Reachable is true then I is reachable in T and Model (T) (I).Path is the sequence of directions corresponding to the path from the root of T to I. < stands for prefix order on paths.

tree from Fig. 1. To express this invariant, we use the model of the underlying binary tree. The value stored at node J belonging to the subtree rooted at node I (where path inclusion from the root is used to determine that J belongs to the subtree rooted at node I) is smaller (resp. greater) than the value stored at node I if J belongs to the subtree rooted at the left (resp. right) child of I.

Red-Black Trees: The invariant of red-black trees states that a red node can only have black children. It is given in Fig. 4. An example of colors that would fit the tree from Fig. 3 is also given in Fig. 4. This corresponds to property (1) of red-black trees as presented in Sect. 2.3. Verifying property (2) would require implementing a new inductive model function over binary trees, like the one we defined for reachability. As it would be very similar to the work presented here, and would essentially double the effort, we did not attempt it.

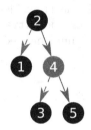

```
(for all I in Index_Type ⇒
  (if Parent (T.Struct, I) = Empty
    or else T.Color (Parent (T.Struct, I)) = Red
  then T.Color (I) = Black))
```

Fig. 4. Type invariant of red-black trees. (Color figure online)

3.2   Implementation

Our implementation of red-black trees differs on two accounts from the straighforward implementation of the algorithm. First, as stated above, we used an array as the underlying memory for trees, instead of dynamically allocating nodes. This is to comply with a restriction of SPARK which does not allow pointers, but only references and addresses. The rationale for this restriction is that pointers make automatic proof very difficult due to possible aliasing. Hence trees are bounded by the size of the underlying array. As the algorithm for balancing red-black trees requires splitting and merging trees, we had the choice of either copying arrays for generating new trees, or sharing the same array between disjoint trees (coming from the splitting of a unique tree). For obvious efficiency reasons, we chose the latter. Hence we are defining a type **Forest** for possibly representing disjoint binary trees sharing the same underlying array.

The other distinguishing feature of our implementation is the layered design. Each module defining a type with an invariant also needs to provide functions for manipulating objects of the type while preserving their invariant. As an example, binary trees are not updated by direct assignments in the implementation of search trees, but using two new functions, **Extract** and **Plug**, which split and merge disjoint trees while preserving the forest invariant.

At the next layer, search trees are defined as records with two components: a binary tree along with an additional array of values. For search trees, we only need to consider forests that hold one tree identified through its root. Only intermediate values will hold true forests with multiple roots, while the tree is being rotated. The module defining search trees provides basic set functions, namely inserting a value into the tree and testing a value for membership in the tree. It also provides balancing functions for the upper layer of red-black trees. They allow rotating nodes of a search tree to the left or to the right while preserving the order between values. An example of such a rotation is given in Fig. 5. Defining these balancing functions inside the implementation of search trees rather than inside the implementation of red-black trees allows keeping all order-related concerns in the search tree layer. Indeed, balancing functions do not preserve balance, as they are to be called on unbalanced trees, but they do preserve order. Note that implementing the balancing functions at this level avoids the need for lifting low-level tree handling functions such as `Plug` and `Extract` at the next layer. All the functions defined on search trees are implemented using functions over binary trees.

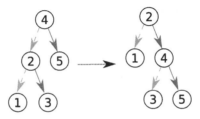

Fig. 5. Example of application of Right_Rotate.

Red-black trees are implemented in the same way as search trees by adding an array of colors to a search tree and using balancing functions to rebalance the tree after an insertion.

3.3   Specification

Functional specifications of the insertion and membership functions that operate on red-black trees consist in simple contracts (preconditions and postconditions) presented in Fig. 6. These contracts use a model function `Values` that returns the set of values in the tree. `Mem` returns true if and only if the element is in the tree and `Insert` adds a new element in the tree.

The most complex specifications have to do with the four properties to maintain over red-black trees:

1. A red-black tree is always a valid binary tree (we can navigate it from the root in the expected way).

```
function Values (T : Rbt) return Value_Set with
   Post ⇒ (if Size (T) = 0 then Is_Empty (Values ' Result));

function Mem (T : Rbt; V : Natural) return Boolean with
   Post ⇒ Mem' Result = Mem (Values (T), V);

procedure Insert (T : in out Rbt; V : Natural) with
   Pre  ⇒ Size (T) < Max,
   Post ⇒ (if Mem (T'Old, V) then Values (T) = Values (T'Old)
           else Is_Add (Values (T'Old), V, Values (T)));
```

Fig. 6. Specification of red-black trees.

2. There is no memory leak (if we have inserted fewer than **Max** elements, there is still room enough in the data structure to insert a new element).
3. The values stored in the tree are ordered (it is a valid search tree).
4. The tree stays balanced (we only verify this property partially, that is, that red nodes can only have black children).

As already discussed, each property is specified at the most appropriate layer. The first property is enforced at the level of binary trees. The invariant on binary trees (see Sect. 3.1) ensures that the fields of a node (Parent, Position, Left, and Right) are consistent. This is not enough to ensure that all the allocated nodes in the forest belong to well-formed binary trees though, as it does not rule out degenerate, root-less, cyclic structures that would arise from linking the root of a binary tree as the child of one of its leafs. Still, this is enough to ensure that red-black trees are always well formed, as red-black trees always have a root. Note that the fact that every node in the forest is part of a well formed binary tree is ensured at the level of binary trees by enforcing that such degenerate structures can never be created in the contracts of functions operating on binary trees.

The second property is enforced at the level of search trees. It is specified as a postcondition of every function operating on search trees. Figure 7 shows the part of the postcondition of **Right_Rotate** ensuring that it has not introduced any dangling node. It uses the function **Model** described in Sect. 3.1 to reason about node reachability.

```
procedure Right_Rotate (T : in out Search_Tree; I : Index_Type) with
   Post ⇒
      ─── The size of the tree is preserved
      Size (T) = Size (T)'Old

      ─── Nodes in the tree are preserved
      and (for all J in Index_Type ⇒
            Model (T) (J).Reachable = Model (T'Old) (J).Reachable);
```

Fig. 7. Postcondition of **Right_Rotate** dealing with absence of memory leaks.

The third and fourth properties are expressed in the type invariant of respectively search trees and red-black trees as explained in Sect. 3.1.

Apart from these top-level specifications, many more specifications are needed on subprograms at lower layers (binary trees and search trees) in order to be able to prove the properties at higher layers (respectively search trees and red-black trees). This is inherent to the modular style of verification supported by GNATprove. For example, as `Right_Rotate` on search trees calls `Plug` and `Extract` on binary trees, the contracts for these functions need to provide enough information to verify both the absence of memory leaks as stated in the postcondition of `Right_Rotate` and the preservation of the order of values as stated in the invariant of search trees.

3.4   Proof Principles

Verifying our implementation of red-black trees has proved to be challenging, and above the purely automatic proving capabilities of GNATprove. There are several reasons for this:

- The imperative, pointer-based implementation of red-black trees makes it difficult to reason about disjointness of different trees/subtrees in the forest.
- Reasoning about reachability in the tree structure involves inductive proofs, which automatic provers are notoriously bad at.
- Reasoning about value ordering involves using transitivity relations, to deduce that ordering for two pairs of values (X, Y) and (Y, Z) can be extended to the pair (X, Z). This requires in general to find a suitable intermediate value Y, which usually eludes automatic provers.
- The size of the formulas to verify, number of verification conditions, and number of paths in the program are large enough to defy provers scalability.

To work around these limitations, we used auto-active verification techniques, which, as described in Sect. 2.2, can guide automatic provers without requiring a proof assistant. We explain some of these techniques in this section.

Intermediate Lemmas: One of the classical techniques in manual proof consists in factoring some useful part of a proof in an intermediate lemma so that it can be verified independently and used as many times as necessary. In auto-active verification, this can be done by introducing a procedure with no output, which, when called, will cause the deductive engine to verify its precondition and assume its postcondition. In Fig. 8, we show an intermediate lemma which can be used

```
procedure Prove_Model_Distinct (F : Forest; T1, T2 : Index_Type) with
   --   Trees rooted at different indexes in the forest are disjoint.
   Pre  ⇒ T1 ≠ T2
      and then Valid_Root (F, T1)
      and then Valid_Root (F, T2),
   Post ⇒ (for all I in Index_Type ⇒
              (not Model (F, T1) (I).Reachable
               or not Model (F, T2) (I).Reachable));
```

Fig. 8. Intermediate lemma stating disjointness of trees in a forest.

to verify that two trees of a single forest with different roots are disjoint. A caller of this function will have to verify that T1 and T2 are different valid roots in F and as a consequence we know that there can be no node reachable from both roots in F. Naturally, the lemma is not assumed, its actual proof is performed when verifying the procedure Prove_Model_Distinct.

Reasoning by Induction: Though some automatic provers are able to discharge simple inductive proofs, inductive reasoning still requires manual interaction in most cases. In auto-active style, an inductive proof can be done using loop invariants. GNATprove splits the verification of a loop invariant in two parts. First, it verifies that the invariant holds in the first iteration of the loop and then that it holds in any following iteration knowing that it held in the previous one. This behavior is exactly what we want for a proof by induction. For example, Fig. 9 demonstrates how the intermediate lemma presented in Fig. 8 can be verified using a loop to perform an induction over the size of the path from the root T1 to any node reachable from T1 in F. The loop goes from 1 to the maximum size of any branch in the forest F. We have written the property we wanted to prove as a loop invariant. To verify this procedure, GNATprove will first check that the invariant holds in the first iteration of the loop, that is, that T1 itself cannot be reached from T2. Then, it will proceed by induction to show that this holds for any node reachable from T1 in F.

```
procedure Prove_Model_Distinct
    (F : Forest; T1, T2 : Index_Type) is
begin
    for N in Index_Type loop
        pragma Loop_Invariant
            (for all I in Index_Type ⇒
                (if Model (F, T1) (I).Reachable
                    and Length (Model (F, T1) (I).Path) < N
                    then not Model (F, T2) (I).Reachable));
    end loop;
end Prove_Model_Distinct;
```

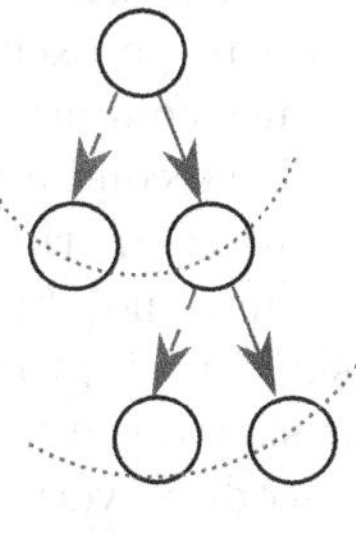

Fig. 9. Proof by induction over the path length from the root to a node in the tree.

Providing Witnesses: When reasoning about value ordering, it is common to use transitivity. For example, when searching for a value in a search tree, we only compare the requested value with values stored along a single path in the tree, that is, the path where it was expected to be stored. All other values are ruled out by transitivity of the order relation: if value X is not found on this path, it cannot be equal to another value Z in the tree, as X and Z are on two opposite sides of the value Y at the root of the subtree containing both X and Z. Unfortunately, due to how they handle universal quantification, automatic provers used in GNATprove are usually unable to come up with the appropriate intermediate value to use in the transitivity relation. To achieve the proofs, we provided provers with the appropriate term whenever necessary. For example, function Find_Root in Fig. 10 computes the first common ancestor of two nodes in a search tree.

```
function Find_Root (F : Forest; R, I, J : Index_Type) return Index_Type with
  Post ⇒
    ──  The node returned is in the tree
    Model (F, R) (Find_Root'Result).Reachable

    ──  The node returned is on the path of I
    and Model (F, R) (Find_Root'Result).Path ≤ Model (F, R) (I).Path

    ──  The node returned is on the path of J
    and Model (F, R) (Find_Root'Result).Path ≤ Model (F, R) (J).Path

    ──  The common ancestor of I and J is either I, or J, or an ancestor
    ──  node such that the paths of I and J diverge at this point.
    and (I = Find_Root'Result
         or else J = Find_Root'Result
         or else Get (Model (F, R) (I).Path,
                      Length (Model (F, R) (Find_Root'Result).Path) + 1)
             ≠ Get (Model (F, R) (J).Path,
                      Length (Model (F, R) (Find_Root'Result).Path) + 1));
```

Fig. 10. Function that computes a witness for transitivity applications.

3.5   Ghost Code

In this experiment, we made an extensive use of ghost code, that is, code meant only for verification, that has no effect on the program behavior. We used it for two different purposes. The first use of ghost code is for specifying complex properties about our algorithms, in particular through model functions. As ghost code can be executed in SPARK, these ghost model functions can be used to produce complex test oracles that can be exercised in the test campaign.

The second use of ghost code in our experiment is for auto-active verification. In particular, the procedures used to encode intermediate lemmas are ghost, as they have no effect. What is more, we strived to keep all verification-only code inside ghost procedures so that it can be removed by the compiler and will not slow down the execution of the program. It is all the more important since the code is very inefficient, involving multiple loops and model constructions. As functional behaviors are complex, coming up with contracts for these ghost procedures can be painful, and produce huge, hard to read specifications. To alleviate this problem, we can benefit from a feature of GNATprove which inlines local subprograms with no contracts, allowing the proof to go through with less annotation burden. In this way, we can choose, on a case-by-case basis, if it is worthwhile to turn a chunk of auto-active proof into an intermediate lemma with its own contract, allowing for a modular verification, or if we prefer to have the tool automatically inline the proof wherever we call the ghost procedure.

4   Development and Verification Data

All the execution times and verification times reported in this section were obtained on a Core i7 processor with 2,8 GHz and 16 GB RAM.

The code implementing the core algorithm for red-black trees, even when split in three modules for binary trees, search trees and red-black trees, is quite small, only 286 lines overall. But this code only accounts for 14% of the total lines of code, when taking into account contracts (22%) and more importantly ghost code (64%). Table 1 summarizes the logical lines of code as counted by the tool GNATmetric. It took roughly two weeks to develop all the code, contracts and ghost code to reach 100% automatic proof.

Table 1. Number of lines of code for operational code, contracts and ghost code.

	Code	Contracts	Ghost	Total
Binary trees	92 (10%)	250 (28%)	548 (62%)	890
Search trees	127 (12%)	188 (17%)	780 (71%)	1095
Red-black trees	67 (52%)	18 (14%)	45 (35%)	130
Total	286 (14%)	456 (22%)	1373 (64%)	2115

There are few simple top-level contracts for red-black trees (see Table 2). Many more contracts and assertions are needed for auto-active verification, in the form of subprogram contracts, type invariants, type default initial conditions, loop invariants and intermediate assertions which split the work between automatic provers and facilitate work of individual provers.

Table 2. Number of conjuncts (and-ed subexpressions) in contracts on types, on subprograms, in loop invariants and in assertions. Numbers in parentheses correspond to conjuncts for contracts on externally visible subprograms.

	On types	On subprograms	On loops	Assertions	Total
Binary trees	10	155 (73)	42	12	219
Search trees	2	138 (60)	20	68	228
Red-black trees	2	4 (4)	8	10	24
Total	14	297 (177)	70	90	471

Taking both tables into account, it is clear that verification of search trees was the most costly in terms of overall efforts, with a large part of ghost code (71%) and many intermediate assertions needed (68 conjuncts). Verification of red-black trees on the contrary was relatively straighforward, with less ghost code than operational code (35% compared to 52%) and few intermediate assertions needed (10 conjuncts). This matches well the cognitive effort required to understand the correction of search trees compared to red-black trees. Note that the verification of red-black trees would probably have needed roughtly the same effort as binary trees if the second propery of red-black trees had been considered. Overall, ghost code accounts for a majority (64%) of the code, which can be explained by the various uses of ghost code to support automatic proof as described in Sect. 3.4.

The automatic verification that the code (including ghost code) is free of run-time errors and that it respects its contracts takes less than 30 min, using 4 cores and two successive runs of GNATprove at proof levels 2 and 3. As automatic provers CVC4, Z3 and Alt-Ergo are called in sequence on unproved Verification Conditions (VCs), it is not surprising that CVC4 proves a majority of VCs (3763), while Z3 proves 103 VCs left unproved by CVC4 and Alt-Ergo proves the last 3 remaining VCs, for a total of 3869 VCs issued from 2414 source code checks (1185 run-time checks, 231 assertions and 998 functional contracts).

As the code has been fully proved to be free of run-time errors and that all contracts have been proved, it is safe to compile it with no run-time checks, and only the precondition on insertion in red-black trees activated (since this might be violated by an external call). Disabling run-time checks is done through a compiler switch (-gnatp) and only enabling preconditions in red-black trees is done through a configuration pragma in the unit. Inserting one million integers in a red-black tree from 1 to 1 million leads to a violation of the balancing in 999,998 cases, which requires 999,963 left rotations and no right rotations. The running time for performing these 1 million insertions is 0.65 s without run-time checks, and 0.70 s with run-time checks (which are few due to the use of Ada range types for array indexes), or 0.65 μs (respectively 0.70 μs) per insertion.

Enabling all contracts and assertions at run-time is also possible during tests. Here, ghost code is particularly expensive to run, as constructing the model for a binary tree is at worst quadratic in the size of the tree, and contracts contain quantifications on the maximal size of the tree that call functions which themselves quantify over the same size in their own contracts or code. In addition, the expensive operation of constructing the model is performed repeatedly in contracts, as SPARK does not yet provide a let-expression form. As a result, inserting one element in a tree of size one takes 2 min.

5   Related Work

There have been several previous attempts at verifying red-black trees implementations. In particular, red-black trees are used in the implementation of ordered sets and maps in the standard library of the Coq proof assistant [1,7]. As part of these libraries, the implementations have been proven correct using interactive proofs in Coq. These implementations notably differ from our work because they are written in a functional style, using recursive data types instead of pointers and recursive functions instead of loops. Similar libraries are provided for the Isabelle proof assistant [13]. Functional implementations of red-black trees have also been verified outside of proof assistants, using characteristic formulas [3], or in the Why3 programming language as part of VACID-0 competition [16]. This last implementation differs from the previous ones in that it is mostly auto-active, even if it uses Coq for a few verification conditions.

Verifying imperative implementations of red-black trees is more challenging as it involves reasoning about the well-formedness of the tree structure, which comes for free in the functional implementations. As part of VACID-0, attempts have been made at verifying red-black trees in C using VCC and in Java using KeY [2]. Both attempts seem to have been left in preliminary stages though.

More recently, imperative implementations of red-black trees in C and Java have been verified using more specialized logics. Enea et al. obtained an automatic verification of a C implementation of red-black trees using separation logic, a logic specialized for the verification of heap manipulating programs [6]. In the same way, Stefănescu et al. were able to verify several implementations of red-black trees in particular in Java and C using matching logic [20]. As used in this work, matching logic provides a very precise, low-level view of the heap structure, allowing for powerful proofs on this kind of programs. Both works use specialized tools, which are specifically designed for verifying low-level, heap manipulating programs but which have never been used, to the best of our knowledge, to verify higher-level software.

6   Conclusion

In this article, we have explained how, using auto-active techniques, we could achieve formal verification of key functional properties of an imperative implementation of red-black trees in SPARK. This is not an example of what should be a regular use of the SPARK toolset but rather a successful demonstration of how far we can go using such technology.

However, the techniques presented on this example can be reused with significant benefits on a much smaller scale. In particular, we have shown that inductive proofs can be achieved rather straightforwardly using auto-active reasoning. The multi-layered approach, using type invariants and model functions to separate concerns, can also be reused to reason about complex data structures.

To popularize the use of auto-active techniques, we are also working on integrating simple interactive proof capabilities in GNATprove. This would allow applying the same techniques in a simpler, more straightforward way, and also to avoid polluting the program space with ghost code which is never meant to be executed.

Acknowledgements. We would like to thank our colleague Ben Brosgol and the anonymous reviewers for their useful comments.

References

1. Appel, A.W.: Efficient verified red-black trees (2011). https://www.cs.princeton.edu/~appel/papers/redblack.pdf
2. Bruns, D.: Specification of red-black trees: showcasing dynamic frames, model fields and sequences. In: Wolfgang, A., Richard, B. (eds.) 10th KeY Symposium (2011)
3. Charguéraud, A.: Program verification through characteristic formulae. ACM Sigplan Not. **45**(9), 321–332 (2010)
4. Cormen, T.H., Leiserson, C.E., Rivest, R.L., Stein, C.: Introduction to Algorithms, 3rd edn. The MIT Press, Cambridege (2009)

5. Dross, C., Moy, Y.: Abstract software specifications and automatic proof of refinement. In: Lecomte, T., Pinger, R., Romanovsky, A. (eds.) RSSRail 2016. LNCS, vol. 9707, pp. 215–230. Springer, Cham (2016). doi:10.1007/978-3-319-33951-1_16

6. Enea, C., Sighireanu, M., Wu, Z.: On automated lemma generation for separation logic with inductive definitions. In: Finkbeiner, B., Pu, G., Zhang, L. (eds.) ATVA 2015. LNCS, vol. 9364, pp. 80–96. Springer, Cham (2015). doi:10.1007/978-3-319-24953-7_7

7. Filliâtre, J.-C., Letouzey, P.: Functors for proofs and programs. In: Schmidt, D. (ed.) ESOP 2004. LNCS, vol. 2986, pp. 370–384. Springer, Heidelberg (2004). doi:10.1007/978-3-540-24725-8_26

8. Filliâtre, J.-C., Paskevich, A.: Why3 — where programs meet provers. In: Felleisen, M., Gardner, P. (eds.) ESOP 2013. LNCS, vol. 7792, pp. 125–128. Springer, Heidelberg (2013). doi:10.1007/978-3-642-37036-6_8. https://hal.inria.fr/hal-00789533

9. Furia, C.A., Nordio, M., Polikarpova, N., Tschannen, J.: AutoProof: auto-active functional verification of object-oriented programs. Int. J. Softw. Tools Technol. Transfer 1–20 (2016). http://dx.doi.org/10.1007/s10009-016-0419-0

10. Hawblitzel, C., Howell, J., Kapritsos, M., Lorch, J.R., Parno, B., Roberts, M.L., Setty, S., Zill, B.: IronFleet: proving practical distributed systems correct. In: Proceedings of the 25th Symposium on Operating Systems Principles, SOSP 2015, pp. 1–17. ACM, New York (2015). http://doi.acm.org/10.1145/2815400.2815428

11. Hawblitzel, C., Howell, J., Lorch, J.R., Narayan, A., Parno, B., Zhang, D., Zill, B.: Ironclad apps: end-to-end security via automated full-system verification. In: Proceedings of the 11th USENIX Conference on Operating Systems Design and Implementation, OSDI 2014, pp. 165–181. USENIX Association, Berkeley (2014). http://dl.acm.org/citation.cfm?id=2685048.2685062

12. Kosmatov, N., Marché, C., Moy, Y., Signoles, J.: Static versus dynamic verification in Why3, Frama-C and SPARK 2014. In: Margaria, T., Steffen, B. (eds.) ISoLA 2016. LNCS, vol. 9952, pp. 461–478. Springer, Cham (2016). doi:10.1007/978-3-319-47166-2_32. https://hal.inria.fr/hal-01344110

13. Lammich, P., Lochbihler, A.: The isabelle collections framework. In: Kaufmann, M., Paulson, L.C. (eds.) ITP 2010. LNCS, vol. 6172, pp. 339–354. Springer, Heidelberg (2010). doi:10.1007/978-3-642-14052-5_24

14. Leino, K.R.M.: Dafny: an automatic program verifier for functional correctness. In: Clarke, E.M., Voronkov, A. (eds.) LPAR 2010. LNCS (LNAI), vol. 6355, pp. 348–370. Springer, Heidelberg (2010). doi:10.1007/978-3-642-17511-4_20. http://dl.acm.org/citation.cfm?id=1939141.1939161

15. Leino, K.R.M., Moskal, M.: Usable auto-active verification. In: Usable Verification Workshop (2010). http://fm.csl.sri.com/UV10/

16. Leino, K.R.M., Moskal, M.: VACID-0: verification of ample correctness of invariants of data-structures, edition 0 (2010)

17. McCormick, J.W., Chapin, P.C.: Building High Integrity Applications with SPARK. Cambridge University Press, Cambridge (2015)

18. O'Neill, I.: SPARK - a language and tool-set for high-integrity software development. In: Boulanger, J.L. (ed.) Industrial Use of Formal Methods: Formal Verification. Wiley, Hoboken (2012)

19. Polikarpova, N., Tschannen, J., Furia, C.A.: A fully verified container library. In: Bjørner, N., de Boer, F. (eds.) FM 2015. LNCS, vol. 9109, pp. 414–434. Springer, Cham (2015). doi:10.1007/978-3-319-19249-9_26

20. Stefănescu, A., Park, D., Yuwen, S., Li, Y., Roşu, G.: Semantics-based program verifiers for all languages. In: Proceedings of the 2016 ACM SIGPLAN International Conference on Object-Oriented Programming, Systems, Languages, and Applications, pp. 74–91. ACM (2016)
21. Tafat, A., Marché, C.: Binary heaps formally verified in Why3. Research report 7780, INRIA, October 2011. http://hal.inria.fr/inria-00636083/en/

Analysing Security Protocols Using Refinement in iUML-B

Colin Snook[(✉)], Thai Son Hoang, and Michael Butler

ECS, University of Southampton, Southampton, U.K.
{cfs,t.s.hoang,mjb}@ecs.soton.ac.uk

Abstract. We propose a general approach based on abstraction and refinement for constructing and analysing security protocols using formal specification and verification. We use class diagrams to specify conceptual system entities and their relationships. We use state-machines to model the protocol execution involving the entities' interactions. Features of our approach include specifying security principles as invariants of some abstract model of the overall system. The specification is then refined to introduce implementable mechanisms for the protocol. A gluing invariant specifies why the protocol achieves the security principle. Security breaches arise as violations of the gluing invariant. We make use of both theorem proving and model checking techniques to analyse our formal model, in particular, to explore the source and consequence of the security attack. To demonstrate the use of our approach we explore the mechanism of a security attack in a network protocol.

Keywords: Virtual LAN · Security · Event-B · iUML-B

1 Introduction

Ensuring security of protocols is a significant and challenging task in the context of autonomous cyber-physical systems. In this paper, we investigate the use of formal models of protocols in order to discover and analyse possible security threats. In particular, we are interested in the role of formal models in identifying security flaws, exploring the nature of attacks that exploit these flaws and proposing measures to counter flaws in systems that are already deployed.

Our contribution is a general approach based on abstraction and refinement for constructing and analysing security protocols. The approach is suitable for systems containing multiple conceptual entities (for example, data packets, devices, information tags, etc.). We use class diagrams to specify the relationships between entities and state-machines to specify protocols involved in their interactions. Security principles are defined as constraints on the system entities and their relationships. We use refinements of these models, to gradually introduce implementation details of the protocols that are supposed to achieve these security properties. The use of abstract specification and refinement allows us to separate the security properties from the protocol implementation. In particular,

© Springer International Publishing AG 2017
C. Barrett et al. (Eds.): NFM 2017, LNCS 10227, pp. 84–98, 2017.
DOI: 10.1007/978-3-319-57288-8_6

possible security flaws are detected as violations of the gluing invariants that link the abstract and concrete models. Further analysis helps to pinpoint the origin and nature of attacks that could exploit these flaws. The approach has been developed within the Enable-S3 project [4] which aims to provide cost-efficient cross-domain verification and validation methods for autonomous cyber-physical systems. Within Enable-S3, we are applying the approach on case studies in the avionics and maritime domains. The case-studies involve secure authentication and communications protocols as part of larger autonomous systems.

We illustrate our approach with an analysis of *Virtual Local Area Network* (VLAN) operation including the principle of tagging packets. We explore a known security flaw of these systems, namely double tagging. We use the Event-B method and iUML-B class diagrams and state-machines as the modelling tool.

The rest of the paper is structured as follows. Section 2 gives some background on the case study, the methods and tools that we use. The main content of the paper is in Sect. 3 describing the development using iUML-B and analysis of the VLAN model. Finally, we summarise our approach in Sect. 4 and conclude in Sect. 5. For more information and resources, we refer the reader to our website: http://eprints.soton.ac.uk/id/eprint/403533. The website contains the Event-B model of the VLAN.

2   Background

2.1   VLAN Tagging

A *Local Area Network* (LAN) consists of devices that communicate over physical data connections that consist of multiple steps forming routes via intermediate network routing devices called switches. The 'trunk' connections between switches are used by multiple routes. A VLAN restricts communication so that only devices that share the same VLAN as the sender, can receive the communication thus providing a way to group devices irrespective of physical topology. In order to achieve this, switches attach a tag to message packets in order to identify the sender's VLAN. The tag is removed before being sent to the receiving device. Typically, a system uses one VLAN identity to represent a default VLAN. This is known as the *native* VLAN. A packet intended for the native VLAN does not require tagging. The IEEE 802.1Q standard [6] is the most common protocol for ethernet-based LANs and includes a system for VLAN tagging and associated handling procedures. The standard permits multiple VLAN tags to be inserted so that the network infrastructure can use VLANs internally as well as supporting client VLAN tagging. A well-known security attack exploits double tagging by hiding a tag for a supposedly inaccessible VLAN behind a tag for the native VLAN. The receiving switch sees the unnecessary native VLAN tag and removes it before sending the packet on to the next switch. This switch then sees the tag for the inaccessible VLAN and routes the packet accordingly so that the packet infiltrates the targeted VLAN. Double tagging attacks can be avoided by not using (i.e. de-configuring) the native VLAN.

2.2   Event-B

Event-B [1] is a formal method for system development. Main features of Event-B include the use of *refinement* to introduce system details gradually into the formal model. An Event-B model contains two parts: *contexts* and *machines*. Contexts contain *carrier sets*, *constants*, and *axioms* constraining the carrier sets and constants. Machines contain *variables* v, *invariants* $I(v)$ constraining the variables, and *events*. An event comprises a guard denoting its enabled-condition and an action describing how the variables are modified when the event is executed. In general, an event e has the following form, where t are the event parameters, $G(t, v)$ is the guard of the event, and $v := E(t, v)$ is the action of the event[1].

$$\text{e} \mathrel{\widehat{=}} \textbf{any } t \textbf{ where } G(t, v) \textbf{ then } v := E(t, v) \textbf{ end} \qquad (1)$$

A machine in Event-B corresponds to a transition system where *variables* represent the states and *events* specify the transitions. Contexts can be *extended* by adding new carrier sets, constants, axioms, and theorems. Machine **M** can be *refined* by machine **N** (we call **M** the abstract machine and **N** the concrete machine). The state of **M** and **N** are related by a gluing invariant $J(v, w)$ where v, w are variables of **M** and **N**, respectively. Intuitively, any "behaviour" exhibited by **N** can be simulated by **M**, with respect to the gluing invariant J. Refinement in Event-B is reasoned event-wise. Consider an abstract event e and the corresponding concrete event f. Somewhat simplifying, we say that e is refined by f if f's guard is stronger than that of e and f's action can be simulated by e's action, taking into account the gluing invariant J. More information about Event-B can be found in [5]. Event-B is supported by the Rodin platform (Rodin) [2], an extensible toolkit which includes facilities for modelling, verifying the consistency of models using theorem proving and model checking techniques, and validating models with simulation-based approaches.

2.3   iUML-B

iUML-B [8–10] provides a diagrammatic modelling notation for Event-B in the form of state-machines and class diagrams. The diagrammatic models are contained within an Event-B machine and generate or contribute to parts of it. For example a state-machine will automatically generate the Event-B data elements (sets, constants, axioms, variables, and invariants) to implement the states while Event-B events are expected to already exist to represent the transitions. Transitions contribute further guards and actions representing their state change, to the events that they elaborate. An existing Event-B set may be associated with the state-machine to define its instances. In this case the state-machine is 'lifted' so that it has a value for every instance of the associated set. State-machines are typically refined by adding nested state-machines to states.

---

[1] Actions in Event-B are, in the most general cases, non-deterministic [5].

Class diagrams provide a way to visually model data relationships. Classes, attributes and associations are linked to Event-B data elements (carrier set, constant, or variable) and generate constraints on those elements. For the VLAN we use class diagrams extensively to model the sets of entities and their relationships and we use state-machines to constrain the sequences of events and to declare state dependant invariant properties.

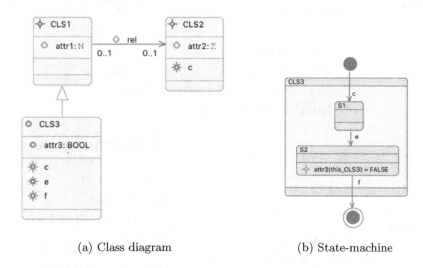

(a) Class diagram   (b) State-machine

Fig. 1. Example iUML-B diagrams

Figure 1 shows an abstract example of an iUML-B model to illustrate the features we have used in the VLAN. We give the corresponding translation into Event-B in Fig. 2. In Fig. 1a, there are three classes; *CLS1*, *CLS2*, which elaborate carrier sets, and *CLS2*, which is a sub-class of *CLS1* and elaborates a variable. An *attribute* or *association* of a class can have a combination of the following properties: *surjective*, *injective*, *total*, and *functional*. Attributes *attr1* of *CLS1* and *attr3* of *CLS3* are total and functional, while *attr2* of *CLS2* is functional. An injective association *rel* defined between *CLS1* and *CLS2* elaborates a constant. Figure 1b shows an example of a state-machine, which is lifted to the carrier set *CLS1* for its instances. This is also the instances set for the class *CLS1* and a state of the state-machine is named after its variable sub-class, *CLS3*. Further sub-states *S1* and *S2* are modelled as variable subsets of *CLS3*. The state of an instance is represented by its membership of these sets. The state-machine transitions are linked to the same events as the methods of *CLS3*. Hence the state-machine constrains the invocation of class methods for a particular instance of the class. The contextual instance is modelled as a parameter *this_CLS3* which can be used in additional guards and actions in both the class diagram and the state-machine.

The transition c, from the initial state to *S1* also enters parent state *CLS3* and therefore represents a constructor for the class *CLS3*. The class method c is

sets : $CLS1, CLS2$ **constants** : $attr1, attr2, rel$

axioms :
$rel \in CLS1 \rightarrowtail CLS2$
$attr1 \in CLS1 \rightarrow \mathbb{N}$
$attr2 \in CLS2 \rightarrow \mathbb{Z}$

variables :
$CLS3$,
$S1$,
$S2$
$attr3$

invariants :
$CLS3 \subseteq CLS1$
$S1 \subseteq CLS3$
$S2 \subseteq CLS3$
$partition(CLS3, S1, S2)$
$attr3 \in CLS3 \rightarrow BOOL$
$\forall this\_CLS3 \cdot (this\_CLS3 \in S2) \Rightarrow$
$\qquad (attr3(this\_CLS3) = FALSE)$

INITIALISATION : **begin**
$CLS3 := \varnothing$
$S1 := \varnothing$
$S2 := \varnothing$
$attr3 := \varnothing$
end

c :
any $this\_CLS2, this\_CLS3$ **where**
$this\_CLS2 \in CLS2$
$this\_CLS3 \notin CLS3$
$rel(this\_CLS3) = this\_CLS2$
then
$S1 := S1 \cup \{this\_CLS3\}$
$CLS3 := CLS3 \cup \{this\_CLS3\}$
$attr3 := attr3 \vartriangleleft \{this\_CLS3 \mapsto FALSE\}$
end

e :
any $this\_CLS3, b$ **where**
$this\_CLS3 \in CLS3$
$this\_CLS3 \in S1$
$b \in BOOL$
$attr2(rel(this\_CLS3)) > 0$
then
$S1 := S1 \setminus \{this\_CLS3\}$
$S2 := S2 \cup \{this\_CLS3\}$
$attr3(this\_CLS3) := b$
end

Fig. 2. Event-B translation of the iUML-B example

also defined as a constructor and automatically generates an action to initialise the instance of $attr3$ with its defined initial value. The same event c is also given as a method of class $CLS2$ in order to generate a contextual instance $this\_CLS2$ which is used in an additional (manually entered) guard to define a value for the association rel of the super-class. The transition and method e is a normal method of class $CLS3$, which is available when the contextual instance exists in $CLS3$ and $S1$, and changes state by moving the instance from $S1$ to $S2$. The other guards and actions shown in this event concerning parameter b and attribute $attr2$, have been added as additional guards and actions of the transition or method. These are not shown in the diagram as they are entered using the diagram's properties view. The state invariant shown in state $S2$ applies to any instance while it is in that state. The Event-B version of the invariant is quantified over all instances and an antecedent added to represent the membership of $S2$. In the rest of this paper we do not explain the translation to Event-B.

2.4   Validation and Verification

Consistency of Event-B models is provided via means of proof obligations, e.g., invariant preservation by all events. Proof obligations can be discharged automatically or manually using the theorem provers of Rodin. Another important tool for validation and verification of our model is ProB [7]. ProB provides model checking facility to complement the theorem proving technique for verifying Event-B models. Features of the ProB model checker include finding invariant violations and deadlock for multiple refinement levels simultaneously. Furthermore, ProB also offers an animator enabling users to validate the behaviour of the models by exploring execution traces. The traces can be constructed interactively by manual selection of events or automatically as counter-examples from the model checker. Here, an animation trace is a sequence of event execution with parameters' value. The animator shows the state of the model after each event execution in the trace.

3   Development

In this section, we discuss the development of the model. The model consists of three refinement levels. The abstract level captures the essence of the security property which is proven for the abstract representation of events that make new packets and move them around the network. The first refinement introduces some further detail of the network system and is proven to be a valid refinement of the first model. That is, it maintains the security property. Both of these first levels are un-implementable because they refer directly to a conceptual property of a packet which is the VLAN that the packet was intended for. In reality it is not possible to tell from a raw packet, which VLAN it was originally created for. The second refinement introduces tagging as a means to implement a record of this conceptual property. The refinement models nested tagging and the behaviour of a typical switch which, apart from tagging packets depending on their source, also removes tags for the native LAN. The automatic provers are unable to prove that removing tags satisfies the gluing invariant. This is the well-known security vulnerability to double tagging attacks. Adding a constraint to, effectively, disallow the native LAN from being configured as a VLAN, allows the provers to discharge this proof obligation. This corresponds to the usual protective measure against double tagging attacks.

3.1   M0: An Abstract Model of VLAN Security

We aim to make the first model minimally simple while describing the essential security property. We use a class diagram (Fig. 3) to introduce some 'given' sets for data packets (class PKT) and VLANs (class $VLAN$). The constant association PV describes the $VLAN$ that each packet is intended for. (Note that this is a conceptual relationship representing an intention and hence the implementation cannot access it). We abstract away from switches and devices and

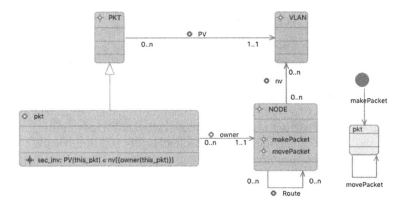

Fig. 3. Abstract model of VLAN security requirement

introduce a set of nodes, class *NODE*, to represent both. The communications topology is given by the constant association, *Route*, which maps nodes to nodes in a many to many relationship.

The set of VLANs that a particular node is allowed to see, is given by the constant association *nv*. For now this is a many to many relationship but in later refinements we will find that, while switches are allowed to see all VLANs, devices may only access the packets of one VLAN.

The class *pkt* represents the subset of packets that currently exist (whereas, *PKT* represented all possible packets that might exist currently or in the past or future). A packet that exists, always has exactly one owner node. The method makePacket takes a non-existing packet from *PKT* and adds it to *pkt* and initialises the new packet's *owner* to the contextual node instance. The method movePacket changes the *owner* of an existing packet to a new node that is non-deterministically selected from the nodes that the current owner node is directly linked to via *Route*.

The class invariant, sec_inv, in class *pkt* describes the security property[2]:

$$\forall this\_pkt \cdot this\_pkt \in pkt \ \Rightarrow \ PV(this\_pkt) \in nv[\{owner(this\_pkt)\}] \ , \qquad (2)$$

i.e., the VLAN for which this packet is intended, belongs to the VLANs that its owner is allowed to see. For this invariant to hold we need to restrict the method movePacket so that it only moves packets to a new owner that is allowed to see the VLAN of the packet. For now we do this with a guard, $PV(p) \in nv[\{n\}]$, where p is the packet and n is the destination node. However, this guard must be replaced in later refinements because it refers directly to the conceptual property *PV* and is therefore not implementable. We also ensure that makePacket only creates packets with a *PV* value that its maker node is allowed to see.

---

[2] A concise summary of the Event-B mathematical notation can be found at http://wiki.event-b.org/images/EventB-Summary.pdf.

We use a state-machine (Fig. 3) to constrain the sequence of events that can be performed on a packet. The state-machine is lifted to the set PKT of all packets, At this stage we only require that makePacket is the initial event that brings a packet into existence, and this can be followed by any number of movePacket events.

3.2 M1: Introducing Switches and Devices

In M0, to keep things simple we did not distinguish between switches and devices. However, they have an important distinction since switches are allowed to see all VLAN packets. The design will utilise this distinction so we need to introduce it early on. In **M1** (Fig. 4) we introduce two new classes, *Switch* and *Device*, as subtypes of *NODE*.

Since switches are implicitly associated with all VLANS (i.e. trusted), we do not need to model which VLANs they are allowed to access. Therefore, we replace nv with a functional association dv whose domain (source) is restricted to *Device*. It is a total function, rather than a relation, because a device has access to exactly one VLAN and again we model this as a constant function since we do not require it to vary.

Switches are not allowed to create new packets so we move makePacket to *Device*. Since, when moving a packet, the destination kind affects the security checks, we split movePacket into two alternatives: movePacketToSwitch which does not need any guard concerning PV and movePacketToDevice where we replace the guard, $PV(p) \in nv[\{n\}]$, with $PV(p) = dv(n)$ to reflect the data refinement. Note however, that the new guard still refers to PV.

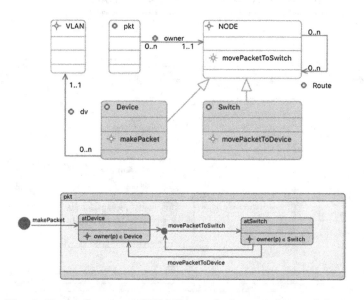

Fig. 4. First refinement of VLAN introducing switches and devices

The refinement introduces the need for some further constraints on the
sequence of events for a particular package. We introduce sub-states *atDevice*
and *atSwitch* (Fig. 4) to show that a packet can only be moved to a device from
a switch. Note that these states could be derived from *owner* (hence the invariants in states *atDevice* and *atSwitch*) however, the state diagram helps visualise
the process relative to a packet which will become more significant in the next
refinement level.

3.3 M2: Introducing Tagging

We can now introduce the tagging mechanism that allows switches to know
which VLAN a packet is intended for. Our aim is that, in this refined model,
switches should not use the *PV* relationship other than for proving that the tag
mechanism achieves an equivalent result. We introduce a new given set, *TAG*,
(Fig. 5) which has a total functional association *TV* with *VLAN*. This function

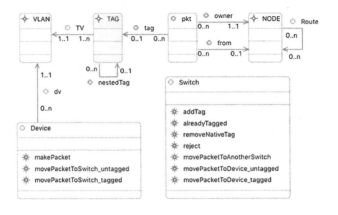

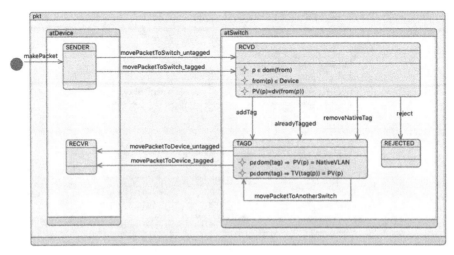

Fig. 5. Second refinement of VLAN introducing tagging

represents the VLAN identifier within a tag, which is part of the implementation, i.e., guards that reference TV are implementable. We add a variable partial function association, tag, from pkt to TAG, which represents the tagging of a packet.

In typical LAN protocols, already tagged packets can be tagged again to allow switches to use VLANs for internal system purposes. Although, for simplification, we omit this internal tagging, we allow tags to be nested so that we can model a double tagging attack by a device. Therefore we model nested tags with a variable partial functional association, $nestedTag$ from TAG to itself. When a packet arrives at a switch from a device, the switch can tell which VLAN it belongs to from the port that it arrived on. However, for simplicity, we avoid introducing ports in this refinement. Instead we model this information via a variable functional association $from$ from pkt to $NODE$. Hence a switch can determine which VLAN a packet, p, is for via $dv(from(p))$. Port configuration could easily be introduced in a subsequent refinement without altering the main points of this article. A significant behaviour of switches that relates to security is how they deal with packets for the native VLAN. Therefore, in the Event-B context for **M2**, we introduce a specific instance of $VLAN$ called $NativeVLAN$.

The behaviour (Fig. 5) is refined to add procedures for handling tagged packets. State $atSwitch$ is split into three sub-states, $RCVD$ for packets that have just been received from a device, $TAGD$ for packets from a device that have been successfully processed and $REJECTED$ for packets that are found to be invalid. A device may now send an untagged packet to a switch (transition movePacketToSwitch_untagged) and allow the switch to determine appropriate tagging, or it may tag the packet itself (transition movePacketToSwitch_tagged) in which case the switch will check the tag. In the latter case the tag may be valid or invalid and may have nested tags.

After receiving a packet, p, at the state $RCVD$, the new owner switch processes it by taking one of the following transitions:

- addTag : if p is not already tagged, a tag,tg, such that $TV(tg) = dv(from(p))$, is added and the packet is accepted by moving it to state $TAGD$.
- alreadyTagged : if p is already tagged correctly (i.e., $TV(tg) = dv(from(p))$) and not tagged as the native VLAN (i.e. $TV(tg) \neq NativeVLAN$) the packet is accepted as is.
- removeNativeTag : if p is correctly tagged for the native VLAN (i.e., $TV(tg) = dv(from(p)) = NativeVLAN$), the tag is removed and the packet is accepted. The tag is removed in such as way as to leave p tagged with a nested tag if any.
- reject : if p is incorrectly tagged (i.e., $TV(tg) \neq dv(from(p))$), it is rejected by moving it to state $REJECTED$ which has no outgoing transitions.

After processing packet, p, the switch can either pass it on to another switch or, if available, pass it to a device via one of the following transitions:

- movePacketToDevice_untagged : if p is not tagged, and the switch is connected to a device, n, on the native VLAN (i.e. $dv(n) = NativeVLAN$),

– movePacketToDevice_tagged : if p is tagged and the switch is connected to a device, n, which is on the VLAN indicated by the tag (i.e. $dv(n) = TV(tag(p))$).

It is these two transitions that refine movePacketToDevice, which need to establish the security invariant using tags rather than the unimplementable guard concerning PV. This has been done as indicated above by the conditions on $dv(n)$. It can be seen by simple substitution, that the state invariants of $TAGD$ enable the prover to establish that the new guards are at least as strong as the abstract one $(PV(p) = dv(n))$. We also need to prove that these state invariants are satisfied by the incoming transitions of state $TAGD$. A state invariant $PV(p) = dv(from(p))$ is added to $RCVD$ in order to allow the prover to establish this. Again, this can be checked using simple substitutions of the guards of addTag, alreadyTagged and removeNativeTag using this state invariant. The other two state invariants for $RCVD$ are merely to establish well-definedness of the function applications. The state invariants of state $RCVD$ are clearly established by the actions of incoming transitions movePacketToSwitch_untagged and movePacketToSwitch_tagged.

3.4 Analysis

We analyse the protocol using both theorem proving and model checking techniques. Given the model in Sect. 3.3, the automatic provers discharge all proof obligations except for one. The prover cannot establish that the transition removeNativeTag establishes the state-invariant

$$p \in dom(tag) \Rightarrow TV(tag(p)) = PV(p) \tag{3}$$

of state $TAGD$. In general, a failed invariant preservation proof identifies the property (the invariant) that may be at risk and the transition (event) that may violate it. We say 'may' because lack of proof does not necessarily indicate a problem. It can be a result of insufficient prover power. We therefore use the ProB model checker to confirm the problem.

As with any model checker, we instantiate the context of the system, in this case, the network topology. The network topology under consideration can be seen in Fig. 6. The switches, i.e., $SWCH1$ and $SWCH2$ have access to all VLANs, namely, $VLAN1$, and $VLAN2$. The native VLAN $NativeVLAN$ is defined to be

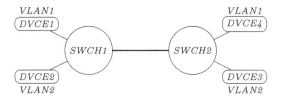

Fig. 6. Network topology for analysis

VLAN1. Devices *DVCE1*, *DVCE4* belong to *VLAN1* and devices *DVCE2* and *DVCE3* both belong to *VLAN2*. We define two packets *PK1* and *PK2* where *PK1* is intended for *VLAN1* and *PK2* is for *VLAN2*, i.e.,

$$PV = \{PK1 \mapsto VLAN1, PK2 \mapsto VLAN2\} \ .$$

Finally, we define two tags *TAG1*, and *TAG2* corresponding to *VLAN1* and *VLAN2*, respectively. A tag with nested tag is numbered accordingly, for example, *TAG12* is for *VLAN1* and has an inner tag for *VLAN2*. Our subsequent analysis is based on this particular setting.

Firstly, we want to identify whether the state-invariant (3) can indeed be violated. We model check the whole refinement-chain from **M0** to **M2**. ProB indeed identifies a counter-example trace which leads to the violation of the invariant as follow.

$$\dots$$

$$\longrightarrow \quad \textsf{makePacket}(PK1, DVCE1) \tag{4}$$

$$\longrightarrow \quad \textsf{movePacketToSwitch\_tagged}(PK1, SWCH1, TAG12, DVCE1) \tag{5}$$

$$\dots \dots$$

$$\longrightarrow \quad \textsf{removeNativeTag}(PK1, SWCH1) \tag{6}$$

In the trace, *DVCE1* creates *PK1* (4) before moving it to *SWCH1* with tag *TAG12* (5). When *SWCH1* removes the native tag *TAG12* from *PK1* (6), resulting in *TAG2*, the state-invariant (3) becomes invalid since *PK1* is intended for *VLAN1*, but it is now tagged with *TAG2*, which is identified for *VLAN2*.

However, the violation could be caused by an unnecessarily strong gluing invariant. To verify whether the security invariant (2) is indeed violated in **M2**, we model check **M2** without **M0** and **M1** but with the security invariant copied from **M0** to **M2** in place of the gluing invariant. Once again, ProB returns a counter-example trace which is an extension of the previous trace, i.e.,

$$\dots$$

$$\longrightarrow \quad \textsf{makePacket}(PK1, DVCE1) \tag{7}$$

$$\longrightarrow \quad \textsf{movePacketToSwitch\_tagged}(PK1, SWCH1, TAG12, DVCE1) \tag{8}$$

$$\dots \dots$$

$$\longrightarrow \quad \textsf{removeNativeTag}(PK1, SWCH1) \tag{9}$$

$$\dots \dots$$

$$\longrightarrow \quad \textsf{moveUntaggedPacketToDevice\_tagged}(DVCE2, PK1, SWCH1) \tag{10}$$

After removing the native tag of *PK1* (9), the packet is moved from *SWCH1* to *DVCE2* (10). At this time, *PK1* has arrived to a device (*DVCE2*) which does not have permission to receive any packet for *VLAN1*.

Note that there are three different points in the process leading to the security breach:

– the point where the security attack is initiated (8),
– the point where the design assumptions are violated and (9),
– the point where the security is breached (10).

Coming back to the original failed invariant preservation proof obligation, we can now confirm that it is indeed possible for the invariant to be violated[3]. Examination of the pending goal that the prover is attempting to prove reveals more detail about the problem.

$$TV((\{p\} \times nestedTag[tag[\{p\}]])(p)) = PV(p),$$

It shows that the prover has replaced the packet's tag with its nested tag in the design property, and is attempting to show that the VLAN of the nested tag is also for the correct VLAN for the packet. From the theorem prover, therefore, we know that

– the switch's procedure of removing the native tag causes a problem,
– the problem is that the nested tag becomes the packets main tag and does not necessarily indicate the correct VLAN.

When a constraint, $NativeVLAN \notin ran(dv)$, i.e., no device can be configured to use the native VLAN, is added to the model the proof obligation is immediately discharged since the guard of the transition removeNativeTag can easily be shown to be false. This constraint corresponds to the recommended protective action to prevent double tagging attacks.

Overall, the theorem provers can identify the security flaw in a design or protocol. They do not need to find an example attack but can pinpoint the exact nature of the flaw directly. This is because proof obligations are generated from the actions of individual events. While the provers indicates the nature of the violation of the design assumption, they do not reveal the complete sequence from attack to security breach. The model-checker, while being restricted to example instantiations, is able to illustrate the process from initial attack through to security breach.

4   Summary of Approach

To summarise, our approach is as follows:

1. Create an iUML-B Class diagram model of the entities and relationships that are essential concepts of the system. Add a state-machine to model the required behaviour of the system. Only model sufficient concepts to express the security property. Do not model the mechanism that implements the security.

---

[3] This is because removing the native tag may reveal an invalid nested tag (the known security flaw exploited by double tagging attacks).

2. Express the security property as an invariant over the entities in the model. Make sure that the model preserves the invariant.
3. Refine the iUML-B model (possibly over several iterations) to introduce the mechanism that will ensure the system is secure. Do not constrain the behaviour of elements unless the security system has control over this behaviour. That is, allow attacks to occur within the model.
4. Animate each refinement level to ensure that the model behaves in a useful way. This is important to *validate* that our formal model captures the behaviour of the real system.
5. If any POs are not proven check the type of PO and the goal to see whether there is a mistake in the model. Correct the model as necessary.
6. If unproven POs remain for the gluing invariant, this may mean that the security mechanism has a flaw. Analyse the problem as follows:

- Examine the PO. Note the event that it relates to and examine the goal of the prover. This can often be used to interpret what is going wrong or whether a manual proof is possible.
- Run the model-checker to establish that there really is a problem. If the model checker can not find a trace to the violation, a manual proof may be possible.
- Remove the gluing invariant and copy the security property invariant from the abstract model and run the model checker (without previous refinement levels). If it does not find a trace that violates the security property, the gluing invariant may be too strong.
- If a trace to the security property is found there is a flaw in the protocol. The trace can be examined to analyse the nature of the attack, the flaw in the security mechanism and how it leads to the security violation.

In the example presented in this paper, the abstract model (step 1) **M0** was developed in Sect. 3.1, and the security invariant (step 2) was introduced in the same section. The refinement process (step 3) involved an intermediate refinement **M1** in Sect. 3.2 and a final refinement **M2** in Sect. 3.3. At each refinement level, animation with ProB (step 4) and examination of unproven POs (step 5), helped us to arrive at a correct and useful model. A security flaw was detected and analysed (step 6) as described in Sect. 3.4.

5   Conclusion

Our investigation into a known example of a security vulnerability indicates that formal modelling with strong verification tools can be extremely beneficial in understanding security problems. The tools at our disposal include an automatic theorem prover as well as a model checker. In our previous work on safety-critical systems we have found that these tools exhibit great synergy and this is also the case when analysing security protocols.

We use iUML-B class diagrams and state-machines as a diagrammatic representation of the Event-B formalism. The diagrams help us create, visualise and communicate the models leading to a better understanding of the systems.

Although we use animation to informally validate system behaviour, we have not yet done any rigorous analysis of liveness properties. A future aim of our research is to incorporate liveness reasoning into our approach.

This refinement-based approach can be applied to any problem that involves sets of entities that are interacting in some way via a procedure or protocol. For example, an authentication protocol such as Needham-Schroder could be modelled abstractly as a class of *agents* sending *messages* and receiving them with property *perceived sender* based on an *actualSender*. This could then be refined to replace direct references to the *actual sender*, with encrypted *nonces*.

Finally, we envisage that without refinement, formulating the gluing invariant that links the specification to the implementation would, in general, be challenging. Here the role of the gluing invariant is essential as its violation helps the designer to identify the point where the design assumptions are offended, causing the actual security breach. A similar observation has been made in [3].

Acknowledgement. This work is funded by the Enable-S3 Project, http://www.enable-s3.eu.

References

1. Abrial, J.-R.: Modeling in Event-B: System and Software Engineering. Cambridge University Press, Cambridge (2010)
2. Abrial, J.-R., Butler, M., Hallerstede, S., Hoang, T.S., Mehta, F., Voisin, L.: Rodin: an open toolset for modelling and reasoning in Event-B. Softw. Tools Technol. Transf. **12**(6), 447–466 (2010)
3. Butler, M.: On the use of data refinement in the development of secure communications systems. Form. Asp. Comput. **14**(1), 2–34 (2002)
4. Enable-S3 consortium. Enable-S3 project website. http://www.enable-s3.eu. Accessed 04 Dec 2016
5. Hoang, T.S.: An introduction to the Event-B modelling method. In: Romanovsky, A., Thomas, M. (eds.) Industrial Deployment of System Engineering Methods, pp. 211–236. Springer, Heidelberg (2013)
6. IEEE. 802.1Q-2014 - Bridges and Bridged Networks. http://www.ieee802.org/1/pages/802.1Q-2014.html. Accessed 02 Dec 2016
7. Leuschel, M., Butler, M.: ProB: an automated analysis toolset for the B method. Softw. Tools Technol. Transf. (STTT) **10**(2), 185–203 (2008)
8. Said, M.Y., Butler, M., Snook, C.: A method of refinement in UML-B. Softw. Syst. Model. **14**(4), 1557–1580 (2015)
9. Colin, S.: iUML-B statemachines. In: Proceedings of the Rodin Workshop 2014, pp. 29–30, Toulouse, France (2014). http://eprints.soton.ac.uk/365301/
10. Snook, C., Butler, M.: UML-B: Formal modeling and design aided by UML. ACM Trans. Softw. Eng. Methodol. **15**(1), 92–122 (2006)

On Learning Sparse Boolean Formulae
for Explaining AI Decisions

Susmit Jha[(✉)], Vasumathi Raman, Alessandro Pinto, Tuhin Sahai,
and Michael Francis

United Technologies Research Center, Berkeley, USA
jha@csl.sri.com, {pintoa,sahait,francism}@utrc.utc.com

Abstract. In this paper, we consider the problem of learning Boolean formulae from examples obtained by actively querying an oracle that can label these examplesz as either positive or negative. This problem has received attention in both machine learning as well as formal methods communities, and it has been shown to have exponential worst-case complexity in the general case as well as for many restrictions. In this paper, we focus on learning *sparse* Boolean formulae which depend on only a small (but unknown) subset of the overall vocabulary of atomic propositions. We propose an efficient algorithm to learn these sparse Boolean formulae with a given confidence. This assumption of sparsity is motivated by the problem of mining explanations for decisions made by artificially intelligent (AI) algorithms, where the explanation of individual decisions may depend on a small but unknown subset of all the inputs to the algorithm. We demonstrate the use of our algorithm in automatically generating explanations of these decisions. These explanations will make intelligent systems more understandable and accountable to human users, facilitate easier audits and provide diagnostic information in the case of failure. The proposed approach treats the AI algorithm as a black-box oracle; hence, it is broadly applicable and agnostic to the specific AI algorithm. We illustrate the practical effectiveness of our approach on a diverse set of case studies.

1 Introduction

The rapid integration of robots and other intelligent agents into our industrial and social infrastructure has created an immediate need for establishing trust between these agents and their human users. The long-term acceptance of AI will depend critically on its ability to explain its actions, provide reasoning behind its decisions, and furnish diagnostic information in case of failures. This is particularly true for systems with close human-machine coordination such as self-driving cars, care-giving and surgical robots. Decision-making and planning algorithms central to the operation of these systems currently lack the ability to explain the choices and decisions that they make. It is important that intelligent agents become capable of responding to inquiries from human users. For example, when

---

S. Jha—The author is currently at SRI International.

C. Barrett et al. (Eds.): NFM 2017, LNCS 10227, pp. 99–114, 2017.
DOI: 10.1007/978-3-319-57288-8_7

riding in an autonomous taxi, we might expect to query the AI driver using questions similar to those we would ask a human driver, such as "why did we not take the Bay Bridge", and receive a response such as "there is too much traffic on the bridge" or "there is an accident on the ramp leading to the bridge or in the middle lane of the bridge." These explanations are essentially propositional formulae formed by combining the user-observable system and the environment states using Boolean connectives.

Even though the decisions of intelligent agents are the consequence of algorithmic processing of perceived system and environment states [24,30], the straight-forward approach of reviewing this processing is not practical. First, AI algorithms use internal states and intermediate variables to make decisions which may not be observable or interpretable by a typical user. For example, reviewing decisions made by the A* planning algorithm [20] could reveal that a particular state was never considered in the priority queue. But this is not human-interpretable, because a user may not be familiar with the details of how A* works. Second, the efficiency and effectiveness of many AI algorithms relies on their ability to intelligently search for optimal decisions without deducing information not needed to accomplish the task, but some user inquiries may require information that was not inferred during the original execution of the algorithm. Third, artificial intelligence is often a composition of numerous machine learning and decision-making algorithms, and explicitly modelling each one of these algorithms is not practical. Instead, we need a technique which can treat these algorithms as black-box oracles, and obtain explanations by observing their output on selected inputs. These observations motivate us to formulate the problem of generating explanations as an oracle-guided learning of Boolean formula where the AI algorithm is queried multiple times on carefully selected inputs to generate examples, which in turn are used to learn the explanation.

Given the observable system and environment states, S and E respectively, typical explanations depend on only a small subset of elements in the overall vocabulary $V = S \cup E$, that is, if the set of state variables on which the explanation ϕ depends is denoted by $support(\phi) \subseteq V$, then $|support(\phi)| << |V|$. This support or its exact size is not known a priori. Thus, the explanations are sparse formulae over the vocabulary V. The number of examples needed to learn a Boolean formula is exponential in the size of the vocabulary in the general case [8,18,19]. Motivated by the problem of learning explanations, we propose an efficient algorithm that exploits sparsity to efficiently learn *sparse* Boolean formula. Our approach builds on recent advances in oracle-guided inductive formal synthesis [16,17]. We make the following three contributions:

- We formulate the problem of finding explanations for decision-making AI algorithms as the problem of learning sparse Boolean formulae.
- We present an efficient algorithm to learn sparse Boolean formula where the size of required examples grows logarithmically (in contrast to exponentially in the general case) with the size of the overall vocabulary.
- We illustrate the effectiveness of our approach on a set of case-studies.

2 Motivating Example

We now describe a motivating example to illustrate the problem of providing human-interpretable explanations for the results of an AI algorithm. We consider the A* planning algorithm [20], which enjoys widespread use in path and motion planning due to its optimality and efficiency. Given a description of the state space and transitions between states as a weighted graph where weights are used to encode costs such as distance and time, A* starts from a specific node in the graph and constructs a tree of paths starting from that node, expanding paths in a best-first fashion until one of them reaches the predetermined goal node. At each iteration, A* determines which of its partial paths is most promising and should be expanded. This decision is based on the estimate of the cost-to-go to the goal node. We refer readers to [20] for a detailed description of A*. Typical implementations of A* use a priority queue to perform the repeated selection of intermediate nodes. The algorithm continues until some goal node has the minimum cost value in the queue, or until the queue is empty (in which case no plan exists). Figure 1 depicts the result of running A* on a 50×50 grid, where cells that form part of an obstacle are colored red. The input map (Fig. 1(a)) shows the obstacles and free space. A* is run to find a path from lower right corner to upper left corner. On the output map (Fig. 1(b)), cells on the returned optimal path are colored dark blue. Cells which ever entered A*'s priority queue are colored light cyan, and those that never entered the queue are colored yellow.

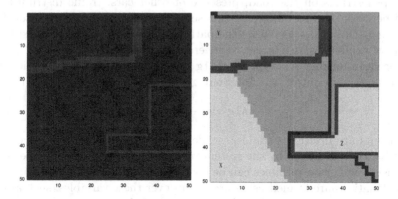

Fig. 1. (a) Input map to A* (b) Output showing final path and internal states of A* (Color figure online)

Consider the three cells X, Y, Z marked in the output of A* in Fig. 1(b). An observer might want to enquire why points X, Y or Z were not selected for the optimal path generated by A*. Given the output and logged internal states of the A* algorithm, we know that Y was considered as a candidate cell and discarded due to non-optimal cost whereas X was never even considered as a candidate. But, this is not a useful explanation because a non-expert observing the behavior of a robot cannot be expected to understand the concept of a priority queue, or the details of how A* works. Looking at point Z, we notice that neither X nor Z was ever inserted into the priority queue; hence, both were never considered as candidate cells on the optimal path. When responding to a user query about why X and Z were not selected in the optimal path, we cannot differentiate between the two even if all internal decisions and states of the A* algorithm were logged. So, we cannot provide the intuitively expected explanation that Z is not reachable due to certain obstacles, while X is reachable but has higher cost than the cells that were considered. This is an example of a scenario where providing explanation requires new information that the AI algorithm might not have deduced while solving the original decision making problem.

3   Problem Definition

The class of AI algorithms used in autonomous systems include path planning algorithms, discrete and continuous control, computer vision and image recognition algorithms. All of these algorithms would be rendered more useful by the ability to explain themselves. Our goal is to eventually develop an approach to generate explanations for the overall system, but we focus on individual components in this paper rather than the overall system. For example, the path planner for a self-driving car takes inputs from machine learning and sensor-fusion algorithms, which in turn receive data from camera, LIDAR and other sensors. The processed sensor data often has semantic meaning attached to it, such as detection of pedestrians on the road, presence of other cars, traffic distribution in a road network, and so on. Given this semantic information, the reason for a particular path being selected by the path planner is often not obvious: this is the sort of explanation we target to generate automatically.

A decision-making AI algorithm Alg can be modelled as a function that computes values of output variables out given input variables in, that is,

$$\text{Alg} : \text{in} \rightarrow \text{out}$$

The outputs are decision variables, while the inputs include environment and system states as observed by the system through the perception pipeline. While the decision and state variables can be continuous and real valued, the inquiries and explanations are framed using predicates over these variables, such as comparison of a variable to some threshold. Let the vocabulary of atomic predicates used in the inquiry from the user and the provided explanation from the system be denoted by $\mathcal{V}$. We can separate the vocabulary $\mathcal{V}$ into two subsets: $\mathcal{V}_Q$ used to formulate the user inquiry and $\mathcal{V}_R$ used to provide explanations.

$$\mathcal{V}_Q = \{q_1, q_2, \ldots q_m\}, \mathcal{V}_R = \{r_1, r_2, \ldots r_n\} \text{ where } q_i, r_i : \text{in} \cup \text{out} \rightarrow \text{Bool}$$

Intuitively, $\mathcal{V}$ is the shared vocabulary that describes the interface of the AI algorithm and is understood by the human-user. For example, the inquiry vocabulary for a planning agent may include propositions denoting selection of a waypoint in the path, and the explanation vocabulary may include propositions denoting presence of obstacles on a map. An *inquiry* ϕ_Q from the user is an observation about the output (decision) of the algorithm, and can be formulated as a Boolean combination of predicates in the vocabulary $\mathcal{V}_Q$. Hence, we can denote it as $\phi_Q(\mathcal{V}_Q)$ where the predicates in $\mathcal{V}_Q$ are over the set **in** $\cup$ **out**, and the corresponding grammar is:

$$\phi_Q := \phi_Q \wedge \phi_Q \mid \phi_Q \vee \phi_Q \mid \neg \phi_Q \mid q_i \text{ where } q_i \in \mathcal{V}_Q$$

Similarly, the *response* $\phi_R(\mathcal{V}_R)$ is a Boolean combination of the predicates in the vocabulary $\mathcal{V}_R$ where the predicates in $\mathcal{V}_R$ are over the set **in** $\cup$ **out**, and the corresponding grammar is:

$$\phi_R := \phi_R \wedge \phi_R \mid \phi_R \vee \phi_R \mid \neg \phi_R \mid r_i \text{ where } r_i \in \mathcal{V}_R$$

Definition 1. *Given an AI algorithm* **Alg** *and an inquiry* $\phi_Q(\mathcal{V}_Q)$, $\phi_R(\mathcal{V}_R)$ *is a necessary and sufficient explanation when* $\phi_R(\mathcal{V}_R) \iff \phi_Q(\mathcal{V}_Q)$ *where* $\mathcal{V}_R, \mathcal{V}_Q$ *are predicates over* **in** $\cup$ **out** *as explained earlier, and* **out** = **Alg**(**in**). $\phi_R(\mathcal{V}_R)$ *is a sufficient explanation when* $\phi_R(\mathcal{V}_R) \Rightarrow \phi_Q(\mathcal{V}_Q)$.

If the algorithm **out** = **Alg**(**in**) could be modelled explicitly in appropriate logic, then the above definition could be used to generate explanations for a given inquiry using techniques such as satisfiability solving. However, such an explicit modelling of these algorithms is currently outside the scope of existing logical deduction frameworks, and is impractical for large and complicated AI systems even from the standpoint of the associated modelling effort. The AI algorithm **Alg** is available as an executable function; hence, it can be used as an oracle that can provide an outputs for any given input. This motivates oracle-guided learning of the explanation from examples using the notion of confidence associated with it.

Definition 2. *Given an AI algorithm* **Alg** *and an inquiry* $\phi_Q(\mathcal{V}_Q)$, $\phi_R(\mathcal{V}_R)$ *is a necessary and sufficient explanation with confidence* κ *when* $Pr(\phi_R(\mathcal{V}_R) \iff \phi_Q(\mathcal{V}_Q)) \geq \kappa$ *where* $\mathcal{V}_R, \mathcal{V}_Q$ *are predicates over* **in** $\cup$ **out** *as explained earlier,* **out** = **Alg**(**in**) *and* $0 \leq \kappa \leq 1$. $\phi_R(\mathcal{V}_R)$ *is a sufficient explanation with confidence* κ *when* $Pr(\phi_R(\mathcal{V}_R) \Rightarrow \phi_Q(\mathcal{V}_Q)) \geq \kappa$.

The oracle used to learn the explanation is implemented using the AI algorithm. It runs the AI algorithm on a given input in_i to generate the decision output out_i, and then marks the input as a positive example if $\phi_Q(out_i)$ is true, that is, the inquiry property holds on the output. It marks the input as a negative example if $\phi_Q(out_i)$ is not true. We call this an *introspection oracle*, and it marks each input as either positive or negative.

Definition 3. *An* introspection oracle $\mathcal{O}_{\phi_Q,\text{Alg}}$ *for a given algorithm* **Alg** *and inquiry* ϕ_Q *takes an input* in_i *and maps it to a positive or negative label, that is,* $\mathcal{O}_{\phi_Q,\text{Alg}} : \text{in} \rightarrow \{\oplus, \ominus\}$.

$\mathcal{O}_{\phi_Q,\text{Alg}}(in_i) = \oplus$ *if* $\phi_Q(\mathcal{V}_Q(out_i))$ *and* $\mathcal{O}_{\phi_Q,\text{Alg}}(in_i) = \ominus$ *if* $\neg\phi_Q(\mathcal{V}_Q(out_i))$, *where* $out_i = \text{Alg}(in_i)$, *and* $\mathcal{V}_Q(out_i)$ *is the evaluation of the predicates in* $\mathcal{V}_Q$ *on* out_i

We now formally define the problem of learning Boolean formula with specified confidence κ given an oracle to label examples.

Definition 4. *The problem of oracle-guided learning of Boolean formula from examples is to identify (with confidence κ) the target Boolean function ϕ over a set of atomic propositions $\mathcal{V}$ by querying an oracle $\mathcal{O}$ that labels each input in_i (which is an assignment to all variables in $\mathcal{V}$) as positive or negative $\{\oplus, \ominus\}$ depending on whether $\phi(in_i)$ holds or not, respectively.*

We make the following observations which relates the problem of finding explanations for decisions made by AI algorithms to the problem of learning Boolean formula.

Observation 1. *The problem of generating explanation ϕ_R for the AI algorithm* Alg *and an inquiry ϕ_Q is equivalent to the problem of oracle-guided learning of Boolean formula using oracle $\mathcal{O}_{\phi_Q, \text{Alg}}$ as described in Definition 4.*

$\phi[r_i]$ denotes the restriction of the Boolean formula ϕ by setting r_i to true in ϕ and $\phi[\overline{r_i}]$ denotes the restriction of ϕ by setting r_i to false. A predicate r_i is in the support of the Boolean formula ϕ, that is, $r_i \in \text{support}(\phi)$ if and only if $\phi[r_i] \neq \phi[\overline{r_i}]$.

Observation 2. *The explanation ϕ_R over a vocabulary of atoms $\mathcal{V}_R$ for the AI algorithm* Alg *and a user inquiry ϕ_Q is a sparse Boolean formula, that is, $|\text{support}(\phi_R)| << |\mathcal{V}_R|$.*

These observations motivate the following problem definition for learning sparse Boolean formula.

Definition 5. *Boolean function ϕ is called k-sparse if $|\text{support}(\phi_R)| \leq k$. The problem of oracle-guided learning of k-sparse Boolean formula from examples is to identify (with confidence κ) the target k-sparse Boolean function ϕ over a set of atomic propositions $\mathcal{V}$ by querying an oracle $\mathcal{O}$ that labels each input in_i (which is an assignment to all variables in $\mathcal{V}$) as positive or negative $\{\oplus, \ominus\}$ depending on whether $\phi(in_i)$ holds or not, respectively.*

Further, the explanation of decisions made by an AI algorithm can be generated by solving the problem of oracle-guided learning of k-sparse Boolean formula. In the following section, we present a novel approach to efficiently solve this problem.

4   Learning Explanations as Sparse Boolean Formula

Our proposed approach to solve the k-sparse Boolean formula learning problem has two steps:

1. In the first step, we find the support of the explanation, that is, support $(\phi_R) \subseteq \mathcal{V}_R$. This is accomplished using a novel approach which requires a small number of runs (logarithmic in $|\mathcal{V}_R|$) of the AI algorithm Alg.

2. In the second step, we find the Boolean combination of the atoms in $\mathcal{V}_{\phi_R}$ which forms the explanation ϕ_R. This is accomplished by distinguishing input guided learning of propositional logic formula which we have earlier used for the synthesis of programs [16].

Before delving into details of the above two steps, we introduce additional relevant notations. Recall that the vocabulary of explanation is $\mathcal{V}_R = \{r_1, r_2, \ldots, r_n\}$. Given any two inputs in_1 and in_2, we define the *difference* between them as follows.

$$\texttt{diff}(in_1, in_2) = \{i \mid r_i(in_1) \neq r_i(in_2)\}.$$

Next, we define a *distance* metric d on inputs as the size of the difference set, that is,

$$d(in_1, in_2) = |\texttt{diff}(in_1, in_2)|$$

Intuitively, $d(in_1, in_2)$ is the Hamming distance between the n-length vectors that record the evaluation of the atomic predicates r_i in $\mathcal{V}_R$. We say that two inputs in_1, in_2 are *neighbours* if and only if $d(in_1, in_2) = 1$. We also define a partial order $\preceq$ on inputs as follows:

$$in_1 \preceq in_2 \text{ iff } r_i(in_1) \Rightarrow r_i(in_2) \text{ for all } 1 \leq i \leq n$$

Given an input in and a set $J \subseteq \{1, 2, \ldots, n\}$, a *random J-preserving mutation* of in, denoted $\texttt{mutset}(in, J)$, is defined as:

$$\texttt{mutset}(in, J) = \{in' | in' \in in \text{ and } r_j(in') = r_j(in) \text{ for all } j \in J\}$$

Finding the Support: We begin with two random inputs in_1, in_2 on which the oracle $\mathcal{O}_{\phi_Q, \texttt{Alg}}$ returns different labels, say it returns positive on in_1 and negative on in_2 without loss of generality. Finding such in_1, in_2 can be done by sampling the inputs and querying the oracle until two inputs disagree on the outputs. The more samples we find without getting a pair that disagree on the label, the more likely it is that the Boolean formula being used by the oracle to label inputs is a constant (either $\texttt{true}$ or $\texttt{false}$). We later formalize this as a probabilistic confidence. Given the inputs in_1, in_2, we find $J = \texttt{diff}(in_1, in_2) = \{i_1, i_2, \ldots, i_l\}$ on which the inputs differ with respect to the vocabulary $\mathcal{V}_R = \{r_1, r_2, \ldots, r_n\}$. We partition J into two subsets $J_1 = \{i_1, i_2, \ldots, i_{\lfloor l/2 \rfloor}\}$ and $J_2 = \{i_{\lfloor l/2 \rfloor + 1}, i_{\lfloor l/2 \rfloor + 2}, \ldots, i_l\}$. The two sets J_1 and J_2 differ in size by at most 1. The set of inputs that are halfway between the two inputs w.r.t the Hamming distance metric d defined earlier is given by the set $\texttt{bisect}(in_1, in_2)$ defined as:

$$\texttt{bisect}(in_1, in_2) = \{in' | \forall j \in J_1 \, r_j(in') \text{ iff } r_j(in_1), \forall j \in J_2 \, r_j(in') \text{ iff } r_j(in_2)\}$$

Satisfiability solvers can be used to generate an input in' from $\texttt{bisect}(in_1, in_2)$. The oracle $\mathcal{O}_{\phi_Q, \texttt{Alg}}$ is run on in' to produce the corresponding label. This label will match either the label for the input in_1 or that of the input in_2. We discard the input whose label matches in' to produce the next pair of inputs, that is,

$$\texttt{introspect}(in_1, in_2) = \begin{cases} (in_1, in') & \text{if } \mathcal{O}_{\phi_Q, \texttt{Alg}}(in') \neq \mathcal{O}_{\phi_Q, \texttt{Alg}}(in_2) \\ (in', in_2) & \text{if } \mathcal{O}_{\phi_Q, \texttt{Alg}}(in') \neq \mathcal{O}_{\phi_Q, \texttt{Alg}}(in_1) \end{cases}$$
$$\text{where } in' \in \texttt{bisect}(in_1, in_2)$$

Starting from an initial pair of inputs on which $\mathcal{O}_{\phi_Q, \texttt{Alg}}$ produces different labels, we repeat the above process, considering a new pair of inputs at each iteration until we have two inputs in_1, in_2 that are neighbours, with $\texttt{diff}(in_1, in_2) = \{j\}$. Hence, $r_j \in \mathcal{V}_R$ is in the support of the explanation ϕ_R. We add this to the set of variables $\mathcal{V}_{\phi_R}$. We repeat the above process to find the next variable to add to the support set. For example, consider a 2-sparse Boolean formula $x_1 \vee x_2$ over the vocabulary set x_1, x_2, x_3, x_4, x_5. Given two random samples $(\texttt{T}, \texttt{F}, \texttt{T}, \texttt{F}, \texttt{F})$ and $(\texttt{F}, \texttt{F}, \texttt{F}, \texttt{T}, \texttt{T})$ - the first is labelled positive by oracle $\mathcal{O}$ and the second is negative. The $\texttt{diff}$ set is $\{1, 3, 4, 5\}$ and the $\texttt{bisect}$ produces a new example $(\texttt{T}, \texttt{F}, \texttt{T}, \texttt{T}, \texttt{T})$ which is labelled positive. So, the next pair is $(\texttt{T}, \texttt{F}, \texttt{T}, \texttt{T}, \texttt{T})$ and $(\texttt{F}, \texttt{F}, \texttt{F}, \texttt{T}, \texttt{T})$. The $\texttt{bisect}$ now produces new example $(\texttt{T}, \texttt{F}, \texttt{F}, \texttt{T}, \texttt{T})$ which is labelled positive. Now, the $\texttt{diff}$ set is a singleton set $\{1\}$. So, x_1 is in the support set of ϕ_R. This is repeated to find the full support $\{x_1, x_2\}$. The efficiency of the introspection process to obtain each variable is summarized in Lemma 1.

Lemma 1. *The introspective search for each new variable $r_j \in \mathcal{V}_{\phi_R}$ takes at most $O(\ln n)$ queries to $\mathcal{O}_{\phi_Q, \texttt{Alg}}$.*

Proof. The size of the difference set $J = \texttt{diff}(in_1, in_2)$ for any inputs in_1, in_2 is at most n for a vocabulary ϕ_R of size n. The i-th call to $\texttt{introspect}$ reduces the size of the difference set as follows: $|J(i)| \leq |J(i-1)|/2 + 1$. Thus, the number of calls to $\texttt{introspect}$ before the difference set is singleton and the two inputs are neighbours, obtained by solving the above recurrence equation, is $O(\ln n)$.

This introspective search for variables in the support set $\mathcal{V}_{\phi_R}$ is repeated till we cannot find a pair of inputs in_1, in_2 on which the oracle produces different outputs. We check this condition probabilistically using Lemma 2.

Lemma 2. *If m random samples $in_1, in_2, \ldots, in_m$ from $\texttt{mutset}(in, J)$ produce the same output as input 'in' for the oracle $\mathcal{O}_{\phi_Q, \texttt{Alg}}$ where ϕ_R is k-sparse, then the probability that all mutations $in' \in \texttt{mutset}(in, J)$ produce the same output is at least κ, where $m = 2^k \ln(1/(1 - \kappa))$.*

Proof. If all the mutations $in' \in \texttt{mutset}(in, J)$ do not produce the same output, then the probability of the Oracle $\mathcal{O}_{\phi_Q, \texttt{Alg}}$ differing from the output of in for any random sample in' is at least $1/2^k$ since the size of the set $\texttt{mutset}(in, J)$ is at most $s = 2^k$. So,

$$(1 - 1/s)^m \geq 1 - \kappa \quad \Leftarrow e^{(-1/s)m} \geq 1 - \kappa \; (\text{ since } 1 - x \leq e^{-x})$$
$$\Leftrightarrow (-1/s)m \geq \ln(1 - \kappa) \Leftrightarrow m \leq s \; \ln(1/(1 - \kappa))$$

We can now define $\mathtt{sample}(\mathcal{O}_{\phi_Q,\mathtt{Alg}}, in, J, \kappa)$ that samples $m = 2^k \ln(1/(1 - \kappa))$ inputs from the set $\mathtt{mutset}(in, J)$ and generates two inputs on which the oracle $\mathcal{O}_{\phi_Q,\mathtt{Alg}}$ disagrees and produces different outputs. If it cannot find such a pair of inputs, it returns $\bot$. The overall algorithm for finding the support of the explanations ϕ_R with probability κ is presented in Algorithm 1.1 using the oracle $\mathcal{O}_{\phi_Q,\mathtt{Alg}}$. It is a recursive algorithm which is initially called with a randomly generated input in and an empty set J. Notice that the support of a sufficient explanation can be found by making the recursive call on only one of the two inputs, that is, $\mathtt{getSupport}(\mathcal{O}_{\phi_Q,\mathtt{Alg}}, in_1, J, \kappa)$ or $\mathtt{getSupport}(\mathcal{O}_{\phi_Q,\mathtt{Alg}}, in_2, J, \kappa)$ instead of both.

Algorithm 1.1. Introspective computation of $\mathcal{V}_{\phi_R}$: $\mathtt{getSupport}(\mathcal{O}_{\phi_Q,\mathtt{Alg}}, in, J, \kappa)$

---

if $\mathtt{sample}(\mathcal{O}_{\phi_Q,\mathtt{Alg}}, in, J, \kappa) = \bot$ then
    return {} // The J-restricted Boolean formula is constant with probability κ.
else
    $(in_1, in_2) \Leftarrow \mathtt{sample}(\mathcal{O}_{\phi_Q,\mathtt{Alg}}, in, J, \kappa)$
    while $|\mathtt{diff}(in_1, in_2)| \neq 1$ do
        $in_1, in_2 \Leftarrow \mathtt{introspect}(in_1, in_2)$
    r_i is the singleton element in $\mathtt{diff}(in_1, in_2)$, $J \Leftarrow J \cup \{i\}$
    return $\{r_i\} \cup \mathtt{getSupport}(\mathcal{O}_{\phi_Q,\mathtt{Alg}}, in_1, J, \kappa) \cup \mathtt{getSupport}(\mathcal{O}_{\phi_Q,\mathtt{Alg}}, in_2, J, \kappa)$

Theorem 1. *The introspective computation of the support set $\mathcal{V}_{\phi_R}$ of variables of the k-sparse Boolean formula ϕ_R defined over the vocabulary of size n using at most $O(2^k \ln(n/(1 - \kappa)))$ examples.*

Proof. Each variable in $\mathcal{V}_{\phi_R}$ can be found using an introspective search that needs at most $O(\ln n)$ examples according to Lemma 1. So, the $\mathtt{while}$ loop in Algorithm 1.1 makes at most $O(\ln n)$ queries. In Lemma 2, we showed that the maximum number of examples needed for $\mathtt{sample}$ is $O(2^k \ln(1/(1 - \kappa)))$. The recursion is repeated at most $O(2^k)$ times. Thus, the overall algorithms needs at most $O(2^{2k} (\ln(1/(1 - \kappa)) + \ln n))$, that is, $O(2^{2k} \ln(n/(1 - \kappa)))$ examples.

Learning Boolean Formula ϕ_R: Learning a Boolean formula that forms the explanation ϕ_R for the given query ϕ_Q is relatively straight-forward once the variables $\mathcal{V}_{\phi_R}$ which form the support of the Boolean formula have been identified. Efficient techniques have been developed to solve this problem in the context of program synthesis, and we adopt a technique based on the use of distinguishing inputs proposed by us in [16]. The algorithm starts with a single random input in_1. The oracle $\mathcal{O}_{\phi_Q,\mathtt{Alg}}$ is queried with the example and it is marked positive or negative depending on the label returned by the oracle. A candidate explanation ϕ_R^c is generated which is consistent with the positive and negative examples seen so far. Then, the algorithm tries to find an alternative consistent explanation ϕ_R^a. If such an alternate explanation ϕ_R^a cannot be found, the algorithm terminates with ϕ_R^c as the final explanation. If ϕ_R^a is found, we find an input which distinguishes ϕ_R^c and ϕ_R^a and query the oracle with this new input in order to mark it as positive or negative. This refutes one of the two explanation formulae R^c and R^a. We keep repeating the process until we converge to a single Boolean formula. Algorithm 1.2 summarizes this learning procedure.

Theorem 2. *The overall algorithm to generate k-sparse explanation ϕ_R for a given query ϕ_Q takes $O(2^k \ln(n/(1 - \kappa)))$ queries to the oracle, that is, the number of examples needed to learn the Boolean formula grows logarithmically with the size of the vocabulary n.*

Algorithm 1.2. Learning ϕ_R given the vocabulary $\mathcal{V}_{\phi_R}$ and oracle $\mathcal{O}_{\phi_Q,\text{Alg}}$

Randomly sample an input in_0
if $\mathcal{O}_{\phi_Q,\text{Alg}}(in_0) = \oplus$ **then**
    $E^+ \Leftarrow E^+ \cup \{in_0\}$
else
    $E^- \Leftarrow E^- \cup \{in_0\}$
$\phi_R^c = $ Boolean formula consistent with E^+, E^-
while Alternative ϕ_R^a consistent with E^+, E^- exists **do**
    Generate distinguishing input in that satisfies $(\phi_R^c \wedge \neg \phi_R^a) \vee (\phi_R^a \wedge \neg \phi_R^c)$
    if $\mathcal{O}_{\phi_Q,\text{Alg}}(in) = \oplus$ **then**
        $E^+ \Leftarrow E^+ \cup \{in\}$
    else
        $E^- \Leftarrow E^- \cup \{in\}$
    $\phi_R^c = $ Boolean formula consistent with E^+, E^-
return ϕ_R^c

Proof. The first-step to compute the support set $\mathcal{V}_{\phi_R}$ of the explanation ϕ_R takes $O(2^k \ln(n/(1-\kappa)))$ queries and after that, the learning of explanation ϕ_R takes $O(2^k)$ queries. So, the total number of queries needed is $O(2^k \ln(n/(1 - \kappa)))$.

Thus, our algorithm adopts a binary search like procedure using the Hamming distance metric d to find the support of the Boolean formula over a vocabulary of size n using a number of examples that grow logarithmically in n. After the support has been found, learning the Boolean formula can be accomplished using the formal synthesis based approach that depends only on the size of the support set and not on the vocabulary size n. Algorithms that do not exploit sparsity have been previously shown to need examples that grow exponentially in n [18,19] in contrast to the logarithmic dependence on n of the algorithm proposed here. The proposed algorithm is very effective for sparse Boolean formula, that is, $k << n$, which is often the case with explanations.

5 Experiments

We begin by describing the results on the motivating example of A* presented in Sect. 2. The vocabulary is $\mathcal{V}_Q = \{on_{ij} \text{ for each cell } i, j \text{ in the grid}\}$ where

on_{ij} denotes the decision that i,j-th cell was selected to be on the final path, and $\neg on_{ij}$ denotes the decision that the i,j-th cell was not selected to be on the final path. The vocabulary $\mathcal{V}_R = \{obst_{ij}\}$ for each cell i,j in the grid where $obst_{ij}$ denotes that the cell i,j has an obstacle and $\neg obst_{ij}$ denote that the cell i,j is free. The explanation query is: "Why were no points in $25 \leq i \leq 50, j = 40$ (around z) not considered on the generated path?" The inquiry framed using $\mathcal{V}_Q$ is $\bigwedge_{25 \leq i \leq 50} \neg(on_{i,40})$. A sufficient explanation for this inquiry is $obst_{42,32} \wedge obst_{37,32}$ with κ set to 0.9. This is obtained in 2 min 4 s (48 examples). The second query is for the area around x: $\bigwedge_{0 \leq i \leq 20} \neg(on_{i,44})$ and the sufficient explanation obtained is $obst_{2,17} \wedge obst_{2,18}$ in 2 min 44 s (57 examples). The third query for area around y is $\bigwedge_{0 \leq i \leq 5} \neg(on_{i,5})$ and the corresponding explanation is $obst_{4,17} \wedge obst_{4,18}$ which was obtained in 1 min 48 s (45 examples). Given the 177 obstacles, a naive approach of enumerating all possible explanations would require 1.9×10^{153} runs of A* which is clearly infeasible in each of these three cases. Even if we assumed that the number of explanations is 2 (but did not know which two variables are in the support set), there are more than $15,000$ cases to be considered.

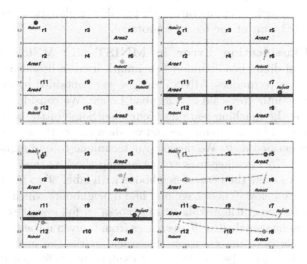

Fig. 2. Execution of reactive strategy for particular sequence of door closings. Each Robot i is initially assigned to goal Area i, but they can swap if needed to achieve the global goal (each marked Area must eventually get one robot). Brown lines indicate closed doors preventing the robots' motion. Time steps depicted are 0, 3, 4 and 24. (Color figure online)

Explaining Reactive Strategy [26]: We also applied our approach to a reactive switching protocol for multi-robot systems generated according to the approach described in [26]. The task involves 4 robots operating in the workspace depicted in Fig. 2. In the beginning, each robot is assigned the corresponding area to surveil (i.e. Robot i is assigned to Area i). Starting from their initial positions, they must reach this region. However, in response to the opening and closing of doors in the environment at each time step, they are allowed to swap goals. As can be seen from the Fig. 2, robots 1 and 2 swap goals because the top door closes, and robots 3 and 4 swap goals because the bottom door is closed. They stand by these decisions even though the doors later reopen. The simulation takes 24 time steps for all the robots to reach their final goals. The vocabulary is $V_Q = \{$final$_{ij}$ for each robot i and area $j\}$, where final$_{ij}$ denotes that robot i ended up in area j. The vocabulary $V_R = \{$door$_{\text{top},t}$, door$_{\text{bot},t}$, door$_{\text{left},t}$, door$_{\text{right},t}\}$, where door$_{\text{top},t}$ denotes that the door between the top and middle row of areas is closed at time t, door$_{\text{left},t}$ denotes that the door between the left and middle column of areas is closed at time t, etc. We pose the query, "Why did Robot 1 end up in Area 2?", i.e. final$_{12}$. Starting with the original input sequence and one in which no door-related events occur, the generated explanation is door$_{\text{bot},3}$, which is obtained in 0.76 s, and 7 introspective runs of the protocol on mutated inputs (door activity sequences). The second query was, "Why did Robot 3 not end up in Area 3?", or ¬final$_{33}$. This took 0.61 s and 6 runs to generate", door$_{\text{top},4}$. Given that there are 4 doors and 24 time steps, a naive approach of enumerating all possible explanations would require $(2^4)^{24} = 7.9 \times 10^{28}$ runs of the reactive protocol.

Explaining Classification Error in MNIST [21]: MNIST database of scanned images of digits is a common benchmark used in literature to evaluate image classification techniques. MNIST images were obtained by normalization of original images into greyscale 28×28 pixel image. We consider a k-NN classifier for k = 9 as the machine learning technique. Some of the test images are incorrectly identified by this technique and we show one of these images in Fig. 3 where 4 is misidentified as 9. We deploy our technique to find explanations for this error. The k-NN classifier uses voting among the k-nearest neighbours to label test data. We show the nearest neighbour with label '9' to the misclassified image in the figure below. This image of 4 had 6 neighbours which were labelled '9'. The oracle for generating explanations works as follows: If the number of neighbours of the image labelled '9' decreases from 6 (even if the final label from the k-NN classifier does not change), the oracle marks the image as positive, and negative, otherwise. The vocabulary of explanation is formed by 4×4 pixel blocks (similar to superpixels in [29]) being marked completely dark or clear (this corresponds to predicate abstraction of greyscale pixels). The set of atomic propositions in the support of the explanation is illustrated in the third figure by manually picking assignment values to support variables for purpose of illustration. The last two figures show images which are filtered by two conjunctions in the generated explanation. The generation of the explanation took 3 min 48 s and required 58 examples where we initialized the algorithm with the images of 4 and 9 in the figure below.

Fig. 3. Left to right: Misclassified image of '4', closest image of '9', changing all pixels corresponding to support of explanations, changing pixels for one of the sufficient explanation, changing pixels for another sufficient explanation

6 Related Work

Our approach relies on learning logical explanations in the form of sparse Boolean formula from examples that are obtained by carefully selected introspective simulations of the decision-making algorithm. The area of active learning Boolean formula from positive and negative examples has been studied in literature [1,18] in both exact and probably approximately correct (PAC) setting. Exact learning Boolean formula [3,19] requires a number of examples exponential in the size of the vocabulary. Under the PAC setting, learning is guaranteed to find an approximately correct concept given enough independent samples [2,23,25]. It is known that k-clause conjunctive normal form Boolean formula are not PAC learnable with polynomial sample-size, even though monomials and disjunctive normal form representations are PAC learnable [8,25]. Changing the representation from CNF to DNF form can lead to exponential blow-up. In contrast, we consider only sparse Boolean formula and our goal is to learn the exact Boolean formula with probabilistic confidence, and not its approximation. Efficient learning techniques exist for particular classes of Boolean formulae such as monotonic and read-one formulae [12,15], but explanations do not always take these restricted forms, and hence, our focus on sparse Boolean formulae is better suited for this context.

Another related research area is the newly emerged field of formal synthesis, which combines induction and deduction for automatic synthesis of systems from logical or black-box oracle specifications [16]. Unlike active learning, formal synthesis is also concerned with defining techniques for the generation of interesting examples and not just its inductive generalization, much like our approach. While existing formal synthesis techniques have considered completion of templates by inferring parameters [4,28,32], composition of component Boolean functions or uplifting to bitvector form [7,13,16,35], inferring transducers and finite state-machines [5,6,11], and synthesis of invariants [31,33], our work is the first to consider sparsity as a structural assumption for learning Boolean formulae.

The need for explanations of AI decisions to increase trust of decision-making systems has been noted in the literature [22]. Specific approaches have been introduced to discover explanations in specific domains such as MDPs [9], HTNs [14] and Bayesian networks [36]. Explanation of failure in robotic systems by detecting problems in the temporal logic specification using formal requirement analysis was shown to be practically useful in [27]. Inductive logic programming [10] has also been used to model domain-specific explanation generation rules. In contrast, we propose a domain-independent approach to generate explanations by treating the decision-making AI algorithm as an oracle. Domain-independent approaches have also been proposed in the AI literature for detecting sensitive input components that determine the decision in a classification problem [29,34]. While these approaches work in a quantitative setting, such as measuring sensitivity from the gradient of a neural network classifier's ouput, our approach is restricted to the discrete, qualitative setting. Further, we not only detect sensitive inputs (support of Boolean formulae) but also generate the explanation.

7   Conclusion and Future Work

We proposed a novel algorithm that uses a binary-search like approach to first find the support of any sparse Boolean formula followed by a formal synthesis approach to learn the target formula from examples. We demonstrate how this method can be used to learn Boolean formulae corresponding to the explanation of decisions made by an AI algorithm. This capability of self-explanation would make AI agents more human-interpretable and decrease the barriers towards their adoption in safety-critical applications of autonomy. We identify two dimensions along which our work can be extended. First, our approach currently uses a predicate abstraction to Boolean variables for learning explanations. We plan to extend our technique to a richer logical language such as signal temporal logic for explanations involving real values. Second, we need to extend our approach to infer multiple valid explanations in response to an inquiry. This work is a first step towards using formal methods, particularly, formal synthesis to aid artificial intelligence by automatically generating explanations of decisions made by AI algorithms.

References

1. Abouzied, A., Angluin, D., Papadimitriou, C., Hellerstein, J.M., Silberschatz, A.: Learning and verifying quantified boolean queries by example. In: ACM Symposium on Principles of Database Systems, pp. 49–60. ACM (2013)
2. Angluin, D., Computational learning theory: survey and selected bibliography. In: ACM Symposium on Theory of Computing, pp. 351–369. ACM (1992)
3. Angluin, D., Kharitonov, M.: When won't membership queries help? In: ACM Symposium on Theory of Computing, pp. 444–454. ACM (1991)
4. Bittner, B., Bozzano, M., Cimatti, A., Gario, M., Griggio, A.: Towards pareto-optimal parameter synthesis for monotonie cost functions. In: FMCAD, pp. 23–30, October 2014
5. Boigelot, B., Godefroid, P.: Automatic synthesis of specifications from the dynamic observation of reactive programs. In: Brinksma, E. (ed.) TACAS 1997. LNCS, vol. 1217, pp. 321–333. Springer, Heidelberg (1997). doi:10.1007/BFb0035397

6. Botinčan, M., Babić, D., Sigma*: Symbolic learning of input-output specifications. In: POPL, pp. 443–456 (2013)
7. Cook, B., Kroening, D., Rümmer, P., Wintersteiger, C.M.: Ranking function synthesis for bit-vector relations. FMSD **43**(1), 93–120 (2013)
8. Ehrenfeucht, A., Haussler, D., Kearns, M., Valiant, L.: A general lower bound on the number of examples needed for learning. Inf. Comput. **82**(3), 247–261 (1989)
9. Elizalde, F., Sucar, E., Noguez, J., Reyes, A.: Generating explanations based on Markov decision processes. In: Aguirre, A.H., Borja, R.M., Garciá, C.A.R. (eds.) MICAI 2009. LNCS (LNAI), vol. 5845, pp. 51–62. Springer, Heidelberg (2009). doi:10.1007/978-3-642-05258-3_5
10. Feng, C., Muggleton, S.: Towards inductive generalisation in higher order logic. In: 9th International Workshop on Machine learning, pp. 154–162 D (2014)
11. Godefroid, P., Taly, A.: Automated synthesis of symbolic instruction encodings from i/o samples. SIGPLAN Not. **47**(6), 441–452 (2012)
12. Goldsmith, J., Sloan, R.H., Szörényi, B., Turán, G.: Theory revision with queries: Horn, read-once, and parity formulas. Artif. Intell. **156**(2), 139–176 (2004)
13. Gurfinkel, A., Belov, A., Marques-Silva, J.: Synthesizing safe bit-precise invariants. In: Ábrahám, E., Havelund, K. (eds.) TACAS 2014. LNCS, vol. 8413, pp. 93–108. Springer, Heidelberg (2014). doi:10.1007/978-3-642-54862-8_7
14. Harbers, M., Meyer, J.-J., van den Bosch, K.: Explaining simulations through self explaining agents. J. Artif. Soc. Soc. Simul. **13**, 10 (2010)
15. Hellerstein, L., Servedio, R.A.: On PAC learning algorithms for rich boolean function classes. Theoret. Comput. Sci. **384**(1), 66–76 (2007)
16. Jha, S., Seshia, S.A.: A theory of formal synthesis via inductive learning. Acta Informatica, pp. 1–34 (2017)
17. Jha, S., A. Seshia, and A. Tiwari. Synthesis of optimal switching logic for hybrid systems. In: EMSOFT, pp. 107–116. ACM (2011)
18. Kearns, M., Li, M., Valiant, L.: Learning boolean formulas. J. ACM **41**(6), 1298–1328 (1994)
19. Kearns, M., Valiant, L.: Cryptographic limitations on learning boolean formulae and finite automata. Journal of the ACM (JACM) **41**(1), 67–95 (1994)
20. LaValle, S.M.: Planning Algorithms. Cambridge University Press, Cambridge (2006)
21. Lecun, Y., Cortes, C.: The MNIST database of handwritten digits. http://yann.lecun.com/exdb/mnist/
22. Lee, J., Moray, N.: Trust, control strategies and allocation of function in human-machine systems. Ergonomics **35**(10), 1243–1270 (1992)
23. Mansour, Y.: Learning boolean functions via the fourier transform. In: Theoretical Advances in Neural Computation and Learning, pp. 391–424 (1994)
24. Nau, D., Ghallab, M., Traverso, P.: Automated Planning: Theory and Practice. Morgan Kaufmann Publishers Inc., San Francisco (2004)
25. Pitt, L., Valiant, L.G.: Computational limitations on learning from examples. J. ACM (JACM) **35**(4), 965–984 (1988)
26. Raman, V.: Reactive switching protocols for multi-robot high-level tasks. In: IEEE/RSJ, pp. 336–341 (2014)
27. Raman, V., Lignos, C., Finucane, C., Lee, K.C.T., Marcus, M.P., Kress-Gazit, H.: Sorry Dave, I'm afraid i can't do that: explaining unachievable robot tasks using natural language. In: Robotics: Science and Systems (2013)
28. Reynolds, A., Deters, M., Kuncak, V., Tinelli, C., Barrett, C.: Counterexample-guided quantifier instantiation for synthesis in SMT. In: Kroening, D., Păsăreanu, C.S. (eds.) CAV 2015. LNCS, vol. 9207, pp. 198–216. Springer, Cham (2015). doi:10.1007/978-3-319-21668-3_12

29. Ribeiro, M.T., Singh, S., Guestrin, C.: Why Should I Trust You?: Explaining the predictions of any classifier. In: KDD, pp. 1135–1144 (2016)
30. Russell, J., Cohn, R.: OODA Loop. Book on Demand, Norderstedt (2012)
31. Sankaranarayanan, S.: Automatic invariant generation for hybrid systems using ideal fixed points. In: HSCC, pp. 221–230 (2010)
32. Sankaranarayanan, S., Miller, C., Raghunathan, R., Ravanbakhsh, H., Fainekos, G.: A model-based approach to synthesizing insulin infusion pump usage parameters for diabetic patients. In: Annual Allerton Conference on Communication, Control, and Computing, pp. 1610–1617, October 2012
33. Sankaranarayanan, S., Sipma, H.B., Manna, Z.: Constructing invariants for hybrid systems. FMSD $32(1)$, 25–55 (2008)
34. Štrumbelj, E., Kononenko, I.: Explaining prediction models and individual predictions with feature contributions. KIS $41(3)$, 647–665 (2014)
35. Urban, C., Gurfinkel, A., Kahsai, T.: Synthesizing ranking functions from bits and pieces. In: Chechik, M., Raskin, J.-F. (eds.) TACAS 2016. LNCS, vol. 9636, pp. 54–70. Springer, Heidelberg (2016). doi:10.1007/978-3-662-49674-9_4
36. Yuan, C., Lim, H., Lu, T.-C.: Most relevant explanation in bayesian networks. J. Artif. Intell. Res. (JAIR) 42, 309–352 (2011)

Event-Based Runtime Verification of Temporal Properties Using Time Basic Petri Nets

Matteo Camilli[1]([✉]), Angelo Gargantini[2], Patrizia Scandurra[2],
and Carlo Bellettini[1]

[1] Department of Computer Science, Università degli Studi di Milano, Milan, Italy
{camilli,bellettini}@di.unimi.it
[2] Department of Management, Information and Production Engineering (DIGIP),
Università degli Studi di Bergamo, Bergamo, Italy
{angelo.gargantini,patrizia.scandurra}@unibg.it

Abstract. We introduce a formal framework to provide an efficient event-based monitoring technique, and we describe its current implementation as the MAHARAJA software tool. The framework enables the quantitative runtime verification of temporal properties extracted from occurring events on JAVA programs. The monitor continuously evaluates the conformance of the concrete implementation with respect to its formal specification given in terms of Time Basic Petri nets, a particular timed extension of Petri nets. The system under test is instrumented by using simple JAVA annotations on methods to link the implementation to its formal model. This allows a separation between implementation and specification that can be used for other purposes such as formal verification, simulation, and model-based testing. The tool has been successfully used to monitor at runtime and test a number of benchmarking case-studies. Experiments show that our approach introduces bounded overhead and effectively reduces the involvement of the monitor at run time by using negligible auxiliary memory. A comparison with a number of state-of-the-art runtime verification tools is also presented.

Keywords: Runtime verification · Formal methods @ runtime · Timing analysis · Temporal properties · Petri nets

1 Introduction

Software systems are increasingly employed in most domains and activities, including safety critical ones. Therefore, the society increasingly relies on software, and unreliable or unpredictable behavior is becoming less and less tolerated. As a consequence, over the past years, the validation of software systems has become an increasingly important and active research area.

Event-based runtime verification [1] is the monitoring of running programs to verify the occurring events against the requirements. A particularly challenging aspect is the monitoring of temporal properties in the presence of strict time

© Springer International Publishing AG 2017
C. Barrett et al. (Eds.): NFM 2017, LNCS 10227, pp. 115–130, 2017.
DOI: 10.1007/978-3-319-57288-8_8

constraints. In fact, monitoring at runtime introduces overheads on the System Under Test (SUT) that may affect the correctness of the verified properties.

In this paper, we introduce a formal event-based runtime verification framework and we describe its current implementation as a JAVA software tool, so called MAHARAJA[1]. This framework enables the monitoring of JAVA programs, by evaluating the conformance of the concrete implementation with respect to its formal specification given in terms of Time Basic (TB) Petri nets [2] (or simply TB nets), a powerful temporal extension of Petri nets (PNs) for modeling concurrent/distributed systems with real-time constraints.

Although descriptive formalisms are very popular in runtime verification [3], the adoption of operational specifications, like in our approach, offers some advantages with respect to declarative specifications [4,5]. They are usually easier to write, visualize, understand, and allow for step-wise model refinement [6]. Moreover, although other operational formalisms such as timed-automata [7] or finite-state-machines [8] support the modeling of temporal or behavioral aspects, PNs-based approaches can be more concise and easier to use [9]. Furthermore, aspects such as messaging, communication protocols, which are commonly used in concurrent or distributed systems, can be difficult to model with the language primitives of timed-automata [10,11]. Finally, despite several state-based, logic-based, and event-based notations have been used for runtime verification [1], our work is the first attempt (to the best of our knowledge) exploiting the expressiveness of the TB nets for verifying temporal properties at runtime.

The MAHARAJA framework requires the SUT to be instrumented by using simple JAVA annotations on methods, in order to link the implementation to its formal model. Then, at runtime, the execution of the events of interest triggers the conformance verification of temporal properties. Rather than using heavy offline computation to predict the generation rate of possibly invalid events to estimate the maximum detection latency [12], we use an online approach that focuses on maintaining the analysis as lightweight as possible. MAHARAJA operates on and in conjunction with the SUT and it performs data collection and processing asynchronously with the SUT execution. The monitor and the SUT run concurrently on separated CPU cores using a buffer-based mechanism for communication. Our approach tries to bound the cost of executing the SUT instrumentation by having a bounded number of instructions executed upon the generation of possible invalid events. This runtime verification procedure is highly scalable because it does not depend on the size of the entire state space (often far larger than the model size [13]). It operates using just an occurring *event* and the *1-step reachability set* of the current model's state, thus using limited extra memory.

The tool has been applied to a number of benchmarking case studies [14] and we experimentally evaluated the runtime overhead, making it possible for a system designer to reason about the timing constraints of the SUT. The experiments show that MAHARAJA introduces limited monitoringoverhead and

---

[1] Monitoring at Runtime of temporAl properties on Java Applications.

limited detection latency, thereby opening up the possibility to adopt a *fast failing* approach or implement a *self-healing* procedure [15] in a latency-aware adaptation setting.

The paper is organized as follows. Section 2 introduces the proper background on TB nets. Section 3 introduces the formalization of our technique and Sect. 4 describes our current software implementation. Section 5 introduces our experimental evaluation of the runtime overhead, making it possible for a system designer to reason about the timing constraints of the SUT. Section 6 compares our monitoring framework with a number of state-of-the-art runtime verification tools, thus showing both advantages and disadvantages of our framework. Finally, Sect. 7 presents our conclusion and future directions of our work.

2   Background on Time Basic Nets

This section briefly introduces the TB nets formalism by means of a running example, i.e., the timed producer/consumer (P/C) model reported in Fig. 1.

TB nets are a formal model for distributed systems with real-time constraints. This modeling formalism is more expressive then other temporal extensions of PNs and it supports both time and functional extensions in a semantically clear and rigorous way [2]. Thus it represents an effective formal model to deal with specification of highly concurrent systems with real-time constraints.

The structure of a TB net [2,16] is a bipartite graph $N = (P, T, F)$, where P is the finite set of places (i.e., system state variables), T is the finite set of transitions (i.e., events causing state changes), $F \subseteq (P \times T) \cup (T \times P)$ is the flow relation. The pre/post-sets of $t \in T$ are $^\bullet t = \{p \in P : (p, t) \in F\}$ and $t^\bullet = \{p \in P : (t, p) \in F\}$, respectively.

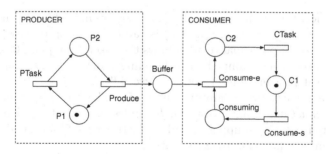

Initial marking: $m_0 : P1\{T_0\}, C1\{T_0\}, T_0 = 0$

Time functions:

PTask	$[P1 + 1000, P1 + 2500]$
Produce	$[P2, P2 + 1000]$
Consume-s	$[C1, C1 + 1000]$
Consume-e	$[max(Buffer, Consuming+1000), max(Buffer, Consuming+1000) + 5000]$
CTask	$[C2 + 1000, C2 + 2000]$

Fig. 1. Producer-consumer TB net model.

The P/C example describes two processes that asynchronously interact through the place Buffer. After producing (respectively, consuming), the two processes perform some local activity (i.e., PTask and CTask).

In TB nets, tokens are enriched by timestamps recording their creation time. Each place can contain a multiset (bag) of tokens[2]. A *marking* (i.e., a representation of the system state) is a mapping $m : P \rightarrow Bag(\mathbb{R}_{\geq 0})$, that associates time-stamps to tokens in places (e.g., m_0 in Fig. 1).

Time constraints are associated with transitions: two (linear or linearizable) functions associated to each transition t define the lower and the upper bounds $([lb, ub]_t)$ of the interval of real values representing its possible firing times (e.g., $[P1 + 1000, P1 + 2500]$ associated with PTask). Tokens produced by the atomic firing of a transition are time-stamped with the same value. The actions of removing and creating tokens are performed instantaneously.

A *binding* of t is a function $b_t : {}^{\bullet}t \rightarrow \mathbb{R}_{\geq 0}$ that represents a set of time-stamps possibly causing t to be fired. The numerical interval $f_{b_t} : [lb(b_t), ub(b_t)]$ holds the possible *firing times* for b_t and it is evaluated by replacing each occurrence of a place p (free variable) with $b_t(p)$.

For instance, consider the transition Consume-e and the following binding: $b_{\text{Consume-e}}$: {Buffer $\rightarrow$ 2000, Consuming $\rightarrow$ 2500}. According to the time function of Consume-e, the firing times range over $[3500, 8500]$.

Starting from the marking m, a binding b_t is *enabled* if and only if $f_{b_t} \neq \emptyset$. A *firing instance* of t is a pair (b_t, τ) composed of an enabled binding and a real value $\tau \in f_{b_t}$. The firing of t results in a new marking m':

$$\forall p \in P, m'(p) = m(p) - i_{b_t}(p) + o_t^{\tau}(p)$$

where $i_{b_t}(p)$ is $1 \cdot b_t(p)$ if $p \in {}^{\bullet}t$, the null bag otherwise, $o_t^{\tau}(p)$ is $1 \cdot \tau$ if $p \in t^{\bullet}$, the null bag otherwise, and $+, -$ operators are extended to bags. This is denoted $m \xrightarrow{(b_t, \tau)} m'$.

For instance, the binding $b_{\text{Consume-s}}$: {C1 $\rightarrow$ 0} is enabled in the marking m_0. Thus, the firing instance $(b_{\text{Consume-s}}, 450)$ is valid. The firing process produces a new marking m_1. In particular, it withdraws the token from place C1 and it puts a fresh new token, time-stamped with the value 450, into Consuming.

The interval f_{b_t} can be interpreted in two different ways. The *weak* semantics states that t *can* fire at any instant in f_{b_t}. The *strong* semantics instead states that t *must* fire at any instant in f_{b_t}, unless it is disabled by a conflicting transition fired before the upper bound of f_{b_t} (refer to [2] for the details). Our running example adopts a strong semantics.

The marking m_n is *reachable* from m_0 if and only if there exists a *path* σ (sequence of firing instances and markings) such that:

$$\sigma = m_0 \xrightarrow{(b_{t_0}, \tau_0)} m_1 \xrightarrow{(b_{t_1}, \tau_1)} m_2, \ldots, m_{n-1} \xrightarrow{(b_{t_{n-1}}, \tau_{n-1})} m_n$$

The transitions associated with the enabled bindings in m are called *enabled transitions* and they are denoted by $enab(m)$.

---

[2] $b \in Bag(X)$ is a map $X \rightarrow \mathbb{N}$, formally expressed as a weighted sum of X elements.

3   Event-Based Runtime Verification

This section introduces the formalization of our event-based monitoring approach. In order to abstract the behavior of a running program $\mathcal{P}$, let us introduce the observable components of $\mathcal{P}$, so called *action methods*.

Definition 1 (Action method). *Given a program $\mathcal{P}$, an action method is a subroutine performing a specific task, such that its execution is observed at runtime.*

The *action methods* are the events of interest that we want to observe and verify with respect to the expected behavior provided in terms of a TB net formal specification. During the execution of $\mathcal{P}$, we extract temporal information from the action methods depending on their own *action time*.

Definition 2 (Action time). *Given a program $\mathcal{P}$ and a set of action methods A, the action time function Γ maps action methods in A to a non empty set of elements in $\mathcal{T} = \{\texttt{initial}, \texttt{final}\}$.*

Intuitively, the *action time* determines the *moment* (i.e., time instant) at which we want to observe the action methods. $\Gamma(a) = \{\texttt{initial}\}$, implies that a is observed at its own invocation time. The temporal information extracted from the execution of a is a timestamp representing the *initial* time. Similarly, if $\Gamma(a) = \{\texttt{final}\}$, a is observed at its own *final* time; if $\Gamma(a) = \{\texttt{initial}, \texttt{final}\}$, a is observed both at invocation and termination time.

Given the observable components and the *action time* function, we use the notion of *timed trace* to abstract the behavior of a running real-time system.

Definition 3 (Timed trace). *Given a program $\mathcal{P}$ and a set of* action methods $A = \{a_0, a_1, \ldots, a_m\}$, *a timed trace is a finite sequence of events* $\pi = e_0, e_1, \ldots, e_n$, *such that each event $e \in \pi$ is a triplet $\langle a, g, v \rangle$, where:*

- *$a \in A$ is the action method that triggers the event. We denote it with $\alpha(e)$.*
- *$g \in \Gamma(a)$ is the moment associated with the event. We denote it with $\gamma(e)$.*
- *$v \in \mathbb{R}_{>0}$ is the timestamp associated with the event. We denote it with $\rho(e)$.*

As an example, consider the code excerpts reported in Fig. 2. They represent a JAVA implementation of the **Producer** and the **Consumer**, respectively, in a simple producer-consumer program. The **Consumer** calls the **consume** method that retrieves and removes a **Data** object from the **Buffer**, waiting if necessary until an element becomes available. Then it performs some additional tasks using the new element through the **consumerTask** method. The **Producer** creates a new **Data** object through the **producerTask** method and then it pushes the element into the **Buffer**.

The set of action methods is defined as $A = \{produce, producerTask, consume, consumerTask\}$, while the action type function is Γ: $\{produce \rightarrow \{\texttt{final}\}$, $producerTask \rightarrow \{\texttt{final}\}$, $consumerTask \rightarrow \{\texttt{initial}\}$, $consume \rightarrow \{\texttt{initial}, \texttt{final}\}\}$.

The rationale behind the Γ function is explained by means of the following example. Both the *produce* (Fig. 2, line 8) and the *producerTask* (line 12) action methods maps to {final} action time. In fact, the two action methods affect the behavior of the program at the end of their own execution: the *producerTask* method creates a new data element that becomes available at the end of the method execution; the *produce* puts the new data element into the buffer data structure and then terminates itself. Therefore, we want to observe only the final time of these action methods. Instead, the *consumerTask* action method (Fig. 2, line 13) processes the new data by launching an external asynchronous task. In this case we are just interested in knowing whether the external task is called in due time. Therefore, the *consumerTask* maps to {initial} action time. Finally, the execution of the *consume* action method (Fig. 2, line 8) causes the program to wait until a new element becomes available, which is consumed and returned at the end of the method execution. Hence, for each (multiple) execution of the *consume* action method, we want to observe both the initial and the final time. In fact, we may want to check that the consumer does not wait for available data more than a specific time limit.

The execution of the producer-consumer program can generate, for instance, the timed trace π reported in (1).

$$\begin{aligned}
\pi = \ & e_0 : \langle consume, \texttt{initial}, 450 \rangle, \\
& e_1 : \langle producerTask, \texttt{final}, 1100 \rangle, \\
& e_2 : \langle produce, \texttt{final}, 1205 \rangle, \\
& e_3 : \langle consume, \texttt{final}, 1650 \rangle, \\
& e_4 : \langle consumerTask, \texttt{initial}, 2886 \rangle.
\end{aligned} \tag{1}$$

It is worth noting that *consume* occurs twice in π. In fact, the Γ function maps the *consume* action method both to initial and final, thus its own execution generates two different events timestamped with the initial and the final time, respectively.

```
1   public class Producer              1   public class Consumer
2       implements Runnable {          2       implements Runnable {
3       @Override                      3       @Override
4       public void run() {            4       public void run() {
5           Data data = producerTask();5           Data data = consume();
6           produce(data);             6           consumerTask(data);
7       }                              7       }
8       private void produce(Data data){8      private Data consume(){
9           Buffer.getInstance()       9           Data data = Buffer.getInstance()
10              .produce(data);        10              .consume();
11      }                              11          return data;
12      private Data producerTask(){   12      }
13          Data data = computeNext(); 13      private void consumerTask(Data data){
14          normalize(data);           14          log(data);
15          return data;               15          load(data);
16      }                              16      }
17  }                                  17  }
```

Fig. 2. Java implementation of the Producer and Consumer.

Another important observation is that the program can perform inside the action methods different nested methods calls not belonging to A, therefore these are not observed at runtime. This allows us to build timed traces with different levels of granularity.

The construction of a *timed trace* is formalized as follows.

Definition 4 (Timed trace construction). *Given a running program* $\mathcal{P}$, *the set of action methods* A *and the action time function* Γ, *the timed trace* π *is constructed from the execution of each* $a \in A$ *such that:*

$$\forall g \in \Gamma(a), \langle a, g, v \rangle \in \pi,$$

where v *is the timestamp associated with the* moment g.

The timed trace constructed following Definition 4 includes only the events of interest defined by the action methods and the action time function.

To formalize the *conformance relation* between a running program $\mathcal{P}$ and its formal specification, let us introduce first the notion of *action method mapping*.

Definition 5 (Action method mapping function). *Given a TB net structure* (P, T, E) *and the set of action methods* A *associated with the program* $\mathcal{P}$, *the action method mapping function* Λ *associates each element* $a \in A$ *and each moment* $g \in \Gamma(a)$ *to a transition* $\Lambda(a, g) \in T$.

We use this mechanism to bind action methods in the implementation to transitions in the model. This way, the conformance verification can be performed by checking that all the events of a timed trace correspond to feasible firing transitions in the formal specification. The formalization is reported below:

Definition 6 (Path Conformance). *Given a timed trace* π *and an execution path* σ *of a TB net model, there exists a conformance relation between* π *and* σ *iff. for each* $e_i \in \pi$, *there exists* $m_i \in \sigma$ *such that:*

(i) $\Lambda(\alpha(e_i), \gamma(e_i)) = t_i$ *(i.e.,* e_i *is mapped to transition* t_i)
(ii) $\rho(e_i) \in f_{b_{t_i}}$ *(i.e., the timestamp of* e_i *belongs to the firing times of* t_i)

Definition 7 (Model Conformance). *Given a timed trace* π *and a TB net model* N *and the* Λ *function, there is a* conformance relation *between* π *and* N *iff. there exists a feasible execution path* σ *of* N, *such that* π *conforms to* σ, *according to* Λ.

For example consider the timed trace π introduced in (1) and the following definition of the mapping function Λ :

$$\Lambda(producerTask, \texttt{final}) = \texttt{PTask} \qquad \Lambda(produce, \texttt{final}) = \texttt{Produce}$$
$$\Lambda(consume, \texttt{initial}) = \texttt{Consume-s} \quad \Lambda(consume, \texttt{final}) = \texttt{Consume-e}$$
$$\Lambda(consumerTask, \texttt{initial}) = \texttt{CTask}$$

In this case, there exists a conformance relation between π and the producer-consumer TB net reported in Fig. 1. In fact, from the initial marking m_0 the transition Consume-s is enabled with the following binding $b_{\text{Consume-s}}$: $\{\text{P1} \rightarrow 0\}$. The timestamp $\rho(e_0) = 450$ belongs to $f_{b_{\text{Consume-s}}}$: $[0, 1000]$, thus we observe a valid event, and we can compute the next marking m_1, reachable from m_0 by firing the Consume-s transition at time 450.

$$m_1 : P1\{T_0\}, Consuming\{T_1\}; T_0 = 0, T_1 = 450.$$

The transition PTask is enabled from m_1 by the binding b_{PTask}: $\{\text{P1} \rightarrow 0\}$. The timestamp 1100, associated with the second event e_1 belongs to $f_{b_{\text{PTask}}}$: $[1000, 2500]$, thus we observe a valid event, and we can compute the next marking m_2, reachable from m_1 by firing the PTask transition at time 1100.

$$m_2 : P2\{T_1\}, Consuming\{T_0\}; T_0 = 450, T_1 = 1100.$$

And so forth, until we process the last action method. The complete path σ, such that π conforms to σ is:

$$m_0 \xrightarrow{(b_{\text{Consume-s}}, 450)} m_1 \xrightarrow{(b_{\text{PTask}}, 1100)} m_2 \xrightarrow{(b_{\text{Produce}}, 1205)} m_3 \xrightarrow{(b_{\text{Consume-e}}, 1650)} m_4 \xrightarrow{(b_{\text{CTask}}, 2886)} m_5$$

4   The MahaRAJA Framework

We implemented the runtime verification technique presented in the previous section as a JAVA library[3]. The main component of the library is the *Monitor*, i.e., a system that observes and analyzes an executing SUT (JAVA program) in order to verify its correctness by comparing the observed behavior (i.e., ordered timed trace) with an expected behavior (i.e., feasible execution path) of the TB model given in input as a PNML file [18]. The model can be easily generated using a graphical user interface that allows the user to create and edit arbitrary complex TB net models through simple drag and drop gestures.

The input program is linked to the formal specification exploiting the mechanism of JAVA annotations to map *action methods* to corresponding *transitions* (i.e., the mapping function introduced in Definition 5). The *Monitor* is executed in a separated thread and is composed of the following modules: the *Observer*, the *Analyzer* and the *Executor*.

The *Observer* module makes use of ASPECTJ [19] to observe code execution and trigger the verification of the *conformance relation*, performed by the *Analyzer* component. The framework defines a set of annotations[4] used to define the Γ *action type* function and the Λ *action methods mapping* function. The following annotations were inserted into the producer-consumer program:

```
@AfterType(trF="Produce")                    @AroundType(trI="Consume-s",trF="Consume-e")
private void produce(Data data){...}         private Data consume(){...}
@AfterType(trF="PTask")                       @BeforeType(trI="CTask")
private Data producerTask(){...}             private void consumerTask(Data data){...}
```

---

[3] The source code, binaries, and some runnable examples can be found at [17].

[4] They are recorded in class files by the compiler and retained by the virtual machine at run time, so they can be read reflectively by the *Observer* component.

Algorithm 1. Conformance verification procedure

```
 1: function VERIFY(m, e)
 2:     conformance = False
 3:     if Λ(e) ∈ enab(m) then
 4:         τ = ρ(e)
 5:         for all ⟨b_t, f_{b_t}⟩ ∈ enab(m) s.t. t = Λ(e) do
 6:             if τ ∈ f_{b_t} then
 7:                 m' = computeNext(m, t, τ)
 8:                 addNext(m')
 9:                 conformance = True
10:             end if
11:         end for
12:     end if
13:     return conformance
14: end function
```

As an example, the `@AroundType` annotation maps the *consume* action method to {`initial`, `final`} action times, thus observable both before and after its own execution. For each invocation we observe two events: the first event is bound to the `trI` transition; the second event is bound to the `trF` transition.

The execution of the methods annotated by `@BeforeType`, `@AfterType` and `@AroundType` are handled by `@Before`, `@After` and `@Around` ASPECTJ advice types [19], respectively, to generate the proper `inital` and/or `final` observable events. The *Observer* module inspects the execution of the SUT by using the facilities of ASPECTJ and generate observable events into the *event queue* by injecting additional code upon the execution of the action methods.

The *Analyzer* module incrementally builds the timed trace π through the *verification procedure* reported in Algorithm 1. For each occurring event e, extracted from the *event queue*, the *Analyzer* launches the verification procedure, passing as argument the current marking $m \in \sigma$ and the current event e. Thus, it verifies that in the input model, the transition t, retrieved by applying the Λ function, is enabled from the current marking m (line 3) and the time $\rho(e)$ belongs to f_{b_t} (line 6). If this condition holds, the *Executor* component updates the trace σ (line 7) creating a new reachable marking with the proper timestamp $\rho(e)$.

It is worth noting that, given an event e and a reachable marking m, there can be multiple enabled bindings for the transition t (line 5). In this case, for each binding, we compute a new reachable marking m' and we put it into the *reachability set* (line 8) representing all the valid next steps of σ. During the construction of the σ path, for each event e it is fundamental to maintain the entire 1-step *reachability set* for the transition t (instead of a single reachable marking), in order to avoid false alarms (i.e., unreal inconsistencies between the code and its specification) during the conformance checking. The VERIFY function is executed for each marking in the *reachability set*. If there does not exist any marking in the *reachability set* such that the *verification procedure* is successful, the *Analyzer* does not verify the *conformance relation* between π and σ, thus a *conformance failure* exception is thrown. This exception contains useful information about the throwing action method, along with the timestamp associated to this event and the set of enabled bindings (i.e., the expected events). The *Analyzer* module do not need to store the full history of both π and σ, thus it requires limited extra memory. Moreover, the verification procedure is scalable with respect to the SUT size, in fact its own time complexity (i.e., $\mathcal{O}(|enab(m)|)$) does not depend on either the model size or the entire state space, but just on the number of enabled bindings in the current marking.

To alleviate possible burst of the monitoring overhead, our framework makes use of the JAVA THREAD AFFINITY [20] library to separate the execution of the SUT and the *Monitor* into different isolated CPU cores, decreasing the latency caused by suspending and resuming important running tasks. Moreover, MAHARAJA let the user define a *tolerance* that should be set to the expected monitor invocation overhead. The *tolerance* allows two levels of risk to be defined: *warning* and *error* corresponding to a timing constraint violation respectively in- and outside the *tolerance* range. By default the *tolerance* is disabled, in fact, its definition involves the evaluation of the monitor invocation overhead, which is not an easy task and it strictly depends on the underlying hardware/software environment.

In order to help the user to increase the confidence about the correctness of the SUT, the MAHARAJA software tool can be used in conjunction with JUNIT to generate different monitored test cases. This way, the user can integrate our runtime verification technique with *assertions* on variables and on specific *goal conditions*, given in terms of *time constraint* (i.e., a logical predicate formed by linear inequalities involving timestamps) on the observed *timed trace* [17].

The next section introduces our experimental results that could also be used as a guide to evaluate the runtime overhead in order to reason about the timing constraints of the SUT.

5 Experimental Validation

We validated the MAHARAJA framework by collecting data at runtime and performing a testing activity on a number of real-time benchmarking examples [14] summarized in Table 1: a simple producer-consumer (P/C) application, a cruise-control (CC) system, an automated teller machine (ATM) software system, an elevator (EL) controller and a factory (FA) automation distributed system.

Table 1. Case studies.

Case study	$|P|$	$|T|$	SLOC	Tasks	Frequency
P/C	5	4	208	3	4,19
CC	11	16	1185	4	2,65
ATM	12	25	1409	3	1,57
EL	18	24	1231	5	1,12
FA	14	12	996	10	1,09

The model size is reported in terms of number of places ($|P|$) and number of transitions ($|T|$). The SLOC column reflects the source lines of code number in the corresponding JAVA SUT. The *tasks* column contains the number of parallel threads (or process in case of distributed computing) composing the SUT. The *frequency* column reports the average number of monitor invocations per second.

The monitoring process ran in parallel with the SUT in a machine equipped with a Intel Xeon E5-2630 at 2.30 GHz CPU, 32 GB of RAM, the Ubuntu 14.04.3 LTS (GNU/Linux 3.13.0-39-generic x86_64) operating system with a completely fair scheduler [21], and the JAVA HotSpot 1.8 64-Bit Server virtual machine using the Garbage-First (G1) collector tuned to avoid full runs[5]. Data about runtime overhead is reported in this section. They were extracted from program executions monitoring $\sim 10^6$ events. The runtime overhead has been assessed considering the following metrics.

- **Monitoring Overhead:** The monitoring overhead is caused by the ASPECTJ instrumentation (AJO) and the monitor invocation overhead (MIO). Table 2 reports the average values (in μs) of these two different components, for each running case study. The average AJO values, introduced by the invocation of ASPECTJ advices, strictly depend on the byte code generated from the annotated program by using the AJC compiler [19]. Generally, we observed a lower AJO within @Before advices (i.e., events with `initial` action time) and a higher AJO within @Arounde advices (i.e., events with both `initial` and `final` action time). The order of magnitude of the measured AJO values is approximately $10\,\mu s$ (see Table 2).
  The MIO (i.e., the time required to enqueue an occurring event into the *event queue*) does not depend on the action time. In general, both the MIO and the AJO have the same order of magnitude, but the average MIO is 50% lower. Thus, the overhead introduced by ASPECTJ dominates the overall monitoring overhead. Although the distribution of the MIO values for different programs are very similar, a different monitor invocation frequency (e.g., the CC frequency is 47% lower than the P/C one) impacts on the average MIO. For instance, the average P/C MIO is lower then the average CC MIO (approximately 16% lower).
- **Jitter:** The *Jitter* represents the deviance between the monitoring overhead values. The results reported in Table 2 show that the order of magnitude of the AJO jitter and the MIO jitter is the same (approximately $10\,\mu s$). We found that the AJO jitter, for all the action method types, is approximately 43% lower than the MIO jitter. While the AJO jitter strictly depends on the behavior of ASPECTJ at runtime, the MIO jitter depends on the state of the *Monitor* during the execution of the action methods. In fact, a suspended *Monitor* causes a burst of the MIO due to the time required by resuming it, during the enqueuing of an acton method into an empty *event queue*.
- **Detection latency:** Bounding the detection latency (DL) makes it possible for the *Monitor* to quickly recognize a conformance failure, thus making the SUT able to promptly react to a degraded situation though a recovery procedure.

---

[5] Additional information about the configurations of MAHARAJA and the JVM is available at [17].

Table 2 reports the average DL in μs. Our experience indicates the following trend: the higher the frequency is, the lower the DL is. This behavior is caused by the overhead of resuming a suspended *Monitor* thread. In fact, a low frequency implies an empty *event queue* almost all the execution time long. In this case, it is very likely to observe the *Monitor* resumption upon an incoming event. Therefore, although different programs lead to similar DL distribution, lower monitor invocation frequency results in more scattered DL values. The results obtained from our experiments show that MAHARAJA reacts to a conformance failure with a DL of the order of 1 ms.

– **Memory Overhead:** The memory overhead is the space used by the JAVA virtual machine to run and maintain the *Monitor* component. Table 2 shows that MAHARAJA requires negligible auxiliary memory (few KBytes on average). Gathered data shows that this value is related to the monitor invocation frequency: the higher is the frequency, the higher is the memory overhead. In fact, a high frequency implies the accumulation of events into the *event queue*.

Table 2. Monitoring overhead experiments results.

Case study		P/C	CC	ATM	EL	FA
AJO (μs)	Before	43.8	48.5	45.0	44.5	50.1
	After	59.0	51.5	47.4	52.3	52.8
	Around	53.4	53.8	53.1	61.4	58.3
AJO Jitter (μs)	Before	28.2	30.9	36.6	37.1	33.0
	After	27.2	24.8	19.6	20.6	20.3
	Around	22.8	12.5	26.2	27.6	34.5
MIO (μs)		28.0	23.6	24.0	23.0	24.1
MIO Jitter (μs)		45.5	45.4	44.8	50.4	45.7
DL (μs)		874.7	1221.9	1243.9	1274.4	1335.6
Memory (KB)		10838	5302	3503	2083	1734

6   Related Work and Comparative Evaluation

This section mentions the main approaches in the field of event-based runtime verification, and reports also a qualitative comparative evaluation of these tools for the runtime verification of JAVA programs. A preliminary quantitative comparison is available at [17].

CoMA [22] is a formal specification-based software tool that can continuously monitor the behaviors of a target JAVA program and recognize undesirable behaviors in the implementation with respect to its formal specification given in terms of Abstract State Machines (ASMs). Java PathExplorer (JPaX) [23] is a system for monitoring the execution of Java programs. The system extracts an execution trace (as a sequence of events) from a running program and verifies that the trace satisfies certain (past and future) LTL properties. Monitored bytecode is instrumented (by using JTrek) and an observer can check during runtime that the properties are never violated. The JAVA Monitoring and Checking (MaC) architecture [24] supplies two different specification languages: the Primitive Event Definition Language (PEDL) and Meta Event Definition Language (MEDL) allowing for a separation between the definition of the primitive events of a system and the system properties. Instrumented programs send an event stream to the event recognizer to identify higher-level activities, which are in turn processed to find property violations. HAWK [25] is a programming-oriented extension of the rule-based EAGLE logic [26] that has been shown capable of defining and implementing a range of finite trace monitoring logics, including future and past time temporal logic, extended regular expressions, and state machines. It is implemented as a Java library able to perform monitoring through a state-by-state comparison, avoiding to store the entire input trace.

Larva [27] is an event-based runtime verification monitoring tool for temporal and contextual properties of Java programs. The technique implemented in Larva makes use of dynamic communicating automata with timers and events (DATE) to describe properties of systems.

Monitored-oriented programming (MOP) [3] allows the source code of the SUT to be annotated with formal property specifications that can be written in any supported formalism. The formal specifications are translated in the target programming language. Thus, the obtained monitoring code can be used either at runtime or offline by checking traces recorded by probes. In this case, the violation handling mechanism is itself part of the design of the SUT, rather than an additional component on top of the system.

The analysis technique in [12] tries to estimate the rate of possible invalid occurring events and the maximum detection latency to realize predictable monitoring schemas. However, this is not always applicable due to different patterns in the occurrence of monitored events for different execution scenarios of the SUT [28]. An alternative approach used to decrease the monitoring overhead is time-triggered monitoring [28,29] which makes use of periodic sampling of the SUT state and different strategies to reduce the monitoring overhead by dynamically adjusting the sampling period.

Table 3 reports a comparative evaluation between MAHARAJA and some representative state-of-the-art runtime verification software tools. The following key features have been taken into account (for a more general comparison see [1]):

- *formalism*: it represents the formalism used to specify the SUT;
- *operational/descriptive*: it represents whether the tool uses a operational or descriptive formalism;
- *state/event-based*: state-based monitoring approaches rely on a state-by-state comparison, where a state stores the relevant data about the SUT;
- *exceptions*: it represents whether or not the user can express properties which include exception handling;
- *real-time*: it refers to the ability to verify quantitative temporal properties;

Table 3. Features comparison of different Java runtime monitoring tools.

Tool	MahaRAJA	Coma	Larva	Java-MOP	Java-MaC	Hawk	JPaX
Formalism	TB nets	ASMs	DATEs	various[a]	PEDL, MEDL	LTL, PLTL	LTL, PLTL
O/D[b]	O	O	O	O, D	D	D	D
S/E[c]	E	S	E	E	E	E	E
Exceptions	✓	✗	✓	✗	✗	✗	✗
Real-time	✓	✗	✓	✗	✓	✗	✗
Variables	✗	✓	✓	✓	✓	✗	✗
Self-awareness	✓	✓	✓	✓	✓	✗	✓
Testing	✓	✗	✗	✓	✗	✗	✗

[a] Depending on the plug-in: Finite State Machines, Regular Expressions, Context Free Grammar, PLTL, LTL, String Rewriting Systems. [b] Operational/Descriptive formalism. [c] State/Event-based approach.

- *variables*: it refers to the ability of monitoring value changes of variables;
- *self-awareness*: it refers to the capability of the monitoring system to return feedback to the SUT upon failure;
- *testing*: it represents the possibility to use the facilities of the monitoring framework to write test cases.

The results of our comparative evaluation show for each selected monitoring tool, the explicit support for the considered features. As we can see, the MAHARAJA framework has some interesting features, not directly supported by other tools. For instance, it allows both the runtime verification and testing of quantitative temporal properties. MAHARAJA does not support the monitoring of variables (Coma, Larva, Java-MOP and Java-MaC have this feature).

7 Conclusion

We presented an event-based runtime verification approach and its supporting tool MAHARAJA to verify temporal properties on JAVA programs. The proposed framework adopts TB nets to represent the desired behavior of the SUT, including real-time requirements. The designer annotates the source code to link JAVA methods to transitions of the model. Then, MAHARAJA exploits ASPECTJ to observe code execution and trigger the conformance verification at runtime. The usefulness of the approach has been assessed by monitoring a number of real-time benchmarking case-studies to discover both modeling and implementation faults. MAHARAJA focuses on the monitoring of timed events and its main limitation is that it does not support the monitoring of variables, although they can be easily checked during testing activity using MAHARAJA in conjunction with JUNIT. Nonetheless, we believe that our approach represents a viable technique for checking temporal properties of JAVA programs with respect to their formal specifications. Our experience shows that the monitoring overhead can be numerically evaluated and we found ASPECTJ as the major bottleneck. For this reason, we plan to replace ASPECTJ with other efficient bytecode transformation techniques [30]. The auxiliary memory used by the instrumentation is negligible and a preliminary quantitative comparison with other representative state-of-the-art runtime verification software tools individuates MAHARAJA as the less invasive [17]. The detection latency is also limited, thus allowing for a prompt recover after a failure.

The quantitative evaluation lead us to consider MAHARAJA as a viable light-weight pluggable tool to support the verification at runtime of real-time self-adaptive systems [15,31]. We will explore this last topic in our future work.

References

1. Delgado, N., Gates, A.Q., Roach, S.: A taxonomy and catalog of runtime software-fault monitoring tools. IEEE Trans. Softw. Eng. **30**(12), 859–872 (2004)
2. Ghezzi, C., Mandrioli, D., Morasca, S., Pezzè, M.: A unified high-level Petri net formalism for time-critical systems. IEEE Trans. Softw. Eng. **17**, 160–172 (1991)
3. Chen, F., D'Amorim, M., Roşu, G.: A formal monitoring-based framework for software development and analysis. In: Davies, J., Schulte, W., Barnett, M. (eds.) ICFEM 2004. LNCS, vol. 3308, pp. 357–372. Springer, Heidelberg (2004). doi:10. 1007/978-3-540-30482-1_31
4. Arcaini, P., Gargantini, A., Riccobene, E.: Combining model-based testing and runtime monitoring for program testing in the presence of nondeterminism. In: 2013 IEEE Sixth International Conference on Software Testing, Verification and Validation Workshops (ICSTW), pp. 178–187, March 2013
5. Liang, H., Dong, J.S., Sun, J., Wong, W.E.: Software monitoring through formal specification animation. Innov. Syst. Softw. Eng. **5**(4), 231–241 (2009)
6. Felder, M., Gargantini, A., Morzenti, A.: A theory of implementation and refinement in timed Petri nets. Theoret. Comput. Sci. **202**(12), 127–161 (1998)
7. Bengtsson, J., Yi, W.: Timed Automata: Semantics, Algorithms and Tools. Springer, Heidelberg (2004)
8. Gurevich, Y.: Sequential abstract-state machines capture sequential algorithms. ACM Trans. Comput. Log. **1**(1), 77–111 (2000)
9. Ramchandani, C.: Analysis of asynchronous concurrent systems by timed Petri nets. Technical report, Cambridge, MA, USA (1974)
10. Iglesia, D.G.D.L., Weyns, D.: MAPE-K formal templates to rigorously design behaviors for self-adaptive systems. ACM Trans. Auton. Adapt. Syst. **10**(3), 15:1–15:31 (2015)
11. Lee, W.J., Cha, S.D., Kwon, Y.R.: Integration and analysis of use cases using modular Petri nets in requirements engineering. IEEE Trans. Softw. Eng. **24**(12), 1115–1130 (1998)
12. Zhu, H., Dwyer, M.B., Goddard, S.: Predictable runtime monitoring. In: Proceedings of the 2009 21st Euromicro Conference on Real-Time Systems, ser. ECRTS 2009, pp. 173–183. IEEE Computer Society, Washington, DC (2011)
13. Valmari, A.: The state explosion problem. In: Reisig, W., Rozenberg, G. (eds.) ACPN 1996. LNCS, vol. 1491, pp. 429–528. Springer, Heidelberg (1998). doi:10. 1007/3-540-65306-6_21
14. Gomaa, H.: Designing Concurrent, Distributed, and Real-Time Applications with UML, 1st edn. Addison-Wesley Longman Publishing Co., Inc., Boston (2000)
15. Camilli, M., Gargantini, A., Scandurra, P.: Specifying and verifying real-time self-adaptive systems. In: 2015 IEEE 26th International Symposium on Software Reliability Engineering (ISSRE), pp. 303–313, November 2015

16. Bellettini, C., Capra, L.: Reachability analysis of time basic Petri nets: a time coverage approach. In: Proceedings of the 13th International Symposium on Symbolic and Numeric Algorithms for Scientific Computing, ser. SYNASC 2011, pp. 110–117. IEEE Computer Society, Washington, DC (2011)
17. Maharaja framework. http://camilli.di.unimi.it/maharaja/. Accessed Dec 2016
18. Hillah, L.M., Kordon, F., Petrucci, L., Trèves, N.: PNML framework: an extendable reference implementation of the Petri net markup language. In: Lilius, J., Penczek, W. (eds.) PETRI NETS 2010. LNCS, vol. 6128, pp. 318–327. Springer, Heidelberg (2010). doi:10.1007/978-3-642-13675-7_20
19. Kiczales, G., Hilsdale, E., Hugunin, J., Kersten, M., Palm, J., Griswold, W.G.: An overview of AspectJ. In: Knudsen, J.L. (ed.) ECOOP 2001. LNCS, vol. 2072, pp. 327–354. Springer, Heidelberg (2001). doi:10.1007/3-540-45337-7_18
20. Chronicle Software: Java Thread Affinity Library (2016). http://chronicle. software/products/thread-affinity/. Accessed Jan 2016
21. Li, T., Baumberger, D., Hahn, S.: Efficient and scalable multiprocessor fair scheduling using distributed weighted round-robin. SIGPLAN Not. **44**(4), 65–74 (2009)
22. Arcaini, P., Gargantini, A., Riccobene, E.: CoMA: conformance monitoring of Java programs by abstract state machines. In: Khurshid, S., Sen, K. (eds.) RV 2011. LNCS, vol. 7186, pp. 223–238. Springer, Heidelberg (2012). doi:10.1007/978-3-642-29860-8_17
23. Havelund, K., Roşu, G.: An overview of the runtime verification tool Java PathExplorer. Formal Methods Syst. Des. **24**(2), 189–215 (2004)
24. Kim, M., Viswanathan, M., Kannan, S., Lee, I., Sokolsky, O.: Java-MaC: a run-time assurance approach for Java programs. Form. Methods Syst. Des. **24**(2), 129–155 (2004)
25. d'Amorim, M., Havelund, K.: Event-based runtime verification of Java programs. SIGSOFT Softw. Eng. Notes **30**(4), 1–7 (2005)
26. Barringer, H., Goldberg, A., Havelund, K., Sen, K.: Rule-based runtime verification. In: Steffen, B., Levi, G. (eds.) VMCAI 2004. LNCS, vol. 2937, pp. 44–57. Springer, Heidelberg (2004). doi:10.1007/978-3-540-24622-0_5
27. Colombo, C., Pace, G.J., Schneider, G.: Dynamic event-based runtime monitoring of real-time and contextual properties. In: Cofer, D., Fantechi, A. (eds.) FMICS 2008. LNCS, vol. 5596, pp. 135–149. Springer, Heidelberg (2009). doi:10.1007/978-3-642-03240-0_13
28. Bonakdarpour, B., Navabpour, S., Fischmeister, S.: Time-triggered runtime verification. Formal Methods Syst. Des. **43**(1), 29–60 (2013)
29. Navabpour, S., Bonakdarpour, B., Fischmeister, S.: Path-aware time-triggered runtime verification. In: Qadeer, S., Tasiran, S. (eds.) RV 2012. LNCS, vol. 7687, pp. 199–213. Springer, Heidelberg (2013). doi:10.1007/978-3-642-35632-2_21
30. Mastrangelo, L., Hauswirth, M.: JNIF: Java native instrumentation framework. In: Proceedings of the International Conference on Principles and Practices of Programming on the Java Platform: Virtual Machines, Languages, and Tools, ser. PPPJ 2014, pp. 194–199. ACM, New York (2014)
31. de Lemos, R., Garlan, D., Ghezzi, C., Giese, H.: Software engineering for self-adaptive systems: assurances (Dagstuhl Seminar 13511). Dagstuhl Rep. **3**(12), 67–96 (2014). http://drops.dagstuhl.de/opus/volltexte/2014/4508

Model-Counting Approaches for Nonlinear Numerical Constraints

Mateus Borges[1]([⊠]), Quoc-Sang Phan[2], Antonio Filieri[1], and Corina S. Păsăreanu[2,3]

[1] Imperial College London, London, UK
m.borges@ic.ac.uk
[2] Carnegie Mellon University Silicon Valley, Mountain View, USA
[3] NASA Ames, Mountain View, USA

Abstract. Model counting is of central importance in quantitative reasoning about systems. Examples include computing the probability that a system successfully accomplishes its task without errors, and measuring the number of bits leaked by a system to an adversary in Shannon entropy. Most previous work in those areas demonstrated their analysis on programs with linear constraints, in which cases model counting is polynomial time. Model counting for nonlinear constraints is notoriously hard, and thus programs with nonlinear constraints are not well-studied. This paper surveys state-of-the-art techniques and tools for model counting with respect to SMT constraints, modulo the bitvector theory, since this theory is decidable, and it can express nonlinear constraints that arise from the analysis of computer programs. We integrate these techniques within the Symbolic Pathfinder platform and evaluate them on difficult nonlinear constraints generated from the analysis of cryptographic functions.

Keywords: Model counting modulo theories · Bitvector arithmetic · Nonlinear constraints · Cryptographic functions

1 Introduction

Model counting is of central importance in quantitative reasoning, with applications in probabilistic inference [7,8], reliability analysis [11], and quantitative information flow [2,3,23,24]. Most previous work in those areas was performed on programs with linear constraints, using model counting tools such as Latte [18]. Model counting for nonlinear constraints is notoriously hard, and thus programs with nonlinear constraints are not well-studied (with only limited support for floating-point values abstracted as real numbers [4]). In this paper we survey state-of-the-art model counting techniques and tools for SMT (satisfiability modulo theories) constraints modulo the bitvector theory, since this theory is decidable and it can express the nonlinear constraints that arise naturally from the analysis of computer programs. Our work is motivated by a security project [1] that aims to develop automated quantitative information

© Springer International Publishing AG 2017
C. Barrett et al. (Eds.): NFM 2017, LNCS 10227, pp. 131–138, 2017.
DOI: 10.1007/978-3-319-57288-8_9

flow analysis techniques for complex applications, including cryptographic functions that are very difficult to analyze. The bitvector theory is particularly useful for these functions which typically use operations on bitvector values.

We integrate the surveyed techniques within Symbolic PathFinder (SPF) [25] and evaluate them on difficult nonlinear constraints generated using symbolic execution. Although we restrict our evaluation to cryptographic functions, our study should be relevant to anybody interested in quantitative reasoning over complex, nonlinear systems.

1.1 Symbolic Execution and SPF

SPF performs symbolic execution over Java byte code programs. Symbolic execution [14] is a systematic analysis technique that executes a program on symbolic, rather than concrete, input values and computes the effects of the program as *functions* of these symbolic inputs. The result of symbolic execution is a set of symbolic paths, each with a path condition PC, which is a conjunction of constraints over the symbolic inputs that characterizes all the inputs that follow that path. All the PCs are disjoint by construction.

1.2 Quantification of Information Leaks

Perfect software security is hard to achieve. Systems often leak information to an adversary who can observe different aspects of program behavior. Research on quantitative information flow aims at quantifying (in number of bits) the expected leakage.

A program can be viewed as a probabilistic function that maps a *high* security input h and a *low* security input l to an *observable* output o. An adversary tries to guess h by providing l and observing the output. The leakage of the program P is defined as the *mutual information* between the secret h and the public output o [19]: $Leakage(P) = \mathcal{H}(o) - \mathcal{H}(o|h)$, where $\mathcal{H}(x)$ denotes the classical Shannon entropy of a random variable x, measuring the "uncertainty" about x. For a deterministic program P, there is no uncertainty about o when h is given. Therefore $\mathcal{H}(o|h) = 0$. The entropy can thus be computed as: $Leakage(P) = \mathcal{H}(o) = -\sum_{i=1,m} p(o_i) \log_2(p(o_i))$.

Intuitively, the leakage gives an estimate on the number of bits in the secret that an adversary can infer by observing the output of the program. If this estimate is small (or zero) then the program can be considered safe. In [2], Backes et al. combined model checking and model counting to compute the leakage when the observable is an output variable. In a similar setting, we used symbolic execution (SPF) combined with Latte to compute an upper bound on the leakage [23].

More recently [3,24], we used SPF and Latte to compute the leakage when the observables are non-functional characteristics of program executions, i.e. side-channels, such as time consumed, number of memory accessed or packets transmitted over a network. In this model, a symbolic path identified by PC_i leads to a concrete observable o_i. Assuming the secret input has uniform distribution, which means the adversary has no *prior* knowledge about it, the probability of observing o_i can be computed using SPF and model counting as follows: $p(o_i) = \sum_{cost(PC_j)=o_i} \sharp(PC_j)/\sharp D$, where $\sharp(PC_j)$ is the number of solutions (computed with model counting) of constraint PC_j and $\#D$ is the size of the input domain D assumed to be (possibly very large but) finite.

In all the previous work mentioned above, Latte was used to perform model counting; it implements the polynomial time Barvinok algorithm to count models for a system of linear integer inequalities. However Latte cannot handle nonlinear constraints. In this paper we study approaches for the fixed-width bitvector theory, which can represent such constraints. In the following, we use the term "bitvector" and "word" interchangeably.

2 Model Counting Techniques and Tools

In this section we evaluate several tool-supported approaches for counting the models of bitvector constraints. These approaches can be classified according to two orthogonal dimensions: exact vs approximate and bit-level vs word-level.

Exact techniques count the exact number of models for a given constraint. Approximate techniques only explore a portion of the solution space, carefully selected to provide probabilistic guarantees on the accuracy ($0 < \epsilon < 1$) and confidence ($0 < \delta < 1$) of the result. In particular, they guarantee that $\Pr\big((1-\epsilon)c \le c^* \le (1 + \epsilon)c\big) \ge 1-\delta$, where c^* is the approximate result and c is the exact (unknown) count. Other randomized approaches not providing formal guarantees (e.g., [26,31]) are not considered in this study.

Bit-level Approaches address the model counting problem for propositional (SAT) formulas, i.e., #SAT. Model counting for bit vector formulas can be performed as follows. A bitvector formula is first converted to a propositional formula using bit blasting to generate an equivalent Boolean circuit based on bit-level behavior of bitvector operations. This Boolean circuit is interpreted as a propositional logic problem and converted in conjunctive normal form (CNF); at this point #SAT approaches can be used to count the number of models. While the procedure is general, the conversion of Boolean circuits into CNF is usually based on the Tseitin transformation [30], which introduces additional Boolean variables in the process. While this transformation guarantees a model for the CNF form is also a model for the initial problem, the introduction of additional variables may lead to different model counts. For this reason, in this paper we use only #SAT tools supporting projection, i.e., able to project the solution space only on the variables appearing in the Boolean circuit, ignoring the ones introduced by Tseitin transformation.

We found five tools for #SAT that support projection and can thus be used in our setting for bitvector counting: SharpCDCL, All-SAT, SharpSAT and Dsharp, which compute exact solutions, and ApproxMC-p, which produces approximate solutions.

- SharpCDCL [15] is an enumeration-based approach; it iteratively invokes the SAT solver to produce at each iteration a new model, keeping trace of the set of models and their number.
- All-SAT [13] and SharpSAT [28] extend the DPLL algorithm to count the number of solutions of a SAT problem. They both use caching mechanisms and use constraint propagation for pruning the DPLL, which avoid the exhaustive exploration of subtrees containing no solutions.
- Dsharp [20] reuses the algorithmic core of SharpSAT, adapting it to work with a deterministic Decomposable Negation Normal Form (d-DNNF) representation of the SAT problem. d-DNNF provides a more compact representation of the constraints in memory that, according to [20], may better support model counting.
- ApproxMC-p [16] takes as input accuracy and confidence targets and produce an approximate count which deviates from the exact count by at most a factor $1 \pm \epsilon$ with probability at least $1 - \delta$. The approach uses universal hash functions to perform a uniform sampling within the domain. The ratio between the number of models for this sample and the sample size is used as an estimate of the ratio of models over the entire problem domain. The samples is automatically decided to achieve ϵ and δ.

Word-Level Approaches aim to avoid the cost of bit blasting by defining counting procedures that operate directly on SMT variables and operations. We investigate a recent tool that provides an approximate counting procedure for bitvectors: SMTApproxMC [7]. SMTApproxMC uses word-level hashing functions to sample a finite number of candidate models and then an SMT solver to check how many of these candidate models satisfy the constraint. The number of models found within the sample are used to build a robust statistical estimator achieving the desired probabilistic guarantees. SMTApproxMC can avoid bit blasting whenever the SMT solver can check a constraint without it (e.g., for linear constraints); however, for nonlinear constraints (all the subjects of this study), SMTApproxMC requires bit blasting.

Chistikov et al. [8] also extend the hashing-based approach used for #SAT (e.g., in [16]) to counting for SMT problems. Hashing functions allow to uniformly sample candidate solutions. Statistics on the sample are used to estimate the total number of models. However, no tool is available and, according to [7], SMTApproxMC is faster.

A related approach is implemented in the MathSAT solver [9], which provides a functionality, called All-SMT, that given a set of Boolean variables V_I, it can enumerate all the models of the problem projected on V_I. The source code of the tool is not available, nor a technical description of the All-SMT feature, thus we do not know the details of the counting algorithm it implements but can only report its execution time. Our own All-SMT solver aZ3 [21,22] is less efficient than MathSAT, so we do not include its experiment results here.

Other Approaches. We have also investigated other techniques for model counting: blocking-clause enumeration, BDD-based enumerations, counting with Gröbner bases and a brute-force enumeration that we use as baseline.

Blocking clause enumeration make the solver find all the models for a problem by iteratively adding the negation of already found models to the initial problem. The iteration terminates when no more solutions can be found. Intuitively, this method can work only for complex problems with few models. We implemented it on top of Z3 SMT solver [10] to practically confirm this intuition.

BDD-based enumeration represents a propositional formula as a binary decision diagram and then counts the paths from its root to the leaf representing the Boolean constant "true". We implemented a prototype based on the BDD library CUDD [27], which builds a BDD corresponding to a constraint bitblasted with Z3. Unfortunately, for all the subjects in this study the execution time exceeded the timeout of 1 h.

Gröbner bases are used in computational algebra to reason about polynomials over finite fields. Boolean variables and and operators from propositional logic can be mapped into corresponding variables and functions over polynomials. Each zero of such polynomials corresponds to exactly one model of the initial propositional formula [12, 29]. Algebraic solvers can be used to find those zeroes. We implemented this technique using PolyBoRi [5], but its execution timed out for all the subjects.

Finally, we also implemented as a reference a brute force approach which encodes the constraints as bitwise operations on unsigned integers in C. The mapping is straightforward from the smtlib representation. The program iterates over the entire domain and count the number of models for a constraint. We compiled the C sources using level 1 optimization in GCC.

3   Evaluation

Subjects. We study modular exponentiation ($modPow(b, e, m) = b^e$ **mod** m) and modular multiplication ($modMul(x, y) = x * y$ **mod** m) implementations. These are core routines for most public-key cryptographic systems, most notably RSA. In the past, some implementations have been found vulnerable to side channel attacks [6, 17], mostly as effect of optimizations. Our goal is to localize side channels by quantifying information leaks with symbolic execution and model counting (see Sect. 1).

For our experiments, we analyzed a set of randomly selected path conditions from two different implementations of the modular operations (the source code is given in the appendix). The first implementation (subjects a-* in the following), taken from [24], optimizes $modPow$ with a reduction step at each iteration, but uses a naive implementation of $modMul$. We analyze the program with the same configurations from [24]: the modulus m can be either 1717, 834443, or 1964903306; both the base b and exponent e are symbolic, with $b \leq m$ and $e \leq 31$.

The second implementation (benchmarks b-*) is more realistic as it uses Java's `BigInteger` class to encode large messages and secrets (this example was provided to us by DARPA at a recent engagement) and uses fast multiplication. Here modulus m is fixed with a 1536-bit value; the base b is also a concrete 1532-bit value; the exponent e is symbolic BigInteger with 40 bits. We analyze both $modPow$ and $modMul$, where both x and y are symbolic 24-bit BigInteger.

Subject	a-1	a-2	a-3	a-4	a-5	a-6	a-7	b-1	b-2	b-3	b-4
N. Ops	11	26	15	37	121	57	117	250	243	1428	1428
Domain Size	10K	10K	10K	25M	25M	59B	59B	4T	4T	32B	32B
N. Solutions	1.7K	7	1.7K	208K	109K	80M	77M	2B	66B	1	1
N. CNF clauses	40K	78K	58K	67K	114K	58K	78K	2K	2K	2K	2K
Execution time											
BitBlasting	15s	30s	24s	25s	44s	23s	30s	1s	1s	1s	2s
SharpCDCL	1s	1s	1s	43m	-	-	-	-	-	1s	1s
All-SAT	1s	8s	2s	31m*	59m*	15m*	19m*	-	-	1s	1s
SharpSAT	5s	2s	11s	29m	53m	-	-	1s	1s	1s	1s
Dsharp	12m	32s	22m	-	-	-	-	1s	1s	1s	1s
ApproxMC (f)	4s	2s	5s	16s	32s	1m	1m	4s	5s	1s	1s
ApproxMC (p)	4s	2s	6s	2m	5m	21m	24m	16s	25s	1s	1s
SMTapproxMC (f)	6m	15m	8m	-	-	-	-	-	-	2m	2m
SMTapproxMC (p)	-	15m	-	-	-	-	-	-	-	2m	2m
MathSAT	2s	2s	5s	38m	54m	-	-	-	-	1s	1s
Z3-BC	12s	3s	18s	-	-	-	-	-	-	1s	1s
Brute Force	1s	1s	1s	1s	1s	8m	8m	-	-	2m	2m

Fig. 1. Execution time comparison.

Experimental Results. Figure 1 summarizes the performance of the different tools. The results indicate that enumeration-based techniques perform well for complex problem with few solutions (SharpCDCL, Z3-BC). Exact techniques based on DPLL (All-SAT and SharpSAT) scale better than enumeration, but fail for the subjects involving complex constraints over large domains, like a-6 and a-7 which have approximately 58k and 78k CNF clauses over a domain of 59B points. Notably, All-SAT produced the correct count only for the first three subjects. For all the others (marked with *), it significantly under-approximated the count. However, the most recent release dates back to 2004 and the tool is not maintained, making difficult to get the tool fixed.

The performance of approximate methods (ApproxMC and SMTApproxMC) depends on the required accuracy ϵ and confidence δ. The correct counts and the approximate ones are shown in a table in the appendix. We run the tools with two different settings: (f) $\epsilon = 0.5$, $\delta = 0.05$ and (p) $\epsilon = 0.1$, $\delta = 0.05$. SMTApproxMC provides a bad performance on our subjects; this is however expected since its internal solver is required to bit blast our nonlinear constraints for each query. From our experience, low-accuracy approximate methods can be used for a preliminary assessment of the number of solutions: if the coarse approximate count is small, exact methods may then be used for an exact solution. Similarly, if the count is close to the domain size, it is possible to count exactly the models of the negation of the problem (which should be only a few). If the count is far from its extreme values (0 and domain size) or if the problem is particularly complex (>50k CNF clauses on our subjects), exact counters will probably fail if the domain is large and a more precise approximate solution can be pursued.

Not surprisingly, the brute force approach is faster than model counting tools when the domain size is small enough ($<10^9$), but it is not a viable solution for larger problems.

4   Conclusion

We surveyed model counting techniques that are applicable to complex nonlinear constraints. We restricted our study to techniques and tools that are capable of providing formal guarantees on the results. Our survey suggests that that the most promising techniques use approximate model counting and bit-level hashing, however the performance of the tools can degrade when increased precision is required. SMT-based model counting is still a very young research area, but its relevance for quantitative analysis can be an effective driver for its development, as program verification has effectively driven the development in SMT solving.

Acknowledgement. This work was funded in part by the National Science Foundation (NSF Grant Nos. CCF-1319858, CCF-1549161) and also by DARPA under agreement number FA8750-15-2-0087. The U.S. Government is authorized to reproduce and distribute reprints for Governmental purposes notwithstanding any copyright notation thereon. Mateus Borges is funded by an Imperial College PhD Scholarship.

References

1. ISSTAC: Integrated Symbolic Execution for Space-Time Analysis of Code. http://www.cmu.edu/silicon-valley/research/isstac
2. Backes, M., Kopf, B., Rybalchenko, A.: Automatic discovery and quantification of information leaks. In: SP 2009, pp. 141–153 (2009)
3. Bang, L., Aydin, A., Phan, Q.S., Păsăreanu, C.S., Bultan, T.: String analysis for side channels with segmented oracles. In: FSE 2016, pp. 193–204. ACM (2016)
4. Borges, M., Filieri, A., d'Amorim, M., Păsăreanu, C.S., Visser, W.: Compositional solution space quantification for probabilistic software analysis. In: PLDI, pp. 123–132. ACM (2014)
5. Brickenstein, M., Dreyer, A.: PolyBoRi: a framework for gröbner-basis computations with boolean polynomials. J. Symb. Comput. **44**(9), 1326–1345 (2009)
6. Brumley, D., Boneh, D.: Remote timing attacks are practical. In: SSYM 2003, pp. 1–1. USENIX Association (2003)
7. Chakraborty, S., Meel, K.S., Mistry, R., Vardi, M.Y.: Approximate probabilistic inference via word-level counting. In: AAAI 2016, pp. 3218–3224 (2016)
8. Chistikov, D., Dimitrova, R., Majumdar, R.: Approximate counting in SMT and value estimation for probabilistic programs. In: Baier, C., Tinelli, C. (eds.) TACAS 2015. LNCS, vol. 9035, pp. 320–334. Springer, Heidelberg (2015). doi:10.1007/978-3-662-46681-0_26
9. Cimatti, A., Griggio, A., Schaafsma, B.J., Sebastiani, R.: The MathSAT5 SMT solver. In: Piterman, N., Smolka, S.A. (eds.) TACAS 2013. LNCS, vol. 7795, pp. 93–107. Springer, Heidelberg (2013). doi:10.1007/978-3-642-36742-7_7
10. Moura, L., Bjørner, N.: Z3: an efficient SMT solver. In: Ramakrishnan, C.R., Rehof, J. (eds.) TACAS 2008. LNCS, vol. 4963, pp. 337–340. Springer, Heidelberg (2008). doi:10.1007/978-3-540-78800-3_24

11. Filieri, A., Păsăreanu, C.S., Visser, W.: Reliability analysis in symbolic pathfinder. In: ICSE, pp. 622–631. IEEE Press (2013)
12. Gao, S.: Counting zeros over finite fields using Gröbner bases. Master's thesis, Carnegie Mellon University (2009)
13. Grumberg, O., Schuster, A., Yadgar, A.: Memory efficient all-solutions SAT solver and its application for reachability analysis. In: Hu, A.J., Martin, A.K. (eds.) FMCAD 2004. LNCS, vol. 3312, pp. 275–289. Springer, Heidelberg (2004). doi:10.1007/978-3-540-30494-4_20
14. King, J.C.: Symbolic execution and program testing. Commun. ACM **19**(7), 385–394 (1976)
15. Klebanov, V., Manthey, N., Muise, C.: SAT-based analysis and quantification of information flow in programs. In: Joshi, K., Siegle, M., Stoelinga, M., D'Argenio, P.R. (eds.) QEST 2013. LNCS, vol. 8054, pp. 177–192. Springer, Heidelberg (2013). doi:10.1007/978-3-642-40196-1_16
16. Klebanov, V., Weigl, A., Weisbarth, J.: Sound probabilistic #SAT with projection. In: QAPL 2016, pp. 15–29 (2016)
17. Kocher, P.C.: Timing attacks on implementations of Diffie-Hellman, RSA, DSS, and other systems. In: Koblitz, N. (ed.) CRYPTO 1996. LNCS, vol. 1109, pp. 104–113. Springer, Heidelberg (1996). doi:10.1007/3-540-68697-5_9
18. Loera, J.A.D., Hemmecke, R., Tauzer, J., Yoshida, R.: Effective lattice point counting in rational convex polytopes. J. Symb. Comput. **38**(4), 1273–1302 (2004)
19. Malacaria, P.: Algebraic foundations for quantitative information flow. Math. Struct. Comput. Sci. **25**, 404–428 (2015)
20. Muise, C., McIlraith, S.A., Beck, J.C., Hsu, E.I.: DSHARP: fast d-DNNF compilation with sharpSAT. In: Kosseim, L., Inkpen, D. (eds.) AI 2012. LNCS (LNAI), vol. 7310, pp. 356–361. Springer, Heidelberg (2012). doi:10.1007/978-3-642-30353-1_36
21. Phan, Q.S.: Model counting modulo theories. Ph.D. thesis, Queen Mary University of London (2015)
22. Phan, Q.S., Malacaria, P.: All-solution satisfiability modulo theories: applications, algorithms and benchmarks. In: ARES 2015, pp. 100–109 (2015)
23. Phan, Q.S., Malacaria, P., Păsăreanu, C.S., d'Amorim, M.: Quantifying information leaks using reliability analysis. In: SPIN 2014, pp. 105–108. ACM (2014)
24. Păsăreanu, C.S., Phan, Q.S., Malacaria, P.: Multi-run side-channel analysis using Symbolic Execution and Max-SMT. In: CSF 2016, pp. 387–400, June 2016
25. Păsăreanu, C.S., Visser, W., Bushnell, D., Geldenhuys, J., Mehlitz, P., Rungta, N.: Symbolic PathFinder: integrating symbolic execution with model checking for Java bytecode analysis. Autom. Softw. Eng. **20**, 1–35 (2013)
26. Rubinstein, R.: Stochastic enumeration method for counting NP-hard problems. Methodol. Comput. Appl. Probab. **15**(2), 249–291 (2013)
27. Somenzi, F.: CUDD: CU decision diagram package release 3.0.0 (2015)
28. Thurley, M.: sharpSAT – Counting models with advanced component caching and implicit BCP. In: Biere, A., Gomes, C.P. (eds.) SAT 2006. LNCS, vol. 4121, pp. 424–429. Springer, Heidelberg (2006). doi:10.1007/11814948_38
29. Tran, Q., Vardi, M.Y.: Groebner bases computation in boolean rings for symbolic model checking. In: MOAS, pp. 440–445. ACTA Press (2007)
30. Tseitin, G.S.: On the complexity of derivation in propositional calculus. In: Siekmann, J.H., Wrightson, G. (eds.) Automation of Reasoning: 2: Classical Papers on Computational Logic, pp. 466–483. Springer, Heidelberg (1983)
31. Wei, W., Selman, B.: A new approach to model counting. In: Bacchus, F., Walsh, T. (eds.) SAT 2005. LNCS, vol. 3569, pp. 324–339. Springer, Heidelberg (2005). doi:10.1007/11499107_24

Input Space Partitioning to Enable Massively Parallel Proof

Ashlie B. Hocking[1]($\boxtimes$), M. Anthony Aiello[1], John C. Knight[1],
and Nikos Aréchiga[2]

[1] Dependable Computing, Charlottesville, VA, USA
{ben.hocking,tony.aiello,john.knight}@dependablecomputing.com
[2] Toyota InfoTechnology Center, Mountain View, VA, USA
narechiga@us.toyota-itc.com

Abstract. Real-world applications often include large, empirically defined discrete-valued functions. When proving properties about these applications, the proof naturally breaks into one case per entry in the first function reached, and again into one case per entry in the next function, and continues splitting. This splitting yields a combinatorial explosion of proof cases that challenges traditional proof approaches. While each proof case represents a mathematical path from inputs to outputs through these functions, the full set of cases is not available up front, preventing a straightforward application of parallelism. Here we describe an approach that slices the input space, creating a partition based on pre-computed mathematical paths such that each slice has only a small number of proof cases. These slices are amenable to massively parallel proof. We evaluate this approach using an example model of an adaptive cruise control, where proofs are conducted in a highly parallel PVS environment.

1 Introduction

Real-world applications from many domains, such as embedded control systems in the automotive domain, depend upon large *discrete-valued functions* (DVFs) [3,4]. Frequently, these systems operate on physical processes for which no sufficiently accurate analytic models are known. For example, the air-fuel ratio of an internal-combustion engine must be accurately and precisely controlled to maximize fuel efficiency and minimize pollutants [5,7]. Since there are factors for which no sufficiently general and accurate analytic models exist, the values used are determined empirically and represented in the control system as DVFs.

Attempting to prove theorems representing safety properties for applications including DVFs results in a large number of proof cases. When multiple DVFs are combined mathematically, the number of proof cases multiplies combinatorially. For realistic applications, merely running a theorem prover sequentially on the proof cases may take decades — even moderate-size examples require months.

© Springer International Publishing AG 2017
C. Barrett et al. (Eds.): NFM 2017, LNCS 10227, pp. 139–145, 2017.
DOI: 10.1007/978-3-319-57288-8_10

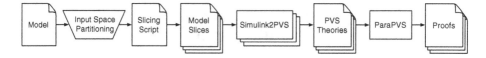

Fig. 1. Overview of the parallelization process

Two approaches to solving this problem naturally arise: (1) replace the DVFs with suitable abstractions and (2) exploit the parallelism inherent in the proof cases to reduce wall-clock time. This paper focuses on exploiting parallelism.

Mathematical interactions amongst distinct DVFs prevent trivial enumeration of proof cases up-front, inhibiting straightforward application of parallelism. Our approach, shown in Fig. 1, enables parallelism by carefully partitioning the input space of the application, yielding proof slices with small and approximately equal numbers of proof cases. We then apply simple optimizations across all slices, significantly reducing the per-slice proof time. Finally, we use a custom tool to invoke the theorem prover in parallel and generate tailored proof reports.

We applied our approach to a SIMULINK model for an example adaptive cruise control system in which the DVFs are represented as lookup tables (LUTs). The approach, which relies on our Simulink2PVS tool [2], yields a 67,000% speedup as compared to sequential proof of the 74,170 proof cases.

2 Input Space Partitioning and Parallel Proof

Proving proof cases in parallel is an obvious approach to dealing a large number of proof cases [1]. If N proof cases can be completed in parallel, then the total speedup is up to a factor of N. Moreover, if N equals the number of proof cases, then the total time required is the time required to prove the slowest proof cases.

Unfortunately, the complete set of proof cases is not available up-front, especially when proof cases arise from the interactions amongst entries in multiple DVFs. An obvious solution is to partition the input space of the application, yielding proof slices that each contain a subset of the proof cases. A naïve partitioning might yield proof slices with input intervals of the same size.

Such a partitioning, however, is unlikely to result in small and equal numbers of proof cases per proof slice. Mathematical interactions amongst entries in the discrete-valued functions may lead to large numbers of proof cases for some slices and small numbers of proof cases for other slices, dramatically reducing the efficacy of parallelization. The input space must be carefully partitioned so that the proof slices have a small and equal number of proof cases. Our approach to generating proof slices is shown in Fig. 2.

1. A map of DVF domain intervals is created for each DVF in the application. For LUTs, these intervals correspond to breakpoints delineating the table data.

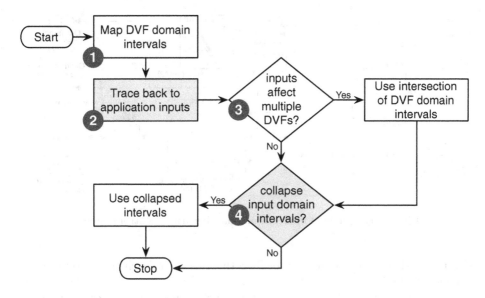

Fig. 2. Proof slice generation

2. The DVF domain intervals are traced back through the application to inputs, to create input domain intervals that form the basis of the input space partitioning. This process requires careful consideration of interactions among inputs. For example, if two inputs are added before entering a DVF, each input domain's upper and lower bounds must be considered. For the smaller input domain, the input domain interval size is governed by the smallest DVF domain interval size. For a given pair of input domain intervals, the DVF domain intervals relevant are those between the sum of the lower bounds and the sum of the upper bounds.
3. Often each input does not affect only one DVF. When multiple DVFs are affected by an input, the intersection of domain intervals is used. For example, if one input directly feeds into two DVFs where the first has breakpoints [0, 3, 9, 12] and the second has breakpoints [0, 4, 9, 12], then the input domain intervals are 0–3, 3–4, 4–9, and 9–12.
4. Input domain intervals are analyzed to determine if they should be collapsed. For example, if there are three input domain intervals such that the first and last create 1 proof case and the middle input domain interval creates 2 proof cases (for a total of 4 proof cases), combining the first and second input domain intervals might still only yield 2 proof cases. This process reduces the total number of proof slices without changing the maximum number of proof cases per slice.

We instantiated this process for the example SIMULINK model shown in Fig. 3. The result of the input-space partitioning is captured in a MATLAB script that generates slices of the original SIMULINK model. Simulink2PVS is executed for

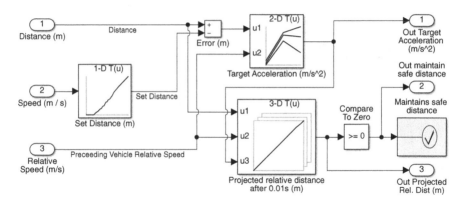

Fig. 3. Hypothetical model of an adaptive cruise control system

each model slice, resulting in a set of PVS theories where each theory represents a single proof slice.

To support running PVS in a highly parallel environment, we created a new tool called ParaPVS that: (a) manages the parallel PVS processes based upon control input, (b) generates custom reports, and (c) can limit the proof to a random subset of the cases (input slices).

3 Reducing Per-Slice Proof Time

Mechanical theorem provers like PVS [6] are often applied to complex proofs. In these applications, the time required for automatic decision procedures to complete the proof is important, but is not a primary goal of the analyst. Instead, the primary goal is completing the proof; much of the time required is identifying a sequence of steps that enable the decision procedures to complete the proof. Once the proof is completed, optimization of the proof steps is not beneficial.

In our parallel application of PVS to proof slices, however, the per-slice proof time is important. Proving N proof slices in parallel offers up to a factor N speedup. Reducing the per-slice proof time by a factor of M offers up to a factor $N \times M$ speedup. In our experience, moreover, M can be a significant factor.

We explored two approaches to reduce per-slice proof time: (1) tailor the proof steps for each proof slice to reduce the time taken by automated decision procedures; and (2) increase the efficiency of the DVF representations.

To tailor the proof for each proof slice, we first used ParaPVS to complete proofs for a random sampling of proof slices. The initial proofs were completed automatically, e.g., by using PVS strategy (grind). We then analyzed results of a random sampling and manually developed more efficient proof strategies for the proof obligations that required the most time. While there is a time cost associated with this process (~1 day), this cost is expected to be roughly constant. These proof strategies always terminate in calls to automatic decision procedures, ensuring that they are generally applicable across all proof slices.

Additionally, we identified an inefficiency in the DVF representation. For a generic DVF, the PVS specification describes the output of the DVF when the input is *outside* the breakpoints and also when the input is *between* the breakpoints. When the input space is partitioned, however, most of the resulting proof slices do not have inputs that lie outside the given breakpoints. To accommodate this, Simulink2PVS was modified to only specify the relevant breakpoint intervals given any lower and upper bounds present on the input data.

4   Case Study

We assess the performance of our approach by application to the model shown in Fig. 3 [8]. This model has three DVFs represented as a 1-D, 2-D and 3-D LUT. The proof of the safety property for this model (that the projected relative distance is non-negative) requires that a total of 74,170 proof cases be completed.

Ideally, the baseline for our assessment would be sequential proof of the safety property for this model. Unfortunately, PVS cannot complete this proof because the number of lines of text in the sequent grows exponentially as the composition of DVFs is expanded, quickly resulting in a sequent that cannot be manipulated.

To provide a baseline, we first applied our input-space partitioning approach, generating a total of 26,880 proof slices. Our input-space partitioning approach is much more efficient than a uniform input-space partitioning approach that generates the same number of proof slices, as shown in Fig. 4. Our approach yields an average of 2.75 cases per slice and a total of 74,170 proof cases, whereas the uniform approach yields 16.04 and a total of over 430,000 proof cases, many of which are contained in more than one slice and are therefore redundant.

We then used ParaPVS to complete the proofs for all proof slices, using 44 PVS processes in parallel. All experiments were performed on a PowerEdge R730 Server with two 22-core 2.2 GHz Xeon hyper-threaded processors and 256 GB of main memory. The result was 98.4 days of CPU time, which we take as our baseline for further comparison. Table 1 presents our results; speedup in the

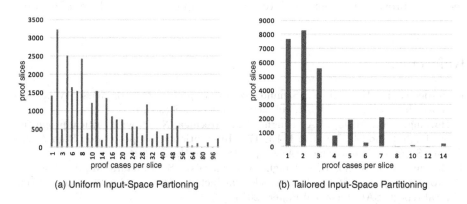

(a) Uniform Input-Space Partioning   (b) Tailored Input-Space Partitioning

Fig. 4. Input-space partitioning comparison

Table 1. Timing results

	Baseline (44 Processes)	Hyper-threading (HT) (88 Processes)	HT + Imp strategies	HT + Imp strategies & representation
CPU time	98.4 days	173.6 days	18.3 days	13.2 days
Elapsed time	53.7 h	47.6 h	4.87 h	3.52 h
Avg time per slice	316.3 s	558.2 s	59.0 s	42.7 s
Speedup	4,400%	4,960%	48,500%	67,000%

table is the ratio of elapsed time to the baseline CPU time of 98.4 days, where CPU time is the sum of the amount of time spent by each process.

Using ParaPVS to complete 88 proof slices in parallel takes advantage of the test platform's hyper-threading, results in only a 1.13× speedup due to a diminishing return of increasing parallelism without additional computation resources. Applying the first per-slice optimization — proof-strategy improvement — yields a 9.78× speedup. Applying the second per-slice optimization — DVF-representation improvement — yields a 1.38× speedup. In total, the proof time is reduced from nearly 100 days to about 3.5 h, a 67,000% speedup.

5   Conclusion

This paper presents a novel approach to dealing with large numbers of proof cases: enabling parallelism through careful partitioning of the application input space, reducing the per-slice proof time, and leveraging a tool for parallel invocation of a theorem prover. Our results demonstrate a speedup of 67,000%.

For moderate-size examples, this approach works; we expect the approach to scale to handle proofs with up to 10^8 proof cases. Further speedup can be achieved by leveraging additional parallelism. Some real-world examples we have seen, however, have proofs with on the order of 10^{30} or more proof cases. These proofs require additional techniques, such as replacement of the DVFs with abstractions that are simple enough to enable efficient proof, yet accurate enough to prove the property of interest. This approach is the subject of ongoing research.

References

1. Bordeaux, L., Hamadi, Y., Samulowitz, H.: Experiments with massively parallel constraint solving. In: IJCAI, vol. 2009, pp. 443–448 (2009)
2. Hocking, A.B., Aiello, M.A., Knight, J.C., Aréchiga, N.: Proving critical properties of Simulink models. In: 2016 IEEE 17th International Symposium on High Assurance Systems Engineering (HASE), pp. 189–196. IEEE (2016)
3. Hocking, A.B., Aiello, M.A., Knight, J.C., Shiraishi, S., Yamaura, M., Aréchiga, N.: Proving properties of simulink models that include discrete valued functions. Technical report, SAE Technical Paper (2016)

4. Jeannin, J.B., Ghorbal, K., Kouskoulas, Y., Gardner, R., Schmidt, A., Zawadzki, E., Platzer, A.: Formal verification of ACAS X, an industrial airborne collision avoidance system. In: Proceedings of the 12th International Conference on Embedded Software, pp. 127–136. IEEE Press (2015)
5. Jin, X., Deshmukh, J.V., Kapinski, J., Ueda, K., Butts, K.: Benchmarks for model transformations and conformance checking. In: 1st International Workshop on Applied Verification for Continuous and Hybrid Systems (ARCH) (2014)
6. Owre, S., Rajan, S., Rushby, J.M., Shankar, N., Srivas, M.: PVS: combining specification, proof checking, and model checking. In: Alur, R., Henzinger, T.A. (eds.) CAV 1996. LNCS, vol. 1102, pp. 411–414. Springer, Heidelberg (1996). doi:10.1007/3-540-61474-5_91
7. Wu, C.W., Chen, R.H., Pu, J.Y., Lin, T.H.: The influence of air-fuel ratio on engine performance and pollutant emission of an si engine using ethanol-gasoline-blended fuels. Atmos. Environ. $38(40)$, 7093–7100 (2004)
8. Yamaura, M., Aréchiga, N., Shiraishi, S.: SimulinkVerificationBenchmark. https://github.com/Toyota-ITC-SSD/SimulinkVerificationBenchmark

Compositional Model Checking of Interlocking Systems for Lines with Multiple Stations

Hugo Daniel Macedo[1,2](✉), Alessandro Fantechi[1,3], and Anne E. Haxthausen[1]

[1] DTU Compute, Technical University of Denmark, Lyngby, Denmark
aeha@dtu.dk
[2] Department of Engineering, Aarhus University, Aarhus, Denmark
hdm@eng.au.dk
[3] DINFO, University of Florence, Firenze, Italy
alessandro.fantechi@unifi.it

Abstract. In the railway domain safety is guaranteed by an interlocking system which translates operational decisions into commands leading to field operations. Such a system is safety critical and demands thorough formal verification during its development process. Within this context, our work has focused on the extension of a compositional model checking approach to formally verify interlocking system models for lines with multiple stations. The idea of the approach is to decompose a model of the interlocking system by applying cuts at the network modelling level. The paper introduces an alternative cut (the linear cut) to a previously proposed cut (border cut). Powered with the linear cut, the model checking approach is then applied to the verification of an interlocking system controlling a real-world multiple station line.

Keywords: Railway interlocking · Compositional verification · Model checking

1 Introduction

A *railway* is a mechanised means of mass movement where diverse vehicles take paths on a shared space/network of tracks. Its main feature is guidance by mechanical contact of wheels on rails. Switch points are introduced to dynamically change the network topology allowing a vehicle to change tracks. Another distinctive feature is the poor braking response time given the physical properties of wheel on rail rolling friction. Such features impose hard restrictions on traffic, vehicle movements, and network configuration.

To regulate traffic, a railway *signalling system* [14] is deployed as an information processing/transmission control loop. The system monitors the status of

H.D. Macedo and A.E. Haxthausen—The authors' research, conducted at DTU Compute, was funded by the RobustRailS project granted by Innovation Fund Denmark.

A. Fantechi—The author's research was funded by Villum Fonden.

© Springer International Publishing AG 2017
C. Barrett et al. (Eds.): NFM 2017, LNCS 10227, pp. 146–162, 2017.
DOI: 10.1007/978-3-319-57288-8_11

vehicles and track elements issuing network re-configuration and vehicle dispatch commands. The usually deployed monitoring scheme assumes that the network under control is divided into sections with train detection equipment and the existence of additional track side elements such as signals. The status (occupied or clear) of train detection sections, position of points, and configuration of track side elements (e.g. the setting of signals) is relayed to the control system. Issued decisions are then transmitted back to each element affecting its configuration (e.g.: issuing a change in point position) and vehicle movements (e.g.: sending dispatch commands to trains through signals).

The technology/operation mode of signalling systems ranges from basic human communication, for instance telecommunications between stakeholders (human controllers, station masters, and vehicle operators), to advanced automation where computers are responsible for the whole control loop. Usually the different systems are used heterogeneously through a network. Several of the recent railway disasters were due to signalling system failures[1] in networks lacking *automated* control.

Automated systems require railway engineers/architects to define the appropriate operation requirements, for instance in the form of routes: each prescribing the path and the required network configuration for safe train traversal along that path. When the system issues a dispatch route command, the network must be reconfigured to comply with such requirements. In addition, the system must ensure the required configuration is maintained during the traversal. And above all, the command must not lead to a safety violation. For that purpose an *interlocking system* takes the responsibility of safely transform each dispatch decision into the control commands that must be executed before a proceed command to a train is issued.

Such responsibility demands for standards in the development of the software controlling interlocking systems. The standard CENELEC 50128 [1] labels such software with the highest safety integrity level (SIL4), and highly recommends the usage of formal methods and formal verification in its development process. However, full formal verification of interlocking systems demands heavy if not infeasible computational resources[2], a phenomenon known as the state explosion problem. The pioneering research in model checking and in applying model checking to the domain of railways [3–5, 7, 9, 20] has developed techniques allowing the verification of models of the interlocking systems controlling larger and highly-complex networks. For example, abstraction techniques can be applied at the domain modelling level before the model checking is performed [9]. Other very efficient techniques applied for real world railways are bounded model checking [8] and k-induction [19]. The state explosion problem can also be tamed using techniques that allow a compositional approach to the model checking task [10]: the model checker must prove that assumptions imply the guarantees of each

---

[1] For instance the July 2016 rural Southern-Italy head-on train collision would have been prevented if automated train detection equipment had been in place.

[2] A model of the interlocking for a fairly simple network may lead to the potential inspection of an astronomical number of states (e.g. in the order of 10^{51} [11]).

contract of the component. The authors report that this technique allowed the verification of a real world station.

Pursuing the same goal, in a previous work [11] we described a compositional approach to the verification of safety properties of models of interlocking systems controlling lines with multiple stations. The approach was developed in the context of the RobustRailS research project[3] extending an automated method for the formal verification of the new Danish interlocking systems [17–19]. The idea in our previous work was based on the observation that decomposing a network at specific points which satisfy a given topological configuration (called *border cut*, see Fig. 1) generates sub-models corresponding to a complete partition of disjoint, connected components of the state space. It is therefore straightforward to combine the results of checking each sub-model to compute the result of checking the monolithic model. This is the case as the routes that can be set inside one sub-model are completely independent from those in the other sub-model.

Fig. 1. Border cut dividing the network topology into two parts.

We have then realised that the *border cut* configuration does not occur in some real world networks, but instead a similar configuration (that we call *linear cut*, see Sect. 3.1), in which the routes of the two sub-models partially overlap, is frequent. Inspired by the already cited compositional approach [10], where a similar route overlap is taken into account, we have modified our compositional approach to consider *linear cut* configurations as the points at which to cut a network into sub-models. This requires a finer analysis of the interferences between sub-models, but again we show that checking each sub-model allows the result of checking the monolithic model to be computed, with significant verification time savings.

The exposition of our results is structured as follows: in Sect. 2 we recall some principles of railway interlocking systems and present the RobustRailS verification method and toolkit on the top of which we have built our compositional approach; in Sect. 3 we present our approach using a divide-and-conquer strategy: we introduce the *linear cut* and explain how our method first uses this to divide a network into sub-networks, then generates sub-models and finally conquer the model checking results for these. The soundness and completeness of the approach is proved in Sect. 4, and in Sect. 5 we report on the results given

---

[3] In Denmark, in the years 2009–2021, new interlocking systems that are compatible with the standardised European Train Control System (ETCS) Level 2 [2] will be deployed in the entire country within the context of the Danish Signalling Programme. In the context of the RobustRailS project accompanying the signalling programme on a scientific level, the approach is applied to the new systems.

by the application of our compositional approach to a typical example and to a real-world line that nearly reached the capacity bounds of the adopted tools when proved as a whole. In both cases the results show that significant gains in verification effort can be achieved. Section 6 summarises the achieved results and discusses possible future extensions and improvements of the work presented here, especially in the direction of addressing interlocking systems that control large stations.

2   The New Danish Route-Based Interlocking Systems

In this section we introduce briefly the new Danish interlocking systems and the domain terminology. The subsequent Sect. 2.1 explains different components of a specification of an interlocking system which is compatible with ERTMS/ETCS Level 2 [2], and Sect. 2.2 explains how the safety properties are verified.

2.1   Specification of Interlocking Systems

The specification of a given route-based interlocking system $I = (N, R)$ consists of two components: (N) a railway network, and (R) an interlocking table.

Railway Networks. A railway network in ETCS Level 2 consists of a number of track and track-side elements of different types[4]: linear sections, points, and marker boards. Figure 2 shows an example layout of a railway network having six linear sections (b10,t10,t12,t14,t20,b14), two points (t11,t13), and eight marker boards (mb10, ..., mb21). These terms, and their functionality within the railway network, will be explained in more detail in the next paragraphs.

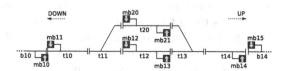

Fig. 2. An example railway network layout.

A *linear section* is a section with up to two neighbours: one in the *up* end, and one in the *down* end. For example, the linear section t12 in Fig. 2 has t13 and t11 as neighbours at its up end and down end, respectively. In Danish railway's terminology, *up* and *down* denote the directions in which the distance from a reference location is *increasing* and *decreasing*, respectively. The reference location is the same for both up and down, e.g., an end of a line. For simplicity, in the examples and figures in the rest of this article, the *up* (*down*) direction is assumed to be the left-to-right (right-to-left) direction.

---

[4] Here we only show types that are relevant for the work presented in this article.

A *point* can have up to three neighbours: one at the *stem*, one at the *plus* end, and one at the *minus* end, e.g., point t11 in Fig. 2 has t10, t12, and t20 as neighbours at its stem, plus, and minus ends, respectively. The ends of a point are named so that the *stem* and *plus* ends form the straight (main) path, and the *stem* and *minus* ends form the branching (siding) path. A point can be switched between two positions: PLUS and MINUS. When a point is in the PLUS (MINUS) position, its *stem* end is connected to its *plus* (*minus*) end, thus traffic can run from its *stem* end to its *plus* (*minus*) end and vice versa. It is not possible for traffic to run from *plus* end to *minus* end and vice versa.

Linear sections and points are collectively called (train detection) sections, as they are provided with train detection equipment used by the interlocking system to detect the presence of trains. Note that sections are bidirectional, i.e., trains are allowed to travel in both directions (but not at the same time).

Along each linear section, up to two *marker boards* (one for each direction) can be installed. A marker board can only be seen in one direction and is used as reference location (for the start and end of routes) for trains going in that direction. For example, in Fig. 2, marker board mb13 is installed along section t12 for travel direction up. Contrary to legacy systems, there are no physical signals in ETCS Level 2, but interlocking systems have a *virtual signal* associated with each marker board. Virtual signals play a similar role as physical signals in legacy systems: a virtual signal can be OPEN or CLOSED, respectively, allowing or disallowing traffic to pass the associated marker board. However, trains (more precisely train drivers) do not see the virtual signals, as opposed to physical signals. Instead, the aspect of virtual signals (OPEN or CLOSED) is communicated to the onboard computer in the train via a radio network. For simplicity, the terms *virtual signals*, *signals*, and *marker boards* are used interchangeably throughout this paper.

Interlocking Tables. An interlocking system constantly monitors the status of track-side elements, and sets them to appropriate states in order to allow trains travelling safely through the railway network under control. The new Danish interlocking systems are route-based. A *route* is a path from a *source* signal to a *destination* signal in the given railway network. A route is called an *elementary route* if there are no signals that are located between its source signal and its destination signal, and that are intended for the same direction as the route.

In railway signalling terminology, *setting* a route denotes the process of allocating the resources – i.e., sections, points, and signals – for the route, and then *locking* it exclusively for only one train when the resources are allocated.

An *interlocking table* specifies the elementary routes in the given railway network and the conditions for setting these routes. The specification of a route r and conditions for setting r include the following information, that will be needed while verifying the expected properties:

- $src(r)$ – the source signal of r,
- $dst(r)$ – the destination signal of r,
- $path(r)$ – the list of sections constituting r's path from $src(r)$ to $dst(r)$,

- *overlap*(r) – a list of the sections in r's *overlap*[5], i.e., the buffer space after dst(r) that would be used in case trains overshoot the route's path,
- *points*(r) – a map from points[6] used by r to their required positions,
- *signals*(r) – a set of protecting signals used for flank or front protection [14] for the route, and
- *conflicts*(r) – a set of conflicting routes which must not be set while r is set.

Table 1 shows an excerpt of an interlocking table for the network shown in Fig. 2. Each row of the table corresponds to a route specification. The column names indicate the information of the route specifications that these columns contain. As can be seen, one of the routes has id 1a, goes from mb10 to mb13 via three sections t10, t11 and t12 on its path, and has no overlap. It requires point t11 (on its path) to be in PLUS position, and point t13 (outside its path) to be in MINUS position (as a protecting point). The route has mb11, mb12 and mb20 as protecting signals, and it is in conflict with routes 1b, 2a, 2b, 3, 4, 5a, 5b, 6b, and 7.

Table 1. Excerpt of the interlocking table for the network of Fig. 2. The overlap column is omitted as it is empty for all routes. (p = PLUS, m = MINUS)

Id	src	dst	path	points	signals	conflicts
1a	mb10	mb13	t10;t11;t12	t11:p;t13:m	mb11;mb12;mb20	1b;2a;2b;3;4;5a;5b;6b;7
..	...	...	...	...	...	...
7	mb20	mb11	t11;t10	t11:m	mb10;mb12	1a;1b;2a;2b;3;5b;6a

2.2 The RobustRailS Verification Method and Toolkit

This section describes shortly the RobustRailS verification method and toolkit that we use as verification technology. For detailed information, see [6,16–19].

The method for modelling and verifying railway interlocking systems is a combination of formal methods and a domain-specific language (DSL) to express network diagrams and interlocking tables. According to this, a toolkit consisting of the following components is provided.

- *An editor and static checker* [6] for editing and checking that a DSL specification $I = (N, R)$ (describing an interlocking system) follows certain well-formedness rules.

---

[5] An overlap section is needed when, for the short distance of a marker board to the end of the section, there is the concrete danger that a braking train stops after the end of the section, e.g. in adverse atmospheric conditions.

[6] These points include points in the path and overlap, and points used for *flank* and *front protection*. Sometimes it is required to protect tracks occupied by a train from another train not succeeding to brake in due space. For details about flank and front protection, see [14].

– The bounded *model checker* of RT-Tester [12,15] which we use for performing k-induction proofs as explained in [19].
– *Generators* transforming a DSL specification $I = (N, R)$ of an interlocking model into inputs to the model checker:
  • a behavioural model m_I (a Kripke structure) of the interlocking system and its environment, defining the state space and possible state transitions, and
  • the required safety properties given as a state invariant (expressing that there are no hazards like train collisions). The invariant is a conjunction of high-level safety properties $\mathcal{H}$ over the variables of the interlocking system model. An $\mathcal{H}$-property is satisfied by an interlocking specification I, written as $\mathcal{H}(I)$, if it is valid in the model of the interlocking system m_I. $\mathcal{H}(I)$ is valid in the model m_I can be written as $m_I \models \forall e : E_N \cdot \mathcal{P}_{\mathcal{H}}(e)$, where E_N is either the subset of all linear sections or all point sections in N and $\mathcal{P}_{\mathcal{H}}(e)$ is a section property related to $\mathcal{H}$.

For details of the models and properties, see [19].

The tools can be used to verify the design of an interlocking system in the following steps:

1. A DSL specification of the configuration data (a network layout and its corresponding interlocking table) is constructed in the following order:
   (a) first the network layout,
   (b) and then the interlocking table (this is either done manually or generated automatically from the network layout).
2. The static checker verifies whether the configuration data is statically well-formed according to the static semantics [18] of the DSL.
3. The generators instantiate a generic behavioural model and generic safety properties with the well-formed configuration data to generate the model input of the model checker and the safety properties.
4. The generated model instance is then checked against the generated properties by the bounded model checker performing a k-induction proof.

The static checking in step (2) is intended to catch errors in the network layout and interlocking table, while the model checking in step (4) is intended to catch safety violations in the control algorithm of the instantiated model.

The tool-chain associated with the method has been implemented using the RT-tester framework [12,15]. The bounded model checker in RT-tester uses the SONOLAR SMT solver [13] to compute counterexamples showing the violations of the base case or induction step. Using this SMT solver rather than a SAT solver allowed us to use very efficient bit-vector operations.

As proof technique in step 4, we used k-induction as this was the most promising (cf. the comparison with other techniques in [19]), however, our compositional method could also be used in combination with other proof techniques.

3 Method

We now proceed to describe the details of how we use the locality features of railway networks to verify large interlocking systems in a compositional manner. The idea is to decompose the model into smaller models that are separately verified for safety properties, and to show that under given conditions such separate verifications are enough to guarantee that the whole network satisfies the safety properties as well. We show that a multi-station interlocking system satisfies such conditions if a suitable (and natural) divide strategy is applied. The strategy provides a completely automated method to verify this class of interlocking systems.

3.1 Linear Cuts on Multiple Station Lines

The typical pattern of a railway is a line connecting multiple stations. Without loss of generality, we can consider a line, denoted $\mathcal{A} \vdash\!\dashv \mathcal{B}$, corresponding to a *network* diagram consisting of two stations denoted by A and B, interconnected by one or several linear sections. More complex multi-station layouts can be obtained by concatenation of such elementary lines.

To divide multiple station lines we search for an interface $\mathcal{I}$, which we define as a linear section[7] with an up and down marker board subject to certain conditions described further below. A cut is then applied producing two sub-networks:

- The $\mathcal{A}$ network defined as the A station and the interface $\mathcal{I}$. An entry marker board is added on the up (B) side of this network.
- The $\mathcal{B}$ network defined as the B station and the interface $\mathcal{I}$. An entry marker board is added on the down (A) side of this network.

With the required configuration of marker boards on the interface and the addition of entry marker boards, the two sub-networks fulfil the required marker board configuration at borders of a railway network.

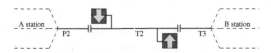

Fig. 3. The multiple station line pattern where sections T2 and T3 connect two stations A and B.

Fig. 4. Resulting $\mathcal{A}$ network.   **Fig. 5.** Resulting $\mathcal{B}$ network.

---

[7] The extension of the interface to divide networks with parallel tracks is straightforward and defines the interface as a set $\mathcal{I}$ of linear sections dividing a network into disjoint and valid connected sub-networks.

For example in Fig. 3 we depict a highlight of a line network diagram in which T2 connects two stations A and B. In the example A contains element P2 and its down neighbours and B contains elements T3 and its up neighbours. Linear section T2 configures a candidate to a linear cut, which results in the two networks illustrated in Figs. 4 and 5, where the linear section (T2) is kept in both as it defines the interface $\mathcal{I}$.

To guarantee that the compositional approach (to be described in next subsection) is sound, the interface $\mathcal{I}$ must satisfy the following *linear cut conditions* *(LCCs)*:

1. there is an up marker board on the upper part of the interface section $\mathcal{I}$ and a down marker board on the down part;
2. the two networks ($\mathcal{A}$ and $\mathcal{B}$) resulting from the cut described above must only have $\mathcal{I}$ in common;
3. no *flank/front protection* requirements for routes in the up (down) sub-network $\mathcal{B}$ ($\mathcal{A}$) depends on elements outside $\mathcal{B}$ ($\mathcal{A}$), except for routes in down (up) direction with destination marker board mounted in $\mathcal{I}$ (i.e. routes that end at the entrance of the A (B) station).

3.2   A Compositional Model Checking Approach

In the division process a network is inspected in search for regions that present candidate patterns to be cut, that is, linear sections of the form T2 of Fig. 3. The search is then recursively applied to the created sub-networks, until either no more suitable cut points can be found or the sub-networks produced are already sufficiently small.

The linear cut allows to automate the compositional verification of multi-station interlocking systems by dividing the network in sub-networks by means of four steps:

1. Search the network for suitable interfaces satisfying the LCCs. For each interface instantiate the $\mathcal{A} \vdash\!\dashv \mathcal{B}$ pattern and divide recursively the network into sub-networks as described in Subsect. 3.1.
2. For each of the resulting sub-networks N_i, complete the specification of a sub-interlocking system using the interlocking table generator mentioned in item 1 of Sect. 2.2. The resulting specifications are called the N_i interlocking specifications.
3. Statically check each of the resulting N_i specifications and generate the models m_{N_i} (called the N_i models) and properties to be verified using the checker and generator mentioned in item 2 and item 3, respectively, of Sect. 2.2.
4. Verify the m_{N_i} models following item 4 of Sect. 2.2.

4   Soundness and Completeness of the Approach

To prove that the decomposition approach is *sound* and *complete* one needs to show that the result of checking any of the high-level safety properties $\mathcal{H}$

(as defined in Subsect. 2.2) for the $\mathcal{A}$ and $\mathcal{B}$ sub-models implies the result of checking the same property $\mathcal{H}$ for the $\mathcal{A} \vdash \mathcal{B}$ monolithic model, and vice versa. (The extension to more than one sub-model is then straightforward). First we prove soundness and then completeness.

4.1 Soundness

Soundness can be rephrased in terms of $\mathcal{H}$'s related invariant $\mathcal{P}_{\mathcal{H}}$. If the invariant holds for every section in the $\mathcal{A}$ interlocking specification and for every section in the $\mathcal{B}$ interlocking specification we can conclude the whole interlocking specification $\mathcal{A} \vdash \mathcal{B}$ satisfies $\mathcal{H}$, meaning its related invariant $\mathcal{P}_{\mathcal{H}}$ holds for every section in the $\mathcal{A} \vdash \mathcal{B}$ interlocking specification.

Given that $\mathcal{H}$-properties are universal quantifications over the sets of linear/point sections[8], a natural strategy to produce such a proof is to decompose the property in terms of the disjoint sets of sections defining the A and B stations, and the interface $\mathcal{I}$. That is, the $\mathcal{H}$ related property $\mathcal{P}_{\mathcal{H}}$ holds for every section in the $\mathcal{A} \vdash \mathcal{B}$ network, if $\mathcal{P}_{\mathcal{H}}$ holds for every section of the network containing the A station, for the interface section $\mathcal{I}$, and for every section of the network containing the B station. In mathematical terms, if we denote by $E_{\mathcal{A}}$ the set of sections of an interlocking specification $\mathcal{A}$, it corresponds to rewrite the formulation of the satisfiability of $\mathcal{H}$ by the model of $\mathcal{A} \vdash \mathcal{B}$, i.e. $m_{\mathcal{A} \vdash \mathcal{B}} \models \forall e : E_{\mathcal{A} \vdash \mathcal{B}} \cdot \mathcal{P}_{\mathcal{H}}(e)$, into:

$$m_{\mathcal{A} \vdash \mathcal{B}} \models (\forall e : A \cdot \mathcal{P}_{\mathcal{H}}(e)) \wedge \mathcal{P}_{\mathcal{H}}(\mathcal{I}) \wedge (\forall e : B \cdot \mathcal{P}_{\mathcal{H}}(e)) \tag{1}$$

The aforementioned rewrite leads one to decompose the proof into three lemmas. The first two relate the local properties satisfied by $\mathcal{A} \vdash \mathcal{B}$ and $\mathcal{A}$ and similarly by $\mathcal{A} \vdash \mathcal{B}$ and $\mathcal{B}$.

Lemma 1. *Consider a line interlocking specification with A and B stations satisfying the $\mathcal{A} \vdash \mathcal{B}$ pattern, the $\mathcal{A}$ and $\mathcal{B}$ interlocking specifications resulting from the application of a linear cut, a high-level safety property $\mathcal{H}$ and its related invariant $\mathcal{P}_{\mathcal{H}}$. We relate the outcome of evaluating $\mathcal{H}(\mathcal{A})$ and $\mathcal{H}(\mathcal{A} \vdash \mathcal{B})$ through the following implication:*

$$m_{\mathcal{A} \vdash \mathcal{B}} \models \forall e : A \cdot \mathcal{P}_{\mathcal{H}}(e) \Leftarrow m_{\mathcal{A}} \models \forall e : A \cdot \mathcal{P}_{\mathcal{H}}(e)$$

Proof. By contradiction. Let us assume that in $m_{\mathcal{A}}$ the property $\mathcal{P}_{\mathcal{H}}$ holds for every section in A and there is a section e in A such that $\mathcal{P}_{\mathcal{H}}(e)$ does not hold in the $m_{\mathcal{A} \vdash \mathcal{B}}$ model. Then, as detailed in [19], there is a state s of $m_{\mathcal{A} \vdash \mathcal{B}}$, where $\mathcal{P}_{\mathcal{H}}(e)$ is false, reachable from the initial state by a sequence of transitions (trace) that we denote as t^*. The state s is characterised by an assignment of values to a vector of variables referring to the elements (sections, signals etc.) of the network. Due to the linear cut definition, such variables refer to elements that

---

[8] In the following, for simplicity, we just quantify over the whole set of sections of a network, intending that we are referring either only to point or only to linear sections according to the nature of $\mathcal{H}$.

are in the $\mathcal{A}$ or in the $\mathcal{B}$ network. Any transition in t^* changes such assignments: following t^* we can find in $m_{\mathcal{A}}$ a corresponding trace $t^{*\prime}$ that makes the same changes to the variables in the state vector of $m_{\mathcal{A}}$, skipping those transitions in t^* that do not change variables in $m_{\mathcal{A}}$. The trace $t^{*\prime}$ therefore ends in a reachable state s' in which the assignments to variables in $m_{\mathcal{A}}$ are the same of those of s, and hence $\mathcal{P}_{\mathcal{H}}(e)$ does not hold, contradicting the hypothesis.

Lemma 2. *The dual case of Lemma 1. Given by substitution of the interlocking specification $\mathcal{A}$ by $\mathcal{B}$, $\mathcal{H}(\mathcal{A})$ by $\mathcal{H}(\mathcal{B})$ and A by B.*

The two lemmas above allow us to transfer checking results on the sections of the two stations A and B to the check of the whole line; however, we still miss the contribution of the interface section, which is copied in both the $\mathcal{A}$ and $\mathcal{B}$ networks. The next lemma has this purpose.

Lemma 3. *(Interfacing lemma) Consider the $\mathcal{A} \vdash \mathcal{B}$ interlocking specification, the $\mathcal{A}$ interlocking specification and the $\mathcal{B}$ interlocking specification resulting from applying a linear cut, a high-level safety property $\mathcal{H}$ and its related invariant $\mathcal{P}_{\mathcal{H}}$. For the interface $\mathcal{I} \in E_{\mathcal{A}} \cap E_{\mathcal{B}}$ we have:*

$$m_{\mathcal{A} \vdash \mathcal{B}} \models \mathcal{P}_{\mathcal{H}}(\mathcal{I}) \Leftarrow m_{\mathcal{A}} \models \mathcal{P}_{\mathcal{H}}(\mathcal{I}) \wedge m_{\mathcal{B}} \models \mathcal{P}_{\mathcal{H}}(\mathcal{I})$$

Proof. By contradiction. Assume $\mathcal{P}_{\mathcal{H}}(\mathcal{I})$ is true in both the $m_{\mathcal{A}}$ and $m_{\mathcal{B}}$ models, but false in the $m_{\mathcal{A} \vdash \mathcal{B}}$ model. Furthermore assume s is the state of $m_{\mathcal{A} \vdash \mathcal{B}}$ falsifying $\mathcal{P}_{\mathcal{H}}(\mathcal{I})$. Thus, there is a trace t^* in $m_{\mathcal{A} \vdash \mathcal{B}}$ leading from the model's initial state to the variable assignment in s. Similarly to what said for Lemma 1 it is then possible to form a trace $t^{*\prime}$ in $m_{\mathcal{A}}$ and a trace $t^{*\prime\prime}$ in $m_{\mathcal{B}}$ from the initial states to two states s' and s'' such that the state vector has an assignment falsifying $\mathcal{P}_{\mathcal{H}}(\mathcal{I})$ in s' or s''. Thus arriving at a contradiction.

Given the proofs of Lemmas 1, 2, and 3, one is in the position to relate the result of the monolithic checking of the $\mathcal{A} \vdash \mathcal{B}$ interlocking specification with the results of the compositional approach in which the $\mathcal{A}$ and $\mathcal{B}$ interlocking specifications are checked.

Theorem 1. *(Soundness) Consider the $\mathcal{A} \vdash \mathcal{B}$ interlocking specification, the $\mathcal{A}$ and $\mathcal{B}$ interlocking specifications resulting from the application of a linear cut, and a high-level safety property $\mathcal{H}$. Then*

$$\mathcal{H}(\mathcal{A} \vdash \mathcal{B}) \Leftarrow \mathcal{H}(\mathcal{A}) \wedge \mathcal{H}(\mathcal{B})$$

which means that if $\mathcal{H}$ is satisfied by $\mathcal{A}$ and by $\mathcal{B}$, one can conclude that it is satisfied by $\mathcal{A} \vdash \mathcal{B}$.

Proof. Assume $\mathcal{H}(\mathcal{A}) \wedge \mathcal{H}(\mathcal{B})$ is true, our goal is to prove $\mathcal{H}(\mathcal{A} \vdash \mathcal{B})$, i.e. (cf. Formula (1)): $m_{\mathcal{A} \vdash \mathcal{B}} \models (\forall e : A \cdot \mathcal{P}_{\mathcal{H}}(e)) \wedge \mathcal{P}_{\mathcal{H}}(\mathcal{I}) \wedge (\forall e : B \cdot \mathcal{P}_{\mathcal{H}}(e))$ which is equivalent to:

$$m_{\mathcal{A} \vdash \mathcal{B}} \models (\forall e : A \cdot \mathcal{P}_{\mathcal{H}}(e)) \wedge m_{\mathcal{A} \vdash \mathcal{B}} \models \mathcal{P}_{\mathcal{H}}(\mathcal{I}) \wedge m_{\mathcal{A} \vdash \mathcal{B}} \models (\forall e : B \cdot \mathcal{P}_{\mathcal{H}}(e))$$

Applying Lemma 1, Lemma 2, and Lemma 3, one obtains:

$$m_{\mathcal{A}} \models (\forall e : A \cdot \mathcal{P}_{\mathcal{H}}(e)) \wedge m_{\mathcal{A}} \models \mathcal{P}_{\mathcal{H}}(\mathcal{I}) \wedge m_{\mathcal{B}} \models \mathcal{P}_{\mathcal{H}}(\mathcal{I}) \wedge m_{\mathcal{B}} \models (\forall e : B \cdot \mathcal{P}_{\mathcal{H}}(e))$$

which is equivalent to: $\mathcal{H}(\mathcal{A}) \wedge \mathcal{H}(\mathcal{B})$.

4.2 Completeness

The following theorem states that the method is complete.

Theorem 2. *(Completeness) Consider the $\mathcal{A} \vdash\!\dashv \mathcal{B}$ interlocking specification, the $\mathcal{A}$ and $\mathcal{B}$ interlocking specifications resulting from the application of a linear cut at an interface $\mathcal{I}$, and a high-level safety property $\mathcal{H}$. Assume that for each internal section b of $\mathcal{A} \vdash\!\dashv \mathcal{B}$ which appears as a border section in one of the subnetworks $\mathcal{A}/\mathcal{B}$ (i.e. b is an $\mathcal{B}/\mathcal{A}$ neighbour to $\mathcal{I}$), there exists a finite trace prefix in $m_{\mathcal{A}\vdash\!\dashv\mathcal{B}}$ leading a train to b from some outer border of the $\mathcal{B}/\mathcal{A}$ network without changing any of the variables that only exist in $m_{\mathcal{A}}/m_{\mathcal{B}}$. Then*

$$\mathcal{H}(\mathcal{A} \vdash\!\dashv \mathcal{B}) \Rightarrow \mathcal{H}(\mathcal{A}) \wedge \mathcal{H}(\mathcal{B})$$

which means that if $\mathcal{H}$ is dissatisfied by $\mathcal{A}$ or by $\mathcal{B}$, one can conclude that it is dissatisfied by $\mathcal{A} \vdash\!\dashv \mathcal{B}$.

Proof. Assume that $\mathcal{H}$ is dissatisfied by $\mathcal{A}/\mathcal{B}$, and let t be the associated counter example (trace). t can now be lifted to a counter example $t_{\mathcal{A}\vdash\!\dashv\mathcal{B}}$ in $m_{\mathcal{A}\vdash\!\dashv\mathcal{B}}$ by first extending the states of t with the additional variables of $m_{\mathcal{A}\vdash\!\dashv\mathcal{B}}$ mapped to their initial states, and then, if the t trace involves a train entering $\mathcal{I}$ from the border b at the $\mathcal{B}/\mathcal{A}$ side of $\mathcal{I}$, this extended trace should be preceded by a trace prefix from $m_{\mathcal{A}\vdash\!\dashv\mathcal{B}}$ leading the train to b from some outer border of $\mathcal{B}/\mathcal{A}$ without changing any of the variables that only exist in $m_{\mathcal{A}}/m_{\mathcal{B}}$.

5 Experiments

In this section we present the results of applying our decomposition approach to an invented line $(\mathcal{A} \vdash\!\dashv \mathcal{B})$ with two stations and to a real world case study with eight stations. Both lines exhibit the pattern of a line with multiple stations which cannot be divided using the *border cut* defined in our previous work [11].

5.1 Experimental Approach

For each of the case studies, we put the method described in Sect. 3.2 in practice by first obtaining sub-networks (in XML format) according to the divide strategy. Then for each sub-network, we use the RobustRailS verification tool [17–19] to generate a model instance and safety properties, and then to verify that the generated safety properties hold in the model.

We also use the RobustRailS verification tool to monolithically verify the railway network (without decomposing it) such that we can compare verification metrics for the compositional approach with verification metrics for the monolithic approach.

While verifying each instance we measure (in seconds) the real time taken to obtain the verification result and what was the total memory (in MB) used by the verification tool. In addition we collect some statistics about the network and model instances as presented in Tables 2 and 3. Such statistics provide a basis for complexity comparison and include: the number of linear and point sections, the number of marker boards (signals), routes, and the potential state space dimension (in logarithmic scale).

All the experiments for both case studies have been performed on a machine with an Intel(R) Xeon(R) CPU E5-1650 @ 3.6 GHz, 125 GB RAM, and running Linux 4.4.0–47.x86_64 kernel.

5.2 Two Stations Case Study

Let us consider as an example the railway line of Fig. 6 denoted $A \vdash\!\dashv B$. In it we find two stations: the set of elements $A = \{T1, P1, A1, A2, P2\}$ defines the A station, whereas the set $B = \{T3, P3, B1, B2, P4, T4\}$ defines the B station. The linear section T2 connects A and B.

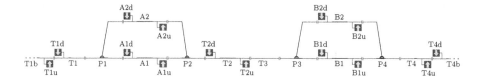

Fig. 6. $A \vdash\!\dashv B$ Network

The RobustRailS tool allows the automatic generation of interlocking tables from a given network layout, and for the $A \vdash\!\dashv B$ network it generates 24 routes. A thorough inspection of the table shows that routes can be categorised into three blocks, partitioning the network into two disjoint networks and a common interface (linear section T2). The inspection of the $A \vdash\!\dashv B$ route table reveals that it makes sense to divide the $A \vdash\!\dashv B$ network into two networks, choosing the linear section T2 as an interface between a network containing the A station and a network containing the B station.

As planned, we have verified the model both compositionally and monolithically; Table 2 shows the verification metrics, first separately for the A and B networks. The metrics for the compositional analysis ($A + B$) are obtained by summing the corresponding metrics for the networks, except for the state space and the memory usage, which are calculated as the respective maximum between the two sub-networks. The table also shows the verification metrics for the monolithic analysis of the network ($A \vdash\!\dashv B$).

Table 2. Verification metrics for the $\mathcal{A} \vdash\!\dashv \mathcal{B}$ case study.

	Linears	Points	Signals	Routes	$log_{10}(|S|)$	Time	Memory
$\mathcal{A}$	6	2	9	13	38	10	186
$\mathcal{B}$	7	2	9	13	41	16	234
$\mathcal{A} + \mathcal{B}$	13	4	18	26	41	26	234
$\mathcal{A} \vdash\!\dashv \mathcal{B}$	10	4	14	24	68	68	556

In all cases the verification tool succeeded to verify the safety properties. As it can be observed the verification time and memory usage of the compositional analysis $(\mathcal{A} + \mathcal{B})$ is, as expected, much better than for the monolithic analysis of $(\mathcal{A} \vdash\!\dashv \mathcal{B})$: The verification time is approximately three times faster and the memory usage (234 MB) is more than halved.

Moreover, if the verification for the $\mathcal{A}$ and $\mathcal{B}$ networks were run in parallel, our compositional approach would achieve a running time of just 16 s. Even though memory consumption would increase in this case, the parallelisation would still use less memory resources (the sum of individual memory usages: 420 MB) than the monolithic case (556 MB).

5.3 EDL: The Real World Case Study

The **EDL** is the first regional line in Denmark to be commissioned in the Danish Signalling Programme. The line spreads over 55 km from the station in Roskilde to Næstved's station, with 8 small to medium sized stations, and the statistics shown in Table 3 gives insight into its composition.

With the definition of the linear cut it is now directly possible to cut the **EDL** network into eight sub-networks, each corresponding to an **EDL** station. Six of the sub-networks (Gadstrup, Havdrup, Herfølge, Tureby, Haslev, and Holme-Olstrup) are of fairly similar complexity, while two (L. Skensved and Køge) are more complex. With such a division we decompose the verification of the interlocking system for **EDL** into the separate verification of the eight stations.

As in the $\mathcal{A} \vdash\!\dashv \mathcal{B}$ case study, the verification tool succeeded to verify the safety properties for the eight sub-interlocking systems and the verification metrics show that for the compositional analysis (see the entry Compositional in Table 3) the verification time is approximately a third (approx. 1.5 h) of that for the monolithic analysis (approx. 4 h). Furthermore, the compositional analysis uses less than half of the memory resources (9243 MB) because we only need as much as the maximum value of memory used to verify each sub-interlocking. Although we are still far from the memory bounds of the used machine in this experiment, such memory reduction is important when checking real world interlocking systems where a single station with a complex network may quickly exhaust the amount of memory available. As already discussed, if run in parallel our compositional approach would achieve a much better running time. Even though memory consumption would increase, the parallelisation would only use

Table 3. Verification metrics for the **EDL** case study.

	Linears	Points	Signals	Routes	$log_{10}(|S|)$	Time	Memory
Gadstrup	14	3	16	21	73	62	567
Havdrup	10	2	12	14	51	19	264
L. Skensved	15	3	16	21	75	72	616
Køge	58	23	62	75	337	5170	9243
Herfølge	6	2	10	14	39	13	210
Tureby	6	2	10	14	39	11	203
Haslev	10	2	12	14	51	14	256
Holme-Ol	12	2	16	20	63	22	352
Compositional	131	39	154	193	337	5383	9243
EDL	110	39	126	179	651	14352	22476

roughly 50% (the sum of the individual memory usages: 11711 MB) of the memory resources than the monolithic case. The parallel verification time is dominated by the time to verify the Køge station, which is the largest of the network: actually, the internal layouts of the stations do not present candidates for linear cuts, so they are not further decomposed in this approach.

6   Conclusion

We have presented a compositional approach to the problem of model checking large railway interlocking systems. This approach, built on top of tools providing support for efficient verification of this kind of systems, is tailored to the characteristics of multi-station interlocking systems, that is, systems that control a line connecting several stations. The approach extends our previous work [11], by a new, realistic division process which can be applied in cases where the previous, simpler approach is not applicable. The approach has successfully been applied to a real world line with eight stations in which case it achieved significant improvements in verification time and memory usage compared to the previous non compositional verification process.

In order to compositionally address more general network layouts the *linear cut* concept put forward in this paper needs to be generalised. An immediate extension is to combine it with the border cut concept introduced in our previous work [11]: such interesting strategy should not demand any special efforts beyond the practicalities involved. But the generalisation of the concepts to the application to interlocking systems controlling large stations, which exhibit highly complex and densely connected networks, requires a novel cut concept, which is the subject of some of our new, ongoing work. In that case the main source of difficulty stems from the fact that a division of a large station into smaller areas implies that some routes have to go through the operated cuts, a situation that is not exhibited by the multiple station lines we have addressed till now.

Actually, we have seen that the interface elements in the linear cut have the destination signals of routes coming from both sides of the interface: in the cut the added markerboard behaves as an abstraction of the removed subnetwork. We are currently studying a similar abstraction principle to support the more complex cut configuration required to address large station interlocking systems.

Another topic for future work could be to formalise the proofs done in Sect. 4 by using a proof assistant like Coq or Isabelle.

Acknowledgement. The authors would like to express their gratitude to Jan Peleska and Linh Hong Vu with whom Anne Haxthausen developed the RobustRailS verification method and tools used in the presented work.

References

1. CENELEC European Committee for Electrotechnical Standardization. EN 50128:2011 - Railway applications - Communications, signalling and processing systems - Software for railway control and protection systems (2011)
2. European Railway Agency. ERTMS - System Requirements Specification - UNISIG SUBSET-026, April 2014. http://www.era.europa.eu/Document-Register/Pages/Set-2-System-Requirements-Specification.aspx
3. Ferrari, A., Magnani, G., Grasso, D., Fantechi, A.: Model checking interlocking control tables. In: Schnieder, E., Tarnai, G. (eds.) FORMS/FORMAT 2010 - Formal Methods for Automation and Safety in Railway and Automotive Systems, pp. 107–115. Springer, Heidelberg (2010)
4. Hvid Hansen, H., Ketema, J., Luttik, B., Mousavi, M.R., Pol, J., Santos, O.M.: Automated verification of executable UML models. In: Aichernig, B.K., Boer, F.S., Bonsangue, M.M. (eds.) FMCO 2010. LNCS, vol. 6957, pp. 225–250. Springer, Heidelberg (2011). doi:10.1007/978-3-642-25271-6_12
5. Haxthausen, A.E., Bliguet, M., Kjær, A.A.: Modelling and verification of relay interlocking systems. In: Choppy, C., Sokolsky, O. (eds.) Monterey Workshop 2008. LNCS, vol. 6028, pp. 141–153. Springer, Heidelberg (2010). doi:10.1007/978-3-642-12566-9_8
6. Haxthausen, A.E., Østergaard, P.H.: On the use of static checking in the verification of interlocking systems. In: Margaria, T., Steffen, B. (eds.) ISoLA 2016. LNCS, vol. 9953, pp. 266–278. Springer, Cham (2016). doi:10.1007/978-3-319-47169-3_19
7. Haxthausen, A.E., Peleska, J., Kinder, S.: A formal approach for the construction and verification of railway control systems. Form. Asp. Comput. **23**(2), 191–219 (2011)
8. Haxthausen, A.E., Peleska, J., Pinger, R.: Applied bounded model checking for interlocking system designs. In: Counsell, S., Núñez, M. (eds.) SEFM 2013. LNCS, vol. 8368, pp. 205–220. Springer, Cham (2014). doi:10.1007/978-3-319-05032-4_16
9. James, P., Moller, F., Nguyen, H.N., Roggenbach, M., Schneider, S., Treharne, H.: Techniques for modelling and verifying railway interlockings. Int. J. Softw. Tools Technol. Transf. **16**(6), 685–711 (2014)
10. Limbrée, C., Cappart, Q., Pecheur, C., Tonetta, S.: Verification of railway interlocking - compositional approach with OCRA. In: Lecomte, T., Pinger, R., Romanovsky, A. (eds.) RSSRail 2016. LNCS, vol. 9707, pp. 134–149. Springer, Cham (2016). doi:10.1007/978-3-319-33951-1_10

11. Macedo, H.D., Fantechi, A., Haxthausen, A.E.: Compositional verification of multistation interlocking systems. In: Margaria, T., Steffen, B. (eds.) ISoLA 2016. LNCS, vol. 9953, pp. 279–293. Springer, Cham (2016). doi:10.1007/978-3-319-47169-3_20

12. Peleska, J.: Industrial-strength model-based testing - state of the art and current challenges. In: Petrenko, A.K., Schlingloff, H. (eds.) 8th Workshop on Model-Based Testing, Rome, Italy, vol. 111, Electronic Proceedings in Theoretical Computer Science, pp. 3–28. Open Publishing Association (2013)

13. Peleska, J., Vorobev, E., Lapschies, F.: Automated test case generation with SMT-solving and abstract interpretation. In: Bobaru, M., Havelund, K., Holzmann, G.J., Joshi, R. (eds.) NFM 2011. LNCS, vol. 6617, pp. 298–312. Springer, Heidelberg (2011). doi:10.1007/978-3-642-20398-5_22

14. Theeg, G., Vlasenko, S.V., Anders, E.: Railway Signalling & Interlocking: International Compendium. Eurailpress, Hamburg (2009)

15. Verified Systems International GmbH. RT-Tester Model-Based Test Case and Test Data Generator - RTT-MBT - User Manual (2013). http://www.verified.de

16. Vu, L.H., Haxthausen, A.E., Peleska, J.: A domain-specific language for railway interlocking systems. In: Schnieder, E., Tarnai, G. (eds.) FORMS/FORMAT 2014–10th Symposium on Formal Methods for Automation and Safety in Railway and Automotive Systems, pp. 200–209. Institute for Traffic Safety and Automation Engineering, Technische Universität Braunschweig (2014)

17. Vu, L.H., Haxthausen, A.E., Peleska, J.: Formal modeling and verification of interlocking systems featuring sequential release. In: Artho, C., Ölveczky, P.C. (eds.) Formal Techniques for Safety-Critical Systems. Communications in Computer and Information Science, vol. 476, pp. 223–238. Springer International Publishing, Cham (2015)

18. Vu, L.H.: Formal development and verification of railway control systems. In the context of ERTMS/ETCS Level 2. Ph.D. thesis, Technical University of Denmark, DTU Compute (2015)

19. Linh Hong, V., Haxthausen, A.E., Peleska, J.: Formal modelling and verification of interlocking systems featuring sequential release. Sci. Comput. Program. **133**, 91–115 (2017)

20. Winter, K.: Symbolic model checking for interlocking systems. In: Flammini, F. (ed.) Railway Safety, Reliability, and Security: Technologies and Systems Engineering. IGI Global (2012)

Modular Model-Checking of a Byzantine Fault-Tolerant Protocol

Benjamin F. Jones[(✉)] and Lee Pike

Galois, Inc., Portland, OR 97204, USA
{bjones,leepike}@galois.com

Abstract. With proof techniques like IC3 and k-induction, model-checking scales further than ever before. Still, fault-tolerant distributed systems are particularly challenging to model-check given their large state spaces and non-determinism. The typical approach to controlling complexity is to construct ad-hoc abstractions of faults, message-passing, and behaviors. However, these abstractions come at the price of divorcing the model from its implementation and making refactoring difficult. In this work, we present a model for fault-tolerant distributed system verification that combines ideas from the literature including calendar automata, symbolic fault injection, and abstract transition systems, and then use it to model-check various implementations of the Hybrid Oral Messages algorithm that differ in the fault model, timing model, and local node behavior. We show that despite being implementation-level models, the verifications are scalable and modular, insofar as isolated changes to an implementation require isolated changes to the model and proofs. This work is carried out in the SAL model-checker.

1 Introduction

Fault-tolerant distributed systems are famously complex, yet are the backbone of life-critical systems, such as commercial avionics. Consequently, this class of systems demands high-assurance of correct design and implementation. Formal verification can help provide that assurance.

The verification of this class of systems has usually been at the algorithmic level, eliding details about a concrete implementation. Historically, it has relied on formal models verified by interactive theorem-proving [1–4]. If formal verification is to be introduced into the workflow of system designers, though, we need more automated methods that scale for implementation-level models. (Mostly) automated proof techniques are required to reduce the need for specialized verification expertise. We also need programmatic verification of *implementations*. System designers create software and hardware implementations to test, simulate, and deploy. Discrepancies between implementations and algorithmic models can arise if the latter is abstracted too much from the former [5], particularly if those abstractions are ad-hoc and system specific. Furthermore, as implementations are modified to explore the design space, it is easy for the formal model and the implementation to become inconsistent, so the verification is no longer about the system deployed.

© Springer International Publishing AG 2017
C. Barrett et al. (Eds.): NFM 2017, LNCS 10227, pp. 163–177, 2017.
DOI: 10.1007/978-3-319-57288-8_12

There are at least two classes of abstractions that separate protocol-level models of fault-tolerant distributed algorithms from their implementations. One is to intertwine the environmental model with the system description. For example, the behaviors of nodes are naturally specified as a transition system in which transitions are guarded by the node's fault state. But faults are part of the environment; an implementation does not typically use its own fault status to choose actions! Another class of abstractions is used to simplify models. For example, message passing might be abstracted with shared state, or a node's local behavior is elided and instead, the output is constrained by a *specification* of the behavior.

In this paper, we present a fault-tolerant distributed systems model, and use that model to verify several variant implementations of the Byzantine fault-tolerant Hybrid Oral Messages algorithm (OMH) [3]. The model combines various ideas from the literature to build scalable and modular formal models suitable for infinite-state model-checking, and it reduces the need for ad-hoc abstractions and optimizations. In Sect. 2, we present the important aspects of the model, including calendar automata, originally developed by Dutertre and Sorea [6], symbolic fault-injection, and abstract transition systems for verification.

We use the model to verify implementation-level models of OMH in which message passing is explicit, nodes are not forced to execute strictly synchronously, and voting is explicit. In short, the models corresponds closely with an implementation of the algorithm. In Sect. 3, we first describe OMH, then an implementation of it that uses the Boyer-Moore Fast Majority Vote algorithm (Fast MJRT) [7]. We then describe a set of modular invariants, such that the invariants only concern specific aspects of the model (e.g., faults, local node behavior, or the passage of time). The verification is interesting in its own right, as it is the first fully parametric (on the number of nodes) model-checked *implementation* of the algorithm.

In Sect. 4, we first show that despite being implementation-level, the model is scalable. Developing invariants requires some user guidance, and isolated changes to an implementation should require isolated modifications to the model and proof. To demonstrate this, we modify the OMH implementation along the dimensions of faults (by adding an omissive-asymmetric fault type [8]), time (by making a time-triggered model), and local behavior (by changing the majority vote to a mid-value selection) and show that in each case, the modifications are small and modular.

Our primary contributions are (1) a model-checking verification of an OMH implementation, and (2) demonstrating that our modeling paradigm allows for modular verification. Additionally, the idea of symbolic fault injection (Sect. 2.2) is novel.

Finally, in Sect. 5 we describe related work, and we make concluding remarks in Sect. 6.

The models and experiments reported herein can be found online.[1]

---

[1] https://github.com/GaloisInc/mmc-paper.

2   Formal Model

Here we describe our formal model specialized for fault-tolerant distributed systems. The model draws on three principal abstractions: calendar automata, symbolic fault injection, and abstract transition systems; we describe each below.

2.1   Calendar Automata

Real-time system verification in general-purpose model-checkers requires an explicit formalism of real-time progression. Trying to encode real-time clocks directly is difficult; in particular, one must avoid Zeno's paradox in which no progress is made because state transitions simply update real-valued variables by an infinite sequence of decreasing amounts whose sum is finite. To avoid this problem, Dutetre and Sorea developed *calendar automata* [6], which is itself inspired by event calendars used in discrete-event simulation. Rather than encoding "how much time has passed since the last event", it encodes "how far into the future is the next scheduled event", and a real-valued variable representing the current time is updated to the next event time.

Define a set of *events* $e_0, e_1, \ldots, e_n \in E$. For now, we do not define events; intuitively, an event is a set of state variables (shortly, we will associate events with messages sent in a distributed system). When an event is *enabled*, the transitions over events are enabled; otherwise, the variables stutter (maintain the same value).

An *event calendar* $\{(e_0, t_0), (e_1, t_1), \ldots, (e_n, t_n)\}$ is a set of ordered pairs (e_i, t_i) called *calendar events* where $e_i \in E$ is an event and $t_i \in \mathbb{R}$ is a *timeout*, the time at which the event is scheduled. We denote element (e_i, t_i) of an event calendar by c_i.

Let *cal* be an event calendar and $c_i, c_j \in cal$ be calendar events. Define an ordering on calendar events such that $c_i \leq c_j$ iff $t_i \leq t_j$, and $min(cal) = \{c_i | \forall c_j \in cal, c_i \leq c_j\}$ are the minimum elements of *cal*.

Let a transition system $\mathcal{M} = (S, I, \rightarrow)$, be a set of states S, a set of initial states $I \subseteq S$, and a transition relation $\rightarrow \subseteq S \times S$. We implicitly assume a set of state variables such that each state $\sigma \in S$ is a total function that maps state variables to values. We sometimes prime a state to denote that it satisfies the transition relation: $\sigma \rightarrow \sigma'$. We also sometimes use a variable assignment notation to describe what state variables are specifically updated: e.g., $\sigma' = \sigma[v := v + 1]$.

We distinguish two special state variables in a transition system: (1) $now \in \mathbb{R}$ denotes the current time in the state, and (2) *cal* is an event calendar.

The following laws must hold of a transition system $\mathcal{M}$ implementing a calendar automaton:

1. Time is initialized to be less than or equal to every calendar timeout: $\forall \sigma \in I$, $\forall (e_i, t_i) \in \sigma(cal)$, $\sigma(now) \leq t_i$.
2. In all states, if the current time is strictly less than every calendar event, then the only enabled transition is a *time progress* update: $\forall \sigma \in S$, $\forall (e_i, t_i) \in \sigma(cal)$, if $\sigma(now) < t_i$, then $\forall \sigma'$ such that $\sigma \rightarrow \sigma'$, $\sigma' = \sigma[now := min(cal)]$.

3. In all states, if the current time equals a timeout, then the only transitions enabled are calendar event updates associated with the timeout: $\forall \sigma \in S$, $\exists (e_i, t_i) \in \sigma(cal)$ such that $\sigma(now) = t_i$ implies $\forall \sigma'$ such that $\sigma \to \sigma'$, $\sigma'(now) = \sigma(now)$, $\sigma'(c_j) = \sigma(c_j)$ for all $c_j \in \sigma(cal)$ such that $c_j \neq c_i$ (recalling that by convention, $c_i = (e_i, t_i)$), and $c_i \notin \sigma'(cal)$.

From the definitions, it follows that in every state, the timeouts are never in the past, and that time is monotonic:

Lemma 1 (Future timeouts). $\forall \sigma \in S$, $(e_i, t_i) \in \sigma(cal)$, $\sigma(now) \leq t_i$.

Lemma 2 (Monotonic time). $\forall \sigma, \sigma' \in S$, if $\sigma \to \sigma'$, then $\sigma'(now) \geq \sigma(now)$.

Proofs of these two lemmas are straightforward and omitted.

In a distributed system, it is convenient to distinguish global actions and local actions. Global actions are principally interprocess communication, while local actions are those carried out by each process to update its local state and produce new messages to broadcast. While both global and local actions can both be modeled as events in a calendar automata, doing so is generally overkill and complicates the model. From the global perspective, individual processes can update their local state atomically.

Again, following Dutetre and Sorea, we associate calendar events with channels in a distributed system [6]. Specializing calendars to message passing does not lose generality since all external communication from an individual process can be abstracted as message passing. Furthermore, fault models can be abstracted to act over channels rather than processes [9]. The calendar introduces real-time constraints on when processes send and receive messages.

Assume processes are indexed from a finite set Id. A *channel* from process i to j is an ordered pair (i, j). Fix a set of messages Msg. Given a channel and a timeout, let *send* be a relation on messages sent on a channel at a given time:

$$send \subseteq Id \times Id \times \mathbb{R} \times Msg$$

So $send(i, j, t, m)$ holds iff i sends to j message m at time t. Likewise, let

$$recv \subseteq Id \times Id \times \mathbb{R} \times Msg$$

be a relation on messages received on a channel at a time, so that $recv(i, j, t, m)$ holds iff the message m received by j from i at time t.

In the absence of faults, we require that messages received were previously sent and not previously received: if $(i, j, t, m) \in recv$, then $\exists t'$ such that $(i, j, t', m) \in recv$ where $t' < t$, and $\neg \exists t''$ such that $t' < t'' < t$ and $(i, j, t'', m) = (i, j, t, m)$. (We address faults in Sect. 2.2.)

Then an event calendar for sending and receiving messages on channels is the union of the *send* and *recv* relations.

The event of receiving a message initiates a process to update its local transition system and generate additional messages to send. When the process is updating its local transition system, the event calendar is paused. That is, updating an event $(i, j, t, m) \in recv$ also includes updating j's transition system.

2.2 Symbolic Fault Injection: A Synchronous Kibitzer

The typical approach to modeling faults is to add new state variables to each process representing its fault state. Then a node chooses actions based on its fault state. As a simple example, we might define a node that sends a good message if it is non-faulty and a bad message otherwise. In pseudo-code using guarded commands, its definition might look like the following:

```
node:
  health: Fault_Type;
  faulty(health)     --> send(bad_msg);
  non_faulty(health) --> send(good_msg);
```

But this approach mixes the specification of a node's behavior with the fault model, an aspect of the environment. Generally, nodes do not contain state variables assigned to their faults, or use their fault-status to determine their behavior![2] The upshot is that combining faults and node state divorces the specification from its implementation.

A second difficulty with model-checking fault-tolerant systems in general is that modeling faults requires adding state and non-determinism. The minimum number of additional states that must be introduced may depend non-obviously on other aspects of the fault model, specific protocol, and system size. Such constraints lead to "meta-model" reasoning, such as the following, in which Rushby describes the number of data values that a particular protocol model must include to model the full range of Byzantine faults (defined later in this section):

> To achieve the full range of faulty behaviors, it seems that a faulty source should be able to send a *different* incorrect value to each relay, and this requires n different values. It might seem that we need some additional incorrect values so that faulty relays can exhibit their full range of behaviors. It would certainly be safe to introduce additional values for this purpose, but the performance of model checking is very sensitive to the size of the state space, so there is a countervailing argument against introducing additional values. A little thought will show that .... Hence, we decide against further extension to the range of values [10].

The second problem is the most straightforward to solve. In infinite-state model-checking, we can use either the integers or the reals as the datatype for values. Fault-tolerant voting schemes, such as a majority vote or mid-value selection (see Sect. 3), require only equality, or a total order, respectively, to be defined for the data.

The solution to the first problem is more involved. Our solution is to introduce what we call a *synchronous kibitzer* that symbolically injects faults into the model. The kibitzer decomposes the state and transitions associated with the fault model from the system itself. For the sake of concreteness in

---

[2] There are exceptions; for example, benign faults may be detected by a node itself (e.g., in a built-in-test).

describing the synchronous kibitzer, we introduce a particular fault model, the hybrid fault model of Thambidurai and Park [11]. This fault model distinguishes Byzantine, symmetric, and manifest faults. It applies to broadcast systems in which a process is expected to broadcast the same value to multiple receivers. A *Byzantine* (or *arbitrary*) fault is one in which a process that is intended to broadcast the same value to other processes may instead broadcast arbitrary values to different receivers (including no value or the correct value). A *symmetric* fault is one in which a process may broadcast the same, but incorrect, value to other processes. Finally, a *manifest* (or *benign*) fault is one in which a process's broadcast fault is detectable by the receivers; e.g., by performing a cyclic redundancy check (CRC) or because the value arrives outside of a predetermined window.

Define a set of fault types

$$\text{Faults} = \{none, byz, sym, man\}.$$

As in the previous section, let Id be a finite set of process indices, and let the variable

$$faults : Id \rightarrow \text{Faults}$$

range over possible mappings from processes to faults.

The hybrid fault model assumes a broadcast model of communication. A $broadcast : Id \rightarrow 2^{Id} \rightarrow \mathbb{R} \rightarrow Msg \rightarrow 2^E$ takes a sender, a set of receivers, a real-time, and a message to send each receiver, and returns a set of calendar events:

$$broadcast(i, R, t, m) = \{m | j \in R \text{ and } send(i, j, t) = m\}$$

With this machinery, we can define the semantics of faults by constraining the relationship between a message broadcast and the values received by the recipients. For a nonfaulty process that broadcasts, every recipient receives the sent message, and for symmetric faults, there is no requirement that the messages sent are the ones received, only that every recipient receives the same value:

$$nonfaulty\_constraint =$$
$$\forall i, j \in Id, t \in \mathbb{R}$$
$$faults(i) = none$$
$$\text{implies } recv(i, j, t) = send(i, j, t)$$

$$sym\_constraint =$$
$$\forall i, j, k \in Id, t \in \mathbb{R}$$
$$(\quad faults(i) = sym$$
$$\text{and } broadcast(i, \{j, k\}, t, m))$$
$$\text{implies } recv(i, j, t) = recv(i, k, t)$$

Byzantine faults are left completely unconstrained.

Thus, faults can be modeled solely in terms of their effects on sending and receiving messages. A node's specification does not have to depend on its fault status directly.

If the *faults* mapping is a constant, then faults are permanently but non-deterministically assigned to nodes. However, we can easily model *transient faults* in which nodes are faulty temporarily by making *faults* a state variable that is updated non-deterministically. Whether we model permanent or transient faults, a *maximum fault assumption* (MFA) describes the maximum number of faults permitted in the system. The *faults* mapping can be non-deterministically updated during execution while satisfying the MFA using a constraint such as $faults \in \{f \mid mfa(f)\}$, where the MFA is defined by the function *mfa*.

2.3 Abstract Transition Systems

Due to the sheer size of implementation-level models, manually examining counterexamples is tedious. To scale up verification, we use abstract transition systems (also known as disjunctive invariants) [12,13]. In this context, an abstract transition system, relative to a given transition system $\mathcal{M} = (S, I, \rightarrow)$, is a set of state predicates $A_1, \ldots, A_n$ over S and a transition system $\mathcal{M}_* = (S_*, I_*, \rightsquigarrow)$ such that:

1. $S_* = \{a_1, \ldots, a_n\}$ is a set of "abstract states" which correspond one-to-one with the state predicates A_i.
2. $\forall s \in I, \exists i : a_i \in I_* \land A_i(s)$.
3. $\forall a_i \in S_* \, \forall \sigma, \sigma' : A_i(\sigma) \land \sigma \rightarrow \sigma' \implies A_{k_1}(\sigma') \lor \ldots \lor A_{k_m}(\sigma')$ where $\{a_{k_1}, \ldots, a_{k_m}\}$ are the abstract states to which $\mathcal{M}_*$ may transition from a_i.

For verification purposes, it is important to note that if $\mathcal{M}$ and $\mathcal{M}_*$ satisfy the requirements above, then $A_1 \lor \ldots \lor A_n$ is an inductive invariant of $\mathcal{M}$. We may use such an invariant freely as a powerful assumption in the proof of other invariants (see Sect. 3.3).

The use of abstract transition systems not only allows us to scale proofs farther, but also to improve traceability and debugging while developing a model. In models like the ones described in Sect. 4.2 where there are on the order of 100 state variables and counterexample traces could be 30 steps long, the designer can be easily lost trying to identify the essence. In such cases, the values of the abstract predicates can serve to focus the designer's attention on one particular mode of the system where the counter example is taking place. At the present we do not have a good method for synthesizing the predicates $A_1, \ldots, A_n$ automatically for general systems; they must be supplied by the user.

3 Modeling and Verification for Oral Messages

The Hybrid Oral Messages (OMH) algorithm [3] is a variant of the classic Oral Messages (OM(m)) algorithm [14], originally developed by Thambidurai and Park [11] to achieve distributed consensus in the presence of a hybrid fault model. However, OMH had a bug, as originally formulated, which was corrected and the mended algorithm was formally verified by Lincoln and Rushby using interactive theorem-proving [3].

First, we briefly describe the algorithm, sketch our instantiation of the model for the particular protocol in Sect. 2, then describe it's invariants.

3.1 OMH(m) Algorithm

OMH is a recursive algorithm that proceeds in rounds of communication. Here we give a recursive specification for OMH(m), parameterized by the number of rounds, m. Consider a finite set of nodes N. Distinguish one node as the *general*, g, and the remaining nodes $L = N \setminus \{g\}$ as the *lieutenants*. We assume the identity of any general or lieutenant cannot be spoofed. Broadcast communication proceeds in rounds. Denote any message that is detectably faulty (e.g., fails a CRC) or is absent, by ERR. Additionally, in the algorithm, nodes report on values they have previously received. In doing so, nodes must differentiate *reporting* ERR from an ERR itself. Let R denote that an error is being reported. Finally, let V be a special, designated value.

The algorithm is recursively defined for $m \geq 0$:

– OMH(0): g broadcasts a value to each lieutenant and the lieutenants return the value received (or ERR).
– OMH(m), $m > 0$:
  1. g broadcasts a value to each lieutenant, l.
  2. Let l_v be the value received by $l \in L$ from g. Then for each l, execute OMH($m-1$), assigning l to be the general and $L \setminus \{l\}$ to be the lieutenants. l sends l_v, or R if $l_v = ERR$.
  3. For each lieutenant $l \in L$, remove all ERR values received in Step 2 from executing OMH($m - 1$). Compute the majority value over the remaining values, or V if there is no majority. If the majority value is R, return E.

In particular, OMH(1) includes two rounds of broadcast communication: one in which the general broadcasts, and one in which the lieutenants exchange their values.

OMH is designed to ensure *validity* and *agreement* properties under suitable hypotheses on the number and type of faults in the system. Validity states that if the general is nonfaulty, then every lieutenant outputs the value sent by the general. Agreement states that each lieutenant outputs the same value. More formally, Let l_i, l_j denote the outputs of lieutenants $i, j \in L$, respectively, and let v be the value the general broadcasts:

$$\forall i. \quad l_i = v \text{ (Validity)} \qquad \Big| \qquad \forall i,j. \quad l_i = l_j \text{ (Agreement)}$$

We described a hybrid fault model in Sect. 2.2. Under that fault model, validity and agreement hold if $2a + 2s + b + 1 \geq n$, where n is the total number of nodes, a is the number of Byzantine (or asymmetric) faults, s is the number of symmetric faults, and b is the number of benign faults. Additionally, the number of rounds m must be greater or equal to the number of Byzantine faults, a [3,11].

3.2   Model Sketch

We have implemented OMH(1) (as well as the variants described in Sect. 4.2) in the Symbolic Analysis Laboratory (SAL) [15]. SAL contains a suite of model-checkers. In our work, we use infinite-state (SMT-based) k-induction [6].

We follow Rushby [10] in "unrolling" the communication among lieutenants into two sets of logical nodes: *relays* and *receivers*. Relays encode the lieutenants' Step 2 of the OMH algorithm, in which they rebroadcast the values received from the general after filtering manifestly bad messages, while the receivers encode the voting step. We refer to the general as the *source*. The unrolling shows that a generalization of the original algorithm holds: the number of relays and receivers need not be the same. We model communication through one-way, typed channels. The source broadcasts a message to each relay which, in turn, each broadcast their messages to all receivers.

The relays and receivers explicitly send and receive messages and store them in local buffers as needed. In addition, the receivers implement the Fast MJRY algorithm [7].

Our SAL model defines seven transition systems in total: clock, source, relay (parametrized over an ID), receiver (parametrized over an ID), observer, abstractor, and abstract_monitor. The first four of these are composed asynchronously, in an intermediate system we label system, and share access to a global calendar consisting of event slots (message, time), one for each channel in the system. The clock transition system is responsible for updating a global variable t (called *now* in Sect. 2.1) representing time according to the rules for calendar automata.

The asynchronous composition of the system relaxes the original specification of the algorithm considerably. For example, in our implementation, a receiver may receive a message from one relay before another relay has received a message from the source. We only require that all relays and receivers have executed before voting. With a general asynchronous model, it is easy to refine it further; for example, we refine it to a time-triggered model in Sect. 4.2.

The observer is a synchronous observer [16] that encodes the validity and agreement properties as synchronously-composed transition systems. State variables denoting validity and agreement are set to be false if the receivers have completed their vote but the respective properties do not hold.

Finally, the abstractor and abstract_monitor encode an abstract transition system for the system, as described in Sect. 2.3.

3.3   Invariants

To make the proof scalable, we specify inductive invariants to be used by SAL's k-induction engine. There are 11 invariants, falling into five categories:

1. *Calendar automata*: Lemmas relating to the calendar automata model. These include lemmas such as time being monotonic, channels missing messages if there is no calendar event, and only nodes associated with a calendar event may execute their local transition systems.

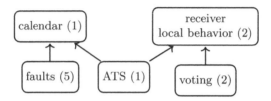

Fig. 1. Invariant classification and dependencies.

2. *Abstract transition sytem (ATS)*: Lemmas relating the ATS states to the implementation states.
3. *Receiver local behavior*: Lemmas describing the modes of behavior of the receivers. The major modes of their behavior are receiving messages, then once it has filled its buffer, it votes, and after voting returns the result. An additional lemma notes that the messages currently received plus missing messages equals the total number of expected messages.
4. *Faults*: Lemmas characterizing the effect of a fault in a single broadcast. Examples include lemmas stating that if a node receives a faulty message, some "upstream" node in the communication path was faulty. Another example is that the faults of messages latched by a node in its buffer match the faults ascribed to the sender in the calendar event.
5. *Voting*: Lemmas proving that the Fast MJRTY algorithm implements a majority vote, if one exists. These lemmas are nearly verbatim transcriptions from the journal proofs for the algorithm [7].

The proof structure is shown in Fig. 1. The number of lemmas per category are shown in parentheses. Arrows denote dependencies. For example, the ATS lemmas depend on both the calendar automata and receiver state-machine lemmas. As can be seen, the proof structure is modular. The calendar lemmas are general and independent of any particular protocol or fault model. Similarly, lemmas about the internal behavior of a receiver is independent of the global protocol behavior. It is also independent of the effect of faults on the system— the only "knowledge" of faults that receiver has is whether a fault is benign or not. Lemmas about the behavior of faults in the system are also independent of the particular protocol being modeled. Likewise, lemmas about the particular voting algorithm used depend only on the receiver's internal behavior. Only the ATS depends on both calendar-specific and local state-machine results, since it is an abstraction of the entire system implementation. Recall, however, that the ATS is a convenience for debugging and can be elided.

4   Experimental Results

Here we present two classes of experimental results. First, we demonstrate the scalability results of the verification, despite the low-level modeling. Then we describe modularity results, demonstrated by making modifications to the model and re-validating the model.

4.1   Scalability

We present benchmarks in Fig. 2. The benchmarks were performed on a server with Intel Xeon E312xx (Sandy Bridge) CPUs. The table provides execution times in seconds, with a timeout limit of one hour, for verifying the model, given a selected number of relays and receivers. The voting logic is in the receivers, so they have substantially more state than the relays, and dominate the execution time. The execution times sums the execution times for verifying each of the eleven lemmas individually, as well as the final agreement and validity theorems. Each proof incurs the full startup, parsing, type-checking, and model-generation time of SAL. Observe the theorems hold even in the degenerate cases of one relay or one receiver.

		\multicolumn{10}{c}{Receivers}
		1	2	3	4	5	6	7	8	9	10
	1	7	9	12	15	21	25	32	40	54	74
	2	17	14	21	30	42	53	74	99	144	-
	3	21	22	40	50	81	102	155	279	-	-
	4	27	34	59	99	141	237	1114	-	-	-
Relays	5	22	94	125	335	**T**	1406	-	-	-	-
	6	36	132	2966	844	2457	-	-	-	-	-
	7	83	487	**T**	**T**	-	-	-	-	-	-
	8	298	**T**	**T**	-	-	-	-	-	-	-
	9	1428	**T**	-	-	-	-	-	-	-	-
	10	**T**	-	-	-	-	-	-	-	-	-

Fig. 2. Benchmark of full proof computation time for OMH(1) implementation. Times are in seconds with a timeout (**T**) limit of one hour. Dashes ('-') denote no benchmark was run.

As a point of comparison, Rushby presents an elegant high-level model of OM(1), also in SAL [10]. For small numbers of relays/receivers, the verification of Rushby's model is much faster, likely due to making only one call to SAL. However, for six relays and two receivers, it takes 449 seconds and timeouts (at one hour) for seven relays and two receivers. Checking Rushby's model requires use of symbolic, BDD-based model-checking techniques which are well-known to scale poorly. On the other hand, our model requires the use of k-induction which scales well, but requires (inductive) invariants to be provided.

4.2   Modular Verification

To demonstrate the modularity of the modelling and verification approach, in this section, we explore variants to the model and report the effort required to implement the modifications and repair the proofs. The results are summarized in Fig. 3 and sketched below. In the table, for each modification, we report how much of the model must be modified. We report on four aspects of the system:

which transition systems are modified (as described in Sect. 3.2), how many definitions have to be added or modified, the number of invariants that have to be added or modified, and which invariant classes (as defined in Sect. 3.3) those lemmas belong to. We modify the implementation along the axes of faults, time, and local node behavior.

	Transition systems (7 total)	Definitions (58 total)	Invariants (11 total)	Invariant classes (5 total)
Omissive Asymmetric Faults	none	1 new, 2 modified	2 modified	faults
Time-Triggered Messaging	source, relays, receivers, ATS	3 new	2 modified, 3 modified	calendar, faults
Mid-Value Selection	receivers	4 new, 3 modified	2 modified	ATS, voting

Fig. 3. Refactoring effort for protocol modifications, measured by which portions of the model have to be modified.

Omissive Asymmetric Faults. Removing faults already described by the fault model is easy. Recall that in our model faults do not appear in the system specification and only operate on the calendar. Removing a fault from the system requires only setting the number of a particular kind of faults to zero in the maximum fault assumption.

Adding new kinds of faults requires more work but is still modular. Consider adding *omissive asymmetric faults*, a restriction of Byzantine faults in which a broadcaster either sends the correct value or a benign fault [8], to the fault model. Doing so requires modifying none of transition systems, because of the synchronous kibitzer. We add a new uninterpreted function definition for omissive asymmetric faults, then modify the type of faults, and their effect on the calendar. Two invariants, both in the class of invariants cover faults, are extended to cover the cases where a sender is omissive asymmetric.

Time-Triggered Messaging. A *time-triggered* distributed system is one in which nodes are independently clocked, but clock constraints allow the model to appear as if it is executing synchronously [17].

Changing the model to be time-triggered principally requires making the source, relays, and receivers driven explicitly by the passage of time (we do not model clock drift or skew). As well, a "receive window" is defined at which messages from non-faulty nodes should be received. Messages received outside the window are marked as coming from manifest-faulty senders. The model requires three new definitions to encode nondeterministic message delay and two are small helper functions. The guards in the relays and receivers are modified to latch messages received outside the receive windows as being manifest faults.

The ATS definition is modified to track the times in the calendar, not just the messages. Two new calendar invariants are introduced, stating that the calendar messages are either empty, or their time-stamps fall within the respective message windows. Then, three invariants classifying faults are relaxed to allow for the possibility of faulty nodes sending benign messages.

Mid-Value Selection. Our OMH(1) model leverages a majority vote in order to tolerate faults. Another choice for the fault masking algorithm used is mid-value selection. This choice is common in applications involving hardware, signal selection, or cases where information about congruence is useful. To implement mid-value selection in our model, we allow messages sent to take values in $\mathbb{R}$ and the receiver transition system is modified in two ways. First, a second buffer is introduced which will hold the sorted contents of the main buffer once voting has commenced. Second, a mid-value select function is called on the sorted buffer and the result is stored as the receiver's vote. The only invariants needing modification were the ATS definition (to account for the values stored by the new buffer and the relation between it and the main buffer) and the voting invariant.

4.3 Proof Effort Remarks

The lemmas described in Sect. 3.3 are constructed by-hand and represent multiple days of effort, but that effort includes both model and protocol construction and generalization as well as verification. The counterexamples returned by SAL are very useful for strengthening invariants, but tedious to analyze—a model with five relays and two receivers contains 90 state variables, and there are known counterexamples to models that size [3]. Once we developed the synchronously-composed ATS observer, the verification effort was sped up considerably.

The invariants are surprisingly modular. One benefit of a model-checking based approach is that it is automated to rerun a proof of a theorem omitting lemmas to see if the proof still holds. This allowed us to explore reducing dependencies between invariants related to different aspects of the system.

The modifications to the implementation described in Sect. 4.2 took at most hours to develop. Moreover, most of the invariants do not concern the specific protocol modeled at all, and we hypothesize that for completely different fault-tolerance protocols, only the modeling aspects related to the protocol behavior and local node behavior would change, and the invariant structure would remain modular.

Moreover, we are agnostic about how lemmas are discovered. As techniques like IC3 scale, they may be discovered automatically. k-induction in infinite-state model-checking blurs the lines between interactive and automated theorem proving. IC3 can even be strengthened using k-induciton [18].

5 Related Work

The Oral Messages algorithm and its variants and its variants have a long history of formal verification. OM(1) was verified in both the PVS and ACL2 interactive theorem-provers [2]. Also in ACL2, an implementation of a circuit design to implement OM(1) is given [1]; the low-level model most closely relates to our level of detail. A refinement-based verification approach is used, and OM(1) is specialized to a fixed number of nodes. Bokor *et al.* describe a message-passing model for synchronous distributed algorithms that is particularly amenable to partial-order reduction for explicit-state model-checking [19]. The model is efficient for up to five nodes, but results are not presented beyond that. Very recently, Jovanović and Dutertre use a "flattened" high-level model of OM(1) as a benchmark for IC3 augmented with k-induction [18].

Moreover, our work is heavily influenced by previous verifications of fault-tolerant and real-time systems in SAL [6,10,13].

6 Conclusions

This work fits within a larger project, in collaboration with Honeywell Labs, to build an *architectural domain-specific language* (ADSL) for specifying and verifying distributed fault-tolerant systems. The ADSL should be able to synthesize both software and/or hardware implementations as well as formal models for verification. Before building such an ADSL, we needed a scalable general formal model to which to compile, leading to the work presented in this paper. We hypothesize that the ADSL will make refactoring even easier, and we can generate invariants or invariant templates useful for verification. Indeed, we have developed a preliminary ADSL that generates C code as well as formal models in SRI's Sally [18], to be described in a future paper.[3]

Beyond building an ADSL, another avenue of research is producing a formal proof that a software implementation satisfies the node specification in our formal model. While our model of node behavior is low-level, there are gaps. For example, our work is in SAL's language of guarded commands [15] and needs to be either refined or verified to be equivalent to a software implementation's semantics. Another aspect is that behavior related to networking, serialization, etc. is left abstract, implicit in the *send* and *recv* functions.

Acknowledgments. This work is partially supported by NASA contract #NNL14AA08C. We are indebted to our collaborators Brendan Hall and Srivatsan Varadarajan at Honeywell Labs, and to Wilfredo Torres-Pomales at NASA Langley for their discussions and insights. Additionally, we acknowledge that this work is heavily inspired by a series of papers authored by John Rushby.

References

1. Bevier, W.R., Young, W.D.: The proof of correctness of a fault-tolerant circuit design. Computational Logic Inc., Technical report 57 (1990). http://computationallogic.com/reports/index.html
2. Young, W.D.: Comparing verification systems: interactive consistency in ACL2. IEEE Trans. Softw. Eng. **23**(4), 214–223 (1997)

---

[3] https://github.com/GaloisInc/atom-sally.

3. Lincoln, P., Rushby, J.: A formally verified algorithm for interactive consistency under a hybrid fault model. In: 23rd Fault Tolerant Computing Symposium, pp. 402–411. IEEE Computer Society (1993)

4. Owre, S., Rushby, J., Shankar, N., von Henke, F.: Formal verification for fault-tolerant architectures: prolegomena to the design of PVS. IEEE Trans. Software Eng. **21**(2), 107–125 (1995)

5. Chandra, T.D., Griesemer, R., Redstone, J.: Paxos made live: an engineering perspective. In: ACM Symposium on Principles of Distributed Computing (PODC), pp. 398–407. ACM (2007)

6. Dutertre, B., Sorea, M.: Modeling and verification of a fault-tolerant real-time startup protocol using calendar automata. In: Lakhnech, Y., Yovine, S. (eds.) FORMATS/FTRTFT -2004. LNCS, vol. 3253, pp. 199–214. Springer, Heidelberg (2004). doi:10.1007/978-3-540-30206-3_15

7. Boyer, R.S., Moore, J.S.: MJRTY-a fast majority vote algorithm. In: Boyer, R.S. (ed.) Automated Reasoning. Automated Reasoning Series, vol. 1, pp. 105–117. Springer, Dordrecht (1991)

8. Azadmanesh, M.H., Kieckhafer, R.M.: Exploiting omissive faults in synchronous approximate agreement. IEEE Trans. Comput. **49**(10), 1031–1042 (2000)

9. Pike, L., Maddalon, J., Miner, P., Geser, A.: Abstractions for fault-tolerant distributed system verification. In: Slind, K., Bunker, A., Gopalakrishnan, G. (eds.) TPHOLs 2004. LNCS, vol. 3223, pp. 257–270. Springer, Heidelberg (2004). doi:10.1007/978-3-540-30142-4_19

10. Rushby, J.: SAL tutorial: analyzing the fault-tolerant algorithm OM(1). Computer Science Laboratory, SRI International, Menlo Park, CA, CSL Technical note. http://www.csl.sri.com/users/rushby/abstracts/om1

11. Thambidurai, P., Park, Y.-K.: Interactive consistency with multiple failure modes. In: Symposium on Reliable Distributed Systems, pp. 93–100. IEEE (1988)

12. Rushby, J.: Verification diagrams revisited: disjunctive invariants for easy verification. In: Emerson, E.A., Sistla, A.P. (eds.) CAV 2000. LNCS, vol. 1855, pp. 508–520. Springer, Heidelberg (2000). doi:10.1007/10722167_38

13. Dutertre, B., Sorea, M.: Timed systems in SAL. In: SRI International, Menlo Park, CA, SDL Technical report SRI-SDL-04-03, July 2004

14. Lamport, L., Shostak, R., Pease, M.: The Byzantine generals problem. ACM Trans. Program. Lang. Syst. **4**(3), 382–401 (1982)

15. Bensalem, S., Ganesh, V., Lakhnech, Y., Muñoz, C., Owre, S., Rueß, H., Rushby, J., Rusu, V., Saïdi, H., Shankar, N., Singerman, E., Tiwari, A.: An overview of SAL. In: NASA Langley Formal Methods Workshop, pp. 187–196 (2000)

16. Rushby, J.: The versatile synchronous observer. In: Iida, S., Meseguer, J., Ogata, K. (eds.) Specification, Algebra, and Software. LNCS, vol. 8373, pp. 110–128. Springer, Heidelberg (2014). doi:10.1007/978-3-642-54624-2_6

17. Kopetz, H.: Real-Time Systems: Design Principles for Distributed Embedded Applications. Kluwer, Philadelphia (1997)

18. Javanović, D., Dutertre, B.: Property-directed k-induction. In: Formal Methods in Computer Aided Design (FMCAD) (2016)

19. Bokor, P., Serafini, M., Suri, N.: On efficient models for model checking message-passing distributed protocols. In: Hatcliff, J., Zucca, E. (eds.) FMOODS/FORTE -2010. LNCS, vol. 6117, pp. 216–223. Springer, Heidelberg (2010). doi:10.1007/978-3-642-13464-7_17

Improved Learning for Stochastic Timed Models by State-Merging Algorithms

Braham Lotfi Mediouni[✉], Ayoub Nouri, Marius Bozga, and Saddek Bensalem

Université Grenoble Alpes, CNRS, VERIMAG, 38000 Grenoble, France
braham-lotfi.mediouni@univ-grenoble-alpes.fr

Abstract. The construction of faithful system models for quantitative analysis, e.g., performance evaluation, is challenging due to the inherent systems' complexity and unknown operating conditions. To overcome such difficulties, we are interested in the automated construction of system models by learning from actual execution traces. We focus on the timing aspects of systems that are assumed to be of stochastic nature. In this context, we study a state-merging procedure for learning stochastic timed models and we propose several enhancements at the level of the learned model structure and the underlying algorithms. The results obtained on different examples show a significant improvement of timing accuracy of the learned models.

1 Introduction

A necessary condition for a successful system design is to rely on faithful models that reflect the actual system behavior. In spite of the long experience designers have on building system models, their construction remains a challenging task, especially with the increasing complexity of recent systems. For performance models, this is even harder because of the inherent complexity and the induced stochastic behavior that is usually combined with time constraints.

Machine Learning (ML) is an active field of research where new algorithms are constantly developed and improved in order to address new challenges and new classes of problems (see [13] for a recent survey). Such an approach allows to automatically build a model out of system observations, i.e., given a learning sample S, a ML algorithm infers an automaton that, in the limit[1], represents the language L of the actual system [2]. We believe that ML can be used to automatically build system models capturing performance aspects, especially the timing behavior and the stochastic evolution. Those system models may be useful for documenting legacy code, and for performing formal analyses in order to enhance the system performance, or to integrate new functionalities [11].

Despite the wide development of ML techniques, only few works were interested in learning stochastic timed models [9,10,12,14]. In this paper, we study the RTI+ algorithm [14] and we propose improvements that enhance its accuracy. This algorithm learns a sub-class of timed automata [1] augmented with

---

[1] By considering a sufficient number of observations [4].

© Springer International Publishing AG 2017
C. Barrett et al. (Eds.): NFM 2017, LNCS 10227, pp. 178–193, 2017.
DOI: 10.1007/978-3-319-57288-8_13

probabilities, called Deterministic Real-Time Automata (DRTA). Given a timed learning sample S (traces of timestamped actions of the system), the algorithm starts by building a tree representation of S, called Augmented Prefix Tree Acceptor (APTA). Then, based on statistical tests, it performs state-merging and splitting operations until no more operations are possible. In this algorithm, clock constraints are captured as time intervals over transitions and are built in a coarse fashion. These time intervals are actually considered to be the largest possible, which makes the learning procedure converge faster. However, this introduces a lot of generalization in the built APTA, by allowing timing behaviors that are not part of the actual system language L. Furthermore, we identified that such behaviors cannot be refined during the learning process. The learned model is thus not accurate from a timing point of view.

In this work, we propose a more accurate learning procedure by investigating better compromises between the time generalization introduced in the APTA and its size (and consequently its learning time). We introduce three new APTA models representing different levels of time generalization; the first model is the exact representation of the learning sample, i.e., with no generalization, while the two others introduce some generalization which is less than the original RTI+. We implemented the new variants of the RTI+ algorithm and validated them on different examples. The obtained results show that the learned models are more accurate than the original implementation, albeit the learning time is generally higher.

Outline. In Sect. 2, we discuss some related works on learning stochastic timed models. Section 3 introduces notations and key definitions used in the rest of the paper. We recall the RTI+ learning algorithm and study underlying time representation issues in Sect. 4. In Sect. 5, we present the three improvements we propose for RTI+ and discuss them. Section 6 presents experiments and results of the improved algorithms. Conclusions are drawn in Sect. 7.

2   Related Works

In the literature, several algorithms have been proposed for automata learning [2,3,7,14], mostly in the deterministic case. In the last decades, an increasing interest has been shown for learning probabilistic models, partly due to the success of verification techniques such as probabilistic and statistical model checking [5,6]. Despite this development, only few works considered the problem of learning stochastic timed models [9,10,12,14].

Most of the algorithms proposed in this setting are based on the state-merging procedure made popular by the Alergia algorithm [3]. Moreover, many of them consider Continuous-Time Markov Chains (CTMCs) as the underlying model. For instance, in [12], an algorithm is proposed for model-checking black-box systems. More recently, the AAlergia algorithm [8], initially proposed for learning Discrete-Time Markov Chains and Markov Decision Processes, was extended to learn CTMCs [9]. This work is an extension of Alergia to learn models having timed in/out actions.

Other algorithms such as RTI+ [14] and BUTLA [7] focus on learning timed automata augmented with probability distributions on discrete transitions and uniform probabilities over timing constraints. Both follow a state-merging procedure but consider different statistical tests for checking states compatibility.

In [10], authors focus on learning more general stochastic timed models, namely Generalized Semi-Markov Processes, following the same state-merging procedure. This algorithm relies on new statistical clocks estimators, in addition to the state compatibility criterion used in Alergia.

3   Background

Let Σ be a finite alphabet, Σ^* the set of words over Σ and ϵ the empty word. Let $\mathbb{T}$ be a time domain and $\mathbb{T}^*$ the set of time sequences over $\mathbb{T}$. In our work, we consider integer time values, i.e., $\mathbb{T} \subseteq \mathbb{N}$. For a set of clocks $\mathcal{C}$, let $CC(\mathcal{C})$ denote the set of clock constraints over $\mathcal{C}$. Let $\mathcal{I}$ be the intervals domain, where $I \in \mathcal{I}$ is an interval of the form $[a; b]$, $a, b \in \mathbb{T}$ such that $a \leq b$, and represents the set of integer values between a and b. Let ω be an untimed word over Σ and τ a time sequence over $\mathbb{T}$. We write $\omega \leq \omega'$ (resp. $\tau \leq \tau'$) whenever ω (resp. τ) is a prefix of ω' (resp. τ'). We also write ωu (resp. τv) for the concatenation of ω (resp. τ) and $u \in \Sigma^*$ (resp. $v \in \mathbb{T}^*$). $|\omega|$ (resp. $|\tau|$) is the size of ω (resp. τ).

3.1   Deterministic Real-Time Automata (DRTA)

A Real-Time Automaton (RTA) is a timed automaton with a single clock that is systematically reset on every transition.

Definition 1 (Real-Time Automaton (RTA)). *An RTA is a tuple $\mathcal{A} = \langle \Sigma, L, l_0, \mathcal{C}, T, inv \rangle$ where: (1) Σ is the alphabet, (2) L is a finite set of locations, (3) $l_0 \in L$ is the initial location, (4) $\mathcal{C} = \{c\}$ contains a single clock, (5) $T \subseteq L \times \Sigma \times CC(\mathcal{C}) \times \mathcal{C} \times L$ is a set of edges with a systematic reset of the clock c, (6) $inv : L \longrightarrow CC(\mathcal{C})$ associates invariants to locations.*

For more convenience, transitions are denoted as $l \xrightarrow{\sigma, I} l'$, where $\sigma \in \Sigma$ and $I \in \mathcal{I}$ is a time interval including both transition guards and location invariants. For simplicity, we also omit the systematic reset.

An RTA is deterministic (DRTA) if, for each location l and a symbol σ, the timing constraints of any two transitions starting from l and labeled with σ are disjoint, i.e., $\forall l \in L, \forall \sigma \in \Sigma, \forall t_1, t_2 \in T, t_1 = \langle l, \sigma, I_1, l_1 \rangle$ and $t_2 = \langle l, \sigma, I_2, l_2 \rangle, (I_1 \cap I_2 \neq \emptyset) \Leftrightarrow (t_1 = t_2)$. A DRTA generates timed words over $\Sigma \times \mathbb{T}$. Each timed word is a sequence of timed symbols $(\omega, \tau) = (\sigma_1, \tau_1)(\sigma_2, \tau_2)...(\sigma_m, \tau_m)$, representing an untimed word ω together with a time sequence τ. A set of n timed words constitute a *learning sample* $S = \{(\omega, \tau)^i, i \in [1; n], \omega \in \Sigma^*, \tau \in \mathbb{T}^*\}$. We denote by $\mathbb{T}^S$ the set of time values appearing in S.

A Prefix Tree Acceptor (PTA) is a tree representation of the learning sample S where locations represent prefixes of untimed words in S. Timing information is captured in a PTA in form of intervals $I \in \mathcal{I}$ over transitions. This structure is called Augmented PTA (APTA). In the latter, each transition $l \xrightarrow{\sigma, I} l'$ is annotated with a frequency that represents the number of words in S having l' as a prefix. An APTA can be seen as an acyclic DRTA annotated with frequencies. Let $\mathcal{N} : T \longrightarrow \mathbb{N}$ be this annotation function. Given a DRTA $\mathcal{A}$, a pair $(\mathcal{A}, \mathcal{N})$ is an *annotated* DRTA, denoted $DRTA^+$.

3.2 Stochastic Interpretation of a DRTA

A DRTA starts at the initial location l_0 with probability 1. It moves from a location to another using transitions in T. At each location l, a transition is chosen among the set of available transitions T_l. Selecting a transition consists of choosing a timed symbol (σ_i, τ_i). A probabilistic strategy φ that associates a probability function to each location l over the set of transitions T_l is used to make this choice: $\varphi : L \times T \longrightarrow [0, 1]$, such that $\Sigma_{t \in T_l} \varphi(l, t) = 1, \forall l \in L$. For the chosen transition $l \xrightarrow{\sigma, I} l'$, the choice of the time value is done uniformly over the time interval I. Figure 1 shows an example where two transitions labeled A and B are possible from location 1. The strategy φ associates probability 0.6 to A and 0.4 to B. Then, uniform choices on the associated time intervals are performed.

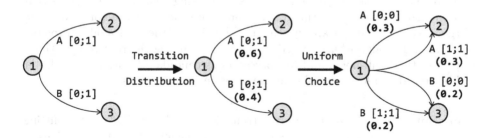

Fig. 1. Probabilistic strategy with uniform choice

4 The RTI+ Learning Procedure

RTI+ [14] is a state-merging algorithm for learning DRTA models from a sample of timed words. The algorithm first builds a PTA then reduces it by merging locations having similar behaviors, according to a given compatibility criterion. Compared to other state-merging algorithms, RTI+ relies on a time-split operation to identify the different timed behaviors and to split them into disjoint ones. The algorithm is able to learn a stochastic DRTA, i.e., a $DRTA^+$ where the strategy is obtained from the associated annotation function $\mathcal{N}$.

4.1   Building the APTA

The timed learning sample is represented as an APTA where all the time intervals span over $\mathbb{T}$. Initially, the built APTA only contains a root node consisting of the empty word ϵ. RTI+ proceeds by adding a location in the tree for each prefix of untimed words in S. Then, a transition labeled with σ is created from location l to location l' if the prefix of l' is obtained by concatenating the prefix of l and symbol σ. Finally, transitions are augmented with the largest time constraint $[0; max(\mathbb{T}^S)]$, where $max(\mathbb{T}^S) = Max\{a \in \mathbb{T}^S\}$. The annotation function $\mathcal{N}$ is built at the same time and represents transitions frequencies. In this work, we denote this construction as *generalized-bound APTA*.

Definition 2 (Generalized-bound APTA). *A generalized-bound APTA is a $DRTA^+$ $(\langle \Sigma, L, l_0, \mathcal{C}, T, inv \rangle, \mathcal{N})$ where:*

- $L = \{\omega \in \Sigma^* \mid \exists(\omega', \tau') \in S, \omega \leq \omega'\}$, $l_0 = \epsilon$,
- T *contains transitions of the form* $t = \langle \omega, \sigma, [0; max(\mathbb{T}^S)], \omega' \rangle$ *s.t.* $\omega\sigma = \omega'$, *and* $\mathcal{N}(t) = |\{(\omega'u, \tau) \in S, u \in \Sigma^*\}|$.

4.2   The Learning Process

The learning process aims to identify the $DRTA^+$ that represents the target language while reducing the size of the initial APTA. At each iteration, the algorithm first tries to identify the timing behavior of the system, by using time-split operations. The second step consists of merging compatible locations that show similar stochastic and timed behaviors. Locations that are not involved in merge or split operations are marked as belonging to the final model (promote operation). The algorithm proceeds by initially marking the root of the APTA as part of the final model and its successors as candidate locations. The latter will be considered for time-split, merge or promote operations.

Time-Split Operation. For a given transition $t = \langle l, \sigma, [a; b], l' \rangle \in T$, splitting t at a specific time value $c \in [a; b]$ consists of replacing t by two transitions t_1 and t_2 with disjoint time intervals $[a; c]$ and $[c+1; b]$, respectively. This operation alters the subtree of l' such that the corresponding timed words that used to trigger transition t with time values in $[a; c]$ (resp. $[c + 1; b]$) are reassigned to the subtree pointed by transition t_1 (resp. t_2).[2]

Merge Operation. Given a marked location l (belongs to the final model) and a candidate location l', this operation is performed by first redirecting the transitions targetting l', to l and then by folding the subtree of l' on l (see footnote 2).

---

[2] For further details, see: http://www-verimag.imag.fr/~nouri/drta-learning/Appendice.pdf.

4.3   Compatibility Evaluation

The compatibility criterion used in RTI+ is the Likelihood Ratio (LR) test. Intuitively, this criterion measures a distance between two hypotheses with respect to specific observations. In our case, the considered hypotheses are two $DRTA^+$ models: H with m transitions and H' with m' transitions ($m < m'$), where H is the model after a merge operation (resp. before a split) and H' is the model before a merge (resp. after a split). The observations are the traces of S.

We define the likelihood function that estimates how S is likely to be generated by each model (H or H'). It represents the product of the probability to generate each timed word in S^3. Note that the ith timed word $(\omega, \tau)^i$ in S corresponds to a unique path p^i in the $DRTA^+$. The probability to generate $(\omega, \tau)^i$ is the product of the probabilities of each transition in $p^i = s_1 s_2 ... s_{|\omega|}$:

$$f((\omega, \tau)^i, H) = \prod_{j=1}^{|\omega|-1} \pi((\omega_j, \tau_j)^i, s_j)$$

Where $\pi((\omega_j, \tau_j)^i, s_j)$ corresponds to the probability to transit from the location s_j to s_{j+1} in H with the jth timed symbol $(\omega_j, \tau_j)^i$. Given a learning sample S of size n, the likelihood function of H is $Likelihood(S, H) = \prod_{i=1}^{n} f((\omega, \tau)^i, H)$. The likelihood ratio is then computed as follows

$$LR = \frac{Likelihood(S, H)}{Likelihood(S, H')}$$

Let Y be a random variable following a χ^2 distribution with $m' - m$ degrees of freedom, i.e., $Y \rightsquigarrow \chi^2(m' - m)$. Then, $y = -2ln(LR)$ is asymptotically χ^2 distributed. In order to evaluate the probability to obtain y or more extreme values, we compute the p-value $pv = P(Y \geq y)$. If $pv < 0.05$, then we conclude that H and H' are significantly different, with 95% confidence.

The compatibility criterion concludes that a time-split operation is accepted whenever it identifies a new timing behavior, that is, the model after split is significantly different from the model before split ($pv < 0.05$). In contrast, a merge is rejected whenever the model after merge is significantly different from the model before merge since the merged locations are supposed to have similar stochastic and timed behaviors.

4.4   Shortcomings

The RTI+ algorithm relies on the generalized-bound APTA as initial representation of the learning sample S. As pointed out before, this kind of APTA augments an untimed PTA with the largest possible time intervals, without considering the values that concretely appear in S. This introduces an *initial generalization* that leads the APTA to accept words that do not actually belong to S and might

---

[3] Since the timed words in S are generated independently.

not belong to the target language L. In Example 1, we show that this initial generalization cannot be refined later in the learning process. More concretely, we observe that the time intervals that do not appear in S are not isolated and removed from the $DRTA^+$.

Example 1. Let us consider the following learning sample $S = \{(A,5)(B,5);$ $(A,4)(A,3); (A,3)(B,5); (B,1)(A,5); (B,3)(B,5); (B,5)(A,1)\}$. The left-hand model in Fig. 2 presents the initial $DRTA^+$ (H) of S on which we evaluate a time-split operation. The latter is expected to identify the empty interval $[0;2]$ on transition $t = \langle 1, A, [0;5], 2 \rangle$, since no timed word in S takes this transition with time values in $[0;2]$. The right-hand figure represents the model assuming a split of transition t at time value 2 (H'). The LR test returns $pv = 1$ which leads to reject the time-split operation, and hence, the empty interval $[0;2]$ is not identified during the learning process.

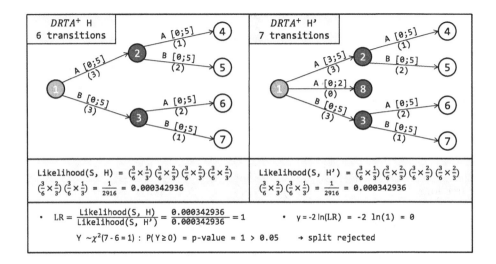

Fig. 2. Identifying empty intervals with time-split operation

The generalized-bound APTA introduces empty time intervals that cannot be removed during the learning process. To overcome this issue, we propose, in the next section, new representations of the learning sample S.

5   Learning More Accurate Models

A faithful representation of the learning sample consists of building an APTA that accepts only words in S by taking into account the time values. This can be done at different granularities, which results on different tradeoffs between the introduced initial generalization and the APTA size. We propose three different APTA models denoted unfolded, constructive-bound and tightened-bound APTAs.

5.1 Unfolded APTA

This APTA model fits perfectly the traces in S, that is, accepts exactly the timed words in S. Hence, it does not introduce any initial generalization. To build such a model, we need to consider both symbols and time values. The APTA initially contains the empty word. Locations are added for every timed prefix and corresponding transitions are created such that each transition only accepts a single time value, i.e., time intervals are equalities of the form $[a; a] \in \mathcal{I}$.

Definition 3 (Unfolded APTA). *An unfolded APTA is a $DRTA^+$ where:*

- $L = \{(\omega, \tau) \in \Sigma^* \times \mathbb{T}^* |\ \exists(\omega', \tau') \in S, \omega \leq \omega', \tau \leq \tau'\}$,
- T *contains transitions of the form* $t = \langle(\omega, \tau), \sigma, [a; a], (\omega', \tau')\rangle$ *such that: (1)* $\omega\sigma = \omega'$, *(2)* $\tau a = \tau'$, *and* $\mathcal{N}(t) = |\{(\omega'u, \tau'v) \in S, u \in \Sigma^*, v \in \mathbb{T}^*\}|$.

5.2 Constructive-Bound APTA

A more compact representation of S compared to the unfolded APTA can be obtained by reducing the size of the initial APTA. At each location, a reduction of the number of transitions is performed by grouping all the contiguous time values for the same symbol into a single transition where the time interval I is the union of the different time intervals.

Definition 4 (Constructive-bound APTA). *A constructive-bound APTA is a $DRTA^+$ where:*

- $L = \{(\omega, \{I_i\}_{i=1}^{|\omega|}), \omega \in \Sigma^*, I_i \in \mathcal{I} \mid \forall i \in [1; |\omega|], \forall c \in I_i, \exists(\omega', \tau') \in S, \forall j < i, \tau'_j \in I_j, c = \tau'_i, \omega \leq \omega'\} \cup \{l_0 = (\epsilon, \emptyset)\}$,
- T *contains transitions of the form* $t = \langle(\omega, \{I_i\}_{i=1}^{|\omega|}), \sigma, I, (\omega', \{I'_i\}_{i=1}^{|\omega'|})\rangle$ *such that: (1)* $\omega\sigma = \omega'$, *(2)* $\forall i \in [1; |\omega|], I_i = I'_i$ *and* $I'_{|\omega'|} = I'_{|\omega|+1} = I$, *and* $\mathcal{N}(t) = |\{(\omega'u, \tau'v) \in S, \forall i \in [1; |\omega'|], \tau'_i \in I'_i, u \in \Sigma^*, v \in \mathbb{T}^*\}|$.

In Definition 4, each location corresponds to a subset of timed words that have a common untimed prefix where each symbol (of the prefix) apprears with contiguous time values. A location is labeled by the given untimed prefix ω and the sequence of intervals $\{I_i\}_{i=1}^{|\omega|}$ corresponding to each symbol of ω. I_i is the interval grouping the contiguous time values for the symbol σ_i of ω. All time values of these intervals are present in at least one timed word in S. A transition is added between locations l and l' such that: (1) the concatenation of the untimed prefix relative to l and symbol σ produces the untimed prefix relative to l', and (2) adding I to the interval sequence of l gives the interval sequence of l'.

5.3 Tightened-Bound APTA

The minimal size of APTA is obtained by allowing the minimal number of transitions from each location. This minimal number is obtained by assigning at most one transition for each symbol of Σ. The initial generalization is reduced (compared to the generalized-bound APTA) by identifying the minimum (resp. the maximum) time value t_{min} (resp. t_{max}) among all the time values for each location l and symbol σ. Then, a single transition is created from l with symbol σ and a time interval $[t_{min}; t_{max}]$. We call this APTA model a *tightened-bound* APTA. It has the same structure as the generalized-bound APTA but with tighter bounds. The time interval $[t_{min}; t_{max}]$ of each transition is computed locally depending on the corresponding timed words in S.

Definition 5 (Tightened-bound APTA). *A tightened-bound APTA is a $DRTA^+$ where:*

- $L = \{\omega \in \Sigma^* \mid \exists(\omega', \tau') \in S, \omega \le \omega'\}$, $l_0 = \epsilon$,
- T *contains transitions of the form* $t = \langle \omega, \sigma, [t_{min}; t_{max}], \omega' \rangle$ *such that: (1)* $\omega\sigma = \omega'$, *(2)* $t_{min} = Min\{\tau_{|\omega'|} \mid (\omega'u, \tau) \in S\}$, *(3)* $t_{max} = Max\{\tau_{|\omega'|} \mid (\omega'u, \tau) \in S\}$, *and* $\mathcal{N}(t) = |\{(\omega'u, \tau) \in S\}|$, *where* $u \in \Sigma^*$.

5.4 Evaluation

In this section, we discuss the proposed APTA models with respect to their ability to faithfully represent S and to their size. We consider the following sample $S = \{(A,5)(B,5); (A,4)(A,3); (A,3)(B,5); (B,3)(A,5); (B,3)(B,5); (B,1)(A,1)\}$. Figure 3 depicts the three types of APTAs representing S.

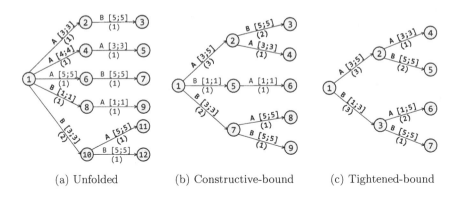

(a) Unfolded   (b) Constructive-bound   (c) Tightened-bound

Fig. 3. The three APTA models for the sample S

Initial Generalization. The unfolded APTA does not introduce any initial generalization (Fig. 3a). The constructive-bound APTA is a more compact representation of S compared to the unfolded APTA with less generalization than the generalized-bound APTA. Some generalization is introduced due to the possible combination of grouped time values. In other words, the time values of the time intervals appear in S, but the language generated by the APTA overapproximates S since it accepts more time sequences. For instance, in Fig. 3b, the timed word (A,3)(A,3) is accepted although not in S. This is due to the combination of time values coming from the timed words (A,4)(A,3) and (A,3)(B,5).

The tightened-bound APTA introduces two kinds of generalization. The first is due to the combination of grouped time values, as for the constructive-bound APTA. The second one is caused by the presence of empty intervals. An example is given in Fig. 3c where transitting from the root is possible using the timed symbol (B,2) which is not in S. This latter generalization is similar to the one we pointed out for the generalized-bound APTA albeit with more restrictive time intervals, since the empty intervals $[0; t_{min} - 1]$ and $[t_{max} + 1; max(\mathbb{T}^S)]$ are initially removed. The relationship between these models and the generalization they introduce is summarized in Fig. 4.

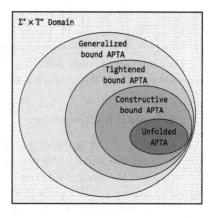

Fig. 4. Generalization introduced by the different *APTAs*

APTA Size. In terms of the size of initial representation, the unfolded APTA is the largest. The APTA size depends on the size of Σ and $\mathbb{T}^S$. The worst case is encountered when all the traces in S are of the same length N and when S contains all the combinations of symbols and time values. The resulting complete tree, in this case, represents the upper bound on the exponential number of locations and can be expressed as

$$MaxSize_{(unfolded)} = \frac{1 - (|\Sigma| \times |\mathbb{T}^S|)^{N+1}}{1 - (|\Sigma| \times |\mathbb{T}^S|)}$$

This maximum number of locations is reduced in the constructive-bound APTA by grouping contiguous time values. However, this improvement is meaningless in the case where all the time values are disjoint. For a given interval $[0; max(\mathbb{T}^S)]$, the maximum number of disjoint intervals is encountered when all the time values are disjoint and is equal to $(max(\mathbb{T}^S) + 1)$ *div* 2. The worst case number of locations of a complete tree of depth $N + 1$ is

$$MaxSize_{(constructive)} = \frac{1 - (|\Sigma| \times ((max(\mathbb{T}^S) + 1) \ div \ 2))^{N+1}}{1 - (|\Sigma| \times ((max(\mathbb{T}^S) + 1) \ div \ 2))}$$

The number of locations, in this case, is highly dependent on the size of Σ and less on the size of $\mathbb{T}^S$. This latter can be removed by allowing only one interval for each symbol at each location. This is the case of the generalized-bound APTA and the tightened-bound APTA which return the minimum number of locations.

6   Experiments

In this section, we evaluate the learned model according to its ability to accept the words belonging to L and to reject the others. This gives insight into how accurate the learned model is. A $C++$ implementation of the proposed algorithms and the considered examples can be found in http://www-verimag.imag. fr/~nouri/drta-learning. The same page also contains additional materials such as algorithms and formal definitions of the elementary operations, in addition to a discussion about the proposed models' accuracy.

6.1 Evaluation Procedure

The accuracy of the learned model can be quantified using two metrics: the precision and the recall. The precision is calculated as the proportion of words that are correctly recognized (true positives) in the learned model H' over all the words recognized by H', while the recall represents the proportion of words that are correctly recognized in H' over all the words recognized by the initial model H. The precision and the recall can be combined in a single metric called F1 score. A high F1 score corresponds to a high precision and recall, and conversely.

$$Precision(H', H) = \frac{|\{(\omega, \tau) \in \Sigma^* \times \mathbb{T}^* \mid (\omega, \tau) \in \mathcal{L}(H) \wedge (\omega, \tau) \in \mathcal{L}(H')\}|}{|\mathcal{L}(H')|}$$

$$Recall(H', H) = \frac{|\{(\omega, \tau) \in \Sigma^* \times \mathbb{T}^* \mid (\omega, \tau) \in \mathcal{L}(H) \wedge (\omega, \tau) \in \mathcal{L}(H')\}|}{|\mathcal{L}(H)|}$$

$$F1\_score(H', H) = 2 \times \frac{prec(H', H) \times recall(H', H)}{prec(H', H) + recall(H', H)}$$

Based on these metrics, we distinguish four degrees of generalization for the learned models (see Fig. 5):

1. The maximum F1 score is obtained when the exact target language $L(H)$ is learned.
2. A precision of 1 and a recall strictly lower than 1 characterize an under-approximation, i.e., the learned model H' recognizes a subset of words of $L(H)$.
3. A recall of 1 and a precision strictly lower than 1 characterize an over-approximation, i.e., the learned model H' accepts all the words of $L(H)$ in addition to extra words not in $L(H)$.
4. A precision and a recall strictly lower than 1 characterize a cross-approximation, i.e., $L(H')$ contains only a subset of words in $L(H)$ plus additional words not in $L(H)$.

Our experimental setup shown in Fig. 6, consists of three modules responsible for trace generation, model learning and model evaluation. Since we are trying to evaluate how accurate the learning algorithm is, the initial model H, designed as a $DRTA^+$, is only known by the trace generator and the model evaluator, while the model learner has to guess it. The trace generator produces a timed learning sample S and a test sample. The latter contains timed traces that do not appear in S. This sample is used to evaluate the learned model with respect to new traces that were not used during the learning phase.

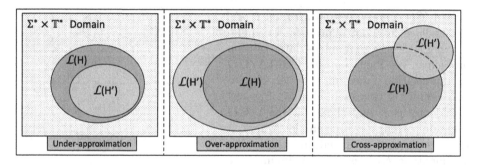

Fig. 5. Degrees of generalization of the learned language $L(H')$ with respect to the target language $L(H)$

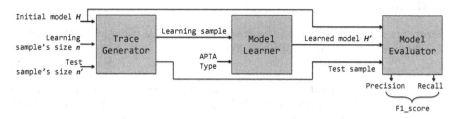

Fig. 6. Experimental setup to validate the improved learning procedure

6.2   Benchmarks

We run our experimental setup on three examples, namely, *Periodic A*, *Periodic A-B* and *CSMA/CD communication medium model*.

Periodic A is a synthetic periodic task A that executes for 1 to 3 time units in a period of 5 time units. The goal of this benchmark is to check if the algorithm is able to learn the periodicity and the duration of a single task. Two less constrained variants of this model are also considered. In both of them, we remove the periodicity of the task by setting a predefined waiting time of 5 time units after the task A finishes. In the first variant, called aperiodic contiguous-time (**ap_cont A**), the execution time of the task A can take contiguous time values in $[1; 3]$. In the second one, called aperiodic disjoint (**ap_dis A**), the execution time takes the disjoint time values 0, 2 and 4. Our goal is to check if the algorithm is able to detect the unused time values 1 and 3.

Periodic A-B consists of two sequential tasks A and B, taking execution time values, respectively, in intervals $[1;3]$ and $[1;2]$ with a periodicity of 5 time units. In this example, the learning algorithm is faced with dependencies between clock constraints for the task A, the task B and their periodicities, which is a more complex setting.

CSMA/CD communication Medium Model is a media access control protocol for single-channel networks that solves data collision problems. We focus on the **CSMA/CD** communication medium model for a 2-station network presented in [5]. Figure 7 represents the underlying **CSMA/CD** communication medium model where λ represents the propagation time. We assume that t_{max} is the maximum time elapsing between two consecutive events.

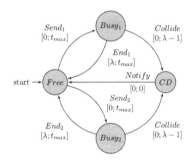

Fig. 7. CSMA/CD communication medium model for a 2-station network

6.3   Results

Experiments have been done on the described examples using a learning sample of size 200 and a test sample of size 1000.

The Synthetic Examples. Table 1 summerizes the results for **periodic A** (and variants) and **periodic A-B**. Since all the learned models have a 100% recall, only the precision is discussed in the sequel. The obtained results show that the original RTI+ learns an over-approximating model with a poor precision for all the considered examples. In contrast, as shown by the F1 score, the exact model is learned using the unfolded APTA for **periodic A** and its variants. Both the constructive and the tightened-bound APTAs do not learn the exact **periodic A** model (although more accurate than RTI+). They actually fail to identify the periodicity of task A. For **ap_cont A**, the constructive and the tightened-bound APTAs learn the exact model. However, for **ap_dis A**, the constructive-bound approach learns the exact model, while the tightened-bound one returns a model with a low precision since it does not detect the unused time values 1 and 3.

For the **periodic A-B** example, none of the variants was able to learn an accurate model: the obtained precision is at most 2.27% (using the constructive-bound APTA). They all fail to capture dependencies over clock constraints. Nevertheless, the precision is still better than the original RTI+ (0.18%).

Figure 8 shows the impact of bigger time periods in the **periodic A** example on the quality of the learned model (Fig. 8a) and the learning time (Fig. 8b). We observe that increasing the period makes it more difficult to learn accurate models; Increasing the period decreases the precision as shown in Fig. 8a and increases the learning time as shown in Fig. 8b. For instance, the original RTI+ with generalized-bound APTA is quite fast but its precision tends to zero. Using constructive and tightened-bound APTAs improves the precision with a similar learning time. Finally, relying on the unfolded APTA produces very precise models but induces an important learning time when the period exceeds 15 time units.

Table 1. Accuracy results for the synthetic benchmarks with the four APTAs

Benchmark		Periodic A	Ap_dis A	Ap_cont A	Periodic AB
Generalized-bound	Precision	11%	0.8%	0.6%	0.18%
	Recall	100%	100%	100%	100%
	F1 score	0.1982	0.0159	0.0119	0.0036
Unfolded	Precision	100%	100%	100%	1.97%
	Recall	100%	100%	100%	100%
	F1 score	1.0000	1.0000	1.0000	0.0386
Constructive-bound	Precision	16.4%	100%	100%	2.27%
	Recall	100%	100%	100%	100%
	F1 score	0.2818	1.0000	1.0000	0.0444
Tightened-bound	Precision	16.9%	3.01%	100%	2.18%
	Recall	100%	100%	100%	100%
	F1 score	0.2891	0.0584	1.0000	0.0427

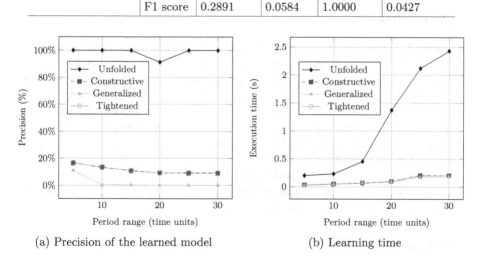

(a) Precision of the learned model   (b) Learning time

Fig. 8. Impact of varying the task A period on the precision/the learning time

The CSMA/CD Example. Table 2 summarizes the experiments done on **CSMA/CD**. On the one hand, one can notice that RTI+, like in the previous cases, learns an over-approximating model with a poor precision (6.20%) but in a short time (∼6 s). Moreover, the generalized-bound APTA, initially having 2373 locations, is reduced to a final model with only 4 locations which represents a high reduction. On the other hand, the proposed APTAs produce significantly different models that cross-approximate the original **CSMA/CD**. For instance, the tightened-bound APTA learns a very precise model (93.70%). However, the model is obtained in more than 8 hours and has 370 locations. Using the constructive-bound APTA gives a model with less precision (85.80%) in a lower execution time (∼3 h). Finally, the unfolded APTA gives a model with

Table 2. Experimental results for **CSMA/CD** using the four APTA models

APTA type	Precision	Recall	F1 score	Time	APTA size	DRTA size	Reduction
Generalized	6.20%	100.00%	0.1168	~6 s	2373	4	99.83%
Unfolded	49.40%	96.70%	0.6539	~9 min	3586	19	99.47%
Constructive	85.80%	52.00%	0.6475	~3 h	2652	207	92.19%
Tightened	93.70%	49.90%	0.6512	~8 h	2373	370	84.41%

a 49.40% precision and a 96.70% recall, which corresponds to the best F1 score (0.6539). Furthermore, compared to constructive and tightened-bound APTAs, the learning time for the unfolded APTA is lower (~9 min). Hence, we conclude that, for this example, the unfolded APTA provides a good tradeoff between accuracy and learning time.

7   Conclusion

In this work, we proposed different variants of the RTI+ algorithm for learning models with both stochastic and timed behaviors. We formally defined three APTA models with different levels of generalization and representation sizes. We validated our proposal by performing different experiments that showed that using the new APTA variants provides more accurate models regarding the time behaviors. However, we observed that a higher learning time is generally required, depending on the desired accuracy. In the future, we are planning to improve our algorithms to better handle models with dependencies over clock constraints such as in the **periodic A-B** example. We are investigating a new compatibility criterion that takes into account such dependencies and that is able to isolate empty time intervals.

References

1. Alur, R., Dill, D.L.: A theory of timed automata. Theoret. Comput. Sci. **126**(2), 183–235 (1994)
2. Angluin, D.: Learning regular sets from queries and counterexamples. Inf. Comput. **75**(2), 87–106 (1987)
3. Carrasco, R.C., Oncina, J.: Learning stochastic regular grammars by means of a state merging method. In: Carrasco, R.C., Oncina, J. (eds.) ICGI 1994. LNCS, vol. 862, pp. 139–152. Springer, Heidelberg (1994). doi:10.1007/3-540-58473-0_144
4. De la Higuera, C.: Grammatical Inference: Learning Automata and Grammars. Cambridge University Press, Cambridge (2010)
5. Kwiatkowska, M., Norman, G., Sproston, J., Wang, F.: Symbolic model checking for probabilistic timed automata. Inf. Comput. **205**(7), 1027–1077 (2007)
6. Legay, A., Delahaye, B., Bensalem, S.: Statistical model checking: an overview. In: Barringer, H., Falcone, Y., Finkbeiner, B., Havelund, K., Lee, I., Pace, G., Roşu, G., Sokolsky, O., Tillmann, N. (eds.) RV 2010. LNCS, vol. 6418, pp. 122–135. Springer, Heidelberg (2010). doi:10.1007/978-3-642-16612-9_11

7. Maier, A., Vodencarevic, A., Niggemann, O., Just, R., Jaeger, M.: Anomaly detection in production plants using timed automata. In: 8th International Conference on Informatics in Control, Automation and Robotics. pp. 363–369 (2011)
8. Mao, H., Chen, Y., Jaeger, M., Nielsen, T.D., Larsen, K.G., Nielsen, B.: Learning probabilistic automata for model checking. In: 2011 Eighth International Conference on Quantitative Evaluation of Systems (QEST), pp. 111–120. IEEE (2011)
9. Mao, H., Chen, Y., Jaeger, M., Nielsen, T.D., Larsen, K.G., Nielsen, B.: Learning deterministic probabilistic automata from a model checking perspective. Mach. Learn. **105**(2), 255–299 (2016)
10. de Matos Pedro, A., Crocker, P.A., de Sousa, S.M.: Learning stochastic timed automata from sample executions. In: Margaria, T., Steffen, B. (eds.) ISoLA 2012. LNCS, vol. 7609, pp. 508–523. Springer, Heidelberg (2012). doi:10.1007/978-3-642-34026-0_38
11. Nouri, A., Bozga, M., Molnos, A., Legay, A., Bensalem, S.: ASTROLABE: a rigorous approach for system-level performance modeling and analysis. ACM Trans. Embed. Comput. Syst. **15**(2), 31:1–31:26 (2016)
12. Sen, K., Viswanathan, M., Agha, G.: Learning continuous time markov chains from sample executions. In: Proceedings of the First International Conference on The Quantitative Evaluation of Systems, pp. 146–155. QEST 2004, IEEE Computer Society, Washington, DC (2004)
13. Verwer, S.E., Eyraud, R., De La Higuera, C.: PAutomaC: a probabilistic automata and hidden markov models learning competition. Mach. Learn. **96**(1–2), 129–154 (2014)
14. Verwer, S.E.: Efficient identification of timed automata: theory and practice. Ph.D. thesis, TU Delft, Delft University of Technology (2010)

Verifying Safety and Persistence Properties of Hybrid Systems Using Flowpipes and Continuous Invariants

Andrew Sogokon[1]([✉]) [iD], Paul B. Jackson[2] [iD], and Taylor T. Johnson[1] [iD]

[1] Institute for Software Integrated Systems, Vanderbilt University,
Nashville, TN, USA
{andrew.sogokon,taylor.johnson}@vanderbilt.edu
[2] Laboratory for Foundations of Computer Science, University of Edinburgh,
Edinburgh, Scotland, UK
Paul.Jackson@ed.ac.uk

Abstract. We propose a method for verifying persistence of nonlinear hybrid systems. Given some system and an initial set of states, the method can guarantee that system trajectories always eventually evolve into some specified target subset of the states of one of the discrete modes of the system, and always remain within this target region. The method also computes a time-bound within which the target region is always reached. The approach combines flow-pipe computation with deductive reasoning about invariants and is more general than each technique alone. We illustrate the method with a case study concerning showing that potentially destructive stick-slip oscillations of an oil-well drill eventually die away for a certain choice of drill control parameters. The case study demonstrates how just using flow-pipes or just reasoning about invariants alone can be insufficient. The case study also nicely shows the richness of systems that the method can handle: the case study features a mode with non-polynomial (nonlinear) ODEs and we manage to prove the persistence property with the aid of an automatic prover specifically designed for handling transcendental functions.

1 Introduction

Hybrid systems combine discrete and continuous behaviour and provide a very general framework for modelling and analyzing the behaviour of systems such as those implemented in modern embedded control software. Although a number of tools and methods have been developed for verifying properties of

This material is based upon work supported by the UK Engineering and Physical Sciences Research Council under grants EPSRC EP/I010335/1 and EP/J001058/1, the National Science Foundation (NSF) under grant numbers CNS 1464311 and CCF 1527398, the Air Force Research Laboratory (AFRL) through contract number FA8750-15-1-0105, and the Air Force Office of Scientific Research (AFOSR) under contract number FA9550-15-1-0258.

© Springer International Publishing AG 2017
C. Barrett et al. (Eds.): NFM 2017, LNCS 10227, pp. 194–211, 2017.
DOI: 10.1007/978-3-319-57288-8_14

hybrid systems, most are geared towards proving bounded-time safety properties, often employing set reachability computations based on constructing over-approximating enclosures of the reachable states of ordinary differential equations (e.g. [7, 13, 14, 21]). Methods capable of proving unbounded-time safety properties often rely (explicitly or otherwise) on constructing *continuous invariants* (e.g. [25, 42], and referred to in short as *invariants*). Such invariants may be thought of as a generalization of *positively invariant sets* (see e.g. [5]) and which are analogous to inductive invariants used in computer science to reason about the correctness of discrete programs using Hoare logic.

We argue in this paper that a combined approach employing bounded time reachability analysis and reasoning about invariants can be effective in proving *persistence* and *safety* properties in non-polynomial (nonlinear) hybrid systems. We illustrate the combined approach using a detailed case study with non-polynomial ODEs for which neither approach individually was sufficient to establish the desired safety and persistence properties.

Methods for bounded time safety verification cannot in general be applied to prove safety for all time and their accuracy tends to degrade for large time bounds, especially for nonlinear systems. Verification using invariants, while a powerful technique that can prove strong properties about nonlinear systems, relies on the ability to find invariants that are sufficient for proving the unbounded time safety property. In practice, many invariants for the system can be found which fall short of this requirement, often for the simple reason that they do not include all the initial states of the system. We show how a combined approach employing both verification methods can, in some cases, address these limitations.

Contributions

In this paper we (I) show that bounded time safety verification based on flowpipe construction can be naturally combined with invariants to verify persistence and unbounded time safety properties, addressing some of the limitations of each verification method when considered in isolation. (II) To illustrate the approach, we consider a simplified torsional model of a conventional oil well drill string that has been the subject of numerous studies by Navarro-López et al. [34]. (III) We discuss some of the challenges that currently stand in the way of fully automatic verification using this approach. Additionally, we provide a readable overview of the methods employed in the verification process and the obstacles that present themselves when these methods are applied in practice.

2   Safety and Persistence for Hybrid Automata

2.1   Preliminaries

A number of formalisms exist for specifying hybrid systems. The most popular framework at present is that of hybrid automata [3, 19], which are essentially discrete transition systems in which each discrete state represents an operating mode inside which the system evolves continuously according to an ODE under some evolution constraint. Additionally, transition guards and reset maps are used to specify the discrete transition behaviour (i.e. switching) between the operating modes. A sketch of the syntax and semantics of hybrid automata is as follows.

Definition 1 (Hybrid automaton [26]**).** *Formally, a hybrid automaton is given by* $(Q, Var, f, Init, Inv, T, G, R)$, *where*

- $Q = \{q_0, q_1, \ldots, q_k\}$ *is a finite* set of discrete states (modes),
- $Var = \{x_1, x_2, \ldots, x_n\}$ *is a finite* set of continuous variables,
- $f : Q \times \mathbb{R}^n \to \mathbb{R}^n$ *gives the vector field defining continuous evolution inside each mode,*
- $Init \subset Q \times \mathbb{R}^n$ *is the set of initial states,*
- $Inv : Q \to 2^{\mathbb{R}^n}$ *gives the* mode invariants *constraining evolution for every discrete state,*
- $T \subseteq Q \times Q$ *is the transition relation,*
- $G : T \to 2^{\mathbb{R}^n}$ *gives the guard conditions for enabling transitions,*
- $R : T \to 2^{\mathbb{R}^n \times \mathbb{R}^n}$ *gives the reset map.*

A *hybrid state* of the automaton is of the form $(q, \boldsymbol{x}) \in Q \times \mathbb{R}^n$. A *hybrid time trajectory* is a sequence (which may be finite or infinite) of intervals $\tau = \{I_i\}_{i=0}^N$, for which $I_i = [\tau_i, \tau_i']$ for all $i < N$ and $\tau_i \leq \tau_i' = \tau_{i+1}$ for all i. If the sequence is finite, then either $I_N = [\tau_N, \tau_N']$ or $I_N = [\tau_N, \tau_N')$. Intuitively, one may think of τ_i as the times at which discrete transitions occur. An *execution* (or a *run* or *trajectory*) of a hybrid automaton defined to be $(\tau, q, \varphi_t^i(\boldsymbol{x}))$, where τ is a hybrid time trajectory, $q : \langle \tau \rangle \to Q$ (where $\langle \tau \rangle$ is defined to be the set $\{0, 1, \ldots, N\}$ if τ is finite and $\{0, 1, \ldots\}$ otherwise) and $\varphi_t^i(\boldsymbol{x})$ is a collection of diffeomorphisms $\varphi_t^i(\boldsymbol{x}) : I_i \to \mathbb{R}^n$ such that $(q(0), \varphi_0^0(\boldsymbol{x})) \in Init$, for all $t \in [\tau_i, \tau_i')$ $\dot{\boldsymbol{x}} = f(q(i), \varphi_t^i(\boldsymbol{x}))$ and $\varphi_t^i(\boldsymbol{x}) \in Inv(i)$. For all $i \in \langle \tau \rangle \setminus \{N\}$ it is also required that transitions respect the guards and reset maps, i.e. $e = (q(i), q(i+1)) \in T$, $\varphi_{\tau_i'}^i(\boldsymbol{x}) \in G(e)$ and $(\varphi_{\tau_i'}^i(\boldsymbol{x}), \varphi_{\tau_{i+1}}^{i+1}(\boldsymbol{x})) \in R(e)$.

We consider MTL[1] formulas satisfied by trajectories. The satisfaction relation is of form $\rho \models^p \phi$, read as *"trajectory ρ at position p satisfies temporal logic formula ϕ"*, where positions on a trajectory are identified by pairs of form (i, t) where $i \leq N$ and time $t \in I_t$. We use the MTL modality $\Box_I \phi$ which states that formula ϕ always holds in time interval I in the future. Formally, this can be defined as $\rho \models^p \Box_I \phi \equiv \forall p' \geq p$ s.t. $(p'.2 - p.2) \in I. \rho \models^{p'} \phi$, where $(i', t') \geq (i, t) \equiv i' > i \lor (i' = i \land t' \geq t)$. Similarly we can define the modality $\Diamond_I \phi$ which states that formula ϕ eventually holds at some time in the time interval I in the future. An MTL formula is valid for a given hybrid automaton if it is satisfied by all trajectories of that automaton starting at position $(0, 0)$. For clarity when writing MTL formulas, we assume trajectories are not restricted to

---

[1] Metric Temporal Logic; see e.g. [22].

start in *Init* states and instead introduce *Init* predicates into the formulas when we want restrictions.

Alternative formalisms for hybrid systems, such as *hybrid programs* [41], enjoy the property of having a compositional semantics and can be used to verify properties of systems by verifying properties of their parts in a theorem prover [15,44]. Other formal modelling frameworks for hybrid systems, such as *Hybrid CSP* [24], have also found application in theorem provers [60,62].

2.2 Bounded Time Safety and Eventuality

The *bounded-time safety verification problem* (with some finite time bound $t > 0$) is concerned with establishing that given an initial set of states Init $\subseteq Q \times \mathbb{R}^n$ and a set of safe states Safe $\subseteq Q \times \mathbb{R}^n$, the state of the system may not leave Safe within time t along any valid trajectory τ of the system. In the absence of closed-form solutions to the ODEs, this property may be established by verified integration, i.e. by computing successive over-approximating enclosures (known as *flowpipes*) of the reachable states in discrete time steps. Bounded-time reachability analysis can be extended to full hybrid systems by also computing/over-approximating the discrete reachable states (up to some finite bound on the number of discrete transitions).

A number of bounded-time verification tools for hybrid systems have been developed based on verified integration using interval enclosures. For instance, *iSAT-ODE*, a verification tool for hybrid systems developed by Eggers et al. [13] relies on the verified integration tool *VNODE-LP* by Nedialkov [37] for computing the enclosures. Other examples include *dReach*, a reachability analysis tool for hybrid systems developed by Kong et al. [21], which uses the *CAPD* library [1]. Over-approximating enclosures can in practice be very precise for small time horizons, but tend to become conservative when the time bound is large (due to the so-called *wrapping effect*, which is a problem caused by the successive build-up of over-approximation errors that arises in interval-based methods; see e.g. [38]). An alternative verified integration method using *Taylor models* was introduced by Makino and Berz (see [4,38]) and can address some of these drawbacks, often providing tighter enclosures of the reachable set. Implementations of the method have been reported in *COSY INFINITY*, a scientific computing tool by Makino and Berz [29]; *VSPODE*, a tool for computing validated solutions to parametric ODEs by Lin and Stadtherr [23]; and in *Flow**, a bounded-time verification for hybrid systems developed by Chen et al. [7].

Because flowpipes provide an over-approximation of the reachable states at a given time, verified integration using flowpipes can also be used to reason about *liveness* properties such as *eventuality*, i.e. when a system is guaranteed to eventually enter some *target set* having started off at some point in an initial set. The bounded-time safety and eventuality properties may be more concisely expressed by using MTL notation, i.e. by writing Init $\rightarrow \Box_{[0,t]}$ Safe, and Init $\rightarrow \Diamond_{[0,t]}$ Target, where Init describes the initial set of states, Safe $\subseteq Q \times \mathbb{R}^n$ is the set of safe states and Target $\subseteq Q \times \mathbb{R}^n$ is the target region which is to be eventually attained.

Remark 2. The bounded time eventuality properties we consider in this paper are more restrictive than the general (unbounded time) case. For instance, consider a continuous 2-dimensional system governed by $\dot{x}_1 = x_2, \dot{x}_2 = 0$ and confined to evolve in the region where $x_2 > 0$. If one starts this system inside a state where $x_1 = 0$, it will eventually evolve into a state where $x_1 = 1$ by following the solution, however one may not put a finite bound on the time for this to happen. Thus, while $x_1 = 0 \rightarrow \Diamond_{[0,\infty)} x_1 = 1$ is true for this system the bounded time eventuality property $x_1 = 0 \rightarrow \Diamond_{[0,t]} x_1 = 1$, will not hold for any finite $t > 0$.

2.3   Unbounded Time Safety

A safety property for unbounded time may be more concisely expressed using an MTL formula:

$$\text{Init} \rightarrow \Box_{[0,\infty)} \text{ Safe.}$$

A proof of such a safety assertion is most commonly achieved by finding an appropriate *invariant*, $I \subseteq Q \times \mathbb{R}^n$, which contains no unsafe states (i.e. $I \subseteq \text{Safe}$) and such that the state of the system may not escape from I into an unsafe state along any valid trajectory of the system. Invariance is a special kind of safety assertion and may be written as $I \rightarrow \Box_{[0,\infty)} I$. A number of techniques have been developed for proving invariance properties for continuous systems without the need to compute solutions to the ODEs [17,25,41,49,53,58].

2.4   Combining Unbounded Time Safety with Eventuality to Prove Persistence

In linear temporal logic, a *persistence* property states that a formula is 'eventually always' true. For instance, using persistence one may express the property that a system starting in any initial state always eventually reaches some target set and then always stays within this set. Using MTL notation, we can write this as:

$$\text{Init} \rightarrow \Diamond_{[0,\infty)} \Box_{[0,\infty)} \text{ Target.}$$

Persistence properties generalize the concept of stability. With stability one is concerned with showing that the state of a system always converges to some particular equilibrium point. With persistence, one only requires that the system state eventually becomes always trapped within some set of states.

In this paper we are concerned with a slightly stronger form of persistence, where one ensures that the target set is always reached within some specified time t:

$$\text{Init} \rightarrow \Diamond_{[0,t]} \Box_{[0,\infty)} \text{ Target.}$$

We observe that a way of proving this is to find a set $I \subseteq \text{Target}$ such that:

1. Init $\rightarrow \Diamond_{[0,t]} I$ holds, and
2. I is an invariant for the system.

This fact can be stated more formally as a rule of inference:

$$\text{(Persistence)} \quad \frac{\text{Init} \to \Diamond_{[0,t]} I \qquad I \to \Box_{[0,\infty)} I \qquad I \to \text{Target}}{\text{Init} \to \Diamond_{[0,t]} \Box_{[0,\infty)} \text{Target}}.$$

Previous Sects. 2.2 and 2.3 respectively surveyed how the eventuality premise Init $\to \Diamond_{[0,t]} I$ and invariant premise $I \to \Box_{[0,\infty)} I$ can be established by a variety of automated techniques. In Sect. 5 we explore automation challenges further and remark on ongoing work addressing how to automatically generate suitable invariants I.

2.5 Using Persistence to Prove Safety

Finding appropriate invariants to prove unbounded time safety as explained above in Sect. 2.3 can in practice be very difficult. It might be the case that invariants $I \subseteq$ Safe for the system can be found, but also ensuring that Init $\subseteq I$ is infeasible. Nevertheless it might be the case that one of these invariants I is always eventually reached by trajectories starting in Init and all those trajectories are contained within Safe. In such cases, Safe is indeed a safety property of the system when starting from any point in Init. More precisely, if one can find an invariant I as explained above in Sect. 2.4 to show the persistence property: Init $\to \Diamond_{[0,t]} \Box_{[0,\infty)}$ Safe, and further one can show for the same time bound t that: Init $\to \Box_{[0,t]}$ Safe, then one has: Init $\to \Box_{[0,\infty)}$ Safe. As a result, one may potentially utilize invariants that were by themselves insufficient for proving the safety property.

Remark 3. The problem of showing that a state satisfying $\Box_{[0,\infty)}$ Safe is reached in finite time t, while ensuring that the formula $\Box_{[0,t]}$ Safe also holds (i.e. states satisfying ¬Safe are avoided up to time t) is sometimes called a *reach-avoid problem* [61].

Even if one's goal is to establish bounded-time rather than unbounded-time safety properties, this inference scheme could still be of use, as it could significantly reduce the time bound t needed for bounded time reachability analysis. In practice, successive over-approximation of the reachable states using flow-pipes tends to become conservative for large values of t. In highly non-linear systems one can realistically expect to compute flowpipes only for very modest time bounds (e.g. in chaotic systems flowpipes are guaranteed to 'blow up', but invariants may still sometimes be found). Instead, it may in some cases be possible to prove the safety property by computing flowpipes up to some small time bound, after which the system can be shown to be inside an invariant that implies the safety property for all times thereafter.

3 An Example Persistence Verification Problem

Stick-slip oscillations are commonly encountered in mechanical engineering in the context of modelling the effects of dynamic friction. Informally, the phenomenon manifests itself in the system becoming "stuck" and "unstuck" repeatedly, which results in unsteady "jerky" motions. In engineering practice, stick-slip oscillations can often degrade performance and cause failures when operating expensive machinery [36]. Although the problem of demonstrating absence of stick-slip oscillations in a system is primarily motivated by safety considerations, it would be misleading to call this a *safety verification problem*. Instead, the problem may broadly be described as that of demonstrating that the system (in finite time) enters a state in which no stick-slip motion is possible and remains there indefinitely. Using MTL one may write:

$$\text{Init} \rightarrow \Diamond_{[0,t]} \Box_{[0,\infty)} \text{ Steady,}$$

where Steady describes the states in which harmful oscillations cannot occur. The formula may informally be read as saying that "from any initial configuration, the system will eventually evolve within time t into a state region where it is always steady".

As an example of a system in which eventual absence of stick-slip oscillations is important, we consider a well-studied [34] model of a simplified conventional oil well drill string. The system can be characterized in terms of the following variables: φ_r, the angular displacement of the top rotary system; φ_b, the angular displacement of the drilling bit; $\dot{\varphi}_r$, the angular velocity of the top rotary system; and $\dot{\varphi}_b$, the angular velocity of the drilling bit. The continuous state of the system $\boldsymbol{x}(t) \in \mathbb{R}^3$ can be described in terms of these variables, i.e. $\boldsymbol{x}(t) = (\dot{\varphi}_r, \ \varphi_r - \varphi_b, \ \dot{\varphi}_b)^T$. The system has two control parameters: W_{ob} giving the weight applied on the drilling bit, and $u = T_m$ giving the surface motor torque. The dynamics is governed a non-linear system of ODEs $\dot{\boldsymbol{x}} = f(\boldsymbol{x})$, given by:

$$\dot{x}_1 = \frac{1}{J_r}\left(-(c_t + c_r)x_1 - k_t x_2 + c_t x_3 + u\right), \tag{1}$$

$$\dot{x}_2 = x_1 - x_3, \tag{2}$$

$$\dot{x}_3 = \frac{1}{J_b}\left(c_t x_1 + k_t x_2 - (c_t + c_b)x_3 - T_{f_b}(x_3)\right). \tag{3}$$

The term $T_{f_b}(x_3)$ denotes the friction modelling the bit-rock contact and is responsible for the non-polynomial non-linearity. It is given by

$$W_{ob} R_b \left(\mu_{c_b} + (\mu_{s_b} - \mu_{c_b})e^{-\frac{\gamma_b}{\nu_f}|x_3|}\right) \text{sgn}(x_3),$$

where $\text{sgn}(x_3) = \frac{x_3}{|x_3|}$ if $x_3 \neq 0$ and $\text{sgn}(x_3) \in [-1,1]$ if $x_3 = 0$. Constants used in the model [34] are as follows: $c_b = 50 \, \text{Nms/rad}, k_t = 861.5336 \, \text{Nm/rad}, J_r = 2212 \, \text{kg m}^2, J_b = 471.9698 \, \text{kg m}^2, R_b = 0.155575 \, \text{m}, c_t = 172.3067 \, \text{Nms/rad}, c_r = 425 \, \text{Nms/rad}, \mu_{cb} = 0.5, \mu_{sb} = 0.8, \gamma_b = 0.9, \nu_f = 1 \, \text{rad/s}$. Even though at first glance the system looks like a plain continuous system with a single set of differential equations, it is effectively a hybrid system with at least 3 modes, where the drilling bit is: "rotating forward" ($x_3 > 0$), "stopped" ($x_3 = 0$), and "rotating backward" ($x_3 < 0$). A sub-mode of the stopped mode models when the drill bit is stuck. In this sub-mode, the torque components on the drill bit due to c_t, c_b and k_t are insufficient to overcome the static friction $W_{ob}R_b\mu_{c_b}$, and $\mathrm{sgn}(x_3)$ is further constrained so as to ensure $\dot{x}_3 = 0$.

Once the drill is in operation, so-called *stick-slip oscillations* can cause damage when the bit repeatedly becomes stuck and unstuck due to friction in the bottom hole assembly. In the model this behaviour would correspond to the system entering a state where $x_3 = 0$ repeatedly. The objective is to verify the eventual absence of stick-slip oscillations in the system initialised at the origin (i.e. at rest) for some given choice of the control parameters W_{ob} and u. Previous work by Navarro-López and Carter [34] explored modelling the simplified model of the drill as a hybrid automaton and simulated the resulting models in Stateflow and Modelica.

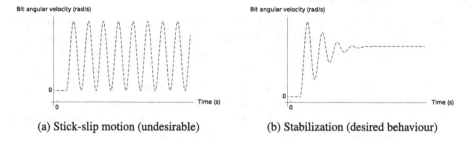

(a) Stick-slip motion (undesirable)   (b) Stabilization (desired behaviour)

Fig. 1. Simulations can exhibit stabilization with positive bit angular velocity and stick-slip bit motion.

Simulations, such as those obtained in [34], using different models and control parameters for the drill can suggest stick-slip oscillations or their absence (illustrated in Fig. 1) in a particular model, however the task of verifying their eventual absence cannot be adequately addressed with simulation alone. In practice however, simulation is incredibly useful in providing some degree of confidence in the overall result, which is very important to know before attempting verification.

A simulation of the system with a concrete choice for the control parameters $W_{ob} = 50,000\,\mathrm{N}$ and $u = 6,000\,\mathrm{Nm}$, shown as a trajectory in the 3-dimensional state space in Fig. 3a, suggests that the system does not exhibit stick-slip oscillations, because the trajectory is observed to start at the origin, escape the surface $(x_3 = 0)^2$ and stabilize around a point where the angular velocity of the drilling bit is positive ($x_3 > 0$).

4   Verifying Persistence

The property of interest, i.e. the eventual absence of stick-slip oscillation that we observe in the simulation, may be phrased as the following formula in metric

---

[2] The system exhibits *sliding behaviour* on a portion of this surface known as the *sliding set*. See [34].

temporal logic: $x_1 = 0 \wedge x_2 = 0 \wedge x_3 = 0 \rightarrow \Diamond_{[0,t]} \square_{[0,\infty)} x_3 > 0$, which informally asserts that the system initialised at the origin will *eventually* (diamond modality) enter a state where it is *always* (box modality) the case that $x_3 > 0$. In the following sections we describe a method for proving this assertion. Following our approach, we break the problem down into the following two sub-problems:

1. Finding an appropriate invariant I in which the property $\square_{[0,t]} x_3 > 0$ holds. For this we employ continuous/positive invariants, discussed in the next section.
2. Proving that the system reaches a state in the set I in finite time when initialised at the origin, i.e. $x_1 = 0 \wedge x_2 = 0 \wedge x_3 = 0 \rightarrow \Diamond_{[0,t]} I$.[3]

4.1   Continuous Invariant

Finding continuous invariants that are sufficient to guarantee a given property is in practice remarkably difficult. Methods for automatic continuous invariant generation have been reported by numerous authors [16,18,25,30,49,52–54,59, 63], but in practice often result in "coarse" invariants that cannot be used to prove the property of interest, or require an unreasonable amount of time due to their reliance on expensive real quantifier elimination algorithms.

Stability analysis (involving a linearisation; see [56] for details) can be used to suggest a polynomial function $V : \mathbb{R}^n \rightarrow \mathbb{R}$, given by

$$V(x) = 50599.6 - 14235.7x_1 + 1234.22x_1^2 - 4351.43x_2 + 342.329x_1x_2$$
$$+ 288.032x_2^2 - 3865.81x_3 + 367.657x_1x_3 + 18.2594x_2x_3 + 241.37x_3^2,$$

for which we can reasonably conjecture that $V(x) \leq 1400$ defines a positively invariant set under the flow of our non-linear system. Geometrically, this represents an ellipsoid that lies above the surface defined by $x_3 = 0$ in the state space (see Fig. 3b). In order to prove the invariance property, it is sufficient to show that the following holds:[4]

$$\forall x \in \mathbb{R}^3. V(x) = 1400 \rightarrow \nabla V \cdot f(x) < 0. \tag{4}$$

Unfortunately, in the presence of non-polynomial terms[5] a first order sentence will in general not belong to a decidable theory [51], although there has recently been progress in broadening the scope of the popular CAD algorithm [9] for real quantifier elimination to work with restricted classes of non-polynomial problems [57].

In practice, this conjecture is easily proved in under 5 s using MetiTarski, an automatic theorem prover, developed by L.C. Paulson and co-workers at the University of Cambridge, designed specifically for proving universally quantified first order conjectures featuring transcendental functions (such as sin, cos, ln, exp, etc). The interested reader may find more details about the MetiTarski system in [2,40].

---

[3] Files for the case study are available online. http://www.verivital.com/nfm2017.
[4] Here ∇ denotes the *gradient* of V, i.e. the vector of partial derivatives $(\frac{\partial V}{\partial x_1}, \ldots, \frac{\partial V}{\partial x_n})$.
[5] E.g. those featured in the right-hand side of the ODE, i.e. $f(x)$.

Remark 4. Although Wolfram's *Mathematica* 10 computer algebra system also provides some functionality for proving first-order conjectures featuring non-polynomial expressions using its Reduce[] function, we were unable (on our system[6]) to prove conjecture (4) this way after over an hour of computation, after which the Mathematica kernel crashed.

The automatic proof of conjecture (4) obtained using MetiTarski (provided we trust the system) establishes that $V(\boldsymbol{x}) \leq 1400$ defines a positively invariant set, and thus we are guaranteed that solutions initialised inside this set remain there at all future times. In order to be certain that no outgoing discrete transitions of the hybrid system are possible when the system is evolving inside $V(\boldsymbol{x}) \leq 1400$, we further require a proof of the following conjecture featuring only polynomial terms:

$$\forall \, \boldsymbol{x} \in \mathbb{R}^3. \ V(\boldsymbol{x}) \leq 1400 \to x_3 > 0. \tag{5}$$

An automatic proof of this conjecture may be obtained using an implementation of a decision procedure for first-order real arithmetic.

4.2   Verified Integration

In order to show that the system does indeed enter the positively invariant ellipsoid $V(\boldsymbol{x}) \leq 1400$ in finite time, it is not sufficient to observe this in a simulation (as in Fig. 3b), which is why we use a tool employing *verified integration* based on Taylor models. *Flow** (implemented by Chen et al. [7]) is a bounded-time safety verification tool for hybrid systems that computes Taylor models to analyze continuous reachability. The tool works by computing successive over-approximations (flowpipes) of the reachable set of the system, which are internally represented using Taylor models (but which may in turn be over-approximated by a bounding hyper-box and easily rendered).

Figure 2a shows the bounding boxes of solution enclosures computed from the point initial condition at the origin using Flow* with adaptive time steps and Taylor models of order 13, a time bound of 12.7 and the same control parameters used in the simulation (i.e. $u = 6,000\,\mathrm{Nm}$, $W_{ob} = 50,000\,\mathrm{N}$). We observe that once solutions escape to the region where $x_3 > 0$, they maintain a positive x_3 component for the duration of the time bound.

The last flowpipe computed by Flow* for this problem can be bounded inside the hyper-rectangle BoundBox characterized by the formula

$$\mathrm{BoundBox} \equiv \frac{39}{10} \leq x_1 \leq 4 \wedge \frac{51}{10} \leq x_2 \leq \frac{26}{5} \wedge \frac{7}{2} \leq x_3 \leq \frac{37}{10}.$$

Once more, using a decision procedure for real arithmetic, we can check that the following sentence is true:

$$\forall \, \boldsymbol{x} \in \mathbb{R}^3. \ \mathrm{BoundBox} \to V(\boldsymbol{x}) \leq 1400.$$

If we are able to establish the following facts:

---

[6] Intel i5-2520M CPU @ 2.50 GHz, 4 GB RAM, running Arch Linux kernel 4.2.5-1.

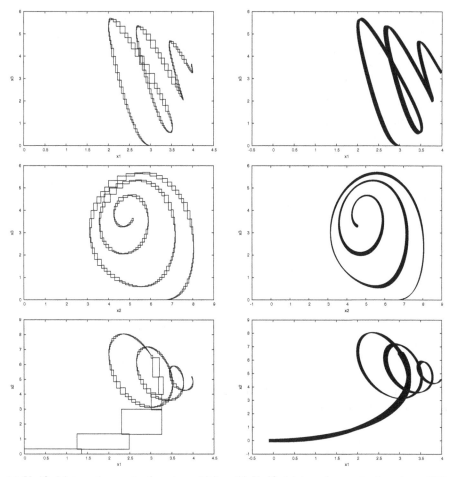

(a) Verified integration up to time $t = 12.7$ from a point initial condition at the origin.

(b) Verified integration up to time $t = 12.2$ from an interval initial condition.

Fig. 2. Verified integration using Flow*.

1. $I \rightarrow \square_{[0,\infty)} I$ (I is a continuous invariant),
2. $I \rightarrow$ Steady   (inside I, there are no harmful oscillations), and
3. Init $\rightarrow \lozenge_{[0,t]} I$ (the system enters the region I in finite time),

then we can conclude that Init $\rightarrow \lozenge_{[0,t]} \square_{[0,\infty)}$ Steady is also true and the system does not exhibit harmful stick-slip oscillations when started inside Init. By taking Init to be the origin $x_1 = 0 \wedge x_2 = 0 \wedge x_3 = 0$, I to be the positively invariant sub-level set $V(\boldsymbol{x}) \leq 1400$ and Steady to be $x_3 > 0$, we are able to conclude the temporal property:

$$x_1 = 0 \wedge x_2 = 0 \wedge x_3 = 0 \rightarrow \lozenge_{[0,t]} \square_{[t,\infty)} x_3 > 0.$$

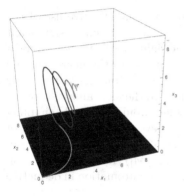
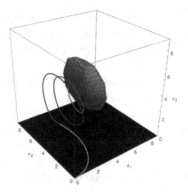

(a) Simulation showing stabilization with positive bit angular velocity.

(b) Simulation showing eventual entry into an
ellipsoidal invariant.

Fig. 3. Simulation of the hybrid system initialised at the origin with $W_{ob} = 50,000\,\text{N}$ and $u = 6000\,\text{Nm}$. The trajectory is contained by the flowpipes shown in Fig. 2a and is observed to enter the positively invariant ellipsoid $V(x) \leq 1400$, illustrating the persistence property of eventual absence of stick-slip oscillations.

Verified integration using Taylor models also allows us to consider *sets* of possible initial conditions, rather than initial points (illustrated in Fig. 2b). This is useful when there is uncertainty about the system's initial configuration; however, in practice this comes with a significant performance overhead for verified integration.

5 Outlook and Challenges to Automation

Correctness of reachability analysis tools based on verified integration is a soundness critical to the overall verification approach, which makes for a strong case in favour of using formally verified implementations. At present few are available, e.g. see recent work by Immler [20] which presented a formally verified continuous reachability algorithm based on adaptive Runge-Kutta methods. Verified implementations of Taylor model-based reachability analysis algorithms for continuous and hybrid systems would clearly be very valuable. One alternative to over-approximating reachable sets of continuous systems using flowpipes is based on simulating the system using a finite set of sampling trajectories and employs *sensitivity analysis* to address the coverage problem. This technique was explored by Donzé and Maler in [10]. A similar approach employing *matrix measures* has more recently been studied by Maidens and Arcak [27,28].

As an alternative to using verified integration, a number of deductive methods are available for proving eventuality properties in continuous and hybrid systems (e.g. [42,55]). These approaches can be much more powerful since they allow one to work with more general classes of initial and target regions that are necessarily out of scope for methods based on verified integration (e.g. they can work with initial sets that are unbounded, disconnected, etc.) Making effective use of the deductive verification tools currently in existence typically requires significant input and expertise on part of the user (finding the right invariants being one of the major stumbling blocks in practice), in stark contrast to the near-complete level of automation offered by tools based on verified integration. Methods for automatic continuous invariant generation are crucial to the mechanization of the overall verification approach. Progress on this problem would be hugely enabling for non-experts and specialists alike, as it would relieve them from the task of manually constructing appropriate invariants, which often requires intuition and expertise. Work in this area is ongoing (see e.g. [25,43,54]). Indeed, progress on this problem is also crucial to providing a greater level of automation in deductive verification tools.

6 Related Work

Combining elements of qualitative and quantitative reasoning[7] to study the behaviour of dynamical systems has previously been explored in the case of planar systems by Nishida et al. [39]. The idea of combining bounded-time reachability analysis with qualitative analysis in the form of discrete abstraction was investigated by Clarke et al. in [8]. Similar ideas are employed by Carter [6] and Navarro-López in [35], where the concept of *deadness* is introduced and used as a way of disproving liveness properties. Intuitively, deadness is a formalization of an idea that inside certain regions the system cannot be live, i.e. some desired property may never become true as the system evolves inside a "deadness region". These ideas were used in a case study [6, Chap. 5] also featuring the drill system studied in [34], but with a different set of control parameters and in which the verification objective was to prove the existence of a *single trajectory* for which the drill eventually gets "stuck", which is sufficient to disprove the liveness (oscillation) property.

Region stability is similar to our notion of persistence [45], which requires all trajectories to eventually reach some region of the state space. Sound and complete proof rules for establishing region stability have been explored and automated [47], as have more efficient encodings of the proof rule that scale better in dimensionality [31]. However, all algorithms we are aware of for checking region stability require linear or simpler (timed or rectangular) ODEs [11,31,45–48]. Strong attractors are basins of attraction where every state in the state space eventually reaches a region of the state space [45]. Some algorithms do not check region stability, but actually check stronger properties such as strong attraction, that imply region stability [45]. In contrast to these works, our method checks the weaker notion of persistence for nonlinear ODEs.

She and Ratschan studied methods of proving set eventuality in continuous systems under constraints using Lyapunov-like functions [50]. Duggirala and

---

[7] E.g. numerical solution computation with "qualitative" features, such as invariance of certain regions.

Mitra also employed Lyapunov-like function concepts to prove inevitability properties in hybrid systems [12]. Möhlmann et al. developed Stabhyil [33], which can be applied to nonlinear hybrid systems and checks classical notions of Lyapunov stability, which is a strictly stronger property than persistence. In [32] Möhlmann et al. extended their work and applied similar ideas, using information about (necessarily invariant) sub-level sets of Lyapunov functions to terminate reachability analysis used for safety verification. Prabhakar and Soto have explored abstractions that enable proving stability properties without having to search for Lyapunov functions, albeit these are not currently applicable to nonlinear systems [48]. In summary, in contrast to other works listed above, our approach enables proving persistence properties in conjunction with safety properties for nonlinear, non-polynomial hybrid systems and does not put restrictions on the form or the type of the invariant used in conjunction with bounded time reachability analysis.

7 Conclusion

This paper explored a combined technique for safety and persistence verification employing continuous invariants and reachable set computation based on constructing flowpipes. The approach was illustrated on a model of a simplified oil well drill string system studied by Navarro-López et al., where the verification objective is to prove absence of damaging stick-slip oscillations. The system was useful in highlighting many of the existing practical challenges to applying and automating the proposed verification method. Many competing approaches already exist for verifying safety in hybrid systems, but these rarely combine different methods for reachability analysis and deductive verification, which our approach combines. We demonstrate that a combination of different approaches can be more practically useful than each constituent approach taken in isolation.

Acknowledgements. The authors wish to thank to the anonymous reviewers for their careful reading and valuable suggestions for improving this paper.

References

1. CAPD library. http://capd.ii.uj.edu.pl/
2. Akbarpour, B., Paulson, L.C.: MetiTarski: an automatic theorem prover for real-valued special functions. J. Autom. Reason. **44**(3), 175–205 (2010)
3. Alur, R., Courcoubetis, C., Henzinger, T.A., Ho, P.-H.: Hybrid automata: an algorithmic approach to the specification and verification of hybrid systems. In: Grossman, R.L., Nerode, A., Ravn, A.P., Rischel, H. (eds.) HS 1991–1992. LNCS, vol. 736, pp. 209–229. Springer, Heidelberg (1993). doi:10.1007/3-540-57318-6_30
4. Berz, M., Makino, K.: Verified integration of ODEs and flows using differential algebraic methods on high-order Taylor models. Reliab. Comput. **4**(4), 361–369 (1998)
5. Blanchini, F.: Set invariance in control. Automatica **35**(11), 1747–1767 (1999)

6. Carter, R.A.: Verification of liveness properties on hybrid dynamical systems. Ph.D. thesis, University of Manchester, School of Computer Science (2013)
7. Chen, X., Ábrahám, E., Sankaranarayanan, S.: Flow*: an analyzer for non-linear hybrid systems. In: Sharygina, N., Veith, H. (eds.) CAV 2013. LNCS, vol. 8044, pp. 258–263. Springer, Heidelberg (2013). doi:10.1007/978-3-642-39799-8_18
8. Clarke, E.M., Fehnker, A., Han, Z., Krogh, B.H., Ouaknine, J., Stursberg, O., Theobald, M.: Abstraction and counterexample-guided refinement in model checking of hybrid systems. Int. J. Found. Comput. Sci. 14(4), 583–604 (2003)
9. Collins, G.E.: Quantifier elimination for real closed fields by cylindrical algebraic decompostion. In: Brakhage, H. (ed.) GI-Fachtagung 1975. LNCS, vol. 33, pp. 134–183. Springer, Heidelberg (1975). doi:10.1007/3-540-07407-4_17
10. Donzé, A., Maler, O.: Systematic simulation using sensitivity analysis. In: Bemporad, A., Bicchi, A., Buttazzo, G. (eds.) HSCC 2007. LNCS, vol. 4416, pp. 174–189. Springer, Heidelberg (2007). doi:10.1007/978-3-540-71493-4_16
11. Duggirala, P.S., Mitra, S.: Abstraction refinement for stability. In: Proceedings of 2011 IEEE/ACM International Conference on Cyber-Physical Systems, ICCPS, pp. 22–31, April 2011
12. Duggirala, P.S., Mitra, S.: Lyapunov abstractions for inevitability of hybrid systems. In: HSCC, pp. 115–124. ACM, New York (2012)
13. Eggers, A., Ramdani, N., Nedialkov, N.S., Fränzle, M.: Improving the SAT modulo ODE approach to hybrid systems analysis by combining different enclosure methods. Softw. Syst. Model. 14(1), 121–148 (2015)
14. Frehse, G., Guernic, C., Donzé, A., Cotton, S., Ray, R., Lebeltel, O., Ripado, R., Girard, A., Dang, T., Maler, O.: SpaceEx: scalable verification of hybrid systems. In: Gopalakrishnan, G., Qadeer, S. (eds.) CAV 2011. LNCS, vol. 6806, pp. 379–395. Springer, Heidelberg (2011). doi:10.1007/978-3-642-22110-1_30
15. Fulton, N., Mitsch, S., Quesel, J.-D., Völp, M., Platzer, A.: KeYmaera X: an axiomatic tactical theorem prover for hybrid systems. In: Felty, A.P., Middeldorp, A. (eds.) CADE 2015. LNCS (LNAI), vol. 9195, pp. 527–538. Springer, Cham (2015). doi:10.1007/978-3-319-21401-6_36
16. Ghorbal, K., Platzer, A.: Characterizing algebraic invariants by differential radical invariants. In: Ábrahám, E., Havelund, K. (eds.) TACAS 2014. LNCS, vol. 8413, pp. 279–294. Springer, Heidelberg (2014). doi:10.1007/978-3-642-54862-8_19
17. Ghorbal, K., Sogokon, A., Platzer, A.: A hierarchy of proof rules for checking differential invariance of algebraic sets. In: D'Souza, D., Lal, A., Larsen, K.G. (eds.) VMCAI 2015. LNCS, vol. 8931, pp. 431–448. Springer, Heidelberg (2015). doi:10.1007/978-3-662-46081-8_24
18. Gulwani, S., Tiwari, A.: Constraint-based approach for analysis of hybrid systems. In: Gupta, A., Malik, S. (eds.) CAV 2008. LNCS, vol. 5123, pp. 190–203. Springer, Heidelberg (2008). doi:10.1007/978-3-540-70545-1_18
19. Henzinger, T.A.: The Theory of Hybrid Automata, pp. 278–292. IEEE Computer Society Press, Washington, DC (1996)
20. Immler, F.: Verified reachability analysis of continuous systems. In: Baier, C., Tinelli, C. (eds.) TACAS 2015. LNCS, vol. 9035, pp. 37–51. Springer, Heidelberg (2015). doi:10.1007/978-3-662-46681-0_3
21. Kong, S., Gao, S., Chen, W., Clarke, E.: dReach: δ-reachability analysis for hybrid systems. In: Baier, C., Tinelli, C. (eds.) TACAS 2015. LNCS, vol. 9035, pp. 200–205. Springer, Heidelberg (2015). doi:10.1007/978-3-662-46681-0_15
22. Koymans, R.: Specifying real-time properties with metric temporal logic. Real-Time Syst. 2(4), 255–299 (1990)

23. Lin, Y., Stadtherr, M.A.: Validated solutions of initial value problems for parametric ODEs. Appl. Numer. Math. **57**(10), 1145–1162 (2007)
24. Liu, J., Lv, J., Quan, Z., Zhan, N., Zhao, H., Zhou, C., Zou, L.: A calculus for hybrid CSP. In: Ueda, K. (ed.) APLAS 2010. LNCS, vol. 6461, pp. 1–15. Springer, Heidelberg (2010). doi:10.1007/978-3-642-17164-2_1
25. Liu, J., Zhan, N., Zhao, H.: Computing semi-algebraic invariants for polynomial dynamical systems. In: EMSOFT, pp. 97–106. ACM (2011)
26. Lygeros, J., Johansson, K.H., Simić, S.N., Zhang, J., Sastry, S.S.: Dynamical properties of hybrid automata. IEEE Trans. Autom. Control **48**(1), 2–17 (2003)
27. Maidens, J.N., Arcak, M.: Reachability analysis of nonlinear systems using matrix measures. IEEE Trans. Autom. Control **60**(1), 265–270 (2015)
28. Maidens, J.N., Arcak, M.: Trajectory-based reachability analysis of switched nonlinear systems using matrix measures. In: CDC, pp. 6358–6364, December 2014
29. Makino, K., Berz, M.: Cosy infinity version 9. Nucl. Instrum. Methods Phys. Res., Sect. A **558**(1), 346–350 (2006)
30. Matringe, N., Moura, A.V., Rebiha, R.: Generating invariants for non-linear hybrid systems by linear algebraic methods. In: Cousot, R., Martel, M. (eds.) SAS 2010. LNCS, vol. 6337, pp. 373–389. Springer, Heidelberg (2010). doi:10.1007/978-3-642-15769-1_23
31. Mitrohin, C., Podelski, A.: Composing stability proofs for hybrid systems. In: Fahrenberg, U., Tripakis, S. (eds.) FORMATS 2011. LNCS, vol. 6919, pp. 286–300. Springer, Heidelberg (2011). doi:10.1007/978-3-642-24310-3_20
32. Möhlmann, E., Hagemann, W., Theel, O.: Hybrid tools for hybrid systems – proving stability and safety at once. In: Sankaranarayanan, S., Vicario, E. (eds.) FORMATS 2015. LNCS, vol. 9268, pp. 222–239. Springer, Cham (2015). doi:10.1007/978-3-319-22975-1_15
33. Möhlmann, E., Theel, O.: Stabhyli: a tool for automatic stability verification of non-linear hybrid systems. In: HSCC, pp. 107–112. ACM (2013)
34. Navarro-López, E.M., Carter, R.: Hybrid automata: an insight into the discrete abstraction of discontinuous systems. Int. J. Syst. Sci. **42**(11), 1883–1898 (2011)
35. Navarro-López, E.M., Carter, R.: Deadness and how to disprove liveness in hybrid dynamical systems. Theor. Comput. Sci. **642**(C), 1–23 (2016)
36. Navarro-López, E.M., Suárez, R.: Practical approach to modelling and controlling stick-slip oscillations in oilwell drillstrings. In: Proceedings of the 2004 IEEE International Conference on Control Applications, vol. 2, pp. 1454–1460. IEEE (2004)
37. Nedialkov, N.S.: Interval tools for ODEs and DAEs. In: SCAN (2006)
38. Neher, M., Jackson, K.R., Nedialkov, N.S.: On Taylor model based integration of ODEs. SIAM J. Numer. Anal. **45**(1), 236–262 (2007)
39. Nishida, T., Mizutani, K., Kubota, A., Doshita, S.: Automated phase portrait analysis by integrating qualitative and quantitative analysis. In: Proceedings of the 9th National Conference on Artificial Intelligence, pp. 811–816 (1991)
40. Paulson, L.C.: MetiTarski: past and future. In: Beringer, L., Felty, A. (eds.) ITP 2012. LNCS, vol. 7406, pp. 1–10. Springer, Heidelberg (2012). doi:10.1007/978-3-642-32347-8_1
41. Platzer, A.: Differential dynamic logic for hybrid systems. J. Autom. Reason. **41**(2), 143–189 (2008)
42. Platzer, A.: Differential-algebraic dynamic logic for differential-algebraic programs. J. Log. Comput. **20**(1), 309–352 (2010)
43. Platzer, A., Clarke, E.M.: Computing differential invariants of hybrid systems as fixedpoints. In: Gupta, A., Malik, S. (eds.) CAV 2008. LNCS, vol. 5123, pp. 176–189. Springer, Heidelberg (2008). doi:10.1007/978-3-540-70545-1_17

44. Platzer, A., Quesel, J.-D.: KeYmaera: a hybrid theorem prover for hybrid systems (system description). In: Armando, A., Baumgartner, P., Dowek, G. (eds.) IJCAR 2008. LNCS (LNAI), vol. 5195, pp. 171–178. Springer, Heidelberg (2008). doi:10. 1007/978-3-540-71070-7_15

45. Podelski, A., Wagner, S.: Model checking of hybrid systems: from reachability towards stability. In: Hespanha, J.P., Tiwari, A. (eds.) HSCC 2006. LNCS, vol. 3927, pp. 507–521. Springer, Heidelberg (2006). doi:10.1007/11730637_38

46. Podelski, A., Wagner, S.: Region stability proofs for hybrid systems. In: Raskin, J.-F., Thiagarajan, P.S. (eds.) FORMATS 2007. LNCS, vol. 4763, pp. 320–335. Springer, Heidelberg (2007). doi:10.1007/978-3-540-75454-1_23

47. Podelski, A., Wagner, S.: A sound and complete proof rule for region stability of hybrid systems. In: Bemporad, A., Bicchi, A., Buttazzo, G. (eds.) HSCC 2007. LNCS, vol. 4416, pp. 750–753. Springer, Heidelberg (2007). doi:10.1007/978-3-540-71493-4_76

48. Prabhakar, P., Garcia Soto, M.: Abstraction based model-checking of stability of hybrid systems. In: Sharygina, N., Veith, H. (eds.) CAV 2013. LNCS, vol. 8044, pp. 280–295. Springer, Heidelberg (2013). doi:10.1007/978-3-642-39799-8_20

49. Prajna, S., Jadbabaie, A.: Safety verification of hybrid systems using barrier certificates. In: Alur, R., Pappas, G.J. (eds.) HSCC 2004. LNCS, vol. 2993, pp. 477–492. Springer, Heidelberg (2004). doi:10.1007/978-3-540-24743-2_32

50. Ratschan, S., She, Z.: Providing a basin of attraction to a target region of polynomial systems by computation of Lyapunov-like functions. SIAM J. Control Optim. **48**(7), 4377–4394 (2010)

51. Richardson, D.: Some undecidable problems involving elementary functions of a real variable. J. Symb. Logic **33**(4), 514–520 (1968)

52. Sankaranarayanan, S.: Automatic invariant generation for hybrid systems using ideal fixed points. In: HSCC, pp. 221–230 (2010)

53. Sankaranarayanan, S., Sipma, H.B., Manna, Z.: Constructing invariants for hybrid systems. FMSD **32**(1), 25–55 (2008)

54. Sogokon, A., Ghorbal, K., Jackson, P.B., Platzer, A.: A method for invariant generation for polynomial continuous systems. In: Jobstmann, B., Leino, K.R.M. (eds.) VMCAI 2016. LNCS, vol. 9583, pp. 268–288. Springer, Heidelberg (2016). doi:10. 1007/978-3-662-49122-5_13

55. Sogokon, A., Jackson, P.B.: Direct formal verification of liveness properties in continuous and hybrid dynamical systems. In: Björner, N., de Boer, F. (eds.) FM 2015. LNCS, vol. 9109, pp. 514–531. Springer, Cham (2015). doi:10.1007/978-3-319-19249-9_32

56. Sogokon, A., Jackson, P.B., Johnson, T.T.: Verifying safety and persistence properties of hybrid systems using flowpipes and continuous invariants. Technical report, Vanderbilt University (2017)

57. Strzeboński, A.W.: Cylindrical decomposition for systems transcendental in the first variable. J. Symb. Comput. **46**(11), 1284–1290 (2011)

58. Taly, A., Tiwari, A.: Deductive verification of continuous dynamical systems. In: Kannan, R., Kumar, K.N. (eds.) FSTTCS. LIPIcs, vol. 4, pp. 383–394. Schloss Dagstuhl - Leibniz-Zentrum für Informatik, Wadern (2009)

59. Tiwari, A.: Generating box invariants. In: Egerstedt, M., Mishra, B. (eds.) HSCC 2008. LNCS, vol. 4981, pp. 658–661. Springer, Heidelberg (2008). doi:10.1007/978-3-540-78929-1_58

60. Wang, S., Zhan, N., Zou, L.: An improved HHL prover: an interactive theorem prover for hybrid systems. In: Butler, M., Conchon, S., Zaïdi, F. (eds.) ICFEM 2015. LNCS, vol. 9407, pp. 382–399. Springer, Cham (2015). doi:10.1007/978-3-319-25423-4_25
61. Xue, B., Easwaran, A., Cho, N.J., Fränzle, M.: Reach-avoid verification for nonlinear systems based on boundary analysis. IEEE Trans. Autom. Control (2016)
62. Zhao, H., Yang, M., Zhan, N., Gu, B., Zou, L., Chen, Y.: Formal verification of a descent guidance control program of a lunar lander. In: Jones, C., Pihlajasaari, P., Sun, J. (eds.) FM 2014. LNCS, vol. 8442, pp. 733–748. Springer, Cham (2014). doi:10.1007/978-3-319-06410-9_49
63. Zhao, H., Zhan, N., Kapur, D.: Synthesizing switching controllers for hybrid systems by generating invariants. In: Liu, Z., Woodcock, J., Zhu, H. (eds.) Theories of Programming and Formal Methods. LNCS, vol. 8051, pp. 354–373. Springer, Heidelberg (2013). doi:10.1007/978-3-642-39698-4_22

A Relational Shape Abstract Domain

Hugo Illous[1,2(✉)], Matthieu Lemerre[1], and Xavier Rival[2]

[1] CEA, LIST, Software Reliability and Security Laboratory,
P.C. 174, 91191 Gif-sur-Yvette, France
{hugo.illous,matthieu.lemerre}@cea.fr
[2] Inria Paris/CNRS/École Normale Supérieure/PSL Research University,
Paris, France
xavier.rival@ens.fr

Abstract. Static analyses aim at inferring semantic properties of programs. While many analyses compute an over-approximation of reachable states, some analyses compute a description of the input-output relations of programs. In the case of numeric programs, several analyses have been proposed that utilize relational numerical abstract domains to describe relations. On the other hand, designing abstractions for relations over memory states and taking shapes into account is challenging. In this paper, we propose a set of novel logical connectives to describe such relations, which are inspired by separation logic. This logic can express that certain memory areas are unchanged, freshly allocated, or freed, or that only part of the memory was modified. Using these connectives, we build an abstract domain and design a static analysis that over-approximates relations over memory states containing inductive structures. We implement this analysis and report on the analysis of a basic library of list manipulating functions.

1 Introduction

Generally, static analyses aim at computing semantic properties of programs. Two common families of analyses are *reachability analyses*, that compute an over-approximation for the *set of reachable states* of programs, and *relational analyses*, that compute an over-approximation for the relations between input and output states. In general, sets of states are easier to abstract than state relations, which often makes reachability analyses simpler to design. On the other hand, abstracting relations brings several advantages:

– First, state relations allow to make the analyses modular [3,6,10,17,22] and compositional. Indeed, to analyze a sequence of two sub-programs, relational analyses can simply analyze each sub-program separately, and compose the resulting state relations. When sub-programs are functions, relational analyses may analyze each function separately, and compute one summary per function, so that the analysis of a function call does not require re-analyzing the body of the function, which is an advantage for scalability.

© Springer International Publishing AG 2017
C. Barrett et al. (Eds.): NFM 2017, LNCS 10227, pp. 212–229, 2017.
DOI: 10.1007/978-3-319-57288-8_15

– Second, some properties can be expressed on state relations but not on sets of states, which makes relational analyses intrinsically more expressive. For example, contract languages [1, 21] let functions be specified by formulas that may refer both to the input and to the output states. Such properties cannot be expressed using abstractions of sets of states, thus are beyond the scope of reachability analyses.

In general, the increased expressiveness of relational analyses requires more expressive abstractions. Let us discuss, as an example the case of numeric programs. A common way to express relations between input and output states consists in defining for each variable x a primed version x' that describes the value of x in the output state whereas the non primed version denotes the value of x in the input state. In this context, non-relational numerical abstract domain such as intervals [8] cannot capture any interesting relation between input and output states. On the other hand, relational numerical abstract domains such as convex polyhedra [7] can effectively capture relations between input and output states, as shown in [22]: for instance, when applied to a program that increments x by one, this analysis can infer the relation $x' = x + 1$.

In the context of programs manipulating complex data structures, relational analysis could allow to compute interesting classes of program properties. For instance, such analyses could express and verify that some memory areas were not physically modified by a program. Reachability analyses such as [5, 15, 24] cannot distinguish a program that inputs a list and leaves it unmodified from a program that inputs a list, copies it into an identical version and deallocates it, whereas a relational analysis could. More generally, it is often interesting to infer that a memory region is not modified by a program.

Separation logic [23] provides an elegant description for sets of states and is at the foundation of many reachability analyses for heap properties. In particular, the separating conjunction connective $*$ expresses that two regions are disjoint and allows local reasoning. On the other hand, it cannot describe state relations.

In this paper, we propose a logic inspired by separation logics and that can describe such properties. It provides connectives to describe that a memory region has been left unmodified by a program fragment, or that memory states can be split into disjoint sub-regions that undergo different transformations. We build an abstract domain upon this logic, and apply it to design an analysis for programs manipulating simple list or tree data structures. We make the following contributions:

– In Sect. 2, we demonstrate the abstraction of state relations using a specific family of heap predicates;
– In Sect. 4, we set up a logic to describe heap state relations and lift it into an abstract domain that describe concrete relations defined in Sect. 3;
– In Sect. 5, we design static analysis algorithms to infer heap state relations from abstract pre-condition;
– In Sect. 6, we report on experiments on basic linked data structures (lists and trees);
– Finally, we discuss related works in Sect. 7 and conclude in Sect. 8.

2 Overview and Motivating Example

We consider the example code shown in Fig. 1, which implements the insertion of an element inside a non empty singly linked list containing integer values. When applied to a pointer to an existing non empty list and an integer value, this function traverses it partially (based on a condition on the values stored in list elements —that is elided in the figure). It then allocates a new list element, inserts it at the selected position and copies the integer argument into the **data** field. For instance, Fig. 2(a) shows an input list containing elements $0, 8, 6, 1$ and an output list where value 9 is inserted as a new element in the list. We observe that all elements of the input list are left physically unmodified except the element right before the insertion point. We now discuss abstractions of the behaviors of this program using abstractions for sets of states and abstractions for state relations.

```
1  typedef struct list { struct list * next; int data; } list;
2  void insert_non_empty( list *l, int v ){
3    assume(l != NULL); list *c = l;
4    while( c->next != NULL && ... ){
5      c = c->next;
6    }
7    list *e = new( {next, data} ); // allocate 2 fields block
8    e->next = c->next; c->next = e; e->data = v;
9  }
```

Fig. 1. A list insertion program

Reachability Analysis. First, we consider an abstraction based on separation logics with inductive predicates as used in [5,15]. We assume that the predicate **list**(α) describes heap regions that consist of a well-formed linked list starting at address α (α is a symbolic variable used in the abstraction to denote a concrete address). This predicate is intuitively defined by induction as follows: it means either the region is empty and α is the null pointer, or the region is not empty, and consists of a list element of address α and with a **next** field containing a value described by symbolic variable β and a region that can be described by **list**(β). Thus, the valid input states for the insertion function can be abstracted by the abstract state shown in the top of Fig. 2(b). The analysis of the function needs to express that the insertion occurs somewhere in the middle of the list. This requires a list segment predicate **listseg**(α, α'), that is defined in a similar way as for **list**: it describes region that stores a sub list starting at address α and the last element of which has a **next** field pointing to address α' (note that the empty region can be described by **listseg**(α, α)). Using this predicate, we can now also express an abstraction for the output states of the insertion function: the abstract state shown in the bottom of Fig. 2(b) describes the states where the new element was inserted in the middle of the structure (the list starts with a segment, then the predecessor of the inserted element, then the inserted element, and finally the list tail). We observe that this abstraction allows to express and to verify that the function is memory safe, and returns a well-formed list. Indeed, it captures the fact that no null or dangling pointer is ever dereferenced. Moreover, all states described by the abstract post-condition consist of a well-formed list, made of a segment, followed by two elements and a list tail. On the other hand, it does not say anything about the location of the list in the output state with respect to the list in the input state. More precisely, it cannot capture the fact that the elements of addresses a_0, a_1, a_3 are left unmodified physically. This is a consequence of the fact that each abstract state in Fig. 2(b) independently describes a set of concrete heaps.

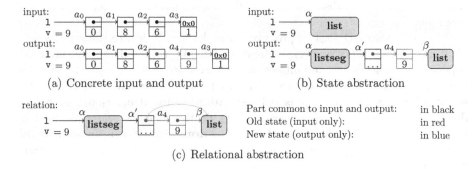

(a) Concrete input and output   (b) State abstraction

(c) Relational abstraction

Fig. 2. Abstractions (Color figure online)

Relational Analysis. To abstract *state relations* instead of sets of states, we now propose to define a new structure in Fig. 2(c), that partially overlays the abstractions of input and output states. First, we observe that the tail of the list is not modified at all, thus, we describe it with a single predicate $\mathbf{Id}(\mathbf{list}(\beta))$, that denotes pairs made of input state and an output state, that are *physically equal* and can both be described by $\mathbf{list}(\beta)$. The same kind of predicate can be used to describe that the initial segment has not changed between the two states. Second, we need to define a counterpart for separating conjunction at the relation level. Indeed, the effect of the insertion function can be decomposed as its effect on the initial segment (which is left unchanged), its effect on the tail (which is also left unchanged) and its effect on the insertion point (where a new element is allocated and a **next** pointer is modified). This relation separating conjunction is noted $*_R$. To avoid confusion, from now on, we write $*_S$ for the usual separating conjunction. Last, the insertion function allocates a new element and modifies the value of the **next** field of an existing element. To account for this, we need a new connective $[\cdot \dashrightarrow \cdot]$ which is applied to two abstract states: if $h_0^\sharp, h_1^\sharp$ are abstract heaps (described by formulas in the usual separation logic with inductive predicates), then $[h_0^\sharp \dashrightarrow h_1^\sharp]$ describes the transformation of an input state described by $h_0^\sharp$ into an output state described by $h_1^\sharp$. This is presented with different colors in the figure. In Sect. 4, we formalize this logics and the abstraction that it defines. The analysis by forward abstract interpretation [8] starts with the identity relation at function entry, and computes relations between input and output states step by step. The analysis algorithms need to unfold inductive predicates to materialize cells (for instance to analyze the test at line 4), and to fold inductive predicates in order to analyze loops. In addition to this, it also needs to reason over Id, $[\cdot \dashrightarrow \cdot]$ and $*_R$ predicates, and perform operations similar to unfolding and folding on them. Section 5 describes the analysis algorithms.

3   Concrete Semantics

Before defining the abstraction, we fix notations for concrete states and programs.

We let $\mathbb{X}$ denote the set of program variables and $\mathbb{V}$ denote the set of values (that includes the set of numeric addresses). A field $\in \mathbb{F}$ (noted as $\mathtt{next}, \mathtt{data}, \ldots$) denotes both field names and offsets. A memory state $\sigma \in \mathbb{M}$ is a partial function from addresses to values. We write $\mathbf{dom}(\sigma)$ for the domain of σ, that is the set of addresses for which it is defined. Additionally, if σ_0, σ_1 are such that $\mathbf{dom}(\sigma_0) \cap \mathbf{dom}(\sigma_1) = \emptyset$, we let $\sigma_0 \circledast \sigma_1$ be the memory state obtained by merging σ_0 and σ_1 (its domain is $\mathbf{dom}(\sigma_0) \cup \mathbf{dom}(\sigma_1)$). If a_i is an address and v_i a value, we write $[a_0 \mapsto v_0; \ldots; a_n \mapsto v_n]$ the memory state where a_i contains v_i (with $0 \le i \le n$).

In the following, we consider simple imperative programs, that include basic assignments, allocation and deallocation statements and loops (although our analysis supports a larger language, notably with conditionals and unstructured control flow). Programs are described by the grammar below:

$$
\begin{array}{llll}
\mathtt{L} & ::= \mathtt{x} & (\mathtt{x} \in \mathbb{X}) \mid \mathtt{L\,{-}{>}\,f} & (\mathtt{f} \in \mathbb{F}) & \text{l-values} \\
\mathtt{E} & ::= v & (v \in \mathbb{V}) \mid \mathtt{L} \mid \mathtt{E} \oplus \mathtt{E} & (\oplus \in \{+, -, \le, \ldots\}) & \text{expressions} \\
\mathtt{P} & ::= \mathtt{L} = \mathtt{E}; \mid \mathtt{L} = \mathbf{new}(\{\mathtt{f_0}, \ldots\}); \mid \mathbf{free}(\mathtt{L}); \mid \mathtt{P}; \mathtt{P} \mid \mathbf{while}(\mathtt{E})\mathtt{P} & \text{programs}
\end{array}
$$

We assume the semantics of a program $\mathtt{P}$ is defined as a function $[\![\mathtt{P}]\!]$ that maps a set of input states into a set of output states (thus $[\![\mathtt{P}]\!] : \mathcal{P}(\mathbb{M}) \longrightarrow \mathcal{P}(\mathbb{M})$). We do not provide a full formal definition for $[\![\mathtt{P}]\!]$ as it is classical. Given a program $\mathtt{P}$, we define its *relational semantics* $[\![\mathtt{P}]\!]_\mathcal{R} : \mathbb{M} \to \mathbb{M} \times \mathbb{M}$ by:

$$\forall M \subseteq \mathbb{M}, \; [\![\mathtt{P}]\!]_\mathcal{R}(M) = \{(\sigma_0, \sigma_1) \mid \sigma_0 \in M \wedge \sigma_1 \in [\![\mathtt{P}]\!](\{\sigma_0\})\}$$

In the following, we define an analysis to compute an over-approximation for $[\![\mathtt{P}]\!]_\mathcal{R}$.

4   Abstraction

In this section, we first define *abstract states*, that describe sets of memory states (as in [5]), and then we set up *abstract state relations*, that describe binary relations over memory states. Although our analysis and implementation support more general inductive predicates (such as trees and others), we consider only list inductive predicates in the body of the paper, for the sake of simplicity.

Abstract States. We assume a countable set $\mathbb{A} = \{\alpha, \beta, \ldots\}$ of *symbolic addresses* that abstract values and heap addresses. An abstract state $\sigma^\sharp$ consists of an abstract heap $h^\sharp$ with a conjunction of numerical constraints such as equalities and disequalities. An abstract heap is a separating conjunction of region predicates that abstract *separate* memory regions [23] (as mentioned above, separating conjunction is denoted by $*_s$). A node $n \in \mathbb{N}$ is either a variable address $\&x$ or a symbolic address α. A region predicate is either **emp** describing an empty region, or a points-to predicate $n \cdot f \mapsto n'$ (that describes a heap memory cell at the base address n with the possibly null offset f and with the content n'), or a summary predicate **list**(n) describing a list structure or **listseg**(n, n') for a (possibly empty) list segment from address n to n'. The **list** predicate is defined by induction as follows:

$$\textbf{list}(n) ::= \textbf{emp} \wedge n = \textbf{0x0}$$
$$\vee \quad n \cdot \textbf{next} \mapsto \alpha_n *_s n \cdot \textbf{data} \mapsto \alpha_d *_s \textbf{list}(\alpha_n) \wedge n \neq \textbf{0x0}$$

Segment predicate **listseg** stands for the segment version of **list** and describes a list without a tail; it can also be defined by induction. We write $\overset{unfold}{\longrightarrow}$ for the unfolding relation that syntactically transforms an instance of an inductive predicate into any of the disjuncts of that predicate.

Definition 1 (Abstract state). *Abstract heaps* and *abstract states* are *defined by the grammar below:*

$$c^\sharp \quad ::= n \odot \textbf{0x0} \quad (\odot \in \{=, \neq\}) \mid n = n' \mid c^\sharp \wedge c^\sharp$$
$$h^\sharp(\in \mathbb{H}) ::= \textbf{emp} \mid n \cdot f \mapsto n' \mid \textbf{list}(n) \mid \textbf{listseg}(n, n') \mid h^\sharp *_s h^\sharp$$
$$\sigma^\sharp(\in \Sigma) ::= h^\sharp \wedge c^\sharp \qquad n(\in \mathbb{N}) ::= \alpha \quad (\alpha \in \mathbb{A}) \mid \&x \quad (x \in \mathbb{X})$$

We now define the meaning of abstract heaps and abstract states using *concretization functions* [8], that associate to abstract elements the set of concrete elements they describe. To concretize an abstract heap, we also need to define how the nodes are bound into concrete values in concrete memories. We call *valuation* a function ν that maps nodes into concrete values and addresses.

Definition 2 (Concretization of abstract states). *The concretization function $\gamma_\mathbb{C}$ maps a numeric constraint into a set of valuations whereas $\gamma_\mathbb{H}$ and γ_Σ respectively map an abstract heap and an abstract state into a set of pairs made of memory state and a valuation. They are defined by induction as follows:*

$$\gamma_\mathbb{C}(n \odot \textbf{0x0}) = \{\nu \mid \nu(n) \odot \textbf{0x0}\}$$
$$\gamma_\mathbb{C}(n = n') = \{\nu \mid \nu(n) = \nu(n')\} \qquad \gamma_\mathbb{C}(c_0^\sharp \wedge c_1^\sharp) = \gamma_\mathbb{C}(c_0^\sharp) \cap \gamma_\mathbb{C}(c_1^\sharp)$$
$$\gamma_\mathbb{H}(n \cdot f \mapsto n') = \{[\nu(n) + f \mapsto \nu(n')], \nu)\} \qquad \gamma_\mathbb{H}(\textbf{emp}) = \{([], \nu)\}$$
$$\gamma_\mathbb{H}(\textbf{ind}) = \bigcup \{\gamma_\Sigma(\sigma^\sharp) \mid \textbf{ind} \overset{unfold}{\longrightarrow} \sigma^\sharp\} \quad if \; \textbf{ind} \; is \; \textbf{list}(n) \; or \; \textbf{listseg}(n, n')$$
$$\gamma_\mathbb{H}(h_0^\sharp *_s h_1^\sharp) = \{(\sigma_0 \circledast \sigma_1, \nu) \mid (\sigma_0, \nu) \in \gamma_\mathbb{H}(h_0^\sharp) \wedge (\sigma_1, \nu) \in \gamma_\mathbb{H}(h_1^\sharp)\}$$
$$\gamma_\Sigma(h^\sharp \wedge c^\sharp) = \{(\sigma, \nu) \mid (\sigma, \nu) \in \gamma_\mathbb{H}(h^\sharp) \wedge \nu \in \gamma_\mathbb{C}(c^\sharp)\}$$

Example 1 (Abstract state). The abstract pre-condition of the program of Fig. 1 is $\&1 \mapsto \alpha *_S \text{list}(\alpha) *_S \&v \mapsto \beta$.

Abstract Relations. An *abstract heap relation* describes a set of pairs made of an *input* memory state σ_i and an *output* memory state σ_o. Abstract heap relations are defined by the following connectives:

- the *identity relation* $\text{Id}(h^\sharp)$ describes pairs of memory states that are equal and are both abstracted by $h^\sharp$; this corresponds to the identity transformation;
- the *transformation relation* $[h_i^\sharp \dashrightarrow h_o^\sharp]$ describes pairs corresponding to the transformation of a memory state abstracted by $h_i^\sharp$ into a memory state abstracted by $h_o^\sharp$;
- the *relation separating conjunction* $r_0^\sharp *_R r_1^\sharp$ of two heap relations $r_0^\sharp, r_1^\sharp$ denotes a transformation that can be described by combining independently the transformations described by $r_0^\sharp$ and $r_1^\sharp$ on disjoint memory regions.

Definition 3 (Abstract relations). *The syntax of abstract heap relations and abstract state relations are defined by the grammar below:*

$$r^\sharp (\in \mathbb{R}) ::= \text{Id}(h^\sharp) \mid [h^\sharp \dashrightarrow h^\sharp] \mid r^\sharp *_R r^\sharp \qquad \rho^\sharp (\in \Pi) ::= r^\sharp \wedge c^\sharp$$

The concretization of relations also requires using valuations as it also needs to define the concrete values that nodes denote. It thus returns triples made of two memory states and a valuation.

Definition 4 (Concretization of abstract relations). *The concretization functions γ_R, γ_Π respectively map an abstract heap relation and an abstract state relation into elements of $M \times M \times (N \longrightarrow V)$. They are defined by:*

$$\gamma_R(\text{Id}(h^\sharp)) = \{(\sigma, \sigma, \nu) \mid (\sigma, \nu) \in \gamma_H(h^\sharp)\}$$
$$\gamma_R([h_i^\sharp \dashrightarrow h_o^\sharp]) = \{(\sigma_i, \sigma_o, \nu) \mid (\sigma_i, \nu) \in \gamma_H(h_i^\sharp) \wedge (\sigma_o, \nu) \in \gamma_H(h_o^\sharp)\}$$
$$\gamma_R(r_0^\sharp *_R r_1^\sharp) = \{(\sigma_{i,0} \circledast \sigma_{i,1}, \sigma_{o,0} \circledast \sigma_{o,1}, \nu) \mid$$
$$(\sigma_{i,0}, \sigma_{o,0}, \nu) \in \gamma_R(r_0^\sharp) \wedge \mathbf{dom}(\sigma_{i,0}) \cap \mathbf{dom}(\sigma_{o,1}) = \emptyset$$
$$\wedge (\sigma_{i,1}, \sigma_{o,1}, \nu) \in \gamma_R(r_1^\sharp) \wedge \mathbf{dom}(\sigma_{i,1}) \cap \mathbf{dom}(\sigma_{o,0}) = \emptyset\}$$
$$\gamma_\Pi(r^\sharp \wedge c^\sharp) = \{(\sigma_i, \sigma_o, \nu) \mid (\sigma_i, \sigma_o, \nu) \in \gamma_R(r^\sharp) \wedge \nu \in \gamma_C(c^\sharp)\}$$

We remark that $*_R$ is commutative and associative.

Example 2 (Expressiveness). Let $r_0^\sharp = \text{Id}(\text{list}(n))$ and $r_1^\sharp = [\text{list}(n) \dashrightarrow \text{list}(n)]$. We observe that $r_0^\sharp$ describes only the identity transformation applied to a pre-condition where n is the address of a well-formed list, whereas $r_1^\sharp$ describes any transformation that inputs such a list and also outputs such a list, but may modify its content, add or remove elements, or may modify the order of list elements (except for the first one which remains at address n). This means that $\gamma_R(r_0^\sharp) \subset \gamma_R(r_1^\sharp)$.

More generally, we have the following properties:

Theorem 1 (Properties). *Let* $h^\sharp, h_0^\sharp, h_1^\sharp, h_{i,0}^\sharp, h_{i,1}^\sharp, h_{o,0}^\sharp, h_{o,1}^\sharp$ *be abstract heaps. Then, we have the following properties*

1. $\gamma_\mathbb{R}(\mathtt{Id}(h_0^\sharp *_\mathtt{S} h_1^\sharp)) = \gamma_\mathbb{R}(\mathtt{Id}(h_0^\sharp) *_\mathtt{R} \mathtt{Id}(h_1^\sharp))$
2. $\gamma_\mathbb{R}(\mathtt{Id}(h^\sharp)) \subseteq \gamma_\mathbb{R}([h^\sharp \dashrightarrow h^\sharp])$ *(the opposite inclusion may not hold, as observed in Example 2);*
3. $\gamma_\mathbb{R}([h_{i,0}^\sharp \dashrightarrow h_{o,0}^\sharp] *_\mathtt{R} [h_{i,1}^\sharp \dashrightarrow h_{o,1}^\sharp]) \subseteq \gamma_\mathbb{R}([(h_{i,0}^\sharp *_\mathtt{S} h_{i,1}^\sharp) \dashrightarrow (h_{o,0}^\sharp *_\mathtt{S} h_{o,1}^\sharp)])$ *(the opposite inclusion may not hold).*

Example 3 (Abstract state relation). The effect of the insertion function of Fig. 1 can be described by the abstract state relation $\mathtt{Id}(h_0^\sharp) *_\mathtt{R} [h_1^\sharp \dashrightarrow h_2^\sharp] *_\mathtt{R} [\mathbf{emp} \dashrightarrow h_3^\sharp]$, where $h_0^\sharp = \&1 \mapsto \alpha_0 *_\mathtt{S} \&v \mapsto \beta *_\mathtt{S} \mathbf{listseg}(\alpha_0, \alpha_1) *_\mathtt{S} \mathbf{list}(\alpha_2) *_\mathtt{S} \alpha_1 \cdot \mathbf{data} \mapsto \beta_2)$ (preserved region), $h_1^\sharp = \alpha_1 \cdot \mathbf{next} \mapsto \alpha_2$, $h_2^\sharp = \alpha_1 \cdot \mathbf{next} \mapsto \alpha$ (modified region) and $h_3^\sharp = \alpha \cdot \mathbf{next} \mapsto \alpha_2 *_\mathtt{S} \alpha \cdot \mathbf{data} \mapsto \beta$ (new region).

5   Analysis Algorithms

We now propose a static analysis to compute abstract state relations as described in Definition 3. It proceeds by forward abstract interpretation [8], starting from the abstract relation $\mathtt{Id}(h^\sharp)$ where $h^\sharp$ is a pre-condition, supplied by the user.

More generally, the analysis of a program P is a function $[\![P]\!]_\mathcal{R}^\sharp$ that inputs an abstract state relation describing a previous transformation $\mathcal{T}$ done on the input *before* running P and returns a relation describing that transformation $\mathcal{T}$ followed by the execution of P. Thus, $[\![P]\!]_\mathcal{R}^\sharp$ should meet the following soundness condition:

$$\forall \rho^\sharp \in \Pi, \ \forall (\sigma_0, \sigma_1) \in \gamma_\Pi(\rho^\sharp), \ \forall \sigma_2 \in \mathbb{M},$$
$$(\sigma_1, \sigma_2) \in [\![P]\!]_\mathcal{R} \implies (\sigma_0, \sigma_2) \in \gamma_\Pi([\![P]\!]_\mathcal{R}^\sharp(\rho^\sharp))$$

5.1   Basic Abstract Post-conditions

We start with the computation of abstract post-condition for assignments, allocation and deallocation, on abstract relations that do not contain inductive predicates. As an example, we consider the analysis of an assignment L = E, starting from an abstract pre-condition relation $r^\sharp$. To compute the effect of this assignment on $r^\sharp$, the analysis should update it so as to reflect the modification of L in the output states of the pairs denoted by $r^\sharp$. We first consider the case where $r^\sharp$ is a transformation relation.

Case of a Transformation Relation. We assume $r^\sharp = [h_0^\sharp \dashrightarrow h_1^\sharp]$. Then, if $h_2^\sharp$ is an abstract state that describes the memory states after the assignment L = E, when it is executed on a state that is in $\gamma_\mathtt{H}(h_1^\sharp)$, then a valid definition for $[\![L = E]\!]_\mathcal{R}^\sharp(r^\sharp)$ is $[h_0^\sharp \dashrightarrow h_2^\sharp]$. An algorithm for computing such a $h_2^\sharp$ can be found in [5]. It first evaluates L into a points-to predicate $n \cdot f \mapsto n'$ describing the cell that L represents, then evaluates E into a node n'' describing the value of the right hand side and finally replaces $n \cdot f \mapsto n'$ with $n \cdot f \mapsto n''$. As a consequence, we have the following definitions for the two main cases of assignments:

$$[\![x = y \mathrel{-}\!\!> f]\!]_{\mathcal{R}}^{\sharp}([h_0^{\sharp} \dashrightarrow (h_1^{\sharp} *_S \&x \mapsto \alpha_0 *_S \&y \mapsto \alpha_1 *_S \alpha_1 \cdot f \mapsto \alpha_2)])$$
$$= [h_0^{\sharp} \dashrightarrow (h_1^{\sharp} *_S \&x \mapsto \alpha_2 *_S \&y \mapsto \alpha_1 *_S \alpha_1 \cdot f \mapsto \alpha_2)]$$
$$[\![x \mathrel{-}\!\!> f = y]\!]_{\mathcal{R}}^{\sharp}([h_0^{\sharp} \dashrightarrow (h_1^{\sharp} *_S \&x \mapsto \alpha_0 *_S \alpha_0 \cdot f \mapsto \alpha_1 *_S \&y \mapsto \alpha_2)])$$
$$= [h_0^{\sharp} \dashrightarrow (h_1^{\sharp} *_S \&x \mapsto \alpha_0 *_S \alpha_0 \cdot f \mapsto \alpha_2 *_S \&y \mapsto \alpha_2)]$$

Case of a Separating Conjunction Relation. We now assume that $r^{\sharp} = r_0^{\sharp} *_R r_1^{\sharp}$. If the assignment can be fully analyzed on $r_0^{\sharp}$ (i.e., it does not read or modify $r_1^{\sharp}$), then the following definition provides a sound transfer function, that relies on the same principle as the Frame rule [23] for separation logic:

$$\text{if } [\![L = E]\!]_{\mathcal{R}}^{\sharp}(r_0^{\sharp}) \text{ is defined, then } [\![L = E]\!]_{\mathcal{R}}^{\sharp}(r_0^{\sharp} *_R r_1^{\sharp}) = [\![L = E]\!]_{\mathcal{R}}^{\sharp}(r_0^{\sharp}) *_R r_1^{\sharp}$$

When $L = E$ writes in $r_0^{\sharp}$ and reads in $r_1^{\sharp}$, we get a similar definition as above. For instance:

$$[\![x = y \mathrel{-}\!\!> f]\!]_{\mathcal{R}}^{\sharp}([h_0^{\sharp} \dashrightarrow (\&x \mapsto \alpha_0)] *_R [h_1^{\sharp} \dashrightarrow (\&y \mapsto \alpha_1 *_S \alpha_1 \cdot f \mapsto \alpha_2)])$$
$$[h_0^{\sharp} \dashrightarrow (\&x \mapsto \alpha_2)] *_R [h_1^{\sharp} \dashrightarrow (\&y \mapsto \alpha_1 *_S \alpha_1 \cdot f \mapsto \alpha_2)]$$

Case of an Identity Relation. We now assume that $r^{\sharp} = \text{Id}(h^{\sharp})$. As observed in Theorem 1, $\gamma_{\Pi}(\text{Id}(h^{\sharp})) \subseteq \gamma_{\Pi}([h^{\sharp} \dashrightarrow h^{\sharp}])$. We derive from the previous two paragraphs and from this principle the following definitions:

$$[\![x = y \mathrel{-}\!\!> f]\!]_{\mathcal{R}}^{\sharp}(\text{Id}(h^{\sharp} *_S \&x \mapsto \alpha_0 *_S \&y \mapsto \alpha_1 *_S \alpha_1 \cdot f \mapsto \alpha_2))$$
$$= \text{Id}(h^{\sharp} *_S \&y \mapsto \alpha_1 *_S \alpha_1 \cdot f \mapsto \alpha_2) *_R [(\&x \mapsto \alpha_0) \dashrightarrow (\&x \mapsto \alpha_2)]$$
$$[\![x \mathrel{-}\!\!> f = y]\!]_{\mathcal{R}}^{\sharp}(\text{Id}(h^{\sharp} *_S \&x \mapsto \alpha_0 *_S \alpha_0 \cdot f \mapsto \alpha_1 *_S \&y \mapsto \alpha_2))$$
$$= \text{Id}(h^{\sharp} *_S \&x \mapsto \alpha_0 *_S \&y \mapsto \alpha_2) *_R [(\alpha_0 \cdot f \mapsto \alpha_1) \dashrightarrow (\alpha_0 \cdot f \mapsto \alpha_2)]$$

Other Transfer Functions. Condition tests boil down to numeric constraints intersections. The analysis of allocation needs to account for the creation of cells in the right side of relations whereas deallocation needs to account for the deletion of cells that were present before. Thus, for instance:

$$[\![x = \mathbf{new}(\{f_0, \ldots, f_n\})]\!]_{\mathcal{R}}^{\sharp}(r^{\sharp} *_R [h^{\sharp} \dashrightarrow (\&x \mapsto \alpha)])$$
$$= r^{\sharp} *_R [h^{\sharp} \dashrightarrow (\&x \mapsto \beta)] *_R [\mathbf{emp} \dashrightarrow (\beta \cdot f_0 \mapsto \beta_0 *_S \ldots *_S \beta \cdot f_n \mapsto \beta_n)]$$
$$\text{where } \beta, \beta_0, \ldots, \beta_n \text{ are fresh}$$
$$[\![\mathbf{free}(x)]\!]_{\mathcal{R}}^{\sharp}(r^{\sharp} *_R \text{Id}(\&x \mapsto \alpha *_S \alpha \cdot f_0 \mapsto \alpha_0) *_R [h_i^{\sharp} \dashrightarrow (h_o^{\sharp} *_S \alpha \cdot f_1 \mapsto \alpha_1)])$$
$$= r^{\sharp} *_R \text{Id}(\&x \mapsto \alpha) *_R [(\alpha \cdot f_0 \mapsto \alpha_0) \dashrightarrow \mathbf{emp}] *_R [h_i^{\sharp} \dashrightarrow h_o^{\sharp}]$$

5.2 Materialization and General Abstract Post-conditions

In Sect. 5.1, we considered only abstract states without inductive predicates, to first provide a simpler definition of abstract post-conditions. We now lift this restriction. For example, the analysis of the program in Fig. 1 starts with $\mathtt{Id}(\&1 \mapsto \alpha *_{\mathsf{S}} \mathbf{list}(\alpha) *_{\mathsf{S}} \&v \mapsto \beta)$, and then has to analyze a reading of 1 -> next.

If we consider an abstract state relation of the form $[\mathtt{h}^{\sharp} \dashrightarrow \mathbf{list}(\mathtt{n})]$, and an assignment that reads or writes a field at base address n, the inductive predicate $\mathbf{list}(\mathtt{n})$ should first be *unfolded* [5]: before the post-condition operators of Sect. 5.1 can be applied, this predicate first needs to be substituted with the disjunction of cases it is made of, as defined in Sect. 4. This process is known in reachability shape analyses as a technique to materialize cells [5,15,24]. It results in disjunctive abstract states. For instance, the concretization of the abstract state relation $[\mathtt{h}^{\sharp} \dashrightarrow \mathbf{list}(\mathtt{n})]$ is included in the union of the concretizations of $[\mathtt{h}^{\sharp} \dashrightarrow \mathbf{emp}] \wedge \mathtt{n} = \mathbf{0x0}$ and $[\mathtt{h}^{\sharp} \dashrightarrow (\mathtt{n} \cdot \mathbf{next} \mapsto \alpha_n *_{\mathsf{S}} \mathtt{n} \cdot \mathbf{data} \mapsto \alpha_d *_{\mathsf{S}} \mathbf{list}(\alpha_n))] \wedge \mathtt{n} \neq \mathbf{0x0})$. This disjunctive abstract states allows to analyze a read or write into a field at address n.

However, this naive extension of unfolding may be imprecise here. Let us consider the unfolding at node n in the abstract state relation $[\mathtt{n} \cdot \mathbf{next} \mapsto \alpha *_{\mathsf{S}} \mathtt{n} \cdot \mathbf{data} \mapsto \beta \dashrightarrow \mathbf{list}(\mathtt{n})]$. The above technique will generate two disjuncts, including one where $\mathtt{n} = \mathbf{0x0}$. However, n cannot be equal to the null pointer here, since n is the base address of a regular list element in the left side of the $[. \dashrightarrow .]$ abstract relation. Therefore, unfolding should take into account information in both sides of abstract relations for the sake of analysis precision.

In the following, we let $\mathbf{unfold}_{\Sigma}(\mathtt{n}, \sigma^{\sharp})$ denote the set of disjuncts produced by unfolding an inductive predicate at node n in abstract state $\sigma^{\sharp}$, if any. For instance, $\mathbf{unfold}_{\Sigma}(\mathtt{n}, \mathbf{list}(\mathtt{n}))$ is $\{(\mathbf{emp} \wedge \mathtt{n} = \mathbf{0x0}), (\mathtt{n} \cdot \mathbf{next} \mapsto \alpha_n *_{\mathsf{S}} \mathtt{n} \cdot \mathbf{data} \mapsto \alpha_d *_{\mathsf{S}} \mathbf{list}(\alpha_n)) \wedge \mathtt{n} \neq \mathbf{0x0}\}$. If there is no inductive predicate attached to node n in $\sigma^{\sharp}$, we let $\mathbf{unfold}_{\Sigma}(\alpha, \sigma^{\sharp}) = \{\sigma^{\sharp}\}$. This operator is sound in the sense that, $\gamma_{\Sigma}(\sigma^{\sharp})$ is included in $\cup\{\gamma_{\Sigma}(\sigma_u^{\sharp}) \mid \sigma_u^{\sharp} \in \mathbf{unfold}_{\Sigma}(\mathtt{n}, \sigma^{\sharp})\}$.

Using $\mathbf{unfold}_{\Sigma}$, we define the function $\mathbf{unfold}_{\Pi}$ that performs unfolding at a given node and in an abstract state relation as follows:

- $\mathbf{unfold}_{\Pi}(\mathtt{n}, \mathtt{Id}(\mathtt{h}^{\sharp})) = \{\mathtt{Id}(\mathtt{h}_u^{\sharp}) \wedge c_u^{\sharp} \mid (\mathtt{h}_u^{\sharp} \wedge c_u^{\sharp}) \in \mathbf{unfold}_{\Sigma}(\mathtt{n}, \mathtt{h}^{\sharp})\}$;
- if the node n carries inductive predicate in $r_0^{\sharp}$ then $\mathbf{unfold}_{\Pi}(\mathtt{n}, r_0^{\sharp} *_{\mathsf{R}} r_1^{\sharp}) = \{(r_{0,u}^{\sharp} *_{\mathsf{R}} r_1^{\sharp}) \wedge c_{0,u}^{\sharp} \mid (r_{0,u}^{\sharp} \wedge c_{0,u}^{\sharp}) \in \mathbf{unfold}_{\Pi}(\mathtt{n}, r_0^{\sharp})\}$;
- $\mathbf{unfold}_{\Pi}(\mathtt{n}, [\mathtt{h}_i^{\sharp} \dashrightarrow \mathtt{h}_o^{\sharp}]) = \{[\mathtt{h}_{i,u}^{\sharp} \dashrightarrow \mathtt{h}_{o,u}^{\sharp}] \wedge (c_{i,u}^{\sharp} \wedge c_{o,u}^{\sharp}) \mid (\mathtt{h}_{i,u}^{\sharp} \wedge c_{i,u}^{\sharp}) \in \mathbf{unfold}_{\Sigma}(\mathtt{n}, \mathtt{h}_i^{\sharp}) \wedge (\mathtt{h}_{o,u}^{\sharp} \wedge c_{o,u}^{\sharp}) \in \mathbf{unfold}_{\Sigma}(\mathtt{n}, \mathtt{h}_o^{\sharp})\}$;
- $\mathbf{unfold}_{\Pi}(\mathtt{n}, r^{\sharp} \wedge c^{\sharp}) = \{r_u^{\sharp} \wedge (c^{\sharp} \wedge c_u^{\sharp}) \mid (r_u^{\sharp} \wedge c_u^{\sharp}) \in \mathbf{unfold}_{\Pi}(\mathtt{n}, r^{\sharp})\}$.

We note that conjunctions of numerical constraints over node may yield to unfeasible elements being discarded in the last two cases: for instance, in the $[\cdot \dashrightarrow \cdot]$ case, unfolding will only retain disjuncts where both sides of the arrow express compatible conditions over n.

We can prove by case analysis that this unfolding operator is sound:

$$\gamma_{\Pi}(\rho^{\sharp}) \subseteq \bigcup\{\gamma_{\Pi}(\rho_u^{\sharp}) \mid \rho_u^{\sharp} \in \mathbf{unfold}_{\Pi}(\mathtt{n}, \rho^{\sharp})\}$$

Example 4 (Abstract state relation unfolding and post-condition). Let us consider the analysis of the insertion function of Fig. 1. This function should be applied to states where l is a non null list pointer (the list should have at least one element), thus, the analysis should start from $\text{Id}(\&\text{l} \mapsto \alpha *_{\text{S}} \text{list}(\alpha)) \wedge \alpha \neq \textbf{0x0}$ (in this example, we omit v for the sake of concision). Before the loop entry, the analysis computes the abstract state relation $\text{Id}(\&\text{l} \mapsto \alpha *_{\text{S}} \text{list}(\alpha)) *_{\text{R}}$ $[\textbf{emp} \dashrightarrow (\&\text{c} \mapsto \alpha)] \wedge \alpha \neq \textbf{0x0}$. To deal with the test c->next != NULL (and the assignment c = c->next), the analysis should materialize the cell at node α. This unfolding is performed under the Id connective, and produces:

$$\text{Id}(\&\text{l} \mapsto \alpha *_{\text{S}} \alpha \cdot \text{next} \mapsto \alpha_0 *_{\text{S}} \alpha \cdot \text{data} \mapsto \beta_0 *_{\text{S}} \text{list}(\alpha_0))$$
$$*_{\text{R}} [\textbf{emp} \dashrightarrow (\&\text{c} \mapsto \alpha)] \wedge \alpha \neq \textbf{0x0}$$

In turn, the effect of the condition test and of the assignment in the loop body can be precisely analyzed from this abstract state relation.

5.3   Folding and Lattice Operations

Like classical shape analyses [5,15], our analysis needs to *fold* inductive predicates so as to (conservatively) decide inclusion and join abstract states. We present folding algorithms in the following paragraphs.

Conservative Inclusion Checking. Inclusion checking is used to verify logical entailment, to check the convergence of loop iterates, and to support the join/widening algorithm. It consists of a conservative function $\textbf{isle}_{\text{H}}$ over abstract states and a conservative function $\textbf{isle}_{\text{R}}$ over abstract state relations, that either return **true** (meaning that the inclusion of concretizations holds) or **false** (meaning that the analysis cannot conclude whether inclusion holds).

Their definition relies on a conservative algorithm, that implements a proof search, based on the rules shown in Fig. 3 (for clarity, we omit the numerical constraints inclusion checking). In this system of rules, if $h_0^{\sharp} \sqsubseteq_{\text{H}} h_1^{\sharp}$ (resp., $r_0^{\sharp} \sqsubseteq_{\text{R}} r_1^{\sharp}$), then $\gamma_{\text{H}}(h_0^{\sharp}) \subseteq \gamma_{\text{H}}(h_1^{\sharp})$ (resp., $\gamma_{\text{R}}(r_0^{\sharp}) \subseteq \gamma_{\text{R}}(r_1^{\sharp})$). The rules $(\sqsubseteq_{=}), (\sqsubseteq_{\text{seg}})$ and $(\sqsubseteq_{*_{\text{S}}})$ are specific to reasoning of abstract states, and are directly inspired from [5] (they allow to reason over equal abstract regions, over segments, and over separating conjunction). The rule $(\sqsubseteq_{\text{unfold}})$ allows to reason by unfolding of inductive predicates, at the level of relations. Finally, the rules $(\sqsubseteq_{\text{Id}}), (\sqsubseteq_{\dashrightarrow-\text{intro}}), (\sqsubseteq_{\text{Id}-\text{weak}}), (\sqsubseteq_{*_{\text{R}}})$ and $(\sqsubseteq_{\dashrightarrow-\text{weak}})$ allow to derive inclusion over abstract state relations, and implement the properties observed in Theorem 1. The proof search algorithm starts from the goal to prove and attempt to apply these rules so as to complete an inclusion derivation. We observe that abstract states are equivalent up to a renaming of the internal nodes (the nodes that are not of the form &x), thus, the implementation also takes care of this renaming, although the rules of Fig. 3 do not show it, as this issue is orthogonal to the reasoning over abstract state relations which is the goal of this paper (indeed, this requires complex renaming functions that are made fully explicit in [5]). The rules can be proved sound one by one, thus they define a sound inclusion checking procedure:

$$\frac{h^{\sharp} \text{ is of the form } n \cdot f \mapsto n' \text{ or } \mathbf{list}(n) \text{ or } \mathbf{listseg}(n, n')}{h^{\sharp} \sqsubseteq_{\mathbb{H}} h^{\sharp}} \quad (\sqsubseteq_{=})$$

$$\frac{h^{\sharp} \sqsubseteq_{\mathbb{H}} \mathbf{list}(n')}{\mathbf{listseg}(n, n') *_{S} h^{\sharp} \sqsubseteq_{\mathbb{H}} \mathbf{list}(n)} \quad (\sqsubseteq_{seg}) \qquad \frac{h^{\sharp}_{0,0} \sqsubseteq_{\mathbb{H}} h^{\sharp}_{1,0} \qquad h^{\sharp}_{0,1} \sqsubseteq_{\mathbb{H}} h^{\sharp}_{1,1}}{h^{\sharp}_{0,0} *_{S} h^{\sharp}_{0,1} \sqsubseteq_{\mathbb{H}} h^{\sharp}_{1,0} *_{S} h^{\sharp}_{1,1}} \quad (\sqsubseteq_{*_S})$$

$$\frac{r^{\sharp}_{u} \in \mathbf{unfold}_{\Pi}(n, r^{\sharp}_{1}) \qquad r^{\sharp}_{0} \sqsubseteq_{\mathbb{R}} r^{\sharp}_{u} \qquad r^{\sharp}_{1} \text{ contains } \mathbf{list}(n) \text{ or } \mathbf{listseg}(n, n')}{r^{\sharp}_{0} \sqsubseteq_{\mathbb{R}} r^{\sharp}_{1}} \quad (\sqsubseteq_{unfold})$$

$$\frac{h^{\sharp}_{0} \sqsubseteq_{\mathbb{H}} h^{\sharp}_{1}}{\mathbf{Id}(h^{\sharp}_{0}) \sqsubseteq_{\mathbb{R}} \mathbf{Id}(h^{\sharp}_{1})} \quad (\sqsubseteq_{\mathbf{Id}}) \qquad \frac{h^{\sharp}_{i,0} \sqsubseteq_{\mathbb{H}} h^{\sharp}_{i,1} \qquad h^{\sharp}_{o,0} \sqsubseteq_{\mathbb{H}} h^{\sharp}_{o,1}}{[h^{\sharp}_{i,0} \dashrightarrow h^{\sharp}_{o,0}] \sqsubseteq_{\mathbb{R}} [h^{\sharp}_{i,1} \dashrightarrow h^{\sharp}_{o,1}]} \quad (\sqsubseteq_{\dashrightarrow - intro})$$

$$\frac{r^{\sharp} *_{\mathbb{R}} [h^{\sharp} \dashrightarrow h^{\sharp}] \sqsubseteq_{\mathbb{R}} [h^{\sharp}_{i} \dashrightarrow h^{\sharp}_{o}]}{r^{\sharp} *_{\mathbb{R}} \mathbf{Id}(h^{\sharp}) \sqsubseteq_{\mathbb{R}} [h^{\sharp}_{i} \dashrightarrow h^{\sharp}_{o}]} \quad (\sqsubseteq_{\mathbf{Id} - weak}) \qquad \frac{r^{\sharp}_{0,0} \sqsubseteq_{\mathbb{R}} r^{\sharp}_{1,0} \qquad r^{\sharp}_{0,1} \sqsubseteq_{\mathbb{R}} r^{\sharp}_{1,1}}{r^{\sharp}_{0,0} *_{\mathbb{R}} r^{\sharp}_{0,1} \sqsubseteq_{\mathbb{R}} r^{\sharp}_{1,0} *_{\mathbb{R}} r^{\sharp}_{1,1}} \quad (\sqsubseteq_{*_{\mathbb{R}}})$$

$$\frac{r^{\sharp} *_{\mathbb{R}} [h^{\sharp}_{i,0} *_{S} h^{\sharp}_{i,1} \dashrightarrow h^{\sharp}_{o,0} *_{S} h^{\sharp}_{o,1}] \sqsubseteq_{\mathbb{R}} [h^{\sharp}_{i} \dashrightarrow h^{\sharp}_{o}]}{r^{\sharp} *_{\mathbb{R}} [h^{\sharp}_{i,0} \dashrightarrow h^{\sharp}_{o,0}] *_{\mathbb{R}} [h^{\sharp}_{i,1} \dashrightarrow h^{\sharp}_{o,1}] \sqsubseteq_{\mathbb{R}} [h^{\sharp}_{i} \dashrightarrow h^{\sharp}_{o}]} \quad (\sqsubseteq_{\dashrightarrow - weak})$$

Fig. 3. Inclusion checking rules

Theorem 2 (Soundness of inclusion checking). *If* $h^{\sharp}_{0}, h^{\sharp}_{1} \in \mathbb{H}$ *and* $r^{\sharp}_{0}, r^{\sharp}_{1} \in \mathbb{R}$ *then:*

$$\mathbf{isle}_{\mathbb{H}}(h^{\sharp}_{0}, h^{\sharp}_{1}) = \mathbf{true} \implies \gamma_{\mathbb{H}}(h^{\sharp}_{0}) \subseteq \gamma_{\mathbb{H}}(h^{\sharp}_{1})$$
$$\mathbf{isle}_{\mathbb{R}}(r^{\sharp}_{0}, r^{\sharp}_{1}) = \mathbf{true} \implies \gamma_{\mathbb{R}}(r^{\sharp}_{0}) \subseteq \gamma_{\mathbb{R}}(r^{\sharp}_{1})$$

Example 5 (Inclusion checking). Let us consider the following abstract state relations, and discuss the computation of $\mathbf{isle}_{\mathbb{R}}(r^{\sharp}_{0}, r^{\sharp}_{1})$:

$$r^{\sharp}_{0} = \mathbf{Id}(n \cdot \mathbf{next} \mapsto \alpha_{0} *_{S} \mathbf{list}(\alpha_{0})) *_{\mathbb{R}} [n \cdot \mathbf{data} \mapsto \alpha_{1} \dashrightarrow n \cdot \mathbf{data} \mapsto \alpha_{2}]$$
$$r^{\sharp}_{1} = [\mathbf{list}(n) \dashrightarrow \mathbf{list}(n)]$$

Using first rule ($\sqsubseteq_{\mathbf{Id} - weak}$) then rule ($\sqsubseteq_{\dashrightarrow - weak}$), this goal gets reduced into checking the inclusion $[h^{\sharp}_{0} \dashrightarrow h^{\sharp}_{1}] \sqsubseteq_{\mathbb{R}} r^{\sharp}_{1}$, where $h^{\sharp}_{0} = n \cdot \mathbf{next} \mapsto \alpha_{0} *_{S} \mathbf{list}(\alpha_{0}) *_{S} n \cdot \mathbf{data} \mapsto \alpha_{1}$ and $h^{\sharp}_{1} = n \cdot \mathbf{next} \mapsto \alpha_{0} *_{S} \mathbf{list}(\alpha_{0}) *_{S} n \cdot \mathbf{data} \mapsto \alpha_{2}$. In turn, this inclusion follows from rule ($\sqsubseteq_{unfold}$).

Join/Widening Operators. In the following, we define abstract operators $\mathbf{wid}_{\mathbb{H}}$, $\mathbf{wid}_{\mathbb{R}}$ that respectively operate over abstract states and abstract state relations, and compute an over-approximation for concrete unions. They also ensure termination and serve as widening. The algorithm to compute these two functions heavily relies on the inclusion checking that was discussed in the previous paragraph. Indeed, the widening functions compute results that are more approximate than their arguments. To achieve this, they search for syntactic patterns in their arguments and produce outputs that inclusion checking proves more general. This process is performed region by region on both arguments of the widening, as formalized in [5, Fig. 7]. We discuss in the following a list of such widening rules:

– when both arguments of widening are equal to a same base predicate, widening is trivial, and returns the same base predicate, thus for instance:

$$\mathbf{wid}_{\mathbb{H}}(n \cdot f \mapsto \alpha, n \cdot f \mapsto \alpha) = n \cdot f \mapsto \alpha$$
$$\mathbf{wid}_{\mathbb{H}}(\mathbf{list}(\alpha), \mathbf{list}(\alpha)) = \mathbf{list}(\alpha)$$

– when applied to two abstract relations that consist of the same connective, the widening functions simply calls themselves recursively on the sub-components:

$$\mathbf{wid}_{\mathbb{R}}(\mathrm{Id}(h_0^\sharp), \mathrm{Id}(h_1^\sharp)) = \mathrm{Id}(\mathbf{wid}_{\mathbb{H}}(h_0^\sharp, h_1^\sharp))$$
$$\mathbf{wid}_{\mathbb{R}}([h_{i,0}^\sharp \dashrightarrow h_{o,0}^\sharp], [h_{i,1}^\sharp \dashrightarrow h_{o,1}^\sharp]) = [\mathbf{wid}_{\mathbb{H}}(h_{i,0}^\sharp, h_{i,1}^\sharp) \dashrightarrow \mathbf{wid}_{\mathbb{H}}(h_{o,0}^\sharp, h_{o,1}^\sharp)]$$
$$\mathbf{wid}_{\mathbb{R}}(r_{0,0}^\sharp *_{\mathbb{R}} r_{0,1}^\sharp, r_{1,0}^\sharp *_{\mathbb{R}} r_{1,1}^\sharp) = \mathbf{wid}_{\mathbb{R}}(r_{0,0}^\sharp, r_{1,0}^\sharp) *_{\mathbb{R}} \mathbf{wid}_{\mathbb{R}}(r_{0,1}^\sharp, r_{1,1}^\sharp)$$

– when applied to an $\mathrm{Id}(\cdot)$ predicate and another abstract relation, widening first tries to maintain the $\mathrm{Id}(\cdot)$ predicate, and, if this fails, tries to weaken it into an $[\cdot \dashrightarrow \cdot]$ predicate:

if $\mathbf{isle}_{\mathbb{H}}(h_0^\sharp, h^\sharp) = \mathbf{true}$ then,
$$\mathbf{wid}_{\mathbb{R}}(\mathrm{Id}(h_0^\sharp), r^\sharp) = \begin{cases} \mathrm{Id}(h^\sharp) & \text{if } \mathbf{isle}_{\mathbb{R}}(r^\sharp, \mathrm{Id}(h^\sharp)) = \mathbf{true} \\ [h^\sharp \dashrightarrow h^\sharp] & \text{otherwise, if } \mathbf{isle}_{\mathbb{R}}(r^\sharp, [h^\sharp \dashrightarrow h^\sharp]) = \mathbf{true} \end{cases}$$

– when applied to an $[\cdot \dashrightarrow \cdot]$ predicate, the widening tries to weaken the other argument accordingly:

if $\mathbf{isle}_{\mathbb{H}}(h_{i,0}^\sharp, h_i^\sharp) = \mathbf{true}$ and $\mathbf{isle}_{\mathbb{H}}(h_{o,0}^\sharp, h_o^\sharp) = \mathbf{true}$
and $\mathbf{isle}_{\mathbb{R}}(r^\sharp, [h_i^\sharp \dashrightarrow h_o^\sharp]) = \mathbf{true}$ then,
$$\mathbf{wid}_{\mathbb{R}}([h_{i,0}^\sharp \dashrightarrow h_{o,0}^\sharp], r^\sharp) = [h_i^\sharp \dashrightarrow h_o^\sharp]$$

Each of these operations is sound, and the results computed by widening are also sound:

Theorem 3 (Soundness of widening). *If* $h_0^\sharp, h_1^\sharp \in \mathbb{H}$ *and* $r_0^\sharp, r_1^\sharp \in \mathbb{R}$ *then:*

$$\gamma_{\mathbb{H}}(h_0^\sharp) \cup \gamma_{\mathbb{H}}(h_1^\sharp) \subseteq \gamma_{\mathbb{H}}(\mathbf{wid}_{\mathbb{H}}(h_0^\sharp, h_1^\sharp)) \qquad \gamma_{\mathbb{R}}(r_0^\sharp) \cup \gamma_{\mathbb{R}}(r_1^\sharp) \subseteq \gamma_{\mathbb{R}}(\mathbf{wid}_{\mathbb{R}}(r_0^\sharp, r_1^\sharp))$$

Furthermore, termination of widening follows from an argument similar to [5].

Example 6 (Widening). We consider the analysis of the program of Fig. 1, and more specifically, the widening after the first abstract iteration over the loop:

$$\mathbf{wid}_{\mathbb{R}}(\mathrm{Id}(\&\mathrm{l} \mapsto \alpha *_{\mathbb{S}} \mathbf{list}(\alpha) *_{\mathbb{S}} \&\mathrm{v} \mapsto \beta) *_{\mathbb{R}} [\mathbf{emp} \dashrightarrow \&\mathrm{c} \mapsto \alpha],$$
$$\mathrm{Id}(\&\mathrm{l} \mapsto \alpha *_{\mathbb{S}} \alpha \cdot \mathbf{data} \mapsto \alpha_d *_{\mathbb{S}} \alpha \cdot \mathbf{next} \mapsto \alpha_n *_{\mathbb{S}} \mathbf{list}(\alpha_n) *_{\mathbb{S}} \&\mathrm{v} \mapsto \beta)$$
$$*_{\mathbb{R}} [\mathbf{emp} \dashrightarrow \&\mathrm{c} \mapsto \alpha_n])$$
$$= \mathrm{Id}(\&\mathrm{l} \mapsto \alpha *_{\mathbb{S}} \mathbf{listseg}(\alpha, \alpha') *_{\mathbb{S}} \mathbf{list}(\alpha') *_{\mathbb{S}} \&\mathrm{v} \mapsto \beta) *_{\mathbb{R}} [\mathbf{emp} \dashrightarrow \&\mathrm{c} \mapsto \alpha']$$

This abstract widening performs some generalization and introduces a list segment inductive predicate, that over-approximates an empty segment in the left argument, and a segment of length one. It also involves some renaming of symbolic nodes (as observed in the previous paragraph, the concretization of an abstract states is unchanged under symbolic nodes renaming).

5.4   Analysis

The abstract semantics $[\![.]\!]^\sharp_{\mathcal{R}}$ relies on the abstract operations defined in Sect. 5.1, on the unfolding of Sect. 5.2 to analyze basic statements, and on the folding operations defined in Sect. 5.3 to cope with control flow joins and loop invariants computation. Soundness follows from the soundness of the basic operations.

Theorem 4 (Soundness). *The analysis is sound in the sense that, for all program P and for all abstract state relation $\rho^\sharp$:*

$$\forall(\sigma_0, \sigma_1) \in \gamma_\Pi(\rho^\sharp), \ \forall\sigma_2 \in \mathbb{M}, (\sigma_1, \sigma_2) \in [\![P]\!]_{\mathcal{R}} \implies (\sigma_0, \sigma_2) \in \gamma_\Pi([\![P]\!]^\sharp_{\mathcal{R}}(\rho^\sharp))$$

6   Experimental Evaluation

In this section, we report on the implementation of our analysis and try to evaluate:

1. whether it can prove precise and useful relational properties, and
2. how it compares with a more classical reachability shape analysis.

Our implementation supports built-in inductive predicates to describe singly linked lists and binary trees. It provides both the analysis described in this paper, and a basic reachability shape analysis in the style of [5], and supporting the same inductive predicates. It was implemented as a Frama-C [19] plugin consisting of roughly 7800 lines of OCaml. We have ran both the reachability shape analysis and relational shape analysis on series of small programs manipulating lists and trees listed in Table 1. These tests are selected to test specifically the relational domain (and not a full analysis). This allows us to not only assess the results of the analysis computing abstract state relations, but also to compare them with an analysis that infers abstract states.

First, we discuss whether the analysis computing abstract state relations computes the expected relations, that describes the most precisely the transformation implemented by the analyzed function. As an example, in the case of an insertion at the head of a list, we expect the abstract relation below, that expresses that the body of the list was not modified:

$$[\&1 \mapsto \alpha \dashrightarrow \&1 \mapsto \beta] *_{\mathsf{R}} [\mathbf{emp} \dashrightarrow \beta \cdot \mathbf{next} \mapsto \alpha *_{\mathsf{S}} \beta \cdot \mathbf{data} \mapsto \delta] *_{\mathsf{R}} \mathrm{Id}(\mathbf{list}(\alpha))$$

We observe that the state relation computed in all test cases except the list reverse and map are the most precise. For example, with the function map that traverses a list and modifies only its **data** fields, the relation obtained is:

$$\mathrm{Id}(\&1 \mapsto \alpha) *_{\mathsf{R}} [(\mathbf{listseg}(\alpha, \beta)) \dashrightarrow (\mathbf{listseg}(\alpha, \beta))]$$

This relation shows that both input and output lists start at the address α and end at the address β. This is not enough to prove that the lists contain the same addresses linked in the same order.

Table 1. Experiment results (sll: singly linked lists; tree: binary trees; time in milliseconds averaged over 1000 runs on a laptop with Intel Core i7 running at 2.3 GHz, with 16 GB RAM, for the reachability and relational analyses; the last column states whether the relational shape analysis computed the expected abstract relation)

Structure	Function	Time (in ms)		Loop iterations	Relational property
		Reach	Relat.		
sll	allocation	0.53	1.27	2	Yes
sll	deallocation	0.34	0.99	2	Yes
sll	traversal	0.53	0.83	2	Yes
sll	insertion (head)	0.32	0.33	0	Yes
sll	insertion (random pos)	1.98	2.75	2	Yes
sll	insertion (random)	2.33	3.94	2	Yes
sll	reverse	0.52	2.36	2	Partial
sll	map	0.66	1.17	2	Partial
tree	allocation	0.94	2.21	2	Yes
tree	search	1.06	1.76	2	Yes

Second, we compare the runtime of the relational analysis and of the reachability analysis. We observe that the slow-down is at most 4× (reverse), and is about 2× in most cases. An exception is the list head insertion, which incurs no slowdown. This is due to the fact this analysis does not require computing an abstract join. While these test cases are not large, these results show that the analysis computing abstract state relations has a reasonable overhead compared to a classical analysis, yet it computes stronger properties. Furthermore, it would be more adapted to a modular interprocedural analysis.

7   Related Works

Our analysis computes an abstraction of the relational semantics of programs so as to capture the effect of a function or other blocks of code using an element of some specifically designed abstract domain. This technique has been applied to other abstractions in the past, and often applied to design *modular* static analyses [10], where program components can be analyzed once and separately. For numerical domains, it simply requires duplicating each variable into two instances respectively describing the old and the new value, and using a relational domain to the inputs and outputs. For instance, [22] implements this idea using convex polyhedra and so as to infer abstract state relations for numerical programs. It has also been applied to shape analyses based on Three Valued Logic [24] in [17]. This work is probably the closest to ours, but it relies on a very different abstraction using a TVLA whereas we use a set of abstract predicates based on separation logic. It uses the same variable duplication trick as mentioned above. Our analysis also has a notion of overlaid old/new predicates, but these are described heap regions, inside separation logic formulas. Desynchronized separation [11] also introduces a notion of overlaid state in separation logic, but does not support inductive predicates as our analysis does. Instead, it allows to reason on abstractions of JavaScript open objects seen as dictionaries. Also, [13,14] can express relations between heaps in different states using temporal logic extensions and automatas. In the context of functional languages, [18] allows to write down relations between function inputs and outputs, and relies on a solver to verify that constraints hold and [25] computes shape specifications by learning. Modular analyses that compute invariants by separate analysis of program components [4,6,12] use various sorts of abstractions for the behavior of program components. A common pattern is to use tables of couples made of an abstract pre-condition and a corresponding abstract post-condition, effectively defining a sort of cardinal power abstraction [9]. This technique has been used in several shape analyses based on separation logic [2,3,16,20]. We believe this tabular approach could benefit from abstractions of relations such as ours to infer stronger properties, and more concise summaries.

8 Conclusion

In this paper, we have introduced a set of logical connectives inspired by separation logic, to describe state relations rather than states. We have built upon this logic an abstract domain, and a static analysis based on abstract interpretation that computes conservative state relations. Experiments prove it effective for the analysis of basic data structure library functions.

Acknowledgements. We thank Arlen Cox for fruitful discussions, and Francois Berenger, Huisong Li, Jiangchao Liu and the anonymous reviewers for their comments on an earlier version of this paper. This work has received funding from the European Research Council under the EU's seventh framework programme (FP7/2007-2013), grant agreement 278673, Project MemCAD, and from Bpifrance, grant agreement P3423-189738, FUI Project P-RC2.

References

1. Baudin, P., Filliâtre, J.-C., Marché, C., Monate, B., Moy, Y., Prevosto, V.: ACSL: ANSI C specification language (2008)
2. Calcagno, C., Distefano, D., O'Hearn, P.W., Yang, H.: Footprint analysis: a shape analysis that discovers preconditions. In: Nielson, H.R., Filé, G. (eds.) SAS 2007. LNCS, vol. 4634, pp. 402–418. Springer, Heidelberg (2007). doi:10.1007/978-3-540-74061-2_25
3. Calcagno, C., Distefano, D., O'Hearn, P., Yang, H.: Compositional shape analysis by means of bi-abduction. In: Symposium on Principles of Programming Languages (POPL), pp. 289–300. ACM (2009)

4. Castelnuovo, G., Naik, M., Rinetzky, N., Sagiv, M., Yang, H.: Modularity in lattices: a case study on the correspondence between top-down and bottom-up analysis. In: Blazy, S., Jensen, T. (eds.) SAS 2015. LNCS, vol. 9291, pp. 252–274. Springer, Heidelberg (2015). doi:10.1007/978-3-662-48288-9_15

5. Chang, B.-Y.E., Rival, X.: Relational inductive shape analysis. In: Symposium on Principles of Programming Languages (POPL), pp. 247–260. ACM (2008)

6. Chatterjee, R., Ryder, B.G., Landi, W.A.: Relevant context inference. In: Symposium on Principles of Programming Languages (POPL), pp. 133–146. ACM (1999)

7. Cousot, P., Halbwachs, N.: Automatic discovery of linear restraints among variables of a program. In: Symposium on Principles of Programming Languages (POPL), pp. 84–97. ACM (1978)

8. Cousot, P., Cousot, R.: Abstract interpretation: a unified lattice model for static analysis of programs by construction or approximation of fixpoints. In: Symposium on Principles of Programming Languages (POPL) (1977)

9. Cousot, P., Cousot, R.: Systematic design of program analysis frameworks. In: Symposium on Principles of Programming Languages (POPL). ACM (1979)

10. Cousot, P., Cousot, R.: Modular static program analysis. In: Horspool, R.N. (ed.) CC 2002. LNCS, vol. 2304, pp. 159–179. Springer, Heidelberg (2002). doi:10.1007/3-540-45937-5_13

11. Cox, A., Chang, B.-Y.E., Rival, X.: Desynchronized multi-state abstractions for open programs in dynamic languages. In: Vitek, J. (ed.) ESOP 2015. LNCS, vol. 9032, pp. 483–509. Springer, Heidelberg (2015). doi:10.1007/978-3-662-46669-8_20

12. Dillig, I., Dillig, T., Aiken, A., Sagiv, M.: Precise and compact modular procedure summaries for heap manipulating programs. In: Conference on Programming Language Design and Implementation (PLDI), pp. 567–577. ACM (2011)

13. Distefano, D., Katoen, J.-P., Rensink, A.: Who is pointing when to whom? In: Lodaya, K., Mahajan, M. (eds.) FSTTCS 2004. LNCS, vol. 3328, pp. 250–262. Springer, Heidelberg (2004). doi:10.1007/978-3-540-30538-5_21

14. Distefano, D., Katoen, J.-P., Rensink, A.: Safety and liveness in concurrent pointer programs. In: Boer, F.S., Bonsangue, M.M., Graf, S., Roever, W.-P. (eds.) FMCO 2005. LNCS, vol. 4111, pp. 280–312. Springer, Heidelberg (2006). doi:10.1007/11804192_14

15. Distefano, D., O'Hearn, P.W., Yang, H.: A local shape analysis based on separation logic. In: Hermanns, H., Palsberg, J. (eds.) TACAS 2006. LNCS, vol. 3920, pp. 287–302. Springer, Heidelberg (2006). doi:10.1007/11691372_19

16. Gulavani, B.S., Chakraborty, S., Ramalingam, G., Nori, A.V.: Bottom-up shape analysis. In: Palsberg, J., Su, Z. (eds.) SAS 2009. LNCS, vol. 5673, pp. 188–204. Springer, Heidelberg (2009). doi:10.1007/978-3-642-03237-0_14

17. Jeannet, B., Loginov, A., Reps, T., Sagiv, M.: A relational approach to interprocedural shape analysis. ACM Trans. Program. Lang. Syst. (TOPLAS) **32**(2), 5 (2010)

18. Kaki, G., Jagannathan, S.: A relational framework for higher-order shape analysis. In: International Colloquium on Function Programming, pp. 311–324. ACM (2014)

19. Kirchner, F., Kosmatov, N., Prevosto, V., Signoles, J., Yakobowski, B.: Frama-C: a software analysis perspective. Form. Asp. Comput. **27**(3), 573–609 (2015)

20. Le, Q.L., Gherghina, C., Qin, S., Chin, W.-N.: Shape analysis via second-order bi-abduction. In: Biere, A., Bloem, R. (eds.) CAV 2014. LNCS, vol. 8559, pp. 52–68. Springer, Cham (2014). doi:10.1007/978-3-319-08867-9_4

21. Leavens, G.T., Baker, A.L., Ruby, C.: JML: a java modeling language. In: Formal Underpinnings of Java Workshop (at OOPSLA 1998), pp. 404–420 (1998)

22. Popeea, C., Chin, W.-N.: Inferring disjunctive postconditions. In: Okada, M., Satoh, I. (eds.) ASIAN 2006. LNCS, vol. 4435, pp. 331–345. Springer, Heidelberg (2007). doi:10.1007/978-3-540-77505-8_26

23. Reynolds, J.: Separation logic: a logic for shared mutable data structures. In: Symposium on Logics in Computer Science (LICS), pp. 55–74. IEEE (2002)

24. Sagiv, M., Reps, T., Wilhelm, R.: Parametric shape analysis via 3-valued logic. ACM Trans. Program. Lang. Syst. (TOPLAS) 24(3), 217–298 (2002)

25. Zhu, H., Petri, G., Jagannathan, S.: Automatically learning shape specifications. In: Conference on Programming Language Design and Implementation (PLDI), pp. 491–507. ACM (2016)

Floating-Point Format Inference
in Mixed-Precision

Matthieu Martel[✉]

Laboratoire de Mathématiques et Physique (LAMPS),
Université de Perpignan Via Domitia, Perpignan, France
matthieu.martel@univ-perp.fr

Abstract. We address the problem of determining the minimal precision on the inputs and on the intermediary results of a program containing floating-point computations in order to ensure a desired accuracy on the outputs. The first originality of our approach is to combine forward and backward static analyses, done by abstract interpretation. The backward analysis computes the minimal precision needed for the inputs and intermediary values in order to have a desired accuracy on the results, specified by the user. The second originality is to express our analysis as a set of constraints made of first order predicates and affine integer relations only, even if the analyzed programs contain non-linear computations. These constraints can be easily checked by an SMT Solver. The information collected by our analysis may help to optimize the formats used to represent the values stored in the floating-point variables of programs. Experimental results are presented.

1 Introduction

Issues related to numerical accuracy are almost as old as computer science. An important step towards the design of more reliable numerical software was the definition, in the 1980's, of the IEEE754 Standard for floating-point arithmetic [2]. Since then, work has been carried out to determine the accuracy of floating-point computations by dynamic [3,17,29] or static [11,13,14] methods. This work has also been motivated by a few disasters due to numerical bugs [1,15].

While existing approaches may differ strongly each other in their way of determining accuracy, they have a common objective: to compute approximations of the errors on the outputs of a program depending on the initial errors on the data and on the roundoff of the arithmetic operations performed during the execution. The present work focuses on a slightly different problem concerning the relations between precision and accuracy. Here, the term *precision* refers to the number of bits used to represent a value, i.e. its format, while the term *accuracy* is a bound on the absolute error $|x - \hat{x}|$ between the represented $\hat{x}$ value and the exact value x that we would have in the exact arithmetic.

We address the problem of determining the minimal precision on the inputs and on the intermediary results of a program performing floating-point computations in order to ensure a desired accuracy on the outputs. This allows compilers

© Springer International Publishing AG 2017
C. Barrett et al. (Eds.): NFM 2017, LNCS 10227, pp. 230–246, 2017.
DOI: 10.1007/978-3-319-57288-8_16

to select the most appropriate formats (for example IEEE754 half, single, double or quad formats [2,23]) for each variable. It is then possible to save memory, reduce CPU usage and use less bandwidth for communications whenever distributed applications are concerned. So, the choice of the best floating-point formats is an important compile-time optimization in many contexts. Our approach is also easily generalizable to the fixed-point arithmetic for which it is important to determine data formats, for example in FPGAs [12,19].

The first originality of our approach is to combine a forward and a backward static analysis, done by abstract interpretation [8,9]. The forward analysis is classical. It propagates safely the errors on the inputs and on the results of the intermediary operations in order to determine the accuracy of the results. Next, based on the results of the forward analysis and on assertions indicating which accuracy the user wants for the outputs at some control points, the backward analysis computes the minimal precision needed for the inputs and intermediary results in order to satisfy the assertions. Not surprisingly, the forward and backward analyses can be applied repeatedly and alternatively in order to refine the results until a fixed-point is reached.

The second originality of our approach is to express the forward and backward transfer functions as a set of constraints made of propositional logic formulas and relations between affine expressions over integers (and only integers). Indeed, these relations remain linear even if the analyzed program contains non-linear computations. As a consequence, these constraints can be easily checked by a SMT solver (we use Z3 in practice [4,21]). The advantage of the solver appears in the backward analysis, when one wants to determine the precision of the operands of some binary operation between two operands a and b, in order to obtain a certain accuracy on the result. In general, it is possible to use a more precise a with a less precise b or, conversely, to use a more precise b with a less precise a. Because this choice arises at almost any operation, there is a huge number of combinations on the admissible formats of all the data in order to ensure a given accuracy on the results. Instead of using an ad-hoc heuristic, we encode our problem as a set of constraints and we let a well-known, optimized solver generate a solution.

This article is organized as follows. We briefly introduce some elements of floating-point arithmetic, a motivating example and related work in Sect. 2. Our abstract domain as well as the forward and backward transfer functions are introduced in Sect. 3. The constraint generation is presented in Sect. 4 and experimental results are given in Sect. 5. Finally, Sect. 6 concludes.

2 Preliminary Elements

In this section we introduce some preliminary notions helpful to understand the rest of the article. Elements of floating-point arithmetic are introduced in Sect. 2.1. Further, an illustration of what our method does is given in Sect. 2.2. Related work is discussed in Sect. 2.3.

2.1   Elements of Floating-Point Arithmetic

We introduce here some elements of floating-point arithmetic [2,23]. First of all, a *floating-point number* x in base β is defined by

$$x = s \cdot (d_0.d_1 \ldots d_{p-1}) \cdot \beta^e = s \cdot m \cdot \beta^{e-p+1} \tag{1}$$

where $s \in \{-1, 1\}$ is the sign, $m = d_0 d_1 \ldots d_{p-1}$ is the *significand*, $0 \leq d_i < \beta$, $0 \leq i \leq p - 1, p$ is the *precision* and e is the exponent, $e_{min} \leq e \leq e_{max}$.

A floating-point number x is *normalized* whenever $d_0 \neq 0$. Normalization avoids multiple representations of the same number. The IEEE754 Standard also defines denormalized numbers which are floating-point numbers with $d_0 = d_1 = \ldots = d_k = 0, k < p - 1$ and $e = e_{min}$. Denormalized numbers make underflow gradual [23]. The IEEE754 Standard defines binary formats (with $\beta = 2$) and decimal formats (with $\beta = 10$). In this article, without loss of generality, we only consider normalized numbers and we always assume that $\beta = 2$ (which is the most common case in practice). The IEEE754 Standard also specifies a few values for p, e_{min} and e_{max} which are summarized in Fig. 1. Finally, special values also are defined: nan (Not a Number) resulting from an invalid operation, $\pm\infty$ corresponding to overflows, and $+0$ and -0 (signed zeros).

Format	Name	p	e bits	e_{min}	e_{max}
Binary16	Half precision	11	5	-14	$+15$
Binary32	Single precision	24	8	-126	$+127$
Binary64	Double precision	53	11	-1122	$+1223$
Binary128	Quadruple precision	113	15	-16382	$+16383$

Fig. 1. Basic binary IEEE754 formats.

The IEEE754 Standard also defines five rounding modes for elementary operations over floating-point numbers. These modes are towards $-\infty$, towards $+\infty$, towards zero, to the nearest ties to even and to the nearest ties to away and we write them $\circ_{-\infty}, \circ_{+\infty}, \circ_0, \circ_{\sim_e}$ and $\circ_{\sim_a}$, respectively. The semantics of the elementary operations $\diamond \in \{+, -, \times, \div\}$ is then defined by

$$f_1 \diamond_\circ f_2 = \circ(f_1 \diamond f_2) \tag{2}$$

where $\circ \in \{\circ_{-\infty}, \circ_{+\infty}, \circ_0, \circ_{\sim_e}, \circ_{\sim_a}\}$ denotes the rounding mode. Equation (2) states that the result of a floating-point operation $\diamond_\circ$ done with the rounding mode $\circ$ returns what we would obtain by performing the exact operation $\diamond$ and next rounding the result using $\circ$. The IEEE754 Standard also specifies how the square root function must be rounded in a similar way to Eq. (2) but does not specify the roundoff of other functions like sin, log, etc.

We introduce hereafter two functions which compute the *unit in the first place* and the *unit in the last place* of a floating-point number. These functions are used further in this article to generate constraints encoding the way roundoff errors are propagated throughout computations. The ufp of a number x is

$$\mathsf{ufp}(x) = \min\left\{i \in \mathbb{N} \ : \ 2^{i+1} > x\right\} = \lfloor \log_2(x) \rfloor. \tag{3}$$

The ulp of a floating-point number which significand has size p is defined by

$$\mathsf{ulp}(x) = \mathsf{ufp}(x) - p + 1. \tag{4}$$

The ufp of a floating-point number corresponds to the binary exponent of its most significant digit. Conversely, the ulp of a floating-point number corresponds to the binary exponent of its least significant digit. Note that several definitions of the ulp have been given [22].

2.2   Overview of Our Method

Let us consider the program of Fig. 2 which implements a simple linear filter. At each iteration t of the loop, the output y_t is computed as a function of the current input x_t and of the values x_{t-1} and y_{t-1} of the former iteration. Our program contains several annotations. First, the statement `require_accuracy(`y_t`, 10)` on the last line of the code informs the system that the programmer wants to have 10 accurate binary digits on y_t at this control point. In other words, let $y_t = d_0.d_1 \dots d_n \cdot 2^e$ for some $n \geq 10$, the absolute error between the value v that y_t would have if all the computations where done with real numbers and the floating-point value $\hat{v}$ of y_t is less than $2^{e-11} : |v - \hat{v}| \leq 2^{e-9}$.

Note that accuracy is not a property of a number but a number that states how closely a particular floating-point number matches some ideal true value.

```
x_{t-1}:=[1.0,3.0]#16;
x_t:=[1.0,3.0]#16;
y_{t-1}:=0.0;
while(c) {
    u:=0.3 * y_{t-1};
    v:=0.7 * (x_t + x_{t-1});
    y_t:=u + v;
    y_{t-1}:=y_t;
};
require_accuracy(y_t,10);
```

```
x_{t-1}^{|9|}:=[1.0,3.0]^{|9|}; x_t^{|9|}:=[1.0,3.0]^{|9|};
y_{t-1}^{|10|}:=0.0^{|10|};
while(c) {
    u^{|10|}:=0.3^{|10|} *^{|10|} y_{t-1}^{|10|};
    v^{|10|}:=0.7^{|11|} *^{|10|} (x_t^{|9|} +^{|10|} x_{t-1}^{|9|});
    y_t^{|10|}:=u^{|10|} +^{|10|} v^{|10|};
    y_{t-1}^{|10|}:=y_t^{|10|}; };
require_accuracy(y_t,10);
```

```
x_{t-1}^{|16|}:=[1.0,3.0]^{|16|};
x_t^{|16|}:=[1.0,3.0]^{|16|};
y_{t-1}^{|52|}:=0.0^{|52|};
u^{|52|}:=0.3^{|52|} *^{|52|} y_{t-1}^{|52|};
v^{|15|}:=0.7^{|52|} *^{|15|} (x_t^{|16|} +^{|16|} x_{t-1}^{|16|});
y_t^{|15|}:=u^{|52|} +^{|15|} v^{|15|};
y_{t-1}^{|15|}:=y_t^{|15|};
```

```
x_{t-1}^{|9|}:=[1.0,3.0]^{|9|}; x_t^{|9|}:=[1.0,3.0]^{|9|};
y_{t-1}^{|8|}:=0.0^{|8|};
u^{|10|}:=0.3^{|8|} *^{|10|} y_{t-1}^{|8|};
v^{|10|}:=0.7^{|11|} *^{|10|} (x_t^{|9|} +^{|10|} x_{t-1}^{|9|});
y_t^{|10|}:=u^{|10|} +^{|10|} v^{|10|};
y_{t-1}^{|10|}:=y_t^{|10|};
require_accuracy(y_t,10);
```

Fig. 2. Top left: initial program. Top right: annotations after analysis. Bottom left: forward analysis (one iteration). Bottom right: backward analysis (one iteration).

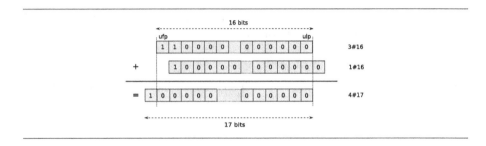

Fig. 3. Example of forward addition: `3.0#16 + 1.0#16 = 4.0#17`.

For example, using the basis $\beta = 10$ for the sake of simplicity, the floating-point value 3.149 represents π with an accuracy of 3. It itself has a precision of 4. It represents the real number 3.14903 with an accuracy of 4.

An abstract value $[a, b]_p$ represents the set of floating-point values with p accurate bits ranging from a to b. For example, in the code of Fig. 2, the variables x_{t-1} and x_t are initialized to the abstract value $[1.0, 3.0]_{16}$ thanks to the annotation `[1.0,3.0]#16`. Let $\mathbb{F}_p$ be the of set of all floating-point numbers with accuracy p. This means that, compared to exact value v computed in infinite precision, the value $\hat{v} = d_0.d_1 \ldots d_n \cdot 2^e$ of $\mathbb{F}_p$ is such that $|v - \hat{v}| \leq 2^{e-p+1}$. By definition, using the function ufp introduced in Eq. (3), for any $x \in \mathbb{F}_p$ the roundoff error $\varepsilon(x)$ on x is bounded by $\varepsilon(x) < 2^{\mathsf{ulp}(x)} = 2^{\mathsf{ufp}(x)-p+1}$. Concerning the abstract values, intuitively we have the concretization function

$$\gamma([a, b]_p) = \{x \in \mathbb{F}_p \ : \ a \leq x \leq b\}. \tag{5}$$

These abstract values are special cases of the values used in other work [18] in the sense that, in the present framework, the errors attached to floating-point numbers have form $[-2^u, 2^u]$ for some integer u instead of arbitrary intervals with real bounds. Restricting the form of the errors enables one to simplify drastically the transfer functions for the backward analysis and the generation of constraints in Sect. 4. In this article, we focus on the accuracy of computations and we omit other problems related to runtime-errors [3,5]. In particular, overflows are not considered and we assume that any number with p accurate digits belongs to $\mathbb{F}_p$. In practice, a static analysis computing the ranges of the variables and rejecting programs which possibly contain overflows is done before our analysis.

In our example, x_t and x_{t-1} belong to $[1.0, 3.0]_{16}$ which means, by definition, that these variables have a value $\hat{v}$ ranging in $[1.0, 3.0]$ and such that the error between $\hat{v}$ and the value v that we would have in the exact arithmetic is bounded by $2^{\mathsf{ufp}(x)-15}$. Typically, in this example, this information would come from the specification of the sensor related to x. By default, the values for which no accuracy annotation is given (for instance the value of y_{t-1} in the example of Fig. 2) are considered as exact numbers rounded to the nearest in double precision. In this format numbers have 53 bits of significand (see Fig. 1). The last bit being rounded, these numbers have 52 accurate bits in our terminology and, consequently, by default values belong to $\mathbb{F}_{52}$ in our framework. Based on the accuracy of the inputs, our forward analysis computes the accuracy of all the other variables and expressions. The program in the left bottom corner of Fig. 2 displays the result of the forward analysis on the first iteration of the loop. Let $\overrightarrow{\oplus}$ denote the forward addition (all the operations used in the current example are formally defined in Sect. 3). For example, the result of $x_t + x_{t-1}$ has 16 accurate digits since

$$\overrightarrow{\oplus}(1.0\#16, 1.0\#16) = 2.0\#16, \quad \overrightarrow{\oplus}(1.0\#16, 3.0\#16) = 4.0\#17,$$

$$\overrightarrow{\oplus}(3.0\#16, 1.0\#16) = 4.0\#17, \quad \overrightarrow{\oplus}(3.0\#16, 3.0\#16) = 6.0\#16.$$

This is illustrated in Fig. 3 where we consider the addition of these values at the bit level. For the result of the addition $\overrightarrow{\boxplus}$ between intervals, we take the most pessimistic accuracy: $\overrightarrow{\boxplus}([1.0,3.0]\#16,[1.0,3.0]\#16) = [2.0,6.0]\#16$.

The backward analysis is performed after the forward analysis and takes advantage of the accuracy requirement at the end of the code (see the right bottom corner of Fig. 2 for an unfolding of the backward analysis on the first iteration of the loop). Since, in our example, 10 bits only are required for y_t, the result of the addition u+v also needs 10 accurate bits only. By combining this information with the result of the forward analysis, it is then possible to lower the number of bits needed for one of the operands. Let $\overleftarrow{\oplus}$ be the backward addition. For example, for $x_t + x_{t-1}$ in the assignment of v, we have:

$$\overleftarrow{\oplus}(2.0\#10, 1.0\#16) = 1.0\#8, \quad \overleftarrow{\oplus}(2.0\#10, 3.0\#16) = -1.0\#8,$$

$$\overleftarrow{\oplus}(6.0\#10, 1.0\#16) = 5.0\#9, \quad \overleftarrow{\oplus}(6.0\#10, 3.0\#16) = 3.0\#8.$$

Conversely to the forward function, the interval function now keeps the largest accuracy arising in the computation of the bounds:

$$\overleftarrow{\boxplus}([2.0,6.0]\#10,[1.0,3.0]\#16) = [1.0,3.0]\#9.$$

By processing similarly on all the elementary operations and after computation of the loop fixed point, we obtain the final result of the analysis displayed in the top right corner of Fig. 2. This information may be used to determine the most appropriate data type for each variable and operation, as shown in Fig. 4. To obtain this result we generate a set of constraints corresponding to the forward and backward transfer functions for the operations of the program. There exists several ways to handle a backward operation: when the accuracy on the inputs x and y computed by the forward analysis is too large wrt. the desired accuracy on the result, one may lower the accuracy of either x or y or both.

```
volatile half x_{t-1}, x_t;
half u, v, y_t;
float y_{t-1}, tmp;
y_{t-1}:=0.0;
while(c) {
  u:=0.3 * y_{t-1};
  tmp:=x_t + x_{t-1};
  v:=0.7 * tmp;
  y_t:=u + v;
  y_{t-1}:=y_t;
};
```

Fig. 4. Final program with generated data types for the example of Fig. 2.

Since this question arises at each binary operation, we would face to a huge number of combinations if we decided to enumerate all possibilities. Instead, we generate a disjunction of constraints corresponding to the minimization of the accuracy of each operand and we let the solver search for a solution. The control flow of the program is also encoded with constraints. For a sequence of statements, we relate the accuracy of the former statements to the accuracy of the latter ones. Each variable x has three parameters: its forward, backward and final accuracy, denoted $\mathrm{acc}_F(x)$, $\mathrm{acc}_B(x)$ and $\mathrm{acc}(x)$ respectively. We must always have

$$0 \leq \mathrm{acc}_B(x) \leq \mathrm{acc}(x) \leq \mathrm{acc}_F(x). \tag{6}$$

For the forward analysis, the accuracy of some variable may decrease when passing to the next statement (we may only weaken the pre-conditions). Conversely, in the backward analysis, the accuracy of a given variable may increase when we jump to a former statement in the control graph (the post-conditions may only be strengthened). For a loop, we relate the accuracy of the variables at the beginning and at the end of the body, in a standard way.

The key point of our technique is to generate simple constraints made of propositional logic formulas and of affine expressions among integers (even if the floating-point computations in the source code are non-linear). A static analysis computing safe ranges at each control point is performed before our accuracy analysis. Then the constraints depend on two kinds of integer parameters: the ufp of the values and their accuracies acc_F, acc_B and acc. For instance, given control points ℓ_1, ℓ_2 and ℓ_3, the set C of constraints generated for $3.0\#16^{\ell_1} +^{\ell_3} 1.0\#16^{\ell_2}$, assuming that we require 10 accurate bits for the result are:

$$C = \left\{ \begin{array}{l} \mathrm{acc}_F(\ell_1) = 16, \ \mathrm{acc}_F(\ell_2) = 16, \ r^{\ell_3} = 2 - \max(\mathrm{acc}_F(\ell_1) - 1, \mathrm{acc}_F(\ell_2)), \\ (1 - \mathrm{acc}_F(\ell_1)) = \mathrm{acc}_F(\ell_2) \Rightarrow i^{\ell_3} = 1, \ (1 - \mathrm{acc}_F(\ell_1)) \neq \mathrm{acc}_F(\ell_2) \Rightarrow i^{\ell_3} = 0, \\ \mathrm{acc}_F(\ell_3) = r^{\ell_3} - i^{\ell_3}, \ \mathrm{acc}_B(\ell_3) = 10 \\ \mathrm{acc}_B(\ell_1) = 1 - (2 - \mathrm{acc}_B(\ell_3)), \ \mathrm{acc}_B(\ell_2) = 1 - (2 - \mathrm{acc}_B(\ell_3)) \end{array} \right\}.$$

For the sake of conciseness, the constraints corresponding to Eq. (6) have been omitted in C. For example, for the forward addition, the accuracy $\mathrm{acc}_F(\ell_3)$ of the result is the number of bits between $\mathrm{ufp}(3.0 + 1.0) = 2$ and the ufp u of the error which is

$$u = \max\left(\mathrm{ufp}(3.0) - \mathrm{acc}_F(\ell_1), \mathrm{ufp}(1.0) - \mathrm{acc}_F(\ell_2)\right) + i$$
$$= \max\left(1 - \mathrm{acc}_F(\ell_1), 0 - \mathrm{acc}_F(\ell_2)\right) + i,$$

where $i = 0$ or $i = 1$ depending on some condition detailed later. The constraints generated for each kind of expression and command are detailed in Sect. 4.

2.3   Related Work

Several approaches have been proposed to determine the best floating-point formats as a function of the expected accuracy on the results. Darulova and Kuncak use a forward static analysis to compute the propagation of errors [11]. If the computed bound on the accuracy satisfies the post-conditions then the analysis is run again with a smaller format until the best format is found. Note that in this approach, all the values have the same format (contrarily to our framework where each control-point has its own format). While Darulova and Kuncak develop their own static analysis, other static techniques [13,29] could be used to infer from the forward error propagation the suitable formats. Chiang et al. [7] have proposed a method to allocate a precision to the terms of an arithmetic expression (only). They use a formal analysis via Symbolic Taylor Expansions and error analysis based on interval functions. In spite of our linear constraints, they solve a quadratically constrained quadratic program to obtain annotations.

Other approaches rely on dynamic analysis. For instance, the Precimonious tool tries to decrease the precision of variables and checks whether the accuracy requirements are still fulfilled [24,27]. Lam et al. instrument binary codes in order to modify their precision without modifying the source codes [16]. They also propose a dynamic search method to identify the pieces of code where the precision should be modified. Finally, another related research axis concerns the compile-time optimization of programs in order to improve the accuracy of the floating-point computation in function of given ranges for the inputs, without modifying the formats of the numbers [10,26].

3 Abstract Semantics

In this section, we give a formal definition of the abstract domain and transfer functions presented informally in Sect. 2. The domain is defined in Sect. 3.1 and the transfer functions are given in Sect. 3.2.

3.1 Abstract Domain

Let $\mathbb{F}_p$ be the set floating-point numbers with accuracy p (we assume that the error between $x \in \mathbb{F}_p$ and the value that we would have in the exact arithmetic is less than $2^{\mathsf{ufp}(x)-p+1}$) and let $\mathbb{I}_p$ be the set of all intervals of floating-point numbers with accuracy p. As mentioned in Sect. 2.2, we assume that no overflow arises during our analysis and we omit to specify the lower and upper bounds of $\mathbb{F}_p$. An element $i^\sharp \in \mathbb{I}_p$, denoted $i^\sharp = [\underline{f}, \overline{f}]_p$, is then defined by two floating-point numbers and an accuracy p. We have

$$\mathbb{I}_p \ni [\underline{f}, \overline{f}]_p = \{f \in \mathbb{F}_p : \underline{f} \le f \le \overline{f}\} \text{ and } \mathbb{I} = \bigcup_{p \in \mathbb{N}} \mathbb{I}_p. \tag{7}$$

Our abstract domain is the complete lattice $\mathcal{D}^\sharp = \langle \mathbb{I}, \sqsubseteq, \sqcup, \sqcap, \bot_\mathbb{I}, \top_\mathbb{I} \rangle$ where elements are ordered by $[a, b]_p \sqsubseteq [c, d]_q \iff [a, b] \subseteq [c, d]$ and $q \le p$. In other words, $[a, b]_p$ is more precise than $[c, d]_q$ if it is an included interval with a greater accuracy. Let $\circ_{r,m}(x)$ denote the rounding of x at precision r using the rounding mode m. Then the join and meet operators are defined by

$$[a,b]_p \sqcup [c,d]_q = [\circ_{r,-\infty}(u), \circ_{r,+\infty}(v)]_r \text{ with } r = \min(p,q), \; [u,v] = [a,b] \cup [c,d] \quad (8)$$

and

$$[a,b]_p \sqcap [c,d]_q = [u,v]_r \text{ with } r = \max(p,q), \; [u,v] = [a,b] \cap [c,d]. \quad (9)$$

In addition, we have $\perp_{\mathbb{I}} = \emptyset_{+\infty}$ and $\top_{\mathbb{I}} = [-\infty, +\infty]_0$ and we have $[a,b]_p \sqcap [c,d]_q = \perp_{\mathbb{I}}$ whenever $[a,b] \cap [c,d] = \emptyset$. Let $\alpha : \wp(\mathbb{F}) \to \mathbb{I}$ be the abstraction function which maps a set of floating-point numbers X with different accuracies p_i, $1 \le i \le n$ to a value of $\mathbb{I}$. Let $x_{min} = \min(X)$, $x_{max} = \max(X)$ and $p = \min \{q \; : \; x \in X \text{ and } x \in \mathbb{F}_q\}$ the minimal accuracy in X. We have,

$$\alpha(X) = [\circ_{p,-\infty}(\min(X)), \circ_{p,+\infty}(\max(X))]_p \quad \text{where } p = \min \{q \; : \; X \cap \mathbb{F}_q \ne \emptyset\}. \quad (10)$$

Let $\gamma : \mathbb{I} \to \wp(\mathbb{F})$ and $i^\sharp = [a,b]_p$. The concretization function $\gamma(i^\sharp)$ is defined as:

$$\gamma(i^\sharp) = \bigcup_{q \ge p} \{x \in \mathbb{F}_q \; : \; a \le x \le b\}. \quad (11)$$

Using the functions α and γ of Eqs. (10) and (11), we define the Galois connection $\langle \wp(\mathbb{F}), \subseteq, \cup, \cap, \emptyset, \mathbb{F} \rangle \xrightleftharpoons[\alpha]{\gamma} \langle \mathbb{I}, \sqsubseteq, \sqcup, \sqcap, \perp_{\mathbb{I}}, \top_{\mathbb{I}} \rangle$ [8].

3.2   Transfer Functions

In this section, we introduce the forward and backward transfer functions for the abstract domain $\mathcal{D}^\sharp$ of Sect. 3.1. These functions are defined using the *unit in the first place* of a floating-point number introduced in Sect. 2.1. First, we introduce the forward transfer functions corresponding to the addition $\overrightarrow{\oplus}$ and product $\overrightarrow{\otimes}$ of two floating-point numbers $x \in \mathbb{F}_p$ and $y \in \mathbb{F}_q$. The addition and product are defined by

$$\overrightarrow{\oplus}(x_p, y_q) = (x+y)_r \text{ where } r = \mathsf{ufp}(x+y) - \mathsf{ufp}\big(\varepsilon(x_p) + \varepsilon(y_q)\big), \quad (12)$$

$$\overrightarrow{\otimes}(x_p, y_q) = (x \times y)_r \text{ where } r = \mathsf{ufp}(x \times y) - \mathsf{ufp}\big(y \cdot \varepsilon(x_p) + x \cdot \varepsilon(y_q) + \varepsilon(x_p) \cdot \varepsilon(y_q)\big). \quad (13)$$

In Eqs. (12) and (13), $x+y$ and $x \times y$ denote the exact sum and product of the two values. In practice, this sum must be done with enough accuracy in order to ensure that the result has accuracy r, for example by using more precision than the accuracy of the inputs. The errors on the addition and product may be bounded by $e_+ = \varepsilon(x_p) + \varepsilon(y_q)$ and $e_\times = y \cdot \varepsilon(x_p) + x \cdot \varepsilon(y_q) + \varepsilon(x_p) \cdot \varepsilon(y_q)$, respectively. Then the most significant bits of the errors have weights $\mathsf{ufp}(e_+)$ and $\mathsf{ufp}(e_\times)$ and the accuracies of the results are $\mathsf{ufp}(x+y) - \mathsf{ufp}(e_+)$ and $\mathsf{ufp}(x \times y) - \mathsf{ufp}(e_\times)$, respectively.

We introduce now the backward transfer functions $\overleftarrow{\oplus}$ and $\overleftarrow{\otimes}$. We consider the operation between x_p and y_q whose result is z_r. Here, z_r and y_q are known while x_p is unknown. We have

$$\overleftarrow{\oplus}(z_r, y_q) = (z-y)_p \text{ where } p = \mathsf{ufp}(z-y) - \mathsf{ufp}\big(\varepsilon(z_r) - \varepsilon(y_q)\big), \quad (18)$$

$$\overleftarrow{\otimes}(z_r, y_q) = (z \div y)_p \text{ where } p = \mathsf{ufp}(z \div y) - \mathsf{ufp}\left(\frac{y \cdot \varepsilon(z_r) - z \cdot \varepsilon(y_q)}{y \cdot (y + \varepsilon(y_q))}\right). \tag{19}$$

The correctness of the backward product relies on the following arguments. Let $\varepsilon(x), \varepsilon(y)$ and $\varepsilon(z)$ be the exact errors on x, y and z respectively. We have $\varepsilon(z) = x \cdot \varepsilon(y) + y \cdot \varepsilon(x) + \varepsilon(x) \cdot \varepsilon(y)$ and then $\varepsilon(x) \cdot (y + \varepsilon(y)) = \varepsilon(z) - x \cdot \varepsilon(y) = \varepsilon(z) - \frac{z}{y} \cdot \varepsilon(y)$. Finally, we conclude that $\varepsilon(x) = \frac{y \cdot \varepsilon(z_r) - z \cdot \varepsilon(y_q)}{y \cdot (y + \varepsilon(y_q))}$.

We end this section by extending the operations to the values of the abstract domain $\mathcal{D}^\sharp$ of Sect. 3.1. First, let $p \in \mathbb{N}$, let $m \in \{-\infty, +\infty, \sim_e, \sim_a, 0\}$ be a rounding mode and let $\circ_{p,m} : \mathbb{F} \to \mathbb{F}_p$ be the rounding function which returns the roundoff of a number at precision p using the rounding mode m. We write $\overrightarrow{\boxplus}$ and $\overleftarrow{\boxplus}$ the forward and backward addition and $\overrightarrow{\boxtimes}$ and $\overleftarrow{\boxtimes}$ the forward and backward products on $\mathcal{D}^\sharp$. These functions are defined in Fig. 5. The forward functions $\overrightarrow{\boxplus}$ and $\overrightarrow{\boxtimes}$ take two operands $[\underline{x}, \overline{x}]_p$ and $[\underline{y}, \overline{y}]_q$ and return the resulting abstract value $[\underline{z}, \overline{z}]_r$. The backward functions take three arguments: the operands $[\underline{x}, \overline{x}]_p$ and $[\underline{y}, \overline{y}]_q$ known from the forward pass and the result $[\underline{z}, \overline{z}]_r$ computed by the backward pass [20]. Then $\overleftarrow{\boxplus}$ and $\overleftarrow{\boxtimes}$ compute the backward value $[\underline{x'}, \overline{x'}]_{p'}$ of the first operand. The backward value of the second operand can be obtained by inverting the operands $[\underline{x}, \overline{x}]_p$ and $[\underline{y}, \overline{y}]_q$. An important point in these formulas is that, in forward mode, the resulting intervals inherit from the minimal accuracy computed for their bounds while, in backward mode, the maximal accuracy computed for the bounds is assigned to the interval.

$$\overrightarrow{\boxplus}\big([\underline{x}, \overline{x}]_p, [\underline{y}, \overline{y}]_q\big) = [\circ_{r,-\infty}(\underline{z}), \circ_{r,+\infty}(\overline{z})]_r \text{ with } \begin{cases} \underline{z}_{r_1} = \overrightarrow{\oplus}(\underline{x}_p, \underline{y}_q), \\ \overline{z}_{r_2} = \overrightarrow{\oplus}(\overline{x}_p, \overline{y}_q), \ r = \min(r_1, r_2). \end{cases} \tag{14}$$

$$\overrightarrow{\boxtimes}\big([\underline{x}, \overline{x}]_p, [\underline{y}, \overline{y}]_q\big) = [\circ_{r,-\infty}(\underline{z}), \circ_{r,+\infty}(\overline{z})]_r \text{ with } \begin{cases} a_{r_1} = \overrightarrow{\otimes}(\underline{x}_p, \underline{y}_q), \ b_{r_2} = \overrightarrow{\otimes}(\underline{x}_p, \overline{y}_q), \\ c_{r_3} = \overrightarrow{\otimes}(\overline{x}_p, \underline{y}_q), \ d_{r_4} = \overrightarrow{\otimes}(\overline{x}_p, \overline{y}_q), \\ \underline{z} = \min(a_{r_1}, b_{r_2}, c_{r_3}, d_{r_4}), \\ \overline{z} = \max(a_{r_1}, b_{r_2}, c_{r_3}, d_{r_4}), \\ r = \min(r_1, r_2, r_3, r_4). \end{cases} \tag{15}$$

$$\overleftarrow{\boxplus}\big([\underline{x}, \overline{x}]_p, [\underline{y}, \overline{y}]_q, [\underline{z}, \overline{z}]_r\big) = [\underline{x'}, \overline{x'}]_{p'} \text{ with } \begin{cases} \underline{u}_{r_1} = \overleftarrow{\oplus}(\underline{z}, \overline{y}_q), \ \overline{u}_{r_2} = \overleftarrow{\oplus}(\overline{z}, \underline{y}_q), \\ \underline{x'} = \max(\underline{u}, \underline{x}), \ \overline{x'} = \min(\overline{u}, \overline{x}), \\ p' = \max(r_1, r_2) \ . \end{cases} \tag{16}$$

$$\overleftarrow{\boxtimes}\big([\underline{x}, \overline{x}]_p, [\underline{y}, \overline{y}]_q, [\underline{z}, \overline{z}]_r\big) = [\underline{x'}, \overline{x'}]_{p'} \text{ with } \begin{cases} a_{r_1} = \overleftarrow{\otimes}(\underline{z}_r, \underline{y}_q), \ b_{r_2} = \overleftarrow{\otimes}(\underline{z}_r, \overline{y}_q), \\ c_{r_3} = \overleftarrow{\otimes}(\overline{z}_r, \underline{y}_q), \ d_{r_4} = \overleftarrow{\otimes}(\overline{z}_r, \overline{y}_q), \\ \underline{u} = \min(a_{r_1}, b_{r_2}, c_{r_3}, d_{r_4}), \\ \overline{u} = \max(a_{r_1}, b_{r_2}, c_{r_3}, d_{r_4}), \\ \underline{x'} = \max(\underline{u}, \underline{x}), \ \overline{x'} = \min(\overline{u}, \overline{x}), \\ p' = \max(r_1, r_2, r_3, r_4). \end{cases} \tag{17}$$

Fig. 5. Forward and backward transfer functions for the addition and product on $\mathcal{D}^\sharp$.

4   Constraint Generation

In this section, we introduce our system of constraints. The transfer functions of Sect. 3 are not directly translated into constraints because the resulting system would be too difficult to solve, containing non-linear constraints among non-integer quantities. Instead, we reduce the problem to a system of constraints made of linear relations between integer elements only. Sections 4.1 and 4.2 introduce the constraints for arithmetic expressions and programs, respectively.

4.1   Constraints for Arithmetic Expressions

In this section, we introduce the constraints generated for arithmetic expressions. As mentioned in Sect. 2, we assume that a range analysis is performed before the accuracy analysis and that a bounding interval is given for each variable and each value at any control point of the input programs.

Let us start with the forward operations. Let $x_p \in \mathbb{F}_p$ and $y_q \in \mathbb{F}_q$ and let us consider the operation $\vec{\oplus}(x_p, y_q) = z_r$. We know from Eq. (12) that $r_+ = \mathsf{ufp}(x+y) - \mathsf{ufp}(\varepsilon_+)$ with $\varepsilon_+ = \varepsilon(x_p) + \varepsilon(y_q)$. We need to over-approximate ε_+ in order to ensure r_+. Let $a = \mathsf{ufp}(x)$ and $b = \mathsf{ufp}(b)$. We have $\varepsilon(x) < 2^{a-p+1}$ and $\varepsilon(y) < 2^{b-p+1}$ and, consequently, $\varepsilon_+ < 2^{a-p+1} + 2^{b-p+1}$. We introduce the function ι defined by $\iota(u,v) = \begin{cases} 1 \text{ if } u = v, \\ 0 \text{ otherwise} \end{cases}$. We have

$$\mathsf{ufp}(\varepsilon_+) < \max(a-p+1, b-q+1) + \iota(a-p, b-q)$$
$$\leq \max(a-p, b-q) + \iota(a-p, b-q)$$

and we conclude that

$$r_+ = \mathsf{ufp}(x+y) - \max(a-p, b-q) - \iota(a-p, b-q). \tag{20}$$

Note that, since we assume that a range analysis has been performed before the accuracy analysis, $\mathsf{ufp}(x+y)$, a and b are known at constraint generation time. For the forward product, we know from Eq. (13) that $r_\times = \mathsf{ufp}(x \times y) - \mathsf{ufp}(\varepsilon_\times)$ with $\varepsilon_\times = x \cdot \varepsilon(y_q) + y \cdot \varepsilon(x_p) + \varepsilon(x_p) \cdot \varepsilon(y_q)$. Again, let $a = \mathsf{ufp}(x)$ and $b = \mathsf{ufp}(b)$. We have, by definition of ufp, $2^a \leq x < 2^{a+1}$ and $2^b \leq y < 2^{b+1}$. Then $\varepsilon_\times$ may be bound by

$$\varepsilon_\times < 2^{a+1} \cdot 2^{b-q+1} + 2^{b+1} \cdot 2^{a-p+1} + 2^{a-p+1} \cdot 2^{b-q+1}$$
$$= 2^{a+b-q+2} + 2^{a+b-p+2} + 2^{a+b-p-q+2}.$$

Since $a+b-p-q+2 < a+b-p+2$ and $a+b-p-q+2 < a+b-q+2$, we may get rid of the last term of the former equation and we obtain that

$$\mathsf{ufp}(\varepsilon_\times) < \max(a+b-p+2, a+b-q+2) + \iota(p,q)$$
$$\leq \max(a+b-p+1, a+b-q+1) + \iota(p,q).$$

We conclude that

$$r_\times = \mathsf{ufp}(x \times y) - \max(a + b - p + 1, a + b - q + 1) - \iota(p, q). \tag{21}$$

Note that, by reasoning on the exponents of the values, the constraints resulting from a product become linear. We consider now the backward transfer functions. If $\overleftarrow{\oplus}(z_r, y_q) = x_{p_+}$ then we know from Eq. (18) that $p_+ = \mathsf{ufp}(z - y) - \mathsf{ufp}(\varepsilon_+)$ with $\varepsilon_+ = \varepsilon(z_r) - \varepsilon(y - q)$. Let $c = \mathsf{ufp}(z)$, we over-approximate ε_+ using the relations $\varepsilon(z_r) < 2^{c-r+1}$ and $\varepsilon(y_q) > 0$. So, $\mathsf{ufp}(\varepsilon_+) < c - r + 1$ and

$$p_+ = \mathsf{ufp}(z - y) - c + r \tag{22}$$

Finally, for the backward product, using Eq. (19) we know that if $\overleftarrow{\otimes}(z_r, y_q) = x_{p_\times}$ then $p_\times = \mathsf{ufp}(x) - \mathsf{ufp}(\varepsilon_\times)$ with $\varepsilon_\times = \frac{y \cdot \varepsilon(z) - z \cdot \varepsilon(y)}{y \cdot (y + \varepsilon(y))}$. Using the relations $2^b \le y < 2^{b+1}$, $2^c \le z < 2^{c+1}$, $\varepsilon(y) < 2^{b-q+1}$ and $\varepsilon(z) < 2^{c-r+1}$, we deduce that $y \cdot \varepsilon(z) - z \cdot \varepsilon(y) < 2^{b+c-r+2} - 2^{b+c-q+1}$ and that $\frac{1}{y \cdot (y + \varepsilon(y))} < 2^{-2b}$. Consequently, $\varepsilon_\times < 2^{-2b} \cdot (2^{b+c-r+2} - 2^{b+c-q+1}) \le 2^{c-b-r+1} - 2^{c-b-q}$ and it results that

$$p_\times = \mathsf{ufp}(x) - \max(c - b - r + 1, c - b - q). \tag{23}$$

4.2 Systematic Constraint Generation

To explain the constraint generation, we use the simple imperative language of Eq. (24) in which a unique label $\ell \in \mathsf{Lab}$ is attached to each expression and command to identify without ambiguity each node of the syntactic tree.

$$e ::= c\#p^\ell \mid x^\ell \mid e_1^{\ell_1} +^\ell e_2^{\ell_2} \mid e_1^{\ell_1} -^\ell e_2^{\ell_2} \mid e_1^{\ell_1} \times^\ell e_2^{\ell_2}$$

$$c ::= x :=^\ell e^{\ell_1} \mid c_1^{\ell_1} ;_\ell c_2^{\ell_2} \mid \mathsf{if}^\ell e^{\ell_0} \mathsf{then}\ c_1^{\ell_1} \mathsf{else}\ c_2^{\ell_2} \tag{24}$$
$$\mid \mathsf{while}^\ell e^{\ell_0} \mathsf{do}\ c_1^{\ell_1} \mid \mathsf{require\_accuracy}(x, n)^\ell$$

As in Sect. 2, $c\#p$ denotes a constant c with accuracy p and the statement $\mathsf{require\_accuracy}(x, n)^\ell$ indicates that x must have at least accuracy n at control point ℓ. The set of identifiers occurring in the source program is denoted Id. Concerning the arithmetic expressions, we assign to each label ℓ of the expression three variables in our system of constraints, $\mathsf{acc}_F(\ell)$, $\mathsf{acc}_B(\ell)$ and $\mathsf{acc}(\ell)$ respectively corresponding to the forward, backward and final accuracies and we systematically generate the constraints $0 \le \mathsf{acc}_B(\ell) \le \mathsf{acc}(\ell) \le \mathsf{acc}_F(\ell)$.

For each control point in an arithmetic expression, we assume given a range $[\underline{\ell}, \overline{\ell}] \subseteq \mathbb{F}$, computed by static analysis and which bounds the values possibly occurring at Point ℓ at run-time. Our constraints use the unit in the first place $\mathsf{ufp}(\underline{\ell})$ and $\mathsf{ufp}(\overline{\ell})$ of these ranges. Let $\Lambda : \mathsf{Id} \to \mathsf{Id} \times \mathsf{Lab}$ be an environment which relates each identifier x to its last assignment x^ℓ: Assuming that $x :=^\ell e^{\ell_1}$ is the last assignment of x, the environment Λ maps x to x^ℓ (we will use join operators when control flow branches will be considered). Then $\mathcal{E}[e]\ \Lambda$ generates the set of constraints for the expression e in the environment Λ. These constraints, defined in Fig. 6, are derived from equations of Sect. 4.1. For commands, labels are used

$$\mathcal{E}[\ c\#p^{\ell}\ ]\Lambda = \{\mathrm{acc}_F(\ell) = p\}$$

$$\mathcal{E}[\ x^{\ell}\ ]\Lambda = \{\mathrm{acc}_F(\ell) = \mathrm{acc}_F(\Lambda(x)),\ \mathrm{acc}_B(\ell) = \mathrm{acc}_B(\Lambda(x))\}$$

$$\mathcal{E}[e_1^{\ell_1} +^{\ell} e_2^{\ell_2}]\Lambda = C[e_1^{\ell_1}]\Lambda \ \cup \ C[e_2^{\ell_2}]\Lambda \ \cup \ F_+(\ell_1, \ell_2, \ell) \ \cup \ O_+(\ell_1, \ell_2, \ell)$$

$$\mathcal{E}[e_1^{\ell_1} \times^{\ell} e_2^{\ell_2}]\Lambda = C[e_1^{\ell_1}]\Lambda \ \cup \ C[e_2^{\ell_2}]\Lambda \ \cup \ F_\times(\ell_1, \ell_2, \ell) \ \cup \ O_\times(\ell_1, \ell_2, \ell)$$

$$\mathcal{O}_+(\ell_1, \ell_2, \ell) = \left|\begin{array}{l} \mathcal{B}_+(\ell_1, \ell_2, \ell) \ \cup \ \mathcal{B}_+(\ell_2, \ell_1, \ell) \\ \cup \ \{(\mathrm{acc}(\ell_1) \leq \mathrm{acc}_F(\ell_1) \ \wedge \ \mathrm{acc}(\ell_2) \geq \mathrm{acc}_B(\ell_2)) \\ \qquad \vee \ (\mathrm{acc}(\ell_2) \leq \mathrm{acc}_F(\ell_2) \ \wedge \ \mathrm{acc}(\ell_1) \geq \mathrm{acc}_B(\ell_1))\} \end{array}\right.$$

$$\mathcal{O}_\times(\ell_1, \ell_2, \ell) = \left|\begin{array}{l} \mathcal{B}_\times(\ell_1, \ell_2, \ell) \ \cup \ \mathcal{B}_\times(\ell_2, \ell_1, \ell) \\ \cup \ \{(\mathrm{acc}(\ell_1) \leq \mathrm{acc}_F(\ell_1) \ \wedge \ \mathrm{acc}(\ell_2) \geq \mathrm{acc}_B(\ell_2)) \\ \qquad \vee \ (\mathrm{acc}(\ell_2) \leq \mathrm{acc}_F(\ell_2) \ \wedge \ \mathrm{acc}(\ell_1) \geq \mathrm{acc}_B(\ell_1))\} \end{array}\right.$$

$$\mathcal{F}_+(\ell_1, \ell_2, \ell) = \left\{\begin{array}{l} \overline{r}^{\ell} = \mathrm{ufp}(\overline{\ell}) - \max(\overline{\ell_1} - \mathrm{acc}_F(\ell_1), \overline{\ell_2} - \mathrm{acc}_F(\ell_2)), \\ \underline{r}^{\ell} = \mathrm{ufp}(\underline{\ell}) - \max(\underline{\ell_1} - \mathrm{acc}_F(\ell_1), \underline{\ell_2} - \mathrm{acc}_F(\ell_2)), \\ \overline{i}^{\ell} = (\mathrm{ufp}(\overline{\ell_1}) - \mathrm{acc}_F(\ell_1) = \mathrm{ufp}(\overline{\ell_2}) - \mathrm{acc}_F(\ell_2))?\ 1\ :\ 0, \\ \underline{i}^{\ell} = (\mathrm{ufp}(\underline{\ell_1}) - \mathrm{acc}_F(\ell_1) = \mathrm{ufp}(\underline{\ell_2}) - \mathrm{acc}_F(\ell_2))?\ 1\ :\ 0, \\ \mathrm{acc}_F(\ell) = \min(\underline{r}^{\ell} - \underline{i}^{\ell}, \overline{r}^{\ell} - \overline{i}^{\ell}) \end{array}\right.$$

$$\mathcal{B}_+(\ell_1, \ell_2, \ell) = \left\{\begin{array}{l} \overline{s}^{\ell_1} = \mathrm{ufp}(\overline{\ell_1}) - (\mathrm{ufp}(\overline{\ell}) - \mathrm{acc}_B(\ell)), \\ \underline{s}^{\ell_1} = \mathrm{ufp}(\underline{\ell_1}) - (\mathrm{ufp}(\underline{\ell}) - \mathrm{acc}_B(\ell)),\ \mathrm{acc}_B(\ell_1) = \max(\underline{s}^{\ell_1}, \overline{s}^{\ell_1}) \end{array}\right\}$$

$$\mathcal{F}_\times(\ell_1, \ell_2, \ell) = \left\{\begin{array}{l} r_1^{\ell} = \mathrm{ufp}(\overline{\ell_1} \times \overline{\ell_2}) - \max\left(\mathrm{ufp}(\overline{\ell_1}) + \mathrm{ufp}(\overline{\ell_2}) - \mathrm{acc}_F(\ell_1), \mathrm{ufp}(\overline{\ell_1}) + \mathrm{ufp}(\overline{\ell_2}) - \mathrm{acc}_F(\ell_2)\right), \\ r_2^{\ell} = \mathrm{ufp}(\underline{\ell_1} \times \underline{\ell_2}) - \max\left(\mathrm{ufp}(\underline{\ell_1}) + \mathrm{ufp}(\underline{\ell_2}) - \mathrm{acc}_F(\ell_1), \mathrm{ufp}(\underline{\ell_1}) + \mathrm{ufp}(\underline{\ell_2}) - \mathrm{acc}_F(\ell_2)\right), \\ r_3^{\ell} = \mathrm{ufp}(\underline{\ell_1} \times \overline{\ell_2}) - \max\left(\mathrm{ufp}(\underline{\ell_1}) + \mathrm{ufp}(\overline{\ell_2}) - \mathrm{acc}_F(\ell_1), \mathrm{ufp}(\underline{\ell_1}) + \mathrm{ufp}(\overline{\ell_2}) - \mathrm{acc}_F(\ell_2)\right), \\ r_4^{\ell} = \mathrm{ufp}(\overline{\ell_1} \times \underline{\ell_2}) - \max\left(\mathrm{ufp}(\overline{\ell_1}) + \mathrm{ufp}(\underline{\ell_2}) - \mathrm{acc}_F(\ell_1), \mathrm{ufp}(\overline{\ell_1}) + \mathrm{ufp}(\underline{\ell_2}) - \mathrm{acc}_F(\ell_2)\right), \\ i^{\ell} = (\mathrm{acc}_F(\ell_1) = \mathrm{acc}_F(\ell_2))?\ 1\ :\ 0,\ \mathrm{acc}_F(\ell) = \min\left(r_1^{\ell} - i^{\ell}, r_2^{\ell} - i^{\ell}, r_3^{\ell} - i^{\ell}, r_4^{\ell} - i^{\ell}\right) \end{array}\right\}$$

$$\mathcal{B}_\times(\ell_1, \ell_2, \ell) = \left\{\begin{array}{l} s_1^{\ell_1} = \mathrm{ufp}(\overline{\ell_1}) - \max\left(\mathrm{ufp}(\overline{\ell}) - \mathrm{ufp}(\overline{\ell_2}) + 1 - \mathrm{acc}_B(\ell), \mathrm{ufp}(\overline{\ell}) - \mathrm{ufp}(\overline{\ell_2}) - \mathrm{acc}_F(\ell_2)\right), \\ s_2^{\ell_1} = \mathrm{ufp}(\underline{\ell_1}) - \max\left(\mathrm{ufp}(\underline{\ell}) - \mathrm{ufp}(\underline{\ell_2}) + 1 - \mathrm{acc}_B(\ell), \mathrm{ufp}(\underline{\ell}) - \mathrm{ufp}(\underline{\ell_2}) - \mathrm{acc}_F(\ell_2)\right), \\ s_3^{\ell_1} = \mathrm{ufp}(\underline{\ell_1}) - \max\left(\mathrm{ufp}(\underline{\ell}) - \mathrm{ufp}(\overline{\ell_2}) + 1 - \mathrm{acc}_B(\ell), \mathrm{ufp}(\underline{\ell}) - \mathrm{ufp}(\overline{\ell_2}) - \mathrm{acc}_F(\ell_2)\right), \\ s_4^{\ell_1} = \mathrm{ufp}(\overline{\ell_1}) - \max\left(\mathrm{ufp}(\overline{\ell}) - \mathrm{ufp}(\underline{\ell_2}) + 1 - \mathrm{acc}_B(\ell), \mathrm{ufp}(\overline{\ell}) - \mathrm{ufp}(\underline{\ell_2}) - \mathrm{acc}_F(\ell_2)\right), \\ \mathrm{acc}_B(\ell_1) = \max(s_1^{\ell_1}, s_2^{\ell_1}, s_3^{\ell_1}, s_4^{\ell_1}) \end{array}\right\}$$

Fig. 6. Constraint generation for arithmetic expressions.

$$\mathcal{C}[x :=^{\ell} e^{\ell_1}]\ \Lambda = (C, \Lambda[x \mapsto x^{\ell}])$$
$$\text{where } C = \left(\mathcal{E}[e^{\ell_1}]\ \Lambda\right) \cup \left\{\mathrm{acc}_F(x^{\ell}) = \mathrm{acc}_F(\ell_1),\ \mathrm{acc}_B(x^{\ell}) = \mathrm{acc}_B(\ell_1)\right\}$$

$$\mathcal{C}[c_1^{\ell_1}\ ;\ c_2^{\ell_2}]\ \Lambda = (C_1 \cup C_2, \Lambda_2) \text{ where } (C_1, \Lambda_1) = \mathcal{C}[c_1]\ \Lambda,\ (C_2, \Lambda_2) = \mathcal{C}[c_2]\ \Lambda_1$$

$$\mathcal{C}[\mathtt{while}^{\ell}\ e^{\ell_0}\ \mathtt{do}\ c^{\ell_1}]\ \Lambda = (C_1 \cup C_2, \Lambda') \text{ where } \left|\begin{array}{l} (C_1, \Lambda_1) = \mathcal{C}[c^{\ell_1}]\ \Lambda',\ \forall x \in \mathrm{Id},\ \Lambda'(x) = x^{\ell}, \\ C_2 = \bigcup_{x \in \mathrm{Id}} \left\{\begin{array}{l} \mathrm{acc}_F(x^{\ell}) \leq \mathrm{acc}_F(\Lambda(x)), \\ \mathrm{acc}_F(x^{\ell}) \leq \mathrm{acc}_F(\Lambda_1(x)), \\ \mathrm{acc}_B(x^{\ell}) \geq \mathrm{acc}_B(\Lambda(x)), \\ \mathrm{acc}_B(x^{\ell}) \geq \mathrm{acc}_B(\Lambda_1(x)) \end{array}\right. \end{array}\right.$$

$$\mathcal{C}[\mathtt{if}^{\ell}\ e^{\ell_0}\ \mathtt{then}\ c^{\ell_1}\ \mathtt{else}\ c^{\ell_2}]\ \Lambda = (C_1 \cup C_2 \cup C_3, \Lambda')$$
$$\text{where } \left|\begin{array}{l} (C_1, \Lambda_1) = \mathcal{C}[c_1^{\ell_1}]\ \Lambda, (C_2, \Lambda_2) = \mathcal{C}[c_1^{\ell_1}]\ \Lambda,\ \forall x \in \mathrm{Id},\ \Lambda'(x) = x^{\ell}, \\ C_3 = \bigcup_{x \in \mathrm{Id}} \left\{\begin{array}{l} \mathrm{acc}_F(x^{\ell}) = \min\left(\mathrm{acc}_F(\Lambda_1(x)), \mathrm{acc}_F(\Lambda_2(x))\right), \\ \mathrm{acc}_B(x^{\ell}) = \max\left(\mathrm{acc}_B(\Lambda_1(x)), \mathrm{acc}_B(\Lambda_2(x))\right) \end{array}\right. \end{array}\right.$$

$$\mathcal{C}[\mathtt{require\_accuracy}(x, n)^{\ell}]\ \Lambda = \{\mathrm{acc}_B(\Lambda(x)) = n\}$$

Fig. 7. Constraint generation for commands.

to distinguish many assignments of the same variable or to implement joins in conditions and loops. Given a command c and an environment Λ, $\mathcal{C}[c]\ \Lambda$ returns a pair (C, Λ') made of a set C of constraints and of a new environment Λ'. $\mathcal{C}$ is defined by induction on the structure of commands in Fig. 7. These constraint join values at control flow junctions and propagate the accuracies as described in Sect. 2. In forward mode, accuracy decreases while in backward mode accuracy increases (we weaken pre-conditions and strengthen post-conditions).

5   Experimental Results

In this section we present some experimental results obtained with our prototype. Our tool generates the constraints defined in Sect. 4 and calls the Z3 SMT solver [21] in order to obtain a solution. Since, when they exist, solutions are not unique in general, we add an additional constraint related to a cost function φ to the constraints of Figs. 6 and 7. The cost function $\varphi(c)$ of a program c computes the sum of all the accuracies of the variables and intermediary values stored in the control points of the arithmetic expressions, $\varphi(c) = \sum_{x \in \mathrm{Id}, \ell \in \mathrm{Lab}} \mathrm{acc}(x^\ell) + \sum_{\ell \in \mathrm{Lab}} \mathrm{acc}(\ell)$. Then, by binary search, our tool searches the smallest integer P such that the system of constraints $(\mathcal{C}[c] \, \Lambda_\perp) \cup \{\varphi(c) \leq P\}$ admits a solution (we aim at using an optimizing solver in future work [6,25,28]). In our implementation we assume that, in the worst case, all the values are in double precision, consequently we start the binary search with $P \in [0, 52 \times n]$ where n is the number of variables and intermediary values stored in the control points. When a solution is found for some P, a new iteration of the binary search is run with a smaller P. Otherwise, a new iteration is run with a larger P.

We consider three sample codes displayed in Fig. 8. The first program computes the determinant $\det(M)$ of a 3×3 matrix $M = \begin{pmatrix} a & b & c \\ d & e & f \\ g & h & i \end{pmatrix}$. We have $\det(M) = (a \cdot e \cdot i + d \cdot h \cdot c + g \cdot b \cdot f) - (g \cdot e \cdot c + a \cdot h \cdot f + d \cdot b \cdot i)$. The matrix coefficients belong to the ranges $\begin{pmatrix} [-10.1, 10.1] & [-10.1, 10.1] & [-10.1, 10.1] \\ [-20.1, 20.1] & [-20.1, 20.1] & [-20.1, 20.1] \\ [-5.1, 5.1] & [-5.1, 5.1] & [-5.1, 5.1] \end{pmatrix}$ and we require that the variable det containing the result has accuracy 10 which corresponds to a fairly rounded half precision number. By default, we assume that in the original program all the variables are in double precision. Our tool infers that all the computations may be carried out in half precision.

The second example of Fig. 8 concerns the evaluation of a degree 9 polynomial using Horner's scheme: $p(x) = a_0 + (x \times (a_1 + x \times (a_2 + \ldots)))$. The coefficients $a_i, 0 \leq i \leq 9$ belong to $[-0.2, 0.2]$ and $x \in [-0.5, 0.5]$. Initially all the variables are in double precision and we require that the result is fairly rounded in single precision. Our tool then computes that all the variables may be in single precision but p which must remain in double precision. Our last example is a proportional differential controller. Initially the measure m is given by a sensor which sends values in $[-1.0, 1.0]$ and which ensures an accuracy of 32. All the other variables are assumed to be in double precision. As shown in Fig. 8, many variables may fit inside single precision formats.

For each program, we give in Fig. 9 the number of variables of the constraint system as well as the number of constraints generated. Next, we give the total

```
a:=b:=c:=[-10.1,10.1];          a|5|:=b|5|:=c|6|:=[-10.1,10.1]|6|;        half a,b,c,d,e;
d:=e:=f:=[-20.1,20.1];          d|5|:=e|5|:=f|6|:=[-20.1,20.1]|6|;        half f,g,h,i,det;
g:=h:=i:=[-5.1,5.1];            g|5|:=h|5|:=i|6|:=[-5.1,5.1]|6|;          //init a,b,c,d,e,
det:=(a * e * i +               det|10|:=(a|5|*|6|e|5|*|8|i|6|+|9|        //   f,g,h and i
    d * h * c + g * b * f)       d|5|*|6|h|5|*|8|c|6|+|9|g|5|*|6|b|5|*|8|f|6|)   det:=(a * e * i +
    - (g * e * c +               -|10|(g|5|*|8|e|5|*|8|c|6|+|9|               d * h * c +
    a * h * f + d * b * i);       a|5|*|6|h|5|*|8|f|6|+|9|d|5|*|6|b|5|*|8|i|6|);  g * b * f)
require_accuracy              require_accuracy(det,10);                   - (g * e * c +
        (det,10);                                                          a * h * f +
                                                                           d * b * i);
```

```
a:=array                      a|23|:=array(10,[-0.2,0.2]|23|);       float a[10];
    (10,[-0.2,0.2]#53);        x|23|:=[0.0,0.5]|23|;                 float x,tmp;
x:=[0.0,0.5]#53;               p|23|:=0.0|23|; i := 0;               double p;
p:=0.0; i:=0;                  while(i<10) {                         // init a and x
while(i<10) {                    p|24|:=p|23|*|23|x|23|+|24|a[i]|23|;  p:=0.0; i:=0;
    p:=p * x + a[i];           };                                    while(i<10) {
};                             require_accuracy(p,23);                  tmp:=p * x;
require_accuracy(p,23);                                                  p:=tmp + a[i];};
```

```
m:=[-1.0,1.0]#32;             m|21|:=[-1.0,1.0]|21|;                 volatile float m;
kp:=0.194; kd:=0.028;          kp|21|:=0.194|21|;kd|20|:=0.028|20|;  float kp,kd,p,d,r;
invdt:=10.0; c:=0.5;           invdt|20|:=10.0|20|;                  float invdt,c,e0;
e0:=0.0;                       c|21|:=0.5|21|;e0|21|:=0.0|21|;       double e,tmp;
while (true) {                 while (true) {                        kp:=0.194;kd:=0.028;
    e:=c - m;                    e|21|:=c|21|-|21|m|22|;             invdt:=10.0; c:=0.5;
    p:=kp * e;                   p|22|:=kp|21|*|22|e|21|;            e0:=0.0 ;
    d:=kd*invdt*(e-e0);          d|23|:=kd|20|*|22|invdt|20|         while (true) {
    r:=p + d;                        *|23|(e|21|-|22|e0|21|);          e:=c-m;p:=kp*e;
    e0:=e;                       r|23|:=p|22|+|23|d|23|;e0|21|:=e|21|;};   tmp:=e - e0;
};                             require_accuracy(r,23);                 d:=kd * invdt;
require_accuracy(r,23);                                                 d:=d * tmp;
                                                                        r:=p + d; e0:=e;};
```

Fig. 8. Examples of mixed-precision inference. Source programs, inferred accuracies and formats. Top: 3×3 determinant. Middle: Horner's scheme. Bottom: a PD controller.

Program	#Var.	#Constr.	Time(s)	#Bits-Init.	#Bits-Optim.	Z3-Calls
Linear filter	239	330	0.31	1534	252	12
Determinant	604	775	0.45	2912	475	14
Horner	129	179	0.18	884	346	11
PD Controller	388	530	0.49	2262	954	12

Fig. 9. Measures of efficiency of the analysis on the codes of Figs. 2 and 8.

execution time of the analysis (including the generation of the system of constraints and the calls to the SMT solver done by the binary search). Then we give the number of bits needed to store all the values of the programs, assuming that all the values are stored in double precision (column #Bits-Init.) and as computed by our analysis (column #Bits-Optim.) Finally, the number of calls to the SMT solver done during the binary search is displayed. Globally, we can observe that the numbers of variables and constraints are rather small and very tractable for the solver. This is confirmed by the execution times which are very short. The improvement, in the number of bits needed to fulfill the requirements, compared to the number of bits needed if all the computations are done in double precision, ranges from 57% to 83% which is very important.

6   Conclusion

We have defined a static analysis which determines the floating-point formats needed to ensure a given accuracy. This analysis is done by generating a set of linear constraints between integer variables only, even if the programs contain non-linear computations. These constraints are easy to solve by a SMT solver.

Our technique can be easily extended to other language structures. For example, since all the elements of an array must have the same type, we just need to join all the elements in a same abstract value to obtain a relevant result. Similarly, functions are also easy to manage since only one type per argument and returned value need. Our analysis is built upon a range analysis performed before. Obviously, the precision of this analysis impacts the precision of the floating-point format determination and the inference of sharp ranges given by relational domains, improves the quality of the results. In future work, we aim at exploring the use a solver based on optimization modulo theories [6,25,28] instead of the non-optimizing solver coupled to a binary search used presently.

References

1. Patriot missile defense: Software problem led to system failure at Dhahran, Saudi Arabia. Technical Report GAO/IMTEC-92-26, General Accounting office (1992)
2. ANSI/IEEE: IEEE Standard for Binary Floating-Point Arithmetic (2008)
3. Barr, E.T., Vo, T., Le, V., Su, Z.: Automatic detection of floating-point exceptions. In: POPL 2013, pp. 549–560. ACM (2013)
4. Barrett, C.W., Sebastiani, R., Seshia, S.A., Tinelli, C.: Satisfiability modulo theories. In: Handbook of Satisfiability. Frontiers in Artificial Intelligence and Applications, vol. 185, pp. 825–885. IOS Press (2009)
5. Bertrane, J., Cousot, P., Cousot, R., Feret, J., Mauborgne, L., Miné, A., Rival, X.: Static analysis by abstract interpretation of embedded critical software. ACM SIG-SOFT Softw. Eng. Notes **36**(1), 1–8 (2011)
6. Bjørner, N., Phan, A.-D., Fleckenstein, L.: νZ - an optimizing SMT solver. In: Baier, C., Tinelli, C. (eds.) TACAS 2015. LNCS, vol. 9035, pp. 194–199. Springer, Heidelberg (2015). doi:10.1007/978-3-662-46681-0_14
7. Chiang, W., Baranowski, M., Briggs, I., Solovyev, A., Gopalakrishnan, G., Rakamaric, Z.: Rigorous floating-point mixed-precision tuning. In: POPL, pp. 300–315. ACM (2017)
8. Cousot, P., Cousot, R.: Abstract interpretation: a unified lattice model for static analysis of programs by construction or approximation of fixpoints. In: Principles of Programming Languages, pp. 238–252. ACM Press (1977)
9. Cousot, P., Cousot, R.: A gentle introduction to formal verification of computer systems by abstract interpretation. NATO Science Series III: Computer and Systems Sciences, pp. 1–29. IOS Press (2010)
10. Damouche, N., Martel, M., Chapoutot, A.: Intra-procedural optimization of the numerical accuracy of programs. In: Núñez, M., Güdemann, M. (eds.) FMICS 2015. LNCS, vol. 9128, pp. 31–46. Springer, Cham (2015). doi:10.1007/978-3-319-19458-5_3
11. Darulova, E., Kuncak, V.: Sound compilation of reals. In: Symposium on Principles of Programming Languages, POPL 2014, pp. 235–248. ACM (2014)

12. Gao, X., Bayliss, S., Constantinides, G.A.: SOAP: structural optimization of arithmetic expressions for high-level synthesis. In: International Conference on Field-Programmable Technology, pp. 112–119. IEEE (2013)

13. Goubault, E.: Static analysis by abstract interpretation of numerical programs and systems, and FLUCTUAT. In: Logozzo, F., Fähndrich, M. (eds.) SAS 2013. LNCS, vol. 7935, pp. 1–3. Springer, Heidelberg (2013). doi:10.1007/978-3-642-38856-9_1

14. Goubault, E., Putot, S.: Static analysis of finite precision computations. In: Jhala, R., Schmidt, D. (eds.) VMCAI 2011. LNCS, vol. 6538, pp. 232–247. Springer, Heidelberg (2011). doi:10.1007/978-3-642-18275-4_17

15. Halfhill, T.R.: The truth behind the Pentium bug. Byte, March 1995

16. Lam, M.O., Hollingsworth, J.K., de Supinski, B.R., LeGendre, M.P.: Automatically adapting programs for mixed-precision floating-point computation. In: Supercomputing, ICS 2013, pp. 369–378. ACM (2013)

17. Lamotte, J.L., Chesneaux, J.M., Jézéquel, F.: CADNA_C: a version of CADNA for use with C or C++ programs. Comput. Phys. Commu. **181**(11), 1925–1926 (2010)

18. Martel, M.: Semantics of roundoff error propagation in finite precision calculations. High.-Order Symb. Comput. **19**(1), 7–30 (2006)

19. Martel, M., Najahi, A., Revy, G.: Code size and accuracy-aware synthesis of fixed-point programs for matrix multiplication. In: Pervasive and Embedded Computing and Communication Systems, pp. 204–214. SciTePress (2014)

20. Miné, A.: Inferring sufficient conditions with backward polyhedral under-approximations. Electr. Notes Theor. Comput. Sci. **287**, 89–100 (2012)

21. Moura, L., Bjørner, N.: Z3: an efficient SMT solver. In: Ramakrishnan, C.R., Rehof, J. (eds.) TACAS 2008. LNCS, vol. 4963, pp. 337–340. Springer, Heidelberg (2008). doi:10.1007/978-3-540-78800-3_24

22. Muller, J.M.: On the definition of ulp(x). Technical report 2005–09, Laboratoire d'Informatique du Parallélisme, Ecole Normale Supérieure de Lyon (2005)

23. Muller, J.M., Brisebarre, N., de Dinechin, F., Jeannerod, C.P., Lefèvre, V., Melquiond, G., Revol, N., Stehlé, D., Torres, S.: Handbook of Floating-Point Arithmetic. Birkhäuser Boston, Boston (2010)

24. Nguyen, C., Rubio-Gonzalez, C., Mehne, B., Sen, K., Demmel, J., Kahan, W., Iancu, C., Lavrijsen, W., Bailey, D.H., Hough, D.: Floating-point precision tuning using blame analysis. In: International Conference on Software Engineering (ICSE). ACM (2016)

25. Nieuwenhuis, R., Oliveras, A.: On SAT modulo theories and optimization problems. In: Biere, A., Gomes, C.P. (eds.) SAT 2006. LNCS, vol. 4121, pp. 156–169. Springer, Heidelberg (2006). doi:10.1007/11814948_18

26. Panchekha, P., Sanchez-Stern, A., Wilcox, J.R., Tatlock, Z.: Automatically improving accuracy for floating point expressions. In: PLDI, pp. 1–11. ACM (2015)

27. Rubio-Gonzalez, C., Nguyen, C., Nguyen, H.D., Demmel, J., Kahan, W., Sen, K., Bailey, D.H., Iancu, C., Hough, D.: Precimonious: tuning assistant for floating-point precision. In: International Conference for High Performance Computing, Networking, Storage and Analysis, pp. 27:1–27:12. ACM (2013)

28. Sebastiani, R., Tomasi, S.: Optimization modulo theories with linear rational costs. ACM Trans. Comput. Log. **16**(2), 12:1–12:43 (2015)

29. Solovyev, A., Jacobsen, C., Rakamarić, Z., Gopalakrishnan, G.: Rigorous estimation of floating-point round-off errors with symbolic Taylor expansions. In: Bjørner, N., de Boer, F. (eds.) FM 2015. LNCS, vol. 9109, pp. 532–550. Springer, Cham (2015). doi:10.1007/978-3-319-19249-9_33

A Verification Technique for Deterministic Parallel Programs

Saeed Darabi[✉], Stefan C.C. Blom, and Marieke Huisman

University of Twente, Enschede, The Netherlands
{s.darabi,s.c.c.blom,M.Huisman}@utwente.nl

Abstract. A commonly used approach to develop parallel programs is to augment a sequential program with compiler directives that indicate which program blocks may potentially be executed in parallel. This paper develops a verification technique to prove correctness of compiler directives combined with functional correctness of the program. We propose syntax and semantics for a simple core language, capturing the main forms of deterministic parallel programs. This language distinguishes three kinds of basic blocks: parallel, vectorized and sequential blocks, which can be composed using three different composition operators: sequential, parallel and fusion composition. We show that it is sufficient to have contracts for the basic blocks to prove correctness of the compiler directives, and moreover that functional correctness of the sequential program implies correctness of the parallelized program. We formally prove correctness of our approach. In addition, we define a widely-used subset of OpenMP that can be encoded into our core language, thus effectively enabling the verification of OpenMP compiler directives, and we discuss automated tool support for this verification process.

1 Introduction

A common approach to handle the complexity of parallel programming is to write a sequential program augmented with parallelization compiler directives that indicate which part of code might be parallelized. A parallelizing compiler consumes the annotated sequential program and automatically generates a parallel version. This approach is often called *deterministic parallel programming*, as the parallelization of a deterministic sequential program augmented with correct compiler directives is always deterministic. Deterministic parallel programming is supported by different languages and libraries such as OpenMP [18] and is often used for financial and scientific applications [3,11,16,19].

Although it is relatively easy to write parallel programs in this way, careless use of compiler directives can easily introduce data races and consequently non-deterministic program behaviour. This paper proposes a static technique to prove that parallelization as indicated by the compiler directives does not introduce such non-determinism. Moreover it also shows how our technique reduces functional verification of the parallelized program to functional verification of the sequential program. We develop our verification technique over

© Springer International Publishing AG 2017
C. Barrett et al. (Eds.): NFM 2017, LNCS 10227, pp. 247–264, 2017.
DOI: 10.1007/978-3-319-57288-8_17

a core deterministic parallel programming language called PPL (for Parallel Programming Language). To show practical usability of our approach, we present how a commonly used subset of OpenMP can be encoded into PPL and then be verified in our approach. We also discuss tool support for this process.

In essence, PPL is a language for the composition of code blocks. We identify three kinds of *basic blocks*: a *parallel block*, a *vectorized block* and a *sequential block*. Basic blocks are composed by three binary block composition operators: *sequential composition*, *parallel composition* and *fusion composition* where the fusion composition allows two parallel basic blocks to be merged into one. An operational semantics for PPL is presented.

Our verification technique requires each basic block to be specified by an *iteration contract* [6] that describes which memory locations are read and written by a thread. Moreover, the program itself should be specified by a global contract. To verify the program, we show that the block compositions are memory safe (i.e. data race free) by proving that for all *independent iterations* (i.e. the iterations that might run in parallel) all accesses to shared memory are non-conflicting, meaning that they are disjoint or they are read accesses. If all block compositions are memory safe, then it is sufficient to prove that the sequential composition of all the basic blocks w.r.t. program order is memory safe and functionally correct, to conclude that the parallelized program is functionally correct.

The main contributions of this paper are the following:

- A core language, PPL, and an operational semantics which captures the main forms of parallelization constructs in deterministic parallel programming.
- A verification approach for reasoning about data race freedom and functional correctness of PPL programs.
- A soundness proof that all verified PPL programs are indeed data race free and functionally correct w.r.t. their contracts.
- Tool support that addresses the complete process of encoding of OpenMP into PPL and verification of PPL programs.

This paper is organized as follows. After some background information, Sect. 3 explains syntax and semantics of PPL. Section 4 presents our verification technique for reasoning about PPL programs and also discusses soundness of our verification approach. Section 5 explains how our approach is applied to verification of OpenMP programs. Finally, we conclude with related and future work.

2   Background

We present some background information on OpenMP, Permission-based Separation Logic and the notion of iteration contract.

2.1   OpenMP

This section illustrates the most important OpenMP features by an example. We verify this example later in Sect. 5 where the program contract and the iteration

```
1   /*@ Program Contract (PC) @*/          10   for(int i =0;i<L;i++) //Loop L2
2   void adm(int L,int a[],int b[],int c[],  11   /*@ Iteration  Contract 2 (IC₂) @*/
3   int d[]){                                12      { c[i]=c[i]+b[i]; }
4   #pragma omp parallel {                   13   #pragma omp for
5   #pragma omp for schedule(static) nowait  14   for(int i =0; i<L; i++) //Loop L3
6   for(int i =0;i<L;i++) //Loop L1          15   /*@ Iteration  Contract 3 (IC₃)  @*/
7   /*@ Iteration  Contract 1 (IC₁) @*/      16      { d[i]=a[i]*b[i]; }
8      { c[i]=a[i]; }                        17   }}
9   #pragma omp for schedule(static) nowait
```

Fig. 1. OpenMP example

contracts are added. The example in Fig. 1 is a sequential C program augmented by OpenMP compiler directives (*pragmas*). The pivotal parallelization annotation in OpenMP is *omp parallel* which determines the parallelizable code block (called *parallel region*). Threads are forked upon entering a parallel region and joined back into a single thread at the end of the region.

The example shows a parallel region with three for-loops L1, L2, and L3. The loops are marked as *omp for* meaning that they are parallelizable (i.e. their iterations are allowed to be executed in parallel). To precisely define the behaviour of threads in the parallel region, *omp for* annotations are extended by *clauses*. For example the combined use of the *nowait* and *schedule(static)* clauses indicates that it is safe to *fuse* the parallel loops L1 and L2, meaning that the corresponding iterations of L1 and L2 are executed by the same thread without waiting. The clause *nowait* implies that it is safe to eliminate the implicit barrier at the end of *omp for*. The clause *schedule(static)* ensures that the OpenMP compiler assigns the same thread to corresponding iterations of the loops. In OpenMP all variables which are not local to a parallel region are considered as *shared* by default unless they are explicitly declared as private (using *private* clause) when they are passed to a parallel region.

2.2 Permission-Based Separation Logic

Our verification technique is based on Permission-based Separation Logic [7, 10]. Separation logic [21] is an extension of Hoare logic [14], originally proposed to reason about pointer programs. Separation logic is also suited for modular verification of concurrent programs [17]: two threads working on disjoint parts of the heap do not interfere and thus can be verified in isolation.

The basis of our specification language is a separation logic for C [22], extended with fractional permissions [7,10] to denote the right to either read from or write to a location. Any fraction in the interval $(0, 1)$ denotes a *read permission*, while 1 denotes a *write permission*. Permissions can be split and combined, but soundness of the logic prevents the sum of the permissions for a location over all threads to exceed 1. This guarantees that if permission specifications can be verified, the program is data race free. The set of permissions that a thread holds are often called its *resources*. In earlier work, we have shown that this logic is suitable to reason about kernel programs [5] and parallel loops [6].

Formulas F in our logic are built from first-order logic formulas b, permission predicates $\mathsf{Perm}(l, f)$, conditional expressions $(\cdot? \cdot : \cdot)$, separating conjunction $\star$, and universal separating conjunction $\bigstar$ over a finite set I. The syntax of formulas is formally defined as follows:

$$F ::= b \mid \mathsf{Perm}(l, f) \mid b?F : F \mid F \star F \mid \bigstar_{i \in I} F(i)$$

where b is a side-effect free boolean expression, l is a side-effect free expression of type location, and f is a side-effect free expression of type fraction. The semantics of formulas is given in the extended version of this paper [12].

2.3   Iteration Contract

An *iteration contract* specifies the variables read and written by one iteration of the loop. In [6], we prove that if the iteration contract can be proven correct without any further specifications, the iterations are independent and the loop is parallelizable. If a loop has dependences, we can add additional specifications that capture these dependences, and describe how resources are transferred to another iteration of the loop. For example the iteration contract of L1 consists of: a precondition $\mathsf{Perm}(c[i], 1) \star \mathsf{Perm}(a[i], 1/4)$ and a post-condition $\mathsf{Perm}(c[i], 1) \star \mathsf{Perm}(a[i], 1/4) \star (c[i] == a[i])$.

3   Syntax and Semantics of Deterministic Parallelism

This section presents the abstract syntax and semantics of PPL, our core language for deterministic parallelism.

3.1   Syntax

Figure 2 presents the PPL syntax. The basic building block of a PPL program is a *block*. Each block has a single entry point and a single exit point. Blocks are composed using three binary composition operators: *parallel composition* $\parallel$, *fusion*

Parallel Programming Language:

Block ::= $\big($Block $\parallel$ Block$\big)$ $\mid$ $\big($Block $\oplus$ Block$\big)$ $\mid$ $\big($Block $\mathbin{;} $ Block$\big)$ $\mid$ Par(N) S $\mid$ S
S   ::= $s;$S $\mid$ skip
s ::= ass $\mid$ if (b) {S} else {S} $\mid$ while (b) {S} $\mid$ Vec(N) V
V   ::= $b \Rightarrow$ ass;V $\mid$ skip
ass   ::= $v := e$ $\mid$ $v :=$ mem(e) $\mid$ mem$(e) := v$
b ::= boolean expression over private memory
e ::= arithmetic expression over private memory
v ::= thread local variable

Fig. 2. Abstract syntax for parallel programming language

composition ⊕ and *sequential composition* ⨾. The entry block of the program is the outermost block. *Basic blocks* are: a *parallel* block Par (N) S; a *vectorized* block Vec (N) V; and a *sequential* block S, where N is a positive integer variable that denotes the number of parallel threads, i.e., the block's *parallelization level*, S is a sequence of statements and V is a sequence of guarded assignments $b \Rightarrow$ ass. We assume a restricted syntax for fusion composition such that its operands are parallel basic blocks with the same parallelization levels. Each basic block has a local read-only variable tid ∈ [0...N) called *thread identifier* where N is the block's parallelization level. We generalize the term *iteration* to refer to the computations of a single thread in a basic block. So a parallel or vectorized block with parallelization level N has N iterations. For simplicity, but without loss of generality, threads have access to a single shared array which we refer to as *heap*. We assume all memory locations in the heap are allocated initially. A thread may update its local variables by performing a local computation ($v := e$), or by reading from the heap ($v := \text{mem}(e)$). A thread may update the heap by writing one of its local variables to it ($\text{mem}(e) := v$).

3.2   Semantics

The behaviour of PPL programs is described using a small step operational semantics. Throughout, we assume existence of the finite domains: VarName, the set of variable names, Val, the set of all values, which includes the memory locations, Loc, the set of memory locations and [0...N) for thread identifiers. We write ++ to concatenate two statement sequences (S ++ S). To define the program state, we use the following definitions.

$h \in \text{Heap} \triangleq \text{Loc} \rightarrow \text{Val}$ heap, modeled as a single shared array

$\gamma \in \text{Store} \triangleq \text{VarName} \rightarrow \text{Val}$ program store, accessible to all threads

$\sigma \in \text{PrivateMem} \triangleq \text{VarName} \rightarrow \text{Val}$ private memory, accessible to a single thread

Now we define BlockState. We distinguish various kinds of block states: an initial state Init, composite block states ParC and SeqC, a state in which a parallel basic block should be executed Par, a local state Local in which a vectorized or a sequential basic block should be executed, and a terminated block state Done.

EB ∈ BlockState $\triangleq$

    Init(Block)| initial block states

    ParC(EB, EB)| SeqC(EB, Block)| composite block states

    Par(𝕃𝕊)| parallel basic block states

    Local(LS)| thread local states

    Done   terminated block state

The Init state consists of a block statement Block. The ParC state consists of two block states, and the SeqC state contains a block state and a block statement Block; they capture all the states that a parallel composition and a sequential composition of two blocks might be in, respectively. The basic block state Par captures all the states that a parallel basic block Par (N) S might be in during its execution. It contains a mapping 𝕃𝕊 ∈ [0...N) → LocalState, that maps each thread to its local state, which models the parallel execution of the threads. There are three kinds of local states: a vectorized state Vec, a sequential state Seq, and a terminated sequential state Done.

LS ∈ LocalState $\triangleq$

Vec(Σ, E, V, σ, S)|	vectorized basic block states
Seq(σ, S)|	sequential basic block states
Done	terminated sequential basic block states

The Vec block state captures all states that a vectorized basic block Vec (N) V might be in during its execution. It consists of $\Sigma \in [0 \dots N) \rightarrow$ PrivateMem, which maps each thread to its private memory, the body to be executed V, a private memory σ, and a statement S. As vectorized blocks may appear inside a sequential block, keeping σ and S allows continuation of the sequential basic block after termination of the vectorized block. To model vectorized execution, the state contains an auxiliary set E $\subseteq [0 \dots N)$ that models which threads have already executed the current instruction. Only when E equals $[0 \dots N)$, the next instruction is ready to be executed. Finally, the Seq block state consists of private memory σ and a statement S.

We model the *program state* as a triple of block state, program store and heap (EB, γ, h) and *thread state* as a pair of local state and heap (LS, h). The program store is constant within a block and it contains all global variables (e.g. the initial address of arrays). To simplify our notation, each thread receives a copy of the program store as part of its private memory when it initializes. The operational semantics is defined as a transition relation between program states: $\rightarrow_p \subseteq$ (BlockState $\times$ Store $\times$ Heap) $\times$ (BlockState $\times$ Store $\times$ Heap), (Fig. 3), using an auxiliary transition relation between thread local states $\rightarrow_s \subseteq$ (LocalState $\times$ Heap) $\times$ (LocalState $\times$ Heap), (Fig. 4), and a standard transition relation $\rightarrow_{ass} \subseteq$ (PrivateMem $\times$ S $\times$ Heap) $\times$ (PrivateMem $\times$ Heap) to evaluate assignments, (Fig. 5). The semantics of expression e and boolean expression b over private memory σ, written $\mathcal{E}[\![e]\!]_\sigma$ and $\mathcal{B}[\![b]\!]_\sigma$ respectively, is standard and not discussed any further. We use the standard notation for function update: given a function $f : A \rightarrow B$, $a \in A$, and $b \in B$:

$$f[a := b] = x \mapsto \begin{cases} b & , \ x = a \\ f(x), & \text{otherwise} \end{cases}$$

Program execution starts in a program state (Init(Block), γ, h) where Block is the program's entry block. Depending on the form of Block, a transition is made into an appropriate block state, leaving the heap unchanged. The evaluation of a ParC state non-deterministically evaluates one of its block states (i.e. EB$_1$ or EB$_2$), evaluation of a sequential block is done by evaluating the local state. The evaluation of a SeqC state evaluates its block state EB step by step when this evaluation is done, the subsequent block is initiated.

The evaluation of a parallel basic block is defined by the rules **Par Step** and **Par Done**. To allow all possible interleavings of the threads in the block's thread pool, each thread has its own local state LS, which can be executed independently, modeled by the mapping $\mathbb{LS}$. A thread in the parallel block terminates

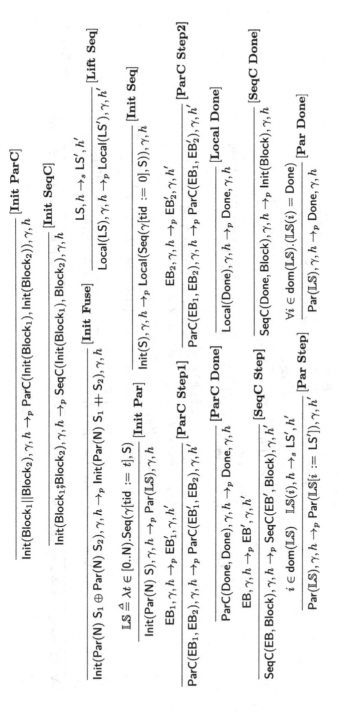

Fig. 3. Operational semantics for program execution

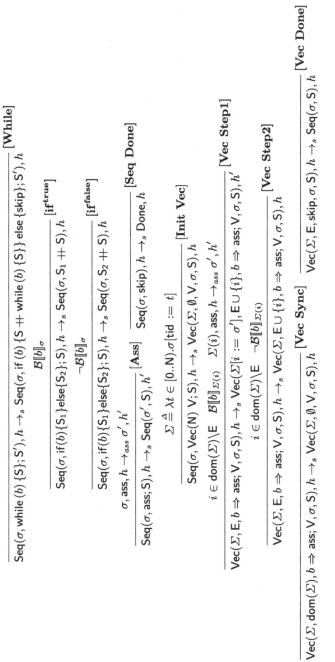

Fig. 4. Operational semantics for thread execution

$$\frac{}{\sigma, v := e, h \rightarrow_{ass} \sigma[v := \mathcal{E}\llbracket e \rrbracket_\sigma], h} \text{ [LAss]}$$

$$\frac{}{\sigma, v := \mathsf{mem}(e), h \rightarrow_{ass} \sigma[v := h(\mathcal{E}\llbracket e \rrbracket_\sigma)], h} \text{ [rdsh]} \qquad \frac{}{\sigma, \mathsf{mem}(e) := v, h \rightarrow_{ass} \sigma, h[\mathcal{E}\llbracket e \rrbracket_\sigma := v]} \text{ [wrsh]}$$

Fig. 5. Operational semantics for assignments

if there is no more statement to be executed and a parallel block terminates if all threads executing the block are already terminated.

The evaluation of sequential basic block's statements as defined in Fig. 4 is standard except when it contains a vectorized basic block. A sequential basic block terminates if there is no instruction left to be executed (**Seq Done**). The execution of a vectorized block (defined by the rules **Init Vec**, **Vec Step**, **Vec Sync** and **Vec Done** in Fig. 4) is done in lock-step, i.e. all threads execute the same instruction and no thread can proceed to the next instruction until all are done, meaning that they all share the same program counter. As explained, we capture this by maintaining an auxiliary set, E, which contains the identifier of the threads that have already executed the vector instruction (i.e. the guarded assignment $b \Rightarrow \mathsf{ass}$). When a thread executes a vector instruction, its thread identifier is added to E (rules **Vec Step**). The semantics of vector instructions (i.e. guarded assignments) is the semantics of assignments if the guard evaluates to true and it does nothing otherwise. When all threads have executed the current vector instruction, the condition $\mathsf{E} = \mathsf{dom}(\Sigma)$ holds, and execution moves on to the next vector instruction of the block (with an empty auxiliary set) (rule **Vec Sync**). The semantics of assignments as defined in Fig. 5 is standard and does not require further discussion.

4   Verification Approach

This section discusses our verification technique for reasoning about PPL programs, as well as soundness of our verification approach.

4.1   Verification

For the verification of PPL programs, we assume that each basic block is specified by an iteration contract. We distinguish two kinds of formulas in an iteration contract: resource formulas (in permission-based separation logic) and functional formulas (in first-order logic). For an individual basic block if its iteration contract is proven correct, then the basic block is data race free and it is functionally correct w.r.t. its iteration contract. To verify the correctness of the program, using standard permission-based separation logic rules, the contracts of all composite blocks should be given. However, our verification approach requires only the basic blocks to be specified at the cost of an extra proof obligation that ensures that the heap accesses of all iterations which are not ordered sequentially are non-conflicting (i.e. they are disjoint or they are read accesses). If this condition holds, correctness of the PPL program can be derived from the correctness of a linearised variant of the program. The rest of this section discusses the formalization of our approach.

To verify a program, we require each basic block of the program to be specified by an iteration contract which consists of: a resource contract $rc(i)$, and a functional contract $fc(i)$, where i is the block's iteration variable. The functional contract consists of a precondition $P(i)$, and a postcondition $Q(i)$. We also require the program to be globally specified by a contract G which consists of the program's resource contract $RC_{\mathcal{P}}$ and the program's functional contract $FC_{\mathcal{P}}$ with the program's precondition $P_{\mathcal{P}}$ and the program's postcondition $Q_{\mathcal{P}}$.

Let $\mathbb{P}$ be the set of all PPL programs and $\mathcal{P} \in \mathbb{P}$ be an arbitrary PPL program assuming that each basic block in $\mathcal{P}$ is identified by a unique label. We define $\mathbb{B}_{\mathcal{P}} = \{b_1, b_2, \ldots, b_n\}$, as the finite set of basic block labels of the program $\mathcal{P}$. For a basic block b with parallelization level m, we define a finite set of iteration labels $I_b = \{0^b, 1^b, \ldots, (m-1)^b\}$ where i^b indicates the ith iteration of the block b. Let $\mathbb{I}_{\mathcal{P}} = \bigcup_{b \in \mathbb{B}_{\mathcal{P}}} I_b$ be the finite set of all iterations of the program $\mathcal{P}$.

To state our proof rule, we first define the set of all iterations which are not ordered sequentially, the *incomparable iteration pairs*, $\mathfrak{I}_{\perp}^{\mathcal{P}}$ as:

$$\mathfrak{I}_{\perp}^{\mathcal{P}} = \{(i^{b_1}, j^{b_2}) | i^{b_1}, j^{b_2} \in \mathbb{I}_{\mathcal{P}} \wedge b_1 \neq b_2 \wedge i^{b_1} \not\prec_e j^{b_2} \wedge j^{b_2} \not\prec_e i^{b_1}\}$$

where $\prec_e \subseteq \mathbb{I}_{\mathcal{P}} \times \mathbb{I}_{\mathcal{P}}$ is the least partial order which defines an extended happens-before relation. The extension addresses the iterations which are happens-before each other because their blocks are fused. We define $\prec_e$ based on two partial orders over the program's basic blocks: $\prec \subseteq \mathbb{B}_{\mathcal{P}} \times \mathbb{B}_{\mathcal{P}}$ and $\prec_{\oplus} \subseteq \mathbb{B}_{\mathcal{P}} \times \mathbb{B}_{\mathcal{P}}$. The former is the standard happens-before relation of blocks where they are sequentially composed by $\,\fatsemi\,$ and the latter is an happens-before relation w.r.t. fusion composition $\oplus$. They are defined by means of an auxiliary partial order generator function $\mathcal{G}(\mathcal{P}, \delta) : \mathbb{P} \times \{\fatsemi, \oplus\} \to \mathbb{B}_{\mathcal{P}} \times \mathbb{B}_{\mathcal{P}}$ such that: $\prec = \mathcal{G}(\mathcal{P}, \fatsemi)$ and $\prec_{\oplus} = \mathcal{G}(\mathcal{P}, \oplus)$. We define $\mathcal{G}$ as follows:

$$\mathcal{G}(\mathcal{P}, \delta) = \begin{cases} \mathbb{G} \cup \{(b', b'') | b' \in \mathbb{B}_{\mathcal{P}'} \wedge b'' \in \mathbb{B}_{\mathcal{P}''}\}, & \text{if } \mathcal{P} = \mathcal{P}' \bullet \mathcal{P}'' \wedge \delta = \bullet \\ \mathbb{G}, & \text{if } \mathcal{P} = \mathcal{P}' \bullet \mathcal{P}'' \wedge \delta \neq \bullet \\ \emptyset, & \text{if } \mathcal{P} \in \{\mathsf{Par(N)\ S}, \mathsf{S}\} \end{cases}$$

where $\mathbb{G} = \mathcal{G}(\mathcal{P}', \delta) \cup \mathcal{G}(\mathcal{P}'', \delta)$.

The function $\mathcal{G}$ computes the set of all iteration pairs of the input program $\mathcal{P}$ which are in relation w.r.t. the given composition operator δ. This computation is basically a syntactical analysis over the input program. Now we define the extended partial order $\prec_e$ as:

$$\forall i^b, j^{b'} \in \mathbb{I}_{\mathcal{P}}.i^b \prec_e j^{b'} \Leftrightarrow (b \prec b') \vee \left((b \prec_{\oplus} b') \wedge (i = j)\right)$$

This means that the iteration i^b happens-before the iteration $j^{b'}$ if b happens-before b' (i.e. b is sequentially composed with b') or if b is fused with b' and i and j are corresponding iterations in b and b'.

We extend the program logic that we introduced in [6] with the proof rule **b-linearise**. We first define the *block level linearisation* (*b-linearisation* for

$$\frac{\left(\forall(i^b, j^{b'}) \in \mathfrak{I}^P_\bot.(RC_\mathcal{P} \to rc_b(i) \star rc_{b'}(j))\right) \quad \{RC_\mathcal{P} \star P_\mathcal{P}\}blin(\mathcal{P})\{RC_\mathcal{P} \star Q_\mathcal{P}\}}{\{RC_\mathcal{P} \star P_\mathcal{P}\}\mathcal{P}\{RC_\mathcal{P} \star Q_\mathcal{P}\}} \text{ [b–linearise]}$$

Fig. 6. Proof rule for b-linearisation reduction of PPL programs.

short) $blin : \mathbb{P} \to \mathbb{P}_\S$ as a program transformation which substitutes all non-sequential compositions by a sequential composition. We define $\mathbb{P}_\S$ as a subset of $\mathbb{P}$ in which only sequential composition $\S$ is allowed as composition operator.

Figure 6 presents the rule **b-linearise**. In the rule, $rc_b(i)$ and $rc_{b'}(j)$ are the resource contracts of two different basic blocks b and b' where $i^b \in I_b$ and $j^{b'} \in I_{b'}$. Application of the rule results in two new proof obligations. The first ensures that all heap accesses of all incomparable iteration pairs (the iterations that may run in parallel) are non-conflicting (i.e. all block compositions in $\mathcal{P}$ are memory safe). This reduces the correctness proof of $\mathcal{P}$ to the correctness proof of its b-linearised variant $blin(\mathcal{P})$ (the second proof obligation). Then the second proof obligation is discharged in two steps: (1) proving the correctness of each basic block against its iteration contract (using the proof rule introduced in [6]) and (2) proving the correctness of $blin(\mathcal{P})$ against the program contract.

4.2 Soundness

Next we show that a PPL program with provably correct iteration contracts and a global contract that is provable in our logic extended with the rule **b-linearise** is indeed data race free and functionally correct w.r.t. its specifications. To show this, we prove soundness of the **b-linearise** rule, as well as data race freedom of all verified programs.

For the soundness proof, we show that for each *program execution* there exists a corresponding *b-linearised execution* with the same functional behaviour (i.e. they end in the same terminal state if they start in the same initial state) if all independent iterations are non-conflicting. From the rule's assumption, we know that if the precondition holds for the initial state of the b-linearised execution (which is also the initial state of the program execution) then its terminal state satisfies the postcondition. As both executions end in the same terminal state, the postcondition thus also holds for the program execution. To prove that there exists a matching b-linearised execution for each program execution, we first show that any valid program execution can be normalized w.r.t. program order and second that any normalized execution can be mapped to a b-linearised execution. To formalize this argument, we first define: an *execution*, an *instrumented execution*, and a *normalized execution*.

We assume all program's blocks including basic and composite blocks have a block label and program's statements are labelled by the label of the block to which they belong. Also there exists a total order over the block labels.

Definition 1 *(Execution)*. *An* execution *of a program* $\mathcal{P}$ *is a finite sequence of state transitions* $\mathsf{Init}(\mathcal{P}), \gamma, h \to^*_p \mathsf{Done}, \gamma, h'$.

To distinguish between valid and invalid executions, we instrument our operational semantics with *heap masks*. A heap mask models the access permissions to every heap location. It is defined as a map from locations to fractions $\pi : \mathsf{Loc} \to \mathsf{Frac}$ where Frac is the set of fractions ($[0, 1]$). Any fraction $(0, 1)$ is read and 1 is write permission. The instrumented semantics ensures that each transition has sufficient access permissions to the heap locations that it accesses. We first add a heap mask π to all block state constructors (Init, ParC, SeqC and so on) and local state constructors (Vec, Seq and Done). Then we extend the operational semantics rules such that in each block initialization state with heap mask π an extra premise should be discharged, which states that there are $n \geq 2$ heap masks $\pi_1, \ldots, \pi_n$, one for each newly initialized state such that $\Sigma_i^n \pi_i \leq \pi$. The heap masks are carried along by the computation and termination transitions without any extra premises, while in the termination transitions heap masks of the terminated blocks are forgotten as they are not required after termination. As an example, we provide the instrumented versions of the rules **Init ParC**, **ParC Done**, **rdsh**, and **wrsh**.

$$\frac{\pi_1 + \pi_2 \leq \pi}{\mathsf{Init}(\mathsf{Block}_1 \| \mathsf{Block}_2, \pi), \gamma, h \to_{p,i} \mathsf{ParC}(\mathsf{Init}(\mathsf{Block}_1, \pi_1), \mathsf{Init}(\mathsf{Block}_2, \pi_2), \pi), \gamma, h} \; [\text{Init ParC}]$$

$$\frac{}{\mathsf{ParC}(\mathsf{Done}(\pi_1), \mathsf{Done}(\pi_2), \pi), \gamma, h \to_{p,i} \mathsf{Done}(\pi), \gamma, h} \; [\text{ParC Done}]$$

$$\frac{l = \mathcal{E}[\![e]\!]_\sigma \quad \pi(l) > 0}{\sigma, v := \mathsf{mem}(e), h, \pi \to_{ass,i} \sigma[v := h(l)], h, \pi} \; [\text{rdsh}] \qquad \frac{l = \mathcal{E}[\![e]\!]_\sigma \quad \pi(l) = 1}{\sigma, \mathsf{mem}(e) := v, h, \pi \to_{ass,i} \sigma, h[l := v], \pi} \; [\text{wrsh}]$$

where $\to_{p,i}$ and $\to_{ass,i}$ denote program and assignment transition relations in the instrumented semantics respectively. If a transition cannot satisfy its premises it blocks.

Definition 2 *(Instrumented Execution)*. *An* instrumented execution *of a program $\mathcal{P}$ is a finite sequence of state transitions $\mathsf{Init}(\mathcal{P}, \pi), \gamma, h \to_{p,i}^* \mathsf{Done}(\pi), \gamma, h'$ where the set of all instrumented executions of $\mathcal{P}$ is written as $\mathbb{IE}_\mathcal{P}$.*

Lemma 1. *Assuming that (1) $\vdash \forall (i^b, j^{b'}) \in \mathfrak{I}_\perp^\mathcal{P}.RC_\mathcal{P} \to rc_b(i) \star rc_{b'}(j)$ and (2) $\forall b \in \mathbb{B}_\mathcal{P}.\{\bigstar_{i \in [0...N_b)} rc_b(i)\} \mathsf{Block}_b \{\bigstar_{i \in [0...N_b)} rc_b(i)\}$ are valid for a program $\mathcal{P}$ (i.e. every basic block in $\mathcal{P}$ respects its iteration contract), for any execution E of the program $\mathcal{P}$, there exists a corresponding instrumented execution.*

Proof. Given an execution E, we assign heap masks to all program states that the execution E might be in. The program's initial state is assigned by a heap mask $\pi \leq 1$. Assumption (1) implies that all iterations which might run in parallel are non-conflicting which implies that for all **Init ParC** transitions, there exist π_1 and π_2 such that $\pi_1 + \pi_2 \leq \pi'$ where π' is the heap mask of the state in which **Init ParC** evaluates. In all computation transitions the successor state receives a copy of the heap mask of its predecessor. Assumption (2) implies that all iterations of all parallel and vectorized basic blocks are non-conflicting. This implies that for an arbitrary **Init Par** or **Init Vec** transition which initializes a basic block b, there exists $\pi_1, \ldots, \pi_n$ such that $\Sigma_i^n \pi_i \leq \pi_b$ holds in b's initialization transition and in all computation transitions of an arbitrary iteration i of the block b the premises of **rdsh** and **wrsh** transitions is satisfiable by π_i.   □

Lemma 2. *All instrumented executions of a program $\mathcal{P}$ are data race free.*

Proof. The proof proceeds by contradiction. Assume that there exists an instrumented execution that has a data race. Thus, there must be two parallel threads such that one writes to and the other one reads from or writes to a shared heap location e. Because all instrumented executions are non-blocking, the premises of all transitions hold. Therefore, $\pi_1(e) = 1$ holds for the first thread, and $\pi_2(e) > 0$ for the second thread either it writes or reads. Also because the program starts with one single main thread, both threads should have a single common ancestor thread z such that $\pi_x(e) + \pi_y(e) \leq \pi_z(e)$ where x and y are the ancestors of the first and the second thread respectively. A thread only gains permission from its parent; therefore $\pi_1(e) + \pi_2(e) \leq \pi_z(e)$ holds. Permission fractions are in the range $[0, 1]$ by definition, therefore $\pi_1(e) + \pi_2(e) \leq 1$ holds. This implies that if $\pi_1(e) = 1$, then $\pi_2(e) \leq 0$ which is a contradiction.   □

A normalized execution is an instrumented execution that respects the program order, which is defined using an auxiliary labelling function $\mathcal{L} : \mathbb{T} \to \mathbb{B}_{\mathcal{P}}^{all} \times \mathbb{L}$ where $\mathbb{T}$ is the set of all transitions, $\mathbb{L}$ is the set of labels $\{I, C, T\}$, and $\mathbb{B}_{\mathcal{P}}^{all}$ is the set of block labels (including both composite and basic block labels).

$$\mathcal{L}(t) = \begin{cases} (LB(\text{block}), I), & \text{if } t \text{ initializes a block block} \\ (LB(s), C), & \text{if } t \text{ computes a statement } s \\ (LB(\text{block}), T), & \text{if } t \text{ terminates a block block} \end{cases}$$

where LB returns the label of each block or statement in the program. We assume the precedence order $I < C < T$ over $\mathbb{L}$. We say transition t with label (b, l) is less than t' with label (b', l') if $(b \leq b') \vee (b > b' \to (l' = T \wedge b \in LB_{sub}(b')))$ where $LB_{sub}(b)$ returns the label set of all blocks of which b is composed.

Definition 3 *(Normalized Execution). An instrumented execution labelled by $\mathcal{L}$ is* normalized *if the labels of its transitions are in non-decreasing order.*

We transform an instrumented execution to a normalized one by safely commuting the transitions whose labels do not respect the program order.

Lemma 3. *For each instrumented execution of a program $\mathcal{P}$, there exists a normalized execution such that they both end in the same terminal state.*

Lemma 4. *For each normalized execution of a program $\mathcal{P}$, there exists a b-linearised execution $blin(\mathcal{P})$, such that they both end in the same terminal state.*

The extended version of this paper [12] presents the proofs of Lemmas 3 and 4.

Definition 4 *(Validity of Hoare Triple). The Hoare triple $\{RC_{\mathcal{P}} \star P_{\mathcal{P}}\} \mathcal{P} \{RC_{\mathcal{P}} \star Q_{\mathcal{P}}\}$ is* valid *if for any execution E (i.e. $\mathsf{Init}(\mathcal{P}), \gamma, h \to_p^* \mathsf{Done}, \gamma, h'$) if $\gamma, h, \pi \vDash RC_{\mathcal{P}} \star P_{\mathcal{P}}$ is valid in the initial state of E, then $\gamma, h', \pi \vDash RC_{\mathcal{P}} \star Q_{\mathcal{P}}$ is valid in its terminal state.*

The validity of $\gamma, h, \pi \vDash RC_{\mathcal{P}} \star P_{\mathcal{P}}$ and $\gamma, h', \pi \vDash RC_{\mathcal{P}} \star Q_{\mathcal{P}}$ is defined by the semantics of formulas presented in the extended version of this paper [12].

Theorem 1. *The rule **b-linearise** is sound.*

Proof. Assume (1). $\vdash \forall (i^b, j^{b'}) \in \mathfrak{I}_{\perp}^{\mathcal{P}}.RC_{\mathcal{P}} \rightarrow rc_b(i) \star rc_{b'}(j)$ and (2). $\vdash \{RC_{\mathcal{P}} \star P_{\mathcal{P}}\}$ $blin(\mathcal{P})\{RC_{\mathcal{P}} \star Q_{\mathcal{P}}\}$. From assumption (2) and the soundness of the program logic used to prove it [6], we conclude (3). $\forall b \in \mathbb{B}_{\mathcal{P}}.\{\bigstar_{i \in [0...N_b)} rc_b(i)\}\mathsf{Block}_b$ $\{\bigstar_{i \in [0...N_b)} rc_b(i)\}$. Given a program $\mathcal{P}$, implication (3), assumption (1) and, Lemma 1 imply that there exists an instrumented execution *IE* for $\mathcal{P}$. Lemma 3 and Lemma 4 imply that there exists an execution E' for the b-linearised variant of $\mathcal{P}$, $blin(\mathcal{P})$, such that both *IE* and E' end in the same terminal state. The initial states of both *IE* and E' satisfy the precondition $\{RC_{\mathcal{P}} \star P_{\mathcal{P}}\}$. From assumption (2) and the soundness of the program logic used to prove it [6], $\{RC_{\mathcal{P}} \star Q_{\mathcal{P}}\}$ holds in the terminal state of E' which thus also holds in the terminal state of *IE* as they both end in the same terminal state. $\qquad\square$

Finally, we show that a verified program is indeed data race free.

Proposition 1. *A verified program is data race free.*

Proof. Given a program $\mathcal{P}$, with the same reasoning steps mentioned in the Theorem 1, we conclude that there exists an instrumented execution *IE* for $\mathcal{P}$. From Lemma 2 all instrumented executions are data race free. Thus, all executions of a verified program are data race free. $\qquad\square$

5   Verification of OpenMP Programs

Finally, this section discusses the practical applicability of our approach, by showing how it can be used for verification of OpenMP programs. We demonstrate this in detail on the OpenMP program presented in Sect. 2.1. More OpenMP examples are available online[1]. Below we precisely identify a commonly used subset of OpenMP programs that can be verified in our approach.

We verify OpenMP programs in the following three steps: (1) specifying the program (i.e. providing an iteration contract for each loop and writing the program contract for the outermost OpenMP parallel region), (2) encoding of the specified OpenMP program into its PPL counterpart (carrying along the original OpenMP specifications), (3) checking the PPL program against its specifications. Steps two and three have been implemented as part of the VerCors toolset [4, 23]. The details of the encoding algorithm are discussed in the extended version of this paper [12].

Figure 7 shows the required contracts for the example discussed in Sect. 2.1. There are four specifications. The first one is the program contract which is attached to the outermost parallel block. The others are the iteration contracts of the loops L1, L2 and L3. The *requires* and *ensures* keywords indicate pre

---

[1] See the online version of the VerCors toolset at http://www.utwente.nl/vercors/.

Program Contract (PC):
/*@ invariant   a != NULL && b != NULL && c != NULL && d != NULL && L>0;
invariant \length(a)==L && \length(b)==L && \length(c)==L && \length(d)==L;
context \forall*   int k; 0 <= k && k < L; Perm(a[k],1/2);
context \forall*   int k; 0 <= k && k < L; Perm(b[k],1/2);
context \forall*   int k; 0 <= k && k < L; Perm(c[k],1);
context \forall*   int k; 0 <= k && k < L; Perm(d[k],1);
ensures \forall   int k; 0 <= k && k < L; c[k]==a[k]+b[k] && d[k]==a[k]*b[k];@*/

Iteration Contract 1 (IC_1) of loop L1:	Iteration Contract 2 (IC_2) of loop L2:
/*@ context Perm(c[i],1) ** Perm(a[i],1/4);	/*@ context Perm(c[i],1) ** Perm(b[i],1/4);
ensures c[i]==a[i]; @*/	ensures c[i]==\old(c[i])+b[i]; @*/

Iteration Contract 3 (IC_3) of loop L3:
/*@ context Perm(d[i],1) ** Perm(a[i],1/4) ** Perm(b[i],1/4);
ensures d[i]==a[i]*b[i];   @*/

Fig. 7. Required contracts for verification of the running OpenMP example

and post-conditions of each contract and the *context* keyword is a shorthand for
both requiring and ensuring the same predicate. We use $**$ and \forall* to denote
separating conjunction $\star$ and universal separating conjunction $\bigstar_{i \in I}$ receptively.
Before verification, we encode the example into the following PPL program $\mathcal{P}$:

/*@ Program Contract @*/

$$\mathcal{P} \begin{cases} \underbrace{(\mathsf{Par(L)} \ /\text{*@}IC_1\text{@*/} \ c[i]=a[i]; \oplus \mathsf{Par(L)} \ /\text{*@}IC_2\text{@*/} \ c[i]=c[i]+b[i];)}_{B_1 \qquad\qquad\qquad\qquad\qquad B_2} \\ \qquad\qquad\qquad\qquad || \\ \underbrace{\mathsf{Par(L)} \ /\text{*@}IC_3\text{@*/} \ d[i]=a[i]*b[i];}_{B_3} \end{cases}$$

Program $\mathcal{P}$ contains three parallel basic blocks B_1, B_2 and B_3 and is verified
by discharging two proof obligations: (1) ensures that all heap accesses of all
incomparable iteration pairs (i.e. all iteration pairs except the identical iterations of B_1 and B_2) are non-conflicting implying that the fusion of B_1 and B_2
and parallel composition of $B_1 \oplus B_2$ and B_3 are memory safe (2) consists of
first proving that each parallel basic block by itself satisfies its iteration contract
$\forall b \in \{1, 2, 3\}.\{\bigstar_{i \in [0...L)} IC_b(i)\} B_b \{\bigstar_{i \in [0...L)} IC_b(i)\}$, and second proving the correctness of the b-linearised variant of $\mathcal{P}$ against its program contract $\{RC_\mathcal{P} \star P_\mathcal{P}\}$
$B_1 \, \mathring{,} \, B_2 \, \mathring{,} \, B_3 \{RC_\mathcal{P} \star Q_\mathcal{P}\}$.

We have implemented a slightly more general variant of PPL in the tool
that supports variable declarations and method calls. To check the first proof
obligation in the tool we quantify over pairs of blocks which allows the number
of iterations in each block to be a parameter rather than a fixed number.

Captured Subset of OpenMP. We define a core grammar which captures a
commonly used subset of OpenMP [1]. This defines also the OpenMP programs
that can be encoded into PPL and then verified using our approach. Figure 8
presents the OMP grammar which supports the OpenMP annotations: omp parallel, omp for, omp simd, omp for simd, omp sections, and omp single. An OMP

```
OMP    ::= #pragma omp parallel [clause]* {Job+}                  |
Job     ::= #pragma omp for [clause]* {for-loop {SpecS}}           |
            #pragma omp simd [clause]* {for-loop {SpecS}}          |
            #pragma omp for simd [clause]* {for-loop {SpecS}} |
            #pragma omp sections [clause]* {Section+}              |
            #pragma omp single {SpecS |OMP}
Section ::= #pragma omp section {SpecS |OMP}                       |
SpecS   ::= a list of sequential statements with a contract
clause  ::= allowed OpenMP clause
```

Fig. 8. OpenMP core grammar

program is a finite and non-empty list of Jobs enclosed by omp parallel. The body of omp for, omp simd, and omp for simd, is a for-loop. The body of omp single is either an OMP program or it is a sequential code block SpecS. The omp sections block is a finite list of omp section sub-blocks where the body of each omp section is either an OMP program or it is a sequential code block SpecS.

6   Related Work

Botincan et al. propose a proof-directed parallelization synthesis which takes as input a sequential program with a proof in separation logic and outputs a parallelized counterpart by inserting barrier synchronizations [8,9]. Hurlin uses a proof-rewriting method to parallelize a sequential program's proof [15]. Compared to them, we prove the correctness of parallelization by reducing the parallel proof to a b-linearised proof. Moreover, our approach allows verification of sophisticated block compositions, which enables reasoning about state-of-the-art parallel programming languages (e.g. OpenMP) while their work remains rather theoretical.

Raychev et al. use abstract interpretation to make a non-deterministic program (obtained by naive parallelization of a sequential program) deterministic by inserting barriers [20]. This technique over-approximates the possible program behaviours which ends up in a determinization whose behaviour is implied by a set of rules which decide between feasible schedules rather than the behaviour of the original sequential program. Unlike them, we do not generate any parallel program. Instead we prove that parallelization annotations can safely be applied and the parallelized program is functionally correct and exhibits the same behaviour as its sequential counterpart. Barthe et al. synthesize SIMD code given pre and postconditions for loop kernels in C++ STL or C# BCL [2]. We alternatively enable verification of SIMD loops, by encoding them into vectorized basic blocks. Moreover, we address the parallel or sequential composition of those loops with other forms of parallelized blocks.

Dodds et al. introduce a higher-order variant of Concurrent Abstract Predicates (CAP) to support modular verification of synchronization constructs for deterministic parallelism [13]. Their proofs use nested region assertions and higher-order protocols, but they do not address the semantic difficulties introduced by these features which make their reasoning unsound.

7   Conclusion and Future Work

We have presented the PPL language which captures the main forms of deterministic parallel programming. Then, we proposed a verification technique to reason about data race freedom and functional correctness of PPL programs. We illustrated the practical applicability of our technique by discussing how a commonly used subset of OpenMP can be encoded into PPL and then verified.

As future work, we plan to look into adapting annotation generation techniques to automatically generate iteration contracts, including both resource formulas and functional properties. This will lead to fully automatic verification of deterministic parallel programs. Moreover, our technique can be extended to address a larger subset of OpenMP programs by supporting more complex OpenMP patterns for scheduling iterations and *omp task* constructs. We also plan to identify the subset of atomic operations that can be combined with our technique that allows verification of the widely-used reduction operations.

References

1. Aviram, A., Ford, B.: Deterministic OpenMP for race-free parallelism. In: HotPar 2011, Berkeley, CA, USA, p. 4 (2011)
2. Barthe, G., Crespo, J.M., Gulwani, S., Kunz, C., Marron, M.: From relational verification to SIMD loop synthesis. In: ACM SIGPLAN Notices, vol. 48, pp. 123–134 (2013)
3. Berger, M.J., Aftosmis, M.J., Marshall, D.D., Murman, S.M.: Performance of a new CFD flow solver using a hybrid programming paradigm. J. Parallel Distrib. Comput. **65**(4), 414–423 (2005)
4. Blom, S., Huisman, M.: The VerCors tool for verification of concurrent programs. In: Jones, C., Pihlajasaari, P., Sun, J. (eds.) FM 2014. LNCS, vol. 8442, pp. 127–131. Springer, Cham (2014). doi:10.1007/978-3-319-06410-9_9
5. Blom, S., Huisman, M., Mihelčić, M.: Specification and verification of GPGPU programs. Sci. Comput. Program. **95**, 376–388 (2014)
6. Blom, S., Darabi, S., Huisman, M.: Verification of loop parallelisations. In: Egyed, A., Schaefer, I. (eds.) FASE 2015. LNCS, vol. 9033, pp. 202–217. Springer, Heidelberg (2015). doi:10.1007/978-3-662-46675-9_14
7. Bornat, R., Calcagno, C., O'Hearn, P., Parkinson, M.: Permission accounting in separation logic. In: POPL, pp. 259–270 (2005)
8. Botincan, M., Dodds, M., Jagannathan, S.: Resource-sensitive synchronization inference by abduction. In: POPL, pp. 309–322 (2012)
9. Botinčan, M., Dodds, M., Jagannathan, S.: Proof-directed parallelization synthesis by separation logic. ACM Trans. Program. Lang. Syst. **35**, 1–60 (2013)
10. Boyland, J.: Checking interference with fractional permissions. In: Cousot, R. (ed.) SAS 2003. LNCS, vol. 2694, pp. 55–72. Springer, Heidelberg (2003). doi:10.1007/3-540-44898-5_4
11. Che, S., Boyer, M., Meng, J., Tarjan, D., Sheaffer, J.W., Lee, S.-H., Skadron, K.: Rodinia: a benchmark suite for heterogeneous computing. In: Workload Characterization, IISWC 2009, pp. 44–54 (2009)
12. Darabi, S., Blom, S.C.C., Huisman, M.: A verification technique for deterministic parallel programs (extended version). Technical report TR-CTIT-17-01, Centre for Telematics and Information Technology, University of Twente (2017)

13. Dodds, M., Jagannathan, S., Parkinson, M.J.: Modular reasoning for deterministic parallelism. In: ACM SIGPLAN Notices, pp. 259–270 (2011)
14. Hoare, C.: An axiomatic basis for computer programming. Commun. ACM **12**(10), 576–580 (1969)
15. Hurlin, C.: Automatic parallelization and optimization of programs by proof rewriting. In: Palsberg, J., Su, Z. (eds.) SAS 2009. LNCS, vol. 5673, pp. 52–68. Springer, Heidelberg (2009). doi:10.1007/978-3-642-03237-0_6
16. Jin, H.-Q., Frumkin, M., Yan, J.: The OpenMP implementation of NAS parallel Benchmarks and its performance (1999)
17. O'Hearn, P.W.: Resources, concurrency and local reasoning. Theoret. Comput. Sci. **375**(1–3), 271–307 (2007)
18. OpenMP Architecture Review Board: OpenMP API specification for parallel programming. http://openmp.org/wp/. Accessed 28 Nov 2016
19. LLNL OpenMP Benchmarks. https://asc.llnl.gov/CORAL-benchmarks/. Accessed 28 Nov 2016
20. Raychev, V., Vechev, M., Yahav, E.: Automatic synthesis of deterministic concurrency. In: Logozzo, F., Fähndrich, M. (eds.) SAS 2013. LNCS, vol. 7935, pp. 283–303. Springer, Heidelberg (2013). doi:10.1007/978-3-642-38856-9_16
21. Reynolds, J.: Separation logic: a logic for shared mutable data structures. In: Logic in Computer Science, pp. 55–74. IEEE Computer Society (2002)
22. Tuch, H., Klein, G., Norrish, M.: Types, bytes, and separation logic. In: Hofmann, M., Felleisen, M. (eds.) POPL, pp. 97–108. ACM (2007)
23. VerCors project homepage, 28 September 2016. http://www.utwente.nl/vercors/

Systematic Predicate Abstraction Using Variable Roles

Yulia Demyanova[1], Philipp Rümmer[2(✉)], and Florian Zuleger[1]

[1] Vienna University of Technology, Vienna, Austria
demy@forsyte.at
[2] Uppsala University, Uppsala, Sweden
philipp.ruemmer@it.uu.se

Abstract. Heuristics for discovering predicates for abstraction are an essential part of software model checkers. Picking the right predicates affects the runtime of a model checker, or determines if a model checker is able to solve a verification task at all. In this paper we present a method to systematically specify heuristics for generating program-specific abstractions. The heuristics can be used to generate initial abstractions, and to guide abstraction refinement through templates provided for Craig interpolation. We describe the heuristics using variable roles, which allow us to pick domain-specific predicates according to the program under analysis. Variable roles identify typical variable usage patterns and can be computed using lightweight static analysis, for instance with the help of off-the-shelf logical programming engines. We implemented a prototype tool which extracts initial predicates and templates for C programs and passes them to the Eldarica model checker in the form of source code annotations. For evaluation, we defined a set of heuristics, motivated by Eldarica's previous built-in heuristics and typical verification benchmarks from the literature and SV-COMP. We evaluate our approach on a set of more than 500 programs, and observe an overall increase in the number of solved tasks by 11.2%, and significant speedup on certain benchmark families.

1 Introduction

Analysis tools, in particular software model checkers, achieve automation by mapping systems with infinite state space to *finite-state abstractions* that can be explored exhaustively. One of the most important classes of abstraction is *predicate abstraction* [13], defined through a set of predicates capturing relevant data or control properties in a program. Picking the right predicates, either upfront or dynamically during analysis [5], is essential in this setting to ensure rapid convergence of a model checker, and is in practice achieved through a combination of "systematic" methods (for CEGAR, in particular through Craig interpolation) and *heuristics*. For instance, SLAM extracts refinement predicates from counterexamples using domain-specific heuristics [16]; YOGI uses machine learning

---

Y. Demyanova and F. Zuleger were supported by the Austrian National Research Network S11403-N23 (RiSE) of the Austrian Science Fund (FWF).

C. Barrett et al. (Eds.): NFM 2017, LNCS 10227, pp. 265–281, 2017.
DOI: 10.1007/978-3-319-57288-8_18

to choose the default set of heuristics for picking predicates [19]; CPAchecker uses domain types to decide whether to represent variables explicitly or using BDDs [2], and to choose refinement predicates [4]; and ELDARICA uses heuristics to guide the process of Craig interpolation [18]. Similar heuristics can be identified in tools based on abstract interpretation, among others.

The goal of the present paper is to systematise the definition of abstraction heuristics, and this way enable easier and more effective adaptation of analysis tools to specific domains. In order to effectively construct program abstractions, it is essential for an analysis tool to have (semantic) information about variables and data-structures used in the program. We propose a methodology in which heuristics are defined with the help of *variable roles* [9], which are features capturing typical variable usage patterns and which can be computed through lightweight static analysis. Knowledge about roles of variables can be used to generate problem-specific parameters for model checkers, or other analysis tools, and thus optimise the actual later analysis process.

As a case study, we describe how variable roles can be used to infer code annotations for the CEGAR-based model checker ELDARICA [20]. ELDARICA has two main parameters controlling the analysis process: *initial predicates* for predicate abstraction, and *templates* guiding Craig interpolation during counterexample-based refinement [18]. Both parameters can be provided in the form of source-code annotations. We focus on the analysis of C programs defined purely over integer scalar variables, i.e., not containing arrays, pointers, heap-based data structures and bitvectors. By manually inspecting a (small) sample of such programs from SV-COMP [3], we were able to identify a compact set of relevant variable roles, and of heuristics for choosing predicates and templates based on those roles. To evaluate the effectiveness of the heuristics, we compared the performance of ELDARICA (with and without the heuristics), and of other model checkers on a set of over 500 programs taken from the literature and SV-COMP. We observe an increase in the number of solved tasks by 11.2% when using our heuristics, and speedups on certain benchmark families.

Contributions of the paper are: 1. We introduce a methodology for defining abstraction heuristics using variable roles; 2. we define 8 roles and corresponding heuristics for efficiently analysing C programs with scalar variables; 3. we implement our approach and perform an extensive experimental evaluation.

Related Work. Patterns of variable usage were studied in multiple disciplines, e.g. in teaching programming languages [21] (where the patterns were called *variable roles*), in type systems for inferring equivalence relations for types [22], and others. In [9] a set of patterns, also called variable roles, was defined using data-flow analysis, based on a set of C benchmarks[1]. In [7,8] variable roles were used to build a portfolio solver for software verification. Similarly to variable roles, code patterns recognised with light-weight static analyses are used in the bug-finding tool Coverity [11] to devise heuristics for ranking possible bugs. Domain types in CPACHECKER [4] can be viewed as a restricted class of variable

---

[1] http://ctuning.org/wiki/index.php/CTools:CBench.

roles. Differently from this work, where variable roles guide the generation of interpolants, the domain types are used in [4] to choose the "best" interpolant from a set of generated interpolants. In addition, our method generates role-based initial predicates, while the method of [4] does not.

There has been extensive research on tuning abstraction refinement techniques, in such a way that convergence of model checkers is ensured or improved. This research in particular considers various methods of Craig interpolation, and controls features such as interpolant strength, interpolant size, the number of distinct symbols in interpolants, or syntactic features like the magnitude of coefficients; for a detailed survey we refer the reader to our previous work [18].

1.1   Introductory Examples of Domain-Specific Abstraction

We introduce our approach on two examples. These and all further examples in this paper are taken from the benchmarks of the software competition SV-COMP'16 [3]. We simplified some of the examples for demonstration purposes.

```
1 extern char nondet_char();
2 void main() {
3    int id1 = nondet_char();
4    int id2 = nondet_char();
5    int id3 = nondet_char();
6    int max1=id1, max2=id2, max3=id3;
7    int i=0, cnt=0;
8
9    assume(id1!=id2 && id1!=id3 &&
10       id2!=id3);
11
12   while (1) {
13      if (max3 > max1) max1 = max3;
14      if (max1 > max2) max2 = max1;
15      if (max2 > max3) max3 = max2;
16
17      if (i == 1) {
18         if (max1 == id1) cnt++;
19         if (max2 == id2) cnt++;
20         if (max3 == id3) cnt++;
21      }
22      if (i>=1) assert(cnt==1);
23      i++;
24   }
25 }
```

(1) Roles input, dynamic enumeration and extremum

```
1 extern int nondet_int();
2 int main() {
3    int n = nondet_int();
4    int k, i, j;
5
6    for (k=0,i=0; i<n; i++,k++);
7    for (j=n; j>0; j--,k--) {
8       assert(k > 0);
9    }
10   return 0;
11 }
```

(2) Role local counter

Fig. 1. Motivation examples illustrating variable roles.

Motivation Example 1. The code in Fig. 1.1 initializes variables max1, max2 and max3 to id1, id2 and id3 respectively, which are in turn initialized non-deterministically. The assume statement at lines 9–10 is an ELDARICA-specific directive, which puts a restriction that control reaches line 12 only if id1!=id2 && id1!=id3 && id2!=id3 evaluates to true. In the loop the value max{id1,id2,id3}, which is the maximum of id1, id2 and id3 is calculated: At the first iteration, max1 is assigned the value max{id1,id3}, and max2 and max3 are assigned the value max{id1,id2,id3}. After the second iteration max1, max2 and max3 all store the value max{id1,id2,id3}. Since id1, id2 and id3 have distinct values, only one of the conditions in lines 18–20 evaluates to true. The assertion checks that the value of exactly one of variables max1, max2 and max3 remains unchanged after two iterations, namely max_i, where i=$\arg\max_j\{id_j\}$.

It takes ELDARICA 27 CEGAR iterations and 19 sec to prove the program safe. However, for 88 out of 108 original programs from SV-COMP with this pattern in category "Integers and Control Flow", of which the code in Fig. 1.1 is a simplified form[2], ELDARICA does not give an answer within the time limit of 15 min. Predicate abstraction needs to generate for these programs from 116 to 996 predicates, depending on the number of values, for which the maximum is calculated. Since predicates are added step-wise in the CEGAR loop, checking these benchmarks is time consuming. We therefore suggest a method of generating the predicates upfront.

In order to prove that exactly one condition in lines 18–20 evaluates to true and cnt is incremented by one, predicate abstraction needs to track the values assigned to variables max1, max2 and max3 with 9 predicates: max1==id1, max1==id2, max1==id3, etc. Additionally, in order to precisely evaluate conditions in lines 13–15, abstraction needs to track the ordering of variables id1, id2 and id3 with 6 predicates which compare variables id1, id2 and id3 pairwise: id1<id2, id1>id2, and so on.

To generate the above mentioned 15 predicates our algorithm uses the following variable roles. Variable is *input* if it is assigned a return value of an external function call. This pattern is often used in SV-COMP to initialize variables non-deterministically, e.g. id1=nondet_char(), where variables id1, id2, id3 are inputs. Variables which are assigned only inputs are run-time analogues of compile-time enumerations. A variable is *dynamic enumeration* if it is assigned only constant values or input variables, i.e. variables max1, max2 and max3 are dynamic enumerations. For each dynamic enumeration x which takes values v1,...,vn, our algorithm generates n equality predicates: x==v1, ..., x==vn.

Variable x is *extremum* if it is used in the pattern if(comp_expr)x = y, where comp_expr is a comparison operator > or < applied to y and some expression expr, e.g. y>expr. For every variable x which is both dynamic enumeration and extremum, our algorithm generates pairwise comparisons for all pairs of input values v1,...,vn assigned to x, e.g. v1<v2, v1>v2, and so on.

ELDARICA proves the program in Fig. 1.1 annotated with the 15 predicates in 8 sec and 0 CEGAR iterations, and it takes ELDARICA from 21 to 858 sec (and from 0 to 4 CEGAR iterations) to prove 53 programs from SV-COMP with

---

[2] E.g. seq-mthreaded/pals_opt-floodmax.3_true-unreach-call.ufo.BOUNDED-6.pals.c.

this pattern annotated analogously. For the remaining 55 benchmarks with this pattern from SV-COMP the number of abstract states becomes too large for ELDARICA to be checked within the time limit.

Motivation Example 2. The code in Fig. 1.2 increments variables i and k in the loop at line 6 until i reaches n, and decrements variables j and k in the loop at lines 7–9 until j reaches 0. The assertion checking that the value of variable k remains positive in the loop can be proven using the predicates k>=i and k>=j. These predicates are difficult to find, e.g., the baseline version of ELDARICA [20] keeps generating a sequence of pairs of predicates (i<=1,k<=1), (i<=2,k<=2), etc. As demonstrated by this example, heuristics are needed to guide interpolation towards finding suitable refinement predicates. The community has suggested various heuristics for the above example, e.g., the most recent version of ELDARICA [18] proves the program safe in 5 sec and 6 CEGAR iterations.

We suggest to generate predicate templates *demand-driven* from the code under analysis. For the above example, we propose a heuristic which tracks the dependencies between loop counters: The heuristic searches for variables x assigned in a loop in a statement matching the pattern x=x+expr, where expr is an arbitrary expression. For each pair x1 and x2 of such variables the heuristic generates a predicate template x1-x2. This template restricts the search space of the interpolation solver to predicates of the form x1-x2>=n, $n \in \mathbb{N}$. To formalise the heuristic we introduce the following role: *local counter* is a variable assigned in a loop in a statement x=x+expr, where expr is an arbitrary expression. Note that we do not restrict expr to be a constant, in contrast to *induction variables* [1], since the heuristic is a trade-off between generality and computational cost and performs well in practice.

Methodology for Choosing Roles. To choose roles and role-based predicates and templates, we investigated benchmarks of the competition SV-COMP'16 from categories "Integers and Control Flow" and "Loops" and loop invariant generation benchmarks (appr. 30 benchmarks altogether) on which ELDARICA did not give an answer within the time limit of 15 min. We manually inspected the code of these benchmarks and annotated the benchmarks with a minimum set of predicates and templates so that ELDARICA checks the benchmarks within the time limit. We then derived new variable roles which captured specific code patterns in which the annotated variables were used.

2   Predicate Abstraction and Refinement

We outline the algorithm implemented by predicate abstraction-based software model checkers, in particular the ELDARICA tool [20] used as test-bed. As the core procedure, ELDARICA applies predicate abstraction [13] and counterexample-guided abstraction refinement [5] to check the satisfiability of *Horn constraints* expressing safety properties of a software program [14,15,20]. The procedure has two main parameters that can be used to tune the abstraction process:

– **initial predicates** Π_0 for predicate abstraction (see Sect. 2.1);
– **interpolation templates** T that guide Craig interpolation towards meaningful predicates during abstraction refinement (see Sect. 2.2).

The pair (Π_0, T) can be computed with the help of variable roles, as outlined in the previous section. It is important to note that neither parameter has any effect on *soundness* of a model checker, only termination is affected.

2.1 Solving Horn Clauses with Predicate Abstraction

A *Horn clause* is a formula of the form $\varphi \wedge B_1 \wedge \cdots \wedge B_n \to H$, with constraint φ, body literals $B_1 \wedge \cdots \wedge B_n$ containing uninterpreted *relation symbols*, and head literal H. ELDARICA has a C/C++ front-end that translates software programs to sets HC of Horn clauses. In this setting, relation symbols represent state invariants Inv_c associated with a control location c of a program, and Horn clauses express 1. pre-conditions $Pre(\bar{s}) \to Inv_c(\bar{s})$ for program entry points c; 2. Floyd-style inductiveness conditions $T(\bar{s}, \bar{s}') \wedge Inv_c(\bar{s}) \to Inv_{c'}(\bar{s}')$, for transitions between control locations c, c'; and 3. safety assertions $\neg P(\bar{s}) \wedge Inv_c(\bar{s}) \to false$ for control locations c. The translation from software programs to Horn clauses HC is defined such that the program is *safe* if and only if the clauses HC are *satisfiable*, i.e., if and only if the predicates Inv_c can be interpreted in such a way that all clauses become valid.

Model checkers like HSF [14] or ELDARICA [20] construct solutions of Horn clauses in disjunctive normal form by building an *abstract reachability graph* (ARG) over a set of given predicates. For this, a Horn solver maintains a mapping $\Pi : \mathcal{R} \to \mathcal{P}_{fin}(For)$ from relation symbols $p \in \mathcal{R}$ to finite sets of predicates. The solver starts from some initial mapping $\Pi = \Pi_0$; for instance, mapping every relation symbol to an empty set of predicates. The solver will then attempt to construct a closed ARG by means of fixed-point computation, which can either succeed (in which case a solution of the Horn clauses has been derived), or fail because some assertion clause $\varphi \wedge p_1(\bar{t}_1) \wedge \cdots \wedge p_n(\bar{t}_n) \to false$ is violated during the construction. In the latter case, a connected acyclic ARG fragment can be extracted that leads from entry clauses (clauses $\varphi \to H$ without relation symbols in the body) to the violated assertion clause. A theorem prover is then used to verify that the counterexample is genuine; spurious counterexamples are eliminated by generating additional predicates by means of Craig interpolation, leading to an extended mapping $\Pi = \Pi_1$ and refined abstraction.

2.2 Craig Interpolation with Templates

Predicate abstraction-based model checkers rely on theorem provers to find suitable interpolants, or interpolants containing the right predicates, in a generally infinite lattice of interpolants for every extracted counterexample (represented as acyclic ARG fragments). ELDARICA uses *interpolation abstraction* [18] as a semantic way to guide the interpolation procedure towards "good" interpolants; in this method, interpolation queries are instrumented to restrict the symbols that can occur in interpolants, ranking the interpolants with the help of *templates*. It has previously been shown that interpolation abstraction can significantly improve the performance of Horn solvers [18].

In the scope of this paper, we focus on templates in the form of *terms*. As an example, consider the binary interpolation query $A \wedge B$ with $A = (x = 1 \wedge y = 2)$ and $B = (x > y)$. The interpolation problem has multiple solutions I (with the property that $A \Rightarrow I$ and $B \Rightarrow \neg I$), including $I_1 = (x = 1 \wedge y = 2)$ and $I_2 = (y = x + 1)$. In a software model checker, clearly I_2 is preferable, since it abstracts from concrete values of the variables. Interpolation abstraction can be used to distinguish between I_1 and I_2, by preventing theorem provers, e.g., to compute I_1 as an interpolant. For this, template terms are used to capture the expressions that an interpolant might contain. In the example, given templates $\{x, y\}$, a theorem prover could compute either of I_1, I_2; with the template $\{x - y\}$, a theorem prover could return $(x - y = -1) \equiv I_2$, but no longer I_1.

In ELDARICA, software programs can be annotated to express preference of certain interpolants. For instance, line 4 of the code in Fig. 1.2 can be annotated to express that the differences i-k and j-k are preferred templates:

```
4 int k, /*@ terms_tpl {i-k} @*/ i, /*@ term_tpl{j-k} @*/ j;
```

Annotations are attached to variable declarations, and are then applied when computing interpolants at control points in the scope of the variable. If no interpolant can be constructed using this template, a conventional interpolant will be used. Besides manual annotation, ELDARICA also has a set of inbuilt heuristics to choose meaningful templates automatically [18].

3   Role-Based Predicates and Templates

Specification Language for Roles. In this section we describe a framework for the specification and computation of role-based initial predicates and predicate templates. Roles are usage patterns of variables, we introduce and formalize them as data-flow analyses in our previous work [9]. Here we re-formulate roles as logic queries on the control-flow graph (CFG) of a program. We choose logic programming as a formalism for two reasons: first, its notation is well known, and second, we can use of-the-shelf logic engines for the computation of roles. Specifically, we use the syntax and standard fixed point semantics of Datalog.

Preliminaries on Datalog. A rule in Datalog is of the form $A_0 \text{:-} L_1, \ldots, L_n$. The head of a rule A_0 is an atom. The body of a rule $\{L_i\}$ is a set of literals, and each literal L_i is of the form A or $\text{not } A$ for an atom A, where the connective **not** corresponds to default negation. An atom takes boolean values and is of the form 1. $\text{p}(\text{t}_1, \ldots, \text{t}_m)$, or 2. $\text{t}_0\text{=f}(\text{t}_1, \ldots, \text{t}_k)$, or 3. $\text{t}_1 \text{ op } \text{t}_2$, where p is a predicate symbol, f is a function symbol, t_j are term symbols and op is a comparison operator (e.g. $>$, $!=$, etc.). Atom $\text{t}_0\text{=f}(\text{t}_1, \ldots, \text{t}_k)$ always evaluates to **true** and assigns to term t_0 the result of function $\text{f}(\text{t}_1, \ldots, \text{t}_k)$. Each term t_j is a constant symbol (i.e. a function symbol with arity 0), a variable, or an integer. Predicate and function symbols start with a small letter, and variables start with a capital letter. A rule is evaluated as follows: if every literal L_i in the body evaluates to `true`, then the atom A_0 in the head evaluates to `true`. A rule with empty body is called a fact.

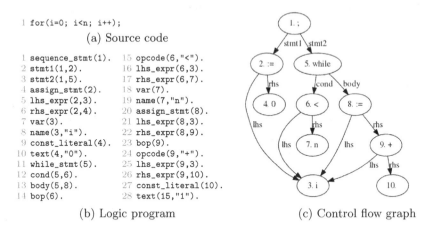

```
1 for(i=0; i<n; i++);
```
(a) Source code

```
 1 sequence_stmt(1).      15 opcode(6,"<").
 2 stmt1(1,2).            16 lhs_expr(6,3).
 3 stmt2(1,5).            17 rhs_expr(6,7).
 4 assign_stmt(2).        18 var(7).
 5 lhs_expr(2,3).         19 name(7,"n").
 6 rhs_expr(2,4).         20 assign_stmt(8).
 7 var(3).                21 lhs_expr(8,3).
 8 name(3,"i").           22 rhs_expr(8,9).
 9 const_literal(4).      23 bop(9).
10 text(4,"0").           24 opcode(9,"+").
11 while_stmt(5).         25 lhs_expr(9,3).
12 cond(5,6).             26 rhs_expr(9,10).
13 body(5,8).             27 const_literal(10).
14 bop(6).                28 text(15,"1").
```
(b) Logic program

(c) Control flow graph

Fig. 2. Translation of C code to a logic program

Translation of C Code to a Logic Program. We assume a C program to be given as a logic program, where each node and edge in the control-flow graph is translated to one or more facts in the logic program. For example, the code in Fig. 2a is translated to a logic program in Fig. 2b (see the CFG in Fig. 2c). In particular, the loop condition `i<n` is represented with nodes 6, 3 and 7 in the CFG and lines 7–8 and 14–19 in the logic program. Below we will denote a node corresponding to variable x in the control-flow graph with $node_x$.

We define roles *local counter*, *extremum*, *input* and *dynamic enumeration* in Fig. 3. Specifically, in Fig. 3a we define role local counter which is used to generate templates, and in Fig. 3b we define roles which are used to generate initial predicates. Due to the lack of space we introduce the remaining roles and the generated predicates and templates informally in Table 1. We explain the definitions of roles in Sect. 3.1, and the generation of predicates and templates for these roles in Sect. 3.2.

3.1   Definition of Roles

Role Local Counter. Role local counter (line 2–4 in Fig. 3) is defined in the scope of one loop. The set of variables to which this role is ascribed is encoded with a binary relation `local_cnt` with a parameter corresponding to the resp. loop statement `WhileStmt`. The parameter is needed, because we later define a template for pairs of local counters, such that the counters have the same parameter. A variable X is ascribed role local counter if there is a loop statement

```
 1 % local counter
 2 local_cnt(X,WhileStmt):- while_stmt(WhileStmt),
 3   sub_stmt(WhileStmt,AsgnStmt), assigned(X,SumExpr,AsgnStmt),
 4   bop(SumExpr), opcode(SumExpr,"+"), operand(SumExpr,X).
 5
 6 % difference templates for local counters
 7 tpl(TplStr):-local_cnt(X,WhileStmt),local_cnt(Y,WhileStmt),
 8   X!=Y, name(X,Xname), name(Y,Yname), TplStr=@concat(Xname,"-",Yname).
```

(a) Role *local counter* and templates.

```
 1 % extremum
 2 extremum(X):- if_stmt(IfStmt), condition(IfStmt,Cond), bop(Cond),
 3   opcode(Cond,Opcode), strict_rel_opcode(Opcode), operand(Cond,Y),
 4   var(Y), assigned(X,Y,AsgnStmt), then(IfStmt,AsgnStmt).
 5
 6 % input
 7 input(X):- assigned(X,CallExpr,AsgnStmt), call_expr(CallExpr),
 8   function(CallExpr,Func), not body(Func).
 9
10 % dynamic enumerations
11 dyn_enum(X):- var(X), not not_dyn_enum(X).
12 % the complement of dyn_enum
13 not_dyn_enum(X):- assigned(X,Y,AsgnStmt), var(Y), not_dyn_enum(Y).
14 not_dyn_enum(X):- assigned(X,Expr,AsgnStmt), not var(Expr),
15   not dyn_enum_expr(Expr).
16 % cases for dynamic enumerations
17 dyn_enum_expr(Expr):- const_literal(Expr).
18 dyn_enum_expr(Expr):- input(Expr).
19
20 % predicates for dynamic enumerations
21 pred(PredStr):- dyn_enum(X), assigned(X,Y), var(Y),
22   name(X,Xname), name(Y,Yname), PredStr=@concat(Xname,"==",Yname).
23
24 % ordering predicates for dynamic enumerations
25 pred(PredStr):- extremum(X), dyn_enum(X), assigned(X,Y),
26   var(Y), assigned(X,Z), var(Z), Y!=Z, name(Y,Yname),
27   name(Z,Zname), PredStr=@concat(Yname,"<",Zname).
```

(b) Roles *dynamic enumeration, input* and *extremum*, and initial predicates.

Fig. 3. Simplified specification of roles and role-based templates and initial predicates.

WhileStmt, in the body of which X is assigned the sum of X and some other expression. Term sub_stmt(Stmt,SubStmt) encodes that in the control flow graph SubStmt is a descendant of Stmt. Term assigned(X,Expr,AsgnStmt) encodes that variable X is assigned expression Expr in statement AsgnStmt. Term operand(Expr,Bop) encodes that Expr is an operand of binary operator Bop. For example, for code in Fig. 2a the evaluation of the rule derives the fact

Table 1. Informal description of remaining roles with examples.

Role name	#	Description of role	Π / T	Example	
				Code	Generated predicates Π /templates T
Assertion condition	1	Variable is used in pattern `assert(expr)`	$\Pi = \{$expr$\}$	`assert( cnt==1)`	$\Pi =\{$cnt==1$\}$
	2	Statement `assert(expr)` is nested in an `if` statement with condition `cond`	$\Pi = \{$cond$\}$	`if(x<1) assert(0)`	$\Pi = \{$x<1$\}$
Parity variable	3	Variable `x` is used in remainder operator `x%c`	$T = \{$x%c$\}$	`x%2`	$T =\{$x%2$\}$
	4	Variable `x` is incremented in a loop by constant c, s.t. `c!=1`	$T = \{$x%c$\}$	`for(i=0;i<n; i+=2)`	$T =\{$x%2$\}$
Loop iterator	5	Variable `x` is modified in a loop and is used in the loop condition `cond`	$\Pi = \{$cond$\}$	`while(i<n) i++`	$\Pi = \{$i<n$\}$
	6	In addition to 5), `cond` matches pattern `expr1!=expr2`	$\Pi =$ $\{$expr1<expr2, expr1>expr2$\}$	`for(i=0; i!=n;i++)`	$\Pi =$ $\{$i<n, i>n$\}$
	7	In addition to 5), `cond` matches pattern `expr1<expr2` (resp. `expr1>expr2`) and loop iterator is changed by 1 in the loop	$\Pi =$ $\{$expr1<=expr2$\}$ (resp. $\{$expr1>=expr2$\})$	`for(i=0;i<n; i++)`	$\Pi = \{$i<=n$\}$
Loop bound	8	Variable `bnd` is compared to loop iterator `it` in loop condition: `it`∘`bnd`, where ∘ $\in \{$<,<=,>,>=,!=,==$\}$; and `bnd` is assigned in statement `bnd=expr`	$\Pi =$ $\{$bnd<=expr, bnd>=expr$\}$	`n=k-2; for(i;i<n; i++);`	$\Pi = \{$n<=k-2, n>=k-2$\}$

`local_cnt(3)` for node node_i=3. For clarity we omit rules for terms `sub_stmt`, `assigned`, `operand` and a rule for the case when the counter is decremented.

Role Extremum. Role extremum (lines 2–4) is ascribed to variable X, denoted with term `extremum(X)`, if there is an if statement `IfStmt`, the condition `Cond` of which is a binary operator greater-than or less-than (encoded with term `strict_rel_opcode(Opcode)`), s.t. `Cond` contains a variable Y which is assigned to X in the body of `IfStmt`. For example, for code `if (max3>max1) max1=max3` (line 13 in Fig. 1.1), the result of evaluating the rule is `extremum(`node_{max1}`)`. Relation `strict_rel_opcode(Opcode)` encodes that its parameter is a greater-than or less-than operator.

Role Input. Role input (lines 7–8) is ascribed to variable X if X is assigned the result of a call `CallExpr` to a function `Func`, the body of which is not defined (encoded with atom not body(Func)). For example, for the C code id1=nondet_char() where nondet_char() is defined as an external function (lines 1 and 3 in Fig. 1.1), evaluation of the rule derives fact input(node$_{id1}$).

Role Dynamic Enumeration. Role dynamic enumeration (lines 11–18) is defined via its complement not_dyn_enum (line 11). Fact not_dyn_enum(X) is generated if variable X is assigned an expression Expr which does not belong to relation dyn_enum_expr (lines 14–15). The unary relation dyn_enum_expr includes constant literals and input variables (lines 17–18). For example, for code in Fig. 1.1 evaluation of rules derives facts dyn_enum(node$_{max1}$), dyn_enum(node$_{max2}$) and dyn_enum(node$_{max3}$).

3.2   Role-Based Predicates and Templates

Our algorithm generates initial predicates $\Pi_{roles} = \{p \mid \text{pred}(p)\}$ and templates $T_{roles} = \{t \mid \text{tpl}(t)\}$, where pred(p) and tpl(t) are the facts derived by the logic program (see line 7 in Fig. 3a and lines 21–22 and 25–27 in Fig. 3b). We now describe the role-based initial predicates and templates in detail.

Local Counter. For every pair of local counters X and Y s.t. X and Y are modified in loop WhileStmt, a template X-Y is derived (lines 7–8). For example, for code in Fig. 1.2 the evaluation of the rule derives templates i-k and j-k.

Dynamic Enumeration. For every pair of a dynamic enumeration X and input Y, s.t. Y is assigned to X, predicate X==Y is derived (lines 21–22). Term @concat encodes a call to a function which concatenates its parameters. For example, for code in Fig. 1.1 the evaluation of the rule derives predicates max1==id1, max2==id2 and max3==id3.

Input Variables. For every pair of input variables Y and Z, s.t. both Y and Z are assigned to dynamic enumeration and extremum X, predicate Y<Z is derived (lines 25–27). For example, for code in Fig. 1.1 the evaluation of rules derives predicates id1<id2, id1>id2, id1<id3, id1>id3, id2<id3 and id2>id3.

4   Evaluation

We implemented our approach in a prototype tool and evaluated the tool on altogether 549 C benchmarks[3].

Benchmarks. Table 2 lists the benchmarks and gives their characteristics. Specifically, the benchmarks contain (listed in the same order as in Table 2):

1. Benchmarks of the competition SV-COMP'16 from the "Integers and Control Flow" category. We excluded the Recursive sub-category and 75 benchmarks which contain C structures and arrays;

---

[3] The tool, the set of used benchmarks and the results of our evaluation are available at http://forsyte.at/software/demy/nfm17.tar.gz.

Table 2. Characteristics of the benchmarks

#	Name	Number of files			Size, KLOC
		Total	Safe	Unsafe	
1	SV-COMP CFI	234	91	143	226.4
2	SV-COMP Loops	95	68	27	6.5
3	VeriMAP	153	133	20	13.2
4	Llreve	21	16	5	0.6
5	HOLA	46	46	0	1.4
	Total	549	354	195	248.0

Table 3. ELDARICA configurations. T_{Eld} denotes the templates generated by built-in heuristics of ELDARICA.

Name	Π_0	T
Eld	$\emptyset$	$\emptyset$
Eld+B	$\emptyset$	T_{Eld}
Eld+R	Π_{roles}	T_{roles}
Eld+BR	Π_{roles}	$T_{roles} \cup T_{Eld}$

2. Benchmarks from the Loops category of SV-COMP'16 (we excluded 50 benchmarks for same reasons);
3. Benchmarks of the verification tool *VeriMAP*[4]. We excluded 234 duplicate benchmarks contained in SV-COMP CFI, and 2 benchmarks, for which the transition relations cannot be expressed with Presburger arithmetic;
4. Simplified versions[5] of the benchmarks of tool llrêve for automated program equivalence checking [12];
5. Loop invariant generation benchmarks of the verication tool HOLA [10].

Tools for Comparison. We evaluate the following configurations of ELDARICA: without interpolation abstraction (to which we refer by Eld), with templates (Eld+B), with roles (Eld+R), and with a combination of templates and roles (Eld+BR). Table 3 lists different choices for the parameters Π_0 and T described in Sect. 2. As a baseline we also compare ELDARICA to SMT solvers Z3 [6] and Spacer [17]. We could not compare to the duality engine of Z3 because of a bug in duality, which was not fixed by the time of paper submission. Finally, we compare ELDARICA to the model checker CPACHECKER, which is not based on Horn clauses. CPACHECKER has very successfully participated in the software competition in the recent years and thus provides an interesting choice for comparison.

Experimental Setup. We performed our experiments on 2.0GHz AMD Opteron PC (31GB RAM, 64KB L1 cache, 512KB L2 cache). We did not restrict the number of cores on which the tasks were performed. We report the wall-clock time measured using the `date` shell utility. For evaluation we set the value of timeout for all tools to 15 min, which is the value of the timeout in the SV-COMP competition. We put no memory limit on the tools.

Overall Improvement of Eldarica. The results of our evaluation are represented in Fig. 4, which shows the number of solved and unsolved tasks, with safe

---

[4] http://map.uniroma2.it/vcgen/benchmark320.tar.gz.
[5] Original benchmarks are accessible at http://formal.iti.kit.edu/projects/improve/ reve and https://www.matul.de/reve.

and unsafe tasks counted separately. Specifically, Fig. 4a gives a summary for all benchmarks, and Figs. 4b-4f show detailed results for each benchmark. In the bar plots on top of each bar is the mean runtime of the respective tool, calculated *without timeouts*. The times for Eld+R include the times for computing roles: the mean and median time of annotating a program for all benchmarks amount to 3.8 sec and 0.8 sec resp. We observe that the best configuration of Eldarica is Eld+R, which solves the highest number of tasks for every benchmark separately and for all benchmarks. The second best configuration for most benchmarks is Eld+B. Overall Eld+R solves 11.2% more tasks than Eld+B: 4.6% more safe and 6.6% more unsafe tasks. *We conclude that the configuration Eld+R improves on the previous configurations of Eldarica (Eld and Eld+B).*

Comparison of Runtimes. Overall, the runtime of Eld+R is comparable to the runtime of other Eldarica's configurations, but for the benchmarks SV-COMP CFI we observe a significant speedup of Eld+R, as shown in Fig. 5. SV-COMP CFI is a specific family of benchmarks because of their big size and a large number of enumeration variables, see e.g. the code in Fig. 1.1. Note that in Fig. 5 we compare Eld+R to Eld, which is the second best configuration, because for these benchmarks no heuristics are needed. The speedup of Eld+R for SV-COMP CFI is caused by a considerable decrease in the number of CEGAR iterations. To demonstrate this, we evaluate the configuration Eld+B with the timeout value of one hour (denoted as Eld+BH in Fig. 4c). We observe that Eld+BH solves 12.8% more unsafe and 9.0% more safe tasks than Eld+B. *To conclude, Eld+R does not increase the runtime on all benchmarks, and even shows a significant speedup for the family of benchmarks from SV-COMP CFI.*

Comparison of Roles with Eldarica's Previous Heuristics. A comparison of Eld+R to Eld+B shows that all but one benchmarks solved by old configurations of Eldarica can also be solved by Eld+R. The one benchmark not solved by Eld+R requires a predicate relating three variables in an equality, which according to our experience does not fall into frequently used patterns. Moreover, as Fig. 4 shows, the configuration Eld+BR, which combines roles and old heuristics of Eldarica, solves 3% less tasks than Eld+R. One possible reason for the slowdown (and consequently the lower number of solved benchmarks) of Eld+BR are redundant predicates generated by built-in heuristics of Eldarica. *These results confirm that our framework not only describes new heuristics but also captures all previous heuristics of Eldarica.*

Improvement on Unsafe Benchmarks. Surprisingly, the initial predicates also help to solve more unsafe benchmarks, as Fig. 4c shows. In principle, these predicates can be found by Eld+B with a higher value of runtime, as demonstrated by the configuration Eld+BH. *We conclude that when variable roles are used, the number of solved unsafe tasks does not decrease in general and even increases for SV-COMP CFI benchmarks.*

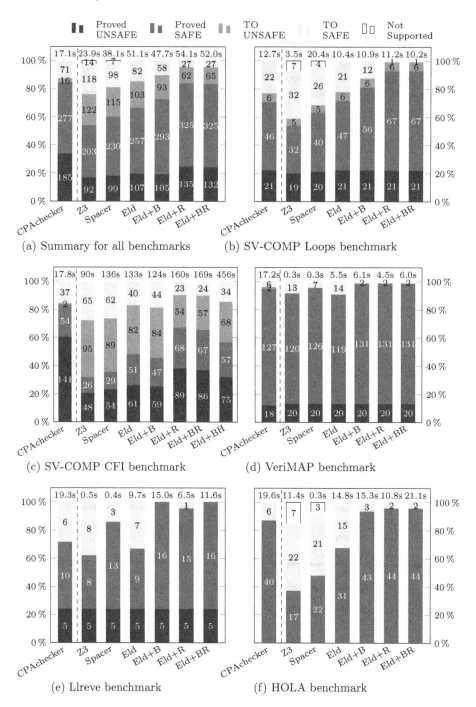

Fig. 4. Bar plots comparing the percentage of proved tasks for CPAchecker, Z3, Spacer and different Eldarica configurations. Inside each bar is the percentage of the resp. answers. On top of each bar is the mean runtime computed *without timeouts* (for solved tasks).

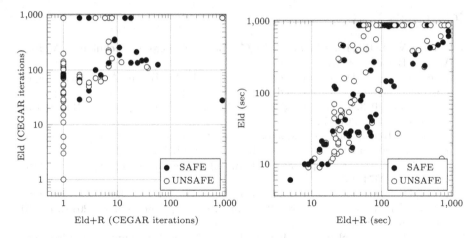

Fig. 5. Scatter plots comparing the number of CEGAR iterations and runtime, both in logarithmic scale, of configurations Eld+R and Eld for benchmark SV-COMP CFI. The mean runtime of Eld+R is 1.5 times smaller than that of Eld, and the average number of CEGAR iterations of Eld+R is 19.0 times smaller than that of Eld, the four values calculated on the tasks solved by both Eld and Eld+R.

Comparison of Eldarica to SMT Solvers. We compare ELDARICA to SMT solvers Z3 and Spacer[6]. We note that a small number of tasks in benchmarks SV-COMP Loops and HOLA cannot be processed by Z3 and Spacer because of existential quantifiers in the SMT translation, which is not in the fragment handled by the PDR engine of Z3. We denote these benchmarks as "Not Supported" in Fig. 4. We observe that, on one hand, all configurations of Eldarica outperform both Z3 and Spacer in the number of solved tasks, in particalar Eld+R solves 30% more tasks than Z3. We note, however, that our method for guiding predicate abstraction uses the structure of a program, which is not preserved on the level of SMT formulae. On the other hand, the mean runtime of Z3 is 2.0 times lower than the mean runtime of Eld+R. *To conclude, Eldarica outperforms Z3 and Spacer in the number of solved tasks, but loses in speed.*

Comparison of Eldarica to CPAChecker. Finally, we compare ELDARICA to the model checker CPACHECKER. We observe that on safe and unsafe tasks the tools show complementary strengths. In particular, CPACHECKER proves more tasks unsafe than ELDARICA on CFI benchmarks, and on other benchmark sets shows comparable to ELDARICA results. For safe benchmarks, however, on all benchmark sets CPACHECKER can prove fewer programs safe than the ELDARICA configurations Eld+B, Eld+R and Eld+BR. *To conclude, ELDARICA with interpolation abstraction outperforms CPACHECKER on safe benchmarks, while CPACHECKER performs better on a family of unsafe benchmarks.*

---

[6] We evaluate the default configuration of Z3 without command-line options. To execute Spacer, we use the command-line option `fixedpoint.xform.slice=false`.

References

1. Aho, A.V., Sethi, R., Ullman, J.D.: Compilers, Principles. Techniques. Addison Wesley, Boston (1986)
2. Apel, S., Beyer, D., Friedberger, K., Raimondi, F., Rhein, A.: Domain types: abstract-domain selection based on variable usage. In: Bertacco, V., Legay, A. (eds.) HVC 2013. LNCS, vol. 8244, pp. 262–278. Springer, Cham (2013). doi:10.1007/978-3-319-03077-7_18
3. Beyer, D.: Reliable and reproducible competition results with benchexec and witnesses (report on SV-COMP 2016). In: Chechik, M., Raskin, J.-F. (eds.) TACAS 2016. LNCS, vol. 9636, pp. 887–904. Springer, Heidelberg (2016). doi:10.1007/978-3-662-49674-9_55
4. Beyer, D., Löwe, S., Wendler, P.: Refinement selection. In: Fischer, B., Geldenhuys, J. (eds.) SPIN 2015. LNCS, vol. 9232, pp. 20–38. Springer, Cham (2015). doi:10.1007/978-3-319-23404-5_3
5. Clarke, E.M., Grumberg, O., Jha, S., Lu, Y., Veith, H.: Counterexample-guided abstraction refinement for symbolic model checking. J. ACM **50**(5), 752–794 (2003)
6. Moura, L., Bjørner, N.: Z3: an efficient SMT solver. In: Ramakrishnan, C.R., Rehof, J. (eds.) TACAS 2008. LNCS, vol. 4963, pp. 337–340. Springer, Heidelberg (2008). doi:10.1007/978-3-540-78800-3_24
7. Demyanova, Y., Pani, T., Veith, H., Zuleger, F.: Empirical software metrics for benchmarking of verification tools. In: Kroening, D., Păsăreanu, C.S. (eds.) CAV 2015. LNCS, vol. 9206, pp. 561–579. Springer, Cham (2015). doi:10.1007/978-3-319-21690-4_39
8. Demyanova, Y., Pani, T., Veith, H., Zuleger, F.: Empirical software metrics for benchmarking of verification tools. Int. J. Form. Methods Syst. Des., 1–28 (2017). doi:10.1007/s10703-016-0264-5. http://link.springer.com/article/10.1007%2Fs10703-016-0264-5
9. Demyanova, Y., Veith, H., Zuleger, F.: On the concept of variable roles and its use in software analysis. In: Formal Methods in Computer-Aided Design (FMCAD), pp. 226–230. IEEE (2013)
10. Dillig, I., Dillig, T., Li, B., McMillan, K.: Inductive invariant generation via abductive inference. ACM SIGPLAN Not. **48**, 443–456 (2013). ACM
11. Engler, D., Chen, D.Y., Hallem, S., Chou, A., Chelf, B.: Bugs as deviant behavior: a general approach to inferring errors in systems code. In: Operating Systems Principles (SOSP), vol. 35. ACM (2001)
12. Felsing, D., Grebing, S., Klebanov, V., Rümmer, P., Ulbrich, M.: Automating regression verification. In: Automated software engineering (ASE), pp. 349–360. ACM (2014)
13. Graf, S., Saidi, H.: Construction of abstract state graphs with PVS. In: Grumberg, O. (ed.) CAV 1997. LNCS, vol. 1254, pp. 72–83. Springer, Heidelberg (1997). doi:10.1007/3-540-63166-6_10
14. Grebenshchikov, S., Lopes, N.P., Popeea, C., Rybalchenko, A.: Synthesizing software verifiers from proof rules. In: Programming Language Design and Implementation (PLDI), pp. 405–416. ACM (2012)
15. Hoder, K., Bjørner, N.: Generalized property directed reachability. In: Cimatti, A., Sebastiani, R. (eds.) SAT 2012. LNCS, vol. 7317, pp. 157–171. Springer, Heidelberg (2012). doi:10.1007/978-3-642-31612-8_13
16. Jhala, R., Majumdar, R.: Software model checking. ACM Comput. Surv. (CSUR) **41**(4), 21 (2009)

17. Komuravelli, A., Gurfinkel, A., Chaki, S., Clarke, E.M.: Automatic abstraction in SMT-based unbounded software model checking. In: Sharygina, N., Veith, H. (eds.) CAV 2013. LNCS, vol. 8044, pp. 846–862. Springer, Heidelberg (2013). doi:10.1007/978-3-642-39799-8_59

18. Leroux, J., Rümmer, P., Subotić, P.: Guiding craig interpolation with domain-specific abstractions. Acta Inform. **53**, 1–38 (2016)

19. Nori, A.V., Rajamani, S.K.: An empirical study of optimizations in YOGI. In: Software Engineering (ICSE), vol. 1, pp. 355–364. ACM (2010)

20. Rümmer, P., Hojjat, H., Kuncak, V.: Disjunctive interpolants for horn-clause verification. In: Sharygina, N., Veith, H. (eds.) CAV 2013. LNCS, vol. 8044, pp. 347–363. Springer, Heidelberg (2013). doi:10.1007/978-3-642-39799-8_24

21. Sajaniemi, J.: An empirical analysis of roles of variables in novice-level procedural programs. In: Human-Centric Computing Languages and Environments (HCC), pp. 37–39. IEEE (2002)

22. Van Deursen, A., Moonen, L.: Type inference for COBOL systems. In: Reverse Engineering (RE), pp. 220–230. IEEE (1998)

specgen: A Tool for Modeling Statecharts in CSP

Brandon Shapiro[1] and Chris Casinghino[2](✉)

[1] Brandeis University, Waltham, MA 02453, USA
bts8394@brandeis.edu
[2] Draper Laboratory, Cambridge, MA 02140, USA
ccasinghino@draper.com

Abstract. We present specgen, a tool for translating statecharts to the Communicating Sequential Processes language (CSP), where they may be explored and verified using FDR, the CSP model checker. We build on earlier algorithms for translating statecharts to CSP by supporting additional features, simplifying the generated models, and implementing a practical tool for statecharts built in Enterprise Architect, a commercially available modeling environment. We demonstrate the tool on a standard example.

1 Introduction

Statecharts are a widely-used technique for graphically representing the high-level behavior of complex systems. Since their introduction by Harel [5], support for various versions of statecharts has been implemented in many commercial tools, including Enterprise Architect and Simulink Stateflow. As the use of statecharts has become widespread, so too have techniques for formally verifying their behavior. Classic examples include modeling via translation to SPIN [10] or to SMV [2].

This paper presents specgen, a tool for translating statecharts to Communicating Sequential Processes (CSP). This makes it possible to explore and verify the behavior of a statechart using FDR, the CSP model checker [4]. CSP and FDR have been used for modeling and formal verification for decades, in both academia and industry [8,9,11].

Translating statecharts to CSP has two main advantages. First, CSP is a rich, expressive language for writing specifications. We may leverage FDR to check these specifications and to interactively explore the behavior of the translated systems. Second, statecharts are themselves a convenient way to represent specifications for more complex systems already implemented in CSP. For example, the second author has also implemented a tool, called cspgen, to translate imperative programs from C source or LLVM IR to CSP [1]. The typical use

This work was sponsored by DARPA/AFRL Contract FA8750-12-C-0261. The views, opinions and/or findings expressed are those of the authors and should not be interpreted as representing the official views or policies of the Department of Defense or the U.S. Government.

C. Barrett et al. (Eds.): NFM 2017, LNCS 10227, pp. 282–287, 2017.
DOI: 10.1007/978-3-319-57288-8_19

of `cspgen` involves taking code written by a domain expert and translating it to CSP, then developing specifications to be checked by FDR. As the domain expert is typically unfamiliar with CSP, statecharts provide an intuitive, graphical common language for these specifications. Having a tool like `specgen` to automatically convert the graphical specification to CSP makes this possible.

The `specgen` tool builds on previous work for modeling statecharts in CSP [12]. We have added support for several additional statechart features and designed a new, simplified algorithm by using new CSP language constructs, as described in Sect. 3. The tool supports statecharts developed with Enterprise Architect and is the first practical implementation of any such translation. The `specgen` distribution also includes several examples, described in Sect. 2, and is available freely under a permissive open-source license [14].

2   The Dining Philosophers: An Example

To illustrate the use of `specgen`, we consider the classic dining philosophers problem [7]. Our distribution of `specgen` includes this example, implemented as a statechart in Enterprise Architect, for 2, 3 and 4 philosophers [14]. Figure 1 shows statecharts representing Philosopher 2 and Fork 2 from the four philosopher system. We elide the full system for space—it consists of four philosophers and forks, similar to those shown, as parallel substates of one top-level node.

We begin our explanation with the statechart for Fork 2. Conceptually, it keeps track of which philosopher has permission to use the fork at any time. It begins in the state Free, indicating that the fork is not in use and may be claimed by either philosopher. Transitions to the Phil2Holds2 and Phil3Holds2 states are guarded by the constraints In(WaitingRight2) and In(WaitingLeft3) respectively. This ensures these transitions are not taken until the relevant philosopher is in

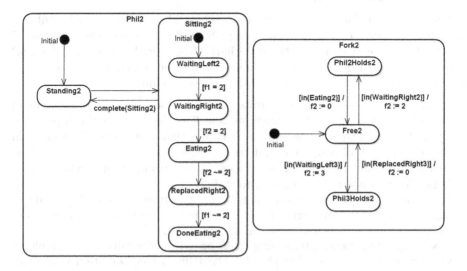

Fig. 1. Statecharts for one philosopher and fork

the state where he is waiting on this fork, so the ownership of the fork is not given to a philosopher until he wants it.

The system also includes four variables, f1, ..., f4, one for each fork. Intuitively, the value in these variables indicates which philosopher, if any, currently has permission to use a given fork. Thus, the transition from state Free2 to state Phil3Holds2 sets variable f2 to 3. These variables are set by the forks, and used by guards in the philosophers. For example, consider node WaitingLeft2 in Phil2. This node models the state where Philosopher 2 is waiting to pick up his left fork (Fork 1). The guard on this transition prevents it from being taken unless f1 = 2, indicating that Philosopher 2 has permission to use Fork 1. Similarly, the transition from Eating2 to ReplacedRight2 is guarded by the requirement that f2 is not 2, indicating that Philosopher 2 no longer has permission to use his right fork. The semantics of statecharts require that all available transitions are taken immediately, ensuring that Fork 2 and Philosopher 2 remain synchronized here.

Finally, we consider the edge from Sitting2 back to Standing2, which is labeled with the *completion event* complete(Sitting2). In statecharts, *events* are named triggers that are often used to represent external events. During execution, a set of enabled events is provided as input, and an edge labeled with an event may only be taken if the event is currently enabled. *Completion events* are special events that are enabled when a node terminates, rather than by input. A node is considered to have terminated when all of its concurrent subnodes have reached states with no out-edges. Here, the event label prevents the philosopher from standing until he is done eating.

It is worth noting that this example is not intended to represent the most efficient or natural implementation of the dining philosophers as a statechart. Rather, we have designed it to highlight several features supported by the tool.

2.1   The Generated Model

When run on an Enterprise Architect statechart like the one described above, specgen produces several files containing CSP definitions, including a top-level process RunSystem that models the statechart's behavior. The behavior of a CSP process is most easily described by finite "traces" of observable events. In the case of RunSystem, the relevant observable events include:

- transition.N.E, indicating a transition between nodes. Here N is the name of the node that contains the transition, and E is the name of the edge itself. Typically, specgen will generate node names that match the name given in the statechart if all nodes have unique names, and will otherwise pick a name based on the full path of a node. Edges are given names like Node1__Node2, indicating a transition from Node1 to Node2.
- tock, indicating the completion of a "step" of the statechart. According to the semantics of statecharts, a step comprises a single transition in every currently-running subchart that can make one.
- read.x.n and write.x.n, indicating reads or writes of a value n in variable x.
- writeerror.x, indicating that the statechart has a race condition where two parallel subcharts attempted to write to the variable x in the same step.

2.2   Finding the Deadlock

The most obvious property to check in the dining philosophers example is deadlock freedom. In our CSP scripts, this property is stated:

```
assert RunSystem \ {| tock |} :[deadlock free]
```

The \ ("hiding") operator here is used to hide the tock events of RunSystem. A statechate continues to take "steps", represented by these events, even if no subchart can make a transition. Intuitively, to detect the deadlock, we must inform FDR that the mere passage of time does not count as progress.

Asking FDR to check this property results in an assertion failure, as expected. Indeed, because the semantics of statecharts require each parallel process to make a transition in each step if able to, this system will always deadlock. FDR also displays the trace that leads to the deadlock. For the three philosopher system, this trace ends with the events:

```
transition.Sitting2.WaitingLeft2__WaitingRight2 ,
transition.Sitting3.WaitingLeft3__WaitingRight3 ,
transition.Sitting1.WaitingLeft1__WaitingRight1
```

We see that the last three events are each philosopher transitioning to his WaitingRight node, indicating that each philosopher has picked up his left fork and is waiting on his right fork.

2.3   More Complicated Properties

FDR, more generally, supports checking *refinement* between two CSP processes. This enables the use of CSP as a rich specification language for properties more interesting than deadlock. Our distribution of specgen includes many worked examples. For the dining philosophers system in particular, we show how to verify that changing the order in which a philosopher picks up his forks eliminates the deadlock, and include a detailed explanation of how to check the property "after sitting, no philosopher stands without eating". We also show how to check for race conditions in variable writes, and include several other statecharts to demonstrate a variety of properties.

2.4   Performance

The time to find the deadlock in FDR is summarized in the table below, organized by the number of philosophers in the system:

Philosophers	2	3	4
Time	2.0 s	6.0 s	117 s

These times are the averages of 5 runs performed on an Intel Xeon E5-2630 v3. The machine had 32 GB of RAM, but all tests consumed less than 6 GB.

Predictably, the time to find the deadlock grows exponentially with the number of philosophers. Checking these translated statecharts is slower than checking more natural implementations of the dining philosophers in CSP, because accurately modeling the semantics of statecharts involves substantial coordination overhead and additional features like per-node timers. As statecharts offer the advantage of wider accessibility, we believe this overhead is sometimes justified.

3   Translation Enhancements

As mentioned in the introduction, specgen builds on an earlier algorithm for modeling statecharts in CSP, by Roscoe and Wu [12]. In addition to providing a practical implementation, we have improved on that paper's translation by including support for two additional statechart features (the "in" guards and completion events described in Sect. 2) and exploiting a newer FDR feature to simplify the generated models. The remainder of this section describes this simplification.

The biggest challenge in modeling statecharts in CSP is representing *priority*. In CSP, a process may select freely among its available actions, but in statecharts certain transitions may be favored over others. For example, nodes must be allowed to take an "idle" step if and only if no transitions are available. Also, transitions out of a state may be favored over transitions within that state when both are available, or vice versa—classic Statemate semantics [6] favor outer transitions while UML favors inner ones [3]. (In specgen we have followed [12] in modeling Statemate, but it would be straightforward to prefer the alternate order, which is more common today).

Roscoe and Wu's translation models these instances of priority with a subtle renaming and synchronization scheme [13]. Happily, modern versions of FDR include a new feature that specgen uses to simplify this: prioritise. This function takes as arguments a process P and an ordered list evs of sets of events. If P may perform events from different sets in evs, then prioritise(P,evs) may perform only events from the first set that contains any of P's events. Combining prioritise with *interrupts*, where a CSP process may be preempted by certain events, also allowed for a simplified encoding of "promoted" actions in statecharts. These actions allow an inner node to transition directly to an outer node, terminating its parallel siblings.

4   Conclusion and Future Work

This paper has described specgen, a tool for translating statecharts to CSP. We demonstrated the use of the tool on a common example, illustrating how to analyze the behavior of a statechart by model-checking its translation with FDR (Sect. 2). Many more examples are available with the specgen distribution, which is available as open-source software [14]. The translation used by the tool is inspired by earlier work by Roscoe and Wu [12], which has been improved and extended (Sect. 3).

We are interested in expanding on this work in several directions. First, the generated model can likely be further optimized for model-checking speed in FDR. In particular, the use of *inductive compression* [13] to reduce the state space created by hidden control events seems particularly promising. Second, it would be interesting to compare our tool directly with other systems for verifying statecharts. Lastly, while the translation is intended to faithfully model one version of statechart semantics, it would be reassuring to formalize and mechanically verify this property with an interactive theorem prover like Coq or Isabelle/HOL.

While specgen is intended as a prototype, we have found it to work surprisingly well on a variety of examples. Readers are encouraged to download the implementation and give it a try.

Acknowledgments. The authors thank Neil Brock, Thomas Gibson-Robinson, Colin O'Halloran and Cody Roux for their advice on this project, and the anonymous reviewers for their helpful feedback.

References

1. Casinghino, C.: cspgen (2016). https://github.com/draperlaboratory/cspgen
2. Chan, W., Anderson, R.J., Beame, P., Burns, S., Modugno, F., Notkin, D., Reese, J.D.: Model checking large software specifications. IEEE Trans. Softw. Eng. **24**(7), 498–520 (1998)
3. Eshuis, R., Wieringa, R.: Requirements-level semantics for UML statecharts. In: Fourth International Conference on Formal Methods for Open Object-Based Distributed Systems, pp. 121–140. Kluwer Academic Publishers (2000)
4. Gibson-Robinson, T., Armstrong, P., Boulgakov, A., Roscoe, A.W.: FDR3 — a modern refinement checker for CSP. In: Ábrahám, E., Havelund, K. (eds.) TACAS 2014. LNCS, vol. 8413, pp. 187–201. Springer, Heidelberg (2014). doi:10.1007/978-3-642-54862-8_13
5. Harel, D.: Statecharts: a visual formalism for complex systems. Sci. Comput. Programm. **8**(3), 231–274 (1987)
6. Harel, D., Naamad, A.: The statemate semantics of statecharts. ACM Trans. Softw. Eng. Methodol. **5**(4), 293–333 (1996)
7. Hoare, C.A.R.: Communicating Sequential Processes. Prentice Hall Inc., Upper Saddle River (1985)
8. Lawrence, J.: Practical application of CSP and FDR to software design. In: Abdallah, A.E., Jones, C.B., Sanders, J.W. (eds.) Communicating Sequential Processes. The First 25 Years. LNCS, vol. 3525, pp. 151–174. Springer, Heidelberg (2005). doi:10.1007/11423348_9
9. Lowe, G.: Casper: a compiler for the analysis of security protocols. J. Comput. Secur. **6**(1–2), 53–84 (1998)
10. Mikk, E., Lakhnech, Y., Siegel, M., Holzmann, G.J.: Implementing statecharts in PROMELA/SPIN. In: Proceedings of the Second IEEE Workshop on Industrial Strength Formal Specification Techniques. IEEE Computer Society (1998)
11. Mota, A., Sampaio, A.: Model-checking CSP-Z: strategy, tool support and industrial application. Sci. Comput. Program. **40**, 59–96 (2001)
12. Roscoe, A.W., Wu, Z.: Verifying statemate statecharts using CSP and FDR. In: Liu, Z., He, J. (eds.) ICFEM 2006. LNCS, vol. 4260, pp. 324–341. Springer, Heidelberg (2006). doi:10.1007/11901433_18
13. Roscoe, A.: Understanding Concurrent Systems, 1st edn. Springer, New York (2010)
14. Shapiro, B., Casinghino, C.: specgen (2016). https://github.com/draperlaboratory/specgen

HyPro: A C++ Library of State Set Representations for Hybrid Systems Reachability Analysis

Stefan Schupp$^{(\boxtimes)}$, Erika Ábrahám, Ibtissem Ben Makhlouf, and Stefan Kowalewski

RWTH Aachen University, Aachen, Germany

Abstract. In this tool paper we introduce HyPro, our free and open-source C++ programming library, which offers implementations for the most prominent state set representations used by flowpipe-construction-based reachability analysis techniques for hybrid systems.

1 Introduction

As *hybrid systems* with mixed discrete-continuous behaviour are often safety-critical applications, a rising interest in their safety verification resulted in the development of powerful tools implementing different approaches to determine the set of system states that are reachable from a given set of initial states. Besides approaches based on, e.g., theorem proving or SMT solving, *flowpipe-construction-based reachability analysis* is a well established method, which over-approximates the set of reachable states of a hybrid system by a union of state sets, each of them being *represented* by a geometric object of a certain shape (like boxes, polytopes, or zonotopes) or symbolically (like support functions or Taylor models). Hybrid systems reachability analysis tools like, e.g., CORA [1], FLOW* [2], HYCREATE [7], HYREACH [8], SOAPBOX [5], and SPACEEX [3] implement different techniques using different geometric or symbolic state set representations, each of them having individual strengths and weaknesses.

The implementation of novel reachability analysis algorithms that use some geometric or symbolic state set representations is still effortful, as datatypes for the underlying state set representations need to be implemented first. In this paper we report on the first release of our free and open-source C++ library HyPro, providing implementations for the most prominent state set representations. Our aim is to offer assistance for the rapid implementation of new algorithms by encapsulating all representation-related issues and allowing the developers to focus on higher-level algorithmic aspects.

The HyPro library specifies a unified interface for different representations, which supports all operations required in reachability analysis as well as conversion methods between the different representations. Besides own

This work was supported by the German Research Council (DFG) in the context of the HyPro project.

C. Barrett et al. (Eds.): NFM 2017, LNCS 10227, pp. 288–294, 2017.
DOI: 10.1007/978-3-319-57288-8_20

implementations for state set representations, the library also offers approaches towards wrapping other existing libraries implementing a certain state set representation.

After some preliminaries in Sect. 2, we describe in Sect. 3 the structure and usage of our library and provide some experimental evaluation in Sect. 4.

2 Hybrid Systems Reachability Analysis

Reachability analysis aims at the computation of the set of states that are reachable in some system from a given set of initial states. Reachability analysis is often used for safety verification by showing that the set of reachable states does not intersect with a pre-defined set of unsafe states.

We are interested in reachability analysis for *hybrid automata* [6], a popular modelling formalism for hybrid systems. Intuitively, they extend discrete automata models, whose nodes resp. transitions model the states (*control modi*) resp. state changes (*jumps*) of the discrete part of the system, by additionally modelling the evolution of continuous quantities (*flowpipe*) between discrete state changes through ordinary differential equation (ODE) systems.

As the reachability problem for hybrid automata is in general undecidable, *over-approximative bounded reachability analysis* can be used to overapproximate reachability along such paths that satisfy some upper bounds on the time elapse between two consecutive jumps (*time horizon*) and on the number of jumps (*jump depth*). Due to the over-approximation, we can prove bounded safety in case of an empty intersection of the reachable state set with the unsafe state set, but no conclusive answer can be given if this intersection is not empty.

Flowpipe-construction-based reachability analysis approaches iteratively compute successors of a given initial state set. To over-approximate flowpipes, they divide a given time horizon into time segments and over-approximate the states reachable within each time segment by a state set, thus "paving" the flowpipe with state sets. For computing jump successors, they determine the intersections of those "paving" state sets with the guards of jumps that exit the current control modus, and apply the jumps' reset transformations to those intersections (see Fig. 1).

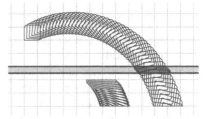

Fig. 1. Flowpipe-construction-based reachability analysis (guard satisfying sets in red, jump successor in green). (Color figure online)

3 The HyPro Library

The library is published at https://github.com/hypro/hypro. In the following we describe its components (see Fig. 2) and its usage. For more details we refer to the online documentation and the user's guide accessible on the above page.

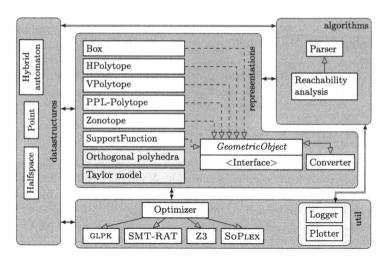

Fig. 2. HYPRO class structure.

Arithmetic Computations. HYPRO is templated in the number type and makes use of **boost** and the following external libraries:

- **cln**, GMP (optional): exact number types **cl_RA** and **mpq_class**;
- CARL: number-type-templated (**cl_RA** or **mpq_class**) exact arithmetic computations, number type conversion;
- EIGEN3: number-type-templated matrix computations; when instantiated with **double**, conservativeness is not assured;
- PPL (optional): efficient but inexact computations with polytopes;
- GLPK: linear optimiser using either floating-point or exact arithmetic, however, its interface does not support the exchange of exact numbers, thus the results are not provably correct;
- SMT-RAT, SOPLEX and Z3 (optional): exact linear optimisers; SMT-RAT and SOPLEX support **mpq_class** in their interfaces, but not Z3, therefore we need to convert **mpq_class**-numbers to strings when calling Z3;
- **log4cplus** (optional): logger functionalities.

Currently, HYPRO can be instantiated with inexact (**double**) or exact (**cl_RA**, **mpq_class**) number types; EIGEN3 will be instantiated the same way. When *inexact*, all representations as well as EIGEN3 use the **double** number type, thus we cannot guarantee over-approximative results; however, as exact optimisation is extremely important for meaningful results for most representations, we still guarantee exact optimisation through a combination of inexact GLPK with an exact optimiser if available (see Fig. 3). When using an *exact* number type, HYPRO assures conservative results if one of the modules SMT-RAT, SOPLEX or Z3 are available and if PPL is not used; as GLPK is faster than the other optimisers but its interface is inexact, we use the same approach as for the **double** representation shown in Fig. 3, but run GLPK in exact modus.

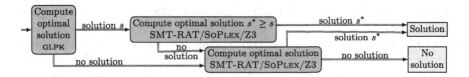

Fig. 3. Increased efficiency by combining inexact and exact computations.

State Set Representations. To implement the computations described in the previous section, we need a suitable data type (*representation*) that supports the *storage* of state sets (subsets of $\mathbb{R}^n$) and certain *operations* on them. The choice of the state set representation is highly relevant, as it strongly influences both computational effort and precision. Our library offers state-set representation by *boxes, (convex) polytopes* [10] in vertex ($\mathcal{V}$) as well as in halfspace ($\mathcal{H}$) representation, *support functions* [9] and *zonotopes* [4]. For these representations, we provide all operations needed for the reachability analysis of *linear* hybrid automata (hybrid automata specified using linear conditions and resets, and linear ODEs): linear transformation, Minkowski sum, intersection, union, and test for emptiness. All the above representations implement a common interface specifying these operations, extended with some additional convenience functions (e.g., functions for determining the dimension of a set or functionalities for output). Some representations also extend this interface with individual functions, only relevant for that representation (e.g., order reduction functions for zonotopes).

We additionally provide a module for *orthogonal polyhedra*, but it is partial as we found no proper way to compute the Minkowski sum and linear transformation. We thank Xin Chen who contributed with a further module for *Taylor models*; however, as Taylor-model-based reachability analysis requires different operations, this module does not implement the global HyPro interface.

Conversion. None of the state set representations is generally optimal in terms of both computational effort and precision in reachability analysis. Switching between representations, although mostly expensive, can pay off during the analysis, for instance to improve the precision of the computed state sets locally. This feature allows for the implementation of backtracking mechanisms and fast look-ahead strategies in a dynamic reachability analysis approach. HyPro implements easy-to-use (exact or over-approximating) conversion operations for all included state set representations; this converter is a template parameter and thus exchangeable by the user, if more specialised methods are desired.

Reduction Techniques. The size of state set representations usually strongly increases during the analysis due to more complex shapes (e.g., when computing Minkowski sum) and number representations (e.g., when computing linear transformation). For boxes and polytopes, HyPro provides efficient and conservative over-approximating number reduction techniques. For zonotopes we offer a conservative order-reduction algorithm to limit the number of generators. For support functions we reduce the operational tree of the object.

Additional Datastructures and Utility Functions. We provide a data type for hybrid automata, a parser for FLOW*-like syntax, utility functions such as a plotter which creates GNUPLOT or TikZ output files for state set visualisation, logging mechanisms to trace executions, and an exemplary reachability analysis algorithm among various other examples showing how to use the library.

Usage. We illustrate the usage of the HyPro library on some simple examples based on the double number type (where also EIGEN3 objects are instantiated with double); for further details see the examples folder and the user's guide.

We can create a state set $\{x \in \mathbb{R}^n \mid Ax \le b\}$ represented by an $\mathcal{H}$-polytope p by specifying an EIGEN3 matrix A, representing the constraints (row-wise) and an EIGEN3 vector b representing the constant parts, as follows:

```
HPolytope<double> p = HPolytope<double>(A, b);
```

The Minkowski sum p of two $\mathcal{H}$-polytopes p1 and p2 can be computed by:

```
HPolytope<double> p = p1.minkowskiSum(p2);
```

A box containing a set V of points of type std::vector<Point<double>> can be converted to a polytope in the $\mathcal{H}$-representation using the Converter class:

```
HPolytope<double> p = Converter::toHPolytope(Box<double>(V));
```

To plot an object (per default in the first two dimensions), we can report its vertices to the singleton class Plotter, and create a GNUPLOT file using the method plot2d():

```
Plotter<double>::getInstance().addObject(p.vertices());
Plotter<double>::getInstance().plot2d();
```

Future Work. Currently we focus on efficiency-related improvements for the presented representations, including the better exploitation of inexact arithmetic. Long-term plans address also extensions with further representations. Regarding efficiency, naturally, we cannot compete with well-established special-purpose libraries like PPL and POLYMAKE for polytope computations. Additionally to PPL, we work on the development of further wrappers for third-party libraries. Last but not least, as representation-related parameter settings are currently global and static, we work on the support of representation- and object-specific settings.

4   Experimental Evaluation

Using our library we implemented a simple reachability analysis algorithm for linear hybrid systems, and used it to evaluate the efficiency of our library on three commonly known benchmarks: (1) the *bouncing ball* (BBall) models the bouncing of an elastic ball dropped from a predefined height (parameters: time step $\delta = 0.01$, time horizon $T = 3$); (2) the *rod reactor* (Rod) models the temperature controller of a nuclear power plant and its cooling dynamics

Table 1. Benchmark results with runtimes in seconds (TO for $\geq$ 20 minutes). Dashes indicate that a tool does not support this kind of state set representation.

		mpq_class			double			SPACEEX	
		GLPK	GLPK+SMT-RAT	GLPK+Z3	GLPK	GLPK+SMT-RAT	GLPK+Z3	LGG	STC
Box	BBall	0.1	0.1	0.1	0.002	0.002	0.03	0.003	0.01
	Rod	63.8	64.8	65.1	0.01	0.06	0.02	0.02	0.2
	5D SW	0.3	0.3	0.3	0.02	0.02	0.02	0.02	0.03
HPoly	BBall	1.2	1.1	8.7	0.2	0.7	4.9	-	-
	Rod	24.3	21.3	136.5	4.8	16.1	131	-	-
	5D SW	54.8	TO	TO	4.3	TO	TO	-	-
VPoly	BBall	1.8	1.5	6.0	TO	(0.7)	(5.5)	-	-
	Rod	100.2	98.7	171.5	TO	(0.3)	(2.6)	-	-
	5D SW	TO	TO	TO	TO	TO	TO	-	-
PPL	BBall	0.07	0.07	0.08	0.05	0.06	0.06	-	-
	Rod	2.7	2.6	2.9	1.8	1.9	1.9	-	-
	5D SW	TO	TO	TO	TO	TO	TO	-	-
SF	BBall	0.6	2.0	15.6	0.02	1.1	43.8	0.2	0.03
	Rod	72.8	101.6	1125.8	0.4	54.4	609.6	1.1	0.9
	5D SW	270.6	279.8	411.1	0.04	2.6	319.3	0.8	0.2
Zono	BBall	TO	TO	TO	0.006	0.007	0.006	-	-
	Rod	4.8	4.9	4.9	0.02	0.02	0.02	-	-
	5D SW	3.8	3.9	3.9	0.004	0.004	0.004	-	-

($\delta = 0.01$, $T = 17$); (3) the *switching 5D linear system* (5D SW) is an artificially created benchmark in 5 dimensions with planar guards ($\delta = 0.001$, $T = 0.2$).

All experiments were carried on an Intel Core i7 (4×4 GHz) CPU with 16 GB RAM. Table 1 shows the results when using mpq_class (exact) and double (inexact) number types, and as representations boxes (Box), $\mathcal{H}$-polytopes (HPoly), $\mathcal{V}$-polytopes which are converted to $\mathcal{H}$-polytopes for intersection computation (VPoly), polytope representation by the PPL library (PPL), support functions (SF) and zonotopes (Zono). For both mpq_class and double, we distinguish GLPK only in exact resp. inexact modus, and glpk+SMT-RAT and glpk+Z3 combining GLPK with an exact solver as in Fig. 3. Inexact-arithmetic results that we (manually) detected to be under-approximating are put in parenthesis; this occurred for VPoly due to inexact EIGEN3computations. For comparison, we present SPACEEX results using support functions (SF) as well as SF with box templates (Box); note that SPACEEX uses double representation and GLPK.

Due to space limitation, we discuss only some timing issues. At least on these few examples, HYPRO in inexact GLPK-only modus is competitive with SPACEEX. A higher computational effort can be observed for exact arithmetic, most prominently for SF, which highly relies on optimisation; the longer running times for

GLPK+Z3 (wrt. SMT-RAT) are due to the string-based interface communication overhead. For 5D SW, the initial set is a single point. Zonotopes, performing well on small initial sets, deliver very good results here.

References

1. Althoff, M., Dolan, J.M.: Online verification of automated road vehicles using reachability analysis. IEEE Trans.Robot. **30**(4), 903–918 (2014)
2. Chen, X., Ábrahám, E., Sankaranarayanan, S.: Flow*: an analyzer for non-linear hybrid systems. In: Sharygina, N., Veith, H. (eds.) CAV 2013. LNCS, vol. 8044, pp. 258–263. Springer, Heidelberg (2013). doi:10.1007/978-3-642-39799-8_18
3. Frehse, G., et al.: SpaceEx: scalable verification of hybrid systems. In: Gopalakrishnan, G., Qadeer, S. (eds.) CAV 2011. LNCS, vol. 6806, pp. 379–395. Springer, Heidelberg (2011). doi:10.1007/978-3-642-22110-1_30
4. Girard, A.: Reachability of uncertain linear systems using zonotopes. In: Morari, M., Thiele, L. (eds.) HSCC 2005. LNCS, vol. 3414, pp. 291–305. Springer, Heidelberg (2005). doi:10.1007/978-3-540-31954-2_19
5. Hagemann, W., Möhlmann, E., Rakow, A.: Verifying a PI controller using SoapBox and Stabhyli: experiences on establishing properties for a steering controller. In: Proceedings of ARCH 2014. EPiC Series in Computer Science, vol. 34. EasyChair (2014)
6. Henzinger, T.: The theory of hybrid automata. In: Proceedings of LICS 1996, pp. 278–292. IEEE Computer Society Press (1996)
7. HyCreate. http://stanleybak.com/projects/hycreate/hycreate.html
8. HyReach. https://embedded.rwth-aachen.de/doku.php?id=en:tools:hyreach
9. Le Guernic, C., Girard, A.: Reachability analysis of linear systems using support functions. Nonlinear Anal.: Hybrid Syst. **4**(2), 250–262 (2010)
10. Ziegler, G.M.: Lectures on Polytopes, vol. 152. Springer Science & Business Media, New York (1995)

Asm2C++: A Tool for Code Generation from Abstract State Machines to Arduino

Silvia Bonfanti[1,2(✉)], Marco Carissoni[1], Angelo Gargantini[1],
and Atif Mashkoor[2]

[1] Università degli Studi di Bergamo, Bergamo, Italy
{silvia.bonfanti,angelo.gargantini}@unibg.it,
m.carissoni1@studenti.unibg.it
[2] Software Competence Center Hagenberg GmbH,
Hagenberg im Mühlkreis, Austria
atif.mashkoor@scch.at

Abstract. This paper presents Asm2C++, a tool that automatically generates executable C++ code for Arduino from a formal specification given as Abstract State Machines (ASMs). The code generation process follows the model-driven engineering approach, where the code is obtained from a formal abstract model by applying certain transformation rules. The translation process is highly configurable in order to correctly integrate the underlying hardware. The advantage of the Asm2C++ tool is that it is part of the Asmeta framework that allows to analyze, verify, and validate the correctness of a formal model.

1 Introduction

The Abstract State Machines (ASM) method [4] is a formal method that is used to guide the rigorous development of software and embedded systems seamlessly from their informal requirements. The ASM method follows a design process based on the refinement principle that allows to capture all details of the system design by a sequence of refined models till the desired level of detail. It combines validation (by simulation and testing) and verification methods at any desired level of detail. The final step of this refinement process consists in realizing the implementation, generally code that is compiled and deployed on the real system. Performing this last step manually increases costs, limits the reuse of a formal specification, is error prone as some faults can be introduced in the code writing process, and can be a barrier for a wider adoption of ASMs. For these reasons, we have devised a methodology supported by the Asm2C++ tool that is able to generate the desired source code from ASMs. In this paper, we target Arduino[1] that is a widespread platform for rapid prototyping of embedded systems and

---

This work is partially supported by the Austrian Ministry for Transport, Innovation and Technology, the Federal Ministry of Science, Research and Economy, and the Province of Upper Austria in the frame of the COMET center SCCH.

[1] https://www.arduino.cc/.

C. Barrett et al. (Eds.): NFM 2017, LNCS 10227, pp. 295–301, 2017.
DOI: 10.1007/978-3-319-57288-8_21

supports C++. It is also suitable for learning the design of embedded systems due to its low cost.

The ultimate aim of the paper is to show the implementation of the model-driven engineering (MDE) paradigm through ASMs: requirements models are platform independent, there is a clear distinction between platform-specific details and original user and system requirements, the code generation process is seamless and automatic, and last but not least, the rigorous quality and correctness assurance is embedded in the development process. As an additional goal, we aim at producing a code which is *readable* such that the code instructions can be easily *traced back* to the specification concepts and constructs. Although this may decrease the code efficiency, we believe that it increases the maintainability and the usability of the Asm2C++ tool.

The paper is organized as follows: In Sect. 2, we present the ASM methodology. The process of code generation is presented in Sect. 3 and by means of a simple example, we illustrate some basic concepts of the proposed translation in Sect. 4. Section 5 presents some related work and Sect. 6 concludes the paper with some future work.

2   Abstract State Machine Methodology

The ASM method guides the development of software from requirements capture to code generation through several steps. Figure 1 shows the process of the ASM-based development. This method is supported by the Asmeta (ASM mETAmodeling) framework[2] [3] which provides a set of tools to help a developer in various development activities. The modelling process is based on refinement, i.e., it starts from an abstract model and adds further details to capture the complete system behaviour described in the requirements document. The correct refinement between two models is automatically proved using the ASMRefProver tool. If a model becomes complex, it is difficult to understand the behaviour only by the textual specification. For this reason, the visualizer AsmetaVis provides a visual notation that helps in the navigation of the model.

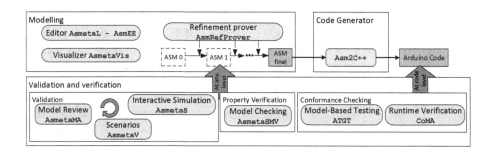

Fig. 1. ASM process: from requirements to code

---

[2] http://asmeta.sourceforge.net/.

The validation and verification (V&V) activities are well-integrated in the process, as shown in Fig. 1, and can be applied to any refined machine. The validation of a model can be achieved in multiple ways: either through the model simulator AsmetaS, through the model validator AsmetaV or through the model reviewer AsmetaMA. The simulator AsmetaS allows to perform two type of simulations: *interactive simulation* (the user inserts the values of parameters by choice) and *random simulation* (the tool randomly chooses the values that depends on the environment). The model validator AsmetaV takes *scenarios* as input files that contain the expected system behaviours. The scenarios are executed to check whether the machine runs correctly. The model reviewer AsmetaMA performs static analysis, it determines whether a model has sufficient *quality* attributes (e.g., minimality, completeness, consistency). The verification tool AsmetaSMV verifies whether the properties, derived from the requirements document, comply with the behaviour of the model. When the final model is available, the Arduino code is automatically generated using the Asm2C++ tool (see Sect. 3). When an actual code of the system implementation is available, *conformance checking* is possible. It is divided in model-based testing (to check the conformance *offline*) and runtime verification (to check the conformance *online*). The former uses the ATGT tool that automatically generates from ASM models tests cases which can be used to test any programming language. The latter, using the CoMA tool, can be used to perform runtime verification: the machine code is checked during the execution.

The language used by Asm2C++ is UASM (Unified Syntax for Abstract State Machine) [2], the new ASM syntax developed by the ASM community to unify various ASMs dialects.

3   Code Generation Process

The translation process shown in Fig. 2 generates the runnable C++ code for Arduino starting from a UASM specification that we assume verified and validated. The first step of the transformation process consists in parsing the textual

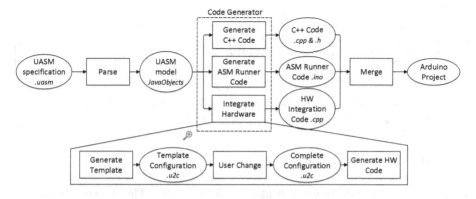

Fig. 2. Transformation process: from specification to code

specification and producing the UASM model, which is given to the code generator. The code generator performs three activities: (1) Generate C++ Code (2) Generate ASM Runner Code (3) Integrate Hardware. The result is merged as an Arduino project.

The first activity translates the ASM model into C++ code. The code is composed of a header (.h) that contains the translation of the ASM signature and a source (.cpp) file that defines how the ASM evolves by translating each ASM rule to a C++ method.

The second activity generates the Arduino code that defines the running policy according to the ASM execution divided in four iterative steps: acquire inputs, perform the main rule, update state, and release outputs. The output, the ASM Runner, is an .ino file that is the default extension for the Arduino C++ code.

The third activity integrates all HW-related aspects into the project: Arduino board version, I/O devices connections, Arduino-specific libraries that must be included, and any other HW-dependent information. The tool automatically generates a template configuration file (with .u2c extension). According to the HW configuration, the user edits this file which is used to generate the HW integration file. This is a C++ source file that works as an adapter between the generated code and the hardware. The output files are finally merged together to compose the Arduino project.

Asm2C++ is built on top of Xtext [6], a framework for the development of domain-specific languages, which provides facilities for parsing and code generation and is fully compatible with the Eclipse Modeling Framework. The code generator has been developed as a model-to-text (M2T) transformation. The transformation was realized by means of Xtend, a Java dialect provided by the Xtext framework with features for code generation. The listing below shows the translation scheme for the SeqBlock rule of the ASM method. A SeqBlock is a list of rules which are executed sequentially and is translated as a list of C++ instructions enclosed by curly brackets. In Xtext syntax, the content within ''' ''' symbols is a template string, while the code inside ≪ ≫ brackets is a variable part of the template expression that will be translated according to the rules parameter.

```
override String caseSeqBlock(SeqBlock rules) {
    return ''' {  ≪translateRules(rules.getRules())≫  } '''
}
```

The detailed information about the Asm2C++ tool can be found at http://asmeta.sourceforge.net/download/asm2c++.html.

4   Illustrative Example

Asm2C++ has been used to implement a small case study. The system is a control panel to be placed on the car dashboard that enables the driver to interact with various car functionalities. The panel is responsible for controlling the following functionalities: 1. Switching on/off the system 2. Climate control 3. Smart headlights activation 4. Radio system. Code examples 1 to 4 in Fig. 4 focus on functionality 1 to show some translation rules. The ASM is translated in the CarPanel class, where domains, functions and rules become respectively data types, properties and methods. As shown in Code 3, the runner cyclically calls four CarPanel methods: 1. Acquire inputs from sensors (getInputs) 2. Perform the main rule (r_Main) 3. Update the ASM state (updateState) 4. Set outputs to actuators (setOutputs). Parallel execution is translated as described in [7], where controlled functions are duplicated and the state is updated only after the main rule.

The implementation process followed the methodology described in Sect. 2. We first defined a ground model that was progressively refined. When the model reached the last refinement step, we generated the runnable Arduino code. Along this process, we proved liveness properties with the model checker and executed some scenarios with the AsmetaV tool. In order to check the compliance between the specification and the code, we ran the same scenarios on the Arduino code, obtaining the same behavior as for the ASM simulation. The real system is shown in Fig. 3.

Fig. 3. CarPanel

```
asm CarPanelFinal
  enum Switch = {OFF, ON}
  controlled carState -> Switch
  initially OFF
  monitored carButton -> Switch
  ...
  rule r_Main =
  if carState = OFF then
    r_SwitchOnCar
  else if carButton = ON then
    carState := OFF
  else
    par
    r_Menu
    r_Headlights
    r_SetTemperature
    ...
    endpar
  endif
  endif
  ...
```

Code (1) UASM

Code (2) CarPanel.h

```
class CarPanel{
  enum Switch {OFF, ON};
  Switch carState[2],carButton;
  public:
  void getInputs();
  void r_Main();
  void updateState();
  void setOutputs();
  ...
};
```

```
#include "CarPanel.h"
CarPanel carPanel;
...
void loop(){
  carPanel.getInputs();
  carPanel.r_Main();
  carPanel.updateState();
  carPanel.setOutputs();
}
```

Code (3) ASM runner

```
#include "CarPanel.h"

// main rule
void CarPanel::r_Main(){
  if (carState[0] == OFF)
    r_SwitchOnCar();
  else if (carButton == ON)
    carState[1] = OFF;
  else{
    r_Menu();
    r_Headlights();
    r_SetTemperature();
    ...
  }
}
// apply the update set
// to the current state
void CarPanel::updateState(){
  carState[0]=carState[1];
}
...
```

Code (4) CarPanel.cpp

Fig. 4. Snippets from model and code

5   Related Work

Automatic code generation from formal specifications is available as a part of tool support for several formal methods. SCADE[3] and MATLAB/Simulink[4] provide this feature as a commercial off-the-shelf solution. The formal method B [1], on the other hand, provides this facility in the form of the Atelier B platform[5], that comes with code generators for different target languages, including C, C++, Java, and Ada, and its Community Edition is freely available without any restriction. EventB2Java is another tool that generates executable code implemented as a plug-in of the Rodin platform [5].

As best of our knowledge, there is no state of the art, reusable and publicly available tool for the ASM method that is capable of automatically generating programming language code from formal specifications written in the ASM method. In the past, [7] introduced a compilation scheme to transform an ASM specification (written in ASM-SL) into C++ code, but this work was done within a company setting. Although some of the key results of the proposed compilation scheme were useful for our work as mentioned in Sect. 4.

6   Conclusions and Future Work

We have presented `Asm2C++`, a tool that is able to generate C++ from formal specifications written as ASMs. This work follows the MDE paradigm: source code is obtained from requirements models by applying a set of M2T transformations. We have already successfully tried the tool with students of advanced programming courses to teach them rapid prototyping and designing of embedded devices.

In the future, we plan to extend the tool with an automatic test cases generator. From the ASM specification, a series of tests could be automatically generated which would be executed on the Arduino board. This would test both the system and the translation from the specification to the code. As, currently, the conformance relation between the specification and the code is coarsely defined, we also intend to formally specify and prove the correctness of the code transformation process.

References

1. Abrial, J.-R.: The B-book: Assigning Programs to Meanings. Cambridge University Press, New York (1996)
2. Arcaini, P., Bonfanti, S., Dausend, M., Gargantini, A., Mashkoor, A., Raschke, A., Riccobene, E., Scandurra, P., Stegmaier, M.: Unified syntax for abstract state machines. In: Butler, M., Schewe, K.-D., Mashkoor, A., Biro, M. (eds.) ABZ 2016. LNCS, vol. 9675, pp. 231–236. Springer, Cham (2016). doi:10.1007/978-3-319-33600-8_14

---

[3] http://www.esterel-technologies.com/products/scade-suite/.

[4] https://www.mathworks.com/products/simulink/.

[5] http://www.atelierb.eu/en/.

3. Arcaini, P., Gargantini, A., Riccobene, E., Scandurra, P.: A model-driven process for engineering a toolset for a formal method. Softw.: Pract. Exp. **41**, 155–166 (2011)
4. Börger, E., Stark, R.F.: Abstract State Machines: A Method for High-Level System Design and Analysis. Springer, New York (2003)
5. Cataño, N., Rivera, V.: EventB2Java: a code generator for event-B. In: Rayadurgam, S., Tkachuk, O. (eds.) NFM 2016. LNCS, vol. 9690, pp. 166–171. Springer, Cham (2016). doi:10.1007/978-3-319-40648-0_13
6. Eysholdt, M., Behrens, H.: Xtext: implement your language faster than the quick and dirty way. In: Proceedings of the ACM International Conference Companion on OOPSLA, pp. 307–309. ACM (2010)
7. Schmid, J.: Compiling abstract state machines to C++. JUCS **7**(11), 1068–1087 (2001)

SPEN: A Solver for Separation Logic

Constantin Enea[1], Ondřej Lengál[2(✉)], Mihaela Sighireanu[1],
and Tomáš Vojnar[2]

[1] Univ. Paris Diderot, IRIF CNRS UMR 8243, Paris, France
[2] FIT, Brno University of Technology, IT4Innovations Centre of Excellence,
Brno, Czech Republic
lengal@fit.vutbr.cz

Abstract. SPEN is a solver for a fragment of separation logic (SL) with inductively-defined predicates covering both (nested) list structures as well as various kinds of trees, possibly extended with data. The main functionalities of SPEN are deciding the satisfiability of a formula and the validity of an entailment between two formulas, which are essential for verification of heap manipulating programs. The solver also provides models for satisfiable formulas and diagnosis for invalid entailments. SPEN combines several concepts in a modular way, such as boolean abstractions of SL formulas, SAT and SMT solving, and tree automata membership testing. The solver has been successfully applied to a rather large benchmark of various problems issued from program verification tools.

1 Introduction

For analyzing programs with dynamic memory, *separation logic* (SL) is an established and fairly popular logic introduced by Reynolds et al. [11]. The high expressivity of SL, its ability to generate compact proofs, and its support for local reasoning motivated development of many tools for automatic reasoning about programs with complex dynamic linked data structures. These tools aim at establishing memory safety properties and/or inferring shape properties of the heap. The tools often build on (semi-)decision procedures for checking *satisfiability* and *entailment* problems in SL.

Our tool SPEN[1] provides (semi-)decision procedures for the most commonly considered *symbolic heaps* fragment of SL, extended with user-defined inductive predicates to specify data structures of an unbounded size. Because unrestricted definitions of inductive predicates make the entailment problem for the fragment undecidable [3], only semi-decision procedures have been proposed, e.g., in [2,4]. Iosif *et al.* [10] identified a rather large class of inductive definitions for which the entailment problem is decidable, although with a high complexity. SPEN focuses on a smaller class of inductive definitions that is, however, expressive enough to specify complex dynamic data structures, such as skip lists, lists of circular lists, AVL trees, or binary search trees.

---

[1] https://github.com/mihasighi/spen.

© Springer International Publishing AG 2017
C. Barrett et al. (Eds.): NFM 2017, LNCS 10227, pp. 302–309, 2017.
DOI: 10.1007/978-3-319-57288-8_22

The chosen class of inductive definitions enables the design of efficient (semi-) decision procedures for satisfiability and entailment [6,8]. The key idea used for satisfiability checking in SPEN is to exploit the semantics of restricted inductive definitions and of separating conjunction to build an equisatisfiable boolean abstraction of the formula. For entailment checking, the idea is to reduce the problem of checking $\varphi \Rightarrow \psi$ to the problem of checking a set of *simple entailments* where the right-hand side is an inductive predicate atom. The compositionality of this reduction leads to high efficiency (the simple entailments can be checked independently) and to a capability to provide fine diagnosis for invalid entailments.

The current version of SPEN improves on the ones reported in [6,8] in several directions. First, we introduced caching of constructions and results obtained from checking simple entailments in order to increase its efficiency. Second, the wrappers calling the SAT and SMT solvers have been refined to generate smaller formulas and to exploit the incrementality feature of underlying solvers. Third, we improved the diagnosis produced by SPEN. For satisfiability checking, SPEN now provides either a model of a satisfiable formula or an unsatisfiable core; for entailment checking, SPEN provides a proof witness for valid entailments and a diagnostic information otherwise.

SPEN has been successfully tested on a quite large benchmark. The first version of SPEN participated in the SL-COMP'14 contest [15] where it won one of its divisions and was second in another one. The later extensions now allow SPEN to handle a richer fragment than those considered in the competition. Moreover, the improvements above lead to better execution times (e.g., by 10% within the SL-COMP'14 division won by the first version of SPEN and by 30% on the division where SPEN was the second).

SPEN is not the only solver for SL. The existing solvers differ in the fragment considered (CYCLIST [2], SLIDE [9]) and/or the techniques used (ASTERIX [12], DRYAD [14], GRASSHOPPER [13], SLEEK [4]). A detailed comparison with these solvers is beyond the scope of this paper—we refer the reader to the survey in [6,8,15].

2   Logic Fragment

SPEN deals with decision problems in a fragment of SL, denoted as $\mathsf{SL^{ID}}$, that combines the *symbolic heaps* fragment of SL [1] with user-defined *inductive predicates* describing various kinds of *lists* (possibly nested, cyclic, or equipped with skip links) or *trees*, possibly extended with data constraints.

Syntax: We write X, Y, Z to denote *location variables*, d to denote *data variables*, and x, y, z for both kinds of variables. We use the vector notation $\vec{x}$ to abbreviate tuples. We denote by ρ the tuples built from pairs of *field labels* and variables that specify structured values. We assume a finite set $\mathcal{P} = \{P_1, \ldots, P_n\}$ of *predicate symbols*, each with an associated arity, and a special location variable nil.

A *symbolic heap formula* ψ is a formula of the form $\exists \vec{x} \cdot \Pi \wedge \Sigma$ where Π is a *pure formula* and Σ is a *spatial formula* with the following syntax:

$$\Pi ::= X = Y \mid X \neq Y \mid \Delta \mid \Pi \wedge \Pi \qquad\qquad \Sigma ::= \mathtt{emp} \mid X \mapsto \rho \mid P(X, \vec{x}) \mid \Sigma * \Sigma$$

Here, Δ is a constraint over data variables. We let it unspecified, though SPEN presently supports the first-order theory over multisets of integers with integer linear constraints. The spatial atoms (i.e., the empty heap, the heap cell allocated at X, resp. the heap region shaped by some predicate $P \in \mathcal{P}$) are composed by the separating conjunction "$*$". An $\mathsf{SL}^{\mathsf{ID}}$ formula φ is a set of symbolic heaps interpreted as a disjunction $\vee_i \psi_i$.

Predicates $P \in \mathcal{P}$ are defined by a set of *inductive rules* of the form $\psi \Rightarrow P(X, \vec{x})$ where $(X, \vec{x})$ is a tuple of distinct variables including all free variables in the symbolic heap ψ (the rule body). X is called the root node of the heap segment defined by P. A rule is called a *base rule* if its spatial part is $\mathtt{emp}$, i.e., an empty heap; otherwise, it is an *inductive rule*.

Fragments: SPEN considers a restricted class of inductive rules such that the defined predicates specify (possibly empty) heap segments connecting (by location fields) the root location X with all locations in the heap or nil. The restrictions have been defined formally in [6,8]. They mainly require, for each inductive predicate P, the presence of a unique base rule and inductive rules where the root X points to a memory cell that contains at least one field from which another heap specified by P starts. The fragment defined in [6], called $\mathsf{SL}_\mathsf{L}^{\mathsf{ID}}$, can describe various kinds of lists that can be singly- or doubly-linked, cyclic, nested, and can have skip links. It does not permit data constraints and inductive tree structures. On the other hand, the fragment $\mathsf{SL}_\mathsf{D}^{\mathsf{ID}}$ defined in [8] permits data constraints and can describe tree structures of bounded width, such as sorted list segments, AVL trees, binary search trees, but not nested cyclic lists.

Decision Problems: For both fragments above, SPEN considers the problems of checking satisfiability of a formula, i.e., checking whether $\models \varphi$ holds, and the validity of an entailment $\varphi \Rightarrow \varphi'$ where the symbolic heaps of φ' can be quantified only over data variables. A simple example of an entailment problem in $\mathsf{SL}_\mathsf{L}^{\mathsf{ID}}$ considered by SPEN is:

$$\exists Y, W. \, X \neq Z \wedge X \mapsto \{(\mathtt{next}, Y)\} * \mathtt{sll}(Y, W) * W \mapsto \{(\mathtt{next}, Z)\} \quad \overset{?}{\Rightarrow} \quad \mathtt{sll}(X, Z),$$

which, intuitively, checks whether a composition of two memory cells specified by the *points-to atoms* $X \mapsto \{(\mathtt{next}, Y)\}$ and $W \mapsto \{(\mathtt{next}, Z)\}$ and the predicate atom $\mathtt{sll}(Y, W)$ describes a set of heaps that are all also models of the predicate $\mathtt{sll}(X, Z)$ defining an acyclic singly-linked list segment between X and Z.

3 Satisfiability Checking

Given a set of inductive defini-
tions $\mathcal{P}$ and a symbolic heap ψ,
the procedures for checking satisfiability in SPEN follow the workflow given in Fig. 1. The satisfiability checking of an SL^{ID} formula φ makes a classic use of this
basic procedure. The crux of the
procedures for both fragments is
the definition of a boolean formula $B[\psi]$, called *boolean abstraction*, such that the data-free part
of ψ is satisfiable iff $B[\psi]$ is satisfiable [6,7].

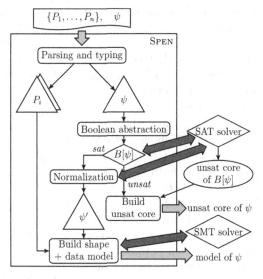

Once the boolean abstraction
$B[\psi]$ is computed, SPEN queries a
SAT solver (currently, MINISAT[2])
for the satisfiability of $B[\psi]$. If
$B[\psi]$ is unsatisfiable, SPEN can

Fig. 1. SPEN workflow for satisfiability checking

return an unsatisfiable core of ψ, deduced from an unsatisfiable core of $B[\psi]$.
If $B[\psi]$ is satisfiable and $\psi \in SL_L^{ID}$, SPEN has the option of returning a model of
ψ obtained from a model of $B[\psi]$ by unfolding predicate atoms corresponding
to non-empty heap segments. The unfolding of predicate atoms is done twice
to emphasize the non-emptiness of the segment. For $\psi \in SL_D^{ID}$, the satisfiability
checking continues by constructing a formula Δ_ψ that conjuncts the data part of
ψ with the data parts obtained by unfolding the non-empty heap segments given
by the model of $B[\psi]$. To check the satisfiability of Δ_ψ, SPEN queries an SMT
solver for the theory of multisets with integer data (currently, SPEN implements
a wrapper for the UFLIA theory of z3 [5]).

If the boolean abstraction $B[\psi]$ is satisfiable, it is then used to normalize the
spatial part of ψ, which is a step used by entailment checking too. This process
saturates the pure part of ψ with (dis-)equalities between locations variables and
removes predicate atoms that correspond to empty heap segments, producing
a normalized formula ψ'.

4 Entailment Checking

To check the validity of an entailment $\varphi_1 \Rightarrow \varphi_2$, SPEN uses a sound procedure to
deal with disjunctive formulas: it checks that for every disjunct ψ_1 in φ_1, there is
a disjunct ψ_2 of φ_2 such that $\psi_1 \Rightarrow \psi_2$. The procedure for deciding the validity
of entailments between symbolic heaps follows the workflows given in Figs. 2 and
3 (the theoretical foundations were established in [6,8]). The two formulas are
first checked for satisfiability and normalized using the procedures from Sect. 3.

---

[2] Available at http://minisat.se.

If one of the two formulas is unsatisfiable, then the validity of the entailment can be already determined, e.g., if ψ_1 is unsatisfiable then the entailment is valid. When both formulas are satisfiable, SPEN offers two different procedures tuned for each fragment of SL^{ID}.

For the fragment SL_L^{ID}, SPEN reduces the entailment problem $\psi_1 \Rightarrow \psi_2$ to a set of entailment queries of the form $\psi_1[a] \Rightarrow a$, called *simple entailments*, where $\psi_1[a]$ is a sub-formula of ψ_1 and a is a (points-to or inductive) spatial atom of ψ_2 (there will be one such entailment for each spatial atom a in ψ_2). Intuitively, the sub-formula $\psi_1[a]$

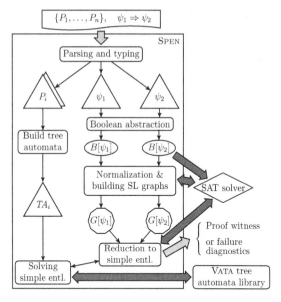

Fig. 2. SPEN workflow for entailment in SL_L^{ID}

describes the region of a heap modelled by ψ_1 that should satisfy a. The procedures for computing $\psi_1[a]$ and testing simple entailments use an intermediary graph representation of symbolic heap formulas, called an *SL-graph* and denoted $G[\psi]$. Basically, nodes of $G[\psi]$ represent sets of aliased variables according to the pure part of ψ, and edges represent dis-equalities and spatial atoms of ψ, e.g., a spatial atom $P(X, Y, \vec{x})$ is represented by a directed edge from X to Y labeled by $P(\vec{x})$. Thus, when a is a predicate atom $P(X, Y, \vec{x})$, $\psi_1[a]$ is obtained from the SL-graph of ψ_1 by selecting the edges reachable from X and co-reachable from Y. The graph selected for $\psi_1[a]$ is transformed into a tree t_1, which is tested for membership in the language of a tree automaton built from the rules defining P for the atom $a = P(X, Y, \vec{x})$.

For the fragment SL_D^{ID}, SPEN implements a proof search strategy for the entailment problem $\psi_1 \Rightarrow \exists \vec{d}. \psi_2$. The strategy computes a sequence of formulas $\exists \vec{d}^1. \psi_1^1, \ldots, \exists \vec{d}^n. \psi_1^n$ such that (1) $\exists \vec{d}^i. \psi_1^i \Rightarrow \exists \vec{d}^{i+1}. \psi_1^{i+1}$ and (2) $\exists \vec{d}^n. \psi_1^n$ is syntactically equivalent to $\exists \vec{d}. \psi_2$. The entailments in point (1) are obtained by applying the inductive rules and lemmas obtained automatically thanks to restriction required on inductive definitions. The procedure requires to check

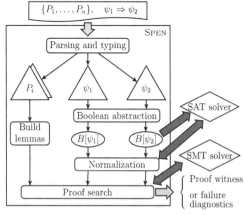

Fig. 3. SPEN workflow for entailment in SL_D^{ID}

Table 1. Experimental results on an Intel(R) Core(TM) i7-2600 CPU at 1.60 GHz

| Fragments | | Benchmark | Size | Time [s] | | SL-COMP'14 results |
SL_L^{ID}	SL_D^{ID}			$SPEN_L$	$SPEN_D$	Time [s] StarExec/solver
✓	✓	sll0_sat	110	11.20	11.28	(I) 1.06/Asterix, (II) 3.27/SPEN
✓	✓	sll0_entl	292	34.45	34.94	(I) 2.98/Asterix, (II) 7.58/SPEN
✓	✓	FDB_entl	43	1.08	1.00	(I) 0.61/SPEN, (II) 43.65/SLEEK
✓		FDB_entl$^+$	55	0.65	—	—

entailments between data constraints, which is done using the previously mentioned wrapper to the SMT solver.

For both procedures, when the input entailment $\psi_1 \Rightarrow \exists \vec{d}. \ \psi_2$ holds, SPEN has the option of providing a proof witness that either indicates the fact that ψ_1 is unsatisfiable or it consists of the normalized forms of ψ_1 and ψ_2 and the mapping of sub-formulas in ψ_1 to atoms of ψ_2. When the input entailment is not valid and the procedure terminates, SPEN provides a diagnosis that explains why the entailment fails.

5 Experimental Results

SPEN has been applied to a benchmark of 578 problems (available in the repository), 90% obtained from verification conditions of iterative programs on complex dynamic data structures. The remaining problems are crafted to test the capabilities of the solver. Tables 1 and 2 provide an overview of results obtained by SPEN on this benchmark.

The benchmark of SL_L^{ID} problems includes three divisions of SL-COMP'14: satisfiability and entailment problems for acyclic singly linked lists (sll0_sat resp. sll0_entl), and entailment checking for formulas describing more complicated types of linked lists, e.g., doubly-linked lists, skip lists, and nested lists (FDB_entl). SPEN spends less than 0.05 s on 90% of the problems with the maximum time of 0.5 s; these times include calls to a SAT solver. The benchmark FDB_entl$^+$ includes the problems not in the SL-COMP'14 benchmark (e.g., formulas describing lists of cyclic lists). The reported times in the last column have been obtained in 2014 on the StarExec[3] platform.

The benchmark of SL_D^{ID} problems (see Table 2) includes verification conditions for proving the correctness of iterative procedures (delete, insert, search) over recursive data structures storing integer data: sorted lists, binary search trees, AVL trees, and red-black trees. SPEN spends less than 0.4 s on each problem,

Table 2. Results for SL_D^{ID}

Benchmark	Size	Time [s]
sll0_sorted	16	0.45
BST	45	1.67
AVL	22	1.21
RBT	21	3.61

---

[3] www.starexec.org, an Intel(R) Xeon(R) CPU E5-2609 at 2.40 GHz of and 10 MB cache.

including calls to SAT and SMT solvers. The first three lines of Table 1 demonstrate that the two approaches implemented in SPEN (based on tree automata—column "SPEN$_L$"—and on proof search—column "SPEN$_D$") are not only complementary but also comparable on the common fragment. The improvements discussed in this paper reduce the execution times by 10% within the division sll0_entl and by 30% within FDB_entl w.r.t. the old version [6].

Acknowledgement. This work was supported by the French ANR project Vecolib, the Czech Science Foundation (project 17-12465S), the BUT FIT project FIT-S-17-4014, the IT4IXS: IT4Innovations Excellence in Science project (LQ1602), and by the European Research Council (ERC) under the European Unions Horizon 2020 research and innovation programme (grant agreement No. 678177).

References

1. Berdine, J., Calcagno, C., O'Hearn, P.W.: A decidable fragment of separation logic. In: Lodaya, K., Mahajan, M. (eds.) FSTTCS 2004. LNCS, vol. 3328, pp. 97–109. Springer, Heidelberg (2004). doi:10.1007/978-3-540-30538-5_9

2. Brotherston, J., Gorogiannis, N., Petersen, R.L.: A generic cyclic theorem prover. In: Jhala, R., Igarashi, A. (eds.) APLAS 2012. LNCS, vol. 7705, pp. 350–367. Springer, Heidelberg (2012). doi:10.1007/978-3-642-35182-2_25

3. Calcagno, C., Yang, H., O'Hearn, P.W.: Computability and complexity results for a spatial assertion language for data structures. In: Hariharan, R., Vinay, V., Mukund, M. (eds.) FSTTCS 2001. LNCS, vol. 2245, pp. 108–119. Springer, Heidelberg (2001). doi:10.1007/3-540-45294-X_10

4. Chin, W.-N., David, C., Nguyen, H.H., Qin, S.: Automated verification of shape, size and bag properties via user-defined predicates in separation logic. Sci. Comput. Program. **77**(9), 1006–1036 (2012). Elsevier

5. De Moura, L., Bjørner, N.: Z3: an efficient SMT solver. In: Ramakrishnan, C.R., Rehof, J. (eds.) TACAS 2008. LNCS, vol. 4963, pp. 337–340. Springer, Heidelberg (2008). doi:10.1007/978-3-540-78800-3_24

6. Enea, C., Lengál, O., Sighireanu, M., Vojnar, T.: Compositional entailment checking for a fragment of separation logic. In: Garrigue, J. (ed.) APLAS 2014. LNCS, vol. 8858, pp. 314–333. Springer, Cham (2014). doi:10.1007/978-3-319-12736-1_17

7. Enea, C., Saveluc, V., Sighireanu, M.: Compositional invariant checking for overlaid and nested linked lists. In: Felleisen, M., Gardner, P. (eds.) ESOP 2013. LNCS, vol. 7792, pp. 129–148. Springer, Heidelberg (2013). doi:10.1007/978-3-642-37036-6_9

8. Enea, C., Sighireanu, M., Wu, Z.: On automated lemma generation for separation logic with inductive definitions. In: Finkbeiner, B., Pu, G., Zhang, L. (eds.) ATVA 2015. LNCS, vol. 9364, pp. 80–96. Springer, Cham (2015). doi:10.1007/978-3-319-24953-7_7

9. Iosif, R., Rogalewicz, A., Vojnar, T.: Deciding entailments in inductive separation logic with tree automata. In: Cassez, F., Raskin, J.-F. (eds.) ATVA 2014. LNCS, vol. 8837, pp. 201–218. Springer, Cham (2014). doi:10.1007/978-3-319-11936-6_15

10. Iosif, R., Rogalewicz, A., Simacek, J.: The tree width of separation logic with recursive definitions. In: Bonacina, M.P. (ed.) CADE 2013. LNCS (LNAI), vol. 7898, pp. 21–38. Springer, Heidelberg (2013). doi:10.1007/978-3-642-38574-2_2

11. O'Hearn, P., Reynolds, J., Yang, H.: Local reasoning about programs that alter data structures. In: Fribourg, L. (ed.) CSL 2001. LNCS, vol. 2142, pp. 1–19. Springer, Heidelberg (2001). doi:10.1007/3-540-44802-0_1
12. Pérez, J.A.N., Rybalchenko, A.: Separation logic modulo theories. In: Shan, C. (ed.) APLAS 2013. LNCS, vol. 8301, pp. 90–106. Springer, Cham (2013). doi:10. 1007/978-3-319-03542-0_7
13. Piskac, R., Wies, T., Zufferey, D.: Automating separation logic using SMT. In: Sharygina, N., Veith, H. (eds.) CAV 2013. LNCS, vol. 8044, pp. 773–789. Springer, Heidelberg (2013). doi:10.1007/978-3-642-39799-8_54
14. Qiu, X., Garg, P., Stefanescu, A., Madhusudan, P.: Natural proofs for structure, data, and separation. In: Proceedings of PLDI 2013. ACM Press (2013)
15. Sighireanu, M., Cok, D.: Report on SL-COMP'14. JSAT **9**, 173–186 (2014)

From Hazard Analysis to Hazard Mitigation Planning: The Automated Driving Case

Mario Gleirscher$^{(\boxtimes)}$ (iD) and Stefan Kugele

Technische Universität München, Munich, Germany
{mario.gleirscher,stefan.kugele}@tum.de

Abstract. Vehicle safety depends on (a) the range of identified hazards and (b) the operational situations for which mitigations of these hazards are acceptably decreasing risk. Moreover, with an increasing degree of autonomy, risk ownership is likely to increase for vendors towards regulatory certification. Hence, highly automated vehicles have to be equipped with verified controllers capable of reliably identifying and mitigating hazards in all possible operational situations. To this end, available methods for the design and verification of automated vehicle controllers have to be supported by models for hazard analysis and mitigation.

In this paper, we describe (1) a framework for the analysis and design of *planners* (i.e., high-level controllers) capable of run-time hazard identification and mitigation, (2) an incremental algorithm for constructing *planning models* from hazard analysis, and (3) an exemplary application to the design of a *fail-operational controller* based on a given control system architecture. Our approach equips the safety engineer with concepts and steps to (2a) elaborate scenarios of endangerment and (2b) design operational strategies for mitigating such scenarios.

Keywords: Risk analysis · Hazard mitigation · Safe state · Controller design · Autonomous vehicle · Automotive system · Modeling · Planning

1 Challenges, Background, and Contribution

Automated and autonomous vehicles (AV) are responsible for avoiding mishaps and even for mitigating hazardous situations in as many *operational situations* as possible. Hence, AVs are examples of systems where the identification (2a) and mitigation (2b) of hazards have to be highly automated. This circumstance makes these systems even more complex and difficult to design. Thus, safety engineers require specific models and methods for risk analysis and mitigation.

As an example, we consider *manned road vehicles in road traffic with an autopilot (AP) feature*. Such vehicles are able to automatically conduct a ride only given some valid target and minimizing human intervention. The following *AV-level (S)afety (G)oal* specifies the problem we want to focus on in this paper:

SG: The AV can always reach a *safest possible state* σ wrt. the hazards identified and present in a specific operational situation *os*.

© Springer International Publishing AG 2017
C. Barrett et al. (Eds.): NFM 2017, LNCS 10227, pp. 310–326, 2017.
DOI: 10.1007/978-3-319-57288-8_23

Table 1. Examples of endangerment scenarios and mitigation strategies.

Scenario of endangerment		Possible mitigation strategy		
		Vehicle	Driver	RoadEnv
Vehicle	Subsystem fault	Dependability pattern	Controlled shutdown	car2x com., digital road signs
Driver	Maloperation	Passive safety	Safe reaction (if controllable)	
RoadEnv	Unforeseen obstacle	Emergency braking assistant	Braking or circumvention	Digital road signs, x2car com.
	IT attack	Security pattern	Safe reaction (if controllable)	

Background. Adopted from [4,9], we give a brief overview of terms used in this paper: We perceive a *mishap* as an event of harm, injury, damage, or loss. A *hazard* (or *hazardous state*) is an event that can lead to a mishap. We consider hazards to be factorable. Hence, a hazard can play the role of a *causal factor* of another hazard or a mishap. We denote causal factors, hazards, and mishaps— i.e., the elements of a *causal (event) chain*—by the term *safety risk* (*risk state* or *risk* for short). We perceive the part of a causal chain increasing risk as an *endangerment scenario*, and the part of a causal chain decreasing risk as a *mitigation strategy*. Table 1 exemplifies different *endangerment* scenarios and how these can be *mitigated* using corresponding strategies.

Mitigation strategies can be seen as specific *system-level safety requirements* implemented by a given control system architecture. We assume that a control system architecture consists of *features* deployed on *sensors*, *actuators*, and *software components* running on *networked computing units* (cf. Fig. 4a). By *traditional driver assistance (TDA)*, we refer to driver assistance features already in the field, e.g. *adaptive cruise control (ACC)* and *lane keeping assistance (LKA)*.

We distinguish between the domains *vehicle*, *driver*, and *road environment*. For highly and fully automated driving, not all domains have to be considered. For example, in full automation (e.g. level 5 in [12]), the vehicle has to operate under all road and environmental conditions manageable by a human driver and therefore a driver does not have to be taken into account.

Contribution. Elaborating on previous work in [5,6], we contribute

(1) a framework for modeling, analysis, and design of *planners* (i.e., high-level controllers) capable of run-time hazard identification and mitigation, and
(2) a procedure for constructing *planning models* from hazard analysis.

For this, we formalize the core engineering steps necessary for (2a) the identification and analysis of scenarios of endangerment and (2b) the design of operational mitigation strategies. Using an exemplary AV, we incrementally build up a risk structure involving three hazards in the vehicle domain, as well as several strategies to reach safe states in presence of these hazards. We discuss approaches to model reduction suited for run-time hazard analysis and mitigation planning where efficient identification of operational situations and acting therein play a crucial role.

In this paper, we discuss related work in Sect. 2, our abstraction in Sect. 3, and our modeling framework in Sect. 4. Section 5 shows a procedure for building a hazard mitigation planning model. We present an AV example in Sect. 6, discuss our approach in Sect. 7, and conclude in Sect. 8.

2   Related Work

Among the related formal methods available in robotics planning, embedded systems, and automated vehicle control, we only discuss a few more recent ones and highlight how we can improve over them.

Güdemann and Ortmeier [7] present a language for probabilistic system modeling for safety analysis. Formalized as MARKOV *decision processes (MDP)*, they propose two ways of failure mode modeling (i.e., per-time and per-demand failure modes), and two ways of deductive cause consequence reasoning (i.e., quantitative and qualitative). Their model and reasoning can extend our approach. However, our work (i) adds stronger guidelines on how to build planning models and (ii) puts hazard analysis into the context of autonomous systems and mitigation planning.

Eastwood et al. [3] present an algorithm for finding permissive robot action plans optimal w.r.t. to safety and performance. They employ *partially observable MDPs* (helpful in regarding uncertainty and robot limitations) to model robot behavior, and two abstractions from this model to capture a system's modes and hazards. Our framework uses three layers of abstraction (Σ^s, Σ^p, Σ), operational situations to capture control modes, and a structure to capture hazards. While they directly encode hazard severity for plan selection, our framework allows the planner to calculate the risk priority based on a causal event tree towards mishaps. As opposed to complete behavioral planning, our approach focuses the construction of mitigation planning models. For example, for system faults we can plan mitigations by using adaptation mechanisms of a given control system architecture.

Jha and Raman [8] discuss the synthesis of vehicle trajectories from probabilistic temporal logic assertions. Synthesized trajectories take into account perception uncertainty through approximation of sensed obstacles by combining Gaussian polytopes. In a similar context, Rizaldi and Althoff [10] formalize safe driving policies to derive safe control strategies implementing worst-case braking scenarios in autonomous driving. They apply a hybrid-trace-based formalization of physics required for model checking of recorded [10] and planned [11] strategies. [8,10,11] discuss low-level control for a specific class of driving scenarios, whereas our approach provides for (i) the investigation and combination of many related operational situations, thus, forming a more comprehensive perspective of driving safety, (ii) regarding various kinds of hazards that might play a role in high- and low-level control beyond safe and optimal trajectory planning and collision avoidance.

Wei et al. [14] describe an autonomous driving platform, capable of bringing vehicles to a safe state and stop, i.e., activating a fail-operational mode on critical failure, and a limp-home mode on less critical failure. These are mitigation strategies we can assess in our framework. Their work elaborates on designing a specific class of architectures. Additionally, we provide an approach to systematically evaluate risks and, consequently, derive an architecture design.

Babin et al. [1] propose a system reconfiguration approach developed with the Event-B method in a correct-by-construction fashion using a behavior pattern similar to our approach (particularly, Fig. 2b). Reconfiguration as one way to *mitigate* faults is discussed in this work. Wardziński [13] discusses hazard identification and mitigation for autonomous vehicles by predetermined risk assessment (i.e., with safety barriers) and dynamic risk assessment. For both, he provides argumentation patterns for creating AV safety cases. In addition to his work, the abstraction and the method we propose covers both paradigms in one framework. We provide formal notions of all core concepts.

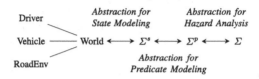

Fig. 1. Abstractions for *state* and *predicate* modeling, and for *hazard analysis*.

3   Abstraction for Run-Time Hazard Mitigation

Figure 1 depicts three *abstractions*—Σ^s, Σ^p, and Σ—for run-time hazard mitigation in AVs. The *state space* Σ^s pertains to the quantization of continuous signals from the physical *world* encompassing the *driver* (`drv`), the *vehicle* (`veh`), and the *road environment* (`renv`). For instance, the quantity *speed* is represented by the discrete state variable `veh.speed`, which in turn is used to formulate predicates to obtain the *abstract state space* Σ^p. For example, a predicate over sensor values $p($`veh.speed`, `veh.loc`, `renv.map`$)$ can encode *exitTunnel*, an invariant constraining the activity of leaving a tunnel. We describe this two-staged abstraction in more detail in [6].

Here, we will work with the *risk state space* Σ whose concepts—actions, hazard phases, their composition and ordering—are discussed below:

Actions. Let $\mathcal{A}$ be a set of actions. We abstract from *control loop behaviors* within and across operational situations by distinguishing four classes of actions: *endangerments* $\mathcal{E}$, *mitigations* $\mathcal{M}$ (see Fig. 2b), *mishaps* $\mathcal{E}_m$, and *ordinary actions* $\mathcal{A}_o$. Note that actions can take place in one or more out of the three domains, `drv`, `veh`, and `renv`, depending on the quantities they modify. We require $\mathcal{E}, \mathcal{M}, \mathcal{A}_o, \mathcal{E}_m \subset \mathcal{A}$.

Definition 1 (Hazard Phases). *Let $\mathcal{H}$ be a set of hazards. Given $h \in \mathcal{H}$, endangerment actions $e^h, e_m^h \in \mathcal{A}$, and $n_h \in \mathbb{N} \setminus \{0\}$ mitigation actions $m_j^h \in \mathcal{A}$, we define the* phases *of a hazard h as the set $P_h = \{0, e^h, e_m^h\} \cup \{m_j^h \mid j \in \mathbb{N} \setminus \{0\} \land j \leqslant n_h\}$ whose elements denote the following:*

0 : *hazard h is (inact)ive,*
e^h : *hazard h has been (act)ivated by an action e^h,*
e_m^h : *(act)ivated hazard h has contributed to a mishap by an action e_m^h, and*
m_j^h : *hazard h has been (mit)igated by an action m_j^h.*

For each hazard h, Fig. 2a depicts P_h as a transition system where $|P_h| = n_h + 3$, the indices $s, e, c, i_1, \ldots, i_n \leqslant n_h$, the state *mit* subsumes $n_h - 1$ phases, *act* subsumes phases e^h and e_m^h. For example, in the vehicle domain, m_s^h can model *degradation* transitions and m_e^h or m_c^h can model *repair* transitions.

From all the sets of hazard phases, we compose a tuple space as follows:

Definition 2 (Risk State Space). *Based on Definition 1, we define the* risk state space *Σ as the set of $|\mathcal{H}|$-tuples*

$$\{(p_{h_1}, \ldots, p_{h_{|\mathcal{H}|}}) \mid \forall i \in \{1, \ldots, |\mathcal{H}|\} : h_i \in \mathcal{H} \land p_{h_i} \in P_{h_i}\}.$$

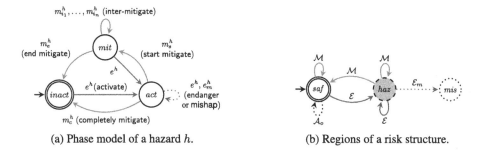

(a) Phase model of a hazard h.   (b) Regions of a risk structure.

Fig. 2. Core concepts for building a risk state space Σ.

We call any subset of Σ a *region*. Let $\sigma, \sigma' \in \Sigma$ with $\sigma = (p_{h_1}, \ldots, p_{h_{|\mathcal{H}|}})$ and $\sigma' = (p'_{h_1}, \ldots, p'_{h_{|\mathcal{H}|}})$. To quantify risk in *scenarios of endangerment* and *mitigation strategies* (Table 1), we define a partial order over Σ:

Definition 3 (Mitigation Order). *Let P_h be a set of phases for hazard h (Definition 1) and $\prec_h = \{(e^h, 0), (e^h, m_j^h), (m_j^h, 0), (e_m^h, e^h) \mid m_j^h \in P_h\}$. By the reflexive transitive closure[1] $\preceq_h = \{(p, p) \mid p \in P_h\} \cup \bigcup_{n \geqslant 1} \prec_h^n$, we define the* mitigation order *$\preceq_m \subseteq \Sigma \times \Sigma$, for states $\sigma, \sigma' \in \Sigma$, as follows:*

$$\sigma \preceq_m \sigma' \Leftrightarrow \forall i \in \{1, \ldots, |\mathcal{H}|\} : p_{h_i} \preceq_h p'_{h_i}.$$

Intuitively, $\sigma \prec_m \sigma'$ denotes "σ' is better or further in mitigation than σ."[2]

---

[1] Here, for a relation R, R^n represents the composition of relations.
[2] We use the convention $\sigma \prec_m \sigma' \equiv \sigma \preceq_m \sigma' \land \sigma \neq \sigma'$.

4   Concepts for Run-Time Hazard Mitigation

In this section, we explain the core concepts of deriving a *risk structure* for a specific *operational situation*. Using the risk state space Σ and actions $\mathcal{A}$, we define the notions of *risk structure*, *risk region*, and *operational situation*:

Definition 4 (Risk Structure). *A risk structure is a weighted labeled transition system $(\Sigma, \mathcal{A}, \Delta, \mathcal{W})$ with*

- *a set Σ called the* risk state space *(Definition 2),*
- *a set $\mathcal{A}$ of actions used as transition labels,*
- *a relation $\Delta \subseteq \Sigma \times \mathcal{A} \times \Sigma$ called* labeled transition relation, *and*
- *a set $\mathcal{W}$ of partial functions $w : (\Sigma \cup \mathcal{A} \cup \Delta) \to \mathbb{W}_w$ called* weights *where the set $\mathbb{W}_w$ can be, e.g. $\mathbb{N}, \mathbb{R}, [0, 1],$ or $\{m, c, f\}$.*[3]

To capture the notions of endangerment scenario and mitigation strategy (Table 1) based on Δ, we consider paths and strategies:

Definition 5 (Paths, Strategies, and Reachability). *By convention, we write $\sigma \xrightarrow{a} \sigma'$ for $(\sigma, a, \sigma') \in \Delta$. Then, for $n, l \in \mathbb{N} \setminus \{0\}$, a path is a sequence $\sigma_0 \xrightarrow{a_0} \ldots \sigma_{n-1} \xrightarrow{a_{n-1}} \sigma_n$. By Δ^l we denote the set of all paths of length l and by $\Delta^\infty = \bigcup_{l>0} \Delta^l$ all paths over Δ. Furthermore, we call a set $S \subset \Delta^\infty$ a strategy. By $\mathsf{reach}_\Delta : \Sigma \to 2^\Sigma$ with $\mathsf{reach}_\Delta(\sigma) = \{\sigma\} \cup \{\sigma' \in \Sigma \mid \exists \sigma \xrightarrow{a} \ldots \xrightarrow{a'} \sigma' \in \Delta^\infty\}$, we denote the set of states reachable in Δ from a state σ.*

Endangerments. We consider an action $a \in \mathcal{A}$ as an *endangerment*, i.e., $a \in \mathcal{E}$, if $\sigma \succ_m \sigma'$ for a transition $(\sigma, a, \sigma') \in \Delta$. The class $\mathcal{E}$ models steps of endangerment scenarios. For example, a can stem from faults in `drv`, `veh`, and `renv`.

Mitigations. We consider an action $a \in \mathcal{A}$ as a *mitigation*, i.e., $a \in \mathcal{M}$, if $\sigma \prec_m \sigma'$ for a transition $(\sigma, a, \sigma') \in \Delta$. The class $\mathcal{M}$ models steps of mitigation strategies. One objective of a good mitigation strategy is to achieve a *stable safe state*.

Operational Situations. States and regions in Σ both correspond to subsets of Σ^s (Sect. 3). To limit the scope of a risk analysis, we use an *operational situation* which combines an *initial region* with a *(reasonably weak) invariant* holding along the driving scenarios in a specific road environment.

Definition 6 (Operational Situation). *An operational situation is a tuple $(\Sigma_0, \{\sigma \in \Sigma^s \mid p(\sigma)\})$ where $\Sigma_0 \subseteq \Sigma$ and p is an invariant over Σ^s including all representations of Σ_0 in Σ^s. Let $\mathcal{O}$ be the set of all operational situations.*

Below, we will work with a risk structure $\mathfrak{R}_{os} = (\Sigma, \mathcal{A}, \Delta, \mathcal{W})$ and assume a fixed operational situation $os \in \mathcal{O}$ associated with $\mathfrak{R}_{os}$. Hence, we use $\mathfrak{R}$ solely.

---

[3] (m)arginal, (c)ritical, (f)atal; for other examples of severity scales, see [4].

Risk Regions. We consider specific subsets of Σ called *risk regions*, particularly, the *safe region saf*, the *hazardous region haz*, and the *mishap region mis* (see Fig. 2b). Safety engineers aim at the design of mitigations which (i) avoid *mis* and (ii) react to endangerments as early and effectively as possible. Then, $\mathcal{E}_m$ reduces to unavoidable actions from so-called *near-mishaps* still in *haz* towards *mis*. For example, we consider a successfully deployed airbag to be in $\mathcal{M}$ such that *mis* is not reached in such an accident (more in Sect. 7).

Our definitions of risk regions depend on $\mathfrak{R}$: First, $mis = \{(p_{h_1}, \ldots, p_{h_{|\mathcal{H}|}}) \in \Sigma \mid \exists i \in \{1, \ldots, |\mathcal{H}|\} \colon p_{h_i} = e_m^{h_i}\}$. We require mishaps to be *final*, i.e., $\forall \sigma \in mis \colon$ $\mathsf{reach}_\Delta(\sigma) = \{\sigma\}$. Second, *saf* and *haz* vary with a given operational situation. Moreover, they can be defined based on, e.g. weights and equivalences. However, $(0, \ldots, 0) \in saf$ and, for an *os*, we start in the safe region iff $\Sigma_0 \subseteq saf$.

Weights. By associating *weights* with elements of $\mathfrak{R}$, we quantify further details on the physical phenomena of the controlled process relevant for risk analysis.

For example, given $\delta = (\sigma, e^h, \sigma') \in \Delta$ with $e^h \in \mathcal{E}$, the *probability of endangerment* $\mathsf{pr}(\delta) \in [0, 1]$ yields the probability that hazard h gets activated in σ' by performing e^h in σ. Furthermore, given $\delta = (\sigma, m_j^h, \sigma') \in \Delta$ with $m_j^h \in \mathcal{M}$,

- the *probability of mitigation* $\mathsf{pr}(\delta) \in [0, 1]$ yields the probability that hazard h gets mitigated in σ' by performing m_j^h in σ.
- the *cost of mitigation* $\mathsf{cs}(\delta) \in \mathbb{N}$ yields the potential effort (i.e., time, energy, other resources) of performing the mitigation m_j^h.

For any mishap $\sigma \in mis$, $\mathsf{sv}(\sigma) \in \{m, c, f\}$ specifies its *severity*. Depending on the abstraction, we can use qualitative (as shown above) or quantitative scales for sv and cs. Anyway, we assume to have operators for sv and cs, e.g. see Fig. 3a.

Weights are typically calculated from measurements of the controlled process. For example, the estimation of $\mathsf{pr}(\sigma, m_j^h, \sigma')$ might be result of a *controllability analysis* of m_j^h in σ (of an operational situation). Moreover, further quantities (e.g. risk priority) might be (i) calculated from weights, (ii) be propagated along Δ, and (iii) lead to an update of weights.

Risk Priority. Given $\sigma \in \Sigma, mis' \subseteq mis$, and a function $\mathsf{rp} : \Sigma \to \{m, c, f\}$, we can compute the *minimum partial risk priority*

$$\mathsf{rp}(\sigma) = \mathsf{Pr}(\sigma \to \Diamond mis') \cdot_{\mathsf{sv}} \min\{\sigma' \in (mis' \cap \mathsf{reach}_\Delta(\sigma)) \mid \mathsf{sv}(\sigma')\} \qquad (1)$$

where $\mathsf{Pr}(\sigma \to \Diamond mis') \in [0, 1]$ denotes the probability[4] that from σ some mishap $\sigma' \in mis'$ is eventually ($\Diamond$) reached in $\mathfrak{R}$. This definition implements a traditional measure of risk analysis (see, e.g. [4]), referring to the *minimum negative outcome* (i.e., damage, injury, harm, loss) possibly reachable from σ in a specific operational situation $os \in \mathcal{O}$. Note that for $\sigma \in mis$, $\mathsf{rp}(\sigma) = \mathsf{sv}(\sigma)$.

---

[4] See, e.g. [2] for details about probabilistic temporal logic and reasoning.

Equivalences Over Σ. For simplification of complex risk structures $\mathfrak{R}$, we can construct equivalence classes over states. From the structure of states in Σ^s, the dynamics in Σ^s, and the elements of the control system architecture (Sect. 1), we give a brief informal overview of equivalences over Σ to be considered:

We speak of *feature equivalence*, $\sigma \approx_f \sigma'$, iff both, σ and σ' map to the same set of *active features* of the control system, i.e., *in-the-loop* no matter whether they are fully operational, faulty, or degraded. Note that out-of-the-loop features can be faulty, deactivated, or in standby mode. Next, we speak of *degradation equivalence*, $\sigma \approx_d \sigma'$, iff $\sigma \approx_f \sigma'$ and both states share the same set of *degraded features*. Furthermore, we speak of *hazard (or fault) equivalence*, $\sigma \approx_h \sigma'$, iff $\forall i \in \{1, \ldots, |\mathcal{H}|\} : p_{h_i} \in P_{h_i} \setminus \{0\} \Leftrightarrow p'_{h_i} \in P_{h_i} \setminus \{0\}$, and, particularly, of *mishap equivalence*, $\sigma \approx_{h_m} \sigma'$, iff $\forall i \in \{1, \ldots, |\mathcal{H}|\} : p_{h_i} = e_m^{h_i} \Leftrightarrow p'_{h_i} = e_m^{h_i}$. Based on $\approx_h$, we finally define:

Definition 7 (Mitigation Equivalence). *Based on Definition 3, two states* $\sigma, \sigma' \in \Sigma$ *are mitigation equivalent, written* $\sigma \approx_m \sigma'$, *iff*

$$\sigma \approx_h \sigma' \wedge \forall i \in \{1, \ldots, |\mathcal{H}|\} : p_{h_i} \succ_h e^{h_i} \Leftrightarrow p'_{h_i} \succ_h e^{h_i}.$$

5 Construction of Risk Structures

In this section, we describe an incremental and forward[5] reasoning approach to building a risk structure $\mathfrak{R}$.

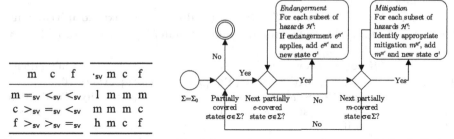

(a) The operators $=_{sv}, <_{sv}, >_{sv}$ and $\cdot_{sv}$ where $\geqslant_{sv} \equiv =_{sv} \wedge >_{sv}$.

(b) Scheme for incremental construction of $\mathfrak{R}$ by constructRS.

Fig. 3. Operators and scheme

Identification of Hazards. Throughout the construction of $\mathfrak{R}$, we assume to have a procedure hazId for the identification of a set of hazards $\mathcal{H}$ based on a fixed control loop design $\mathcal{L}$ of a class of AVs and their environments, and a fixed set $\mathcal{O}' \subset \mathcal{O}$ of operational situations (Definition 6). Failure mode effects and fault-tree analysis (see, e.g. [4]) incorporate widely practiced schemes for hazId.

---

[5] For generation of $\mathfrak{R}$, backward reasoning is the alternative not shown here.

Building the Risk Structure. Figure 3b shows the main steps of a procedure constructRS which, given a set $\mathcal{H}$ and after termination, returns all elements of a *complete* risk structure $\mathfrak{R}$. Here, completeness is relative to $\mathcal{H}$ and means that $\mathfrak{R}$ can no more be extended by (i) states which are reachable by existing actions in $\mathcal{A}$, (ii) actions which allow reaching non-visited states in Σ, (iii) transitions in Δ which are technically possible and probable, and (iv) further knowledge by extending the domains of weights. Based on Fig. 3b, Algorithm 1 refines constructRS for a control loop $\mathcal{L}$ and an operational situation $os \in \mathcal{O}'$.

Algorithm 1. constructRS($\mathcal{L}, os$)

1: $\Sigma = \Sigma_0, \forall \sigma \in \Sigma_0 : \mathsf{rv}_m(\sigma) = \mathsf{rv}_e(\sigma) = \emptyset$
2: **while** $\mathcal{H} = \mathsf{hazld}(\mathcal{L}, os)$ and $\exists \sigma \in \Sigma \setminus mis : \mathcal{H} \setminus (\mathsf{rv}_e(\sigma) \cup \mathsf{rv}_m(\sigma)) \neq \emptyset$ **do**
3:    **for all** $\sigma \in \Sigma \setminus mis$ and $\mathcal{H}' \subseteq \mathcal{H} \setminus \mathsf{rv}_e(\sigma)$ **do**   ▷ **extend endangerments**
4:       **if** $(\sigma', e_j^{\mathcal{H}'}) \leftarrow \mathsf{activate}(\sigma, \mathcal{H}')$ **then** ▷ state/j^{th} action estab. $\mathcal{H}'$ or mishap
5:          $\delta \leftarrow (\sigma, e_j^{\mathcal{H}'}, \sigma')$
6:          **if** $\mathsf{poss}(\delta)$ **then**   ▷ add endangerment?
7:            $(\Sigma, \mathcal{E}, \Delta, \mathsf{rv}_e(\sigma')) \leftarrow (\Sigma \cup \{\sigma'\}, \mathcal{E} \cup \{e_j^{\mathcal{H}'}\}, \Delta \cup \{\delta\}, \emptyset)$
8:            **if** $\sigma' \in mis$ **then**
9:                $\mathsf{sv}(\sigma') \leftarrow \mathsf{estimate}_{\mathcal{L}, os}(sv, \sigma')$ ▷ severity of mishap
10:            **end if**
11:            $\mathsf{pr}(\delta) \leftarrow \mathsf{estimate}_{\mathcal{L}, os}(pr, \delta)$ ▷ probability of endangerment
12:          **end if**
13:       **else**   ▷ activate returns empty tuple
14:          $\mathsf{rv}_e(\sigma) \leftarrow \mathsf{rv}_e(\sigma) \cup \mathcal{H}'$ ▷ i.e., $\mathcal{H}'$ activated and mishap added
15:       **end if**
16:    **end for**
17:    **for all** $\sigma \in \Sigma \setminus mis$ and $\mathcal{H}' \subseteq \mathcal{H} \setminus \mathsf{rv}_m(\sigma)$ **do**   ▷ **extend mitigations**
18:       **if** $(\sigma', m_j^{\mathcal{H}'}) \leftarrow \mathsf{mitigate}(\sigma, \mathcal{H}')$ **then**   ▷ state/j^{th} action mitig. $\mathcal{H}'$ from σ
19:          $\delta \leftarrow (\sigma, m_j^{\mathcal{H}'}, \sigma')$
20:          **if** $\mathsf{poss}(\delta)$ **then**   ▷ add mitigation?
21:            $(\Sigma, \mathcal{M}, \Delta, \mathsf{rv}_m(\sigma')) \leftarrow (\Sigma \cup \{\sigma'\}, \mathcal{M} \cup \{m_j^{\mathcal{H}'}\}, \Delta \cup \{\delta\}, \emptyset)$
22:            $\mathsf{pr}(\delta) \leftarrow \mathsf{estimate}_{\mathcal{L}, os}(pr, \delta)$ ▷ probability of mitigation
23:            $\mathsf{cs}(\delta) \leftarrow \mathsf{estimate}_{\mathcal{L}, os}(cs, \delta)$ ▷ cost of mitigation
24:          **end if**
25:       **else**   ▷ mitigate returns empty tuple
26:          $\mathsf{rv}_m(\sigma) \leftarrow \mathsf{rv}_m(\sigma) \cup \mathcal{H}'$ ▷ i.e., all options for $\mathcal{H}'$ are checked
27:       **end if**
28:    **end for**
29:    $\Sigma \leftarrow \Sigma \setminus \{\sigma \in \Sigma \mid \sigma \notin \bigcup_{\sigma_0 \in \Sigma_0} \mathsf{reach}_\Delta(\sigma_0)\}$ ▷ removing unreachable states
30:    $\ldots$ ▷ further simplifications
31: **end while**
32: **return** $(\Sigma, \mathcal{E} \cup \mathcal{M}, \Delta, \{\mathsf{sv}, \mathsf{pr}, \mathsf{cs}\})$

The **while-loop** (cf. line 2) accounts for the alternation between adding endangerments and mitigations. By using the maps rv_e and rv_m (cf. lines 2, 3, 14, 17, 26), the algorithm keeps track of the *endangerment-* and *mitigation-*coverage of visited states, i.e., for which hazards σ has already been visited.

We assume to have (i) a function $\mathsf{estimate}_{\mathcal{L},os}$ (cf. lines 9, 11, 22, 23) which acts as an oracle for weights (Sect. 4) depending on $(\mathcal{L}, os)$, and (ii) a function poss (cf. lines 6, 20) which acts as an oracle for determining the technical possibility of newly identified transitions.

The first **for-loop** checks for the addition of new transitions to Δ (cf. line 7). The transition constructor $\mathsf{activate}$ returns a state with the given hazard or mishap activated (i.e., phases e^h or e_m^h). Note that $\mathsf{activate}$ can generate $\sigma' \in mis$ reachable via $e_m^{\mathcal{H}'} \in \mathcal{E}_m$.

The second **for-loop** checks for the addition of new transitions to Δ (cf. line 21). The transition constructor $\mathsf{mitigate}$ returns a state with the given hazards $\mathcal{H}'$ mitigated to a new phase $m_{h_i}^h \in P_h$ for each $h \in \mathcal{H}'$.

Note that none of the constructors is idempotent, $\mathsf{mitigate}$ can construct several mitigation phases for each hazard (cf. lines 18, 26) and $\mathsf{activate}$ can construct two activation phases, e^h and e_m^h, both with the corresponding actions (cf. lines 4, 14).

Model Reduction. To keep reasoning efficient, we have to apply reachability-preserving simplifications to $\mathfrak{R}$ (cf. lines 29f), e.g. equivalences such as in Definition 7. The mitigation order (Definition 3) helps in reducing the state space and in merging actions modifying phases of the same hazards (i.e., by hazard equivalence).

Abstraction from Control System Architecture. In both stages of Algorithm 1, we need to analyze the given or envisaged architecture and to identify state variables, e.g. for software modules, at an appropriate level of granularity.

In the endangerment stage (lines 3ff), we can perform dependability analyses to identify events that can activate causal factors. Off-line, we then design specific measures to reach the safe region again, and, on-line, we design generic measures to be refined at run-time.

Moreover, the mitigation stage (lines 17ff) helps to revise a control system architecture, e.g. by adding redundant execution units and degradation paths. Moreover, we can pursue off-line synthesis of respective parts of the control system architecture.

Hazard Mitigation Planning. First, hazId is hybrid in the sense that it (i) performs the sensing of already known endangerment scenarios (e.g. near-collision detection, component fault diagnosis) *on-line*, and (ii) allows the addition of new scenarios from *off-line* hazard analysis.

Second, a simple *planner* would continuously perform shortest weighted path search in $\mathfrak{R}$ to keep a list of all available lowest-risk mitigation paths (Definition 5) and coordinate optimized lower-level controllers.

Based on these two steps, we assume $\mathfrak{R}$ to be continuously updated according to the available information (i.e., adding or modifying endangerments and mitigations according to known scenarios). It is important to have powerful and precise update mechanisms, highly responsive actuation, and short control loop delays. Main issues of signal processing are briefly mentioned in Sect. 7.

The notion of *safest possible state* (**SG**, Sect. 1) is governed by the accuracy of Σ^s (Sect. 3), the completeness of the results of hazId, and the exhaustiveness of $\mathfrak{R}$ for a fixed setting $\mathcal{L}, os$. According to Definition 3, for a pair $(\sigma, \sigma') \in \Sigma \times \Sigma$, we might say that σ' is the *safest possible state* iff we have

$$\nexists \sigma'' \in \mathsf{reach}_{\Delta_\mathcal{M}}(\sigma) \colon \sigma' \prec_m \sigma'' \tag{2}$$

where $\Delta_\mathcal{M} = \Delta \setminus \{(\sigma_1, a, \sigma_2) \in \Sigma \mid a \in \mathcal{E})\}$. Any controller for **SG** would have to find and completely conduct a shortest plan for (σ, σ') to reach σ'.

6   Example: Fail-Operational Driver Assistance

Elaborating on an example in [6], we apply our framework and algorithm to hazard analysis and elaboration of mitigation strategies. We use the abbreviations introduced in Sect. 1.

Identifying an Operational Situation. We consider the situation $os \in \mathcal{O}$: "AV is taking an exit in a tunnel, at a speed between 30 and 90 km/h, with the driver being properly seated, and the next road segments contain a crossing." Figure 4b depicts the corresponding street segment.

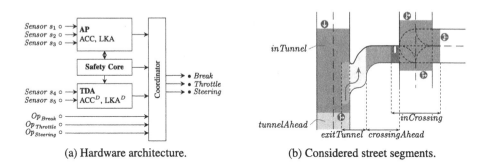

(a) Hardware architecture.   (b) Considered street segments.

Fig. 4. Two cutouts of the road vehicle domain.

Modeling the Road Vehicle Domain. Figure 4a shows a simplified control system architecture used for driver assistance systems. We model the relevant state information according to the abstractions described in Sect. 3. State variables commonly used for road vehicles are listed in Table 2. For Σ^s, we assume to have the variables[6] (prefixed with their domains, in parentheses their types):

---

[6] Variable types and usage depend on the AV sensors and car2X services through which they are measured. We assume individual error estimators for all variables.

Table 2. Exemplary state variables of the different domains.

Domain	State variables	Abbreviation
Driver	Physical presence, consciousness, vigilance, ...	`drv`
Vehicle	Speed, loc(ation), fault conditions, ...	`veh`
RoadEnv	Daylight, weather, traffic, road, ...	`renv`

`veh.loc` (coordinate), `veh.speedvec` (vector of floats), `renv.map` (street map[7]), and `drv.pos` (enumeration). `veh` denotes all variables of this domain. For Σ^p, we identify the following predicates[8]:

$$exitTunnel \equiv \texttt{veh.route} \subset \texttt{renv.map} \cap (P_{\text{exit}} \cup P_{\text{tunnel}})$$
$$crossingAhead \equiv \texttt{veh.route} \cap (\texttt{renv.map} \cap P_{\text{crossing}}) \neq \emptyset$$
$$drvSeated \equiv \texttt{drv.pos} = \text{seated}$$

Furthermore, we use unspecified predicates:

$$inTunnel \equiv p_4(\texttt{veh.loc}, \texttt{renv.map}) \qquad A \equiv p_5(\texttt{veh.faults})$$
$$L \equiv p_6(\texttt{veh.faults}) \qquad R \equiv p_7(\texttt{drv.vigilance})$$
$$inCrossing \equiv p_x(\texttt{veh.loc}, \texttt{renv.map}) \quad tunnelAhead \equiv p_y(\texttt{veh.loc}, \texttt{renv.map})$$

The invariant for os is $p_{os} \equiv exitTunnel \wedge drvSeated \wedge crossingAhead$. Note that the AP is active in the initial state σ_0 associated with os.

Notation. In the following (Figs. 5a, b and 6), for each state, H denotes that the hazard H is active (phase e^H), $\underline{H}$ that H contributed to a mishap (phase e_m^H, only in Table 3), and $\overline{H_i}$ that its ith mitigation phase is active (phase m_i^H). We do not indicate hazards which are in phase 0.

Incremental Forward Construction of the Risk Structure. Refining the regions *haz* and *saf* (Fig. 2b), we construct $\mathfrak{R}$ from three hazards A, L, and R identified by `hazId` (Sect. 5). Table 3 sketches the construction of the first and second increments towards $\mathfrak{R}_2$, including the events $A \equiv$ "AP sensor s_1 fault" and $L \equiv$ "TDA LKA^D software fault."

Figure 5a shows Δ for $\mathfrak{R}_2$. According to Algorithm 1, we try to add the fault condition L to σ_0 and other states in $\mathfrak{R}_1$ (i.e., black states in Fig. 5a). Based on the action f^L, this step yields the states $L, \overline{A}_1 L$, and AL. Then, a mitigation step yields the states $\overline{L}_1$ and $\overline{AL}_1$ and, finally, another step of endangerment analysis based on the action f^A yields $A\overline{L}_1$.

---

[7] With, e.g. topological coordinate system, information about tunneled parts.

[8] Here, P_x refers to a pattern for the street map element class x which acts like a filter on the street map data type. For sake of brevity, we omit details of sensor fusion and street map calculations required for evaluating these predicates.

Table 3. Model after two increments ($\mathfrak{R}_2$). $\|_t$ denotes true parallelism, ; concatenation.

1+2 Description	Model Increment
Σ^s Introduce faults (e.g. from fault model)	`veh.faults`
$\mathcal{H}$ AP sensor s_1 fault	$A \equiv p_5(\texttt{veh.faults})$
$\mathcal{H}$ TDA LKA^D software fault	$L \equiv p_6(\texttt{veh.faults})$
Σ End. phases: Comb. of A and L	$AL \equiv A \wedge L$, $\overline{A}_1 L \equiv \overline{A}_1 \wedge L$
$\overline{A}_1 L \dots$ "LKA^D faulty" $\wedge$ "TDA active" $\wedge$ "AP out of the loop"	
$\mathcal{E}$ Actions establishing A and L (e.g. from architecture analysis)	f^A, f^L $\qquad\qquad \mathcal{E} = \{f^A, f^L\}$
$\mathcal{W}$ Probability of endangerment	e.g. $\mathsf{pr}(f^A) := .01$, $\mathsf{pr}(f^L) := .02$
Severity $\quad\quad AL \dots$ "high-speed collision"	$\underline{AL} \in mis$, $\mathsf{sv}(\underline{AL}) = f$
$\mathcal{M}$ $m_1^A \dots$ "AP fail-op. by degrad. to TDA"	$m_1^A \equiv fo_{TDA}$
$m_2^A \dots$ "deact. ACC" $\|_t$ "driver in loop"	$m_2^A \equiv o\!f\!f_{ACC^D} \|_t on_{Drv}$
$m_3^A \dots$ "AP fail-silent"	$m_3^A \equiv fs_{AP} \|_t on_{Drv}$
$m_1^L \dots$ "TDA fail-silent and warn"	$m_1^L \equiv fs_{L2}; warn_{L2}$
$m_2^L \dots$ "TDA total fail-silent" $\|_t$ "immediate handover to driver"	$m_2^L \equiv fs_* \|_t on_{Drv}$, $m_3^L \equiv m_4^L \equiv m_2^L$
Σ Mitigation phases: $\overline{A}_1 \dots$ "s_1 fault" $\wedge$ "TDA active,"	
$\overline{A}_2 \dots$ "s_1 fault" $\wedge$ "handed to driver" $\wedge$ "TDA active"	
$\overline{A}_3 \dots$ "s_1 fault" $\wedge$ "handed to driver" $\wedge$ "AP out of the loop"	
$\overline{L}_1 \dots$ "TDA out of the loop" $\wedge$ "driver warned"	
$\overline{A}_1 \overline{L}_1 \dots$ "AP and TDA out of the loop" $\wedge$ "handed to driver"	
$\mathcal{W}$ Probability of mitigation	e.g. $\mathsf{pr}(m_3^A) = .50$
Cost of mitigation	e.g. $\mathsf{cs}(m_3^A) = 3$
$\mathfrak{R}$ Simplifications: e.g. $\overline{A}_2 \approx_m \overline{A}_3$ (cf. Definition 7)	

Risk Priority Estimation. From the state $\underline{AL}$ with $\mathsf{sv}(\underline{AL}) = f$, we can derive, e.g. $\mathsf{rp}(\overline{A}_1)$ according to Eq. (1). We can as well derive $\mathsf{rp}(\overline{A}_2) = \mathsf{rp}(\overline{A}_3) = m$ because reaching $\underline{AL}$ by driving assistance control is no more possible.

Equivalences and Model Reduction. In Fig. 5a, for example,

- $\overline{A}_2 \approx_m \overline{A}_3$ because in both states A is mitigated and other hazards are inactive (0, cf. Definition 7),
- $\overline{A}_1 \approx_f \sigma_0$ because in $\overline{A}_1$ the degraded variants of LKA and ACC, i.e., LKA^D and ACC^D, are in the loop,
- $\overline{A}_1 \approx_d \overline{A}_1 L$ because in both states LKA^D and ACC^D are in the loop,
- $\overline{A}_1 L \approx_f AL$ because in both states, LKA and ACC are in the loop, and
- $\overline{A}_1 L \not\approx_h AL$ because ACC (part of AP) is faulty and ACC^D (part of TDA) is fully operational.

Simplifications can be derived from Fig. 5a, where we might (i) merge two states $(\sigma_1, \sigma_2) \in \approx_d$ if $\mathsf{rp}(\sigma_1) = \mathsf{rp}(\sigma_2)$, or (ii) merge two consecutive states on a "safe" mitigation path, e.g. from any $\sigma \in haz$ to σ_0 if actions such as *limp-home*, *shutdown*, and *repair* are feasible from σ.

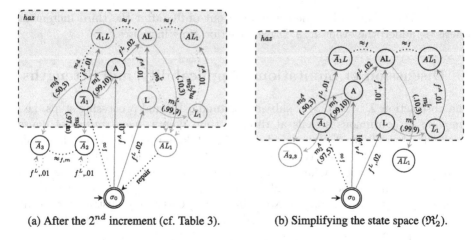

(a) After the 2nd increment (cf. Table 3).   (b) Simplifying the state space ($\mathfrak{R}'_2$).

Fig. 5. Risk structure $\mathfrak{R}_2$ and its simplification $\mathfrak{R}'_2$.

Table 4. Adding endangerments for the third increment ($\mathfrak{R}_3$).

3	Description	Model increment
$\mathcal{H}$	Driver reaction time increases	$R \equiv p_7(\texttt{drv.vigilance})$
Σ	States	$R, LR, AR, ALR, \overline{A}_1R, \overline{A}_1LR, A\overline{L}_1R, \overline{L}_1R$
$\mathcal{E}$	Action e^R ... "driver looks sidewards" $\|_t$ "hands go off steering wheel"	$e^R \qquad \mathcal{E} = \{f^A, f^L, e^R\}$
$\mathcal{M}$		$m_3^L \equiv warn \|_t normalStop$

Figure 5b shows a simplification $\mathfrak{R}'_2$ of $\mathfrak{R}_2$. We omit irrelevant transitions (f^L) and collapse the mitigation-equivalent ($\approx_m$) states $\overline{A}_2$ and $\overline{A}_3$. Consequently, with the states $\overline{A}_{2,3}$ and $\overline{AL}_1$ we get a refinement of saf. According to Eq. (2), $\overline{A}_2$ is a *safest possible state* reachable from A.

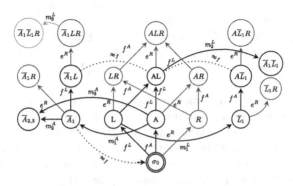

Fig. 6. Risk structure after adding endangerments (in red) for the 3rd increment (weights not shown, cf. Table 4). (Color figure online)

Next, Table 4 and Fig. 6 describe a cut-out of $\mathfrak{R}_3$ after the third increment where we added the event $R \equiv$ "Driver reaction time increases."

7   Discussion of Limitations, Applicability, and Strengths

The abstraction Σ^s (Sect. 3) is subject to standard signal processing steps, i.e., *sampling* of continuous signals at discrete time points, *quantization* of dense domains to form finite domains, and *clamping* of domains. We assume all signals to be sampled faster then their respective NYQUIST period, sufficiently small quantums, and sufficiently large ranges of data types. Furthermore, we expect a mitigation planner to be fast enough (sufficiently low latency) to provide outputs for effective and optimal control. Note that the risk structure abstracts from the low-level parameters necessary for actual control of mitigations which takes place at the level of Σ^s.

The treatment of these issues will determine how accurate mitigations can take place at the right time and duration. In addition, we might consider *higher-order mitigations* to handle adverse impacts of first-order mitigations. However, such impacts have to be identified as hazards to get recognized in $\mathfrak{R}$.

Elaborating on risk regions (Sect. 4), *mis* represents mitigation-less harmful states, however, *haz* includes all states where mitigations are feasible. Consequently, we allow "bad things to happen" as long as we have *partial mitigations*, e.g. an airbag would prevent from reaching *mis* at a certain probability.

8   Conclusion and Future Work

We presented *risk structures* as a model to design high-level controllers capable of run-time hazard mitigation, i.e., of maintaining or reaching the safest states in a given operational situation. We sketched an incremental approach to develop mitigation strategies. Safety measures are a combination of reducing or eliminating endangerments with constructing or strengthening mitigations. Risk structures can help to derive safety requirements for a control system architecture. Moreover, they can lay a basis for the evaluation, choice, and combination of mitigation strategies. Our example highlights challenges to tackle in hazard mitigation of fail-operational automated driving. Finally, we indicate how several formalisms—temporal specification, predicate abstraction, and transition systems—can coherently aid in hazard mitigation planning.

Future Work. Based on risk structures, we aim to *evaluate* criteria such as (i) time, energy, and cost of mitigations, (ii) the role of human intervention, (iii) resilience to change of operational situations, (iv) control system simplicity.

In the next steps, we want to efficiently *automate* the derivation of acceptable mitigation strategies, and synthesize feasible and affordable mitigation strategies. Based on weights, we can define desirable properties of mitigation strategies implemented in $\mathfrak{R}$, e.g. monotonicity.

Definition 8 (Mitigation Monotonicity). *Let $S \subset \Delta^\infty$ be a strategy (Definition 5) and $n \in \mathbb{N} \setminus \{0\}$. We call S mitigation monotonous iff for each path $\sigma_0 \xrightarrow{a_0} \ldots \xrightarrow{a_{n-1}} \sigma_n \in S \colon \forall i \in \{0, \ldots, n-1\} \colon \mathsf{rp}(\sigma_i) \geqslant_{\mathsf{sv}} \mathsf{rp}(\sigma_{i+1})$.*

Intuitively, during planning we seek mitigation paths containing only endangerments, if any, which do not increase risk priority. This might, however, be a definition to be relaxed for practical use by, e.g. allowing rp-distances.

Given that we *use our algorithm off-line*, it is important to make the poss and estimate$_{\mathcal{L},os}$ steps in Algorithm 1 interactive for the safety engineer. Moreover, instead of elaborating *os*-specific risk structures off-line, we aim at using our algorithm to generate such structures on-line given a specific operational situation, and combine this with a transition system switching between operational situations. Given that we *use our algorithm on-line*, it is important to develop simplification rules to be applied to Σ based on the equivalences in Sect. 4.

We plan to evaluate our results in the automotive industry whose aims include checking whether fail-operational extensions of given in-vehicle network architectures for automated driving can be made acceptably safe.

Finally, for a *regulatory agency* to apply our approach to AV, we have to show (i) our approach using a large example involving several operational situations, (ii) how our abstraction can be verified, and (iii) that the limits of controllers do not constrain our approach to achieve safe stable control loops.

Acknowledgments. We are grateful to Maximilian Junker for a thorough review of this work. Moreover, we thank our project partners from the German automotive industry for inspiring discussions and providing a highly innovative practical context for our research. Furthermore, we thank our peer reviewers for suggestions on the use of risk structures, signal processing, and regulatory certification.

References

1. Babin, G., Ait-Ameur, Y., Pantel, M.: Correct instantiation of a system reconfiguration pattern: a proof and refinement-based approach. In: 17th International Symposium on High Assurance Systems Engineering (HASE), pp. 31–38, January 2016
2. Baier, C., Katoen, J.P.: Principles of Model Checking. MIT Press, Cambridge (2008)
3. Eastwood, R., Alexander, R., Kelly, T.: Safe multi-objective planning with a posteriori preferences. In: 17th International Symposium on High Assurance Systems Engineering (HASE), pp. 78–85, January 2016
4. Ericson, C.A.: Hazard Analysis Techniques for System Safety, 2nd edn. Wiley, Hoboken (2015)
5. Gleirscher, M., Kugele, S.: Reaching safe states in autonomous road vehicles. In: 35th Annual International Conference on Computer Safety, Reliability and Security (SAFECOMP). HAL, September 2016. https://hal.laas.fr/hal-01370229. extended abstract
6. Gleirscher, M., Kugele, S.: Defining risk states in autonomous road vehicles. In: IEEE 18th International Symposium on High Assurance Systems Engineering (HASE), Singapore, January 2017

7. Güdemann, M., Ortmeier, F.: A framework for qualitative and quantitative formal model-based safety analysis. In: IEEE 12th International Symposium on High Assurance Systems Engineering (HASE), pp. 132–141, November 2010

8. Jha, S., Raman, V.: Automated synthesis of safe autonomous vehicle control under perception uncertainty. In: Rayadurgam, S., Tkachuk, O. (eds.) NFM 2016. LNCS, vol. 9690, pp. 117–132. Springer, Cham (2016). doi:10.1007/978-3-319-40648-0_10

9. Leveson, N.G.: Engineering a Safer World: Systems Thinking Applied to Safety. Engineering Systems. MIT Press, Cambridge (2012)

10. Rizaldi, A., Althoff, M.: Formalising traffic rules for accountability of autonomous vehicles. In: IEEE 18th International Conference on Intelligent Transportation Systems, pp. 1658–1665, September 2015

11. Rizaldi, A., Immler, F., Althoff, M.: A formally verified checker of the safe distance traffic rules for autonomous vehicles. In: Rayadurgam, S., Tkachuk, O. (eds.) NFM 2016. LNCS, vol. 9690, pp. 175–190. Springer, Cham (2016). doi:10.1007/978-3-319-40648-0_14

12. SAE International: J3016: Taxonomy and Definitions for Terms Related to On-Road Motor Vehicle Automated Driving Systems. Technical report, January 2014

13. Wardziński, A.: Safety assurance strategies for autonomous vehicles. In: Harrison, M.D., Sujan, M.-A. (eds.) SAFECOMP 2008. LNCS, vol. 5219, pp. 277–290. Springer, Heidelberg (2008). doi:10.1007/978-3-540-87698-4_24

14. Wei, J., Snider, J.M., Kim, J., Dolan, J.M., Rajkumar, R., Litkouhi, B.: Towards a viable autonomous driving research platform. In: Proceedings of the 2013 IEEE Intelligent Vehicles Symposium (IV), pp. 763–770, June 2013

Event-B at Work: Some Lessons Learnt from an Application to a Robot Anti-collision Function

Arnaud Dieumegard[1(✉)], Ning Ge[1,2], and Eric Jenn[1,3]

[1] IRT Saint-Exupéry, 118 Route de Narbonne, 31432 Toulouse, France
{arnaud.dieumegard, eric.jenn}@irt-saintexupery.com
[2] Systerel Toulouse, La Maison des Lois, 2 Impasse Michel Labrousse,
31036 Toulouse, France
ning.ge@systerel.fr
[3] Thales Avionics, 105 Avenue du Général Eisenhower,
BP 63647, 31036 Toulouse Cedex 1, France

Abstract. The technical and academic aspects of the Event-B method, and the abstract description of its application in industrial contexts are the subjects of numerous publications. In this paper, we describe the experience of development engineers non familiar with Event-B to getting to grips with this method. We describe in details how we used the formalism, the refinement method, and its supporting toolset to develop the simple anti-collision function embedded in a small rolling robot. We show how the model has been developed from a set of high-level requirements and refined down to the software specification. For each phase of the development, we explain how we used the method, expose the encountered difficulties, and draw some practical lessons from this experiment.

Keywords: Formal refinement · Software verification · Formal verification · Anti-collision · Event-B

1 Introduction

The practical implementation details and the difficulties encountered during the application of the Event-B method by "typical industrial engineers" are usually not widely discussed. Therefore, in the current publication, we share the method *we* have used, the difficulties *we* have encountered, and some lessons *we* have learnt when applying this method to develop one particular function of our small rolling robot [1].

It is worth noting that even though this development was tightly driven by considerations about aeronautical certification, the question of compliance with ARPs [2] or DOs [3–5] objectives using Event-B is not directly addressed here.

The paper is organized as follows. Section 2 outlines our development process. Section 3 introduces our case study: the anti-collision function of a small rover. Section 4 details the elaboration of the software requirements using formal refinement. Section 5 covers related works. We conclude in Sect. 6.

C. Barrett et al. (Eds.): NFM 2017, LNCS 10227, pp. 327–341, 2017.
DOI: 10.1007/978-3-319-57288-8_24

2 Formal Refinement in an Industrial Development Process

Our experiment focuses on the following development activities: (i) formalization of the system specification, (ii) definition of a *refinement strategy*, (iii) application of the refinement strategy to elaborate a set of high-level software requirements compliant with the initial specification. Subsequent software production activities are not detailed and are the subject of an ongoing publication [6]. Other activities such as integration or testing are not addressed.

The development process starts with a set of informal requirements expressed in a natural language. In order to optimize the modelling and validation effort, the initial set of requirements is decomposed into disjoint subsets, the processing of which is realized sequentially. Processing a subset of the requirements involves several phases: *formalization,* where requirements are translated into Event-B constructs; *validation,* where these constructs are validated against the initial user specification; *refinement,* where these constructs are made more concrete; *verification,* where the correctness of these constructs is proved. This process stops when (i) all subsets have been processed and (ii) the set of modelling elements allocated to software is completely defined. The overall development process is depicted on Fig. 1.

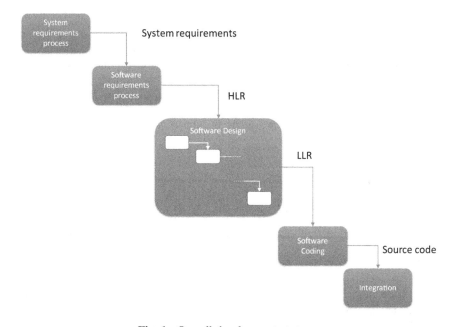

Fig. 1. Overall development strategy

With respect to a typical development process in the aeronautical domain, this part of the overall process covers part of the *system-level specification* and *design activity* (as per ARP4754 [2]) and part of the *software requirement activity* (as per DO-178C [3]).

In our case, we consider the last refinement of the Event-B model to carry high-level requirements (HLR), i.e., "software requirements developed from analysis of system requirements, safety-related requirements, and system architecture" (DO-178C). The software code will be implemented from those HLR; this part of the process is described in [6].

3 The Case Study

3.1 The TwIRTee Rover and the ARP Function

TwIRTee is the three-wheeled robot (or "rover") used as the demonstrator of the INGEQUIP project conducted at the *Institut de Recherche Technologique of Toulouse (IRT Saint-Exupéry)*. It is used to evaluate new methods and tools in the domain of hardware/software co-design [1], virtual integration, and application of formal methods for the development of equipment [6–9]. TwIRTee's architecture, software, and hardware components are representative of aeronautical, spatial and automotive systems.

A rover performs a sequence of *missions* (❶ on Fig. 2) defined by a start time and an ordered set of *waypoints* to be passed-by. Missions are planned *off-line* and transmitted to the rover by a supervision station (❷). To go from the first waypoint to the last, the rover moves on a track materialized by a dark line on the ground. In a more abstract way, a complete mission can be modelled by a *path* in a *graph* where *nodes* represent waypoints, and *edges* represent parts of the track joining two waypoints.

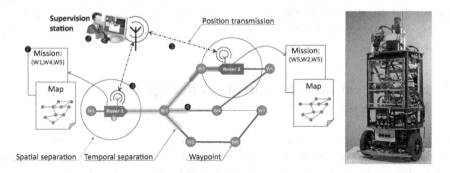

Fig. 2. System overview (Color figure online)

A rover shares the tracks with several identical rovers. In order to prevent collisions, each of them embeds a protection function (or ARP) which purpose is to maintain some specified spatial (❸) and temporal separation (❹) between them. On Fig. 2, temporal separations are represented by light green and light red areas superimposed on the map: basically, rover 2 (resp. rover 1) shall never enter the light green (resp. light red).

In our implementation, the ARP essentially acts by *reducing the rover speed* and, in some specific cases, by performing a simple *avoidance trajectory*. To take the appropriate action, the ARP exploit the following information: the map, the position of all other rovers transmitted by a centralized supervision station (❺), and its own position.

For this paper, we rely on a simplified version of the ARP function where some specification elements such as the rovers positions, speeds, decelerations, etc. are represented as discrete values (no use of Real or Floating Point data). Interested readers can refer to another study [9] conducted on this same function but covering different formal modelling aspects.

3.2   Rodin and Event-B

Event-B [10] is a method to develop systems according to a correct-by-construction approach. It is the system level modelling evolution of the B-method [11] successfully applied in real-size industrial applications [12]. The Event-B method constructs a correct model of a system via a series of refinements of its specification. The correction of a refinement is ensured by proving automatically or manually a set of proof obligations (PO) generated from the model.

The Rodin Platform[1] is an Eclipse-based IDE for Event-B that provides effective support for refinement and mathematical proof. The platform is open source, based on the Eclipse framework. Its development started in 2004 during the RODIN project, and continued within the DEPLOY and ADVANCE projects. The community is still active regarding the development. The extensibility of the platform through the use of plugins is of great interest as it allows to rely among others on (i) analysis tools for verification (SMT solvers, model checkers) or validation (animators, simulators generators) of the models and the refinements, (ii) traceability facilities for link with requirement documents, (iii) code generation tooling, (iv) automated refinements methods easing the refinement work.

4   From System-Level Requirements to High-Level Requirements

In our process, the latest refinement of the Event-B model represents software HLR. As already studied in [10, 13], the development of a refinement strategy is the entry point for the definition of Event-B models. It improves the understanding of the requirements by the designer and the robustness of the development process by providing an intermediate formalization phase between requirements and design. Refinement strategy application produces Event-B refinements.

4.1   Building a Refinement Strategy

Our refinement strategy is based on Abrial [10], Butler et al. [13] and Su et al. [14]. The work started with a thorough analysis of the requirements to identify the variables used

---

[1] http://www.event-b.org/.

in the system and classify them as either **uncontrolled** (environment), **controlled** (system), or **commanded** (operator). Requirements are classified according to the same three categories. The main role of the ARP function is to ensure the absence of collision between rovers by controlling the deceleration of the rover. The controlled variable *deceleration* of the control function is chosen as the first element of focus in the requirements document for the elaboration of the refinement strategy.

Requirements Layering

The refinement strategy defines the order to process the requirements. This order is determined from the dependencies between variables and, consequently, between requirements. In our case study, we identified the *deceleration* feature as dependent of the occurrence of *conflicts* and *emergency braking*. As a first abstraction, *conflicts* might occur at any time and so might *emergency braking*. Our initial layer of refinement was thus only composed of these three variables.

From this entry point, the next requirements layers are produced by gradually introducing new features such as: *fleet of rovers*, *distances between rovers*, *emergency braking* etc. Each feature is attached to a subset of the initial requirements. As some requirements are linked to multiple features, they are attached to multiple layers and their implementation is gradually completed along with the refinement of layers.

Complementary to the previous *horizontal* refinements, *vertical* data refinements are also performed. For instance, the values of the deceleration variable, initially constrained by a simple range in the early refinement, become later constrained by axioms specifying the semantics of deceleration. Similarly, the calculus of the distance between rovers that was simply defined as a value in a range is refined as a shortest path function.

Lessons Learnt

Building a consistent, adequate and applicable refinement strategy is the first step towards the correct understanding of the system and contributes to the correct modelling of the system. If requirement classification is a rather systematic activity, their layering (or sequencing) is more difficult. Layering starts with the identification of an entry point from which the activity starts. Layering may be driven by the identification of the minimal subset of features that ensures the capability to simulate and validate the model at each layer.

4.2   Formalization of Requirements

Formalization starts with the definition of Event-B contexts containing sets, constant variables and constant relations, the definition domain of which are specified as axioms. Then machines are detailed with variables and relations with their definition domain specified as invariants. Variables require the setting of their initial value in the special INITIALIZATION event. Variables shall be used in events specifying the condition under which their value changes (guards) and how their value changes (actions). Event execution modifies the state of the system. Properties expected to be verified by the system shall be added as invariants of the machine and shall hold in every event.

Producing Event-B models from informal specification can be done using multiple approaches. A first approach relies on modelling the states of the system as sets. In that interpretation, state changes are represented by the "movement" of elements from one set to another. This approach has been used for instance in an alternative modelling of our use case in [9] where the study goal was on time and the data refinements relied on the use of real values.

Our modelling approach, depicted in Fig. 3, is inspired from [10]. The function is first abstracted as a hierarchic cyclic state machine comprising two states: the first one updates the state of the environment of the system and the second updates the state of the system itself (i.e., performs the function under design). Transition from one state to the other is triggered by dedicated events (`arp_state_env_start` and `arp_state_fun_start`) updating a state variable `arp_state`. Sub state machines are triggered depending on activation variables (`[mm|fm|cm|em]_ac-tivated`). This approach provides a clear separation between the environment and the system under design, exposes the execution cycle, and so facilitates the production of the executable code from the model. Unfortunately, exposing the execution cycle of the function may also introduce implementation details too early in the refinement process.

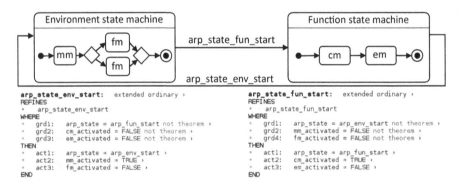

Fig. 3. Event-B model as a circuit

Lessons Learnt

Modelling the system using our approach does suffer from some serious limitations. We assume that all other rovers in the environment do implement the same ARP function as the one under design. For our implementation, this assumption was added as a new environment requirement. Such assumption was not necessary in the alternative modelling approach as every rover in the system was explicitly modelled and each of them implements the same ARP behaviour. Our modelling approach yields an advantage regarding the formal verification: as we do not model all the rovers, a level of universal quantification in the model is removed.

Vertical data refinements produce detailed specifications for variables and for functions. These specifications may be purely declarative or imperative. In the first case, implementation is provided outside of the Event-B world; in the second case,

Event-B is used to "code" the function. In our use case, for instance, an imperative model of the simple "deceleration function" could be easily designed in Event-B. However, this would be much more tedious for the "shortest path function". Thus we have favoured a pure declarative approach in Event-B, leaving the implementation details to programming languages.

The choice of the "set-oriented" or "finite-state-machine-oriented" modelling approach has an impact on efficiency. The use of sets increases abstraction and reduces the modelling effort, but it increases the implementation work. Reciprocally, using the finite state machine approach is less abstract, less compact, more difficult to write, but simplifies the implementation. Additionally, this approach also facilitates the automatic discharging of POs but at the price of adding invariants to propagate the values of variables changed in sub states to the final state of the state machine. Note also that the nature of the variables and the system under design are likely to favor one or the other modelling approaches.

Finally, it is worth noting that *writing* Event-B models does not require more *knowledge* than writing software. While using first order logic and set theory is a shift from classical software engineering methods, this belongs to the mathematical background of any engineer. However, writing Event-B model requires a strong capability of *abstraction* and a capability to describe without being able to execute...

4.3   Verification of Refinements

Verification of formal refinements in the Event-B method relies on the discharging of automatically generated POs. POs can be automatically discharged using predicate provers embedded in the Rodin toolset. Plugins have been developed to leverage the increasing capabilities of SMT solvers such as Alt-Ergo[2], Z3[3], CV4[4], or others. Formal verification is conducted in parallel with formal refinement: as soon as any element is added in an Event-B model, PO are generated and potentially discharged automatically. In some way, this can be related to the automatic syntactic verifications performed by current IDEs.

Refinement Verification in Practice
The number of generated POs increases with the size of the model. Even with automatic verification provided by embedded PP and SMT solvers, some POs remain to be proved "manually". Hopefully, the proof plug-ins in Rodin are easy to use and very intuitive for the users, and thus is of great help when manual proofs are required.

Unfortunately, diagnosing *why* some PO fails to be discharged manually or automatically remains difficult. The reason may be that the property simply does not hold, or that either the automatic prover or the user is not able to carry out the proof. In the latter case, reasons may be the limited capabilities of the human or mechanical prover,

---

[2] http://alt-ergo.lri.fr/.

[3] https://github.com/Z3Prover/z3.

[4] http://cvc4.cs.nyu.edu/web/.

or missing lemmas. Discriminating the various situations is very hard and may require a significant (but hard to estimate) effort.

Rodin embedded prover can be adapted through the definition/modification (with a graphical interface) of profiles. Profiles customization finds its interest in case dependent models as it provides tactics adapted to specific goals to be proved. We relied on profiles customization in our use case in order to add tactics such as "domain rewriting" that were of great help for the automation of the proof work.

Part of the proof work was additionally assisted by adding "helper" invariants. This was unfortunately not enough to fully automate the formal verification, as about 1% of the proofs remained to be done by hand (a total of 2442 POs including 15 proven by hand). Remaining proofs relate to the use of non-linear arithmetic for which automatic provers are not really efficient. We dealt with these proofs by adding theorems adapted to the proof goals and by performing their proof by hand. The necessary work was not complex but is time consuming due to the manual search for missing theorems.

Lessons Learnt

Formal verification is the most time-consuming activity in the refinements process. This work is complex and requires experience and specific skills when automatic proof fails to discharge all POs. Worse, the effort to complete a proof is difficult to estimate. This problem is made even more critical due to the fact that no guidance can be provided to complete a proof. Avoiding manual proof work would thus be a way to avoid such limitation but would require modelling guidance on how to stay on the path of what is automatically provable.

On the other side, proofs performed fully automatically and immediately may cover other difficulties. Hence, our first proofs were performed in no time due to contradictory axioms/invariants/guards. Unfortunately, avoiding such inconsistencies is difficult and detection cannot be done automatically. So we relied on the voluntary insertion of inconsistent axioms/invariants/guards to check for the consistency of the other axioms/invariants/guards.

After a relatively short training on the Event-B method, formalism and proof techniques, it appears to us that modelling systems and proving them using the Rodin toolset is a task that is accessible to engineers with some background in mathematical logics. However, the time needed for the modelling and verification of a system remains difficult to estimate. Worse, the effect of a simple model modification on the proof effort (especially, manual) is difficult to estimate. We really miss appropriate modeling guidance.

4.4   Validation of Formal Requirements

Ideally, the set of requirements is consistent and complete at each refinement level. In reality, it is very likely that some requirements have been ignored, misunderstood, or badly transcoded. As the rework of an Event-B model is fairly expensive, it shall be validated as early and often as possible.

Executing the model has been identified by Event-B experts as the only means to achieve validation [15, 16]. The production of simulators has been the subject of many works [17–19] and tools have been developed for this purpose.

Simulator-Based Validation

In our experiment, we relied on ProB [20] complemented by B-Motion [21] and JeB [22] as validation tools. The last two additionally provide means to graphically represent the execution of the model: this greatly improves stakeholders' ability to validate the Event-B models.

During the phase of requirement analysis, we developed a simulator including movement dynamics of the rovers on a map using ScicosLab[5] as depicted in Fig. 4. The only purpose of the simulator was to validate our understanding of the specification. Such simulator also has the interesting effect of producing simulation scenarios that can be used as test vectors fed to the Event-B simulators [19]. Simulations relying on such values directly contribute to the validation of Event-B models as they rely on pre-validated sets of values. Integration of third party simulators and produced values can be technically done relying on FMI (Functional Model Interface) and the related plugin developed for integration in the Rodin platform [17].

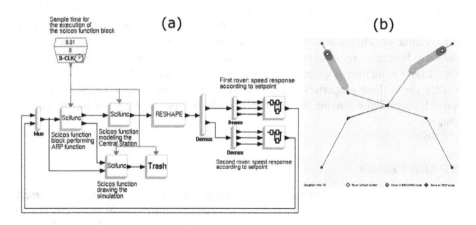

Fig. 4. ScicosLab simulator with graphical display (b) and underlying model (a)

Developing Event-B simulators is easy, especially during the first steps of refinement. However, generating actual input vectors for the simulation can be quite tedious and complex when the variables or constants are specified using non-deterministic expressions.

We relied on JeB [18] for the generation of a web-based simulator and for the generation of values for constants. JeB provides an automatic translation of Event-B models to an executable JavaScript implementation. It is then possible to provide JavaScript functions computing the values for constants (resp. variables and

---

[5] http://www.scicoslab.org/.

parameters). Such functions produce values that are pretty-printed using Event-B notation. These values can then be used in the original Event-B model making JeB a very handy tool for the production of test vectors for complex data (relations pairs etc....). Computed values correction is formally verified using PP and SMT solvers when they are injected in the Event-B model. In our ARP function we produced values for the refined function for the calculus of the deceleration to be applied by the rover using JeB.

In control systems, *liveness properties* or correctness properties such as *deadlock freeness* shall be verified to ensure the responsiveness of the system. Simulation can be used to obtain a first level of confidence on the absence of deadlocks, before resorting to formal proof. Deadlock freeness theorems can be generated using dedicated Rodin plugins, but depending on the model size, their verification may become very challenging. Verifying these properties can also be done using model checking. But this approach suffers from the classical limitations of model checkers. In our experiment, we used a translation to another formalism and toolset (HLL and S3, see [6]) after introducing a scheduling sequence of events to the system under design to tackle more efficiently and automatically the verification of those properties.

Lessons Learnt

Validating a formal model with respect to a set of informal requirements is a difficult task. Hopefully, the Event-B environment provides a set of very helpful animation tools. Animation allows stakeholders to *see* the behavior of the formal model and validate it. Furthermore, it allows to assess reachability and liveness properties that are difficult (and sometime impossible) to express directly on the Event-B model and to formally verify these properties using model checking. However, as for any test-based approach, confidence on the validation depends on the coverage of the validation scenarios.

4.5   Model Review

The review activity in a classical development process aims at ensuring the correct implementation of requirements as code or the correct refinement of requirements, to detect inconsistencies and misinterpreted requirements, and enforce the use of development standard (e.g., code writing standards). Here, we consider three specific goals: ensure a correct encoding of the designer's intent, reduce the verification effort, and support traceability.

Ensure Correct Encoding of Designer Intent

The correct encoding of the designer intent is ensured by the validity, correctness, consistency and completeness of the formal model with respect to the requirements. We provide here multiple elements supporting this goal.

Introduction of verification lemmas is a starting point advocated in many publications to assess the consistency of an Event-B model. As already stated, success in proving obviously false theorems/invariants/guards put in contexts/machine/events allows one to detect inconsistencies in contexts/machine initialisation/event guards and parameters definitions.

Additional automated tooling for checking expressions could also help in our verification process, as an example, checking if bounded logic variables are used in quantified constructs or writing implications in the body of existentially quantified expressions might raise a warning for the designer.

A *proofreading* approach to model review could also be applied to Event-B models by having a reviewer to rewrite chosen guards and invariants using natural language. The reviewer would then check if the natural language expressions are indeed correct rewritings of the associated requirements. The opposite approach could also be done and would be safer (reviewer to write the natural language expression of the guard using FOL) but less straightforward for engineers. Proofreading should be focused on complex guards and invariants that are more likely to contain errors and on invariants stating key properties of the system under design.

Minimize Verification Effort

Verification is one of the most expensive activities in the development of embedded critical systems. Minimizing verification efforts is thus of primary interest.

To facilitate the (possibly automatic) verification process, we have to add additional lemmas to the model. Those lemmas were explicitly identified as "helper" lemmas, so as to ease the work of assessing the correction of the model. After several modifications of the model, some of those lemmas became unnecessary and were removed from the model to lighten the verification. It is worth noting that some tautologies were kept in the model even though they did not bring additional information as they appeared to be very helpful to support "case splitting" and simplify the automatic proof.

The verification effort obviously strongly depends on the ability for the verifier to understand the model. One way to achieve this goal relies on the compliance to a set of well-defined modelling rules compiled in a "modelling standard", in a way similar to what is usually done for software coding. Many rules for code writing such as MISRA-C [23] can be applied to the writing of logical expressions: avoid deep nesting, avoid too long lines of code, line breaks position according to operators, indentation consistency, parenthesizing consistency, avoid having two operator of different precedence at the same level of indentation. Verification effort can also be strongly reduced by an appropriate organization of the models. For instance, in our experiment, we applied the following rule about model elements ordering: "the order of declaration of constants, variables or parameters should match the order of appearance of their respective definition (axioms, invariants, guards)".

It is obvious but worth noting that adding comments in the model significantly contributes to a better understanding of the intent of the designer and of the structure and choices made during the design process. Comments shall be of help and not state obvious information.

Existing tooling may also simplify the models and thus impact its understandability. For instance, the "theory" plugin provides the capability to factorize properties or expressions of the model and thus simplifies the writing (and, later, the understanding) of complex Event-B models.

We have provided here a few examples of good practices for the writing of an Event-B model to produce more readable, reviewable and thus understandable models. There exists many works and standards used in the industry to ensure such properties for code but to our knowledge there is a minimal work done on applying this to logical specification. We plan on tackling these with more details on a dedicated publication.

Traceability

Aeronautics certifications require to trace each design elements to some requirement. The corresponding certification objective is "High-level requirements are traceable to system requirements" (DO178 Annex A, table A-3, objective 6). In our experiment, ensuring traceability during the refinement process first relied on making explicit the mapping between the elements in the informal specification and Event-B constructs. At high level, naming conventions allowed us to link each refinement layer defined by the refinement strategy to its corresponding Event-B machine and context. Newly introduced model element (constant, axiom, variable, invariant, event, guard and action) were commented with the name of the requirement to which it was linked. If an element could not be linked to a requirement, it was marked as "derived" and the corresponding derived requirement was added to the specification.

We decided to use this approach to keep the traceability artefacts visible at all time. An alternative solution would be to rely on the traceability plugin integrated in the Rodin platform (RMF). This solution would simplify the traceability review process and avoid cluttering of the models. Unfortunately, it was not available for the version of Rodin we used in our experiment (such integration is planned to be provided at the time of writing).

Lessons Learnt

We advocate that code review can be applied to Event-B models and may help in (i) demonstrating the correct encoding of the intent of the designer in the formal model; and (ii) minimizing the verification effort by adopting appropriate modelling patterns.

Model review against a well-defined modelling standard is a simple and efficient means to enhance the quality of the model and reduce the number of errors. The benefits of such activity strongly overcome its cost. Hence, it shall be an integral part of the Event-B models development process. We believe that the complexity of such a review activity is affordable for software engineers with basic mathematical knowledge.

Additionally, generating appropriate documentation from Event-B models would also greatly simplify the review work. Indeed, the way of displaying models in the Rodin environment is not really adapted to a proper review activity. For instance, a categorization of model elements and comments according to their purpose/role (traceability, design choices, model element meaning, general information ...) with associated documentation generation would greatly help the review process.

Our approach to deal with traceability was applicable to our use case because of the granularity of our requirements. Tracing more abstract requirements to specific model elements would be difficult to manage and verify that way. Relying on an intermediate level of (semi-)formal requirements as advocated in the use of the "extended problem frame" approach [24] would be more generalizable.

5   Related Works

Research projects have produced a large literature on the methodology and tools around the use of Event-B for system modelling. Project such as DEPLOY, for instance, [24] have provided some very valuable results on the application of Event-B on industrial use cases. In this work, they rely on the "extended problem frames" approach as an intermediate formalism between informal requirements and Event-B models to further formalize relations between requirements elements and thus simplify the formalization work. Model validation is tackled in their approach using traceability and animation through the use of ProB. To assess deadlock freeness, they rely exclusively on ProB.

A complete approach for the design and conception of a pacemaker system [25] and an adaptive cruise control has been developed by Singh [19]. Formalization of requirements is done through the extraction of modes and variables and introduction of refinement charts [25]. Event-B models are then produced, verified and validated [26]. The whole process is also confronted to a potential use in a software certification environment [27].

Our work on the analysis and formalization of requirements does not provide additional elements compared to previously presented state of the art applications. We advocate on relying on animation technologies to improve the understanding of simulation results by stakeholders by providing graphical simulators generated using B-Motion and/or JeB. Simulation input data may be produced through the use of simulators generators like JeB. We propose to additionally rely on a transformation of Event-B models to HLL for verification and validation. A similar approach is advocated in the FORMOSE[6] project relying on UPPAAL [28]. We propose an additional review process to complement validation relying on software review techniques ensuring a better detection of conception errors and misunderstanding of the specification during Event-B models design.

6   Conclusion

This work focuses on the application of the Event-B method on part of the process followed during an industrial development. We give some lessons and proposed some of the simple practices that we applied during this experiment. Relying on the Event-B method for the development of systems provides a framework for the formalization of textual requirements. This is strengthening the traditional error prone formalization step of a software development process. Formal modelling, verification and validation of Event-B models at an early stage provide a very valuable and fast feedback on the correction of requirements.

One important conclusion of our experiment resides in the very fact that we – "standard" software engineers – were able to apply the method on a non-trivial problem in a very reasonable time. This is in particular due to the great maturity of the toolset and the efficiency of the underlying provers. However, this positive conclusion is

---

[6] http://formose.lacl.fr/.

certainly largely due to the natural adequacy of our problem to the method. An additional conclusion of our experiment is that classical verification and validation activities shall be complemented by review activities. They strongly contribute to reduce the number of errors and more generally to enhance the quality of the model.

Before moving to a large scale industrial application, some very important questions remain to be answered: what is the actual usage domain of the method, considering the constraints imposed by the capability of the automatic verification means? How robust is the method to a change in the requirements? What are the good modeling practices to enhance this robustness and to reduce the verification effort? Definitely, it is necessary to evaluate the method on different types of systems to detect weak and strong points for its application.

This work will be pursued to answer these questions, and more specifically to address the applicability of the Event-B method in a DO-178C compliant development process. Additional tooling may be necessary in order to assess requirements coverage and improve review activities. Purpose/role focused documentation generation could serve these activities that needs to be conducted in a certification environment.

References

1. Cuenot, P., Jenn, E., Faure, E., Broueilh, N., Rouland, E.: An experiment on exploiting virtual platforms for the development of embedded equipments. In: 8th European Congress on Embedded Real Time Software and Systems (ERTS 2016) (2016)
2. SAE: SAE ARP4754 Certification Considerations for Highly-Integrated Or Complex Aircraft Systems. Society of Automotive Engineers (SAE), Warrendale, USA (1996)
3. RTCA: DO-178C, Software Considerations in Airborne Systems and Equipment Certification. Special Committee 205 of RTCA (2011)
4. RTCA: DO-333 Formal Methods Supplement to DO-178C and DO-278A. RTCA & EUROCAE, December 2011
5. RTCA: DO-331 Model-Based Development and Verification Supplement to DO-178C and DO-278A. RTCA & EUROCAE, December 2011
6. Ge, N., Dieumegard, A., Jenn, E., Voisin, L.: From Event-B to verified C via HLL, October 2016
7. Clabaut, M., Ge, N., Breton, N., Jenn, E., Delmas, R., Fonteneau, Y.: Industrial grade model checking use cases, constraints, tools and applications. In: 8th European Congress on Embedded Real Time Software and Systems (ERTS 2016), Toulouse, France (2016)
8. Ge, N., Jenn, E., Breton, N., Fonteneau, Y.: Formal verification of a rover anti-collision system. In: Beek, Maurice H., Gnesi, S., Knapp, A. (eds.) FMICS/AVoCS -2016. LNCS, vol. 9933, pp. 171–188. Springer, Cham (2016). doi:10.1007/978-3-319-45943-1_12
9. Singh, N.K., Ait-Ameur, Y., Pantel, M., Dieumegard, A., Jenn, E.: Stepwise formal modeling and verification of self-adaptive systems with Event-B. The automatic rover protection case study. Presented at the ICECCS 2016 (2016)
10. Abrial, J.-R.: Modeling in Event-B - System and Software Engineering. Cambridge University Press, Cambridge (2010)
11. Abrial, J.-R.: The B-book: Assigning Programs to Meanings. Cambridge University Press, New York (1996)

12. Boulanger, J.-L.: Formal Methods Applied to Complex Systems: Implementation of the B Method. Wiley, Hoboken (2014)
13. Butler, M.: Towards a cookbook for modelling and refinement of control problems (2009)
14. Su, W., Abrial, J.-R., Huang, R., Zhu, H.: From requirements to development: methodology and example. In: Qin, S., Qiu, Z. (eds.) ICFEM 2011. LNCS, vol. 6991, pp. 437–455. Springer, Heidelberg (2011). doi:10.1007/978-3-642-24559-6_30
15. Mashkoor, A., Jacquot, J.-P., Souquières, J.: Transformation heuristics for formal requirements validation by animation. In: 2nd International Workshop on the Certification of Safety-Critical Software Controlled Systems-SafeCert 2009 (2009)
16. Hallerstede, S., Leuschel, M., Plagge, D.: Refinement-animation for Event-B — towards a method of validation. In: Frappier, M., Glässer, U., Khurshid, S., Laleau, R., Reeves, S. (eds.) ABZ 2010. LNCS, vol. 5977, pp. 287–301. Springer, Heidelberg (2010). doi:10.1007/978-3-642-11811-1_22
17. Savicks, V., Butler, M., Colley, J., Bendisposto, J.: Rodin multi-simulation plug-in. Presented at the 5th Rodin User and Developer Workshop, Toulouse, France (2014)
18. Yang, F.: A simulation framework for the validation of Event-B specifications. Université de Lorraine (2013)
19. Singh, N.K.: Reliability and safety of critical device software systems. Ecole Centrale de Nantes (2011)
20. Leuschel, M., Butler, M.: ProB: a model checker for B. In: Araki, K., Gnesi, S., Mandrioli, D. (eds.) FME 2003. LNCS, vol. 2805, pp. 855–874. Springer, Heidelberg (2003). doi:10.1007/978-3-540-45236-2_46
21. Ladenberger, L., Bendisposto, J., Leuschel, M.: Visualising Event-B models with B-motion studio. In: Alpuente, M., Cook, B., Joubert, C. (eds.) FMICS 2009. LNCS, vol. 5825, pp. 202–204. Springer, Heidelberg (2009). doi:10.1007/978-3-642-04570-7_17
22. Yang, F., Jacquot, J.-P., Souquières, J.: JeB: safe simulation of Event-B models in Javascript. In: 2013 20th Asia-Pacific Software Engineering Conference (APSEC), vol. 1, pp. 571–576 (2013)
23. MIRA Ltd: MISRA-C:2004 guidelines for the use of the C language in critical systems (2004)
24. Petre, L., Sere, K., Tsiopoulos, L.: Deploy methods: final report. D44, April 2012
25. Méry, D., Singh, N.K.: Formal specification of medical systems by proof-based refinement. ACM Trans. Embed. Comput. Syst. 12(1), 15:1–15:25 (2013)
26. Méry, D., Singh, N.K.: Real-time animation for formal specification. In: Méry, D., Singh, N. K. (eds.) Complex Systems Design & Management 2010, pp. 49–60. Springer, Heidelberg (2010)
27. Méry, D., Singh, N.K.: Trustable formal specification for software certification. In: Margaria, T., Steffen, B. (eds.) ISoLA 2010. LNCS, vol. 6416, pp. 312–326. Springer, Heidelberg (2010). doi:10.1007/978-3-642-16561-0_31
28. Behrmann, G., et al.: UPPAAL 4.0. In: Third International Conference on the Quantitative Evaluation of Systems - (QEST 2006), pp. 125–126 (2006)

Reasoning About Safety-Critical Information Flow Between Pilot and Computer

Seth Ahrenbach[(✉)]

University of Missouri, Columbia, MO 65201, USA
SJK7v7@mail.missouri.edu

Abstract. This paper presents research results that develop a dynamic logic for reasoning about safety-critical information flow among humans and computers. The logic advances previous efforts to develop logics of agent knowledge, which make assumptions that are too strong for realistic human agents. We introduce Dynamic Agent Safety Logic (DASL), based on Dynamic Epistemic Logic (DEL), with extensions to account for safe actions, belief, and the logical relationships among knowledge, belief, and safe action. With this logic we can infer which safety-critical information a pilot is missing when executing an unsafe action. We apply the logic to the Air France 447 incident as a case study and provide a mechanization of the case study in the Coq proof assistant.

1 Introduction

A common theme for aviation mishaps attributed to human error is for a pilot to become overwhelmed by data, lose situational awareness, and provide unsafe inputs to the flight controls. As yet, little work has been done to leverage the power of formal methods to address this problem. This paper remedies that by defining a dynamic logic of belief, knowledge, and safe action. We use the logic to create an axiomatic model of agency suitable for reasoning about safety-critical information flow among pilots and the flight computer. We mechanize this model in the Coq Proof Assistant and apply it to the Air France 447 incident as a case study.[1]

The research contributions of this paper include the development of a dynamic logic that is suitable for reasoning about safety-critical information flow. The dynamic logic is extended beyond most dynamic logics' treatment of action in that it treats both *mere* action and *safe* action, and captures the relationship between the two. The subsequent application and mechanization in Coq explore novel uses of formal methods in aviation safety, beyond mere verification of system component correctness. They introduce the idea of formally analyzing the human component of the safety-critical systems.

Dynamic Logic is a type of modal logic used for reasoning about state transition diagrams of programs [3,8]. A diagram consists of nodes and edges, representing states of the system and labeled transitions between them, respectively.

---

[1] Code: https://github.com/sethkurtenbach/DASL/blob/master/DASL.v.

© Springer International Publishing AG 2017
C. Barrett et al. (Eds.): NFM 2017, LNCS 10227, pp. 342–356, 2017.
DOI: 10.1007/978-3-319-57288-8_25

It is distinguished from other logics by the fact that truth is dynamic, rather than static, in its semantics. Thus, it is capable of representing the way actions change the truth of propositions. It serves as a foundation for a variety of logics similarly concerned with changes in some aspect of the truth as a result of actions. This family of logics has been described as logical dynamics, and includes Public Announcement Logic (PAL) and Dynamic Epistemic Logic (DEL) [5].

Logical dynamics allows researchers to model information flow, rationality, and action in multi-agent systems [5]. In Ahrenbach and Goodloe [1], the authors develop a static modal logic for knowledge, belief, and safety to analyze a family of aviation mishaps involving a type of reasoning error suffered by a single pilot. This paper extends that work by employing dynamic methodologies from logical dynamics to the analysis of mishaps. The use of a dynamic logic rather than a static logic connects safety-critical information and actions in a more natural way, and allows for easier inference from action to information. The application of these methods advances the discipline of logical dynamics by employing them in the real world, beyond toy examples and logic puzzles, and likewise improves the discipline of aviation safety by introducing a formal method suitable for analyzing safety-critical information flow between pilots and machine.

Recent work at the intersection of game theory and logical dynamics focuses on information flow during games. Van Ditmarsch identifies a class of games called *knowledge games*, in which players have diverging information [6]. This slightly relaxes the assumption of classical game theory that players have common knowledge about each other's perfect information. This invites logicians to study the information conveyed by the fact that an action is executed. For example, if agent 1 asks agent 2 the question, "p?", the information conveyed is that 1 does not know whether p, believes that 2 knows whether p, and after the action occurs, this information becomes publicly known. Many actions convey such information, beyond mere speech acts. For example, when a pilot provides flight control inputs, her action conveys information about what she believes about the aircraft's state, namely that it is in a state that safely permits those inputs. Anyone observing her inputs, like the first officer or the flight computer, can make such inferences about her mental picture based on her actions.

This paper proceeds as follows. In Sect. 2 we define the formal model, which consists of a set of axioms in a dynamic modal logic for reasoning about pilot knowledge, belief, and safety. Section 3 mechanizes the model in the Coq Proof Assistant and applies it to case studies, illustrating the logic's use as a formal method for aviation safety. We offer a brief discussion of future work in Sect. 4 and conclude in Sect. 5.

2   Dynamic Agent Safety Logic

The logic for reasoning about information flow in knowledge games is called Dynamic Epistemic Logic (DEL). As its name suggests, it combines elements of epistemic logic and dynamic logic. Epistemic logic is the static logic for reasoning about knowledge, and dynamic logic is used to reason about actions. In dynamic logic semantics, nodes are states of the system or the world, and relations on nodes are transitions via programs or actions from node to node. If we think of each node in dynamic logic as being a model of epistemic logic, then actions become relations on models, representing transitions from one multi-agent epistemic model to another. For example, if we have a static epistemic model $M1$ representing the knowledge states of agents 1 and 2 at a moment, then the action "p?" is a relation between $M1$ and $M2$, a new static epistemic model of 1's and 2's knowledge after the question is asked. All of this is captured by DEL.

We are concerned with an additional element: the *safety* status of an action, and an agent's knowledge and belief about that. To capture this, we extend DEL and call the new logic Dynamic Agent Safety Logic (DASL). The remainder of this section presents DASL's syntax, semantics, and proves its soundness.

2.1   Syntax and Semantics

The Dynamic Agent Safety Logic (DASL) used in this paper has the following syntax.

$$\varphi ::= p \mid \neg\varphi \mid \varphi \wedge \varphi \mid \mathbf{K_i}\,\varphi \mid \mathbf{B_i}\,\varphi \mid [\mathbf{i},(\mathbf{A},\mathbf{a})]\varphi \mid [\mathbf{i},(\mathbf{A},\mathbf{a}),\mathbf{S}]\varphi,$$

where $p \in AtProp$ is an atomic proposition, $\mathbf{i}$ refers to $i \in Agents$, $\mathbf{a}$ is the name of an action, called an action token, belong to a set of such tokens, *Actions*, and $\mathbf{A}$ refers to an action structure. The knowledge operator $\mathbf{K_i}$ indicates that "agent i knows that ..." Similarly, the operator for belief, $\mathbf{B_i}$ can be read, "agent i believes that..." The notion of action tokens and structures will be defined in the semantics. The operators $[\mathbf{i},(\mathbf{A},\mathbf{a})]$ and $[\mathbf{i},(\mathbf{A},\mathbf{a}),\mathbf{S}]$ are the dynamic operators for agent i executing action token a from action structure A in the former case, and doing so safely in the latter case. Note that the $\mathbf{S}$ in $[\mathbf{i},(\mathbf{A},\mathbf{a}),\mathbf{S}]$ stands for 'safety', and is not a variable, whereas the $\mathbf{i},(\mathbf{A},\mathbf{a})$ are variables for agents, action structures, and action tokens, respectively. One can read the action operators as "after i executes a from A, φ holds." We define the dual modal operators $\langle\mathbf{K}_i\rangle$, $\langle\mathbf{B}_i\rangle$, $\langle\mathbf{i},(\mathbf{A},\mathbf{a})\rangle$, and $\langle\mathbf{i},(\mathbf{A},\mathbf{a}),\mathbf{S}\rangle$ in the usual way.

The semantics of DASL involve two structures that are defined simultaneously, one for epistemic models, and one for action structures capturing the transition relation among epistemic models. Additionally, we define numerous helper functions that straddle the division between metalanguage and object language.

Kripke Model. A Kripke model $M \in Model$ is a tuple $\langle W, \{R^i_k\}, \{R^i_b\}, w, V\rangle$. It is a set of worlds, sets of epistemic and doxastic relations on worlds for agents, a world denoting the actual world, and a valuation function V mapping atomic propositions to the set of worlds satisfying them. Most readers will be somewhat familiar with epistemic logic, the logic for reasoning about knowledge. Doxastic logic is a similar logic for reasoning about belief [9].

Action Structure. An action structure $A \in ActionStruct$ is a tuple $\langle Actions, \{\chi_k^i\}, \{\chi_b^i\}, a \rangle$. It is a set of action tokens, sets of epistemic and doxastic relations on action tokens for agents, and an action token, a, denoting an actual action token executed.

An action structure captures the associated subjective events of an action occurring, including how it is observed by various agents, incorporating their uncertainty. The action tokens are the actual objective events that might occur. For example, if I am handed a piece of paper telling me who won the Oscar for Best Actress, and I read it, and you see me read it, then the action structure will include possible tokens in which I read that each nominee has won, and you will consider each of these tokens to be possible. When I read the paper, I consider only one action token to be the one executed. This action structure represents that transition from one epistemic model, in which both of us considers all nominees the potential winner, to an epistemic model in which I know the winner and you still do not know the winner. We can think of the action structure A as the general action "Agent 1 reads the piece of paper" and the tokens as the specific actions "Agent 1 reads that nominee n has won the award."

Model Relation. Just as R_k^i denotes a relation on worlds, $[\![i, (A, a)]\!]$ denotes a relation on Kripke model-world pairs. It represents the relation that holds between M, w and M', w' when agent i executes action (A, a) at M, w and causes the world to transition to M', w'.

Precondition Function. The Precondition function, $pre :: Actions \mapsto \varphi$, maps an action to the formula capturing the conditions under which the action can occur. For example, if we assume agents tell the truth, then an announcement action has as a precondition that the announced proposition is true, as with regular Public Announcement Logic.

Postcondition Function. The Postcondition function, $post :: A \times AtProp \mapsto AtProp$, takes an action structure and an atomic proposition, and maps to the corresponding atomic proposition after the action occurs.

$$post(A, p) = p \text{ if } update(M, A, w, a, i) \models p, \text{else } \neg p.$$

Update Function. The Update function, $update :: (Model \times ActionStruct \times W \times Actions \times Agents) \mapsto (Model \times W)$, takes a Kripke model M, an action structure A, a world from the Kripke model, an action token from the Action structure, and an agent executing the action, and returns a new Kripke model-world pair. It represents the effect actions have on models, and is more complicated than other DEL semantics in that actions can change the facts on the ground in addition to the knowledge and belief relations. It is a partial function that is defined iff a model-world pair satisfies the action's preconditions.

$update(M, A, w, a, i) = (M', w')$ *where*:

1. $M = \langle W, \{R_k^i\}, \{R_b^i\}, w, V \rangle$
2. $A = \langle Actions, \{\chi_k^i\}, \{\chi_b^i\}, a, pre, post \rangle$
3. $M' = \langle W', \{R_k'^i\}, \{R_b'^i\}, w', V' \rangle$
4. $W' = \{(w, a) | w \in W, a \in Actions, \text{ and } w \models pre(a)\}$
5. $R_k'^i = \{((w, a), (v, b)) | w R_k^i v \text{ and } a \chi_k^i b\}$
6. $R_b'^i = \{((w, a), (v, b)) | w R_b^i v \text{ and } a \chi_b^i b\}$
7. $w' = (w, a)$
8. $V'(p) = post(A, p)$

Safety Precondition Function. The Safety Precondition Function, $pre_s :: Actions \mapsto \varphi$, is a more restrictive function than pre. Where pre returns the conditions that dictate whether the action is possible, pre_s returns the conditions that dictate whether the action is safely permissible. This function is the key reason the dynamic approach allows for easy inference from action to safety-critical information.

The logic DASL has the following Kripke semantics.

$$M, w \models p \text{ iff } w \in V(p)$$
$$M, w \models \neg\varphi \text{ iff } M, w \not\models \varphi$$
$$M, w \models \varphi \wedge \psi \text{ iff } M, w \models \varphi \text{ and } M, w \models \psi$$
$$M, w \models \mathbf{K_i}\varphi \text{ iff } \forall v, wR_k^i v \text{ implies } M, v \models \varphi$$
$$M, w \models \mathbf{B_i}\varphi \text{ iff } \forall v, wR_b^i v \text{ implies } M, v \models \varphi$$
$$M, w \models [\mathbf{i}, (\mathbf{A}, \mathbf{a})]\varphi \text{ iff } \forall M', w', (M, w)[\![i, (A, a)]\!](M', w')$$
$$\text{implies } M', w' \models \varphi$$
$$M, w \models [\mathbf{i}, (\mathbf{A}, \mathbf{a}), \mathbf{S}]\varphi \text{ iff } \forall M', w', (M, w)[\![i, (A, a), S]\!](M', w')$$
$$\text{implies } M', w' \models \varphi$$

The definitions of the dynamic modalities make use of a relation between two model-world pairs, which we now define.

$$(M, w)[\![i, (A, a)]\!](M', w') \text{ iff } M, w \models pre(a)$$
$$\text{and } update(M, A, w, a, i) = (M', w')$$
$$(M, w)[\![i, (A, a), S]\!](M', w') \text{ iff } M, w \models pre_s(a)$$
$$\text{and } update(M, A, w, a, i) = (M', w')$$

2.2 Hilbert System

DASL is axiomatized by the following Hilbert system.
All propositional tautologies are axioms.

$\mathbf{K_i}$ is T (knowledge relation is reflexive)
$\mathbf{B_i}$ is KD45 (belief relation is serial, transitive, and Euclidean)
EP1: $\mathbf{K_i}\,\varphi \Rightarrow \mathbf{B_i}\,\varphi$
EP2: $\mathbf{B_i}\,\varphi \Rightarrow \mathbf{B_i}\,\mathbf{K_i}\,\varphi$
EP3: $\mathbf{B_i}\,\varphi \Rightarrow \mathbf{K_i}\,\mathbf{B_i}\,\varphi$
SP: $[\mathbf{i},(\mathbf{A},\mathbf{a})]\varphi \Rightarrow [\mathbf{i},(\mathbf{A},\mathbf{a}),\mathbf{S}]\varphi$
PR: $\langle \mathbf{i},(\mathbf{A},\mathbf{a})\rangle\,\varphi \Rightarrow \mathbf{B_i}\,\langle \mathbf{i},(\mathbf{A},\mathbf{a}),\mathbf{S}\rangle\,\varphi,$

---

plus the inference rules Modus Ponens and Necessitation for $\mathbf{K_i}$ and $\mathbf{B_i}$.

   Above are the axioms characterizing the logic. Knowledge is weaker here than in most epistemic logics, and belief is standard [7]. They are related logically by EP(1–3), which hold that knowledge entails belief, belief entails that one believes that one knows, and belief entails than one knows that one believes. Finally, actions and safe actions are logically related by SP and PR, which hold that necessary consequences of *mere* action are also necessary consequences of *safe* actions, and that a pilot can execute an action only if he believes that he is executing a safe action.

2.3 Soundness

Theorem 1 (Soundness). *Dynamic Agent Safety Logic is sound for Kripke structures with*
(1) reflexive R_k^i relations,
(2) serial, transitive, Euclidean R_b^i relations,
(3) which are partially ordered $(R_k^i \circ R_b^i) \subseteq R_b^i$, $(R_b^i \circ R_k^i) \subseteq R_b^i$, and $R_b^i \subseteq R_k^i$,
(4) $[\![i,(A,a),S]\!] \subseteq [\![i,(A,a)]\!]$ and
(5) $([\![i,(A,a),S]\!] \circ R_b^i) \subseteq [\![i,(A,a)]\!]$.

Proof. (1) *and* (2) correspond to the axioms that $\mathbf{K_i}$ is a T modality and $\mathbf{B_i}$ is a KD45 modality in the usual way. (3) corresponds to EP1, EP2, and EP3. Axioms AP through SB are reduction axioms. This leaves (4), corresponding to SP, and (5) which corresponds to PR. Here we will prove (5). Let M be a Kripke structure satisfying the five conditions above. Let A be an Action structure with a and i as its actual action token and agent.

   We prove (5) via the contrapositive of PR: $\langle \mathbf{B}_i\rangle\,[\mathbf{i},(\mathbf{A},\mathbf{a}),\mathbf{S}]\varphi \Rightarrow [\mathbf{i},(\mathbf{A},\mathbf{a})]\varphi$. Assume $M,w \models \langle \mathbf{B}_i\rangle\,[\mathbf{i}.(\mathbf{A},\mathbf{a}),\mathbf{S}]\varphi$. By the semantics of $\langle \mathbf{B}_i\rangle$, there exists a v, such that $wR_b^i v$ and $v \models [\mathbf{i},(\mathbf{A},\mathbf{a}),\mathbf{S}]\varphi$. From the semantics, it follows that forall M', v', if $(M, v)[\![i, (A, a), S]\!](M', v')$ then $M', v' \models \varphi$. By slightly abusing the notation, and letting $(W, w)R_b^i(W, v)$ be equivalent to $wR_b^i v$, we can create the composed relation $([\![i, (A, a), S]\!] \circ R_b^i)$. It then holds, by condition (5), that $(M, w)([\![i, (A, a), S]\!] \circ R_b^i)(M', v')$ implies $(M, w)[\![i, (A, a)]\!](M', v')$. So, for all M', v', if $(M, w)[\![i, (A, a)]\!](M', v')$, then $M', v' \models \varphi$. So, $M, w \models [i, (\mathbf{A}, \mathbf{a})]\varphi$.

$\square$

3   Case Study and Mechanization

We apply the logic just developed to the formal analysis of the Air France 447 aviation incident. We also mechanize the formalization in the Coq Proof Assistant. Our mechanization follows similar work by Maliković and Čubrilo [12,13], in which they mechanize an analysis of the game of Cluedo using Dynamic Epistemic Logic, based on van Ditmarsch's formalization of the game [6]. It is commonly assumed that games must be adversarial, but this is not the case. Games need only involve situations in which players' payoffs depend on the actions of other players. Similarly, knowledge games need not be adversarial, and must only involve diverging information. Thus, it is appropriate to model aviation incidents as knowledge games of sorts, where players' payoffs depend on what others do, specifically the way the players communicate information with each other. The goal is to achieve an accurate situational awareness and provide flight control inputs appropriate for the situation. Failures to achieve this goal result in disaster, and often result from imperfect information flow. A formal model of information flow in these situations provides insight and allows for the application of formal methods to improve information flow during emergency situations.

3.1   Air France 447

This case study is based on the authoritative investigative report into Air France 447 performed and released by France's Bureau d'Enquêtes et d'Analyses pour la Sécurité de l'Aviation Civile (BEA), responsible for investigating civil aviation incidents and issuing factual findings [4]. The case is mechanized by instantiating, in Coq, the above logic to reflect the facts of the case. One challenge associated with this is that the readings about inputs present in aviation are often real values on a continuum, whereas for our purposes we require discrete values. We accomplish this by dividing the continuum associated with inputs and readings into discrete chunks, similar to how fuzzy logic maps defines predicates with real values [10].

This paper will formalize an excerpted instance from the beginning of the case, involving an initial inconsistency among airspeed indicators, and the subsequent dangerous input provided by the pilot. Formalized in the logic, the facts of the case allow us to infer that the pilot lacked negative introspection about the safety-critical data required for his action. This demonstrates that the logic allows information about the pilot's situational awareness to flow to the computer, via the pilot's actions. It likewise establishes a safety property to be enforced by the computer, namely that a pilot should maintain negative introspection about safety-critical data, and if he fails to do so, it should be re-established as quickly as possible.

According to the official report, at 2 h and 10 min into the flight, a Pitot probe likely became clogged by ice, resulting in an inconsistency between airspeed indicators, and the autopilot disconnecting. This resulted in a change of mode from Normal Law to Alternate Law 2, in which certain stall and control protections ceased to exist. The pilot then made inappropriate control inputs, namely aggressive nose up commands, the only explanation for which is that he mistakenly believed that the aircraft was in Normal Law mode with protections in place to prevent a stall. This situation, and the inference regarding the pilot's mistaken belief, is modeled in the following application and mechanization of the logic.

3.2   Mechanization in Coq

The following mechanization demonstrates progress from the artificially simply toy examples normally analyzed in the literature to richer real-world examples. However, it does not represent the full richness of the approach. The actions and instrument readings mechanized in this paper are constrained to those most relevant to the case study. The approach is capable of capturing the full richness of all instrument reading configurations and actions available to a pilot. To do so, one needs to consult a flight safety manual and formally represent each action available to a pilot, and each potential instrument reading, according to the following scheme.

Before beginning, we note that our use of sets in the following Coq code requires the following argument passed to coqtop before executing: -impredicative-set. In CoqIDE, this can be done by selecting the 'Tools' dropdown, then 'Coqtop arguments'. Type in *-impredicative-set.*

We first formalize the set of agents.

```
Inductive Agents: Set := Pilot | CoPilot | AutoPilot.
```

Next we formalize the set of available inputs. These themselves are not actions, but represent atomic propositions true or false of a configuration.

```
Inductive Inputs : Set :=
            HardThrustPlus  | ThrustPlus
          | HardNoseUp      | NoseUp
          | HardWingLeft    | WingLeft
          | HardThrustMinus | ThrustMinus
          | HardNoseDown    | NoseDown
          | HardWingRight   | WingRight.
```

We represent readings by indicating which *side* of the panel they are on. Typically, an instrument has a left-side version, a right-side version, and sometimes a middle version serving as backup. When one of these instruments conflicts with its siblings, the autopilot will disconnect and give control to the pilot.

```
Inductive Side : Set := Left | Middle | Right.
```

We divide the main instruments into chunks of values they can take, in order to provide them with a discrete representation in the logic. For example, the reading *VertUp1* may represent a nose up reading between 0° and 10°, while *VertUp2* represents a reading between 11° and 20°.

```
Inductive Readings (s : Side) : Set :=
        VertUp1 | VertUp2 | VertUp3 | VertUp4
      | VertDown1 | VertDown2 | VertDown3 | VertDown4
      | VertLevel | HorLeft1 | HorLeft2 | HorLeft3
      | HorRight1 | HorRight2 | HorRight3 | HorLevel
      | AirspeedFast1 | AirspeedFast2 | AirspeedFast3
      | AirspeedSlow1 | AirspeedSlow2 | AirspeedSlow3
      | AirspeedCruise| AltCruise | AltClimb | AltDesc | AltLand.
```

We define a set of potential modes the aircraft can be in.

```
Inductive Mode : Set := Normal | Alternate1 | Alternate2.
```

We define a set of global instrument readings representing the mode and all of the instrument readings, left, right, and middle, combined together. This represents the configuration of the instrumentation.

```
Inductive GlobalReadings : Set := Global (m: Mode)
                                 (rl : Readings Left)
                                 (rm : Readings Middle)
                                 (rr : Readings Right).
```

The set of atomic propositions we are concerned with are those representing facts about the instrumentation.

```
Inductive Atoms : Set :=
     | M (m : Mode)
     | Input (a : Inputs)
     | InstrumentL (r : Readings Left)
     | InstrumentM (r : Readings Middle)
     | InstrumentR (r : Readings Right)
     | InstrumentsG (g : GlobalReadings).
```

Next we follow Maliković and Čubrilo [12,13] in defining a set *prop* of propositions in predicate calculus, distinct from Coq's built in type *Prop*. The definition provides constructors for atomic propositions consisting of particular instrument reading predicate statements, implications, propositions beginning with a knowledge modality, and those beginning with a belief modality. Interestingly, modal logic cannot be directly represented in Coq's framework [11]. We first define propositions in first-order logic, which we then use to define DASL. This appears to be the standard technique for mechanizing modal logics in Coq.

```
Inductive prop : Set :=
 | atm : Atoms → prop
 | imp: prop → prop → prop
 | Forall : forall (A : Set), (A → prop) → prop
 | K : Agents → prop → prop
 | B : Agents → prop → prop
 | Ck : list Agents → prop → prop
 | Cb : list Agents → prop → prop.
```

We use the following notation for implication and universal quantification.

```
Infix "⟹ " := imp (right associativity, at level 85).
Notation "\-/ p" := (Forall _ p) (at level 70, right associativity).
```

We likewise follow Maliković and Čubrilo [12,13] by defining an inductive type *theorem* representing a theorem of DASL. The constructors correspond to the Hilbert system, either as characteristic axioms, or inference rules. The first three represent axioms for propositional logic, then the rule Modus Ponens, then the axioms for the epistemic operator plus its Necessitation rule, then the doxastic operator and its Necessitation rule. Do not confuse the Necessitation rules with material implication in the object language. The final constructors capture the axioms relating belief and knowledge. The axioms for dynamic modal operators are defined separately, and are not included here.

```
Inductive theorem : prop → Prop :=
  |Hilbert_K: forall p q : prop, theorem (p ⟹ q ⟹ p)
  |Hilbert_S: forall p q r : prop,
            theorem ((p⟹ q⟹ r)⟹ (p⟹ q)⟹ (p⟹ r))
  |Classic_NOTNOT : forall p : prop, theorem ((NOT (NOT p)) ⟹ p)
  |MP : forall p q : prop, theorem (p ⟹ q) → theorem p → theorem q
  |K_Nec : forall (a : Agents) (p : prop), theorem p → theorem (K a p)
  |K_K : forall (a : Agents) (p q : prop),
        theorem (K a p ⟹ K a (p ⟹ q) ⟹ K a q)
  |K_T : forall (a : Agents) (p : prop), theorem (K a p ⟹ p)
  |B_Nec : forall (a : Agents) (p : prop), theorem p → theorem (B a p)
  |B_K : forall (a : Agents) (p q : prop),
        theorem (B a p ⟹ B a (p ⟹ q) ⟹ B a q)
  |B_Serial : forall (a : Agents) (p : prop),
            theorem (B a p ⟹ NOT (B a (NOT p)))
  |B_4 : forall (a : Agents) (p : prop), theorem (B a p ⟹ B a (B a p))
  |B_5 : forall (a : Agents) (p : prop),
        theorem (NOT (B a p) ⟹ B a (NOT (B a p)))
  |K_B : forall (a : Agents) (p : prop), theorem (K a p ⟹ B a p)
  |B_BK : forall (a : Agents) (p : prop), theorem (B a p ⟹ B a (K a p)).
```

We use the following notation for *theorem*:

```
Notation "|-- p" := (theorem p) (at level 80).
```

We encode actions as records in Coq, recording the acting pilot, the observability of the action (whether it is observed by other agents or not), the input provided by the pilot, and the preconditions for the action and the safety preconditions for the action, both represented as global atoms.

```
Record Action : Set := act {Ai : Agents; Aj : Agents; pi : PI;
                            input : Inputs; c : GlobalReadings;
                            c_s : GlobalReadings}.
```

The variable c holds the configuration representing the precondition for the action, while the variable c_s holds the configuration for the safety precondition. We encode the precondition and safety precondition functions as follows.

```
Function pre (a:Action) : prop := atm (InstrumentsG (c a)).

Function pre_s (a : Action) : prop := atm (InstrumentsG (c_s a)).
```

In the object language, the dynamic modalities of action and safe action are encoded as follows.

```
Parameter aft_ex_act : Action → prop → prop.
Parameter aft_ex_act_s : Action → prop → prop.
```

Many standard properties of logic, like the simplification of conjunctions, hypothetical syllogism, and contraposition, are encoded as Coq axioms. As an example, here is how we encode simplifying a conjunction into just its left conjunct.

```
Axiom simplifyL : forall p1 p2,
    |-- p1 & p2 → |-- p1.
```

We formalize the configuration of the instruments at 2 h 10 min into the flight as follows.

```
Definition Config_1 := (atm (M Alternate2)) &
                       (atm (InstrumentL (AirspeedSlow3 Left))) &
                       (atm (InstrumentM (AirspeedSlow3 Middle))) &
                       (atm (InstrumentR (AirspeedCruise Right))).
```

The mode is Alternate Law 2, and the left and central backup instruments falsely indicate that the airspeed is very slow, while the right side was not recorded, but because there was a conflict, we assume it remained correctly indicating a cruising airspeed.

The pilot's dangerous input, a hard nose up command, is encoded as follows.

```
Definition Input1 := act Pilot Pilot Pri HardNoseUp
                     (Global Alternate2 (AirspeedSlow3 Left)
                                        (AirspeedSlow3 Middle)
                                        (AirspeedCruise Right))
                     (Global Normal (AirspeedCruise Left)
                                    (AirspeedCruise Middle)
                                    (AirspeedCruise Right)).
```

The action is represented in the object language by taking the dual of the dynamic modality, $\neg[\mathbf{i}, (\mathbf{A}, \mathbf{a})]\neg True$, equivalently $\langle \mathbf{i}, (\mathbf{A}, \mathbf{a}) \rangle True$, indicating that the precondition is satisfied and the action token is executed.

```
Definition Act_1 := NOT (aft_ex_act Input1 (NOT TRUE)).
```

The actual configuration satisfies the precondition for the action, but it is inconsistent with the safety precondition. The safety precondition for the action indicates that the mode should be Normal and the readings should consistently indicate cruising airspeed. However, in Config_1, the conditions do not hold. Thus, the action is unsafe. From the configuration and the action, DASL allows us to deduce that the pilot lacks negative introspection of the action's safety preconditions.

Negative introspection is an agent's awareness of the current unknowns. To lack it is to be unaware of one's unknown variables, so lacking negative introspection about one's safety preconditions is to be unaware that they are unknown.

```
Theorem NegIntroFailMode :
              |-- (Config_1 ⟹
                  Act_1 ⟹
                  ((NOT (K Pilot (pre_s(Action1)))) &
                  (NOT (K Pilot (NOT (K Pilot (pre_s(Action1)))))))).
```

In fact, in general it holds that if the safety preconditions for an action are false, and the pilot executes that action, then the pilot lacks negative introspection of those conditions. We have proven both the above theorem, and the more general theorem, in Coq.

```
Theorem neg_intro_failure :
forall (A Ao : Agents) (pi : PI) (inp : Inputs)
    (m : Mode)
    (rl : Readings Left) (rm : Readings Middle) (rr : Readings Right)
    (ms : Mode)
    (rls : Readings Left) (rms : Readings Middle) (rrs : Readings Right)
    phi,
|-- (NOT
      (aft_ex_act
        (act A Ao pi inp (Global m rl rm rr) (Global ms rls rms rrs))
        (NOT phi)) ⟹
    NOT (atm (InstrumentsG (Global ms rls rms rrs))) ⟹
    (NOT (K A (atm (InstrumentsG (Global ms rls rms rrs)))) &
    (NOT (K A (NOT (K A (atm (InstrumentsG (Global ms rls rms rrs))))))))).
```

This indicates that negative introspection about safety preconditions is a desirable safety property to maintain, consistent with the official report's criticism that the Airbus cockpit system did not clearly display the safety critical information. The logic described in this research accurately models the report's findings that the pilot's lack of awareness about safety-critical information played a key role in his decision to provide unsafe inputs. Furthermore, the logic supports efforts to automatically infer which safety-critical information the pilot is unaware of and effectively display it to him.

4 Future Work

The case study presented in this paper is overly simplified due to space constraints. Future work will undertake the task of extending the approach to other actions in the Air France 447 incident, and the safety-critical information expressed by them. For example, when both pilots provided conflicting inputs to the aircraft, the computer could have inferred that neither was aware of the other's actions. This will illustrate the use of the approach in a multi-agent context. Similarly, as recommended by an anonymous reviewer, we shall apply the approach to other aviation mishaps involving complicated safety-critical information flow, specifically Asiana Airlines Flight 214 [14].

An important extension of the foundational work provided by this paper is the construction of a system that takes advantage of the logic as a runtime safety monitor. It will monitor the pilot's control inputs and current flight configurations, and in the event that an action's safety preconditions do not hold, infer which instrument readings the pilot is unaware of and act to correct this. In order to avoid further information overload, the corrective action taken by the computer should be to temporarily remove or dim the non-safety-critical information from competition for the pilot's attention, until the pilot's unsafe control inputs are corrected, indicating awareness of the safety-critical information. Construction of a prototype of this system is underway.

5 Conclusion

This paper has described Dynamic Agent Safety Logic (DASL), a logic for reasoning about safety-critical information flow. It formalized actions and knowledge in the way common to Dynamic Epistemic Logic, but also formalized the notion of safe actions and beliefs. Additionally, it formalized a more realistic model of human reasoning, capturing a weaker notion of knowledge than most epistemic logics, and modeled the logical relationship between knowledge and belief. It formalized a realistic notion of rationality. The logic was mechanized in the Coq proof assistant and applied to the case of Air France 447 to validate its usefulness as a formal method for aviation safety.

Acknowledgements. Seth Ahrenbach was partially supported by NSF CNS 1553548. The author is grateful for the criticism and suggestions provided by anonymous reviewers, and for the very generous assistance from Alwyn Goodloe, Rohit Chadha, and Chris Hathhorn.

References

1. Ahrenbach, S., Goodloe, A.: Formal analysis of pilot error using agent safety logic. In: Innovations in Systems and Software Engineering (submitted)
2. Barras, B., Boutin, S., Cornes, C., Courant, J., Filliatre, J.C., Gimenez, E., Herbelin, H., Huet, G., Munoz, C., Murthy, C., Parent, C.: The Coq proof assistant reference manual: version 6.1 (Doctoral dissertation, Inria) (1997)
3. Blackburn, P., de Rijke, M., Venema, Y.: Modal Logic. Cambridge University Press, New York (2001)
4. Bureau d'Enquêtes et d'Analyses: Final report on the accident on 1st June 2009 to the Airbus A330-203 registered F-GZCP operated by Air France flight AF 447 Rio de Janeiro-Paris. BEA, Paris (2012)
5. van Benthem, J.: Logical Dynamics of Information and Interaction. Cambridge University Press, New York (2011)
6. Van Ditmarsch, H.: Knowledge games. Bull. Econ. Res. **53**(4), 249–273 (2001)
7. Fagin, R., Halpern, J., Moses, Y., Vardi, M.: Reasoning About Knowledge. The MIT Press, Cambridge (2003)
8. Harel, D., Kozen, D., Tiuryn, J.: Dynamic Logic. MIT Press, Cambridge (2000)
9. Hintikka, J.: Knowledge and Belief. Cornell University Press, Ithaca (1962)
10. Klir, G., Yuan, B.: Fuzzy Sets and Fuzzy Logic, vol. 4. Prentice Hall, New Jersey (1995)
11. Lescanne, P.: Mechanizing common knowledge logic using COQ. Ann. Math. Artif. Intell. **48**(1–2), 15–43 (2006). APA
12. Maliković, M., Čubrilo, M.: Modeling epistemic actions in dynamic epistemic logic using Coq. In: CECIIS 2010 (2010)
13. Maliković, M., Čubrilo, M.: Reasoning about epistemic actions and knowledge in multi-agent systems using Coq. Comput. Technol. Appl. **2**(8), 616–627 (2011)
14. National Transportation Safety Board: Descent below visual glidepath and impact with Seawall Asiana Flight 214, Boeing 777-200ER, HL 7742, San Francisco, California, 6 July 2013 (Aircraft Accident Report NTSB/AAR-14/01). NTSB, Washington, DC (2014)

Compositional Falsification of Cyber-Physical Systems with Machine Learning Components

Tommaso Dreossi[1](✉), Alexandre Donzé[2], and Sanjit A. Seshia[1]

[1] University of California, Berkeley, USA
{dreossi,sseshia}@berkeley.edu
[2] Decyphir, Inc., San Francisco, USA
alex.r.donze@gmail.com

Abstract. Cyber-physical systems (CPS), such as automotive systems, are starting to include sophisticated machine learning (ML) components. Their correctness, therefore, depends on properties of the inner ML modules. While learning algorithms aim to generalize from examples, they are only as good as the examples provided, and recent efforts have shown that they can produce inconsistent output under small adversarial perturbations. This raises the question: can the output from learning components can lead to a failure of the entire CPS? In this work, we address this question by formulating it as a problem of falsifying signal temporal logic (STL) specifications for CPS with ML components. We propose a compositional falsification framework where a temporal logic falsifier and a machine learning analyzer cooperate with the aim of finding falsifying executions of the considered model. The efficacy of the proposed technique is shown on an automatic emergency braking system model with a perception component based on deep neural networks.

Keywords: Cyber-physical systems · Machine learning · Falsification · Temporal logic

1 Introduction

Over the last decade, machine learning (ML) algorithms have achieved impressive results providing solutions to practical large-scale problems (see, e.g., [2,8,10,14]). Not surprisingly, ML is being used in cyber-physical systems (CPS) — systems that are integrations of computation with physical processes. For example, semi-autonomous vehicles employ Adaptive Cruise Controllers (ACC) or Lane Keeping Assist Systems (LKAS) that rely heavily on image classifiers providing input to the software controlling electric and mechanical subsystems (see, e.g., [3]). The safety-critical nature of such systems involving ML raises the

This work is funded in part by the DARPA BRASS program under agreement number FA8750-16-C-0043, NSF grants CNS-1646208 and CCF-1139138, and by TerraSwarm, one of six centers of STARnet, a Semiconductor Research Corporation program sponsored by MARCO and DARPA. The second author did much of the work while affiliated with UC Berkeley.

© Springer International Publishing AG 2017
C. Barrett et al. (Eds.): NFM 2017, LNCS 10227, pp. 357–372, 2017.
DOI: 10.1007/978-3-319-57288-8_26

need for formal methods [18]. In particular, how do we systematically find bugs in such systems?

We formulate this question as the falsification problem for CPS models with ML components (CPSML): given a formal specification φ in signal temporal logic (STL) [12], and a CPSML model M, find an input for which M does *not* satisfy φ. A falsifying input generates a counterexample trace that reveals a bug. To solve this problem, multiple challenges must be tackled. First, the input space to be searched can be intractable. For instance, a simple model of a semi-autonomous car already involves several control signals (e.g., the angle of the acceleration pedal, steering angle) and other sensor input (e.g., images captured by a camera). Second, CPSML are often designed using languages (such as C, C++, or Simulink), for which clear semantics are not given, and involve third-party components that are opaque or poorly-specified. This obstructs the development of formal methods for the analysis of CPSML models and may force one to treat them as gray/black-boxes. Third, the formal verification of ML components is a difficult, and somewhat ill-posed problem due to the complexity of the underlying ML algorithms, large feature spaces, and the lack of consensus on a formal definition of correctness [18]. Hence, we need a technique to systematically analyze ML components within the context of a CPS.

In this paper, we propose a framework for the falsification of CPSML addressing the issues described above. Our technique is compositional in that it divides the search space for falsification into that of the ML component and of the remainder of the system, while establishing a connection between the two. The obtained subspaces are respectively analyzed by a temporal logic falsifier and an ML analyzer that cooperate. This cooperation mainly comprises a series of input space projections, leads to small subsets in which counterexamples are easier to find. Further, our technique can handle any machine learning technique, including the methods based on deep neural networks [8] that have proved effective in many recent applications. The proposed ML analyzer identifies sets of misclassifying features, i.e., inputs that "fool" the ML algorithm. The analysis is performed by considering subsets of parameterized features spaces that are used to approximate the ML components by simpler functions. The information gathered by the temporal logic falsifier and the ML analyzer together reduce the search space, providing an efficient approach to falsification for CPSML models.

Example 1. As an illustrative example, let us consider a simple model of an Automatic Emergency Braking System (AEBS) as a closed-loop control system composed of a controller (automatic brake), a plant (car transmission), and a sensor (obstacle detector) (see Fig. 1). The controller regulates the acceleration and braking of the plant using the velocity of the subject (ego) vehicle and the distance between it and an obstacle. The sensor

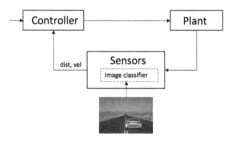

Fig. 1. Automatic Emergency Braking System. An image classifier is used to perceive vehicles in the frame of view.

used to detect the obstacle includes a camera along with an image classifier. In general, this sensor can provide noisy measurements due to incorrect image classifications which in turn can affect the correctness of the overall system.

Suppose we want to verify whether the distance between the subject vehicle and a preceding obstacle is always larger than 5 m. Such a verification requires the exploration of an intractable input space comprising the control inputs (e.g., acceleration and braking pedal angles) and the ML component's feature space (e.g., all the possible pictures observable by the camera). Note that feature space of RGB 1000 × 600 px pictures for an image classifier contains $256^{1000 \times 600 \times 3}$ elements. □

At first, the input space of the model described in Example 1 appears intractable. However, we can observe some interesting aspects of the relationship between the "pure CPS" input space and its ML feature space:

1. Under the assumption of "perfect ML components" (i.e., all feature vectors are correctly classified), we can study the CPSML model on a lower-dimensional input space (the "pure CPS" one) and identify regions of values that satisfy the specification but might be affected by the malfunctioning of some ML modules;
2. Instead of verifying the ML components on their whole feature spaces, we can focus only on those features related to the non-robust input values identified in the previous step, and
3. If we are able to determine misclassifications on the restricted feature space, then we can relate them back to CPSML input space, thus focusing the falsification on a smaller input space.

These three observations constitute the core idea of the compositional falsification method proposed in this paper. Specifically, we use a temporal logic falsifier, Breach [4], in Steps (1) and (3) to partition a given input set into values that do and do not satisfy a given specification, and an ML analyzer in Step (2) to determine subsets of feature vectors that are misclassified by the ML components.

The proposed method, however, presents certain challenges that need to be addressed. First, we need to construct a validity domain of a specification against a CPSML model with (assumed) correct ML components. Second, we need a method to relate the non-robust input areas to the feature space of the ML modules. Third, we need to systematically analyze the ML components with the goal of finding feature vectors leading to misclassifications. We describe in detail in Sects. 3 and 4 how we tackle these challenges.

In summary, the main contributions of this paper are:

- A compositional framework for the falsification of temporal logic properties of CPSML models that works for any machine learning classifier.
- A machine learning analyzer that identifies misclassifications leading to system-level property violations, based on two main ideas:

- An input space parameterization used to abstract the feature space and relate it to the CPSML input space, and
- A classifier approximation method used to identify misclassifications that can lead to unsafe executions of the CPSML.

In Sect. 5, we demonstrate the effectiveness of our approach on an Automatic Emergency Braking System (AEBS) involving an image classifier for obstacle detection based on deep neural networks using leading software packages Caffe [10] and TensorFlow [13].

Related Work

The verification of both CPS and ML algorithms have attracted several research efforts, and we focus here on the most closely related work. Techniques for the falsification of temporal logic specifications against CPS models have been implemented based on nonlinear optimization methods and stochastic search strategies (e.g., Breach [4], S-TaLiRo [1], RRT-REX [5], C2E2 [6]). While the verification of ML programs is less well-defined [18], recent efforts [19] show how even well trained neural networks can be sensitive to small adversarial perturbations, i.e., small intentional modifications that lead the network to misclassify the altered input with large confidence. Other efforts have tried to characterize the correctness of neural networks in terms of risk [21] (i.e., probability of misclassifying a given input) or robustness [7] (i.e., the minimal perturbation leading to a misclassification), while others proposed methods to generate pictures [16] or perturbations [9,15] in such a way to "fool" neural networks. To the best of our knowledge, our work is the first to address the verification of temporal logic properties of CPSML—the combination of CPS and ML systems.

2 Background

2.1 CPSML Models

In this work, we consider models of cyber-physical systems with machine learning components (CPSML). We assume that a system model is given as a gray-box simulator defined as a tuple $M = (S, U, sim)$, where S is a set of system states, U is a set of input values, and $sim : S \times U \times T \to S$ is a simulator that maps a state $\mathbf{s}(t_k) \in S$ and input value $\mathbf{u}(t_k) \in U$ at time $t_k \in T$ to a new state $\mathbf{s}(t_{k+1}) = sim(\mathbf{s}(t_k), \mathbf{u}(t_k), t_k)$, where $t_{k+1} = t_k + \Delta_k$ for a time-step $\Delta_k \in \mathbb{Q}_{>0}$.

Given an initial time $t_0 \in T$, an initial state $\mathbf{s}(t_0) \in S$, a sequence of time-steps $\Delta_0, \ldots, \Delta_n \in \mathbb{Q}_{>0}$, and a sequence of input values $\mathbf{u}(t_0), \ldots, \mathbf{u}(t_n) \in U$, a simulation trace of the model $M = (S, U, sim)$ is a sequence:

$$(t_0, \mathbf{s}(t_0), \mathbf{u}(t_0)), (t_1, \mathbf{s}(t_1), \mathbf{u}(t_1)), \ldots, (t_n, \mathbf{s}(t_n), \mathbf{u}(t_n))$$

where $\mathbf{s}(t_{k+1}) = sim(\mathbf{s}(t_k), \mathbf{u}(t_k), \Delta_k)$ and $t_{k+1} = t_k + \Delta_k$ for $k = 0, \ldots, n$.

The gray-box aspect of the CPSML model is that we assume some knowledge of the internal ML components. Specifically, these components, termed *classifiers*, are functions $f : X \to Y$ that assign to their input *feature vector* $\mathbf{x} \in X$ a *label* $y \in Y$, where X and Y are a feature and label space, respectively. Without loss of generality, we focus on binary classifiers whose label space is $Y = \{0, 1\}$. A ML algorithm selects a classifier using a training set $\{(\mathbf{x}^{(1)}, y^{(1)}), \ldots, (\mathbf{x}^{(m)}, y^{(m)})\}$ where the $(\mathbf{x}^{(i)}, y^{(i)})$ are labeled examples with $\mathbf{x}^{(i)} \in X$ and $y^{(i)} \in Y$, for $i = 1, \ldots, m$. The quality of a classifier can be estimated on a test set of examples comparing the classifier predictions against the labels of the examples. Precisely, for a given test set $T = \{(\mathbf{x}^{(1)}, y^{(1)}), \ldots, (\mathbf{x}^{(l)}, y^{(l)})\}$, the number of false positives $fp_f(T)$ and false negatives $fn_f(T)$ of a classifier f on T are defined as:

$$fp_f(T) = | \{\mathbf{x}^{(i)} \in T \mid f(\mathbf{x}^{(i)}) = 1 \text{ and } y^{(i)} = 0\} |$$
$$fn_f(T) = | \{\mathbf{x}^{(i)} \in T \mid f(\mathbf{x}^{(i)}) = 0 \text{ and } y^{(i)} = 1\} | \tag{1}$$

The error rate of f on T is given by:

$$err_f(T) = (fp_f(T) + fn_f(T))/l \tag{2}$$

A low error rate implies good predictions of the classifier f on the test set T.

2.2   Signal Temporal Logic

We consider Signal Temporal Logic [12] (STL) as the language to specify properties to be verified against a CPSML model. STL is an extension of linear temporal logic (LTL) suitable for the specification of properties of CPS.

A *signal* is a function $s : D \to S$, with $D \subseteq \mathbb{R}_{\geq 0}$ an interval and either $S \subseteq \mathbb{B}$ or $S \subseteq \mathbb{R}$, where $\mathbb{B} = \{\top, \bot\}$ and $\mathbb{R}$ is the set of reals. Signals defined on $\mathbb{B}$ are called *booleans*, while those on $\mathbb{R}$ are said *real-valued*. A *trace* $w = \{s_1, \ldots, s_n\}$ is a finite set of real-valued signals defined over the same interval D.

Let $\Sigma = \{\sigma_1, \ldots, \sigma_k\}$ be a finite set of predicates $\sigma_i : \mathbb{R}^n \to \mathbb{B}$, with $\sigma_i \equiv p_i(x_1, \ldots, x_n) \triangleleft 0$, $\triangleleft \in \{<, \leq\}$, and $p_i : \mathbb{R}^n \to \mathbb{R}$ a function in the variables $x_1, \ldots, x_n$.

An STL formula is defined by the following grammar:

$$\varphi := \sigma \mid \neg\varphi \mid \varphi \wedge \varphi \mid \varphi U_I \varphi \tag{3}$$

where $\sigma \in \Sigma$ is a predicate and $I \subset \mathbb{R}_{\geq 0}$ is a closed non-singular interval. Other common temporal operators can be defined as syntactic abbreviations in the usual way, like for instance $\varphi_1 \vee \varphi_2 := \neg(\neg\varphi_1 \wedge \varphi_2)$, $F_I\varphi := \top U_I \varphi$, or $G_I\varphi := \neg F_I \neg\varphi$. Given a $t \in \mathbb{R}_{\geq 0}$, a shifted interval I is defined as $t + I = \{t + t' \mid t' \in I\}$.

Definition 1 (Qualitative semantics). *Let w be a trace, $t \in \mathbb{R}_{\geq 0}$, and φ be an STL formula. The qualitative semantics of φ is inductively defined as follows:*

$$w, t \models \sigma \text{ iff } \sigma(w(t)) \text{ is true}$$
$$w, t \models \neg\varphi \text{ iff } w, t \not\models \varphi$$
$$w, t \models \varphi_1 \wedge \varphi_2 \text{ iff } w, t \models \varphi_1 \text{ and } w, t \models \varphi_2 \tag{4}$$
$$w, t \models \varphi_1 U_I \varphi_2 \text{ iff } \exists t' \in t + I \text{ s.t. } w, t' \models \varphi_2 \text{ and } \forall t'' \in [t, t'], w, t'' \models \varphi_1$$

A trace w satisfies a formula φ if and only if $w, 0 \models \varphi$, in short $w \models \varphi$. For given signal w, time instant $t \in \mathbb{R}_{\geq 0}$, and STL formula φ, the *satisfaction signal* $\mathcal{X}(w, t, \varphi)$ is $\top$ if $w, t \models \varphi$, $\bot$ otherwise.

Definition 2 (Quantitative semantics). *Let w be a trace, $t \in \mathbb{R}_{\geq 0}$, and φ be an STL formula. The* quantitative semantics *of φ is defined as follows:*

$$
\begin{aligned}
\rho(p(x_1, \ldots, x_n) \lhd 0, w, t) &= p(w(t)) \text{ with } \lhd \in \{<, \leq\} \\
\rho(\neg\varphi, w, t) &= -\rho(\varphi, w, t) \\
\rho(\varphi_1 \wedge \varphi_2, w, t) &= \min(\rho(\varphi_1, w, t), \rho(\varphi_2, w, t)) \\
\rho(\varphi_1 U_I \varphi_2, w, t) &= \sup_{t' \in t+I} \min(\rho(\varphi_2, w, t'), \inf_{t'' [t, t']} \rho(\varphi_1, w, t''))
\end{aligned}
\tag{5}
$$

The *robustness* of a formula φ with respect to a trace w is the signal $\rho(\varphi, w, \cdot)$.

3   Compositional Falsification Framework

In this section, we formalize the falsification problem for STL specifications against CPSML models, define our compositional falsification framework, and show its functionality on the AEBS system of Example 1.

Definition 3 (Falsification of CPSML). *Given a model $M = (S, U, sim)$ and an STL specification φ, find an initial state $\mathbf{s}(t_0) \in S$ and a sequence of input values $\mathbf{u} = \mathbf{u}(t_0), \ldots, \mathbf{u}(t_n) \in U$ such that the trace of states $w = \mathbf{s}(t_0), \ldots, \mathbf{s}(t_n)$ generated by the simulation of M from $\mathbf{s}(t_0) \in S$ under $\mathbf{u}$ does not satisfy φ, i.e., $w \not\models \varphi$. We refer to such $(\mathbf{s}(t_0), \mathbf{u})$ as* counterexamples *for φ. The problem of finding a counterexample is often called* falsification problem.

We now present the compositional framework for the falsification of STL formulas against CPSML models. Intuitively, the proposed method decomposes a given model into two abstractions: a version of the CPSML model under the assumption of perfectly correct ML modules and its actual ML components. The two abstractions are separately analyzed, the first by a temporal logic falsifier that builds the validity domain with respect to the given specification, the second by an ML analyzer that identifies sets of feature vectors that are misclassified by the ML components. Finally, the results of the two analysis are composed and projected back to a targeted input subspace of the original CPSML model where counterexamples can be found by invoking a temporal logic falsifier. Let us formalize this procedure.

Let $M = (S, U, sim)$ be a CPSML model and φ be an STL specification. Let M' be a version of M with perfectly behaving ML components, that is, every feature vector of the ML feature spaces is correctly classified. Let us denote by ml the isolated ML components of the model M.

Under the assumption of correct ML components, the lower-dimensional input space of M' can be analyzed by constructing the validity domain of φ, that is the partition of the input space into the sets U_φ and $U_{\neg\varphi}$ that do and do not satisfy φ, respectively. Note that considering the original model M, a possible misclassification of the ML components ml might affect the elements of U_φ and $U_{\neg\varphi}$. In particular, we are interested in the elements of U_φ that, due to misclassifications of ml, do not satisfy φ anymore. This corresponds to analyze the behavior of the ML components ml on the input set U_φ. We refer to this step as the ML analysis, that can be seen as the procedure of finding a subset $U^{ml} \subseteq U_\varphi$ of input values that are misclassified by the ML components ml. It is important to note that the input space of the CPS model M' and the feature spaces of the ML modules ml are different, thus the ML analyzer must adapt and relate the two different spaces. This important step will be clarified in Sect. 4.

Finally, the intersection $U_\varphi \cap U^{ml}$ of the subsets identified by the decomposed analysis of the CPS model and its ML components targets a small set of input values that are misclassified by the ML modules and are likely to falsify φ. Thus, counterexamples in $U_\varphi \cap U^{ml} \subseteq U$ can be determined by invoking a temporal logic falsifier on φ against M.

Algorithm 1. CPSML falsification scheme

1: **function** COMPFALSFY(M, φ)		$\triangleright$ M CPSML, φ STL specification
2: $\quad [M', ml] \leftarrow$DECOMPOSE$(M)$		$\triangleright$ M' exact ML, ml ML modules
3: $\quad [U_\varphi, U_{\neg\varphi}] \leftarrow$VALIDITYDOMAIN$(M', U, \varphi)$		$\triangleright$ Validity domain of φ w.r.t. M'
4: $\quad U^{ml} \leftarrow$ MLANALYSIS(ml, U_φ)		$\triangleright$ Find misclassified feature vectors
5: $\quad U_{\neg\varphi}^{ml} \leftarrow$FALSIFY$(M, U_\varphi \cap U^{ml}, \varphi)$		$\triangleright$ Falsify on targeted input
6: $\quad$ **return** $U_{\neg\varphi} \cup U_{\neg\varphi}^{ml}$		
7: **end function**		

The compositional falsification procedure is formalized in Algorithm 1. COMPFALSFY receives as input a CPSML model M and an STL specification φ, and returns a set of falsifying counterexamples. At first, the algorithm decomposes M into M' and ml, where M' is an abstract version of M with perfectly working ML modules, and ml are the ML components of M (Line 2). Then, the validity domain of φ with respect to the abstraction M' is computed by VALIDITYDOMAIN (Line 3) and subsets of input that are misclassified by ml are identified by MLANALYSIS (Line 4). Finally, the targeted input set $U_\varphi \cap U^{ml}$, consisting in the intersection of the sets identified by the decomposed analysis, is searched by a temporal logic falsifier on the original model M (Line 5) and a collection of counterexamples is returned.

Example 2. Let us consider the model described in Example 1 and let us assume that the input space U of the model M consists of the initial velocity of the subject vehicle $vel(0)$, the initial distance between the vehicle and the proceeding obstacle $dist(0)$, and the set of pictures that can be captured by the camera. Let $\varphi := G_{[0,T]}(dist(t) \geq \tau)$ be a specification that requires the vehicle to be always farther than τ from the preceding obstacle. Instead of analyzing the whole input space U (including a vast number of pictures), we can adopt our compositional framework to target a specific subset of U. Let M' be the AEBS model with a perfectly working image classifier and ml be the actual classifier. We begin by computing the validity subsets U_φ and $U_{\neg\varphi}$ of φ against M', considering only $vel(0)$ and $dist(0)$ and assuming exact distance measurements during the simulation. Next, we analyze only the image classifier ml on pictures of obstacles whose distances fall in U_φ, say in $[d_m, d_M]$ (see Fig. 2). Our ML analyzer generates only pictures of obstacles whose distances are in $[d_m, d_M]$, finds possible sets of images that are misclassified, and returns the corresponding distances that, when projected back to U, yield the subset $U_\varphi \cap U^{ml}$. Finally, a temporal logic falsifier can be invoked over $U_\varphi \cap U^{ml}$ and a set of counterexamples is returned. $\square$

This example illustrates how the compositional approach relies on tools, such as Breach [4], that compute validity domains and falsify STL specifications, as well as a ML analyzer. In the next section, we introduce our ML analyzer that identifies misclassifications of the ML component relevant to the overall CPSML input space.

4   Machine Learning Analyzer

In this section, we define an ML analyzer that adapts the input of a model to its classifiers feature spaces and identifies subsets of feature vectors for which wrong labels are predicted. The analysis involves the construction of an approximation function used to study the original classifiers. In particular, given a classifier $f : X \to Y$, the ML analyzer determines a simpler function $\tilde{f} : A \to Y$ that approximates f on the abstract domain A. The abstract domain of the function $\tilde{f}$ is analyzed and clusters of misclassifying abstract elements are identified. The concretizations of such elements are subsets of features that are misclassified by the original classifier f.

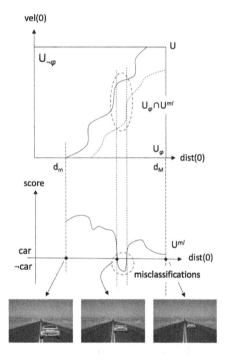

Fig. 2.   Compositional   falsification scheme on AEBS model.

4.1   Feature Space Abstraction

Let $\tilde{X} \subseteq X$ be a subset of the feature space of $f : X \to Y$. Let $\leq$ be a total order on a set A called the abstract set. An abstraction function is an injective function $\alpha : \tilde{X} \to A$ that maps every feature vector $\mathbf{s} \in \tilde{X}$ to an abstract element $\alpha(\mathbf{s}) \in A$. Conversely, the concretization function $\gamma : A \to \tilde{X}$ maps every abstraction $\mathbf{a} \in A$ to a feature $\gamma(\mathbf{a}) \in \tilde{X}$.

The abstraction and concretization functions play a fundamental role in our falsification framework. First, they allow us to map the input space of the CPS model to the feature space of its classifiers. Second, the abstract space can be used to analyze the classifiers on a compact domain as opposite to intractable feature spaces. These concepts are clarified in the following example, where a feature space of pictures is abstracted into a three-dimensional unit hyper-box.

Example 3. Let X be the set of RGB pictures of size 1000×600, i.e., $X = \{0, \ldots, 255\}^{1000 \times 600 \times 3}$. Suppose we are interested in analyzing an image classifier in the automotive context, i.e., on pictures of road scenarios rather than on the whole X. Suppose that we focus on the constrained feature space $\tilde{X} \subseteq X$ composed by the set of pictures of cars overlapped in different positions over a desert road background. We also consider the brightness level of the picture. The x and z positions of the car and the brightness level of the picture can be seen as the dimensions of an abstract set A. In this setting, we can define the abstraction and concretization functions α and γ that relate the abstract set $A = [0,1]^3$ and $\tilde{X}$. For instance, the picture $\gamma(0,0,0)$ sees the car on the left, close to the observer, and low brightness; the picture $\gamma(1,0,0)$ places the car shifted to the right; on the other extreme, $\gamma(1,1,1)$ has the car on the right, far away from the observer, and with a high brightness level. Figure 3 depicts some car pictures of $\tilde{S}$ disposed accordingly to their position in the abstract domain A (the surrounding box). □

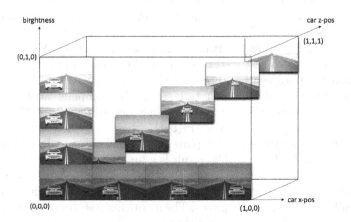

Fig. 3. Example of feature space abstraction A (the surrounding box) and some concretized element of the feature space $\tilde{X}$ (road pictures).

4.2   Approximation of Learning Components

We now describe how the feature space abstraction can be used to construct an approximation that helps the identification of misclassified feature vectors.

Given a classifier $f : X \to Y$ and a constrained feature space $\tilde{X} \subseteq X$, we want to determine an approximated classifier $\tilde{f} : A \to Y$, such that $err_{\tilde{f}}(T) \leq \epsilon$, for some $0 \leq \epsilon \leq 1$ and test set $T = \{(\mathbf{a}^{(1)}, y^{(1)}), \ldots, (\mathbf{a}^{(l)}, y^{(l)})\}$, with $y^{(i)} = f(\gamma(\mathbf{a}^{(i)}))$, for $i = 1, \ldots, l$.

Intuitively, the proposed approximation scheme samples elements from the abstract set, computes the labels of the concretized elements using the analyzed learning algorithm, and finally, interpolates the abstract elements and the corresponding labels in order to obtain an approximation function. The obtained approximation can be used to reason on the considered feature space and identify clusters of potentially misclassified feature vectors.

Algorithm 2. Approximation construction of classifier $f : X \to Y$

1: **function** APPROXIMATION(A, γ, ϵ) ▷ A abstract set $(\gamma : A \to \tilde{X})$, $0 \leq \epsilon \leq 1$
2:     $T_I \leftarrow \emptyset$
3:     **repeat**
4:         $T_I \leftarrow T_I \cup$ SAMPLE(A, f)
5:         $\tilde{f} \leftarrow$ INTERPOLATE(T_I)
6:         $T_E \leftarrow$ SAMPLE(A, f)
7:     **until** $err_{\tilde{f}}(T_E) \leq \epsilon$
8:     **return** $\tilde{f}$
9: **end function**

The APPROXIMATION algorithm (Algorithm 2) formalizes the proposed approximation construction technique. It receives in input an abstract domain A for the concretization function $\gamma : A \to \tilde{X}$, with $\tilde{X} \subseteq X$, the error threshold $0 \leq \epsilon \leq 1$, and returns a function $\tilde{f} : A \to Y$ that approximates f on the constrained feature space $\tilde{X}$. The algorithm consists in a loop that iteratively improves the approximation $\tilde{f}$. At every iteration, the algorithm populates the interpolation test set T_I by sampling abstract features from A and computing the concretized labels accordingly to f (Line 4), i.e., SAMPLE$(A, f) = \{(\mathbf{a}, y) \mid \mathbf{a} \in \tilde{A}, y = f(\gamma(\mathbf{a}))\}$, where $\tilde{A} \subseteq A$ is a finite subset of samples determined with some sampling method. Next, the algorithm interpolates the points of T_I (Line 5). The result is a function $\tilde{f} : A \to Y$ that simplifies the original classifier f on the concretized constrained feature space $\tilde{X}$. The approximation is evaluated on the test set T_E. Note that at each iteration, T_E changes while T_I incrementally grows. The algorithm iterates until the error rate $err_{\tilde{f}}(T_E)$ is smaller than the desired threshold ϵ (Line 7).

The technique with which the samples in T_E and T_I are selected strongly influences the accuracy of the approximation. In order to have a good coverage of the abstract set A, we propose the usage of low-discrepancy sampling methods that, differently from uniform random sampling, cover sets quickly and evenly. In this work, we use the Halton and lattice sequences, that are two common and easy to implement sampling methods. For details see, e.g., [17].

Example 4. We now analyze two image classifiers: the Caffe [10] version of AlexNet [11] and the Inception-v3 model of Tensorflow [13], both trained on the ImageNet database.[1] We sample 1000 points from the abstract domain defined in Example 3 using the lattice sampling techniques. These points encode the x and z displacements of a car in a picture and its brightness level (see Fig. 3). Figure 4(a) depicts the sampled points with their concretized labels. The green circles indicate correct classifications, i.e., the classifier identified a car, the red circles denote misclassifications, i.e., no car detected. The linear interpolation of the obtained points leads to an approximation function. The error rates $err_{\tilde{f}}(T_E)$ of the obtained approximations (i.e., the discrepancies between the predictions of the original image classifiers and their approximations) computed on 300 randomly picked test cases are 0.0867 and 0.1733 for Caffe and Tensorflow, respectively. Figure 4(b) shows the projections of the approximation functions for the brightness value 0.2. The more red a region, the larger the sets of pictures for which the neural networks do not detect a car. For illustrative purposes, we superimpose the projections of Fig. 4(b) over the background used for the picture generation. These illustrations show the regions of the concrete feature vectors in which a vehicle is misclassified.   □

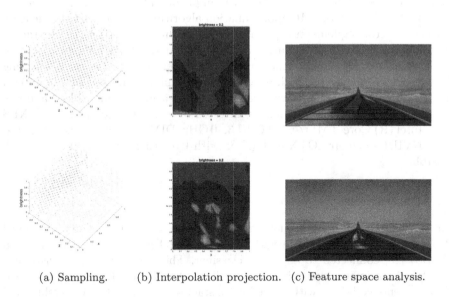

(a) Sampling.   (b) Interpolation projection.   (c) Feature space analysis.

Fig. 4. ML analysis of Caffe (top) and Tensorflow (bottom) on a road scenario. (Color figure online)

The analysis of Example 4 on Caffe and Tensorflow provides useful insights. First, we observe that Tensorflow outperforms Caffe on the considered road pictures since it correctly classifies more pictures that Caffe. Second, we notice

---

[1] http://image-net.org/.

that Caffe tends to correctly classify pictures in which the x abstract component is either close to 0 or 1, i.e., pictures in which the car is not in the middle of the street, but on one of the two lanes. This suggests that the model might not have been trained enough with pictures of cars in the center of the road. Third, using the lattice method on Tensorflow, we were able to identify a corner case misclassification in a cluster of correct predictions (note the isolated red circle with coordinates $(0.1933, 0.0244, 0.4589)$). All this information provides insights on the classifiers that can be useful in the hunt for counterexamples.

5   Experimental Results

5.1   Implementation Details

The presented falsification framework has been implemented in a Matlab toolbox publicly available at https://github.com/tommasodreossi/FalsifCPSML. The tool deals with Simulink models of CPSML and STL specifications. It consists of a temporal logic falsifier and an ML analyzer that interact to falsify the given STL specification against the decomposed Simulink model. As an STL falsifier, we chose the existing tool Breach [4], while the ML analyzer has been implemented from scratch. The ML analyzer implementation includes the feature space abstractor and the ML approximation algorithm (see Sect. 4). The feature space abstractor implements a picture generator that concretizes the abstracted feature vectors. The approximation algorithm, that computes an approximation of the analyzed ML component, gives to the user the possibility of selecting the sampling sequence method, interpolation technique, and setting the desired error rate. Our tool is interfaced with the deep learning frameworks Caffe [10] and Tensorflow [13]. Our tool has been tested on a desktop computer Dell XPS 8900, Intel (R) Core(TM) i7-6700 CPU 3.40 GHz, DIMM RAM 16 GB 2132 MHz, GPU NVIDIA GeForce GTX TITAN X, with Ubuntu 14.04.5 LTS and Matlab R2016b.

5.2   Case Studies

For the experimental evaluations, we consider a closed-loop Simulink model of a semi-autonomous vehicle with an Advanced Emergency Braking System (AEBS) [20] connected to an image classifier. The model mainly consists of a four-speed automatic transmission controller linked to an AEBS that automatically prevents collisions with preceding obstacles and alleviate the harshness of a crash when a collision is likely to happen (see Fig. 5). The AEBS determines a braking mode depending on the speed of the vehicle v_s, the possible presence of a preceding obstacle, its velocity v_p, and the longitudinal distance $dist$ between the two. The distance $dist$ is provided by radars having 30 m of range. For obstacles farther than 30 m, the camera, connected to an image classifier, alerts the AEBS that, in the case of detected obstacle, goes into warning mode.

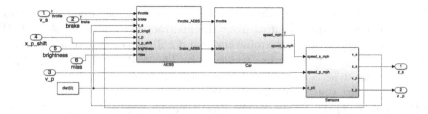

Fig. 5. Simulink model of a semi-autonomous vehicle with AEBS.

Depending on $v_s, v_p, dist$, and the presence of obstacles detected by the image classifier, the AEBS computes the time to collision and longitudinal safety indices, whose values determine a controlled mode among safe, warning, braking, and collision mitigation. In safe mode, the car does not need to brake. In warning mode, the driver should brake to avoid a collision. If this does not happen, the system goes into braking mode, where the automatic brake slows down the vehicle. Finally, in collision mitigation mode, the system, determining that a crash is unavoidable, triggers a full braking action aimed to minimize the damage.

To establish the correctness of the system and in particular of its AEBS controller, we formalize the STL specification $G(\neg(dist(t)) \leq 0)$, that requires $dist(t)$ to always be positive, i.e., no collision happens. The input space is $v_s(0) \in [0, 40]$ (mph), $dist(0) \in [0, 60]$ (m), and the set of all RGB pictures of size 1000×600. The preceding vehicle is not moving, i.e., $v_p(t) = 0$ (mph).

At first, we compute the validity domain of φ assuming that the radars are able to provide exact measurements for any distance $dist(t)$ and the image classifier correctly detects the presence of a preceding vehicle. The computed validity domain is depicted in Fig. 6: green for U_φ and red for $U_{\neg\varphi}$. Next, we identify candidate counterexamples that belong to the satisfactory set (i.e., the inputs that satisfy the specification) but might be influenced by a misclassification of the image classifier. Since the AEBS relies on the classifier only for distances larger than 30 m, we can focus on the subset of the input space with $dist(0) \geq 30$. Specifically, we identify potential counterexamples by analyzing a pessimistic version of the model where the ML component always misclassifies the input pictures

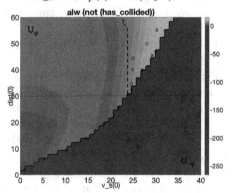

Fig. 6. Validity domain for $G(\neg(dist$ $(t)) \leq 0)$. Proved (red crosses) and disproved (green circles) candidate counterexamples. Dotted (horizontal) line: image classifier activation threshold. Dashed (vertical) line: validity boundary of φ for worst-case misclassifications. (Color figure online)

(see Fig. 6, area with dashed boundary). From this sub-input space, we can identify candidate counterexamples, such as, for instance, $(25, 40)$ (i.e., $v_s(0) = 25$ and $dist(0) = 40$).

Next, let us consider the Caffe image classifier and the ML analyzer presented in Sect. 4 that generates pictures from the abstract feature space $A = [0,1]^3$, where the dimensions of A determine the x and z displacements of a car and the brightness of a generated picture, respectively. The goal now is to determine an abstract feature $\mathbf{a}_c \in A$ related to the candidate counterexample $(25, 40)$, that generates a picture that is misclassified by the ML component and might lead to a violation of the specification φ. The $dist(0)$ component of $\mathbf{u}_c = (25, 40)$ determines a precise z displacement $\mathbf{a}_2 = 0.2$ in the abstract picture. Now, we need to determine the values of the abstract x displacement and brightness. Looking at the interpolation projection of Fig. 4(b), we notice that the approximation function misclassifies pictures with abstract component $\mathbf{a}_1 \in [0.4, 0.5]$ and $\mathbf{a}_3 = 0.2$. Thus, it is reasonable to try to falsify the original model on the input element $v_s(0) = 25, dist(0) = 40$, and concretized picture $\gamma(0.5, 0.2, 0.2)$. For this targeted input, the temporal logic falsifier computed a robustness value for φ of -24.60, meaning that a falsifying counterexample has been found. Other counterexamples found with the same technique are, e.g., $(27, 45)$ or $(31, 56)$ that, associated with the correspondent concretized pictures with $\mathbf{a}_1 = 0.5$ and $\mathbf{a}_3 = 0.2$, lead to the robustness values -23.86 and -24.38, respectively (see Fig. 6, red crosses). Conversely, we also disproved some candidate counterexamples, such as $(28, 50)$, $(24, 35)$, or $(25, 45)$, whose robustness values are $9.93, 7.40$, and 7.67 (see Fig. 6, green circles).

For experimental purposes, we try to falsify a counterexample in which we change the x position of the abstract feature so that the approximation function correctly classifies the picture. For instance, by altering the counterexample $(27, 45)$ with $\gamma(0.5, 0.225, 0.2)$ to $(27, 45)$ with $\gamma(1.0, 0.225, 0.2)$, we obtain a robustness value of 9.09, that means that the AEBS is able to avoid the car for the same combination of velocity and distance of the counterexample, but different x position of the preceding vehicle. Another example, is the robustness value -24.38 of the falsifying input $(31, 56)$ with $\gamma(0.5, 0.28, 0.2)$, that altered to $\gamma(0.0, 0.28, 0.2)$, changes to 12.41.

Finally, we test Tensorflow on the corner case misclassification identified in Sect. 4.2 (i.e., the picture $\gamma(0.1933, 0.0244, 0.4589)$). The distance $dist(0) = 4.88$ related to this abstract feature is below the activation threshold of the image classifier. Thus, the falsification points are exactly the same as those of the computed validity domain (i.e., $dist(0) = 4.88$ and $v_s(0) \in [4, 40]$). This study shows how a misclassification of the ML component might not affect the correctness of the CPSML model.

6 Conclusion

We presented a compositional falsification framework for STL specifications against CPSML models based on the separate analysis of a CPS system and its ML components. We introduced an ML analyzer able to abstract feature spaces, approximate ML classifiers, and provide sets of misclassified feature vectors that can be used to drive the falsification process. We implemented our framework and showed its effectiveness for an autonomous driving controller using perception based on deep neural networks.

This work lays the basis for future advancements. We intend to improve our ML analyzer exploring the automatic generation of feature space abstractions from given training sets. Another direction is to integrate other techniques for generating misclassifications of ML components (e.g. [9,15]) into our approach. One could also apply our ML analyzer outside the falsification context, such as for controller synthesis. Finally, our compositional methodology could be extended to other, non-cyber-physical, systems that contain ML components.

References

1. Annpureddy, Y., Liu, C., Fainekos, G., Sankaranarayanan, S.: S-TALIRO: a tool for temporal logic falsification for hybrid systems. In: Abdulla, P.A., Leino, K.R.M. (eds.) TACAS 2011. LNCS, vol. 6605, pp. 254–257. Springer, Heidelberg (2011). doi:10.1007/978-3-642-19835-9_21

2. Blum, A.L., Langley, P.: Selection of relevant features and examples in machine learning. Artif. Intell. **97**(1), 245–271 (1997)

3. Bojarski, M., et al.: End to end learning for self-driving cars. arXiv:1604.07316 (2016)

4. Donzé, A.: Breach, a toolbox for verification and parameter synthesis of hybrid systems. In: Touili, T., Cook, B., Jackson, P. (eds.) CAV 2010. LNCS, vol. 6174, pp. 167–170. Springer, Heidelberg (2010). doi:10.1007/978-3-642-14295-6_17

5. Dreossi, T., Dang, T., Donzé, A., Kapinski, J., Jin, X., Deshmukh, J.V.: Efficient guiding strategies for testing of temporal properties of hybrid systems. In: Havelund, K., Holzmann, G., Joshi, R. (eds.) NFM 2015. LNCS, vol. 9058, pp. 127–142. Springer, Cham (2015). doi:10.1007/978-3-319-17524-9_10

6. Duggirala, P.S., Mitra, S., Viswanathan, M., Potok, M.: C2E2: a verification tool for stateflow models. In: Baier, C., Tinelli, C. (eds.) TACAS 2015. LNCS, vol. 9035, pp. 68–82. Springer, Heidelberg (2015). doi:10.1007/978-3-662-46681-0_5

7. Fawzi, A., Fawzi, O., Frossard, P.: Analysis of classifiers' robustness to adversarial perturbations. arXiv preprint arXiv:1502.02590 (2015)

8. Hinton, G., et al.: Deep neural networks for acoustic modeling in speech recognition: the shared views of four research groups. IEEE Signal Process. Mag. **29**(6), 82–97 (2012)

9. Huang, X., Kwiatkowska, M., Wang, S., Wu, M.: Safety verification of deep neural networks. CoRR, abs/1610.06940 (2016)

10. Jia, Y., Shelhamer, E., Donahue, J., Karayev, S., Long, J., Girshick, R., Guadarrama, S., Darrell, T.: Caffe: convolutional architecture for fast feature embedding. In: ACM Multimedia Conference, ACMMM, pp. 675–678 (2014)

11. Krizhevsky, A., Sutskever, I., Hinton, G.E.: Imagenet classification with deep convolutional neural networks. In: Advances in Neural Information Processing Systems, pp. 1097–1105 (2012)

12. Maler, O., Nickovic, D.: Monitoring temporal properties of continuous signals. In: Lakhnech, Y., Yovine, S. (eds.) FORMATS/FTRTFT-2004. LNCS, vol. 3253, pp. 152–166. Springer, Heidelberg (2004). doi:10.1007/978-3-540-30206-3_12

13. TensorFlow, M.A., et al.: Large-scale machine learning on heterogeneous systems (2015). Software available from tensorflow.org

14. Michalski, R.S., Carbonell, J.G., Mitchell, T.M.: Machine Learning: An Artificial Intelligence Approach. Springer Science & Business Media, Heidelberg (2013)
15. Moosavi-Dezfooli, S.-M., Fawzi, A., Frossard, P.: Deepfool: a simple and accurate method to fool deep neural networks. In: IEEE Computer Vision and Pattern Recognition, pp. 2574–2582 (2016)
16. Nguyen, A., Yosinski, J., Clune, J.: Deep neural networks are easily fooled: high confidence predictions for unrecognizable images. In: Computer Vision and Pattern Recognition, CVPR, pp. 427–436. IEEE (2015)
17. Niederreiter, H.: Low-discrepancy and low-dispersion sequences. J. Number Theory **30**(1), 51–70 (1988)
18. Seshia, S.A., Sadigh, D., Sastry, S.S.: Towards verified artificial intelligence. CoRR, abs/1606.08514 (2016)
19. Szegedy, C., Zaremba, W., Sutskever, I., Bruna, J., Erhan, D., Goodfellow, I., Fergus, R.: Intriguing properties of neural networks. arXiv:1312.6199 (2013)
20. Taeyoung, L., Kyongsu, Y., Jangseop, K., Jaewan, L.: Development and evaluations of advanced emergency braking system algorithm for the commercial vehicle. In: Enhanced Safety of Vehicles Conference, ESV, pp. 11–0290 (2011)
21. Vapnik, V.: Principles of risk minimization for learning theory. In: NIPS, pp. 831–838 (1991)

Verifying a Class of Certifying Distributed Programs

Kim Völlinger$^{(\boxtimes)}$ and Samira Akili

Humboldt University of Berlin, Berlin, Germany
voellinger@hu-berlin.de

Abstract. A *certifying program* produces in addition to each output a *witness* that certifies the output's correctness. An accompanying *checker* program checks whether the computed witness is correct. Such a checker is usually simpler than the original program, and its verification is often feasible while the verification of the original program is too costly. By verifying the checker and by giving a machine-checked proof that the witness certifies the output's correctness, we get *formal instance correctness*, i.e. a machine-checked proof that a particular input-output pair is correct. This verification method was demonstrated on *sequential* programs. In contrast, we are concerned with the correctness of *distributed* programs which behave fundamentally differently. In this paper, we present a verification method to obtain formal instance correctness for one class of certifying distributed programs. Moreover, we demonstrate our method on the leader election problem using the theorem prover Coq.

Keywords: Certifying distributed program · Formal instance correctness · Coq

1 Introduction

A major problem in software engineering is assuring the quality of software. Well-known methods are testing and formal verification. While testing does not cover all inputs, formal verification is often too costly. We suggest certifying programs – a formal method that is, on the one hand, more rigorous than testing, and on the other hand, less costly than formal verification.

A certifying program verifies the correctness of its output at *runtime*. The idea is to adapt the underlying algorithm of a program at design time to protect its user not only against a faulty implementation but also against a faulty algorithm and a faulty execution (e.g. caused by a hardware failure). To this end, a *certifying program* produces a *witness* in addition to each output that certifies the output's correctness. Since the witness is computed by the untrusted program itself, a simple *checker* program checks whether the witness is correct. Furthermore, there is a verification method for certifying programs to achieve *formal instance correctness* for an output – a machine-checked proof that a particular input-output pair is correct.

© Springer International Publishing AG 2017
C. Barrett et al. (Eds.): NFM 2017, LNCS 10227, pp. 373–388, 2017.
DOI: 10.1007/978-3-319-57288-8_27

In contrast, we are concerned with the correctness of *distributed programs*. Certifying distributed programs behave differently to certifying *sequential* programs; for instance, the witness is distributed over a system and checked by many checkers. In this paper, we present a verification method to achieve formal instance correctness for one class of certifying distributed programs. As a case study, we demonstrate our method on the leader election problem in networks using the theorem prover Coq for program verification and theorem proving. The whole formalization is available on GitHub[1].

1.1   Structure of this Paper

We give the preliminaries in Sect. 2. In Sect. 3, we discuss how to apply the concept of certifying sequential programs to distributed programs. We define a class of certifying distributed algorithms. Our class is particularly interesting since the witness is computed and checked in a distributed manner (Sect. 3.3). Hence, the certification itself is distributed. For this class, we introduce a verification method to obtain formal instance correctness (Sect. 3.4). In Sect. 4, we give a certifying variant of solving the leader election problem in networks and demonstrate our verification method on certifying leader election using the theorem prover Coq. We present related work in Sect. 5, draw our conclusions in Sect. 6 and discuss future work in Sect. 7.

2   Preliminaries

In this section, we recap certifying sequential programs (Sect. 2.1), and a verification method to obtain formal instance correctness for certifying sequential programs (Sect. 2.2).

2.1   Certifying Sequential Programs

The idea of a certifying program is to adapt the underlying algorithm of a program such that it verifies the correctness of its output at runtime [7]. We assume a program that takes an input x from a set X and produces an output y from a set Y. The specification of the program is given by a precondition $\phi \subseteq X$ and a postcondition $\psi \subseteq X \times Y$. Let W be a set of potential witnesses. A *witness predicate* for the specification is a predicate $\Gamma \subseteq X \times Y \times W$ with the *witness property*:

$$\forall x, y, w : (\phi(x) \wedge \Gamma(x, y, w)) \longrightarrow \psi(x, y) \tag{1}$$

If the witness property holds for x, y, w, then the input-output pair (x, y) satisfies the specification, and we call w a *witness* for $\psi(x, y)$.

A (correct) *certifying program* produces in addition to each output a witness such that the witness property is satisfied. However, the idea is that a user of a

---

[1] https://github.com/voellinger/verified-certifying-distributed-algorithms/tree/master/leader-election.

certifying program does not have to trust the program but a (simpler) *checker* program that decides the witness predicate Γ. Figure 1 sums up the concept of a certifying program.

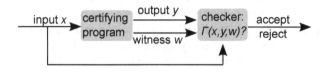

Fig. 1. A certifying program accompanied by its checker.

As an example, we consider the problem of deciding if a graph is bipartite, i.e. if its vertices can be divided in two partitions so that each edge has a vertex in each of both partitions. A certifying variant of a program deciding that a particular graph G is not bipartite additionally produces an odd cycle in G as a *witness*. The *witness predicate* holds if the witness is a cycle of odd length contained in G; it can easily be decided by a *checker* program. The witness certifies the output: an odd cycle contained in G proves that G is not bipartite since an odd cycle itself is not bipartite. Thus, the witness predicate has the *witness property*. For a bipartite graph, the witness could be a bipartition.

There is always a certifying variant of a program, for instance, with a witness that is the computation itself. In general, this is not a good witness, since proving the witness property becomes program verification then. The challenge is to find "good" witnesses.

2.2   Verification of Certifying Sequential Programs

The user of a certifying program has to trust its witness property, and its accompanying checker. A checker is usually much simpler than the original program, and its verification is often feasible while the verification of the original program is too costly. Rizkallah's method is to use the theorem Prover Isabelle to give a machine-checked proof for the witness property, and to verify the checker (e.g. with VCC) [11]. By this combination of certifying programs with theorem proving and program verification, we achieve formal instance correctness for instances for which the checker accepts.

3   Verification Method for a Class of Certifying Distributed Programs

In this section, we give a verification method to obtain formal instance correctness for one class of certifying distributed programs. We begin with what we consider to be a distributed program and with discussing the challenges of applying the concept of certifying sequential programs to distributed programs. Subsequently, we define a class of certifying distributed programs. Finally, for this class, we give a verification method to obtain formal instance correctness.

3.1 Distributed Programs

A distributed system consists of computing components that can communicate with each other by shared memory or message-passing channels. A *distributed algorithm* describes for each component an algorithm such that all components together solve one problem. For instance, there are distributed algorithms to solve problems associated with distributing a computation over a system such as coordination, communication or synchronization of the components. To give some examples, there are distributed algorithms to elect a leader, find a consensus or identify a substructure of the system such as a tree [10]. An implementation of a distributed algorithm is a *distributed program*.

3.2 Challenges of Certifying Distributed Programs

The distributed setting has all the challenges of the sequential setting, and additionally, its own specific challenges [9, Sect. 1.3]. That is why distributed programs are known to be especially hard to verify. While non-termination is considered a fault in sequential programs, some distributed programs should run continuously, e.g. communication protocols. Certification of non-terminating programs poses questions such as when should a non-terminating program compute a witness. For a terminating distributed program, each component holds its output after termination. Hence, the output of the distributed program is distributed over the system. The output's distribution leads to questions such as should there be a witness for each component or one witness for the whole system, and should we verify the correctness of a component's output or of the network's output. Hence, there is not only one way of applying the concept of a certifying sequential program to distributed programs.

3.3 A Class of Certifying Distributed Programs

For defining a class of certifying distributed programs, we focus on networks (i.e. distributed systems with message-passing channels) that are static (i.e. components and channels do not leave the system) and asynchronous (i.e. no global clock exists), and on distributed programs that terminate. After termination, each component holds its local output and the global output of the distributed program is the collective of the local outputs. Our approach is to make such a distributed program certifying by making it compute many local witnesses that together prove the global output's correctness. The local witnesses are computed and checked in a distributed manner at runtime. Hence, we present certifying distributed programs where the certification itself is distributed.

We represent a network by a graph G that is a finite directed connected graph with a vertex set $V = \{1, 2, \ldots, n\}$ and an edge set E that is symmetric. Each vertex presents a component and two directed edges (i, j) and (j, i) present a bidirectional channel between the components i and j. We call such a graph G a *network graph*.

Let G be a network graph. Let X, Y and W be sets containing potential local inputs, local outputs and local witnesses, respectively. A certifying distributed program p of class C computes for a *global input* $\mathbf{x} \in X^n$ a *global output* $\mathbf{y} \in Y^n$, and in addition, a *global witness* $\mathbf{w} \in W^n$. Hence, each component $i \in V$ computes for a *local input* $x_i \in X$ a *local output* $y_i \in Y$ and additionally a *local witness* $w_i \in W$. The specification of p is given by a *(global) precondition* $\phi \subseteq X^n$ and a *(global) postcondition* $\psi \subseteq X^n \times Y^n$.

A *global witness predicate* is a predicate $\Gamma \subseteq X^n \times Y^n \times W^n$ with the *(global) witness property*:

$$\forall \mathbf{x}, \mathbf{y}, \mathbf{w} : \ (\phi(\mathbf{x}) \wedge \Gamma(\mathbf{x}, \mathbf{y}, \mathbf{w})) \longrightarrow \psi(\mathbf{x}, \mathbf{y}) \qquad (2)$$

If the witness property holds for $\mathbf{x}$, $\mathbf{y}$, $\mathbf{w}$, then the global input-output pair $(\mathbf{x}, \mathbf{y})$ satisfies the specification, and we call $\mathbf{w}$ a *global witness* for $\psi(\mathbf{x}, \mathbf{y})$.

We want that the global witness predicate is decided in a distributed manner. That is why we define a local witness predicate. A *local witness predicate* is a predicate $\gamma \subseteq X \times Y \times W$ with the *composition property*:

$$\forall \mathbf{x}, \mathbf{y}, \mathbf{w} : \ (\phi(\mathbf{x}) \wedge (\forall i \in V \ \gamma(x_i, y_i, w_i))) \longrightarrow \Gamma(\mathbf{x}, \mathbf{y}, \mathbf{w}) \qquad (3)$$

For a triple $(x_i, y_i, w_i) \in \gamma$, we call w_i a *local witness* of component i. For the class C, the global witness predicate Γ is checked after termination of p in the way that each component i has a *local checker* that decides the local witness predicate $\gamma(x_i, y_i, w_i)$ for i. Since the checking occurs after termination, we do not have to care about asynchrony.

3.4 Verification Method for Class C

We give a verification method to obtain formal instance correctness, i.e. a proof that a particular input-output pair is correct. Let p be a certifying distributed program of class C. In order to obtain formal instance correctness for p, we have to solve the following proof obligations:

- *Witness Property*: We have to give a machine-checked proof for the implication (2).
- *Composition Property*: We have to give a machine-checked proof of the implication (3).
- *Correctness of the Local Checkers*: We have to prove that the local checker c_i of each component i checks the local witness predicate $\gamma(x_i, y_i, w_i)$, assuming the precondition $\phi(\mathbf{x})$ holds, i.e.
    1. If $\phi(\mathbf{x})$ and $(x_i, y_i, w_i) \in \gamma$, then c_i halts and accepts.
    2. If $\phi(\mathbf{x})$ and $(x_i, y_i, w_i) \notin \gamma$, then c_i halts and rejects.

If we solve these proof obligations, we obtain formal instance correctness for each instance on which all local checkers accept:

Theorem 1. *Let $G = (V, E)$ be a network graph with $|V| = n$. Let X, Y and W be sets. Let $\phi \subseteq X^n$ be a precondition and $\psi \subseteq X^n \times Y^n$ a postcondition. Let $\Gamma \subseteq X^n \times Y^n \times W^n$ be a global witness predicate for ϕ and ψ, and let $\gamma \subseteq X \times Y \times W$ be a local witness predicate for ϕ, Γ, and G. Let $(\mathbf{x}, \mathbf{y}, \mathbf{w}) \in X^n \times Y^n \times W^n$. Let c be a local checker deciding γ. Assuming $\mathbf{x} \in \phi$, if c accepts on (x_i, y_i, w_i) for all $i \in V$, then $(\mathbf{x}, \mathbf{y}) \in \psi$.*

Proof. $(x_i, y_i, w_i) \in \gamma$ for all $i \in V$ since c decides γ. Since γ is a local witness predicate and $\mathbf{x} \in \phi$, it follows from the composition property that $(\mathbf{x}, \mathbf{y}, \mathbf{w}) \in \Gamma$. From Γ being a global witness predicate and $\mathbf{x} \in \phi$, it follows by the witness property that $(\mathbf{x}, \mathbf{y}) \in \psi$.

Notice that the program p itself is not mentioned in the theorem. The machine-checked proofs and the verified local checkers can indeed be combined with any program producing an input, output and witness. Moreover, the reader may wonder why we do not prove: if $(\mathbf{x}, \mathbf{y}) \in \psi$, then there exists a global witness $\mathbf{w}$ such that $(\mathbf{x}, \mathbf{y}, \mathbf{w}) \in \Gamma$. In fact, with such a proof, we would reason about the correctness of p. However, we do not want to establish the correctness of p but to achieve formal instance correctness for p. Verifying formal instance correctness is a different problem than verifying programs.

Verification Within Coq. We use the theorem prover Coq for theorem proving and program verification. Coq [4] is an interactive theorem prover that provides its user with a specification language, a higher-order logic, a richly-typed functional programming language, and some proof automations. Moreover, Coq implements a mechanism to extract programs written in Coq to languages like Haskell and Objective Caml. Coq's programming language is not turing-complete since it allows only structural recursion enforcing that every program halts.

We use Coq for theorem proving in order to solve the proof obligations *witness property* and *composition property*, and for program verification in order to solve the proof obligation *correctness of the local checkers*. Moreover, we extract a verified local checker from Coq to Haskell.

To model a network in Coq, we build upon the graph library *Graph Basics* [3] that defines basic concepts of graph theory such as undirected graphs, trees or connectivity. The purpose of this library is to express mathematical and computational aspects of graph theory in the same formalism. To the best of our knowledge, there is no other graph library for Coq.

3.5   Further Classes of Certifying Distributed Programs

We give a brief outlook of further classes of certifying distributed programs. One modification is to define a different composition property:

$$\forall \mathbf{x}, \mathbf{y}, \mathbf{w} : \ (\phi(\mathbf{x}) \wedge (\exists i \in V \ \gamma(x_i, y_i, w_i))) \longrightarrow \Gamma(\mathbf{x}, \mathbf{y}, \mathbf{w}) \tag{4}$$

Hence, if at least one component satisfies the local witness predicate, then the global witness predicate holds. We used such a composition property for a certifying variant of distributed bipartite testing. Other logical combinations of local witness predicates could be of interest as well.

A different modification is to certify local outputs instead of the global output. Assume all components compute their distance to one component as often done in routing protocols. If one component is buggy, then the local witness predicate cannot hold for all components. However, many components probably hold their actual distance. In this scenario, it would be interesting to verify local outputs. To this end, we need a local witness property. For instance in the form: if the component's local witness predicate holds, then its local input-output pair is correct. Since for many examples such a local witness property is too ambitious, it could also have the form: if for all the components in a subnetwork the local witness predicate hold, then the components of the subnetwork hold their correct local output. Additionally, we need a local specification and more reasoning in general. In that case, we would have to adapt our verification method.

Another modification is to consider non-terminating distributed programs. In this case, the witness and composition property would look significantly different and the checking would become more difficult since it would be done on-line by an reactive checker. Thus, non-termination would also lead to an adapted verification method.

Considering unreliable communication channels or dynamic networks would remarkably complicate the certification and verification. There are many more modifications to take into account but they are outside the scope of this paper.

4   Case Study: Leader Election

As a case study, we consider the leader election problem: all components of a network have to elect exactly one of them as a leader. Usually, a leader is elected for coordination purposes. There are various distributed algorithms that solve leader election. For instance, Lynch gives an asynchronous leader election algorithm for a network of arbitrary topology and components that have unique identifiers [6].

In this section, we first give a certification for leader election that belongs to class C (see Sect. 3.3) and then we give a formalization in Coq.

4.1   Certifying Leader Election

The specification of the leader election problem states that the problem is solved if all components of a network agree on exactly one of them as a leader. Thus, in order to verify the global output's correctness, we have to certify that all components agree on the leader and that the elected leader exists. To certify the agreement on the leader, the global witness consists in each component holding the elected leader of its neighbors. From agreement in all neighborhoods, it follows agreement in the network since neighborhoods overlap. To certify that the elected leader exists, the global witness consists of a spanning tree in the network that is rooted at the leader. In order to check the spanning tree in a distributed manner, we use a characterization of the spanning tree using the distance and the parent function. Note that a component cannot simply check that the elected leader is a component of the network, since it doesn't know all components.

Let $G = (V, E)$ be a network graph with $|V| = n$. The *local input* x_i of a component i is i's neighborhood, i.e. i's neighboring components and i's channels. The *local output* y_i of a component i is $leader_i$ (i's elected leader). The *postcondition* $\psi(\mathbf{x}, \mathbf{y})$ states that there exists $l \in V$ with $leader_i = l$ for all $i \in V$.

The *local witness* w_i of a component i consists of:

– $distance_i$ (i's distance from its elected leader),
– $parent_i$ (i's parent in the spanning tree),
– $distance_{parent_i}$ (the distance that i's parent has from its elected leader) and
– $leader_j$ for all neighbors j of i (the elected leaders of i's neighbors).

The *global witness predicate* $\Gamma(\mathbf{x}, \mathbf{y}, \mathbf{w})$ holds if there exists $l \in V$ ("the elected leader and root of the spanning tree") with $leader_l = l$ such that $distance_l = 0$, $parent_l = l$ and $leader_j = l$ for all neighbors j of l, and if for all $i \in V$ with $leader_i \neq i$ it holds that $distance_i > 0$, $parent_i$ is a neighbor of i, $distance_i = distance_{parent_i} + 1$ and $leader_j = leader_i$ for all neighbors j of i. By the global witness predicate, we can tell that the global witness $\mathbf{w}$ is a spanning tree in G rooted at the elected leader.

The *witness property* states that if all components agree with their neighbors on the leader then all components agree on exactly one leader, and if this elected leader is the root of a spanning tree then the leader exists in the network.

The *local witness predicate* γ states the properties required by the global witness predicate for the neighborhood of a component. There is one clause for the elected leader and another clause for all the other components. Each component i has a *local checker* c_i deciding whether $(x_i, y_i, w_i) \in \gamma$. The *composition property* states that if the local witness predicate holds for all components then the global witness predicate holds.

As an example, Fig. 2 shows a specific network graph and a spanning tree as the global witness in this network. Moreover, for two components the properties required to satisfy their local witness predicates are listed.

For the purpose of this paper, it is not important how a component computes its local witness. However, there are distributed algorithms to compute a spanning tree and Lynch even gives a leader election algorithm that is based on a spanning tree [6].

4.2   Verification in Coq

As a proof-of-concept, we demonstrate our verification method to obtain formal instance correctness (see Sect. 3.4) on certifying leader election using Coq. We

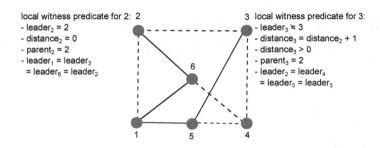

local witness predicate for 2: 2
- leader₂ = 2
- distance₂ = 0
- parent₂ = 2
- leader₁ = leader₃
  = leader₆ = leader₂

3 local witness predicate for 3:
- leader₃ ≍ 3
- distance₃ = distance₂ + 1
- distance₃ > 0
- parent₃ = 2
- leader₂ = leader₄
  = leader₅ = leader₃

Fig. 2. A network graph with six components. A spanning tree is highlighted by dashed lines. For the components 2 and 3, the properties required to satisfy local witness predicates are listed. Component 2 is the elected leader.

begin with the formalization of the network graph and continue with solving the proof obligations *composition property*, *witness property* and *correctness of the local checkers*.

Network Formalization. We formalize the network as an undirected, connected graph provided by the *GraphBasics* library. We define a vertex of the graph as a Component with an unique identifier.

We construct the local input x_i of a component i in such a way that the global input **x** satisfies the precondition. Hence, for the following formalization of the composition property and the witness property, we assume that the precondition holds.

Composition Property. The composition property states that if the local witness predicate holds for each component, then the global witness predicate is satisfied. For certifying leader election, the local witness predicate is a disjunction in which one clause applies for the elected leader and the other clause for all other components (see Sect. 4.1). In Coq, we formalize each clause of the local witness predicate as a single predicate: gamma_root is the local witness predicate of the elected leader and gamma_i is the local witness predicate of all other components.

Each component i holds its values $leader_i$, $parent_i$ and $distance_i$. From a global perspective on the network, we can canonically define the functions *leader*, *parent* and *distance* that each maps a component i to its corresponding value. To instantiate the functions, we added additional properties to the local witness predicate; for instance, we require the mapping between the component i and its function value parent_i by stating the equation parent i = parent_i. In the following Coq formalization of the local witness predicate, we commented on such additional properties with (*x*):

```
Definition gamma_i
(i:Component)(leader_i:Component)(distance_i:nat)
(parent_i:Component) (leader_parent_i:Component)
(distance_parent_i:nat)(leader_neighbors:C_list)
:Prop :=
leader i <> i                                    /\
parent i = parent_i                              /\   (*x*)
a (A_ends i parent_i)                            /\
a (A_ends parent_i i)                            /\
distance i = distance_i                          /\   (*x*)
distance_parent_i = distance parent_i            /\
distance_i = distance_parent_i + 1               /\
leader i = leader_parent_i                       /\   (*x*)
leader_parent_i = leader (parent i)              /\
(forall (k:Component),
In k leader_neighbors -> k = leader i)           /\
(forall (c:Component),
In c (neighbors g i) -> In (leader c) leader_neighbors).


Definition gamma_root
(i:Component)(leader_i:Component)(distance_i:nat)
(parent_i:Component)(leader_neighbors:C_list)
:Prop :=
leader i = leader_i      /\      (*x*)
leader_i = i             /\
parent i = parent_i      /\      (*x*)
parent_i = i             /\
distance i = distance_i  /\      (*x*)
distance_i = 0           /\
(forall (k:Component), In k leader_neighbors ->
k = leader i)            /\
(forall (c:Component) , In c (neighbors g i) ->
In (leader c) leader_neighbors).
```

If the local witness predicate holds for all components, then only in the way that there is one component (**root** – the elected leader) that satisfies the clause gamma_root and all other components satisfy the clause gamma_i. Suppose there is more than one component fulfilling the gamma_root clause. Then there is more than one component that has elected itself as a leader. Since the graph is connected, there is a path between every component. Hence, there must be a path between two components that have a different leader. If we follow the path, there must be a pair of components that contradicts the property that neighbors agree on their leader.

Suppose otherwise that all components fulfill the clause gamma_i, then every component has a parent that is not itself. As there is always an edge between a component and its parent, there are as many edges as components in the subgraph. Hence, this subgraph contains a cycle. Within a cycle the distance property is violated leading to a contradiction.

As a consequence, we fix one component as **root** and formalize the composition property in Coq as follows:

```
Theorem composition_property:
forall (leader_root parent_root: Component)
( distance_root : nat)(leader_neighbors_root : C_list),

(gamma_root root leader_root distance_root parent_root leader_neighbors_root
    ) ->

forall (x:Component)(prop1: v x)(prop2: x <> root)
(leader_i   parent_i leader_parent_i :Component )
(distance_i distance_parent_i: nat)(leader_neighbors_i : C_list),

(gamma_i x leader_i distance_i parent_i leader_parent_i distance_parent_i
    leader_neighbors_i ) ->

distance root = 0                                        /\
distance x = distance (parent x) + 1                     /\
leader root = root                                       /\
leader x <>  x                                           /\
leader x =  leader (parent x)                            /\
parent root = root                                       /\
v (parent x)                                             /\
a (A_ends x (parent x))                                  /\
a (A_ends (parent x) x)                                  /\
(forall (c:Component),
In c (neighbors g x) -> leader c = leader x)             /\
(forall (c:Component),
In c (neighbors g root) -> leader c = leader root).
```

The proof of the composition property in Coq is straightforward and only uses syntactic rewriting.

Witness Property. The witness property states that if the global witness predicate holds, then the leader election problem is solved: the spanning tree witnesses the existence of a leader, and by the agreement between neighbors, there can only be one leader.

As an assumption in Coq, we state that the global witness predicate holds. As a consequence, we can formalize the witness property as follows:

```
Theorem global_witness_property:
exists (l : Component), v l ->
forall (x:Component)(prop1: v x), leader x = l.
```

In order to prove the witness property, we formalize and prove additional properties. We define an inductive type Connection: a Connection is an undirected path between two vertices, consisting of edges that are induced by the parent function. A Connection is constructed from a parent to its child, and has a length.

Moreover, we define the function parent_iteration which takes a component c and a natural number n as input and recursively applies the parent function n-times on c. An *ancestor* of a component is a component that can be obtained by the application of the parent_iteration function on c.

The proof of the witness property rests upon three central lemmata. The first lemma states that there is a Connection between every component and root:

```
Lemma path_to_root:
forall (n:nat) (x:Component) (prop1 : v x),
distance x = n ->
{el : A_list & Connection x root el n }.
```

We conduct a proof by induction on the distance of a component - the length of the Connection. The base case follows from the assumptions. For the induction step, we assume a Connection *co* between root and the parent of a component *x* with length *n*. By definition of Connection, *co* can be extended by the edge between $x's$ parent and *x* to a Connection *co'*. By definition, the length of *co'* is $n + 1$ which equals the distance of *x*.

The second lemma states that a component *x* agrees with all its ancestors on the leader:

```
Lemma parent_is_leader :
forall (n:nat)(x y: Component)(prop1: v x) (prop2:v y),
leader x = leader (parent_iteration n x).
```

We conduct a proof by induction on the argument *n* of the parent_iteration function. The proof is similar to the one presented above.

The third lemma states that if there is a Connection between a component and root, then root is ancestor of the component:

```
Lemma parent_transitive_is_root :
forall  (n:nat) (x: Component)(prop1:v x),
n = distance x ->
{el : A_list & Connection x root el (distance x) } ->
root = (parent_iteration (distance x) x) .
```

By induction, we can establish that if a Connection exists from component *x* to component *y* with length *n*, then *x* is the result of applying the parent_iteration function *n*-times on *y*. Since we already proved that there is a Connection between every component and root, we conclude that root is an ancestor of each component.

We prove the witness property by case analysis. For the first case, we have to prove that root is the leader of root which follows from the assumptions. For the second case, we have to prove that all other components have root as their leader. We first use the lemma parent_is_leader such that we are left with proving that the leader of each ancestor of each component is root. Using the lemma parent_transitive_is_root, we establish that each component has root as its ancestor. As root has itself as leader and all other components have the leader of their ancestors as leader, we conclude that root is leader of each component.

Correctness of the Local Checkers. As the certifying leader election belongs to class *C*, every component has a local checker. The local checker of a component *i* decides its local witness predicate $\gamma(x_i, y_i, w_i)$. Hence, the checker needs *i*'s local input x_i, *i*'s local output y_i and *i*'s local witness w_i.

The local input of a component *i* is the neighborhood of *i* in accordance to the network Graph *G*. For modeling purposes, we define a function that takes the network graph as input and generates a checker c_i for each component i that is initialized with i's local input. Furthermore, we bundle i's local output y_i and local witness w_i in the variable checker_input. We implement the local checker in Coq as follows:

```
Definition checker (l: local_input) (c : checker_input) : bool :=
(((negb (beq c.(leader_i) l.(i)))
beq c.(leader_i) c.(leader_parent_i))                    &&
beq_nat c.(distance_i) ( c.(distance_parent_i)+1 )       &&
In_bool c.(parent_i) l.(neighbors))                      &&
forallb_neigbors c.(leader_neighbors) c.(leader_i)       ||
beq c.(leader_i) l.(i)                                    &&
beq_nat c.(distance_i) 0                                  &&
beq  c.(parent_i) l.(i)                                   &&
forallb_neigbors c.(leader_neighbors) c.(leader_i).
```

Note that a local checker accepts if the disjunction of the clauses gamma_root and gamma_i holds.

To verify correctness of a local checker c_i, we have to prove that c_i only accepts if the local witness predicate holds for i. We formalize the checker correctness as follows:

```
Theorem checker_correctness (l: local_input)
(c: checker_input):
(leaderconsistency l.(i) c.(leader_parent_i))        /\
(distanceconsistency l.(i) c.(distance_parent_i))    /\
(componentconsistency l.(i) c.(leader_i)
c.(parent_i) c.(distance_i)                           /\
(neighborsconsistency l.(i)
c.(leader_neighbors_i)))                              ->

(checker l c = true)                                  <->

((gamma_i l.(i) c.(leader_i)
c.(distance_i) c.(parent_i)
c.(leader_parent_i)  c.(distance_parent_i)
c.(leader_neighbors_i)                                \/

gamma_root l.(i) c.(leader_i) c.(distance_i)
c.(parent_i) c.(leader_neighbors_i) )).
```

The proof of the checker_correctness is straightforward and uses syntactic rewriting. Note that we added the helper predicates leaderconsistency, distanceconsistency, neighborsconsistency and componentconsistency to ensure consistency between two neighbouring components, i.e. to make sure their witnesses match on corresponding values. For example, if a component i chooses a component j as its parent ($parent_i = j$), the value of $distance_{parent_i}$ equals $distance_j$. In a real network, the consistency check requires additional communication between the checkers. We can realize communication in Coq by making the checker's code reactive. As shown in [2], Coq suits to implement interactive software. To model the communication, we can define an inductive type that models the state transitions of the checker caused by incoming or outgoing messages. A similar approach was used to formalize the Border Gateway Protocol (BGP) in Coq [13]. In order to extract checkers from Coq to e.g. Haskell that can run on a real network, we have to integrate communication in our formalization.

Formal Instance Correctness. We solved the proof obligations *composition property, witness property* and *correctness of the local checkers* for certifying leader election using Coq. Thus, we achieved formal instance correctness for certifying leader election.

5 Related Work

Literature offers more than 100 certifying sequential algorithms. A theory of certifying sequential algorithms along with several examples and further reading is given in [7]. Some of these certifying sequential algorithms are implemented in the industrial-level library LEDA (Library for Efficient Data Structures and Algorithms) [8] – a library for combinatorial and geometric computing. In addition, Rizkallah developed a verification method to achieve formal instance correctness for certifying sequential programs and demonstrated her verification method on some programs from the LEDA libraries. Her dissertation [11] points to her further publications on this field. However, all this work was done for *sequential* and not for *distributed* programs. Völlinger and Reisig gave a certification for the shortest path problem in networks as an first example [12]. To the best of our knowledge, there is no other research on certifying *distributed* programs and no verification method to obtain formal instance correctness for certifying distributed programs.

However, some techniques for making a distributed program self-stabilizing share similarities to our approach of making a distributed program certifying. The idea of self-stabilization is that a system in a faulty state stabilizes itself to a correct state. To this end, the components of a system have to detect that the system's state is faulty whereby local detection is desired. As a consequence, there are some similarities to proof labeling schemes [5] as well, since if there exists a (silent) self-stabilizing program, then there exists a proof labeling scheme for that program and vice versa [1]. In contrast, we separate the checking from the computation, rely on witnesses, and integrate proofs for the witness property and the composition property.

6 Conclusion

Since verification of a distributed program is often too costly, we investigated a verification method to obtain formal instance correctness, i.e. a proof that a particular input-output pair is correct. For this purpose, we considered certifying programs. A checker of a certifying program is usually simpler than the original program, and its verification is often feasible while the verification of the original program is too costly. By verifying the checker and by giving a machine-checked proof that the witness certifies the output's correctness, we get formal instance correctness. Rizkallah demonstrated this verification method on certifying *sequential* programs.

In contrast, we are concerned with the correctness of *distributed* programs. In this paper, we defined a class of certifying distributed programs that is particularly interesting since the global witness is computed and checked in a distributed manner (Sect. 3.3). Moreover, we presented a verification method to obtain formal instance correctness for the defined class of certifying distributed programs (Sect. 3.4). Furthermore, we gave a certifying variant of the leader election problem in networks (Sect. 4.1). As a case study, we demonstrated our verification method on certifying leader election using the interactive theorem prover Coq (Sect. 4.2).

7 Future Work

In order to evaluate our verification method, more case studies are of interest. We expect that the library *Graph Basics* would be also helpful for the verification of other certifying distributed programs. However, the library does not offer graphs with weighted edges. Since weighted edges are necessary for the formalization of computing shortest paths in a network, it could be an interesting extension. A first step in this direction is the definition of the inductive type `Connection` that adds the concept of the length of a path.

Moreover, we expect that the formalization of the spanning tree as a global witness can be reused for further case studies, since a lot of our certifying distributed programs rely on a spanning tree.

Another interesting direction would be to investigate further classes of certifying distributed programs and to find a verification method to obtain formal instance correctness for these classes.

References

1. Blin, L., Fraigniaud, P., Patt-Shamir, B.: On proof-labeling schemes versus silent self-stabilizing algorithms. In: Felber, P., Garg, V. (eds.) SSS 2014. LNCS, vol. 8756, pp. 18–32. Springer, Cham (2014). doi:10.1007/978-3-319-11764-5_2
2. Claret, G.: Pluto: a first concurrent web server in Gallina. http://coq-blog.clarus.me/pluto-a-first-concurrent-web-server-in-gallina.html
3. Duprat, J.: A coq toolkit for graph theory (2011). rapport de recherche. Ecole Normale Superieur de Lyon
4. INRIA: The coq proof assistant. http://coq.inria.fr/
5. Korman, A., Kutten, S., Peleg, D.: Proof labeling schemes. Distrib. Comput. **22**(4), 215–233 (2010)
6. Lynch, N.A.: Distributed Algorithms. Morgan Kaufmann Publishers Inc., San Francisco (1996)
7. McConnell, R.M., Mehlhorn, K., Näher, S., Schweitzer, P.: Certifying algorithms. Comput. Sci. Rev. **5**, 119–161 (2011)
8. Mehlhorn, K., Näher, S.: LEDA: A Platform for Combinatorial and Geometric Computing. Cambridge University Press, Cambridge (1999)
9. Peleg, D.: Distributed Computing: A Locality-Sensitive Approach. Society for Industrial and Applied Mathematics, Philadelphia (2000)

10. Raynal, M.: Distributed Algorithms for Message-Passing Systems. Springer, Heidelberg (2013)
11. Rizkallah, C.: Verification of program computations. Ph.D. thesis (2015)
12. Völlinger, K., Reisig, W.: Certification of distributed algorithms solving problems with optimal substructure. In: Calinescu, R., Rumpe, B. (eds.) SEFM 2015. LNCS, vol. 9276, pp. 190–195. Springer, Cham (2015). doi:10.1007/978-3-319-22969-0_14
13. Weitz, K., Woos, D., Torlak, E., Ernst, M.D., Krishnamurthy, A., Tatlock, Z.: Formal semantics and automated verification for the border gateway protocol. In: ACM SIGCOMM Workshop on Networking and Programming Languages (NetPL 2016), Florianopolis, Brazil (2016)

Compact Proof Witnesses

Marie-Christine Jakobs[(✉)] and Heike Wehrheim

Paderborn University, Paderborn, Germany
{marie.christine.jakobs,wehrheim}@upb.de

Abstract. Proof witnesses are proof artifacts showing correctness of programs wrt. safety properties. The recent past has seen a rising interest in witnesses as (a) proofs in a proof-carrying-code context, (b) certificates for the correct functioning of verification tools, or simply (c) exchange formats for (partial) verification results. As witnesses in all theses scenarios need to be stored and processed, witnesses are required to be as small as possible. However, software verification tools – the prime suppliers of witnesses – do not necessarily construct small witnesses.

In this paper, we present a formal account of proof witnesses. We introduce the concept of *weakenings*, reducing the complexity of proof witnesses while preserving the ability of witnessing safety. We develop a weakening technique for a specific class of program analyses, and prove it to be sound. Finally, we experimentally demonstrate our weakening technique to indeed achieve a size reduction of proof witnesses.

Keywords: Software verification · Proof witness · Proof re-use

1 Introduction

In the past years, automatic verification of programs with respect to safety properties has reached a level of maturity that makes it applicable to industrial-size programs. The annual software verification competition SV-COMP [4] demonstrates the advances of program verification, in particular its scalability. Software verification tools prove program correctness, most often for safety properties written into the program in the form of assertions. When the verification tool terminates, the result is typically a yes/no answer optionally accompanied by a counterexample. While this is the obvious result a verification tool should deliver, it became clear in recent years that all the information computed about a program during verification is too valuable to just be discarded at the end. Such information should better be stored in some form of *proof.*

Proofs are interesting for several reasons: (A) Proofs can be used in a proof-carrying code (PCC) context [25] where a program is accompanied by its proof of safety. Verifying this proof allows to more easily recheck the safety of the program, e.g., when its provider is untrusted. (B) A proof can testify that the verification tool worked correctly, and checking the proof gives confidence in its soundness [5]. (C) Verification tools are sometimes unable to complete proving (e.g., due to timeouts). A proof can then summarize the work done until the

© Springer International Publishing AG 2017
C. Barrett et al. (Eds.): NFM 2017, LNCS 10227, pp. 389–403, 2017.
DOI: 10.1007/978-3-319-57288-8_28

tool stopped (see e.g. [6]) so that other tools can continue the work. All these scenarios use proofs as *witnesses* of the (partial) correctness of the program.

For these purposes, witnesses need to be small. If the witness is very large, the gain of having a witness and thus not needing to start proving from scratch is lost by the time and memory required to read and process the witness. Our interest is thus in compact proof witnesses. However, the proof artifacts that software verification tools produce are often even larger than the program itself.

Large proofs are a well-known problem in PCC approaches (e.g. [1,2,22,24, 26,29]). To deal with the problem, Necula and Lee [24] (who employ other types of proofs than automatic verification tools produce) use succinct representations of proofs. A different practice is to store only parts of a proof and recompute the remaining parts during proof validation like done by Rose [28] or Jakobs [22]. An alternative approach employs techniques like lazy abstraction [9,20] to directly construct small proofs. Further techniques as presented by Besson et al. [2] and Seo et al. [29] try to remove irrelevant information from proofs that are fixpoints. The latter two approaches have, however, only looked at proofs produced by path-insensitive program analyses.

In this paper, we first of all present a formal account of proof witnesses. We do so for verification tools generating for the safety analysis some form of abstract state space of the program, either by means of a path insensitive or a path sensitive analysis. We call this *abstract reachability graph* in the sequel, following the terminology for the software verification tool CPACHECKER [8]. We formally state under what circumstances proof witnesses can actually soundly testify program safety. Based on this, we study *weakenings* of proof witnesses, presenting more compact forms of proofs while preserving being a proof witness. Next, we show how to compute weakenings for a specific category of program analyses. Finally, we experimentally show our weakening technique to be able to achieve size reduction of proof witnesses. To this end, we evaluated our weakening technique on 395 verification tasks taken from the SV-COMP [3] using explicit-state software model checking as analysis method for verification. Next to proof size reduction, we also evaluate the combination of our approach with lazy refinement [9] plus examine its performance in a PCC setting [22].

2   Background

Witnesses are used to certify safety of programs. In this section, we start with explaining programs and their semantics. For this presentation, we assume to have programs with assignments and assume statements (representing if and while constructs) and with integer variables only[1]. We distinguish between boolean expressions used in assume statements, and abbreviate assume bexpr simply by *bexpr*, and arithmetic expressions *aexpr* used in assignments. The set *Ops* contains all these statements, and the set *Var* is the set of variables occuring in a program. Following Configurable Software Verification [7] – the technique the tool CPACHECKER, in which we integrated our approach, is based on –,

---

[1] Our implementation in CPACHECKER [8] supports programs written in C.

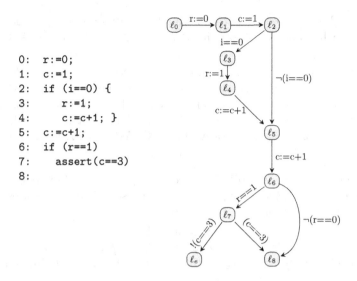

```
0:  r:=0;
1:  c:=1;
2:  if (i==0) {
3:      r:=1;
4:      c:=c+1; }
5:  c:=c+1;
6:  if (r==1)
7:      assert(c==3)
8:
```

Fig. 1. Program isZero (i input variable) and its control-flow automaton

we model a program by a *control-flow automaton* (CFA) $P = (L, E_{CFA}, \ell_0, L_{err})$. The set L represents program locations, ℓ_0 is the initial program location, and $E_{CFA} \subseteq L \times Ops \times L$ models the control-flow edges. The set $L_{err} \subseteq L$ of error locations defines which locations are unsafe to reach. In the program, these safety properties are written as **assert** statements. Note that all safety properties can be encoded this way [23], and that we assume that all properties of interest are encoded at once.

Figure 1 gives a small (completely artificial) program called isZero (which we use later for explanation) and its control-flow automaton. Here, location ℓ_e is the only error location. The program is called isZero since it tests whether the input i is zero (which is recorded as value 1 in r). The assertion checks whether the number of assignments to r or checks on r is 3 when r is 1. This number is accumulated in the variable c.

The semantics of a program $P = (L, E_{CFA}, \ell_0, L_{err})$ is defined by a labeled transition system $(L \times C, E_{CFA}, \rightarrow)$ made up of a set of concrete states C plus locations L, the labels E_{CFA} (the control-flow edges of the program) and a transition relation $\rightarrow \subseteq (L \times C) \times E_{CFA} \times (L \times C)$. We write $(\ell, c) \xrightarrow{e} (\ell', c')$ for $((\ell, c), e, (\ell', c')) \in \rightarrow$. A *concrete state* in C is a mapping $c : Var \rightarrow \mathbb{Z}$. A transition $(\ell, c) \xrightarrow{(\ell, op, \ell')} (\ell', c')$ is contained in the transition relation $\rightarrow$ if either $op \equiv bexpr$, $c(bexpr) = true^2$ and $\forall v \in Var : c(v) = c'(v)$, or $op \equiv x := aexpr$, $c'(x) = c(aexpr)$, and $\forall v \in Var \setminus \{x\} : c(v) = c'(v)$. We call $(\ell_0, c_0) \xrightarrow{e_1} (\ell_1, c_1) \cdots \xrightarrow{e_n} (\ell_n, c_n)$ a *path* of P if $(\ell_i, c_i) \xrightarrow{e_i} (\ell_{i+1}, c_{i+1})$, $1 \leq i < n$, is a transition in T_P. The *set of all paths*, i.e. (partial) program executions,

---

[2] To get $c(bexpr)$ substitute the variables v occurring in $bexpr$ by $c(v)$ and apply standard integer arithmetic.

of program P is denoted by $paths_P$. Finally, a program is *safe* if no program execution reaches an error location, i.e., $\forall (\ell_0, c_0) \xrightarrow{e_1} (\ell_1, c_1) \cdots \xrightarrow{e_n} (\ell_n, c_n) \in paths_P : \ell_n \notin L_{\text{err}}$.

We build our technique for witness compaction on top of the *configurable program analysis* (CPA) framework of Beyer et al. [7] which allows to specify customized, abstract interpretation based program analyses. The advantage of using CPAs is that our results are not just valid for one analysis, but for a whole range of various analyses (namely those specifiable as CPAs). A CPA for a program P is a four-tuple $\mathbb{A} = (D, \rightsquigarrow, \text{merge}, \text{stop})$ containing

1. an *abstract domain* $D = (C, \mathcal{A}, \llbracket \cdot \rrbracket)$ consisting of a set C of concrete states, a complete lattice $\mathcal{A} = (A, \top, \bot, \sqsubseteq, \sqcup, \sqcap)$ on a set of abstract states A and a concretization function $\llbracket \cdot \rrbracket : A \to 2^C$, with

$$\llbracket \top \rrbracket = C \text{ and } \llbracket \bot \rrbracket = \emptyset,$$
$$\forall a, a' \in A : a \sqsubseteq a' \text{ implies } \llbracket a \rrbracket \subseteq \llbracket a' \rrbracket,$$
$$\forall a, a' \in A : \llbracket a \rrbracket \cup \llbracket a' \rrbracket \subseteq \llbracket a \sqcup a' \rrbracket, \forall a, a' \in A : \llbracket a \sqcap a' \rrbracket \subseteq \llbracket a \rrbracket \cap \llbracket a' \rrbracket,$$

2. a *transfer function* $\rightsquigarrow \subseteq A \times E_{CFA} \to A$ defining the abstract semantics: $\forall a \in A, e \in E_{CFA}$ s.t. $\rightsquigarrow(a, e) = a'$

$$\{c' \mid c \in \llbracket a \rrbracket \land \exists \ell, \ell' : (\ell, c) \xrightarrow{e} (\ell', c')\} \subseteq \llbracket a' \rrbracket,$$

3. a *merge operator* merge and a *termination check operator* stop steering the construction of the abstract state space, and satisfying (a) $\forall a, a' \in A : a' \sqsubseteq \text{merge}(a, a')$ and (b) $\forall a \in A, S \subseteq A : \text{stop}(a, S) \implies \exists a' \in S : a \sqsubseteq a'$. Both of these operators will play no role in the following, and are thus not further discussed here.

Based on a given analysis $\mathbb{A}$, an abstract state space of a given program is then constructed in the form of an *abstract reachability graph* (ARG). To this end, the initial abstract state $a_0 \in \mathcal{A}$ is fixed to be $\top$, and the root of the ARG becomes (ℓ_0, a_0). The ARG is then further constructed by examining the edges of the CFA and computing successors of nodes under the transfer function of the analysis $\mathbb{A}$. The stop operator fixes when to end such an exploration. An ARG for a program $P = (L, E_{CFA}, \ell_0, L_{\text{err}})$ is thus a graph $G = (N, E_{ARG}, root)$ with nodes being pairs of locations and abstract values, i.e., $N \subseteq L \times A$ and edges $E_{ARG} \subseteq N \times E_{CFA} \times N$. We say that two nodes $n_1 = (\ell_1, a_1)$ and $n_2 = (\ell_2, a_2)$ are *location equivalent*, $n_1 =_{loc} n_2$, if $\ell_1 = \ell_2$. We lift the ordering on elements in A to elements in $L \times A$ by saying that $(\ell_1, a_1) \sqsubseteq (\ell_2, a_2)$ if $\ell_1 = \ell_2$ and $a_1 \sqsubseteq a_2$. We write $n \xrightarrow{e} n'$, $e \in E_{CFA}$, if $(n, e, n') \in E_{ARG}$, and $n \xrightarrow{e} n'$ if $n = (\ell, a)$, $n' = (\ell', a')$, $e = (\ell, op, \ell') \in E_{CFA}$ and $a \xrightarrow{e} a'$.

3   Proof Witnesses and Weakenings

Abstract reachability graphs represent overapproximations of the state space of the program. They are used by verification tools for inspecting safety of the program: if no error location is reachable in the ARG, it is also unreachable in the program, and the tool can then testify safety. Thus, ARGs are excellent candidates for proof witnesses. However, our definition of an ARG only fixes the syntactical appearance and allows ARGs that are not necessarily proper proof witnesses (and real overapproximations), e.g., our definition allows that an ARG could simply have ignored the exploration of certain edges in the CFA.

Definition 1. *An ARG G constructed by an analysis $\mathbb{A}$ is a proof witness for program P if the following properties hold:*

Rootedness. *The root node root $(\ell_0, \top)$,*
Soundness. *All successor nodes are covered:*

$$\forall n \in N : n \overset{e}{\leadsto} n' \text{ implies } \exists n'' : n \overset{e}{\to} n'' \wedge n' \sqsubseteq n'',$$

Safety. *No error nodes are present:* $\forall(\ell, \cdot) \in N : \ell \notin L_{err}.$

(Sound) verification tools construct ARGs which are indeed proof witnesses (unless the program is not safe). When such an ARG is used as a proof witness, safety of the program can then be checked by validating the above three properties for the ARG. Such checks are often less costly than building a new ARG from scratch. This makes proof witnesses excellent candidates for proofs in a proof-carrying code setting.

Proposition 1. *If an ARG G is a proof witness for program P, then P is safe.*

However, ARGs are often unnecessarily complex witnesses. They often store information about program variables that is either too detailed or even not needed at all. Our interest is thus in finding *smaller* witnesses. In terms of the analysis, too much detail means that the information stored for program locations is unnecessarily low in the lattice ordering $\sqsubseteq$. We build our compaction technique on the following assumption about the size of witnesses.

> *Assumption.* The weaker (i.e., the higher in the lattice ordering) the abstract values stored for program locations, the more compact the witness.

As an example justifying this assumption take the weakest element $\top$: as it represents the whole set of concrete states, it brings us no specific information at all and can thus also be elided from a witness. This assumption is also taken in the work of Besson et al. [2]. We base the following approach on the assumption – which our experiments also confirm – and define weakenings for proof witnesses.

Definition 2. *A function $w : L \times A \to L \times A$ is a weakening function for a domain $D = (C, A, \llbracket \cdot \rrbracket)$ and program $P = (L, E_{CFA}, \ell_0, L_{err})$ if it satisfies the following two properties:*

- $(\ell, a) \sqsubseteq w(\ell, a)$ *(weakening)*,
- $w(\ell, a) =_{loc} (\ell, a)$ *(location preserving)*.

A weakening function for D and P is consistent with the transfer function *if the following holds:*

- *for all $e \in E_{CFA}$, $n \in L \times A$: $w(n) \overset{e}{\leadsto}$ implies $n \overset{e}{\leadsto}$,*
- *for all $n_1 \in L \times A$: if $w(n_1) = n_1'$ and $n_1' \overset{e}{\leadsto} n_2'$, then for n_2 s.t. $n_1 \overset{e}{\leadsto} n_2$: $n_2' \sqsubseteq w(n_2)$.*

While formally being similar to widenings [13] used in program analysis during fixpoint computation, weakenings serve a different purpose. And indeed, widening functions are too limited for being weakenings as they do not take the program under consideration into account.

Weakening functions are applied to ARGs just by applying them to all nodes and edges: for an ARG G, $w(G) = (w(N), w(E), w(root))$, where $w(E) = \{(w(n_1), e, w(n_2)) \mid (n_1, e, n_2) \in E_{ARG}\}$. Note that $w(root) = root$ since the root already uses the top element in the lattice.

Theorem 1. *If an ARG G is a proof witness for program P and w is a weakening function for D and P consistent with the transfer function, then $w(G)$ is a proof witness for program P as well.*

Proof. We use the following notation: $G = (N, E, root)$ is the ARG, $w(G) = (w(N), w(E), w(root)) = (N', E', root')$ its weakening. We need to show the three properties of proof witnesses to be valid in $w(G)$.

Soundness. The most interesting property is soundness. We need to show that $\forall n_1' \overset{e}{\leadsto} n_2', n_1' \in N'$, there is an $n_3' \in N' : n_1' \overset{e}{\to} n_3' \wedge n_2' \sqsubseteq n_3'$.
Let $n_1 \in N$ be the node with $w(n_1) = n_1'$.

$$w(n_1) \overset{e}{\leadsto} n_2'$$
$$\Rightarrow \{ \, w \text{ consistent with transfer function} \, \}$$
$$\exists \hat{n} : n_1 \overset{e}{\leadsto} \hat{n}$$
$$\Rightarrow \{ \, \text{soundness of } G \, \}$$
$$\exists n_2 \in N : n_1 \overset{e}{\to} n_2 \wedge \hat{n} \sqsubseteq n_2$$
$$\Rightarrow \{ \, \text{construction of } G' \, \}$$
$$w(n_1) \overset{e}{\to} w(n_2) \text{ in } G'$$
$$\Rightarrow \{ \, w \text{ consistent with transfer function} \, \}$$
$$n_2' \sqsubseteq w(n_2)$$

Thus, choose $n_3' := w(n_2)$.

Rootedness, Safety. Both follow by w being a weakening function, and $w(G)$ being constructed by applying w on all nodes of the ARG.

4 Variable-Separate Analyses

The last section introduced proof witnesses, and showed that we get a smaller, yet proper proof witness when using a weakening consistent with the transfer function. Next, we show how to define such weakening functions for a specific sort of program analyses $\mathbb{A}$. In the following, we study analyses that use mappings of program variables to abstract values as its abstract domain D. We call such analyses *variable-separate* because they separately assign values to variables. Examples of variable-separating analyses are constant propagation and explicit-state model checking (both assigning concrete values to variables), interval analysis (assigning intervals to variables), sign analysis (assigning signs to variables), or arithmetical congruence (assigning a congruence class $\bar{c}_m$ to variables, i.e., variable value is congruent to c modulo m).

Definition 3. *A variable-separate analysis consists of a base domain $(B, \top_B, \bot_B, \sqsubseteq_B, \sqcup_B, \sqcap_B)$ that is a complete lattice equipped with an evaluation function $eval_B$ on variable-free expressions such that*

- $eval_B(bexpr) \in 2^{\{true, false\}} \setminus \emptyset$ *and*
- $eval_B(aexpr) \in B$,

for $vars(aexpr) = vars(bexpr) = \emptyset$.
  B is lifted to the variable-separate analysis with domain $A = B^{Var}$ where

- $a_1 \sqsubseteq_A a_2$ *is obtained by pointwise lifting of $\sqsubseteq_B$:*
  $\forall v \in Var : a_1(v) \sqsubseteq_B a_2(v)$,
- *expression evaluation is obtained by replacing variables with their values:*
  $a(expr) = eval_B(expr[v \mapsto a(v) \mid v \in vars(expr)])$,
- *$a_1 \overset{bexpr}{\rightsquigarrow} a_2$ if $true \in a_1(bexpr)$ and*

$$a_2 = a_1 \sqcap \bigsqcap_{a \in A, true \in a(bexpr)} a,$$

- *$a_1 \overset{x:=aexpr}{\rightsquigarrow} a_2$ if $a_2(y) = a_1(y)$ for $y \neq x$ and $a_2(x) = a_1(aexpr)$.*

Note that the execution of an assume statement $(bexpr)$ further constrains the successor state to those satisfying $bexpr$. The analysis uses the meet operator $\sqcap$ for this. As an example analysis in our experiments, we use explicit-state model checking [15]. It tracks precise values of variables, however, if combined with lazy refinement [9] it does not track all but just some variables, and therefore does not plainly build the complete state space of a program.

Example 1. Explicit-state model checking uses the flat lattice $B = \mathbb{Z} \cup \{\top, \bot\}$ with $\bot \sqsubseteq b$ and $b \sqsubseteq \top$ for all $b \in B$, all other elements are incomparable. The operators $\sqcup$ and $\sqcap$ are the least upper bound and greatest lower bounds operators, respectively. Assigning $\top$ to a variable amounts to not tracking the value of that variable or the analysis failed to determine a precise, concrete value. The evaluation function computes the usual arithmetic semantics (denoted $\llbracket expr \rrbracket$), except on $\top$ elements (which can appear in expressions when variables are instantiated according to an abstract value).

$$eval_B(bexpr) \ni \begin{cases} true & \text{if } \exists z_i \in \mathbb{Z} : \llbracket bexpr[\top_i \mapsto z_i] \rrbracket = true \\ false & \text{if } \exists z_i \in \mathbb{Z} : \llbracket bexpr[\top_i \mapsto z_i] \rrbracket = false \end{cases}$$

Here, we write $[\![expr[\top_i \mapsto z_i]]\!]$ for replacing all $\top$ occurrences in $expr$ by (possibly different) elements from $\mathbb{Z}$.

$$eval_B(aexpr) = \begin{cases} [\![aexpr]\!] & \text{if no } \top \text{ in } aexpr \\ \top & \text{else} \end{cases}$$

Figure 2 shows the ARG computed for program isZero when using explicit-state model checking without lazy refinement. We directly elide variables which are mapped to $\top$ as these will not be stored in a proof witness.

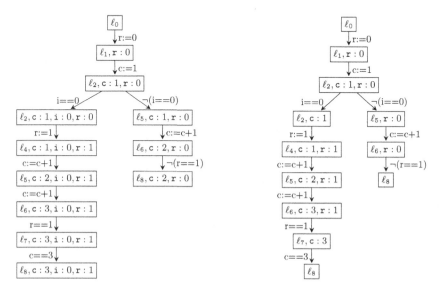

Fig. 2. ARG of program isZero using explicit-state model checking

Fig. 3. Weakened witness of program isZero

For variable-separate analyses, we obtain weakenings by computing the set of variables *relevant* at an ARG node. This is similar to the computation of live variables [27], where, however, the variables to be tracked are tailored towards not introducing new paths in the weakening that were not present in the ARG. The computation of relevant variables has similarities with program slicing [30] as we compute backward dependencies of variables. For $(\ell, a) \in N$, we define

- $init(\ell, a) := \{v \in vars(op) \mid \exists e = (\ell, op, \ell') \in E_{CFA}, (\ell, a) \not\xrightarrow{e}\}$,

- $trans_{(\ell,op,\ell')}(V_{\ell'}) := \begin{cases} (V_{\ell'} \setminus \{x\}) \cup vars(aexpr) \\ \quad \text{if } op \equiv x := aexpr \wedge x \in V_{\ell'} \\ V_{\ell'} \cup vars(bexpr) \\ \quad \text{if } op \equiv bexpr \wedge vars(bexpr) \cap V_{\ell'} \neq \emptyset \\ V_{\ell'} \text{ else} \end{cases}$

The definition of *init* aims at keeping those variables for which the ARG has already determined that a syntactically possible outgoing edge is semantically impossible; the definition of *trans* propagates these sets backwards via dependencies. Together, this gives rise to a family of equations $(rel_{(\ell,a)})_{(\ell,a)\in N}$ for the nodes in the ARG:

$$rel_{(\ell,a)} = \left(init(\ell,a) \cup \bigcup_{((\ell,a),e,(\ell',a'))\in E_{ARG}} trans_e(rel_{(\ell',a')})\right) \setminus \{v \in Var \mid a(v) = \top\}$$

Note that we remove all variables from this set that are assigned $\top$ in a, since no knowledge from previous nodes is required to compute this information. We use $(Rel_{(\ell,a)})_{(\ell,a)\in N}$ to stand for the smallest solution to this equation system that can be computed by a fixpoint computation starting with the emptyset of relevant variables for all nodes[3].

Definition 4. *Let* $(Rel_{(\ell,a)})_{(\ell,a)\in N}$ *be the family of relevant variables. We define the weakening wrt.* Rel *for nodes* $(\ell,a) \in N$ *as*

$$\mathsf{weaken}_{Rel}(\ell,a) := (\ell,a') \; with \; a'(v) = \begin{cases} \top_B & if \; v \notin Rel_{(\ell,a)} \\ a(v) & else \end{cases}$$

For all $(\ell,a) \notin N$, *we set* $\mathsf{weaken}(\ell,a) := (\ell,a)$.

Figure 3 shows the weakened ARG for program isZero. We see that in several abstract states fewer variables have to be tracked. Due to $init$, the weakened ARG tracks variables r and c at locations ℓ_6 and ℓ_7. Furthermore, it tracks those values required to determine the values of these variables at those locations.

The key result of this section states that this construction indeed defines a weakening function consistent with the transfer function.

Theorem 2. *Let* G *be an ARG of program* P *constructed by a variable-separate analysis,* $(Rel_n)_{n\in N}$ *the family of relevant variables. Then* weaken_{Rel} *is a weakening function for* G *consistent with* $\leadsto$.

This theorem follows from the following observations and lemmas: (a) $(\ell,a) \sqsubseteq_A \mathsf{weaken}_{Rel}(\ell,a)$ follows from $\top_B$ being the top element in the lattice B, and (b) $\mathsf{weaken}_{Rel}(\ell,a) =_{loc} (\ell,a)$ by definition of weaken.

Lemma 1. *Let* $n \in N$ *be an ARG node,* $e \in E_{CFA}$ *an edge. Then* $\mathsf{weaken}_{Rel}(n) \overset{e}{\leadsto}$ *implies* $n \overset{e}{\leadsto}$.

Proof. Let $e = (\ell,op,\ell')$, $op = bexpr$, $n = (\ell,a)$ (otherwise the CFA would already forbid an edge), $\mathsf{weaken}(\ell,a) = (\ell,a')$. Proof by contraposition.

$$(\ell,a) \overset{e}{\not\leadsto}$$
$$\Rightarrow \{ \text{ definition of init } \}$$
$$init(\ell,a) = vars(bexpr)$$
$$\Rightarrow \{ \text{ definition of Rel } \}$$
$$init(\ell,a) \setminus \{v \in Var \mid a(v) = \top\} \subseteq Rel_{(\ell,a)}$$
$$\Rightarrow \{ \text{ definition of weaken } \}$$
$$a'(bexpr) = a(bexpr) \not\ni true$$
$$\Rightarrow \{ \text{ definition of transfer function } \}$$
$$(\ell,a') \overset{e}{\not\leadsto}$$

---

[3] The fixpoint exists as we have a finite number of variables Var.

Lemma 2. *Let $n_1 \in N$ be a node of the ARG. If* $\mathsf{weaken}(n_1) = n_1'$ *and* $n_1 \overset{e}{\rightsquigarrow} n_2$, *then* $\forall n_2'$ *such that* $n_1' \overset{e}{\rightsquigarrow} n_2'$ *we get* $n_2' \sqsubseteq \mathsf{weaken}(n_2)$.

Proof. Let $n_1 = (\ell_1, a_1), n_2 = (\ell_2, a_2), n_1' = (\ell_1, a_1'), n_2' = (\ell_2, a_2'), e = (\ell_1, op, \ell_2)$. Let furthermore $V_2 = Rel_{(\ell_2, a_2)}$ and $V_1 = Rel_{(\ell_1, a_1)}$.

Case 1. $op \equiv x := aexpr$.

- $x \in V_2$: Then by definition of Rel, $vars(aexpr) \setminus \{v \in Var \mid a_1(v) = \top\} \subseteq V_1$. We have to show $n_2' \sqsubseteq \mathsf{weaken}(n_2)$. We first look at x.

$$a_2'(x)$$
$$= \{ \text{ def. } \rightsquigarrow \}$$
$$a_1'(aexpr)$$
$$= \{ \text{ def. weaken,} \quad vars(aexpr) \setminus \{v \in Var \mid a_1(v) = \top\} \subseteq V_1 \}$$
$$a_1(aexpr)$$
$$= \{ \text{ def. } \rightsquigarrow \}$$
$$a_2(x)$$
$$\sqsubseteq \{ \text{ def. weaken } \}$$
$$\mathsf{weaken}(a_2)(x)$$

Next $y \neq x$, $y \in V_1$.

$$a_2'(y)$$
$$= \{ \text{ definition } \rightsquigarrow, y \neq x \}$$
$$a_1'(y)$$
$$= \{ \text{ def. weaken } \}$$
$$a_1(y)$$
$$= \{ \text{ def. } \rightsquigarrow \}$$
$$a_2(y)$$
$$\sqsubseteq \{ \text{ def. weaken } \}$$
$$\mathsf{weaken}(a_2)(y)$$

Next $y \neq x, y \notin V_1$. Note that by definition of Rel, $y \notin V_2$, hence $a_1'(y) = \top_B = \mathsf{weaken}(a_2)(y)$.
- $x \notin V_2$: We have $a_2'(x) \sqsubseteq \mathsf{weaken}(a_2)(x)$ since $\mathsf{weaken}(a_2)(x) = \top_B$ by definition of weaken. The case for $y \neq x$ is the same as for $x \in V_2$.

Case 2. $op \equiv bexpr$. Similar to case 1, using the fact that if $a_1(y) = a_1'(y)$ then

$$\left(a_1 \sqcap \bigsqcap_{a \in A, true \in a(bexpr)} a\right)(y) = \left(a_1' \sqcap \bigsqcap_{a \in A, true \in a(bexpr)} a\right)(y).$$

5 Experiments

The last section has introduced a technique for computation of weakenings. Next, we experimentally evaluate this weakening technique for the explicit-state model checking analysis. In our experiments, we wanted to study three questions:

Q1. Does weakening reduce the size of proof witnesses?
Q2. Does explicit-state model checking with lazy refinement [9] benefit from weakening?
Q3. Do PCC approaches benefit from ARG weakenings?

To explain question 2: Lazy refinement already aims at "lazily" including new variables to be tracked, i.e., as few as possible. The interesting question is thus whether our weakenings can further reduce the variables. For question 3, we employed an existing ARG-based PCC technique [22]. To answer these questions, we integrated our ARG weakening within the tool CPACHECKER [8] and evaluated it on category `Control Flow and Integer Variables` of the SV-COMP [3]. We excluded all programs that were not correct w.r.t. the specified property, or for which the verification timed out after 15 min, resulting in 395 programs (verification tasks) in total. For explicit-state model checking with and without lazy refinement we used the respective standard value analyses provided by CPACHECKER. Both analyses generate ARGs.

We run our experiments within BenchExec [10] on an Intel® Xeon E3-1230 v5 @ 3.40 GHz and OpenJDK 64-Bit Server VM 1.8.0_121 restricting each task to 5 of 33 GB. To re-execute our experiments, start the extension of BenchExec bundled with CPACHECKER[4] with `pcc-slicing-valueAnalysis.xml`.

Q1. We measure the size reduction of the proof witness for explicit-state model checking by the number of variable assignments $v \mapsto \mathbb{Z}$ stored in the weakened ARG divided by the number of these assignments in the original ARG (1 thus means "same number of variables", <1 = "fewer variables", >1 = "more variables"). In the left of Fig. 4, we see the results where the x-axis lists the verification tasks and the y-axis the size reduction. For the original ARG, the number of variable assignments was between 10 and several millions. Our experiments show that we *always* profit from ARG weakening. On average the proof size is reduced by about 60%.

Q2. The right part of Fig. 4 shows the same comparison as the diagram in the left, but for ARGs constructed by lazy refinement. Lazy refinement already tries to track as few variables as possible, just those necessary for proving the desired property. Still, our approach *always* reduces the proof size, however, not as much as before (which was actually expected).

Q3. Last, we used the weakenings within the PCC framework of [22]. This uses ARGs to construct certificates of program correctness. Although the certificate stores only a subset of the ARG's nodes, the comparison of the number of variable

---

[4] https://svn.sosy-lab.org/software/cpachecker/trunk/ rv 24405.

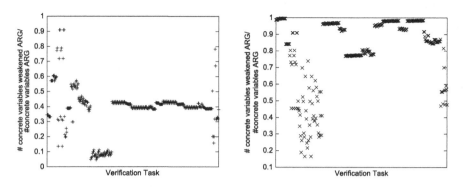

Fig. 4. Comparison of number of variable assignments in original and weakened ARG for explicit-state model checking without (left) and with lazy refinement (right)

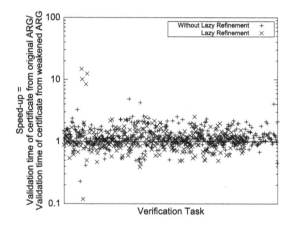

Fig. 5. Comparison of validation times for certificates from original and weakened ARG constructed by explicit-value state model checking with and without lazy refinement

assignments still looks similar to the graphics in Fig. 4. Thus, we in addition focused on the effect of our approach on certificate *validation*. Figure 5 shows the speed-up, i.e., the validation time for the certificate from the original ARG divided by the same time for the certificate from the weakened ARG, both for analyses with and without lazy refinement. In over 70% (50% for lazy refinement) of the cases, the speed-up is greater than 1, i.e., checking the certificate from the weakened ARG is faster. On average, checking the certificate constructed from the weakened ARG is 27% (21% for lazy refinement) faster.

All in all, the experiments show that weakenings can achieve more compact proof witnesses, and more compact witnesses help to speed up their processing.

6   Conclusion

In this paper, we presented an approach for computing weakenings of proof witnesses produced by software verification tools. We proved that our weakenings preserve the properties required for proof witnesses. We experimentally evaluated the technique using explicit-state model checking. The experiments show that the weakenings can significantly reduce the size of witnesses. Weakenings can thus successfully be applied in all areas in which proof witnesses are employed. In the future, we plan for more experiments with other program analyses.

Related Work. Our computation of relevant variables is similar to the computation of variables in slicing [30] or cone-of-influence reduction. Our "slicing criterion" and the dependencies are tailored towards the purpose of preserving properties of proof witnesses.

A number of other approaches exist that try to reduce the size of a proof. First, succinct representations [24,26] were used in PCC approaches. Later, approaches have been introduced, e.g. in [1,22,28], that store only a part of the original proof. Our approach is orthogonal to these approaches. In the experiments we combined our technique with one such approach (namely [22]) and showed that a combination of proof reduction and weakenings is beneficial.

A large number of techniques in verification already try to keep the generated state space small by the analysis itself (e.g. symbolic model checking [12] or predicate abstraction [19]). Giacobazzi et al. [17,18] describe how to compute the coarsest abstract domain, a so called correctness kernel, which maintains the behavior of the current abstraction. Further techniques like lazy refinement [9,20] and abstraction slicing [11] (used in the certifying model checker SLAB [14]) try to reduce the size of the explored state space during verification, and thus reduce the proof size. In our experiments, we combined our technique with lazy refinement for explicit-state model checking [9] and showed that our technique complements lazy refinement.

Two recent approaches aim at reducing the size of inductive invariants computed during hardware verification [16,21]. While in principle our ARGs can be transformed into inductive invariants and thus these approaches would theoretically be applicable to software verification techniques constructing ARGs, it is not directly straightforward how to encode arbitrary abstract domains of static analyses as SAT formulae. We see thus our technique as a practically useful reduction technique for proof witnesses of software verifiers constructing ARGs.

We are aware of only two techniques [2,29] which also replace abstract states in a proof by more abstract ones. Both weaken abstract interpretation results, while we look at ARGs. Besson et al. [2] introduce the idea of a weakest fixpoint, explain fixpoint pruning for abstract domains in which abstract states are given by a set of constraints and demonstrate it with a polyhedra analysis. Fixpoint pruning repeatedly replaces a set of constraints – an abstract state – by a subset of constraints s.t. the property can still be shown. In contrast, we directly compute how to "prune" our abstract reachability graph. Seo et al. [29] introduce the general concept of an abstract value slicer. An abstract value slicer consists of an extractor domain and a backtracer. An extractor from the extractor domain is similar to our weaken operator and the task of the backtracer is related to the task of *trans*. In contrast to us, they do not need something similar to *init* since their abstract semantics never forbids successor nodes (and they just consider path-insensitive analyses).

Summing up, none of the existing approaches can be used for proofs in the form of abstract reachability graphs.

Acknowledgements. This work was partially supported by the German Research Foundation (DFG) within the Collaborative Research Centre "On-The-Fly Computing" (SFB 901). The experiments were run in the VerifierCloud hosted by Dirk Beyer and his group.

References

1. Albert, E., Arenas, P., Puebla, G., Hermenegildo, M.: Reduced certificates for abstraction-carrying code. In: Etalle, S., Truszczyński, M. (eds.) Logic Programming. LNCS, vol. 4079, pp. 163–178. Springer, Heidelberg (2006)
2. Besson, F., Jensen, T., Turpin, T.: Small witnesses for abstract interpretation-based proofs. In: Nicola, R. (ed.) ESOP 2007. LNCS, vol. 4421, pp. 268–283. Springer, Heidelberg (2007). doi:10.1007/978-3-540-71316-6_19
3. Beyer, D.: Status report on software verification. In: Ábrahám, E., Havelund, K. (eds.) TACAS 2014. LNCS, vol. 8413, pp. 373–388. Springer, Heidelberg (2014). doi:10.1007/978-3-642-54862-8_25
4. Beyer, D.: Reliable and reproducible competition results with benchexec and witnesses (report on SV-COMP 2016). In: Chechik, M., Raskin, J.-F. (eds.) TACAS 2016. LNCS, vol. 9636, pp. 887–904. Springer, Heidelberg (2016). doi:10.1007/978-3-662-49674-9_55
5. Beyer, D., Dangl, M., Dietsch, D., Heizmann, M.: Correctness witnesses: exchanging verification results between verifiers. In: Zimmermann et al. [31], pp. 326–337
6. Beyer, D., Henzinger, T.A., Keremoglu, M.E., Wendler, P.: Conditional model checking: a technique to pass information between verifiers. In: FSE, pp. 57:1–57:11. ACM, New York (2012)
7. Beyer, D., Henzinger, T.A., Théoduloz, G.: Configurable software verification: concretizing the convergence of model checking and program analysis. In: Damm, W., Hermanns, H. (eds.) CAV 2007. LNCS, vol. 4590, pp. 504–518. Springer, Heidelberg (2007). doi:10.1007/978-3-540-73368-3_51
8. Beyer, D., Keremoglu, M.E.: CPACHECKER: a tool for configurable software verification. In: Gopalakrishnan, G., Qadeer, S. (eds.) CAV 2011. LNCS, vol. 6806, pp. 184–190. Springer, Heidelberg (2011). doi:10.1007/978-3-642-22110-1_16
9. Beyer, D., Löwe, S.: Explicit-state software model checking based on CEGAR and interpolation. In: Cortellessa, V., Varró, D. (eds.) FASE 2013. LNCS, vol. 7793, pp. 146–162. Springer, Heidelberg (2013). doi:10.1007/978-3-642-37057-1_11
10. Beyer, D., Löwe, S., Wendler, P.: Benchmarking and resource measurement. In: Fischer, B., Geldenhuys, J. (eds.) SPIN 2015. LNCS, vol. 9232, pp. 160–178. Springer, Cham (2015). doi:10.1007/978-3-319-23404-5_12
11. Brückner, I., Dräger, K., Finkbeiner, B., Wehrheim, H.: Slicing abstractions. In: Arbab, F., Sirjani, M. (eds.) FSEN 2007. LNCS, vol. 4767, pp. 17–32. Springer, Heidelberg (2007). doi:10.1007/978-3-540-75698-9_2
12. Burch, J., Clarke, E., McMillan, K., Dill, D., Hwang, L.: Symbolic model checking: 1020 states and beyond. Inf. Comput. **98**(2), 142–170 (1992)

13. Cousot, P., Cousot, R.: Abstract interpretation: a unified lattice model for static analysis of programs by construction or approximation of fixpoints. In: POPL, pp. 238–252. ACM, New York (1977)

14. Dräger, K., Kupriyanov, A., Finkbeiner, B., Wehrheim, H.: SLAB: a certifying model checker for infinite-state concurrent systems. In: Esparza, J., Majumdar, R. (eds.) TACAS 2010. LNCS, vol. 6015, pp. 271–274. Springer, Heidelberg (2010). doi:10.1007/978-3-642-12002-2_22

15. D'Silva, V., Kroening, D., Weissenbacher, G.: A survey of automated techniques for formal software verification. TCAD **27**(7), 1165–1178 (2008)

16. Ghassabani, E., Gacek, A., Whalen, M.W.: Efficient generation of inductive validity cores for safety properties. In: Zimmermann et al. [31], pp. 314–325

17. Giacobazzi, R., Ranzato, F.: Example-guided abstraction simplification. In: Abramsky, S., Gavoille, C., Kirchner, C., Meyer auf der Heide, F., Spirakis, P.G. (eds.) ICALP 2010. LNCS, vol. 6199, pp. 211–222. Springer, Heidelberg (2010). doi:10.1007/978-3-642-14162-1_18

18. Giacobazzi, R., Ranzato, F.: Correctness kernels of abstract interpretations. Inf. Comput. **237**, 187–203 (2014)

19. Graf, S., Saidi, H.: Construction of abstract state graphs with PVS. In: Grumberg, O. (ed.) CAV 1997. LNCS, vol. 1254, pp. 72–83. Springer, Heidelberg (1997). doi:10.1007/3-540-63166-6_10

20. Henzinger, T.A., Jhala, R., Majumdar, R., Sutre, G.: Lazy abstraction. In: POPL, pp. 58–70. ACM, New York (2002)

21. Ivrii, A., Gurfinkel, A., Belov, A.: Small inductive safe invariants. In: Formal Methods in Computer-Aided Design, FMCAD 2014, Lausanne, Switzerland, 21–24 October 2014, pp. 115–122. IEEE (2014)

22. Jakobs, M.-C.: Speed up configurable certificate validation by certificate reduction and partitioning. In: Calinescu, R., Rumpe, B. (eds.) SEFM 2015. LNCS, vol. 9276, pp. 159–174. Springer, Cham (2015). doi:10.1007/978-3-319-22969-0_12

23. Jhala, R., Majumdar, R.: Software model checking. ACM Comput. Surv. **41**(4), 21:1–21:54 (2009)

24. Necula, G., Lee, P.: Efficient representation and validation of proofs. In: LICS, pp. 93–104. IEEE (1998).

25. Necula, G.C.: Proof-carrying code. In: POPL, pp. 106–119. ACM, New York (1997)

26. Necula, G.C., Rahul, S.P.: Oracle-based checking of untrusted software. In: POPL, pp. 142–154. ACM, New York (2001)

27. Nielson, F., Nielson, H.R., Hankin, C.: Principles of program analysis, 1st edn. Springer, Berlin (2005). (corr. 2. print. edn.)

28. Rose, E.: Lightweight bytecode verification. J. Autom. Reason. **31**(3–4), 303–334 (2003)

29. Seo, S., Yang, H., Yi, K., Han, T.: Goal-directed weakening of abstract interpretation results. In: TOPLAS, October 2007, vol. 29(6) (2007)

30. Weiser, M.: Program slicing. In: ICSE, pp. 439–449. IEEE Press, Piscataway (1981)

31. Zimmermann, T., Cleland-Huang, J., Su, Z. (eds.): Proceedings of the 24th ACM SIGSOFT International Symposium on Foundations of Software Engineering, FSE 2016, Seattle, WA, USA, 13–18 November 2016. ACM, New York (2016)

Qualification of a Model Checker for Avionics Software Verification

Lucas Wagner[1]([✉]), Alain Mebsout[2], Cesare Tinelli[2], Darren Cofer[1], and Konrad Slind[1]

[1] Advanced Technology Center, Rockwell Collins, Cedar Rapids, USA
{lucas.wagner,darren.cofer,konrad.slind}@rockwellcollins.com
[2] The University of Iowa, Iowa City, USA
{alain-mebsout,cesare-tinelli}@uiowa.edu

Abstract. Formal methods tools have been shown to be effective at finding defects in safety-critical systems, including avionics systems in commercial aircraft. The publication of DO-178C and the accompanying formal methods supplement DO-333 provide guidance for aircraft manufacturers and equipment suppliers who wish to obtain certification credit for the use of formal methods for software development and verification.

However, there are still a number of issues that must be addressed before formal methods tools can be injected into the design process for avionics systems. DO-178C requires that a tool used to meet certification objectives be *qualified* to demonstrate that its output can be trusted. The qualification of formal methods tools is a relatively new concept presenting unique challenges for both formal methods researchers and software developers in the aerospace industry.

This paper presents the results of a recent project studying the qualification of formal methods tools. We have identified potential obstacles to their qualification and proposed mitigation strategies. We have conducted two case studies based on different qualification approaches for an open source formal verification tool, the Kind 2 model checker. The first case study produced a qualification package for Kind 2. The second demonstrates the feasibility of independently verifying the output of Kind 2 through the generation of proof certificates and verifying these certificates with a qualified proof checker, in lieu of qualifying the model checker itself.

Keywords: Qualification · Certification · Model checking · Software verification

1 Introduction

Civilian aircraft must undergo a rigorous certification process to establish their airworthiness. Certification encompasses the entire aircraft and all of its components, including the airframe, engines, and on-board computing systems. Many of these systems utilize software. Guidance for the certification of airborne

© Springer International Publishing AG 2017
C. Barrett et al. (Eds.): NFM 2017, LNCS 10227, pp. 404–419, 2017.
DOI: 10.1007/978-3-319-57288-8_29

software is provided in *DO-178C: Software Considerations in Airborne Systems and Equipment Certification* [1].

Formal methods tools have been shown to be effective at finding and eliminating defects in safety-critical software [2]. In recognition of this, when DO-178C was published it was accompanied by *DO-333: Formal Methods Supplement to DO-178C and DO-278A* [3]. This document provides guidance on how to acceptably use formal methods to satisfy DO-178C certification objectives. However, there are a number of issues that must be addressed before formal methods tools can be fully integrated into the development process for aircraft software. For example, most developers of aerospace systems are unfamiliar with which formal methods tools are most appropriate for different problem domains. Different levels of expertise are necessary to use these tools effectively and correctly. Further, evidence must be provided of a formal method's soundness, a concept that is not well understood by most practicing engineers. Similarly, most developers of formal methods tools are unfamiliar with certification requirements and processes.

DO-178C requires that a tool used to meet its objectives must be *qualified* in accordance with the tool qualification document *DO-330: Software Tool Qualification Considerations* [4]. The purpose of the tool qualification process is to obtain confidence in the tool functionality. The effort required varies based on the potential impact a tool error could have on system safety. The qualification of formal verification tools poses unique challenges for both tool developers and aerospace software engineers.

Previous NASA-sponsored work has described in detail how one might use various formal methods tools to satisfy DO-178C certification objectives [5]. This paper presents the results of a subsequent study designed to address the qualification of formal methods tools. The goal of the effort was to interpret the guidance of DO-330 and DO-333 and provide critical feedback to the aerospace and formal methods research communities on potential pitfalls and best practices to ensure formal methods tool users and developers alike can successfully qualify their tools.

We are aware of several commercial tool vendors who have successfully qualified formal methods tools. For example, Polyspace by MathWorks and Astreé by AbsInt both have DO-178C qualification kits available. In the early stages of this project we helped to organize a Dagstuhl Seminar on Qualification of Formal Methods Tools [6] to engage both formal methods researchers and certification experts. The seminar included presentations on qualification work for the Alt-Ergo theorem prover [7], SPARK verification tools [8], and the CompCert compiler [9], as well as experience reports on qualification guidance and efforts in other industries. A good summary of tool qualification requirements in other domains is found in [10].

In this paper we examine the qualification of a model checker for use in verification of avionics software. The success of model checking is largely due to the fact that it is a highly automated process, generally requiring less expertise than an interactive theorem prover [11]. One clear strength of model checkers is their ability to return precise error traces witnessing the violation of a given safety property. However, most model checkers are currently unable to return any form of corroborating evidence when they declare a safety property to be satisfied. When used to satisfy certification objectives for aircraft software, a model checking tool would therefore need to qualified.

An alternative is to instrument the model checker so that in addition to its safety claims, it generates a *proof certificate*, which is an artifact embodying a proof of the claims. Such a certificate can then be validated by a qualified certificate checker. By reducing the trusted core to the certificate checker, this approach facilitates the integration of formal method tools into the development processes for aircraft software. It redirects tool qualification requirements from a complex tool, the model checker, to a much simpler one, the certificate checker.

The main contribution of this paper is presentation of these two approaches to qualification as applied to the Kind 2 model checker [12]. Section 2 provides a brief overview of the certification guidance for software in commercial aircraft. Section 3 describes the tool qualification process that is used to establish trust in the tools that are used in avionics software development. Sections 4 and 5 describe two case studies that illustrate different approaches to qualification: direct qualification of the Kind 2 model checker and qualification of the certificate checker for a proof-generating enhancement of the model checker. Section 6 provides conclusions and lessons learned from the project. The complete NASA technical report and qualification artifacts are available at [13].

2   Aircraft Software and Certification

Certification is defined in DO-178C as legal recognition by the relevant certification authority that a product, service, organization, or person complies with its requirements. In the context of commercial aircraft, the relevant certification authority is the FAA in the U.S. or EASA in Europe. The requirements referred to are the government regulations regarding the airworthiness of aircraft operating in the National Airspace System (NAS). In practice, certification consists primarily of convincing representatives of a government agency that all required steps have been taken to ensure the safety, reliability, and integrity of the aircraft. Certification differs from verification in that it focuses on evidence provided to a third party to demonstrate that the required activities were performed completely and correctly, rather on performance of the activities themselves.

The stakeholders in the civil aviation domain (regulators, airframers, equipment manufacturers) have developed a collection of guidance documents defining a certification process which has been accepted as the standard means to comply with regulations. The process includes system development, safety assessment, and design assurance. DO-178C focuses on design assurance for software, and is intended to make sure that software components are developed to meet their requirements without any unintended functionality.

DO-178C does not prescribe a specific development process, but instead identifies important activities and design considerations throughout a development process and defines objectives for each of these activities. It identifies five

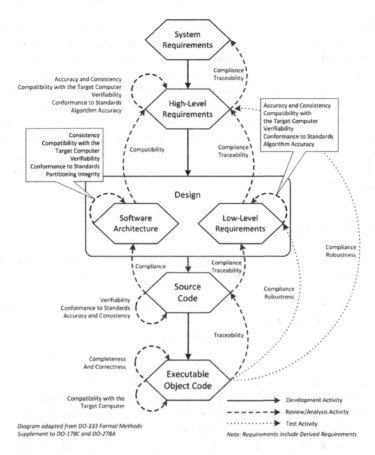

Fig. 1. DO-178C certification activities required for Level A software.

software levels, with each level based on the impact of a software failure on the overall aircraft function. As the software criticality level increases, so does the number of objectives that must be satisfied. Depending on the associated software level, the process can be very rigorous (Level A) or non-existent (Level E). Objectives are summarized in a collection of tables covering each phase of the development process. Figure 1 shows the objectives required for the most critical avionics software, Level A.

One of the foundational principles of DO-178C is requirements-based testing. This means that the verification activities are centered around explicit demonstration that each requirement has been met. A second principle is complete coverage, both of the requirements and of the code that implements them. This means that every requirement and every line of code must be examined in the verification process. Furthermore, several metrics are defined which specify the degree of structural coverage that must be obtained in the verification process, depending on the criticality of the software being verified. A third principle is traceability among all of the artifacts produced in the development process. Together, these objectives provide evidence that all requirements are correctly implemented and that no unintended function has been introduced.

When DO-178C was developed, guidance specific to new software technologies was provided in associated documents called *supplements* which could add, modify, or replace objectives in the core document. New supplements were developed in the areas of model-based development, object-oriented design, and formal methods, as well as an additional document containing expanded guidance on tool qualification. DO-178C and its associated documents were published in 2011 and accepted by the FAA as a means of compliance with airworthiness regulations in 2013.

3   Qualification

Guidance governing tool qualification is provided in Sect. 12.2 of DO-178C. A tool must be qualified if the following two conditions are met:

1. Any of the processes of DO-178C are eliminated, reduced, or automated by the use of a software tool, and
2. The output of the tool is used without being verified.

This means that if a tool is used to identify software defects rather than, for example, demonstrating that source code satisfies its low-level requirements (a DO-178C objective), then qualification is not required. Similarly, if a tool is used to generate test cases, but those test cases will be manually reviewed for correctness, then qualification is not required.

When it is determined that tool qualification is required, the purpose of the qualification process is to ensure that the tool provides confidence at least equivalent to the processes that were eliminated, reduced, or automated by the tool.

Tool qualification is context-dependent. If a tool previously qualified for use on one system is proposed for use on another system, it must be re-qualified in the context of the new system.

DO-330 outlines a process for demonstrating a tool's suitability for satisfying DO-178C objectives that it is being used to eliminate, reduce, or automate. The qualification process is similar to the software verification process defined in DO-178C. Qualification amounts to accomplishing a set of activities with corresponding objectives to:

- Identify the DO-178C objectives that the tool is eliminating, reducing, or automating
- Specify which functions of the tool are being relied upon
- Create a set of requirements that precisely identify those functions
- Develop a set of test cases showing that the tool meets those requirements.

3.1   Tool Qualification Level

As in the certification process itself, there are varying levels of rigor associated with tool qualification. The Tool Qualification Level (TQL) is similar to the software level in DO-178C and defines the level of rigor required by the qualification process. TQL-1 is the most rigorous, while TQL-5 is the least rigorous.

The required TQL is determined by identifying the tool's impact on the software development process. The impact is characterized by determining the impact of a error in the tool. DO-178C provides three criteria to characterize the impact of an error in the tool:

Criterion 1. A tool whose output is part of the airborne software and thus could insert an error.

Criterion 2. A tool that automates verification processes and thus could fail to detect an error, and whose output is used to justify the elimination or reduction of:

- Verification processes other than those automated by the tool, or
- Development processes that could have an impact on the airborne software.

Criterion 3. A tool that, within the scope of its intended use, could fail to detect an error.

A code generator in a model-based development process is an example of a Criterion 1 tool. We expect that most formal methods tools will be used as part of the software verification process and will, therefore, fall into Criteria 2 or 3. That is, they will not be used to generate airborne software, but will be used to verify that the airborne software is correct.

The distinction between Criteria 2 and 3 depends on exactly which processes the tool is eliminating, reducing, or automating. For example, if an abstract interpretation tool determines that division-by-zero cannot occur and this is used to satisfy DO-178C objectives related to the accuracy and consistency of the source code (Objective A-5.6), then the tool is Criterion 3. However, if those results are also used to justify elimination of robustness testing related to division-by-zero in the object code (Objectives A-6.2 and A-6.4), then the tool becomes a Criterion 2 tool. An unofficial rule of thumb is that when a tool addresses objectives from multiple tables of DO-178C (corresponding to different development phases), it is likely a Criterion 2 tool.

The required TQL is determined by the combination of its impact and the DO-178C software level to which the tool is being applied, as shown in Table 1.

In summary, formal methods tools used to satisfy verification process objectives of DO-178C will usually need to be qualified at TQL-5. TQL-4 qualification would only be required if the tool is determined to fall into Criterion 2 and it is being used in the verification of Level A or B software.

Table 1. Determination of tool qualification level.

Software level	Criterion		
	1	2	3
A	TQL-1	TQL-4	TQL-5
B	TQL-2	TQL-4	TQL-5
C	TQL-3	TQL-5	TQL-5
D	TQL-4	TQL-5	TQL-5

3.2 DO-330 and Tool Qualification Objectives

Once the TQL is determined, the required tool qualification objectives are defined by DO-330. Like DO-178C, these objectives are summarized in a collection of tables. Table 2 shows the number of objectives to be satisfied in each area for TQL-4 and TQL-5. Note that objectives for a particular TQL are cumulative, so that the TQL-5 objectives are a subset of the TQL-4 objectives.

Table 2. DO-330 tool qualification objectives.

DO-330 Qualification Objectives	TQL-4	TQL-5
T-0: Tool Operational Processes	7	6
T-1: Tool Planning Processes	2	
T-2: Tool Development Processes	5	
T-3: Verification of Outputs of Tool Requirements Process	8	
T-4: Verification of Outputs of Tool Design Process	1	
T-5: Verification of Outputs of Tool Coding & Integ. Process		
T-6: Testing of Output of Integration Process	2	
T-7: Verification of Outputs of Tool Testing	2	
T-8: Tool Configuration Management	5	2
T-9: Tool Quality Assurance Process	2	2
T-10: Tool Qualification Liaison Process	4	4
Total number of objectives	38	14

Table 2 highlights an important distinction between the qualification objectives. The gray rows (qualification objective tables T-1 through T-7) are objectives related to the development processes of the tool itself. The other rows (T-0 and T-8 through T-10) are objectives related only to the use of the tool. Thus there is a clear distinction between the tool developer context and the tool user context. Furthermore, TQL-5 qualification only requires objectives from the tool user context. This means that TQL-5 qualification is significantly simpler than TQL-4 because it does not require information about how the tool was developed. If a tool was built by a third party, TQL-4 qualification may be difficult to achieve. In particular, since many formal methods tools arise from academic research activities, the artifacts required for TQL-4 qualification may not be available.

Another interesting point is that tool qualification is always performed in the context of a particular aircraft development effort. This means that certain tool functions may not be utilized or addressed in a qualification. For example, qualification of a model checker may only need to cover variables of primitive data types while ignoring composite types such as arrays, records, and tuple types, if those are not relevant for the given application.

Once the proper TQL is determined and the objectives have been identified, qualification is simply a matter of demonstrating that each objective is satisfied. For a TQL-5 qualification, the bulk of this effort is associated with DO-330 Table T-0, Tool Operational Processes, and involves defining and verifying Tool Operational Requirements which describe tool capabilities necessary to satisfy the claimed certification objectives.

4   Case Study: Kind 2 Model Checker

The first case study describes the activities and artifacts necessary to complete a TQL-5 qualification of the Kind 2 model checker based on the guidance in DO-330. Our goal is to provide a concrete example that illustrates the qualification process for a typical formal methods tool and could be used as a pattern by others. We also identify challenges or lessons learned in the process. The qualification package is available as part of the NASA final report for the project.

Kind 2 [14] is an open-source, multi-engine, SMT-based automatic model checker for safety properties of programs written in the synchronous dataflow language Lustre [15]. It takes as input a Lustre file annotated with properties to be proved, and outputs for each property either a confirmation or a counterexample, a sequence of inputs that falsifies the property.

This case study is based on earlier work [5] in which various formal methods were used to satisfy DO-178C and DO-333 objectives for verification of a representative Flight Guidance System (FGS). In one of the examples, the Kind 2 model checker was used to verify that a model of the FGS mode logic satisfies its high-level requirements. This qualification case study extends that work by performing the activities needed to qualify Kind 2 for accomplishing the certification objectives described in the earlier work.

In this example, the mode logic was expressed as a state machine model in Simulink Stateflow, and serves as low-level requirements for the source code that will be generated from it. A Rockwell Collins tool was used to translate this model into Lustre for analysis by the Kind 2 model checker. Textual high-level requirements for the model logic were manually translated to Lustre and merged with the mode logic Lustre model. The overall tool chain is shown in Fig. 2. This case study is limited to qualification of the model checker and ignores (for now) the model translation tools.

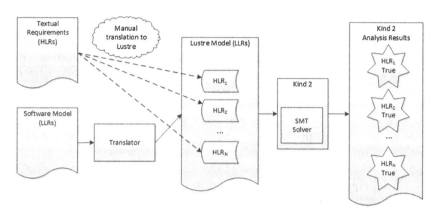

Fig. 2. Verification using qualified Kind 2 model checker.

4.1   Need for Tool Qualification

In this case study Kind 2 is being used to automate processes that satisfy the objectives of Verification of Outputs of Software Design Process (DO-178C Table A-4). This includes, for example:

- **A-4.1** Low-level requirements comply with high-level requirements.
- **A-4.2** Low-level requirements are accurate and consistent.
- **A-4.7** Algorithms are accurate.

Furthermore, the outputs of Kind 2 will not be independently verified. This establishes the need for qualification.

The required TQL is established by determining the impact of Kind 2 on the software development process. In this context the tool:

- Cannot insert an error into the airborne software.
- Could fail to detect an error in the airborne software.
- Is not used to justify the elimination or reduction of other verification processes or development processes that could have an impact on the airborne software.

Therefore, Criterion 3 applies so Kind 2 should be qualified to TQL-5.

4.2   Tool Qualification Objectives

The work performed to satisfy TQL-5 qualification objectives is summarized below:

T-0.1. Tool qualification need is established. (Rationale for tool qualification and determination of the required TQL is described in Sect. 4.1.)

T-0.2. Tool Operational Requirements are defined. Definition of the Tool Operational Requirements (TOR) and their verification in objective T-0.5 are the key qualification activities. The Tool Operational Requirements identify how the tool is to be used within the software life cycle process. This objective requires the identification of the tool usage context, tool interfaces, the tool operational environment, tool inputs and outputs, tool operational requirements, and the operational use of the tool. The focus here is on the tool performance from the perspective of the tool user and what capabilities the tool provides in the software development process.

We have specified 111 TORs that must be verified for Kind 2. These requirements cover:

- The features of the Lustre language used by Kind 2 in this context
- Input validation features
- Properties that must be correctly analyzed as true or false.

Since the requirements will be verified by testing performed on Kind 2, they cover a finite subset of the Lustre grammar. Conservative bounds on the length of inputs are established and validated.

T-0.3. Tool Executable Object Code is installed in the tool operational environment. Identification of the specific versions of the tool and its dependencies, instructions of how to install the tool, and a record of actually installing the tool are required to meet this objective. Qualification was based on Kind 2 version 1.0.1 and the Z3 SMT solver [16] (version 4.4.2).

T-0.5. Tool operation complies with the Tool Operational Requirements. This objective demonstrates that the tool complies with its TORs. This objective is covered in three parts. First, the review and analysis procedures used to verify the TORs are defined. Secondly, we identify a set of tests, referred to as the Tool Operational Test Cases and Procedures, that when executed, demonstrate that Kind 2 meets its TORs. Finally, the results of actually executing the test procedures within the Tool Operational Environment must be collected.

T-0.6. Tool Operational Requirements are sufficient and correct. This objective is satisfied by ensuring that the TORs adequately address the tool usage context, the tool operational environment, the input accepted by the tool, the output produced by the tool, required tool functions, applicable tool user information, and the performance requirements for the tool.

T-0.7. Software life cycle process needs are met by the tool. This objective is satisfied by the review, analysis, and testing results used to satisfy the TORs.

Other Objectives (T-8, T-9, T-10). Tool configuration management, quality assurance, and qualification liaison process. Most of the data required by these objectives are highly dependent on the context and the processes of the applicant organization and can only be meaningfully defined for an actual software development and tool qualification effort.

4.3 Results

The purpose of this qualification package was to provide a complete case study containing a detailed set of tool operational requirements and test procedures. It is anticipated that this qualification package contains all of the necessary information such that it could be used within an avionics certification effort. No barriers were found that would prevent qualification of Kind 2.

One interesting result from the Tool Qualification Liason process is T-10.4 Impact of Known Problems on TORs. During verification of the TORs, some errors were identified. These have either been corrected or will be corrected in the near future. However, such errors do not preclude use of the tool in certification activities, as long as the impact and functional limitations on tool use are identified.

The qualification package and results were reviewed by certification experts at Rockwell Collins and determined to meet the requirements of DO-330. Successfully using it would require an applicant to provide detailed information to support the tool qualification objectives from Table T-8, T-9, and T-10, which are specific to an organization's configuration management, quality assurance, and certification practices respectively. We expect that it could be used as the starting point for tool qualification in an actual avionics software development effort or as a pattern for qualification of another tool.

5 Case Study: Proof-Generating Model Checker

The second qualification case study is based on a proof-generating version of the Kind 2 model checker that is supported by a separate proof checker [14]. In this approach, the proof checker verifies the output of the model checker. This removes the need to qualify a complex tool (the model checker) and instead requires qualification of a much simpler one (the proof checker). By reducing the trusted core to the proof checker, we may be able to reduce the qualification effort required and enhance the overall assurance.

This case study is based on the same software development context as the first, and involves using the model checker to satisfy the same certification objectives for verifying the FGS mode logic. The qualification package developed for the proof checker tool is available as part of the project final report.

5.1 Development of a Proof-Generating Version of Kind 2

For this effort we have used the SMT solver CVC4 [17] with Kind 2. CVC4 is a solver for first-order propositional logic modulo a set of background theories such as integer or real linear arithmetic. Our work relies heavily on the proof production capabilities of CVC4. A unique aspect of CVC4 proofs is that they are fine grained. This means they are very detailed and checking them is only a matter of carefully following and replaying the steps in the proof certificate. In contrast, proofs produced by other solvers require the final proof checker to perform substantial reasoning to reconstruct missing steps.

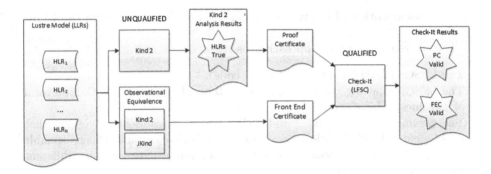

Fig. 3. Verification using Kind 2 and a qualified proof checker.

The proof checker which was qualified in this case study, named Check-It, is an instantiation of the Logical Framework with Side Conditions (LFSC) proof checker [18]. The resulting tool architecture is shown in Fig. 3, which includes both the unqualified Kind 2 model checker and the qualified Check-it proof checker.

Kind 2 is used to generate two separate proof certificates:

– A proof certificate (PC) for safety properties of the transition system corresponding to Lustre model being verified.
– A front-end certificate (FEC) that provides evidence that two independent tools have accepted the same Lustre input model and produced the same first order logic (FOL) internal representation.

The PC summarizes the work of the different analysis engines used in Kind 2. This includes bounded model checking (BMC), k-induction, IC3, as well as additional invariant generation strategies. In practice it takes the form of a k-inductive strengthening of the properties.

This intermediate certificate is checked by CVC4, from which we extract proofs to reconstruct safety arguments using the rules of k-induction. Proofs are produced in the language of LFSC.

To make the whole process efficient and scalable, certificates are first minimized before being checked. An iterative process takes care of this phase by efficiently lowering the bound k and removing any superfluous information contained within the certificate.

The FEC is necessary to ensure that the proof in the PC is actually about the input model provided. Without this step, it is possible that the (unqualified) model checker could produce a valid PC that is unrelated to the input model. The FEC is generated in the form of observational equivalence between two internal representations generated by independently developed front ends. In our case, the two front ends are Kind 2 itself and JKind, a Lustre model checker inspired by Kind but independently developed by Rockwell Collins [19]. Observational equivalence between the two FOL representations is recast as an invariant property. Checking that property yields a second proof certificate from which a global notion of safety can be derived and incorporated in the LFSC proof.

The trusted core of this approach consists of:

- The LFSC checker (5300 lines of C++ code).
- The LFSC signatures comprising the overall proof system in LFSC, for a total of 444 lines of LFSC code.
- The assumption that Kind 2 and JKind do not have identical defects that could escape the observational equivalence check. We consider this reasonable since the tools were produced by different development teams using different programming languages.

5.2 Qualification of Check-It

The approach of using a qualified tool to check the results of an unqualified tool is not unprecedented. FAQ D.7 of DO-330 provides guidance for exactly this "two tool" approach. Recall that qualification of a tool is necessary when it is used to eliminate, reduce, or automate DO-178C processes and when the outputs of the tool are not verified. Kind 2 and Check-It are used to satisfy the same objectives for the FGS mode logic as described in Sect. 4. The outputs of the Kind 2 analysis, a set of proof certificates, are verified using the Check-It proof checking tool. According to the guidance in DO-330 FAQ D.7, this process is acceptable if the Check-It tool is qualified.

Determination of required TQL is the same as in Sect. 4. Check-it is used only to verify proof certificates produced by Kind 2 and so it is a Criterion 3 tool. Therefore, Check-It must be qualified at TQL-5.

The qualification objectives for Check-It were the same as for Kind 2, so we only address the differences here. Since Check-It is simpler than Kind 2, defining its TORs was comparatively straightforward. Inputs to the tool are proof certificates (PC and FEC) that are composed of proof rules defined in six signature files. We have specified 82 TORs that must be verified for Check-It.

Objectives for verification of tool operation were accomplished by a combination of peer review and testing. Test cases cover presence and validity of certificates, compatibility with certificates produced by Kind 2, performance requirements, and proof rule acceptance. Peer review of the proof rules in the signatures files used by Check-It was conducted to identify any potential trust issues. Results from this review were used to identify additional test cases (for example, to preclude the acceptance of unsound rules).

DO-330, FAQ D.7 provides additional information on the use of a qualified tool (Check-It) to check the results of an unqualified tool (Kind 2). This FAQ identifies factors that should be considered to prevent the possibility of errors in both the unqualified tool and the qualified tool. The primary concern is to identify the interaction between tools in the case of various failures in the unqualified tool (for example, if Kind 2 fails to produce a PC or a FEC, or if either is found to be incorrect by Check-It).

The FAQ also identifies four additional concerns that apply in this situation, and which have been addressed in the qualficiation package:

- Coverage of verification objectives for the unqualified tool's output
- Operating conditions of the qualified tool
- Common cause avoidance
- Protection between tools

5.3 Results

To summarize, we found nothing about the "two tool" proof-checking approach that would prevent successful tool qualification. Checking the PC validates the Kind 2 analysis and checking the FEC provides an argument that the emitted PC corresponds to the original Lustre file. If Kind 2 produces incorrect, malformed, or missing certificates Check-It highlights the error. The tools use dissimilar technical approaches, one performing model checking and the other proof checking, minimizing the chance for any common cause failure. The TORs for Check-It were much simpler to define and verify than for Kind 2. However, the proof checking approach was more challenging to explain to certification experts and, consequently, would be inherently riskier to implement. We estimate the overall effort of this approach to be about 75% of the effort required to qualify Kind 2 itself. An added benefit, however, is that the qualified proof checker could be reused with future improved versions of Kind 2 (provided the proof format remains the same), or even with other model checkers which would produce certificates in the same format.

6 Conclusions

In this paper we have explored the qualification of formal methods tools within the context of avionics certification. This effort produced useful examples and artifacts for two qualification case studies, and also provided insight into the qualification process for formal methods tools that should be useful to software developers, tool developers, tool users, and certification experts. Combined with the prior work on Formal Methods Case Studies for DO-333, it provides a comprehensive set of case studies for using and qualifying formal method tools for avionics software development.

The work reveals that qualification at TQL-5 can be a straightforward task. The guidance of DO-330 does not require any activities that are especially difficult or costly for qualification of a model checker. However, the guidance does suggest that tools from the research community may be difficult to qualify at TQL-4 due to the requirements for tool development artifacts including tool requirements, test cases, tool design, and architectural descriptions. Formal methods tool developers who desire to have their tools used in the avionics industry should keep this in mind.

In addition, this work highlights the need for good software engineering practices for formal methods tools used in certification. The relatively high complexity of internal translations, optimizations, and analysis algorithms increases the likelihood that defects will be identified. Bug tracking facilities are absolutely essential for users to understand a tool's limitations.

Lastly, we developed a proof-generating enhancement of the Kind 2 model checker, and explored the impact of this capability on tool qualification. We produced qualification packages for both Kind 2 and for the proof checker for certificates generated by Kind 2. We determined that the "two tool" proof checker approach was viable from a qualification standpoint and provides increased assurance. However, it was not dramatically easier or less costly to qualify and was definitely more difficult to explain and justify to certification experts.

Based purely on cost and perceived risk, we expect that TQL-5 qualfication of a model checker would be the approach preferred by most avionics software developers. The qualified proof checker approach provides significant advantages in terms of greater assurance and modularity, which may be attractive for developers interested in "future-proofing" their verification process. By keeping the model checker separate and free from the need for qualification, improved features and functionality can be more easily incorporated without impacting the qualified (and therefore less flexible) proof checker.

Acknowledgments. This work was funded by NASA contract NNL14AA06C.

References

1. RTCA DO-178C: Software considerations in airborne systems and equipment certification, Washington, DC (2011)
2. Woodcock, J., Larsen, P.G., Bicarregui, J., Fitzgerald, J.S.: Formal methods: practice and experience. ACM Comput. Surv. **41**, 19 (2009)
3. RTCA DO-333: Formal methods supplement to DO-178C and DO-278A, Washington, DC (2011)
4. RTCA DO-330: Software tool qualification considerations, Washington, DC (2011)
5. Cofer, D., Miller, S.: DO-333 certification case studies. In: Badger, J.M., Rozier, K.Y. (eds.) NFM 2014. LNCS, vol. 8430, pp. 1–15. Springer, Cham (2014). doi:10.1007/978-3-319-06200-6_1
6. Cofer, D., Klein, G., Slind, K., Wiels, V.: Qualification of formal methods tools (Dagstuhl seminar 15182). Dagstuhl Rep. **5**, 142–159 (2015)
7. OCamlPro: Alt-ergo (2013). https://alt-ergo.ocamlpro.com/
8. AdaCore: SPARK Pro (2014). http://www.adacore.com/sparkpro/
9. Leroy, X.: A formally verified compiler back-end. J. Autom. Reason. **43**, 363–446 (2009)
10. Camus, J.L., DeWalt, M.P., Pothon, F., Ladier, G., Boulanger, J.L., Blanquart, J.P., Quere, P., Ricque, B., Gassino, J.: Tool qualification in multiple domains: status and perspectives. In: Embedded Real Time Software and Systems, Toulouse, France, 5–7 February, vol. 7991. Springer (2014)
11. Miller, S.P., Whalen, M.W., Cofer, D.D.: Software model checking takes off. Commun. ACM **53**, 58–64 (2010)
12. Champion, A., Mebsout, A., Sticksel, C., Tinelli, C.: The Kind 2 model checker. In: Chaudhuri, S., Farzan, A. (eds.) CAV 2016. LNCS, vol. 9780, pp. 510–517. Springer, Cham (2016). doi:10.1007/978-3-319-41540-6_29

13. NASA: Qualification of Formal Methods Tools Under DO-330 (2017). https:// shemesh.larc.nasa.gov/fm/FMinCert/DO-330-case-studies-RC.html

14. Mebsout, A., Tinelli, C.: Proof certificates for SMT-based model checkers for infinite-state systems. In: FMCAD, Mountain View, California, USA, October 2016. http://cs.uiowa.edu/~amebsout/papers/fmcad2016.pdf

15. Halbwachs, N., Caspi, P., Raymond, P., Pilaud, D.: The synchronous dataflow programming language LUSTRE. In: Proceedings of the IEEE, pp. 1305–1320 (1991)

16. de Moura, L., Bjørner, N.: Z3: an efficient SMT solver. In: Ramakrishnan, C.R., Rehof, J. (eds.) TACAS 2008. LNCS, vol. 4963, pp. 337–340. Springer, Heidelberg (2008). doi:10.1007/978-3-540-78800-3_24

17. Barrett, C., Conway, C.L., Deters, M., Hadarean, L., Jovanović, D., King, T., Reynolds, A., Tinelli, C.: CVC4. In: Gopalakrishnan, G., Qadeer, S. (eds.) CAV 2011. LNCS, vol. 6806, pp. 171–177. Springer, Heidelberg (2011). doi:10.1007/978-3-642-22110-1_14

18. Stump, A., Oe, D., Reynolds, A., Hadarean, L., Tinelli, C.: SMT proof checking using a logical framework. Form. Methods Syst. Des. 41, 91–118 (2013)

19. Gacek, A.: JKind - a Java implementation of the KIND model checker (2014). https://github.com/agacek/jkind

SpeAR v2.0: Formalized Past LTL Specification and Analysis of Requirements

Aaron W. Fifarek[1]([✉]), Lucas G. Wagner[2], Jonathan A. Hoffman[3],
Benjamin D. Rodes[4], M. Anthony Aiello[4], and Jennifer A. Davis[2]

[1] LinQuest Corporation, Dayton, USA
aaron.fifarek@linquest.com
[2] Rockwell Collins, Cedar Rapids, USA
{lucas.wagner,jen.davis}@rockwellcollins.com
[3] Air Force Research Laboratory, Wright-Patterson AFB, USA
jonathan.hoffman.2@us.af.mil
[4] Dependable Computing, Charlottesville, USA
{ben.rodes,tony.aiello}@dependablecomputing.com

Abstract. This paper describes current progress on SpeAR, a novel tool for capturing and analyzing requirements in a domain specific language designed to read like natural language. Using SpeAR, systems engineers capture requirements, environmental assumptions, and critical system properties using the formal semantics of Past LTL. SpeAR analyzes requirements for logical consistency and uses model checking to prove that assumptions and requirements entail stated properties. These analyses build confidence in the correctness of the formally captured requirements.

1 Introduction

This paper presents SpeAR (Specification and Analysis of Requirements) v2.0 [1], an open-source tool for capturing and analyzing requirements stated in a language that is formal, yet designed to read like natural language.

Requirements capture and analysis is a challenging problem for complex systems and yet is fundamental to ensuring development success. Traditionally, requirements suffer from unavoidable ambiguity that arises from reliance on natural language. Formal methods mitigates this ambiguity through mathematical representation of desired behaviors and enables analysis and proofs of properties.

SpeAR allows systems engineers to capture requirements in a language with the formal semantics of Past Linear Temporal Logic (Past LTL) [3] and supports proofs of critical properties about requirements using model checking [2]. Moreover, the SpeAR user interface performs validations, including type-checking, that provide systems engineers with real-time feedback on the well-formedness of requirements. Initial feedback from systems engineers has been positive, emphasizing the readability of the language. Additionally, our use of SpeAR on early case studies has identified errors and omissions in captured requirements.

Approved for Public Release; Distribution Unlimited (Case Number: 88ABW-2016-6046).

C. Barrett et al. (Eds.): NFM 2017, LNCS 10227, pp. 420–426, 2017.
DOI: 10.1007/978-3-319-57288-8_30

2 Related Work

Previous work has investigated the role of formal methods in requirements engineering. Parnas laid the foundation for constraint based requirements with the four variable model: monitored inputs, controlled outputs, and their software representation as inputs and outputs [11]. The Software Cost Reduction (SCR) method builds upon the four variable model using a tabular representation of requirements and constraints [10]. SCR provides tool support for formal analysis, including a consistency checker and model checker. SpeAR also builds upon the four-variable model but expresses requirements in a language that is designed to read like natural language instead of a tabular representation. In contrast to tools like ARSENAL [8] that provide formal analysis of natural language requirements, engineers use SpeAR to capture requirements directly in a formal language, avoiding the introduction of potential ambiguity.

Previous versions of SpeAR [5] used pre-defined specification patterns [4] that were found to be too rigid in practice. SpeAR v2.0 introduces a language providing the formal semantics of Past LTL that is more flexible, allowing users to capture requirements directly, rather than choosing from pre-defined patterns.

3 Formal Requirements Capture

SpeAR captures requirements in a formal language that not only provides the semantics of Past LTL, but is also designed to read like natural language. Previous versions of SpeAR required explicit scoping for temporal operators, using an awkward syntax, for example:

```
while signal > threshold :: always output == ON;
```

SpeAR v2.0 eliminates this syntax and provides English alternatives for most operators, such as `equal to`, `greater than`, `less than or equal to`, `implies`, and `not`. Additionally, SpeAR provides aliases for many operators so that systems engineers can more naturally express their requirements. With these English alternatives, the previous example can be written as:

```
if signal greater than threshold then output equal to ON
```

This syntax is much closer to natural language.

We motivate further discussion of the SpeAR language by describing partial requirements for the thermostat of a simple heating system. As seen in Fig. 1a, the thermostat is represented by a three-state automaton describing reactions to changes in the ambient temperature.

3.1 SpeAR File Stucture

SpeAR promotes grouping requirements according to system components enabling modularity and reuse. Requirements are captured in files laid out in a

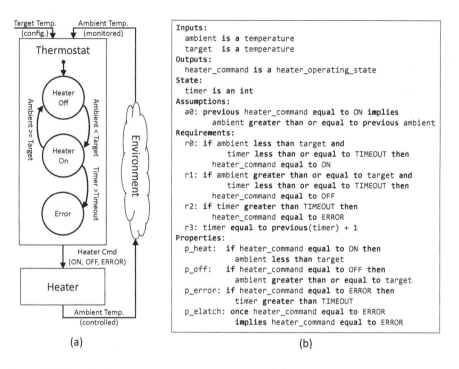

Fig. 1. (a) Simple heating system with associated (b) partial thermostat SpeAR file

common structure. Partial requirements for the thermostat, a component of the heating system, are shown in Fig. 1b.

Inputs, Outputs, State: Inputs represent monitored or observed data from the environment, as well as inputs from other components. Outputs represent data to the environment, as well as outputs to other components. State represents data that is not visible to the environment or to other components. For example, the thermostat monitors the ambient and target temperatures for a room (*inputs*), controls the heater by sending a signal that turns it on or off (*outputs*), and has a counter that tracks heating duration (*state*).

Assumptions: Assumptions identify necessary constraints on inputs from the environment and from other components. For example, the thermostat assumes that the ambient temperature rises when the heater is on (a0). This constraint is an assumption: the thermostat cannot directly control the ambient temperature.

Requirements: Requirements identify constraints that the component must guarantee through its implementation. For example, the thermostat will send a signal to turn the heater on when the ambient temperature is lower than the target temperature (r0).

Properties: Properties represent constraints that the system should satisfy when operating in its intended environment. Properties can be used to validate

Table 1. Past time temporal expressions with SpeAR equivalences

SpeAR	Past LTL
Previous ϕ with initial value *false*	$Y\phi$
Previous ϕ with initial value *true*	$Z\phi$
Historically ϕ	$H\phi$
Once ϕ	$O\phi$
ϕ since ψ	$\phi \, S \, \psi$
ϕ triggers ψ	$\phi \, T \, \psi$

that the requirements define the correct component behavior or to prove that certain undesirable conditions never arise. For example, the heater is only on when the ambient temperature is below the target temperature (p_heat).

3.2 SpeAR Formal Semantics

The formal semantics of SpeAR is as expressive as Lustre [9] and is based upon Past LTL [3] but omits future looking operators. We define this subset as Past-Only LTL, which allows users to express temporal behaviors that begin in the past, with arbitrarily long but finite history, and end at the current step (i.e., transition). Supported temporal operators in SpeAR are shown in Table 1, where φ and ψ are propositions—unlike Past LTL, SpeAR provides support for a general **previous** operator that can be used on all legal types in the model, not just boolean types. In addition to temporal operators, SpeAR provides basic arithmetic, logical, and relational operators.

4 Analysis

In addition to capturing requirements formally, SpeAR provides an analysis platform. SpeAR performs type checking, dimensional analysis of unit computations, and other well-formedness checks on the requirements in real-time. Once requirements have passed these checks, the user can analyze the requirements for logical entailment and logical consistency.

4.1 Logical Entailment

SpeAR enables systems engineers to prove that stated properties are consequences of captured assumptions and requirements. This capability provides early insight into the correctness and completeness of captured requirements.

Formally, SpeAR proves that the conjunction of the Assumptions (A) and Requirements (R) entails each Property (P) as shown in Eq. (1).

$$A_1 \wedge A_2 \wedge \cdots \wedge A_n \wedge R_1 \wedge R_2 \wedge \cdots \wedge R_m \vdash P_i \tag{1}$$

SpeAR proves entailment by (1) translating SpeAR files to an equivalent Lustre model and (2) analyzing the Lustre model using infinite-state model checking. SpeAR presents a counterexample if the requirements do not satisfy a property.

In the thermostat example seen in Fig. 1b, there are four properties: p_heat, p_off, p_error, and p_elatch. Two properties describe the nominal behavior of the system: (1) p_heat asserts the heater is on if the ambient temperature is less than the target temperature, (2) p_off asserts the heater is off if the ambient temperature is greater than or equal to the target temperature. Two properties describe the error behavior of the system: (1) p_error asserts the system is in the error state if a timeout occurs, (2) p_elatch asserts that after the system enters the error state it remains in that state.

Logical entailment allows systems engineers to prove the captured requirements and assumptions satisfy all of the stated properties.

4.2   Logical Consistency

Logical entailment is only valid if the captured requirements and assumptions are not conflicting. When there is a conflict among requirements or assumptions, the logical conjunction of the constraints is false, and thus the logical implication described in Eq. (1) is a vacuous proof (i.e., $false \implies true$).

Currently, SpeAR provides partial analysis to detect logical inconsistency. Logical inconsistency can exist for all steps and inputs, for example when two constraints are always in conflict. Logical inconsistency may also occur only during certain steps or as a result of certain inputs.

SpeAR analyzes requirements for logical inconsistency that is provable within the first N steps, for some user-selected N. This is accomplished by (1) translating SpeAR files to an equivalent Lustre model and (2) searching for a counterexample to the assertion that the conjunction of the assumptions and requirements cannot be true for N consecutive steps, beginning at the initial state, as shown in Eq. (2). Since we use counterexample generation to check consistency, we need a minimum step count to prevent the model checker from merely confirming that the requirements are consistent on the first timestep (a 1-step counterexample).

$$\neg((A_1 \wedge A_2 \wedge \cdots \wedge A_n \wedge R_1 \wedge R_2 \wedge \cdots \wedge R_m) \wedge (Step_{Count} >= N)) \quad (2)$$

If the requirements are proven inconsistent for the first N steps, SpeAR alerts the user to the inconsistency and identifies the set of constraints in conflict. If, however, a counterexample is found to Eq. (2), SpeAR declares the requirements to be consistent even if the constraints are inconsistent at step $N+1$ or for some other set of inputs. This result may mislead the systems engineer to conclude that the requirements are consistent when in fact they are inconsistent. Future versions of SpeAR will address this issue by implementing the stronger concept of realizability [6]—a proof that all requirements and assumptions are consistent for all steps and combinations of inputs that satisfy the assumptions.

5   Conclusion and Future Work

SpeAR is a tool for capturing and analyzing formal requirements in a language that provides the formal semantics of Past LTL and is also designed to read like natural language. In addition to type checking and real-time validation of well-formedness, SpeAR provides two analyses that depend upon model checking: logical entailment and logical consistency. Logical entailment proves that specified properties, which define desired behaviors of the system, are consequences of the set of captured assumptions and requirements. Logical consistency aims to identify conflicting assumptions and requirements.

Systems engineers familiar with, but not experts at, formal methods provided positive initial feedback: SpeAR is more readable than typical formal languages and is worth the effort of learning. Additionally, applying SpeAR to requirements for a stateful protocol revealed a set of unreachable states; a decision was based on a variable whose value was overwritten on the current step. This error represented an incomplete understanding of the requirement that would have been difficult to identify through testing or inspection. After all contributing errors were found and fixed, SpeAR was used to prove that all states were reachable.

While this paper presents current progress on SpeAR v2.0, development and improvement is ongoing. We will expand logical consistency analysis to include realizability, allowing users to prove that the requirements are consistent for all steps and inputs. We will incorporate recent work in inductive validity cores [7] to provide logical traceability analysis, allowing users to identify which requirements and assumptions are used to prove each property—unused requirements and assumptions should be deleted as they overconstrain the system.

We are continuing to refine SpeAR and assess its utility by applying it to the development of unmanned autonomous systems and other research efforts. These results will be presented in future publications.

References

1. https://github.com/lgwagner/SpeAR
2. Baier, C., Katoen, J.P., Larsen, K.G.: Principles of Model Checking. MIT Press, Cambridge (2008)
3. Cimatti, A., Roveri, M., Sheridan, D.: Bounded verification of past LTL. In: Hu, A.J., Martin, A.K. (eds.) FMCAD 2004. LNCS, vol. 3312, pp. 245–259. Springer, Heidelberg (2004). doi:10.1007/978-3-540-30494-4_18
4. Dwyer, M.B., Avrunin, G.S., Corbett, J.C.: Property specification patterns for finite-state verification. In: FMSP 1998 Proceedings of the Second Workshop on Formal Methods in Software Practice, pp. 7–15. ACM, New York (1998)
5. Fifarek, A.W., Wagner, L.G.: Formal requirements of a simple turbofan using the SpeAR framework. In: 22nd International Symposium on Air Breathing Engines. International Society on Air Breathing Engines, University of Cincinnati (2015)
6. Gacek, A., Katis, A., Whalen, M.W., Backes, J., Cofer, D.: Towards realizability checking of contracts using theories. In: Havelund, K., Holzmann, G., Joshi, R. (eds.) NFM 2015. LNCS, vol. 9058, pp. 173–187. Springer, Cham (2015). doi:10.1007/978-3-319-17524-9_13

7. Ghassabani, E., Gacek, A., Whalen, M.W.: Efficient generation of inductive validity cores for safety properties. arXiv e-prints, March 2016

8. Ghosh, S., Elenius, D., Li, W., Lincoln, P., Shankar, N., Steiner, W.: ARSE-NAL: automatic requirements specification extraction from natural language. In: Rayadurgam, S., Tkachuk, O. (eds.) NFM 2016. LNCS, vol. 9690, pp. 41–46. Springer, Cham (2016). doi:10.1007/978-3-319-40648-0_4

9. Halbwachs, N., Caspi, P., Raymond, P., Pilaud, D.: The synchronous data flow programming language LUSTRE. Proc. IEEE **79**(9), 1305–1320 (1991)

10. Heitmeyer, C., Archer, M., Bharadwaj, R., Jeffords, R.: Tools for constructing requirements specification: the SCR toolset at the age of ten. Int. J. Comput. Syst. Sci. Eng. **20**(1), 19–53 (2005)

11. Parnas, D.L., Madey, J.: Functional documents for computer systems. Sci. Comput. Program. **25**, 41–61 (1995)

Just Formal Enough? Automated Analysis of EARS Requirements

Levi Lúcio[1(✉)], Salman Rahman[1], Chih-Hong Cheng[1], and Alistair Mavin[2]

[1] fortiss GmbH, Guerickestraße 25, 80805 München, Germany
{lucio,cheng}@fortiss.org, salman.rahman@tum.de
[2] Rolls-Royce, PO Box 31, Derby, UK
alistair.mavin@rolls-royce.com

Abstract. EARS is a technique used by Rolls-Royce and many other organizations around the world to capture requirements in natural language in a precise manner. In this paper we describe the EARS-CTRL tool for writing and analyzing EARS requirements for controllers. We provide two levels of analysis of requirements written in EARS-CTRL: firstly our editor uses projectional editing as well as typing (based on a glossary of controller terms) to ensure as far as possible well-formedness by construction of the requirements; secondly we have used a controller synthesis tool to check whether a set of EARS-CTRL requirements is realizable as an actual controller. In the positive case, the tool synthesizes and displays the controller as a synchronous dataflow diagram. This information can be used to examine the specified behavior and to iteratively correct, improve or complete a set of EARS-CTRL requirements.

1 Introduction

When writing requirements for software systems in natural language problems such as ambiguity, vagueness, omission and duplication are common [17]. This is due to the large gap between natural language and the languages in which code is expressed. Natural language requirements describe a wide range of concepts of the real, abstract and imaginary worlds. By contrast, programming languages are used to describe precise sequences of operations inside a machine. Natural language can be partial, ambiguous and subjective, whilst code can typically be none of those things.

EARS (Easy Approach to Requirements Syntax) is an approach created at Rolls-Royce to capture requirements in natural language [17]. EARS is based on practical experience, but has been shown to scale effectively to large sets of requirements in diverse domains [15,16]. Application of the approach generates requirements in a small number of patterns. EARS has been shown to reduce or even eliminate many problems inherent in natural language requirements [17]. In spite of its industrial success, we are not aware of any published material describing tool support for EARS. The method is primarily aimed at the early stages of system construction, as a means of providing clear guidance to requirements engineers when using natural language to describe system behavior. Automating the writing and analysis of EARS requirements has not been attempted thus

© Springer International Publishing AG 2017
C. Barrett et al. (Eds.): NFM 2017, LNCS 10227, pp. 427–434, 2017.
DOI: 10.1007/978-3-319-57288-8_31

far. It is however reasonable to expect that, due to the semi-formal nature of the
EARS patterns, automated analysis of EARS specifications can be implemented
to improve software development methodologies already in place at Rolls-Royce
and elsewhere.

In this paper we will describe our initial work in the direction of automating
the analysis of EARS requirements. As domain of application, we have chosen
to focus on the construction of controller software. In particular, the EARS
requirements for the controller running example we present in this study have
been validated by a requirements engineer at Rolls-Royce. Aside from being
industrially relevant, the controller domain lends itself well to analyses and syntheses, given its constrained nature. The contributions described in this paper
are as follows:

- An editor for EARS specifications, called EARS-CTRL, based on the projectional editor MPS (Meta Programming System) [2]. Sentences written in our
  MPS EARS-CTRL editor have the "look and feel" of pure natural language,
  but are in fact templates with placeholders for which meaningful terms are
  proposed to the requirements engineer.
- Automated check of realizability of the requirements as a real controller is
  provided at the push of a button. Additionally, when the controller is realizable, a synchronous dataflow diagram [14] modelling the specified behavior
  is generated. This information can be used iteratively to check whether the
  set of EARS-CTRL requirements correctly express the desired behavior of the
  natural language requirements written in EARS.

2   Running Example

Our running example for this study is a liquid mixing system. The controller
for this system, depicted in Fig. 1, is supposed to behave as follows: when the
start button is pressed, *valve 0* opens until the container is filled with the first

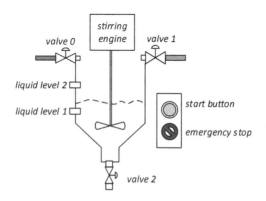

Fig. 1. Liquid mixing system

liquid up to the level detected by the *liquid level 1* sensor. *Valve 0* then closes and *valve 1* opens until the container is filled up with the second liquid up to the level detected by the *liquid level 2* sensor. Once both liquids are poured into the container, they are mixed by the *stirring motor* for a duration of 60 s. When the mixing process is over, *valve 2* opens for 120 s, allowing the mixture to be drained from the container. It is possible to interrupt the process at any point using an *emergency stop* button. Pressing this button closes all valves and stops the *stirring engine*.

3 Expressing and Analyzing Requirements

The first step when writing a set of requirements using EARS-CTRL is to identify the vocabulary to be used. Figure 2 depicts the glossary for the liquid mixing system we have presented in Sect. 2. The glossary defines the name of the controller being built, the names of the components of the system that interface with the controller (together with informal descriptions of their purpose), and the sensors and actuators those components make available. Rules expressing relations between signals are also expressed here.

Glossary For Liquid Mixer

Controller Name: liquid mixer controller

List Of Components:
  emergency button –> to stop the process
  start button –> to start the process
  liquid level 1 sensor –> detects first liquid is loaded
  liquid level 2 sensor –> detects second liquid is loaded
  valve 0 –> valve for first liquid
  valve 1 –> valve for second liquid
  valve 2 –> valve for mixture
  stirring motor –> mixes the two liquids
  60 sec timer –> countdown for mixing
  120 sec timer –> countdown for draining the mixture

List Of Sensors:
  60 second timer expires
  120 sec timer expires
  start button is pressed
  liquidlevel 1 is reached
  liquidlevel 2 is reached
  emergency button is pressed

List of Relations:
  valve 0 : open = not close
  valve 1 : open = not close
  valve 2 : open = not close
  stirring motor : start = not stop

List Of Actuators:
  valve 0 can open
  valve 0 can close
  valve 1 can open
  valve 1 can close
  valve 2 can open
  valve 2 can close
  60 sec timer can start
  120 sec timer can start
  stirring motor can start
  stirring motor can stop

Fig. 2. EARS-CTRL glossary for the container fusing controller

Once the glossary is defined, the EARS-CTRL requirements can be written. Our editor is built using MPS, a projectional meta-editor for DSL development. The projectional capabilities of the editor make it such that requirements can be edited directly as abstract syntax trees projected onto a textual view. In practice this means that each requirement can be added as an instance of a template with placeholders. These placeholders are then filled by the requirements engineer using the terms defined in the glossary.

When   emergency button is pressed **occurs** , **the**   liquid mixer controller **shall** ┃   ┃ valve 2 .
                                                        close ^ListOfResponses (o.i.e.g.examples.Contain
                                                        open ^ListOfResponses (o.i.e.g.examples.Contain

Fig. 3. Example of adding an EARS-CTRL requirement

3.1   Well-Formedness by Construction

In Fig. 4 we depict the action of adding an EARS requirement using our editor. Note that two aspects of well-formedness by construction are enforced at this point: firstly, by using EARS templates instances, we guarantee that the form of the requirement is correct; secondly, the editor provides suggestions for the terms that are added to each of the placeholders as a range of possibilities extracted from the glossary. Figure 3 illustrates some examples for the action associated with the *valve 2* component of the system. Note that in the suggestions associated to this placeholder two constraints are enforced: (a) only actions associated with actuators are proposed, and (b) the actions for component *valve 2* are limited to the ones that are described in the glossary in Fig. 2.

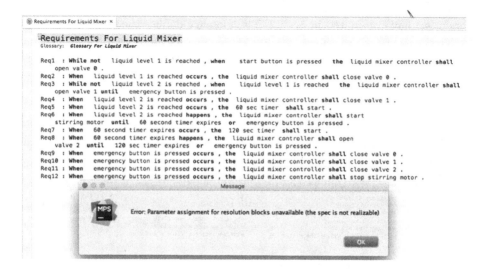

Fig. 4. EARS-CTRL requirements to describe the controller for the liquid mixer system

3.2   Realizability Analysis

Well-formedness by construction, as described in Sect. 3.1, guarantees a certain level of correctness of individual requirements. EARS-CTRL provides additional mechanisms for analyzing the interplay of individual requirements in a specification. In particular, at the press of a button the tool can decide whether the set of requirements is realizable as a concrete controller. Note that non-realizability is typically due to conflicting requirements. This analysis is executed by (a) transforming EARS-CTRL requirements in LTL (Linear Temporal Logic) formulas, and (b) running the GXW synthesis [6] tool autoCode4 [7] via an API to attempt to synthesize a controller for those formulas.

In Fig. 4 we depict a set of requirements[1] for the running example from Sect. 2 that is actually not realizable – as can be understood from the pop-up message in the fig. obtained after running the analysis. When revising the specification, we realized that requirements Req1 and Req9 were in conflict. The reason for this conflict was that, according to Req9, the emergency button can be pressed at any moment thus closing *valve 0*. However, Req1 states that *valve 0* opens when the *start button is pressed*. Thus, logically *valve 0* could be simultaneously open and closed – a contradiction.

Req1 : While not   liquid level 1 is reached , when   start button is pressed   the   liquid mixer controller shall
    open valve 0 until   emergency button is pressed .

Fig. 5. Updated requirement to allow realizing the liquid mixer controller

To eliminate the contradiction we have replaced Req1 in the set of requirements in Fig. 4 by the requirement in Fig. 5.[2] Adding the condition *until emergency button is pressed* to the original version of Req1 disallows *valve 0* being simultaneously open and closed.

When a set of EARS requirements is realizable, EARS-CTRL imports a synchronous dataflow diagram from the autoCode4 tool that describes the behavior of the specified controller. The controller can be visualized inside the EARS-CTRL tool as a block diagram using MPS's graphical rendering capabilities. Due to space limitations, we direct the reader to the project's website [3] for an image of the controller generated for the running example. Note that the synthesized controller is imported into EARS-CTRL as an MPS model, making it possible to further implement automated analyses on this artifact.

3.3 The EARS-CTRL Tool

The EARS-CTRL tool is available as a github project [1]. Note that the tool is distributed as an MPS project and requires MPS [2] to be installed as prerequisite. Together with the functional running example, we distribute with the project the realizable EARS-CTRL requirements for a simple engine controller, a sliding door controller and quiz controller.

4   Related Work

The quest for automatically generating controller implementation from specifications dates back to the ideas of Church [8]. However, it was not until recently

---

[1] For analysability reasons, EARS-CTRL's syntax is slighty different from EARS'. In particular EARS disavows the usage of "until" clauses and composed logical expressions in a requirement.

[2] The requirement in Fig. 5 is an instance of template *While A, when B the system shall C until D*. The corresponding LTL is of the form $C \rightarrow (B \mathbf{W} (D \vee \neg A))$, $\mathbf{W}$ being the weak-until operator.

that researchers investigated practical approaches to the problem. Methodologies such as bounded synthesis [19] or GR-1 [18], and the combination of compositional approaches [10] have proven to be applicable on moderately-sized examples. Based on these results that stand on solid logical foundations, several projects produced research on the generation of logic formulas from natural language, with the goal of achieving reactive control synthesis from natural language. The ARSENAL project starts from specifications written in arbitrary natural language [11] and also uses GR-1 as the underlying synthesis engine. The work of Kress-Gazit et al. focuses on the synthesis of robot controllers [13]. Their methodology is based on using template-based natural language that matches the GR-1 framework. The work of Yan et al. [20] applies to full LTL specifications and includes features such as guessing the I/O partitioning and using dictionaries to automatically derive relations between predicates (such as open(door) = ¬closed(door)), in order to detect inconsistencies in specifications.

The workflow presented in this paper, although also targeting the use of natural language, starts with a methodologically different approach. Conceptually, the tool proposes a formal language with a fixed interpretation, while hiding the formality from end-users; in fact an end-user specifies the required system behavior using only natural language. Therefore, for scenarios such as the relation between open(door) and closed(door), the negation relation is not decided during controller synthesis phase but is given during the requirements design phase. Although our tool supports producing generic LTL formulas, our decision for using the autoCode4 tool and the GXW language subset lies on the rationale that, for iterative validation of requirements, it is necessary that designers understand the structure of controllers. For tools [5,9,12] supporting GR-1 or bounded synthesis, the synthesized controller is commonly a generated via BDD dumping or via creating explicit state-machines which can have thousands of states, making user interaction and inspection difficult. The work presented here largely draws inspiration from and builds on the knowledge obtained when building the AF3 [4] tool for the model-driven development of software.

5   Conclusions and Future Work

Due to the early nature of this work, two main technical issues remain to be addressed: (a) the fact that expressing and analysing complex states such as "the valve is 3/4 closed" or "the quantity of liquid in the container is under quantity X" cannot be reasonably done within EARS-CTRL (due to the boolean representation in autoCode4 of sensors and actuators); and (b) lifting the information provided by the analysis engine autoCode4 for debugging EARS-CTRL requirements is currently manually done.

The work described in this paper is an early analysis of the gap between constrained natural language expressed using EARS and logical specifications that can be automatically transformed into controllers. Note that while the former enables humans to write requirements that are as unambiguous as possible, the latter are developed for computers to process. While these worlds may overlap, they were not necessarily designed to do so.

Ideally, our tool would have as starting point "pure" EARS requirements. However, given the gap mentioned above, we had to slightly adapt "classic" EARS to make it amenable to formal treatment, as briefly mentioned in Sect. 3. The implicit question posed by the title of this paper – whether EARS is *just formal enough* for automated analyses (and syntheses) – is thus partly answered by this work, although additional research is needed. Future efforts will thus concentrate on automatically bridging this gap such that engineers using EARS-CTRL are as unaware as possible of the underlying automatic mechanisms of our tool.

Acknowledgements. This work was developed for the "IETS3" research project, funded by the German Federal Ministry of Education and Research under code 01IS15037A/B.

References

1. EARS-CTRL GitHub project. https://github.com/levilucio/EARS-CTRL.git
2. Meta Programming System. https://www.jetbrains.com/mps/
3. Wiki for the EARS-CTRL project. https://github.com/levilucio/EARS-CTRL/wiki
4. Aravantinos, V., Voss, S., Teufl, S., Hölzl, F., Schätz, B.: AutoFOCUS 3: tooling concepts for seamless, model-based development of embedded systems. In: ACES-MB (Co-located with MoDELS), pp. 19–26 (2015)
5. Bohy, A., Bruyère, V., Filiot, E., Jin, N., Raskin, J.-F.: Acacia+, a tool for LTL synthesis. In: Madhusudan, P., Seshia, S.A. (eds.) CAV 2012. LNCS, vol. 7358, pp. 652–657. Springer, Heidelberg (2012). doi:10.1007/978-3-642-31424-7_45
6. Cheng, C.-H., Hamza, Y., Ruess, H.: Structural synthesis for GXW specifications. In: Chaudhuri, S., Farzan, A. (eds.) CAV 2016. LNCS, vol. 9779, pp. 95–117. Springer, Cham (2016). doi:10.1007/978-3-319-41528-4_6
7. Cheng, C.-H., Lee, E., Ruess, H.: autoCode4: structural reactive synthesis. In: TACAS 2017, accepted for publication, Tool available at: http://autocode4.sourceforge.net
8. Church, A.: Applications of Recursive Arithmetic to the Problem of Circuit Synthesis – Summaries of talks, Institute for Symbolic Logic, Cornell University (1957). Institute for Defense Analysis, Princeton, New Jersey (1960)
9. Ehlers, R.: Unbeast: symbolic bounded synthesis. In: Abdulla, P.A., Leino, K.R.M. (eds.) TACAS 2011. LNCS, vol. 6605, pp. 272–275. Springer, Heidelberg (2011). doi:10.1007/978-3-642-19835-9_25
10. Filiot, E., Jin, N., Raskin, J.-F.: Compositional algorithms for LTL synthesis. In: Bouajjani, A., Chin, W.-N. (eds.) ATVA 2010. LNCS, vol. 6252, pp. 112–127. Springer, Heidelberg (2010). doi:10.1007/978-3-642-15643-4_10
11. Ghosh, S., Elenius, D., Li, W., Lincoln, P., Shankar, N., Steiner, W.: ARSE-NAL: automatic requirements specification extraction from natural language. In: Rayadurgam, S., Tkachuk, O. (eds.) NFM 2016. LNCS, vol. 9690, pp. 41–46. Springer, Cham (2016). doi:10.1007/978-3-319-40648-0_4
12. Jobstmann, B., Galler, S., Weiglhofer, M., Bloem, R.: Anzu: a tool for property synthesis. In: Damm, W., Hermanns, H. (eds.) CAV 2007. LNCS, vol. 4590, pp. 258–262. Springer, Heidelberg (2007). doi:10.1007/978-3-540-73368-3_29

13. Kress-Gazit, H., Fainekos, G.E., Pappas, G.J.: Translating structured English to robot controllers. Adv. Robot. **22**(12), 1343–1359 (2008)

14. Lee, E.A., Messerschmitt, D.G.: Synchronous data flow. Proc. IEEE **75**(9), 1235–1245 (1987)

15. Mavin, A., Wilkinson, P.: Big ears (the return of "easy approach to requirements engineering"). In: RE, pp. 277–282. IEEE (2010)

16. Mavin, A., Wilkinson, P., Gregory, S., Uusitalo, E.: Listens learned (8 lessons learned applying EARS). In: RE, pp. 276–282. IEEE (2016)

17. Mavin, A., Wilkinson, P., Novak, M.: Easy approach to requirements syntax (EARS). In: RE, pp. 317–322. IEEE (2009)

18. Piterman, N., Pnueli, A., Sa'ar, Y.: Synthesis of reactive(1) designs. In: Emerson, E.A., Namjoshi, K.S. (eds.) VMCAI 2006. LNCS, vol. 3855, pp. 364–380. Springer, Heidelberg (2005). doi:10.1007/11609773_24

19. Schewe, S., Finkbeiner, B.: Bounded synthesis. In: Namjoshi, K.S., Yoneda, T., Higashino, T., Okamura, Y. (eds.) ATVA 2007. LNCS, vol. 4762, pp. 474–488. Springer, Heidelberg (2007). doi:10.1007/978-3-540-75596-8_33

20. Yan, R., Cheng, C., Chai, Y.: Formal consistency checking over specifications in natural languages. In: DATE, pp. 1677–1682 (2015)

Author Index

Printed in the United States
By Bookmasters